Network Administration Survival Guide

SUE PLUMLEY

WILEY COMPUTER PUBLISHING

John Wiley & Sons, Inc.
New York • Chichester • Weinheim • Brisbane • Singapore • Toronto

Publisher: Robert Ipsen
Editor: Marjorie Spencer
Assistant Editor: Margaret Hendrey
Managing Editor: Marnie Wielage
Text Design & Composition: Benchmark Productions, Inc.

Designations used by companies to distinguish their products are often claimed as trademarks. In all instances where John Wiley & Sons, Inc., is aware of a claim, the product names appear in initial capital or ALL CAPITAL LETTERS. Readers, however, should contact the appropriate companies for more complete information regarding trademarks and registration.

This book is printed on acid-free paper. ∞

This publication is designed to provide accurate and authoritative information in regard to the subject matter covered. It is sold with the understanding that the publisher is not engaged in professional services. If professional advice or other expert assistance is required, the services of a competent professional person should be sought.

Library of Congress Cataloging-in-Publication Data:
Plumley, Sue.
    Network administration survival guide / Sue Plumley.
        p. cm.
    Includes index.
    ISBN 0-471-29621-X (pbk. : alk. paper)
    1. Computer networks—Management. I. Title.
TK5105.5.P62 1998
004.6—dc21   98-30225
                                                                        CIP

Printed in the United States of America.
10 9 8 7 6 5 4 3 2 1

I dedicate this book to Lou Worrell and Rita Workman, and to all network and system administrators in the trenches.

Advance Praise for
Network Administration Survival Guide

Administrating a modern network can be a painful experience. Sue Plumley has taken the full breadth of network administration and drilled down into the detail that's always left out of network operating system vendor manuals. I've never seen as complete listing of the necessary minutiae of dealing with the minute-to-minute, seemingly never-ending components of responsibly managing a network computing infrastructure. It's a work of art.

—Tom Henderson
Principal Researcher
ExtremeLabs, Inc.
And author of twelve books on systems software and networking

This is a great book for up-and-coming and existing IS professionals, be they administrators or managers. It covers an excellent range of topics with top-level overviews and in-depth descriptions of today's technology.

—Rob Short
Network Administrator
Orbital Sciences

I found the book not just informative and helpful, but easy to read. Too often books on networking become so technical that even a technician like myself finds them too tiresome and difficult to follow. However, this book 'flows' in a logical manner with easy to read dialogue. I congratulate Sue...she did a great job. I have and quite often depend on other books she's written, once again, she didn't let me down. I recommend this book for anyone who needs to know what to watch for in putting up a network for the first time, or making a major change in networking structure.

—Rita Workman
Information Systems Technician & Network Administrator
Raleigh General Hospital
Beckley, West Virginia

Sue's book is right to the point. It covers very important issues that system managers deal with daily. Although it is detailed and comprehensive, it should not scare future system managers away; it will give them the information they need to survive.

—Lou Worrell
HDIS
Raleigh General Hospital
Beckley, West Virginia

CONTENTS

ACKNOWLEDGMENTS

There are so many people to thank for their contributions to this book. First, I want to thank everyone at John Wiley & Sons for their support and patience. Thanks to Marjorie Spencer, whose counseling and friendship inspire and delight me! Thanks too to Margaret Hendrey for her hard work and great patience. I appreciate everyone at Wiley for their dedicated work on this project, including Marnie Wielage for her great attention to detail and her fortitude.

I also want to thank those network and systems managers, administrators, and others who helped me with this book. I learned so much from interviewing people in the field that it would be wrong not to mention their names here. Thanks to Carlos Plumley and Mark Plumley, Humble Opinions; Rich Walker, John Wiley & Sons; Lou Worrell and Rita Workman, Raleigh General Hospital; Rob Short, Orbital; and Art Gonzales, Lockheed Martin.

INTRODUCTION

Networking provides many advantages to your business, such as saving money by sharing expensive printers, easy collaboration between coworkers, protecting sensitive company data while enabling access to multiple users, and so on. Networking your office can save the company money, make work more efficient, insure better communication within the office, and save time for everyone concerned.

Networks also mean a great deal of work; installing, running, troubleshooting, and organizing the computers and networking hardware provides several full-time jobs for network administrators and their assistants. There are also many duties related to data, security, software, operating systems, and other such information.

How do you do it? How can one or two people possibly perform all of the necessary duties to build and manage a network? It's not an easy or simple job. It takes a lot of work and a lot of help to get a network up and running and maintain it so it runs efficiently. You *can* get help. This book provides information and advice for the people who administer networks.

In case you're not sure of your place in the organization, this Introduction defines the various titles given to network people: administrators, managers, specialists, consultants, and so on. The Introduction also summarizes what's in this book.

Who Should Read This Book?

As networking technology has become more popular and more advanced, new definitions and terminology have come into common use. Some terms are easily definable, such as LAN (local area network), email (electronic mail), or palm-top (hand-held) computer; however, other definitions and designations are not so easy to determine.

As a perfect example, what do you call the person who runs the network? Network administrator? Network manager? IT manager? IS supervisor? These titles are used to mean different things and often to mean the same things, and many times the various jobs performed are the same.

Following are different titles used for describing the person who's heading the network; within each section is a brief description of that title's duties. These definitions and specifications came from a variety of sources: want ads, corporation requirements, but mostly from people I interviewed for this book—people who were hired to do one job but found the actual job differed greatly from the description.

If you think the following job descriptions and requirements sound similar, you're right. Many of the duties overlap both in the definitions and in real life. This book is about the person performing these jobs. I prefer to call that person a network administrator.

System Administrator

A system administrator performs or supervises printer installation and system backups, new account creation and account maintenance, peripheral maintenance, operating system installation/maintenance, and support for the network environment. He or she should be knowledgeable in various network operating systems, such as UNIX, NT, NetWare, and even Macintosh.

This person needs good oral and written communication skills and organization skills. He or she provides user and system support for engineering workstations, servers, and terminals. He or she designs, writes, debugs, and installs programs and scripts to help manage the environment and/or automate lower-level sysadmin functions. A system administrator performs hardware and software upgrades, plans the network, troubleshoots problems, installs new machines, upgrades machines, and so on.

Network Administrator

A network administrator is responsible for servers, workstations, backups and restores, disaster recovery, security, service packs, and hardware and software upgrades. He or she performs or delegates user training, user account management, performance monitoring, and growth planning of the network.

Knowledge in UNIX, NT, and NetWare are necessary as well as in network configuration and management. TCP/IP knowledge for use with LAN and WAN management is a must, as are intranet and Web development knowledge.

A network administrator needs leadership ability and extensive knowledge of network and product functions. Consulting and marketing experience is helpful, as are good presentation skills. People skills are perhaps more important than marketing experience.

IT (Information Technology) Manager

The IT manager's job is about 35 percent managing people, 35 percent managing technologies, and 30 percent joining company task forces, working on bidding or strategic planning, working with vendors, or making recommendations about technology and budgets.

The purpose of the IT department is to align new applications with both the user's view and the business process view. Some goals of IT are to create a consistent user interface, hide the application complexity from the user, make sure user interaction is flexible, supply consistent information across all applications, and change IT systems to evolve with changing business requirements.

The IT manager develops, proposes, leads, and executes projects. Communication and organizational skills are a must. Since the IT manager works closely with customers, business partners, and coworkers, people skills are important as well. A BS degree and/or a Microsoft, NetWare, or other technical degree are preferred.

IT Specialist

An IT specialist performs many jobs directly related to keeping the network running. He or she installs servers and workstations; performs backups; installs and configures disks and disk arrays; troubleshoots network problems; and maintains switches, routers, dial-ins, and Internet facilities. An IT specialist may work with CAD users, software and hardware engineers, and participate as a team member of System Administrators. Generally, he or she is on call a great deal of the time. Often a BS degree is required. Additionally, experience in TCP/IP, Internet, dial-in networking, network/system monitors, shell scripts, licensing, and mail is preferred.

IT Consultant

An IT consultant provides technical leadership and hands-on implementation of Internet/intranet projects and networks. He or she may work with system-level security. He or she should have technical competence in UNIX and other various client/server networking systems. Knowledge of Internet technologies at the system infrastructure level; experience with security, firewalls, and encryption technologies; and familiarity with certificates of authority are required. This person should be well versed with various third-party Internet applications and solutions and be able to tackle large-scale Internet projects.

IS (Information Systems) Specialist

An IS specialist designs, develops, tests, and supports software components of various types (such as objects libraries). Knowledge of software development and the maintenance of the software development environment is also required. Preferable are skills in Java, C/C++, RDBMS, UNIX, object-oriented design, Perl, shell scripts, documentation, and verbal communications. A BS in computer science plus experience required.

IS Development and Maintenance Manager

An IS development and maintenance manager supervises the IS team responsible for the evolution, upkeep, and ongoing support of the information systems. An IS manager may manage outside consultants and developers and the installation and customization of specific job-related software and systems. He or she works with software vendors and customers in negotiation, organization, and project planning.

IS Project Manager

An IS project manager position often requires a BS in Business, Computer Science, or other related field. The person should have IS experience in developing and implementing financial systems and in managing development teams. Knowledge of customer support and experience in relational database systems (RDBMS) are a plus. Knowledge about report writing, client/server technology, and Web experience is also preferable.

Furthermore, an IS project manager must have experience in communications and interpersonal and customer support skills. He or she will create a cohesive development staff, design new systems, modify existing systems, and perform all functions in response to client demand.

Realistically Speaking

The number and types of jobs you'll need to perform depend on your company, your network, users, equipment, applications, and such. Realistically speaking, however, the following tasks are what you'll spend a lot of time doing or delegating:

- Writing automated scripts
- Adding new systems to the network
- Going to meetings
- Figuring out network glitches
- Installing programs
- Trying to free up disk space
- Answering user questions
- Moving jobs up in the print queue

If, however, you can delegate these chores, you'll find more time to spend performing the more challenging aspects of your job.

What's in This Book?

This book is a collection of smaller books, each containing information about one aspect of a network administrator's job. The text presents some terminology and explanations of technology, but more importantly, it contains advice, guidelines, and task lists to help you get your job done.

Whether you're upgrading a network or building a new network, you can use this book to get organized. Topics such as planning the installation of your servers, ideas for configuring hardware, tips on preparing users to successfully use the network, and so on, are the focus of this book. No one operating system is featured; however, many various network and client operating systems are discussed. Hardware, IP addressing, troubleshooting, and other reference material is also included for your convenience.

Specifically, this book is broken down as follows:

Network Administration Strategies

Book One *Organization and Planning* Book One includes basic information about client/server networks, network operating systems, network strategies, networking hardware and technologies, and planning and preparing to build or upgrade a network.

Book Two *Server Management* Book Two presents information about server types, server strategies such as centralization and consolidation, hardware and peripheral suggestions, and administration tasks for server implementation.

Book Three *Application Management* Book Three discusses application types, installing applications, determining needs, and so on. It also gives you advice on installing applications on servers or workstations, licensing, naming conventions, and security.

Book Four *Managing Printers* Book Four presents information about network printing, workflow, printer types and print management, server and network preparations, and printing policies suggestions. Also included is advice on writing printer policies and optimizing printer use on the network.

Client Management

Book Five *Configuring Network Clients* Book Five covers assessing users' and company needs, client operating systems, network and PC computers, workstation configuration, and controlling users on the network. Also included is information about integrating various clients and network operating systems and providing training and help for your users.

Book Six *Configuring Internet Clients* Book Six discusses uses for the Internet, connections and hardware for client use, Internet addressing and configuration, and security and policies for Internet users. Additionally, this book covers hardware, software, and configuration for Internet use.

Book Seven *Managing Remote Access* Book Seven includes information about the types of remote access, advantages of remote access, and choosing the appropriate users for remote access. Hardware and terminology used in remote access, virtual private networks, and planning strategies for avoiding problems are also discussed.

Expanding the Network

Book Eight *The Internet, Intranets, and Extranets* Book Eight discusses Internet terminology and technology and network strategies such as what to ask a service provider. It covers hardware and connections and security and suggested policies for your users. Book Eight also contains information on intranets and extranets and implementing them into your network design, as well as a chapter on running a Web server for your business.

Book Nine *Outsourcing* Book Nine presents information on how to find outside experts to help you with your network. It suggests issues you should consider before signing a contract and some advice for items to add to the contract. This book also describes various possibilities for outsourcing, including cabling, remote access, and migration.

Network Maintenance

Book Ten *Backing Up the System* Book Ten discusses backing up servers and workstations on the network. Preparations and planning advice helps you purchase hardware and software plus develop a backup schedule you can live with. Fault tolerance and disaster recovery are also discussed to help you protect your network before it's too late.

Book Eleven *Network Security* Book Eleven presents information about possible risks to your network and your data. Methods of planning and administering the network are also included, as well as policies to help maintain your network and data. Finally, a chapter dedicated to Internet security can help you protect your system from outside sources.

Book Twelve *Optimizing the Network* Book Twelve discusses preventative maintenance and planning advice as well as some system improvements that make the network more efficient. Bandwidth, hardware, and bottlenecks are also discussed.

Reference Material

Appendix A *Network Maps and Models* Appendix A presents illustrations and diagrams of network models and maps. Using these maps, you can learn how to tweak your network design for the most efficiency.

Appendix B *Troubleshooting* Appendix B includes information about network, server, and client problems with suggestions on how to solve these problems. Also presented is information about testing and diagnosing problems, methods of solving problems, and steps to take to prevent problems with your network and equipment.

Appendix C *Task Lists* Appendix C includes several step-by-step lists for administrators wanting to perform specific tasks on the network, such as organize the network, add a new server, manage printing or security, and so on.

Appendix D *IP Addressing* Appendix D describes TCP/IP and IP configuration. Included is information on subnets, gateways, routers, and domains as well as some troubleshooting techniques to help you with setting up, configuring, and maintaining your IP network.

Appendix E *Technologies and Hardware* Appendix E contains information on topologies, backbones, cabling, network devices, and more. The information describes and defines the common networking technologies so you can make reasonable and intelligent decisions when it comes to your own network.

Appendix F *Acronyms* Appendix F defines acronyms common to the computer and networking industry.

Appendix G *Network Operating Systems* Appendix G presents an overview of common network operating systems, including UNIX, Novell NetWare, Windows NT Server, and OS/2. Also included is information about integrating network operating systems.

NETWORK ADMINISTRATION STRATEGIES

Book One

Introduction to Book One

Organizing and planning a network can be the most difficult job you'll face as a network administrator. Whether the network is already established, midway in its construction, or in the planning stages, your most frustrating task may be finding the time to successfully perform your job.

No matter the stage of the network construction, finding the time to properly design your network may be nearly impossible because you'll need to spend time just putting out fires. Perhaps data entry has a printer in need of repair, accounting cannot run an application without more memory, sales has a software problem that is keeping everyone from working. Until you get these situations resolved, you cannot consider topics such as file and directory naming conventions, security policies, backup schedules, and so on. As overwhelming as it is, you *must* find the time to administer the network.

You can try several different solutions to the time management problem. If your budget allows, hire one or more technicians who can deal with the daily operation of client computers and peripherals while you perform the administrative tasks. If you cannot afford to hire help, enlist the assistance of one or more knowledgeable people in each department to help their coworkers with problems and questions. If all else fails, you should talk with your supervisor, administrator, owner, corporate headquarters, or other persons in charge.

Often, these powers that be do not realize the importance of the network or the administration of that network. Before a company can continually realize profits, its owners must understand that the network is the very heart of the business. A company that does not respect this fundamental fact will not continue to run smoothly and prosperously. Following are a few of the advantages of a well-organized network that you can use for ammunition:

With networked computers, your company saves money. Networks enable workgroups to share expensive peripheral equipment—laser printers, fax servers, tape backups, and so on—instead of limiting peripheral use to one or two computers in the office. A network also enables those attached to it to communicate—via email, net-conferencing applications, and so on—with each other; communication between coworkers means more efficient use of company time and resources as well as improved morale.

All of the company's computer resources are equally distributed to users within the company. A powerful file server or database server can supply all users in the company—not just one or two users—with the files they need to complete their work.

Shared resources and information enable people to do their jobs more efficiently and quickly. With additional people working on a project by sharing files and having joint use of the available data, productivity improves greatly.

Purchasing network software is often less expensive than buying several individual copies of a program. Compatibility and upgrading are easier and less expensive when dealing with one copy rather than several individual copies.

Networks offer security safeguards so you can be sure that only those authorized to read or write to sensitive files can access them. Everyone with permission can share the same information and data and even update each other's data simultaneously. Those without permission are denied access to files, data, and resources.

Networks can be expanded to meet almost infinite demands. Add more users, more offices, and even extend the network across cities and countries to serve your company's purpose.

Networks enable various systems. Systems such as mainframes, UNIX boxes, Macintoshes, PCs, and so on can connect through sophisticated gateways so users have ready access to vast information sources.

Naturally, to take full advantage of your network, you must be able to quickly locate users and resources, understand cabling layouts, know the networking equipment, make sense of the server setup, and so on. In other words, your network must be well-organized. An organized network saves time, money, and effort in maintenance and troubleshooting problems and runs efficiently, thus providing more benefits.

In Book One, *Organization and Planning*, you'll learn methods of saving time and expense while getting the most from your network. In addition to advice and tips for network management and administration, you'll also discover information that can help you perform your job more efficiently and effectively.

PRELIMINARY GROUNDWORK

Before you make any decisions, before you order hardware and/or software, before you make any major changes to your company's computer/networking situation, you should assess the current structure and conditions. Following are some general guidelines that this chapter outlines in more detail:

- Appraise the current hardware and software to see if you need to replace or upgrade your equipment and programs.

- Evaluate the needs of the employees, customers, and management so you can best serve those needs with the network.

- Consider the amount of money available for upgrades and new purchases, training, additional staff, and such.

- Think about the amount of space in the offices, the number of users, and the equipment already in place.

- Most importantly, take into account the goals of the company: plans for additional offices and users, remote users, Internet services, and other growth and expansion plans for the future.

Determining Needs

Whether you're building or rebuilding a network, there are certain factors you must consider before you begin. Knowing what you already have and what you need is a large part of the planning. You should enlist the help of managers, supervisors, and users while determining your needs since they will be the ones working with the network resources. Here is a general list of the information you should collect; the following sections outline these questions in more detail.

- What equipment is currently in place?

- What equipment is needed to complete the network?

- How many people will use the network and how many network services will you offer?
- What applications are in place and which applications are needed?
- What are the goals of your company and what is expected from the network?
- What growth potential exists?

Gathering this information may be the largest part of the organization task, but the information will prove invaluable as you plan, design, and organize your network in the months and years to come. Time constraints may prove overwhelming and so you may feel that this part of the job does not take immediate priority. If you cannot possibly take your time to gather this information, you must delegate the job; by assigning only one or two of the tasks at hand to each member of your team, you'll find that gathering data is less overwhelming and more easily achieved. Chapter 3, "Planning Network Strategies," tells you more about applying your inventory to your networking goals.

Taking Inventory

Before you can make any modifications or additions to a network, you must take stock of the existing system. You need to examine the equipment, applications, users, space, location, and budget of the current arrangement and determine the expectations for the new and improved system. This step may take a great deal of time and effort, but it will be worth it in the end; the answers you discover during this stage can help you throughout the following phases of your network organization.

Following are more detailed questions you should ask and answer in preparation for the modification and development of your network.

> **NOTE**
>
> If there is an existing network, locate all of the documentation about the hardware, software, and networking equipment to help in later decisions. If you're just beginning to build your network, make sure you keep accurate records of all equipment, computers, networking hardware, and such as you go. It's much easier to document a network as you build it than after it's up and running.

Is the company located in one office, one building, in several buildings or cities, or around the world? If a network exists, what types of connections are between these locations? What do you want from a connection between build-ings? Will you need great amounts of speed, long connect times, data and video communications, and so on?

What is the current configuration of computers in the company? Are there two standalone computers, a small network using only three or four servers, or a large network with a thousand users and dozens of servers? Will you need to add computers to the system? If so, how many users do you have that need a computer? Write down each user's needs so you can pair the user with the appropriate computer.

What are the peripherals currently in use—CD-ROM drives, modem pools, printer, and so on? Are there UPS devices connected to the servers and/or work-stations? Is there at least one tape drive or other device for making backups? Make note of the needed equipment as well; if you plan connection to the Internet, for example, you'll need specific equipment.

Do you know the networking hardware configurations? For example, what type of cabling, network cards, hubs, and other equipment is used to attach and operate the network? If you're unsure about this information, find someone within the company, or outside of the company, who can tell you about the net-working equipment and draw a network map of the cables, hubs, and such. This step is very important because much troubleshooting, upgrading, and maintenance centers around the networking hardware.

How many users will need to be networked? Attaching 10 users requires a different approach than attaching thousands of users. Are these users knowl-edgeable about the network or will they require training? What are the needs of each user, department, supervisor, and manager as far as a computer is con-cerned? What applications, printing requirements, Internet access, and other features are required by each user? Are there some users who can get by with less? For example, perhaps some users don't need to connect to the network at all or only periodically. On the other hand, there will probably be other users who need constant connection to a server or service. Make note of special needs and conditions.

What type of applications are now in use or will be necessary to run on the network—accounting, email, groupware, or specific vertical applications? Will these applications be available to a few or to everyone? Does your company have specific purposes in mind to accomplish via networking? For instance, is collaboration among coworkers important, will specific customer files be shared, or do users need to attach and access the Internet?

> **NOTE**
>
> Vertical applications are any program written strictly for a certain business; for example, a commercial print shop may use a printing estimation program to help quote customers prices for their print jobs. Other businesses that may use vertical applications are real estate companies, computer consultants, banks, trucking companies, contractors, and so on.

Of the equipment that is now in place, how much will need to be upgraded or replaced? Old 386 PCs, for example, may not be the most efficient computers to run the applications needed over the network. Dot-matrix printers may need to be replaced or supplemented with faster laser printers. Are the servers in place performing adequately, or should they be replaced or upgraded?

What is the budget for upgraded equipment and software and for new purchases? Also consider the expense of training users, hiring additional staff, new applications, and outsourcing work.

What are the goals of the company? Are its current goals being met? If not, how can you best meet those goals by getting the network in place or under control? What are the future goals of the company? Can you prepare for future company growth while planning your network now?

Most importantly, will the administration back you? You must have the support of those in charge to accomplish the task of organizing and/or designing a network. If the boss thinks of you as maintenance personnel or merely a housekeeping team that keeps old and worn computers running, you're not going to have the time, the budget, or the inspiration to appropriately set up a network.

Organizing the Inventory

After you have answered most or all of the previous questions, you'll have a large amount of information to organize. Dividing the information into smaller pieces can help you find the answers to the puzzle more quickly. Now that you've gathered the data, don't waste it; enter it into a word processing or database program, for example, and use it to help determine your purchases and planning. You want to make sure you can rearrange, edit, add to, and delete records and data as you build your inventory through the years.

You can divide the information you've gathered into several categories that may help you make better use of it. For example, you can use categories such as Hardware, Software, Users, Location, Peripherals, and so on. Then you might further organize each category into more topics; Hardware, for example, could be divided into Servers, Clients, Networking, and so on. Within each topic, you don't need to write a book; all you need is to list pertinent information. Be specific and identify each entry as clearly as possible. Following is an example of how you might begin:

Hardware—Servers:

Server 1:

- Gateway 2000 Pentium 6-200MHz
  - 128MB RAM
  - 6.5GB Quantum UDMA hard disk
- Iomega Zip drive
- Mitsumi CD-ROM drive 12x–16x
- 3Com network card
- STB Virge video card
- Running Windows NT Server 4.0
- Service Packs 1, 2, 3
- Primary domain controller and file server
- NTFS file system
- 2 partitions—C=2GB and D=4.5GB

Server 2:

- Gateway 2000 Pentium 6–200MHz
  - 64MB RAM
  - 4.5GB Quantum UDMA hard disk
- Mitsumi CD-ROM drive 12x–16x
- 3Com network card
- STB Virge video card
- Running Windows NT Server 4.0
- Service Packs 1, 2, 3
- Backup domain controller and print server
- NTFS file system
- 2 partitions—C=1GB and D=3.5GB
- Peripherals attached: HP laser printer

As more information is gathered, you can add to these descriptions. For example, you might want to add IRQs (interrupt request) and DMAs (direct memory access) for cards and devices, protocols, client software, and so on. As your system grows and changes, you can easily add to or delete from the list to keep the records up to date. This information assists you when you plan upgrades to hardware and software, troubleshoot problems with the system, and in case you have to replace part of your system in the event of a disaster.

You may also want to document your network with drawn layouts. You can, of course, use an art program to record these drawings, or you can simply sketch the arrangement of computers, buildings, networking hardware, and such in a notebook. These drawings can help you locate machines or other equipment, trace wiring, or troubleshoot points of failure. There's no specific guide to go by in creating a layout, or map, of your network; you just want to make sure the drawing is complete and easy to follow.

Figure 1.1 shows an example of a network segment layout that identifies the server and clients. By identifying each server's job and each workstation's operating system, you make it easy to see the data at a glance. Other informa-

Figure 1.1 Sketch out the server and workstation locations.

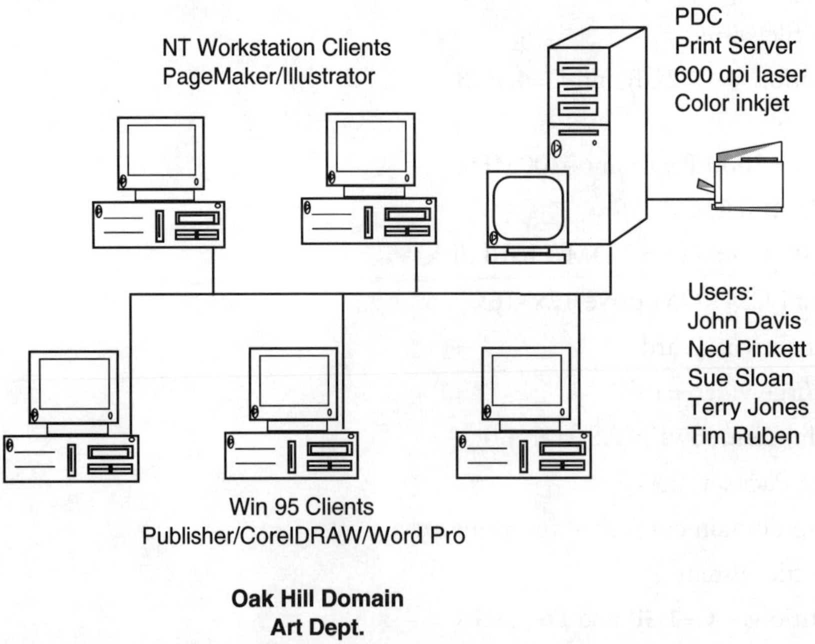

NT Workstation Clients
PageMaker/Illustrator

PDC
Print Server
600 dpi laser
Color inkjet

Users:
John Davis
Ned Pinkett
Sue Sloan
Terry Jones
Tim Ruben

Win 95 Clients
Publisher/CorelDRAW/Word Pro

**Oak Hill Domain
Art Dept.**

tion such as domain and department help identify the location of the networking segment; listing applications, users, and other information is useful as well.

Figure 1.2 shows a network map that describes connections to the servers, locations of switches, routers, and hubs, and network connections. Network maps are particularly useful when tracing equipment problems, checking connections, and upgrading network hardware.

Keeping track of the hardware and software in your company will also enable you to prioritize equipment for upgrade and replacement. Knowing that three workstations are 386s in an office of 486s and Pentiums means you know exactly which computers need to be replaced first. You can better allocate the money in the budget if you can anticipate upgrades and replacements.

When organizing users, you may want to cross-reference each user with the workstation he or she uses most. If users share computers, then simply create a list of users including the appropriate information; for example, the users' duties, most-used applications, passwords, permissions or groups, and so on. This information can help you recreate your users' permissions and rights in case of a disaster, take quick inventory of users who need training or perhaps could perform inhouse training, track users whose employment was terminated, and so on.

Figure 1.2 Draw the network connections and hardware for your network.

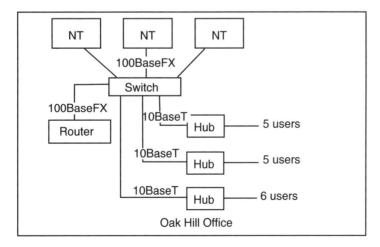

You should keep a record of all applications on the network. You'll need to list the version number, licensing information, upgrade data, and such. When you have a question about whether an application has been upgraded, for instance, it's easier to check your records than to track down the server and the program to check on the version number, especially if the server is located in another building or city.

In your many lists of equipment and other networking facts, don't forget to include information about the following:

Peripherals.   Note any peripheral—printer, modem, CD-ROM, and such—attached to servers and/or workstations. You can, for example, make use of a printer attached to a workstation by allowing several users in a workgroup to print to that printer. This would mean less traffic to a network printer and therefore saves time and bandwidth. You might also want to pool together individual modems to help your users gain fast access to the Internet or to a corporate bulletin board service. A modem pool is more efficient and less expensive to configure than individual modems.

ISP (Internet Service Provider) and Internet settings and connections. List your ISP's or other service provider's phone number, tech support, URL (Universal Resource Locator), and such, as well as any Internet settings for IP addresses, gateways, subnet masks, domain name servers, and so on. Having this information in your records makes it easy to troubleshoot problems and set up new machines.

Networking protocols and connections.   Record information about all protocols used throughout the network. If, for instance, you're using TCP/IP, list all addresses (IP, subnet, and gateway) for each network segment, each device (including hubs and routers), and each computer on the network. You'll be surprised at how many times you'll need to know the addresses of individual devices when you need to troubleshoot a connection.

Figure 1.3 shows an example of IP address assignments created in MS Excel. This spreadsheet makes it easy to find the IP address, user IDs, location of the computer, type of computer, and other connections.

Outsourcing and technical support contacts.   If you or someone else has used an outside company or consultant in setting up any part of the network, applications, Internet access, and so on, you need a complete list including the company's name and address, contact's name and phone number, specific details of what the company did for you, guar-

Figure 1.3 Use a spreadsheet to track your use of IP addresses and other information.

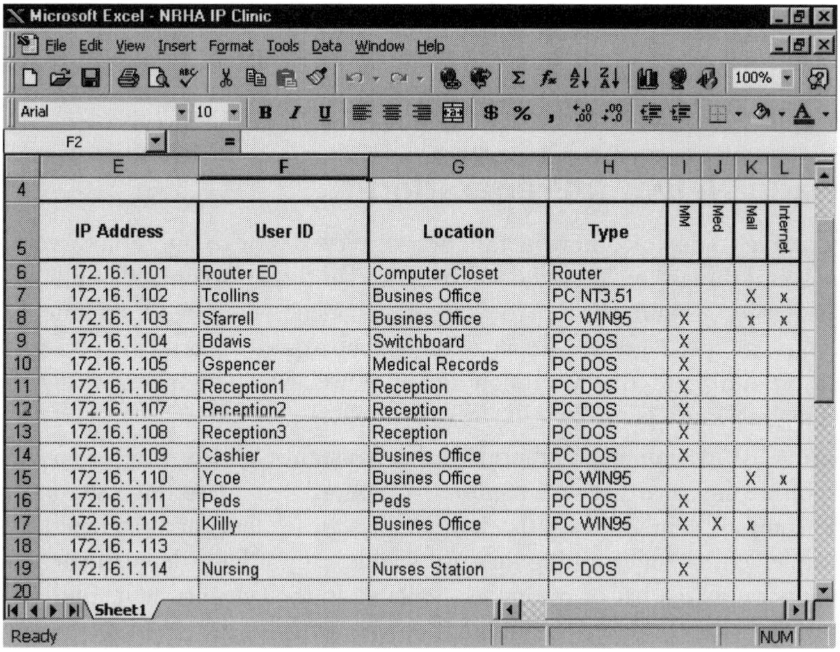

	E	F	G	H	I	J	K	L
					MM	Med	Mail	Internet
5	**IP Address**	**User ID**	**Location**	**Type**				
6	172.16.1.101	Router E0	Computer Closet	Router				
7	172.16.1.102	Tcollins	Busines Office	PC NT3.51			X	x
8	172.16.1.103	Sfarrell	Busines Office	PC WIN95	X		x	x
9	172.16.1.104	Bdavis	Switchboard	PC DOS	X			
10	172.16.1.105	Gspencer	Medical Records	PC DOS	X			
11	172.16.1.106	Reception1	Reception	PC DOS	X			
12	172.16.1.107	Reception2	Reception	PC DOS	X			
13	172.16.1.108	Reception3	Reception	PC DOS	X			
14	172.16.1.109	Cashier	Busines Office	PC DOS	X			
15	172.16.1.110	Ycoe	Busines Office	PC WIN95			X	x
16	172.16.1.111	Peds	Peds	PC DOS	X			
17	172.16.1.112	Klilly	Busines Office	PC WIN95	X	X	x	
18	172.16.1.113							
19	172.16.1.114	Nursing	Nurses Station	PC DOS	X			

antees, limitations, and such. Also, list all technical support and vendor phone numbers for your equipment, software, peripherals, and so on.

Documentation. Gather the documentation for all computers and networking hardware and store it in a central place for easy access. This includes added hard drives, memory, tape drives, floppy drives, and so on; you may need to change jumpers or reference the model number of such hardware at some time.

Backups. Sort out the information about current backups of the system. Find out about the hardware devices, scheduling, storage location, and so on.

Again, this all sounds overwhelming, but delegation is the key. Let a manager gather the information you need for his or her own department. Ask each user to jot down needed information about himself and his computer. Enlist one or more assistants to help you collect and sort the information; then your job will be easier and less time-consuming.

Preparing for Deployment of the Network

When you're preparing for the deployment of the network, you'll have a lot on your mind. There are so many things to remember and to do, that the following lists may help you in your task. You might also consider keeping lists of tasks to do and tasks completed, delegated roles, contacts, and other important information in a notebook or on your computer for easy reference.

Server and Network Preparation

When preparing to deploy a new installation of server(s) or to upgrade servers, there are several things you should do in order to get things organized and lined up for the project. Timing is up to you. If you need the project completed quickly, you can speed up the steps; if time is not quite so critical, you can research a bit and plan your approach in a more deliberate manner. Many of the following tasks can be delegated.

Prepare a list of managers, administrative assistants, and/or interns to help you deploy or otherwise complete preparations.   Use this list to divide some of your duties. For example, assign leaders for preparing and implementing any training that users will need; or have department managers prepare a list of resources available in their departments and a list of resources and peripherals that departments need.

Contact and contract with any support personnel needed for deployment.   Get the help you need from network consultants, technical support contracts, outsource contacts for ISDN (Integrated Services Digital Network) or channel lines, Internet support, and so on. Consider contacting the people you need to help with networking hardware, cabling and wiring, and even remodeling first. Ask questions, find out what you can do to prepare the site, see how long it will take each consultant or technician to do his or her job, and ask what you need to purchase to get the job done. You may need to work around their schedules, so schedule these people first.

Plan networking connections—LAN (Local Area Network), WAN (Wide Area Network), Internet—and steps to complete the task.   Enlist the help of those consultants you've hired, if necessary. Organizing the overall layout of the network will help you decide what equipment is required.

Plan any transitions from your current system, migration of applications, and so on.   This means you must also upgrade any software to a more current version and/or to a client/server version. Make sure you have client software for all applications requiring it, as well. Check into the licensing of all operating systems and applications you plan to use on the network and update licenses as necessary.

Design and build the network for growth, scalability. Think about fault tolerance, load balancing, and so forth. Don't skimp on hardware; your network will grow more quickly than you might think.

Order the server and/or hardware needed to prepare the system. If you plan to replace or upgrade server hardware, workstations, printers, cabling, network cards, and so on, order the equipment so it will be in when you're ready to implement it. Even if you don't need it right away, it doesn't hurt to have it on-site.

Collect applications and data for use on the server. Purchase new software or upgrades; create any new data in databases, Web development programs, or other applications that you need. Set teams to the task of gathering other data and information you may need, such as online catalogs, Web pages, application documentation, and such. Make backups of all current data.

Identify all groups and users who will use data on the server. List users, departments, and applications and resources they need. This will help later in determining groups, permissions, rights, and so on. Delegate this task to, for example, department supervisors or managers.

Notify users of the changes that will take place. A staff that is kept informed of impending changes will less likely panic when all is said and done. You can do this via an assistant, a memo, email, or company meeting; choose the method that best suits your management style.

Prepare documentation for deployment, including technical specifications, troubleshooting tips, contact info, and other pertinent data. Assign a team to compile this data and information and to organize, print, and distribute the information to your employees.

Client Preparation

There are a few additional things you can do when preparing client computers. Some are common sense issues; however, with all you have on your mind right now, you don't want to forget even one detail.

Make sure your hardware is worth connecting to the network. Old computers on their last legs shouldn't be upgraded, they should be replaced. Don't let the budget limit your choices in this area; you'll spend more time trying to keep older hardware running than it's worth.

Make sure workstations have an available slot for the network card, a small but important detail.

Make sure you have all the peripheral software you need to run with your workstations. Obtain drivers for backup tape drives, sound cards, CD-ROM drives, printers, modems or modem server, optical disk drives, and such. Upgrade older equipment, find new drivers, purchase any peripherals you need.

Have users notify you when they need training. This step can help keep you informed without taking too much time to quiz everyone in the company. In your memos or email to your users, announce when you are planning to add a new technology or application and state clearly that anyone needing training should contact the administrative assistant handling the training project.

During the Deployment

During the deployment, there are just a few tasks that can help you keep the workplace organized while things are changing. Keeping your head is the first priority; don't let all of the hectic activity get to you. In addition, follow these suggestions:

Keep users informed of changes, schedules, and other issues related to the network via email, newsletter, memo, and so on. Make sure they know what is going on. Delegate this task to an assistant—sending one email a day to notify users of the day's plans will not take too much time and will truly be appreciated.

Centralize support and administration staff to cut down on paperwork, superfluous work, and so on. Especially during a reorganization or major change in routine, keeping the consultants, technical support, and managers in close contact is important. Also, avoid assigning busy work; cut out all work that's not necessary to business, if only for the time you're deploying the network.

Listen to your users' complaints and problems. As new servers, programs, and workstations go online, users are likely to have problems with the technology, procedures, or equipment. Users should document problems and turn their lists in to specified assistants or managers. Ask for users' ideas for solutions to the problems. Solve problems as quickly as possible and then check up on the solutions to make sure the problems don't come back. This is key to morale and user cooperation.

Make sure support for remote users is as good as it is for inhouse users. People on the road or those working from home are often left by the wayside until you get the office in order. Support remote users from the beginning and solve their problems as if they were in the office with the rest of you.

NETWORK FOUNDATIONS

The first steps to planning your network involve a choice of the type of network and of the operating system. The type of network you choose depends on the amount of data you have to use over the network, data storage techniques, your current system, and how you want to share that data. The network operating system you choose depends on personal preferences, uses you have for the network, your current configuration, and other factors described in this chapter.

Specifically, this chapter covers the following:

- LANs, WANs, enterprise, campus, and global networks

- Networking types, such as mainframes, peer-to-peer, and client server

- Enterprise networking

- Common network operating systems

Networking Types

There are many reasons you might want to install a network for use with your company. Networks help save money, make your employees' time more productive, enable collaboration between coworkers, and can provide a presence for your company on the Internet. If you're planning a network, you want to build the most productive network you can. You have several choices.

You can build your network around a mainframe or minicomputer, a client/server, or a peer-to-peer network. Each network type has its own advantages and disadvantages, benefits and liabilities. Naturally, you could also use any or all of the three network types together to build your own unique networking system, but more than likely with today's technologies, you'll use only one type of network for your business.

LAN, WAN, or Other?

As you plan your new or upgraded network, one of your first decisions is whether to use a LAN or WAN. A LAN (Local Area Network) consists of a group of computers and associated peripheral devices that are connected by a communications channel such as network cabling. The computers in the LAN are capable of sharing files and other resources between several users. Normally, the computers in a LAN are within the same office or building, thus the reference to "local."

A WAN (Wide Area Network) is similar to a LAN; however, a WAN connects users across large distances, such as cities or states or even countries. Another acronym you may hear is MAN (Metropolitan Area Network). A MAN is smaller than a WAN but larger than a LAN and generally refers to a public, high-speed network that's capable of voice and data transmissions.

Other terms tossed around in the networking field are *campus, enterprise,* and *global* networks. A campus network is a network that connects multiple LANs from multiple departments inside a single building or set of buildings. Campus networks don't include WAN services. An enterprise network connects all parts of an organization, often including dissimilar computers. Various systems link together for email, files, and database exchange. Finally, a global network crosses national, commercial, and governmental boundaries to support global activities like international currency trading or environmental protection and assessment.

Mainframe or Minicomputer

If your company already uses a mainframe or minicomputer, like an AS/400, you will likely want to include it in your system because of all the data already housed in the computer. Depending on the work your company does, you may also want to install a mainframe or minicomputer. However, unless you have someone in your company familiar with mainframes or minis, you'll likely use PCs as a base for your network.

NOTE

A mainframe or minicomputer network is also a client/server network.

Peer-to-Peer Networking

Another choice in networking is peer-to-peer. A peer-to-peer network is made up of 2 to 10 workstations cabled together. These workstations can share data, files, resources, and so on. Users can use email and groupware as well. Users can even share applications, although that's not too efficient on a peer-to-peer because the power and memory of each workstation is generally equal to that of the other workstations on the network, and sharing applications drains resources. Figure 2.1 shows the relationship between workstations in a peer-to-peer networking situation, also called a *workgroup*.

Additionally, peer-to-peer limits the number of users you can include on a network. Ten computers are the most that can efficiently work together; adding more computers would slow the performance of all computers on the network. Also, limits in network speed, security, and efficiency make peer-to-peer an unattractive choice for most businesses.

Client/Server Networking

Client/server, or dedicated server, uses at least one central computer as a server. The server is configured to enable easy sharing and storage of files and resources. A server becomes the data management center from which clients can access applications, files, and directories. Finally, the server administers shared

Figure 2.1 Every workstation shares its resources with the others in a peer-to-peer network.

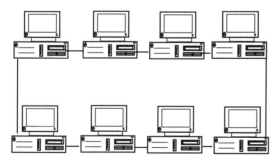

Windows 98 Workstations

resources—like printers, modems, and CD-ROM drives—to clients attached to the network. Figure 2.2 illustrates a simple client/server network. Two servers—an authentication and a backup server—provide all services for the clients; client computers do not communicate with each other.

Client/server networking offers many benefits to your business. No matter what your business goals are, using a client/server system enables better information sharing, communication, and network organization. Email, real-time meetings and chat rooms, document-sharing programs, and such, enable users to send files, ideas, questions, and solutions to each other electronically and quickly.

Control over files, directories, and resources is another benefit of client/server networking. Before a user can access a resource, he or she must have permission to do so, and the administrator is the person who grants permissions. Client/server technology provides the administrator with the tools he or she needs to limit access to shared data and resources so that users' access to critical or sensitive files and directories is limited.

The administrator can also remotely support users of the network. Rather than managing the network from the server, the administrator can use a work-

Figure 2.2 Servers provide workstations with various resources such as printers, files, directories, and so on.

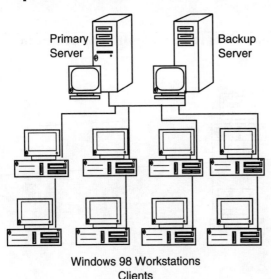

Primary Server

Backup Server

Windows 98 Workstations
Clients

station from which to manage the network and, in many cases, use dial-up remote access from outside of the office.

With client/server networking, multiple users have access to applications that reside on a server. You save money by installing a network copy of the application instead of multiple individual copies. Plus you have control over that application's settings and configuration.

You can use client/server technology to provide and control users' access to the Internet. You can enable everyone to connect or just a few; with the right software, you can even monitor and track users' use of the Net. Client/server networking also enables you to provide resources to customers, users, and others over the Internet and protect your data and resources from users of the Internet.

You can also establish an intranet (internal web site for your company's use only) on which you can publish and update information quickly and efficiently for everyone connected to your network. Publish company rules and guidelines, expense forms, worksheets, customer information, and more to help everyone in the company get the data they need quickly and efficiently.

Another possibility is an extranet, on which you publish files for customers, trading partners, and other specified external users. Advertise your latest services and products, publicize the latest technologies in your business, or broadcast news and interesting facts to those you designate with permission to view the extranet.

> **NOTE**
> Naturally, there are problems that can occur when you use a client/server network, such as security issues, heavy network traffic, slow server response time, server crashes, and such. Many of these problems can be solved by the network operating system you use. NT Server, for example, incorporates various utilities and controls that help you alleviate these and other common client/server problems. There are also many third-party utilities you can purchase to help you manage and control your network.

Choosing a Network Operating System

If you already have an NOS in place, you may want to preserve that system simply because you know it. However, if that NOS is not meeting your needs, you should consider finding one that does. Several network operating systems are

Enterprise Networking

In an enterprise network, all data from any network in your corporation is available to the users on all other networks, as long as the user has appropriate permissions and rights. In an enterprise network, more resources for data, files, images, libraries, and other information are available to more users. Management can watch all aspects of the company—factory, warehouse, customer service, accounting, production, and so on.

In addition to the convenience and often necessity of enterprise networking, administration of such a network can be a nightmare. Problems arise from the management of hundreds of servers and thousands of users. Think about the permissions and rights, replication and backup, print management, and so on for just one small LAN and then multiply that by 10 or 20.

Another consideration with enterprise networking is keeping connections across long distances. ISDN or T1 line problems and network traffic and bottlenecks could keep a team of administrators and technicians busy. Add to these factors the use of different hardware and software across the enterprise; maintenance, upgrades, troubleshooting, compatibility, for example, can all cause problems with communications and everyday functions.

To begin to resolve these obvious problems with enterprise networking, you'll of course need administrators you can depend on in each location. Delegation of power and control is a definite must in this situation. Additionally, a good network operating system can help alleviate some of the enterprise networking obstacles. Configuring an NOS (Network Operating System) for enterprise networking means you'll need a way of establishing security measures between sites, as well as network monitoring utilities, replication capabilities, common protocols, a wide variety of network client types, scalability for growth potential, and centralized management of network resources.

available, such as NT Server, Novell NetWare, and so on. Before you decide on the one you plan to use or upgrade to, consider what it is that you want from your operating system.

Consider first the type of connections you'll make—LAN or WAN, via the Internet, attached to UNIX or Macintosh system, and so on. If you have special needs for the network communications, then you want to choose an NOS that accommodates those needs. For example, you would need a full complement of networking components to attach to different networking systems: TCP/IP protocol for attaching to the Internet, for use with intranet/extranet applications, or for UNIX connectivity. You'll need AppleTalk for Macintosh connectivity; PPTP (Point-to-Point Tunneling Protocol) for VLAN (Virtual LAN) networking; DLC (Data Link Control) for network-attached printers, and so on. The NOS should have Internet services like FTP, Gopher, and World Wide Web; browser compatibility; an HTML editor; and such.

You'll also need administration tools for creating and managing users, system editing and management, event tracking and reporting, remote administration, licensing management, diagnostic tools, backup application, and network client administration. Finally, the NOS should have an easy-to-use interface so your administration will be effortless as well as effective.

NOTE

You may need to choose a specific NOS in order to run a vertical application written specifically for your business. Often, corporations require certain software and that software must run on one NOS only.

Defining an NOS

An NOS (Network Operating System) is the software used to connect computers and other devices, share resources, transfer files, and perform other network services and activities. The NOS is installed to one or more server computers and client software is installed to the workstation computers that will attach to the server(s). Server software makes the computer available to other PCs on the network. Workstation software puts the PC on the network and reroutes data over the network if needed.

An NOS performs the following services:

• Controls the operation of the network—who uses it and when, resources users have access to, and which network resources are available.

Moves data around, redirecting it to a client, server, or other resource.

• Provides the administrative tools you can use to add users, modify resources, and otherwise control the network.

Supports file and record tracking and locking.

Provides security features.

Enables users to share data and resources.

Microsoft's NT Server

NT Server provides a flexible, efficient, and useful client/server network. Windows as a graphical interface is common and popular in the PC world today and it makes network administration easy, especially if you're familiar with Windows.

NT presents many features that are handy with modern networks, such as remote dial-up access, networking protocols and clients, tracking of network events, a performance optimizer, security features, and more. Installation and configuration of NT Server as well as administrative components are fairly easy to learn and control. Following are some more features and advantages of NT Server:

- NT Server is a high-performance file and print server and a powerful applications server. Users can run applications on their local workstations or from NT Server safely and efficiently.

- NT includes an email application, Web browser, a World Wide Web server, and TCP/IP for Internet access.

- Windows is a common platform, meaning there are many compatible products available from both Microsoft and other vendors, such as Lotus, Symantec, and such.

- NT Server works with a variety of client operating systems: MS-DOS, Windows 3.x, Windows 95, Windows NT Workstation, OS/2, UNIX, and Macintosh.

- NT works with a variety of hardware types: Intel, Alpha, MIPS, and RISC-based platforms.

- Scalability enables you to expand the number of clients and servers effectively.

- Built-in tape backup utility enables easy backup of files and data.

NT Server also offers many tools and utilities that ease network administration. These tools enable you to manage user access to the network, manage printers and other resources, log and track security breaches, attach to the Internet, and more.

The User Manager for Domains enables the administrator to enter users for authentication, assign passwords, configure permissions and limitations, and otherwise manage the user's access to the network. Figure 2.3 shows the User Manager for Domains with a listing of users and groups. Groups are made up of

Figure 2.3 Defining users' permissions and limits with the User Manager gives the administrator control over resources.

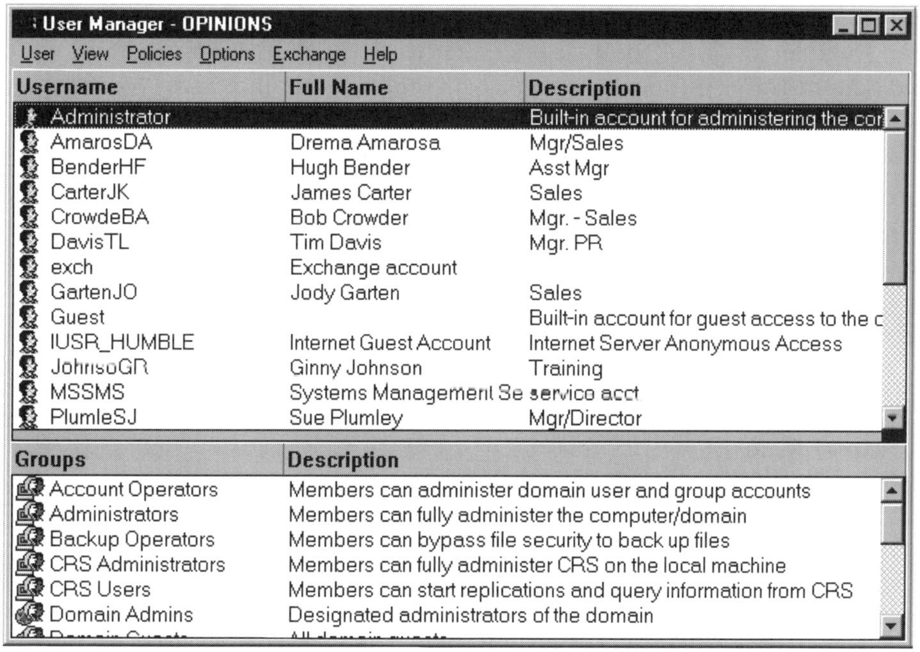

preconfigured and new sets of people with like permissions and limits. By grouping users, the administrator makes it easier to assign rights to multiple people.

NT provides many applications to manage the network. The NT Explorer enables you to display, copy, rename, create, delete, move, and otherwise manage files and directories on the server. The Command prompt allows DOS access to the server and a full set of commands provides the tools needed to work successfully using the DOS interface.

The Internet Explorer is a Web browser included with the operating system. Access Web pages, search engines, hypertext links, and such while exploring the Internet. Microsoft Exchange enables you to communicate over the Internet and over your own network.

Many other features are available with NT Server to make network administration less work than it could be. If you're used to a Windows environment, or if you want to explore a competent and beneficial network operating system, give NT Server a try.

Novell's NetWare

Novell NetWare has been a popular network operating system for years and is the most common NOS used today. NetWare is a 32-bit operating system suitable for large, multisegment networks and includes a set of user and administrator utilities that feature a graphical user interface (versions 4.x and later).

NetWare also has features that ensure the integrity of data on the network, such as protecting data against surface defects, redundant copies of system data, disk duplexing and mirroring, and so on. Novell's NDS (Novell Directory Services) provide a single, network-based view of all services on the network and the NDS database can be distributed through replication for immediate access to the network resources.

Other features included with NetWare are as follows:

- Graphical utilities (in later versions of NetWare) for administering the network.

- Sharing of files and other resources among clients using Windows NT, Windows 95, Windows 3.1, UNIX, OS/2, Macintosh, and DOS.

- GroupWise (included with NetWare 4.x and later), which enables greater collaboration through messaging, calendaring, and information management. Email is possible internally and externally as users access the Internet more and more.

- Multisite LAN and enterprise network management tools that enable the network to expand as your business grows.

- A backup program and virus protection to protect the network from bugs and disasters.

IntraNetWare is a reliable intranet platform that has all the services you need to access the Internet and create your own intranet. It also includes the NetWare distributed services, such as security, multiprotocol routing, messaging, Web publishing, and file and print services. IntraNetWare includes Netscape Navigator as its browser, FTP services, and print services for UNIX.

NetWare also includes many administrative tools that can make managing a network easier. Novell Application Launcher provides easy management of applications on the network and NetWare Multiprotocol Router enables direct connection to the Internet. Novell's Easy Administration Tool makes administrative tasks, such as adding users, printers, groups, and applications, easier.

Banyan VINES

VINES (VIrtual NEtworking Software) is an NOS from Banyan Systems that is based on a special version of UNIX System V operating system. VINES provides all server functions and offers many options for connecting to minicomputers, mainframes, and other network file servers. VINES supports up to four network interface cards per server for any topology. It also manages protocol binding and translations required between the network interface cards for routing to different LAN segments. VINES provides a complete set of administration tools, and workstations can run DOS, Windows, UNIX, OS/2, and Macintosh. VINES is especially handy on large LANs and WANs with multiple file servers.

Banyan's VINES NOS, based on TCP/IP, offers file and print sharing, security standard communications support, and easy resource management. VINES' StreetTalk Explorer is a graphical user interface that enables easy management capabilities. Among its weak points, VINES is limited in scalability, provides only adequate failover or support of fault-tolerant configurations, provides less client support than other NOSs. VINES lacks auditing features and is not certifiable as either B2- or C2-compliant security wise.

Other Network Operating Systems

NT and NetWare are the most popular NOSs; however, there are several other possibilities from which you can choose. IBM LAN Server and UNIX are additional network operating systems you might consider.

IBM's LAN Server supplies file and print services, although directory and security services are limited. Its network management tools are also limited and multiprotocol routing doesn't exist for LAN Server. Although it does supply remote access, LAN Server offers limited host connectivity and fault tolerance, and no document management or storage management services.

UNIX is a 32-bit multitasking operating system that uses the TCP/IP set of protocols. UNIX is available on a variety of hardware, from PCs to Cray super-computers. It is also available in related forms, such as AIX that runs on IBM workstations, A/UX that is a graphical version for Macintosh, and Solaris from SunSoft that runs on Intel processors.

PLANNING NETWORK STRATEGIES

During the planning stages, you need to decide what you want from your network. In Chapter 1, "Preliminary Groundwork," you took inventory of your current system and your needs; now you can apply those needs to your networking goals to form a clear strategy for building a serviceable and profitable network. As part of your networking strategies, you should decide on a set of naming conventions—servers, directories, and so on. You also should plan your users' position on the network along with any limitations or special access.

In this chapter, you learn to do the following:

- Define a network's uses and outline your goals for the network.

- Outline a naming convention for sites, servers, directories, files, and users.

- Organize users of the network by defining position, rights, and limits.

Forming Networking Goals

After gathering and sorting through information about your current network, or after determining what is needed to build a new network (as described in Chapter 1, "Preliminary Groundwork"), you'll have an excellent basis on which to begin work. Decisions about networking types, network operating systems, client operating systems, hardware, software, and so on, will be easier because you know what is needed to make your network efficient and practical. Using your inventory of current equipment and software, you can determine what you need to add to the system by considering what you want from your network.

You must first determine the functions you want your network to perform—sharing files, sharing printers and other peripherals, providing access to the Internet, and so on. Defining network uses will help you decide the type of equipment you need.

Additionally, there are certain goals you will set forth for your network, your users, and yourself. You will, for instance, want your network to be reliable. A network must also be secure. Consider these objectives when planning the layout and equipment for your network.

Defining the Network's Uses

Define the functions of your network to ascertain the hardware and software you will need. Do you want your users to primarily share accounting files? Do you have one office that would benefit from contact with another office in another city? Do you want to sell goods and services over the Internet? Determine how you will use the network and combine that information with your inventory list to plan the changes and additions to your current system.

Following are some common functions of a network. You can use these and add to the list to ascertain your networking needs.

Shared information within workgroups or departments.   List the type of information you want to be shared, such as databases, spreadsheets, accounting, customer information, or even word processing documents.

Improved corporate communications.   Many applications exist for communication within the company. Email promotes a better working relationship between coworkers, and attaching files to email saves workers time and effort. Real-time meeting software enables users to brainstorm ideas, question and suggest concepts, and get feedback from their peers quickly. Groupware applications enable the quick and easy distribution of documents among many users electronically.

Improved customer service.   Disseminate information via email, over an extranet, or over the Internet to your customers; gather data from customers via account status, ordering info, vendor parts lists, for example.

Improved productivity.   Sharing files and resources electronically saves your employees' time and enables them to freely distribute information to each other.

Improved security.   In a network, you can limit access to sensitive data, limit the use of certain files and directories, appoint resources to specific uses, and so on.

Faster backups.   Backing up your data over the network is quick and easy. You can back up data files from one server to another, from a workstation to a server, or from a workstation to another workstation.

Using network connections makes backing up faster than with a tape device. One problem, however, is that unless you're backing up to a computer in another building, your backup is being stored on-site and that increases chances of losing everything, say, in a fire or flood.

Outlining Goals

The ultimate goal of your network is efficiency—users must be able to quickly and consistently access network resources, administration of the network should be simple, there should be only a minimum amount of downtime, and so on. You can use some hardware and software to get the most from your network; you also can apply policies and guidelines to help reach your efficiency goals. Your network should be reliable, consistent, safe and secure, and serviceable to your company. Consider the following when planning to add to your inventory of current hardware and software.

Reliability

Server performance, fault tolerance, and backup and recovery systems are consequential in building and maintaining a reliable network. As you build or replace equipment within your network, consider the benefits of redundancy, backups, and superior equipment. You'll save money in the long run, experience less downtime, and insure an efficient and effective network in your company.

You need a server with the appropriate power and processor, RAM (Random Access Memory), disk space, and so on to run the network operating system efficiently. Consider the growth of your company when purchasing or upgrading a server computer. Purchasing equipment that is a bit more expensive means it will likely last longer and be more reliable; for example, inexpensive RAM chips can often cause problems in your applications and processing. Be careful when choosing a network operating system, as well; find an NOS that provides your network with the appropriate tools and utilities you need to track server performance, manage security, and perform other administrative tasks the way you want it to.

In building fault tolerance into your network, you insure continued system operation in the event of individual equipment failures. Redundant elements—such as RAID (Redundant Array of Inexpensive, or Integrated, Disks), mirroring, or duplicate servers—mean your system can bypass faults automatically and your network keeps working. Supplying a UPS (Uninterruptable Power Supply) for each server, critical peripherals (such as printers), and for certain important workstations can also help to make your network stable. Although it may seem expensive and perhaps even unnecessary to provide redundancy measures, you'll be glad you did the first time a server goes down or a hard drive crashes.

Backup and recovery are perhaps among the most important measures you can take to make your network dependable. Files often become corrupted or lost, mistakes can happen, hard drives go bad, a user may try to sabotage your data, and many other things can go wrong with your data and information. A reliable backup is worth more than your entire system if you cannot get to that one file you need. Create a backup schedule and stick to it. As important as backing up your data is, recovery is just as important. You should test all backups to make sure you'll be able to recover your data. Backing up is important, but only if the backup is dependable.

A reliable, dependable system means a steady workflow, saved time and money, and higher user confidence.

Practical User Management

An efficient network enables users to access resources when they need them. It is important, for example, that the server runs efficiently and contains all applications, services, and such that the user needs. It's also important that each individual user's computer has the appropriate client software, network hardware, and assigned rights or permissions. Additionally, you must deal with new users, changed user configurations, and so on; train users; and anticipate the growth of your user community.

Installation and configuration of desktop equipment is a must; if the network user doesn't have the hardware and/or software he needs, he cannot access the network and valuable work time is lost. Consider upgrades for operating systems, browsers, groupware, suite applications, and such as a necessity for users to keep up with the technology. Also, hardware must be upgraded each time a software upgrade or network upgrade takes place. Don't forget troubleshooting problems users have with the new equipment and/or programs as well.

You will need to maintain user accounts by adding new usernames, deleting usernames that are no longer at your company, updating passwords and permissions, setting profiles, and so on. Maintaining accounts keeps the network and data secure by establishing who may or may not access certain resources.

Additionally, you will want to train users in proper procedures of using the network; this saves time and effort later in having to correct mistakes and disasters. Prepare, for instance, user guidelines governing resources, directories, files, printers, and the like. Supply users with a list of contacts or a help desk they can call for help. Perhaps even prepare inservice classes, schedule training during regular work hours, or pay employees to attend night classes at a local college. The time and money you invest in user training will pay off in fewer problems during the regular work day.

> **NOTE**
>
> When training managers and staff, consider cross-training—sales staff might manage the help desk, network managers might train with the end users, and so on. Benefits of this strategy include improved network management, stronger employee relationships, more effective problem solving, and a boost in morale. Also, in the long run, it will be easier to move employees into other departments as the work flow changes.

Monitor server and other resource performance to insure users get the most from the network equipment. Some NOSs provide monitors to help you with this task, or you can purchase a third-party application that lets you track usage and performance.

And finally, design your network keeping anticipated user growth in mind. Plan for increased server capacity, network traffic, available resources, and such before adding users to the network.

Plan for the Future

You must set up your network with an eye toward the future. Installing one server that handles your current users but cannot handle 10 more users is a waste of time and resources. Consider not only additional users added to your network, but other factors as well. Directory space, file storage, backup storage, application licensing, remote connectivity, Internet access, network traffic, peripheral services, and such will pertain to a growing network. Servers will need added memory and disk space, networking hardware will need to handle more traffic, and new services will be added as your network grows.

Make sure the NOS you choose is scalable, that is, the program can easily handle additions to the network. Naturally, the hardware you purchase also must lend itself to growth and development.

Naming Conventions

On first look, naming conventions may not appear to be one of the major networking strategies that needs to be well planned; however, a little planning now means your network will be better organized when it is set up and especially as it grows. Think about it—if you name your servers, directories, users in an obscure manner, these elements will be harder to find, configure, and control as new servers, directories, and users are added to the network.

Take a little bit of time now to plan how you will name the important elements of the network. First, make a list of those elements that will need to be named. Following are a few ideas:

WAN and its segments

LAN segments

Domains, departments, or buildings

Hubs and routers, cabling closets, and such

Servers (and service accounts)

Directories, files, programs

Printers and other peripherals

Users

Depending on the NOS you choose, your networking configuration, and any server applications you install, you may need to name more or fewer network components than are listed here. For example, if you choose to implement any of the BackOffice servers, you may need to invent Organization, Site, Store, Database, and other name types.

Remember, your goal is to be consistent; create naming conventions that won't be affected by organizational changes and can easily expand with the company and the network.

Site and Server Names

Again, depending on the NOS and servers you install to your network, you may need to name sites (or areas, organizations, buildings, domains, or other such entity) as well as naming servers. If the network grows, the naming form should be similar for several reasons. It helps users locate servers and resources if there is a consistent naming convention; administrators find it easier to locate and manage sites and servers if the naming convention is uniform; and as always, organization is key to a serviceable and successful network.

Consider locations for sites, using the name of a county, city, or region, for example. You may alternatively want to use a building name or number, as long as the network segment or server is likely to remain in that building. You could use the function of the office, or some other unique and easily recognizable scheme for sites as well.

As for server names, you should plan these, too. Server names are generally required to be unique. Try departments, functions, or geographical locations for server names; for example, servers could be named Sales, Graph, Accnt, and so on, or Pitts (for Pittsburgh), Hersh (for Hershey), and Phili (for Philadelphia). You can even add numbers or other identifying letters to names of servers or sites: Email4, Print4, or Files3. Notice the same number of characters are used in each of the names; this is to make the display of servers easier to view, less confusing on screen.

File and Directory Names

When planning directory and file naming conventions, you must consider not only administrative tasks but the user as well. Some directories and files will be constantly in use and if the user cannot easily locate these elements, you'll find you have more administrative duties to perform.

Directories

While planning for the directory structure to suit the users' needs, you must also consider your security requirements. Decide which files and directories are sensitive or private and create a directory structure that limits access to these directories. You'll also use security permissions or rights provided by the NOS to protect these files, but make sure their placement on the server affords protection, too.

Start with a basic outline of directories that are needed on each server. Ask department heads to contribute to the list—which directories do they need to store their department's data, for example. Include applications, such as groupware shared folders, mailboxes, data everyone can access, users' home directories, and so on.

Additionally, consider these suggestions:

Provide enough directories for file storage. Consider providing at least 25MB per user, if possible. Also, think about shared files and folders, chat and meeting areas, and so on.

Create a separate directory for applications, configuration files, drivers, shared data, and personal directories.

Make the structure easy to understand and navigate. The easier users can find the directories they need, the less wasted time and administrative headaches.

Don't go too deep with the directory structure. If users have to open directory after directory after directory, they may get frustrated, make mistakes, or get lost. Keep directory structures shallow.

Be sure that all servers have a similar, or consistent, directory structure. This will allow users to easily navigate any server on the network.

> **NOTE**
>
> Stick with application default directories and file-naming conventions so upgrades and procuring outside technical help will be easier.

Files

File-naming conventions make files on the server easier to display, recognize, and organize. When all file names are, for example, only eight letters long or all files use an extension, the users can pick one file from many much more quickly. You might ask users to name all files by date (day and/or month) or by the initials of the creator plus a numbering scheme; depending on your business, file names could use a customer's name (first five letters of the last name, for instance) or a purchase order or invoice number, or any combination of these ideas.

You must also decide whether to allow users to name files on their workstations their own way or to follow your naming conventions. If you have trouble creating a set of naming conventions, ask managers and/or users to help.

> **NOTE**
>
> Some network operating systems let you use long file names (NT, for example), but remember that not all client computers may be able to take advantage of long file names (DOS, for instance). Consider this when forming your own naming conventions.

Finally, ask yourself the following questions when planning your file naming conventions:

Which files can be stored on individual workstations?

Which applications can be run from servers and which from workstations? Can those files be stored on the workstations?

Do I want users to back up their hard drives to the server?

Are users allowed to install programs to the server?

Usernames

Within most NOSs, users must be entered with a password and a username or nickname. You'll also find the need to enter users for mailboxes, authentication into various servers, and so on. Once again, create a naming convention for all users so names are easy to display and locate on screen and so organizing users will be more efficient.

A common method of identifying usernames is to begin with the first five letters of a last name and then add the first and/or second initial. Sue Plumley would then be PlumlSJ; Hugh Bender would be BendeHR. Besides the convenience of all names being the same length, names displayed alphabetically are easier to locate for modification, deletion, or relocation.

Defining and Organizing Users

A user is anyone who can log on to the network—an administrator, an assistant, a workstation user—anyone to whom you grant access. You can grant access to all resources on the network, to one server, or to only certain files and directories. You can limit user access by limiting the hours he or she can get on the network; you can permit a user to access certain resources, such as a printer or modem.

Although it is early in the project, you must begin to think about your users and how you will handle them once the network operating system is loaded. Before anyone can access the network, you must define that person to the network operating system. The easiest way to begin defining and organizing your users is to start with a list of usernames.

Organizing Users

Your first step is to collect a list of all personnel who will be accessing the network. You can have the manager of each department list his or her staff, or one of your administrative assistants can do the job. If you already have a network in place, you can get the list of users from the current system.

It would be helpful if, beside each user's name, you could list his or her title in the company and a brief description of the job he or she does. This information will help you when you assign rights and permissions. Make sure all employees are listed, including managers, supervisors, administrators, and so on.

Next, have the list organized in a hierarchy, from the top of the company to the bottom. Essentially, have people with similar jobs listed together; for example, all administrative assistants should be listed one after the other. This way, you can apply a group organization to these users without searching the list over and over and missing someone.

Defining Users

When your list is complete, you can define each user and group. Begin with the groups and work your way down to the users. You will find you can assign rights to a group, put individuals in the group, and have no need to add to each individual's list of rights. You'll save time both now and later when you enter the names into the NOS.

Groups

Begin by marking each group of users who have similar duties or needs on the network; in most NOSs, it's easier to assign rights and permissions to a group than to individuals. You assign a group name, group rights, and a group password that you reveal only to members of the group to help limit access to certain tasks and contents on the server.

Name your groups so you can classify users within them; you may have an Assistant's group, a Print Manager's group, an Accounting group, a Sales or Service group, and so on. Next, beside each group's name, list the rights and limits needed for the members of that group to perform their duties. You can list rights, logon hours, dial-in privileges, directories the group can access, and so on. Following is an example of what your list might look like:

Administrative Assistant

Limited control over the server

Create and delete directories

Create shares

Manage printing

All hours accessible

Remote access

Sales Group

Log on and off server

Read and write access to Sale/Cust/Acct2 files

Manage own files and print jobs

Logon hours: M–S 7 A.M. to 7 P.M.

Rights and Permissions

Each NOS provides different rights, permissions, and authorizations to the system and its resources. Additionally, each NOS enables you to mark these limits for your users differently. You'll want to check your NOS's documentation to see how rights are defined; however, following are a few common rights and permissions you may encounter. Use this list to help you plan your groups and users at this time, then modify the list when you enter your groups and users into the system. Generally, rights and permissions can be applied to both groups and users.

Log on to the server. Reserved for administrators and assistants with such privileges as creating and deleting users, managing printers, backing up the system, and so on.

Access the server from the network. Grant this right to anyone who needs a file, directory, or other resource from the server.

Manage security. Reserved for administrators and assistants.

Shut down the system. Reserved for administrators and assistants.

Back up and restore files and directories. Generally granted to a set of assistants who perform full system backups of the servers.

Add users to network. Reserved for administrative assistants who manage users: add and delete usernames, grant permissions to users, and so on.

Read, write, access, execute, change. These are permissions assigned to files and/or directories, thereby limiting access to those who have been granted permissions for those files/directories.

Finally, most NOSs include default groups that have predefined rights and permissions. For example, members of a Print Operator group have the right to manage printers, delete print jobs, change print job priority, and so on.

Members of an Administrators group have permissions and rights to make any and all changes to the server; limit the number of people you assign to this group. Administrators may try to sabotage the system but what's more likely to happen is someone accidentally deletes, modifies, or adds something to the server that proves devastating to business.

Users

After adding users to each group to define their general rights and permissions, you can highlight those users who may have special needs on the network; access to sensitive files, for example. List any additional rights for those users. Then select any users you want to apply special limits to and list those limits; for example, you may want to limit the hours of access or dial-in rights to certain users.

Also consider such issues as passwords, account disqualification and expiration, and such. If you want complete control over your users, you can assign passwords. It is, however, easier to assign everyone the same password and require that each person change the password upon login.

Consider the following password and account policies:

- Require a password to be a certain minimum length, such as five letters, so that it is more difficult to guess.

- Limit the use of the same password over and over, for security's sake.

- Set password expiration dates so users must change their passwords periodically, say every two or three months.

- Lock out a user after a certain number of failed logon attempts, say four or five, to keep hackers out.

- Set auditing on logons so that you have a log of attempts at security breaches.

NOTE

After you get your system up and running, you should have an assistant create some user guidelines for the password and account rules you've defined. For instance, make sure users understand they should not give their password to anyone, that they have limited access hours and resource permissions, and so on. Informed users are more accepting of the policies when they're informed of the policies up front.

NETWORKING TECHNOLOGIES

In preparing to implement a network, you may plan and install the networking hardware yourself. On the other hand, if you're not familiar with cabling, hubs, routers, and other types of equipment you'll need, you may hire a consultant to help plan, purchase, and install your networking hardware. Either way, you should have a basic understanding of the technology's terms, uses, speeds, appropriateness, and so on.

In this chapter, you learn about the following:

- Network cards, hubs, switches, and routers

- Topologies, cabling, and backbones

- Drivers and protocols

- Preparing people

Additionally, I've included some recommendations and considerations for networking and server equipment and configuration.

Networking Hardware

There are many types of networking hardware that you'll need to understand before you start to build your network. You may choose to outsource the cabling and installation of the hardware or you may supervise an inhouse employee. Either way, you should understand the basic concepts of connecting a computer to the network and the equipment required to perform that task. This section outlines and defines the common networking hardware you'll need. This chapter describes more about upgrading and purchasing hardware.

Network Interface Cards

A network interface adapter card (NIC) plugs into the server or workstation to help the operating system control the flow of information over the network. A cable connects the card to the network, which in turn connects all the network interface cards in the network.

You choose a network card depending on its speed, expense, and the topology of the network. You must make sure the NIC is compatible with the computer's operating system (OS) and the NOS. Check the OS and NOS documentation as well as the card's documentation.

You must also match the network interface card to the topology of the network. Topology is the map of the network—the direction in which the cables run between workstations, servers, gateways, and such—and the path data takes to get from one user to another on the network. (See the section, *Networking Software*, later in this chapter.) The NIC must be compatible with the topology you're using on the network.

The four common types of network cards are 10Mbit (Megabit=one million bits), 100Mbit, fiber, and wireless. 10Mbit is used with a 10BaseT topology. The use of 10Mbit technology is declining because of its slow speeds; it's okay for small office use, but still not recommended. 10Mbit is relatively inexpensive.

The 100Mbit card is used with 100BaseT topology and is ten times faster than a 10Mbit card. 100Mbit is perfect for using with large data files, video or sound files, images, and such. The 100Mbit card is more expensive than the 10Mbit and installing the cabling also costs more because 100Mbit cable must be certified.

> **NOTE**
>
> To use a 100Mbit card, the PC must have a PCI (Peripheral Component Interconnect) slot, an Intel specification that defines a local bus allowing up to 10 PCI-compliant expansion cards to be plugged into the computer.

If you're on a tight budget, you can purchase 10/100Mbit cards that can attach to either a 10Mbit or a 100Mbit network. Use the 10Mbit hub to start with and when you need it, you can add the 100Mbit hub to the system to make the network a 100BaseT.

Fiber cards use FDDI (Fiber Distributed Data Interface) networking and follow the ring topology. You'll need a PCI slot for the fiber card, fiber cabling, and fiber hubs. Because of the special equipment, fiber is very expensive to purchase and to install.

Wireless connections enable you to connect without using conventional cabling. Instead, you use infrared or high-frequency radio signals for the connection. High-frequency light waves (infrared) transmit data between two computers up to 80 feet apart using an unobstructed path. High-frequency radio signals transmit between two computers up to 130 feet apart.

Wireless LANs (WLANs) are employed in many vertical markets: retail, healthcare, finance, warehousing, and so on. Wireless technology provides an untethered link to the world network, enabling people to access all of the information their wired counterparts are accustomed to. This type of connection is better used for only special situations where nothing else will do. Wireless connections are expensive and not very dependable.

Hubs, Switches, Bridges, and Routers

In addition to using network interface cards and cabling, you need additional equipment to connect the computers of your network. Depending on the configuration of the network, you might use hubs, routers, bridges, and/or switches.

Hubs

You'll use hubs to connect multiple cables from the workstations. A hub modifies transmission signals and allows the network to be extended to accommodate additional workstations. There are two types of hubs: an *active* hub amplifies transmission signals to extend cable length, and a *passive* hub splits the transmission signal, allowing additional workstations to be added to the network.

Figure 4.1 shows how a hub extends a network. For example, each hub can connect six more computers or five computers and another hub. The switch in the figure works to make sure data moves through the appropriate port to its destination.

Switches

Switches are multiport devices that create temporary paths for routing information over a LAN. Switching provides better performance than routers because it provides more efficient use of the datalink layer and its technology. Switches do not have security, filtering, or WAN options, but switches do deliver faster throughput than any bridge or router on the market.

There are three types of switching: *configuration*, *frame*, and *cell*. Configuration switching is also called *port switching*; it operates at the physical layer and is transparent to upper-layer protocols. Configuration switching enables individual ports to be assigned, when the device is initially attached to the network, to individual segments within a multisegmented network hub.

Figure 4.1 Use hubs to extend the reach of the network.

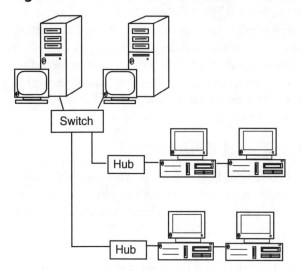

Frame switching operates in the data-link layer and forwards the packet to the output port of the destination computer. It supports both Ethernet and token ring. Ethernet frame switching supports shared or dedicated 10Mbps or 100Mbps connections. Cell switching is a high-speed transfer system designed to carry voice, video, and data traffic. ATM (Asynchronous Transfer Mode) switches can simultaneously support multiple transmissions, eliminating bottlenecks.

Routers

You might also use a *router*, which is an intelligent device that routes data packets to the correct LAN segment. A router comprehends that there are multiple ways of sending a packet between two computers, and based on the network addressing information in the packet, the router decides the most optimal route.

Routers use a set of routing protocols that govern the exchange of data between nodes. Both the sending node and the receiving node must use the same routing protocol to successfully communicate; alternatively, they can use a protocol converter that enables the two nodes to exchange packets. Routers enable data packets to be dispatched between dissimilar networks (Ethernet and token ring, for example) without being translated.

Most routers can also provide dial-in ports for telecommuters or asynchronous dumb terminals and modems, create dial-up connections between LANs and filter traffic, and enable you to remotely manage your network. Figure 4.2

Figure 4.2 Use a router to speed the transmission of data and make transmissions more efficient.

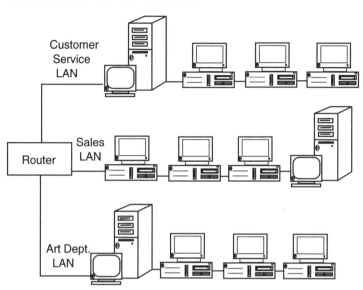

illustrates the use of a router in a network. If, for example, a computer in the Art Department sends data packets to a computer in the Customer Service LAN, the router sends the packets directly to the Customer Service LAN and blocks the Sales LAN from the transmission.

Bridges

A *bridge* is another hardware device that connects computers so they can exchange data. You use a bridge, in particular, to connect networks that use different wiring or network protocols. Figure 4.3 shows how a bridge connects two LANs using different protocols, TCP/IP and IPX.

Adding a bridge to a LAN divides it into two networks. The bridge reads packets and allows them to pass from one network to another only if the address is not in the local segment. Using a bridge reduces the amount of traffic on the LAN and improves performance.

Topologies

Topologies are methods of arranging and connecting computers on a network. Each topology has advantages and disadvantages. Of the available topologies,

Figure 4.3 Use a bridge to transmit data between dissimilar networks.

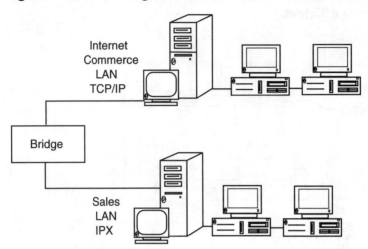

spanning tree (star) and ring are the most efficient and reasonable for modern LANs.

Spanning Tree (Star)

The star topology connects computers through a central hub and the hub distributes signals to all connecting cables. Servers and workstations are connected to the hub, each with a separate cable. The hub modifies transmission signals so each device receives input over the network.

10BaseT and 100BaseT use a modified star topology, or spanning tree (see Figure 4.4). Each hub and its connections form a star, but you can connect to other hubs in a branching design. Use a hub to protect each cable connected to it from all other cables; if one cable is damaged, for example, only one computer on the network is affected. Different sizes of hubs are available: One hub can connect 8 computers or hubs and another may connect 24 or 48 devices. Spanning tree is expensive since hubs cost so much, especially for 100BaseT networks.

Ring Network

In the ring topology, the computer sends a message, or token, that controls the right to transmit. The message is continuously passed from one node to the next in one direction only in a ring around the network.

When a node has data to transmit, it captures the message, adds the message and destination address, then sends the token on. If the address matches a

Which to Use?

The decision on whether to use a bridge, router, or switch depends on your specific needs; however, here are a few clarifications to help you decide.

Switch or Router?

Only one communication at a time can take place in a routing environment; switching enables communications by allowing messages to be routed from one port on the switch to another, so there is no wait time.

Bridge or Router?

Routers differ from bridges in that they calculate the best path for the data to take and they can constantly adjust to changing network conditions. If you used a bridge between a LAN and a remote telephone connection, for example, the bridge would drop the packet if it determined it wasn't meant for the remote connection, instead of sending it back to the LAN as a router would.

Routers are more processing-intensive than bridges and their processing speeds are not usually as high. Routers are also capable of much more sophisticated path selection, thus improving the efficiency of the network.

A *brouter* may be an alternative choice. A brouter is essentially a router that can also bridge. The brouter first checks a packet to see if it fits into the brouter's algorithms for choosing paths; if it doesn't fit, rather than dropping the packet, the brouter bridges the packet using layer two information.

node's address, the message is accepted; if not, the node regenerates the message and places it back on the network, where it travels to the next node in the ring.

Ring networks can cover greater distances than star networks; however, if there is a failure somewhere in the network card, wiring, or other hardware problem, the data cannot pass until the problem is fixed.

Cabling

There are various types of cables, or wires, you can use to connect your network. You can even use wireless connections; however, these are best used in situations where you cannot run cable or when a long-range connection would be too costly. Cables afford better security and throughput than wireless connections.

Coaxial is fairly inexpensive, but it isn't upgradeable and it runs at speeds no greater than 10Mbit. Additionally, if you have to work on one node, every

Figure 4.4 Spanning tree topology uses hubs to extend the network.

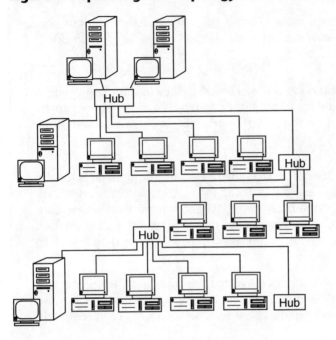

node on the network goes down until the first node is fixed. Coaxial cable is not recommended for most networks.

Twisted-pair cable uses several pairs of wires braided together within a plastic sheath. Electrical signals travel on each wire and are protected from interference by the sheath. Shielded twisted-pair cable (STP) is cable with a foil shield and copper braid surrounding the pairs of wires. STP offers high-speed transmission for long distances and is often associated with token ring networks. Unshielded twisted-pair cable (UTP) contains two or more pairs of twisted copper wires. It's easier to install and less expensive than STP, but it does limit the signaling speeds and uses shorter cable segments.

Of the types of twisted-pair cabling, Category 3 (Cat 3) and Category 5 (Cat 5) are most common. Cat 3 less expensive and less advanced as far as rate of transfer goes. Cat 5 is best for high-speed networking; use Cat 5 with either 10BaseT or 100BaseT.

Fiber optic is a thin glass filament cable that connects to optical equipment on either end. Fiber optic uses light rather than electrical pulses to carry the net-

> **NOTE**
>
> Categories 3, 4, and 5 are also called *levels* and describe performance characteristics of wiring standards. To be safe and to provide for future cabling needs, choose Category 5 UTP, STP, or fiber optic cable for new cable installations.

work signal. The advantage of fiber optic is in its signal strength and its immunity to electrical interference, which gives it the capability of transmitting signals over long distances at very fast speeds. Fiber optic is usually used as a high-speed backbone; a backbone is a cable connecting two or more hubs or two or more LANs.

> **Backbones**
>
> The backbone is the portion of the network that manages the bulk of the traffic. It may connect several different locations or buildings, or other smaller networks. The backbone usually uses a higher-speed protocol than a LAN segment would and often different cabling, such as fiber optic. Two types of backbones are the *collapsed* backbone and the *distributed* backbone.
>
> The collapsed backbone is a segmented network architecture with centralized internetworking. Physical segments from the hubs are *downlinked* via fiber optic cable to central sites, or network centers. This reduces the overall cost of network equipment and its administration. Also, the collapsed backbone design makes the entire network more controllable and easier to manage.
>
> The distributed backbone is a network configuration in which segments are connected by joining each hub with the backbone cable. For example, say there's a three-story building and each floor has its own segment or ring. In a distributed backbone, each segment is connected with a cable to a fourth backbone segment that connects the separate segments' backbones together.

Networking Software

In addition to the networking hardware and the network operating system, you'll also need various networking software to complete the picture.

Hardware drivers are programs that enable hardware to communicate with the rest of the system; without drivers, CD-ROMs, printers, and other peripherals could not work with the other equipment on the network.

Another type of software includes *protocols*. Protocols define the procedures to follow when transmitting and receiving data by defining the format, timing, sequence, and error checking used on the network. Following are descriptions of common networking drivers and protocols.

Drivers

In addition to networking hardware, you'll need some software to insure your peripherals work with the network operating system. Most NOSs supply drivers for peripherals, but you must make sure you have appropriate drivers for your hardware and operating system and that these drivers are the latest drivers developed. Often the drivers that come with an operating system are not the latest and therefore do not work with the most recent server hardware. Check with the manufacturer of the device or the Internet for an updated driver for the following peripherals:

- CD-ROM drives and/or towers

- Sound cards

- UPS

- Backup tape drives

- Optical disk drives

- Print devices

- Modems and/or modem servers

Protocols

There are several types of protocols used in networking; for example, Ethernet and token ring are communications protocols that transfer data from one computer to another. Transport protocols such as TCP/IP or IPX work on a different network layer and insure that messages are delivered, among other things. Following is some common information about these networking protocols.

Communications Protocols

Communications protocols work on the datalink layer of the ISO/OSI (International Standards Organization/Open Systems Interconnection) model for computer-to-computer communications. The data-link layer validates the integrity of the flow of data from one node to another by synchronizing blocks of data and controlling the flow of data. Ethernet is one popular example of a communications protocol; token ring is another.

Ethernet   Ethernet is not only a protocol but it is also a cabling scheme. Its transfer rate is 10Mbit/sec or 100Mbit/sec. Fast Ethernet provides 10 times the bandwidth as Ethernet, plus it includes other features like full-duplex operation and auto-negotiation. Gigabit Ethernet runs 1000Mbps but is considered more of a backbone technology than one for LAN segment connections.

The hardware required for the Ethernet network is fairly inexpensive, except for the hubs and cabling used with the spanning tree topology.

Token Ring   The token ring network and protocol relies on the circulating electronic token passing as its method of communications. A LAN with a ring structure uses token passing to regulate traffic on the network and avoid collision. Token ring runs at 16Mbits and is also more expensive than Ethernet.

Other Communications Protocols   There are two other communications protocols: FDDI and ATM. FDDI is specifically used for fiber optic networks transmitting at a speed of up to 100Mbits per second over a token ring topology. FDDI is suitable for such high-performance clients as engineering workstations, medical imaging, three-dimensional seismic processing, and so on. FDDI also makes a good backbone for linking two LANs together.

ATM (Asynchronous Transfer Mode) is a high-speed networking option usually used for backbones. ATM starts at 25Mbits and goes up to 155Mbits. Speeds of 2.2 Gbits per second are even possible. Although ATM is perfect for integrating disparate networks over large geographical distances, it is very expensive.

Transport Protocols

Transport protocols work on the transport layer of the ISO model for computer-to-computer communications. The transport layer defines protocols for message structure and supervises the validity of the transmission by performing some error checking.

TCP/IP   TCP/IP (Transmission Control Protocol/Internet Protocol) is a set of communications protocols that encompass media access, file transfer, electronic mail, and terminal emulation. TCP/IP is supported by a large number of hardware and software vendors and it's available on many different computers and systems.

Use TCP/IP if you plan to attach your network to the Internet, implement an intranet, or if your network is very large or comprised of many different clients and servers. TCP/IP is routable; however, it isn't easy to configure.

The TCP/IP Protocol Stack

TCP/IP is a set of protocols originally developed in the late 1970s. The set encompasses media access, packet transport, session communications, file transfer, electronic mail, and terminal emulation. TCP/IP is supported by many hardware and software vendors and is available on many different types of computers, from PCs to mainframes.

Following are the most common protocols included with TCP/IP:

TCP (Transmission Control Protocol). A connection-oriented, transport-level protocol.

IP (Internet Protocol). A session-layer protocol that regulates packet forwarding by tracking Internet addresses, routing outgoing messages, and recognizing incoming messages.

PPP (Point-to-Point Protocol). A protocol that provides router-to-router and host-to-network connections over synchronous and asynchronous links.

UDP (User Datagram Protocol). A connectionless, transport-level protocol used with SNMP applications.

SMTP (Simple Mail Transfer Protocol). A protocol for exchanging electronic mail.

FTP (File Transfer Protocol). A protocol for transferring data by dividing information into smaller units and then transferring those units in sequence.

TELNET. A terminal emulation protocol that provides remote terminal-connection services.

SNMP (Simple Network Management Protocol). A standard protocol used to manage and monitor nodes on a network.

NOTE

For more information about TCP/IP, see Stephen Thomas' book, *IPNG and the TCP/IP Protocols: Implementing the Next Generation Internet* (John Wiley & Sons, 1996).

There are many advantages to using TCP/IP. The Domain Name System (DNS) is available; DNS is an electronic addressing system used over the Internet. Point-to-Point Protocol (PPP) is also included with TCP/IP, as is Simple

Network Management Protocol (SNMP) agent for email services. TCP/IP also supports network printing and wide area network browsing. It supports the FDDI, Ethernet, and token ring protocols as well. Finally, TCP/IP includes the following connectivity utilities: finger, FTP, rcp, telnet, and others.

NetBEUI NetBEUI is the Microsoft protocol originally developed for LAN Manager but used with Windows for Workgroups, Windows 95 and 98, NT, and so on. NetBEUI stands for NetBIOS (NETwork Basic Input/Output System) Extended User Interface. NetBIOS is a programming interface for developing client/server applications. NetBIOS can communicate over NetBEUI, TCP/IP, and other protocols.

NetBEUI is perfect for small- to medium-sized networks (2 to 200 computers) in a single location. It's easy to set up and provides good performance. NetBEUI is a fast protocol for a LAN, is self-tuning, affords good error protection, and uses only a small amount of memory. NetBEUI dynamically allocates the memory necessary to process requests made by clients, meaning it uses only memory when it's needed.

NetBEUI also supports dial-up client communications with remote access services so users can dial the server from home or on the road and access the network, and also provides connection-oriented and connectionless data transfer services. It can be used with programs that implement NetBIOS, Network DDE (Dynamic Data Exchange), RPC (Remote Procedure Call) over NetBIOS, and such.

NetBEUI isn't routable, like TCP/IP and IPX, but it does support the token ring form of routing. Routing is a process of directing message packets, or tokens, from a source node to a destination node.

IPX/SPX IPX/SPX (Internet Packet eXchange/Sequenced Packet eXchange) is a protocol generally used with NetWare. NetWare uses the IPX to transfer data between the server and workstation and SPX to provide additional capabilities over IPX, like guaranteeing delivery of data. IPX/SPX can also be used on other network operating systems, such as NT.

Final Considerations

Generally, a network put together hurriedly is a network with a lack of integration among systems and network management tools. Most organizations have diverse hardware, multiple operating systems, and a large number of platform-specific applications. This isn't necessarily the result of poor planning; often it's the result

Some Basic Recommendations

The equipment you choose for networking will depend on your network operating system, your network configuration, the services you plan to provide, number of users, and many other factors. However, following is a simple base from which to start, with a few suggestions for getting the most efficient system you can.

For a server, consider these recommendations:

- Use a Pentium CPU (Central Processing Unit) or Pentium Pro or Alpha.
- Get 128MB RAM at the very least.
- Use PCI cards—ISA (Industry Standard Architecture) or EISA (Extended Industry Standard Architecture) are slower devices.
- Use SCSI hard drives instead of IDE; use disk striping for better I/O (Input/Output) performance and add a RAID controller. SCSI (Small Computer System Interface) throughput is considerably greater than IDE, striping lets you use multiple disks for each I/O transaction, and a RAID card accelerates parity calculations for disk fault-tolerant options. Often RAID 5 controllers are faster than running mere striping.
- Check BIOS (Basic Input/Output System) settings for your motherboard, disk controllers, network cards, and other peripheral devices to make sure they're configured properly.

For the networking hardware:

- Use full-duplex switched 100Mbit networking for all connections if possible, at least for the server backbone. 100Mbit networks offer three times the performance of 10Mbit. Full-duplex operation lets you use all four wiring pairs in Cat 5–8 wire cabling for data transfer.

of too many people governing the network and the lack of a steady budget to purchase equipment needed. The problem is, a great deal of diversity within your network produces many possible points of failure that are hard to troubleshoot.

If you use standard configurations, consistency, and a single network operating system, you'll reduce your administration time, energy, and costs enormously. Upgrade the installed base and retire legacy systems if at all possible; unsupportable configurations and antiquated equipment will just give you headaches. Purchase the highest-performance systems you can to support user requirements. Maintain powerful clients; don't sacrifice performance for manageability.

Also, consider these points:

Centralize and automate management functions.

Use inventory and fault management databases to track problems, history, and resolution logs.

Log and track user problems as they come in.

Use automated backup and software distribution.

Establish desktop and server management policies.

Use a database to track moves, changes, and additions of PCs and servers.

POLICIES AND PROCEDURES

A part of network planning is to devise some policies and procedures that will answer questions as they arise, such as what to do in case of a server crash, or what procedure to follow to repair a printer. Outlining policies before a problem occurs means you'll have the equipment, manpower, and/or game plan ready; thus using less time, effort, and money. Think about policies now as you plan the network so you'll be ready when the network is up and running.

A part of your planning procedure should be to enlist help in implementing your network. There are many ways you can do this, such as delegating tasks and hiring extra help. Establishing a help desk for your users is another way of transferring some of your administrative duties. You should also consider out-sourcing some of the network responsibilities to more experienced and available consultants and technicians.

Finally, another procedure in planning and organization is to prepare the users for the changes to come with the establishment of the network. From the corporate headquarters to the last user, all users should understand why the network is changing and what those changes will mean to them.

In this chapter, you learn the following:

- Some policies to implement in the planning stage to help protect your equipment and network.

- Policies to begin creating for use when the network is up and running.

- How to get help with administrative tasks.

- How to prepare the people you work with for the changes to come.

Preparing Policies

There are certain policies you should implement immediately, as you prepare for the installation or upgrade of your network; and there are policies you will want to implement later, after the network is up and running. All policies should be put in writing and distributed to all users in the company; you may want to email them, send them in the form of a memo, or deliver a hard copy of the policies to your users.

You should also have a meeting with the users, or delegate that responsibility to department managers, to discuss the policies. Explain the reason for the policies and make sure the users understand them. You may also want to take suggestions for new policies from the managers and/or the users.

Planning Policies

As you are planning the network, there are several policies and procedures you might want to distribute. As you read over the following, add any policies or procedures that fit your particular situation.

- All equipment, old and new, should remain in the area to which it was originally assigned. No trading computers or peripherals.

- Users should deliver all software and documentation to a central location.

- Any changes or modifications made to software and/or hardware must be documented during this phase of the deployment.

- Backups are to be made regularly; one copy will be kept off-site while the other copy is kept on-site. Label all backups and test for recovery. Each department is responsible for backing up its own data as an extra precaution.

- Each department is responsible for updating data on its computers and/or server(s), copying drivers and other software needed to install peripherals, and keeping track of all data relating to its work.

- As your workstations and servers go into service, test all installs and configurations before implementing to the entire company.

Security during Planning Stages

Primarily, security related to the planning stage deals with placement of equipment. Keep records and document delivery and location of all new and old equipment. Assign a team to help with this task, if necessary. When new servers are delivered to the office, someone should immediately check them and then place them in a secure area until the computers are set up and ready to be added to the network. A chaotic office with computer boxes crowding the aisles is an easy target for someone needing a new keyboard or monitor.

The same procedures apply to software and peripherals. Make sure assistants staff each department and track incoming equipment and software.

Networking Policies after Implementation

Administrative concerns include human resources, plant operations, user support, project management, daily business support, customer interaction, and business partners' interaction. Hiring, motivating, retaining quality personnel, selecting the right vendors, and supporting the business strategy with technology are all administrative concerns. Each of these tasks requires some sort of policies that govern procedures, processes, conduct, operations, and such.

You don't necessarily need to write all of these policies now; however, you should start planning them as soon as possible. Have department managers jot down ideas as they work; ask users to let the managers know what their problems are with the network, the way things are done within the company, and current policies. You may not find all of their suggestions useful; however, some new and improved policies may result from their efforts.

Disaster recovery is probably one of the most important plans you can make and should be the first policy you devise. If your server(s) should fail, how long would it take to get the company back in full operation? If you've implemented RAID, duplicate servers, or some other form of fault tolerance, you should be able to get your network up and running fairly quickly. If you haven't implemented fault tolerance, you must have a plan for implementing applications, recreating users, attaching clients, setting up the server and the resources, and so on, and you must accomplish these tasks as quickly as possible.

Following is a brief description of other policy subjects to consider:

Security. Decide who can access the LAN, WAN, servers, and/or Internet. Set rights for users—inhouse, remote, and those visiting your Web site, if applicable. Create policies governing sensitive files and data, such as who can access them and who can't, what protections will be put on sensitive data, and what the consequences are for those breaching security. Set a policy for resource permissions—who can use certain resources and who can't, schedules for resource use, limits for use, and so on.

Software deployment. Decide who may install new software and upgrades, which workstations will receive new software first, and where the documentation is to be kept. You might also want to set policy on who decides when it's time to upgrade and who purchases the software.

Maintenance of printers.   Create a policy that states a schedule for regular printer maintenance and cleaning. Decide who performs the maintenance and where is it performed; cleaning a laser printer, for example, is likely to blow black toner everywhere and you don't want that around your computers. Also list who controls the printers and says when they need maintenance, and what do you do when a printer breaks down. State whether replacement printers are available and if so, who should be contacted. Also consider keeping cartridges, toner, and print cables in stock in case something minor happens that can be taken care of in-house.

Backup and recovery.   Assign backup to one person or to a team and make sure within your policy you outline procedures for the backup, testing of the restore, and the restoration of the backup. Testing is so often forgotten and when you desperately need the backup, it's too late to do anything about a bad tape or disk. List in the policy who will back up and when, where the backups will be stored (one copy should be stored off-site), and which files will be backed up.

Servers maintenance.   List how often server drives will be checked, scanned, cleaned, and defragmented. Define any RAID or mirroring procedures, replication schedules included. Determine who will do the upgrades, test upgrades, maintain users, check user directories, clean the files, and so on, as well as schedules and procedures for these tasks.

Email and groupware.   In an email or groupware policy, be careful to outline the type of email or shared documents you will and will not allow; for example, state whether you will allow personal messages and documents, jokes, rumors, nonbusiness-related data, and so on. In groupware-shared folders and documents, outline the types of documents allowed in the folders, who will govern these folders, who is allowed to add or delete documents, and such. Consider, too, setting some sort of email etiquette guidelines.

Users.   Establish guidelines for user logons, passwords, profiles, and account lockout policies. Establish limits for shared directories on servers and users' home directories; for example, don't allow users to back up their entire computer to their home directories on the server or else you'll soon run out of space.

Remote users. State guidelines and policies that pertain to remote users only, such as reasonable working hours, a schedule for contacting the office regularly, backup of their remote computers, access limits to network resources, and such.

Internet. If you plan to provide Internet access to your users, you'll need to establish some limits to maintain productivity. Consider whether Web pages, email, and/or user groups should be accessible to your users. Limit time spent on the Internet each day. Consider applying some or all of your current telephone policies to the Internet access.

Equipment. Define who can and cannot access CD-ROM drives, printers, modems, servers, and such. Limit who can change cables or network cards, even on their own machines. Some users may want to add sound cards and joysticks to their computers, which could cause other parts of their system to malfunction and mean more administrative work for you.

You most likely already have some policies in place that you can apply to new networking policies—equipment purchasing and/or maintenance or guidelines for doing business, for example. Take advantage of any policies already written by revising them to fit similar networking procedures. Review and revise all policies periodically and make sure you redistribute the revised policies to everyone in the company.

Finally, include within your policies a definitive statement of network management philosophy. Let the users know up front whether you're strict or open with the network and resources, for example. Inform them of your general philosophy concerning the network's uses. Then, let your policies reflect that philosophy.

Administrative Help

Realizing your time is limited and much of your work consists of quick fixes, putting out fires, and keeping users happy, or at the very least quiet, you must find ways to perform the administrator's duties if you want a well-organized, effective, and productive network. If you can't do it yourself, there may be other methods of getting the work done, as described in this section.

Another idea for decreasing your work is to create a help desk within your company. Let users who know and understand certain programs, printer features, and other information, help the people in your company who require assistance. Finally, consider outsourcing. If you hire another company that specializes in Web page creation and maintenance to perform that function for your company, you save time and energy.

Help with Administrative Duties

You can delegate many of your duties to managers, assistants, and even interns, if you're creative. Some duties, of course, you must perform yourself; however, if you think about it, there are a lot of tasks you can transfer to others to ease your workload.

Managers or supervisors in your company can perform some duties such as user management, event log monitoring, print management, and so on. Assign the more trusted, mature people to tasks that you can easily oversee when necessary. Allocate one task to each department manager, for example, to lessen your workload while not imposing too much on the manager.

> **NOTE**
>
> If it would make you feel better about asking someone to do extra work, arrange for the managers to receive some sort of privilege or perk for their trouble. If extra pay is not possible, arrange for extra time off, tickets to a show, or some other show of support that will make you both feel better.

You can define administrative assistants in any way that is most helpful to you. You can groom your assistants from the newer employees, especially those who want to help in any way they can. Again, assign one job per assistant so as not to take too much time from his or her normal duties. Assistants can perform a variety of tasks, such as training new users, taking inventory of equipment or software, loading printers with paper or cartridges, collecting information from users with problems, and so on.

Finally, consider an intern program. Interns—students who work part-time while completing a degree—can help you get your network organized while you're grooming a candidate for a full-time position. Intern programs are a small investment of time and money from you.

When interviewing interns, look for a motivated person with some skills in the area you're targeting; most interns will likely have no experience, but your willingness to take them on gives them a foot in the door. You can set up your own program length, structure, and responsibilities to assign. Do make sure you give interns jobs that add value to your company instead of solely mundane tasks (such as tape backups) so they'll be more committed. Let them work on substantial projects—research, for example.

You're probably thinking that training an intern is more trouble than it's worth. Let your assistants do the majority of the training; all you have to do is supervise and suggest. In the long run, you'll get more work from an intern than you might expect.

When preparing to get help with your administrative duties, whether with interns, assistants, or managers, follow these simple guidelines:

- Plan the duties well before proposing them. List the possible projects you'll need completed.

- Develop each individual's skills. If you find someone who is good at organizing, for example, give that person the job of keeping users' directories under control.

- Provide a manager for the assistants and interns, someone who can offer help, training, and troubleshooting information.

- Promote your company, when talking to interns, so at some later point the intern will accept a full-time position with you.

Finally, remember that you are the administrator of the network and there are some chores you should do daily, weekly, and consistently. Included in those chores, keep track of the tasks that have been completed and the tasks that need to be completed. Also, make sure the major decisions for the network are made by the higher-level administrators; don't let lower-level people make too many decisions.

Assign someone to report the status of each department weekly or at the very least, monthly. You should define the management team's roles; design a team structure so that lower-level members report to managers who report to administrative managers and then to you, for example.

> **NOTE**
> Keep track of tasks completed and tasks that need to be completed. Keep the major decisions to the higher-level administrators; don't let lower-level people make too many decisions. Administrators must commit resources, not team members, and assign someone to report status in each department; define management team's roles; consider team skills as well as technical expertise. Design a team structure so that lower-level members report to managers who report to administrative managers and then to you, for example.

Form a Help Desk

A help desk consists of one or more people within your company who are knowledgeable about a subject and willing to help. For your network help desk, you'll need people who know something about printers, browsers, client operating systems, software applications, and networking. No one needs to know about all of these subjects; one person may know about printers and another about Web access; one may know Windows 95 and another the accounting program. This is actually a better scenario because no one person has to answer all questions.

The help desk can be a centrally maintained role or decentralized. For example, if you have thousands of users, you may need to establish an actual area for your help desk and hire knowledgeable people to staff that desk. These people may benefit from keeping a database of all problems reported and the solutions offered; then others can access the database in the future.

If your company is small, you can simply ask those people more experienced in certain networking and computer tasks if they are willing to help others in the company. Have the help people keep a log of problems and solutions, and perhaps even the names of the personnel who called for help. This will help lessen misuse of the system; you can always contact personnel who take advantage and ask them to help themselves a bit more.

Make sure you implement telephone support to take care of users' questions and problems, so calls will be short and to the point. You might try remote-control software (pcAnywhere, for example) for larger help desks.

Help desk staff must know about a variety of technologies and products that are used in your company. Keep resources current; collect all documentation you can. Also, provide training to anyone staffing the help desk.

Help desk people can also double as trainers. Remember though, helping people through their problems is a stressful job; you'll need to keep your people well-trained and keep their morale up. Consider offering advancement opportunities within the help desk and within the company.

Consider Outsourcing

Outsourcing has become more and more popular as technologies multiply in number and complexity. You can hire outside consultants, technicians, Internet service providers, email providers, cabling or networking equipment installers—the list goes on and on. Consider outsourcing some of your networking tasks to qualified experts who can do the job economically and more effectively than you.

> **NOTE**
>
> If you're considering outsourcing, contact the outside help as soon as possible. Let the consultants or technicians you hire to handle some of the network tasks be involved in installing and configuring their part of the network. This will save you time and headaches later.

Naturally, you must be sure you're getting the right people for the job. Ask for and check references, interview intelligently, and keep a constant check of the company even after you hire them. You might even put an assistant in charge of the outsourcing so you're sure the job is done to your specifications. Here are a few other outsourcing suggestions:

Get a contract for all outsourcing work and make sure the agreement suits your purposes.

Document everything and keep good records, notes of meetings, receipts, and such.

Check the contracts carefully; note any escape clauses, financial penalties, and so on.

Notify all departments about the changes outsourcing may cause. Keep your employees informed.

People Preparation

It's extremely important to prepare your users and assistants for what is about to happen. An informed staff will make more allowances for problems, such as with the installation or configuration of computers and programs, network hardware trouble, and so on. Also, if your staff members feel like a part of the transformation, they are more likely to be supportive and helpful instead of stubborn and frustrated.

People in Charge

The people in charge of the company, your boss or perhaps corporate powers that be, must understand the project at hand. It's in your best interest to keep them informed of the networking needs, the inadequacies of the current system, users' attitudes, benefits of the new system, and the progress you're making with the deployment. If the people in charge are not willing to pay for the changes or support you in your work, you'll have a very difficult time completing your task.

> **NOTE**
>
> Think about cross-training. Cross-training is a method by which your sales staff might manage the help desk, or network managers might sit with the end users in a seminar or class. Consider having a knowledge-able user train one of the people in charge to use Windows 95, for example. Let those people who know about a technology or procedure help others, no matter if they're in the same group, level, or department. Benefits to cross-training include improved network management, stronger employee relationships, more effective problem solving, boost in morale, and it makes it easier to move employees into other depart-ments as the work flow changes.

Documentation is the key. You are probably overwhelmed with the amount of planning and organization it takes to get this project going; however, you must take time (or delegate the task) to prepare reports that will convince your boss of the importance of the network and inform him or her of the improvements.

Managers

You must also keep your managers informed of the progress the network is making. Involve managers, supervisors, and administrative assistants as much as possible in decision-making processes; if your managers are involved, they will be happier with the final product and be less likely to complain.

Additionally, you must provide training for those who will govern the network in any way. Say you're using administrative assistants for user account preparation, print management, Web page creation, and so on; have these people find some help with their projects. Taking courses at local or community colleges, attending technological seminars, purchasing books on the subject, or taking classes over the Internet are all possibilities for people to improve their skills and knowledge.

Consider the savings of the proper training. Those who are well-trained can help train users in your company, troubleshoot problems instead of calling on you, and better perform their assigned tasks so you have more time to manage the network. Additionally, morale and self-esteem are increased, thereby mak-ing your staff happier in their jobs.

Users

Finally, you must prepare the users for the changes about to take place. Have man-agers meet with users and discuss the networking changes. Also, managers can ask for suggestions and ideas, problems and possible solutions; then, after refining the list from the users, they turn the ideas in to you for further consideration.

Again, training is a very important issue with the users. You may want to hold seminars yourself or send the users to local seminars that are pertinent to your networking needs. Another option is to have your trained managers and assistants train users by department, teaching small groups how to use the network, a browser, a file or directory structure, and so on.

Have an assistant create a set of guidelines for using the network, as well. Perhaps state password and account lockout policies plus other security considerations, list directories to which users have access, proper email etiquette, or any other subjects pertinent to your company and your networking situation. Once again, prepared and informed users will be more cooperative than those who are left by the wayside wondering what is going on around them.

Book Two

Introduction to Book Two

The server is the heart of your network, providing files, directories, profiles, and a plethora of services to your users. Immediately after you get your network up and running, users quickly become dependent on the servers. Some users will save files to it and share those files with other users; many users will access applications installed to the server; and all users will likely depend on the network printers for hard copies of their work. Internet access, scheduling, email, and other services become the focus of each users' everyday activities.

Whereas a small network may have only one or two servers, larger networks may operate hundreds of servers. Each server can serve a fixed number of users or all users on the network. A server may provide multiple and various services or just one service to the network users. Also, all servers may run the same network operating system, or a few servers may operate on a different NOS. The organization and management of your servers depend on several factors. Book Two outlines those factors and offers advice to help you with your decisions in regard to your network servers.

Following are some of the tasks a server performs:

Authenticates users. When users log on to the network, a server checks the username and password to verify the user's permission to attach. The authentication server contains a list of resources—files, directories, printers, and such—to which the user has rights or permissions to access and any limitations to those resources as defined by the administrator.

Stores files and directories. A server contains files and directories that users can access, view, change, and otherwise manipulate. Only those users with appropriate rights can access and modify files and/or directories.

Manages resources. Resources attached to the network—such as CD-ROMs, modems, and printers—are available to users with permissions to access those resources. A server tracks the use of the resources, limits access to it, and manages its functions over the network.

Stores and runs applications.   Servers manage the use of certain applications—such as databases, accounting programs, and Web servers—for use by the networking clients, at the same time or not.

Manages functions and tracks network problems.   A server includes the tools and utilities to log network problems, system errors, and security breaches.

Accesses the Internet.   Some servers enable and monitor Internet access. Users may access email and newsgroups, browse the Web, provide storefronts for e-commerce, and other services.

Backs up files and data.   Servers enable administrators and users to quickly and easily back up data and files for the entire network.

Enables implementation of an intranet or extranet.   Servers can provide the management tools and power needed to create an intranet over your LAN or an extranet to which your vendors and customers have access.

As you might conclude, managing one or multiple servers is a full-time job and not a job to be taken lightly. The number of tasks an administrator must perform on a daily basis can be overwhelming; add to that maintenance, troubleshooting, upgrading, and other periodic duties and you'll soon see the need to organize and delegate. Book Two, *Server Management,* offers some ideas and tasks for making those jobs more systematic and controllable.

PRELIMINARY GROUNDWORK

Whether you're planning to purchase one or more server computers or to supplement an existing server computer, you need to assess your current situation, think about the future of your network, and make some decisions regarding the use of the server computer(s) in the system. This chapter introduces some server concepts and uses, as well as some guidelines for basing your server decisions on.

Additionally, this chapter includes the following:

- Common services provided by servers

- The difference between using a supercomputer and multiple smaller server computers

- Network operating system necessities

- Guidelines for choosing an NOS

Planning Servers

Servers provide many varied services to your network users. Decisions you make in the planning stage depend upon the number and type of services you want to offer, the number of users on your network, server and networking hardware, networking software, and so on. Your first decision will be to figure out what services you will offer to your users.

Servers can authenticate users, allow access to network resources, and store applications, files, and directories. You might want a print server, Web server, email server, and/or any of several other types of servers. Perhaps you want users to access the Internet or your company's intranet, to share files or access customer data. You'll need to identify the services you want to provide before making other server decisions.

Next, you choose the number of servers you'll need to perform these tasks. Some services may be so hardware intensive that you must provide a dedicated server for that job; other services may be shared on one server. Often, for security reasons, you may need to dedicate a server to a task, such as with a server that attaches to the Internet or one that authenticates your users.

Services

To decide which services you'll need, you must analyze your business, your users, and the goals for your network. Think about how your company now works and what would make it work more efficiently. Consider the projects your users undertake, current methods of performing tasks, future objectives for your company, and so on. Discuss possible services with managers and users; ask them what they need in a network.

Following are some questions you might ask yourself, and others, to help choose the services you'll want from your network, and in parentheses is the type of server that could perform those services. Types of servers are discussed in detail in Chapter 2 of this book, "Terminology and Technology."

- Are you concerned about users accessing sensitive company files? (Authentication server)

- Do you want only certain users to access accounting files? (Authentication server)

- Do some users produce large CAD (Computer Aided Drafting) drawings that must be available to others in the office? (File server)

- Are multimedia files or large text and image files, such as with a company catalog, used a great deal in your office? (File server)

- Do you keep your customer files or product information on the computer? Would it be beneficial for multiple users to access these files to modify and reference? (Database server)

- Would you like to record your company's inventory on the computer? (Database server)

- Are you considering starting a store on the Internet to sell your products? (Transaction server)

- Would your company benefit from having email? (Application server)

- Do several people need to access your accounting program? (Application server)

- Would you like to start an intranet for use by your company only, to publish company guidelines, handbooks, forms, announcements, and such? (Web server)

- Do you want to publish information about your company on the Internet? (Web server)

- Could your users gain from the ability to share documents, opinions, questions, and more over the network? (Groupware server)

- Do you want users in a particular department to collaborate with users in another building? (Groupware server)

- Do you have two expensive laser printers that would serve you better if everyone in the company could use them instead of only two people? (Print server)

- Do you have a color inkjet printer that could be used by several different departments instead of by just one? (Print server)

- Does your business fax advertisements and announcements to your customers? (Fax server)

Number of Servers

When deciding the number of servers you'll need, consider first the number of users that will access the network. Balance that information with the number and types of services to make a final decision about your servers. These decisions aren't final ones; this section is simply providing you with an estimate, with some of the facts you'll need to decide the number of servers you'll require.

Some Examples

Generally, you need only one server if your network is very small, say 2 to 20 users. One server can provide authentication, file and print services, and possibly email. Often the server software you buy will suggest how many users you can apply to one server—some state as many as 200 users per server, and others are not quite so optimistic. It all depends on the server hardware and the amount of access per server.

You can easily start with one server if your network is small and add another server if you need to later. You'll know if you need to add another server if service becomes slow or wait times are too long for users to access data or services. Also, if you use only one server, you should use some alternate method of backup in case the server goes down; for example, RAID or mirroring.

Figure 1.1 shows a small network that uses three servers to provide services to 125 users; each client computer represents 25 computers. The authentication

Figure 1.1 Multiple servers provide various services for a small- to medium-sized network.

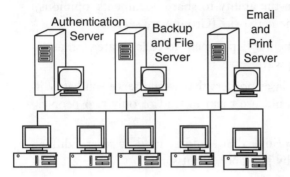

server contains all usernames, passwords, account policies, and so on. The backup server provides a replicated copy of the authentication server, in case of a server crash or other catastrophic event. Also included on the backup server are files that the users share in their day-to-day work. Finally, one server is dedicated to email and print services.

> **NOTE**
> RAID and mirroring are methods of providing an alternate source that can perform the server's duties should the hard drive fail or crash so that your users can continue their work. Data and programs are replicated to another hard disk or even another server that will step in if something happens to the first server.

The more users and services you add to a network, the more servers you need. For example, say you have 200 users. Most will need file and print services, but all will need email services. Many users will want to use the email services for sending attached files and for generally consulting with each other during the business day. In a case such as this, three servers would be quite reasonable—one to provide file services, one for print services, and another to provide email services.

Now say you have 1000 users who all need file, print, email, and Internet services. One server per service may be sufficient, but more than likely you'll need additional servers to supplement services. Again, it also depends on the size and power of your servers.

Supercomputer or Multiple Server Computers

When choosing your computers, you can implement multiple small server computers or fewer powerful supercomputers. A supercomputer is a powerful computer that has massive amounts of RAM, caching, and disk space, with perhaps multiple processors and multiple network adapter cards. A supercomputer can perform many and varied services over the network.

Multiple smaller computers would each have less capacity than a supercomputer. Each smaller server might have one processor and only one or two network cards. Less RAM and disk space means each smaller computer would be able to offer fewer services to its clients.

Figure 1.2 shows one possible supercomputer solution. Two supercomputers are utilized for backup purposes; in case the main computer crashes, all work will not stop on this system because the backup supercomputer can authenticate users and supply files and printing services. An alternate option might be to use smaller server computers as backups, or simply install extra hard drives to the supercomputer to work as backups.

Figure 1.3 illustrates one solution for using multiple smaller server computers. In this building layout, servers and clients are located in different offices, but each server provides services for all users in the building. The authentication and backup authentication servers are located in a secure office with fewer users. The file, mail, and Web servers are located in another office, and so on.

Figure 1.2 Even a supercomputer should have a backup in case of a disaster.

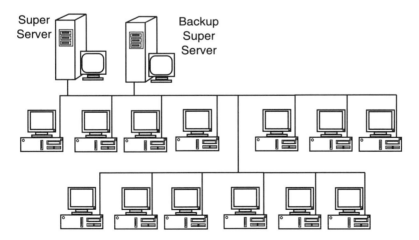

Figure 1.3 Multiple servers divided between offices enable the administrator to delegate server chores to various assistants.

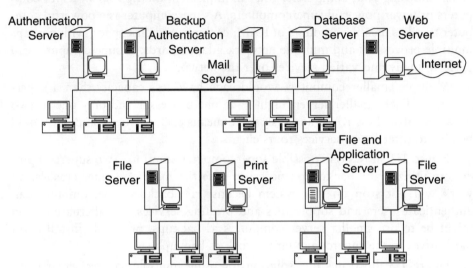

Because of the heavy use of applications, there are multiple file servers and two application servers on the network.

The choice you make depends on your preferences, your budget, and your current equipment. For example, if you already have several smaller server computers and you're going to add to your system, you may not want to add a supercomputer. Following are some advantages and disadvantages of each computer type.

Supercomputer advantages:

• It means less network traffic because there are more users per server and because replication traffic is less or maybe nonexistent.

• It offers better fault-tolerant designs in the hardware, and error correction is easier with more powerful hardware.

• It reduces administration because the network management is centralized.

Supercomputer disadvantages:

• It offers fewer choices of available vendors, and all of the hardware you need may not be available.

• It means you must purchase good network adapter cards and keep one handy because of the high volume of traffic wears and tears on NICs.

- It takes longer to back up and restore the information store and data because its hard drives are so large.
- It means if the computer goes down, the entire system goes down.

Multiple smaller server computers advantages:

- There is less impact on users if the server crashes.
- They offer less expense and more hardware choices.
- Each server can be dedicated or share services.
- This configuration is easier and less expense per purchase than super-computers to gradually increase memory, processors, and to upgrade hardware.

Multiple smaller server computers disadvantages:

- They provide more hardware to maintain and to go down.
- They cost more in administration time and technical support.
- An increase in users or load means multiple servers will need more hardware.
- More computers mean more network overhead and more storage space for replicated data.

In general, when making decisions about the server computer(s), think about your business requirements. You need to make your system more productive and successful. You need to service all users efficiently. And you need to plan for network and company growth.

Choosing a Network Operating System

There are many network operating systems available; your choice will depend on several factors. For example, you or some of your administrative assistants may already have training and certification in a specific NOS. Knowing how to install, configure, and run an NOS is a huge motivation toward the server software you'll use with your network. Perhaps you have previous knowledge of an operating system that you either like or dislike, and base your decision on your experience.

Often, the software you use will determine the network operating system you choose. Many vertical applications—programs written to a business' explicit needs—require one operating system or another. Check with your corporation or your software manufacturers to see if this is the case before purchasing your NOS.

Another factor that may govern your choice is your current hardware and software inventory. Consider any server computers already in operation as well as workstations in place. Older equipment that must be replaced for some network and client operating systems may limit your choices in the NOS you use. However, think about the future of your network in your decisions; you don't want to limit your entire network because of temporary budgeting problems. Try to work out a deployment plan that will enable you to purchase the hardware you'll need.

In making your decision, poll employees, administrative assistants, and other coworkers to find out their needs and thoughts on the subject. Get an estimate of the budget with which you have to work. Consider security, server function, and future networking goals as well. Following is a list of common operating systems:

Microsoft Windows NT Server. Full-featured NOS that provides file and printer access, plus security, tracking, and logging, user management, optimization, Internet access, and more administrative utilities and tools.

Microsoft LAN Manager. Older NOS that provides shared file and printer access.

Novell NetWare/IntranetWare. Full-featured NOS providing file and printer access as well as user management, administration tools, Internet access, security and logging features, and more.

IBM LAN Server. Supplies file and print services, although directory and security services are limited.

IBM OS/2 Warp Server. An NOS that provides file and printer access, user management, security features, and other administrative tools.

Banyan VINES. VINES provides all server functions and offers many options for connecting to minicomputers, mainframes, and other network file servers.

UNIX. A 32-bit multitasking operating system that uses the TCP/IP set of protocols and is available on a variety of hardware, from PCs to Cray supercomputers.

AIX (Advanced Interactive Executive). A UNIX-related NOS that runs on IBM workstations, A/UX that is a graphical version for Macintosh, and Solaris from SunSoft that runs on Intel processors.

> **NOTE**
>
> For more information on specific operating systems, see any of the following books: *The Complete Guide to NetWare 4.11/IntranetWare* by James E. Gaskin (Sybex, 1996), *Essential System Administration: Help for Unix System Administrators* by Aeleen Frisch (O'Reilly & Associates, 1996), or *Documented NT* by Sue Plumley (John Wiley & Sons, 1997).

NOS Necessities

When choosing an NOS, there are certain things you should think about as far as ease of administration and functionality of the network. For example, you'll want diagnostic tools and certain security features. You may also want extra features, such as a Web server or messaging system. Following is a list of NOS necessities; add your own special needs to the list when searching for the appropriate operating system for your network.

- Diagnostic tools for examining the system and network components, such as protocols and clients, ports and connections.

- Utility for recording files on certain occurrences, such as system or application errors and/or security breaches.

- Tools for analyzing the information gathered by logging, diagnostic, and optimization utilities.

- Security features that let you lock out certain accounts, apply password restrictions, and track the use of the network.

- Utilities for creating, modifying, and deleting users and groups.

- Internet support such as a browser, TCP/IP protocols, Web server, and so on.

- Various network clients, protocols, and services as well as client software to load onto workstations.

- Scalability, stability, and an easy-to-use interface.

Integrating Network Operating Systems

If you're building a new network, you probably will have no problem in setting up similar hardware and NOS configurations for all servers. However, if you already have a network up and running, you'll likely need to integrate network

Common Server Operating Environment

You want to establish a common server operating environment for your network if possible. Using the same NOS on all of your servers will make administrative tasks—such as backup and replication, user management, printer management, security, and so on—easier and more efficient. Additionally, using one NOS across the system will make working on the network easier for your users.

Again, to support a more efficient and effective administration of the network, servers within your network should have identical or nearly identical setups—such as application files, directory structures, network drive assignments, and so on. Using the same NOS across the board will help with this task, too. Implementing a similar hardware platform, including peripherals, for all servers will also add to the cost-effectiveness of your network and make the NOS easier to install, configure, and manage.

Finally, if you use one NOS over your system, you can readily assign a team that's responsible for monitoring all servers; downloading applications; testing patches, bug fixes, and updated drivers; record keeping; developing replication procedures; and coordinating the replications.

operating systems to get the services you need on the network. Many of the previously mentioned network operating systems can work together over a network; however, make sure you check the program's documentation before going ahead with installation.

Before making any decisions about keeping your current NOS, consider the costs involved—cost of replacement hardware and software, time it takes to perform migrations, training of users and administrative assistants, and so on. No matter what you decide, probably the best decision is to run your current network in parallel to any new NOS you add so that work can continue, changes for users are gradual, and you can test applications, security, and such on the new server before going online with it.

NOTE

For information about moving from a NetWare system to a Windows NT Server system, see Sue Plumley's book *Migrating from Novell NetWare to Windows NT Server 4* (John Wiley & Sons, 1997).

Server Considerations

When integrating two NOSs over the same network, you'll need to make sure the new NOS meets certain requirements. For example, check that the protocols and clients offered with the new system are compatible with the old. Also regard the following: file system, file and print sharing, security issues, peripheral use, file and

NT, Novell, and LAN Manager

Novell NetWare has long been the most popular network operating system for businesses, small and large. However, as much of the older workstation hardware is being replaced and Windows 95 and 98 are taking over the marketplace, NetWare's popularity has lost a bit to Windows NT Server.

Windows NT's popularity has grown over the last several years because of its easy-to-use graphical interface, practical features, and ability to work with many and varied systems.

Because of NetWare's popularity, Microsoft has made it easy to integrate NT with NetWare on one system. NT comes with a NetWare client (and the IPX/SPX protocol) that enables a user to attach to the NetWare server and access its resources while not sacrificing its ability to attach to the NT server and its resources.

Additionally, Microsoft has added features that make NT and NetWare more compatible, including the Gateway Services, File and Print Services, and a Migration Tool that address specific situations between the two network operating systems.

You can integrate NetWare and NT by adding clients via remote access, to attach NetWare workstations to NT domains, to take advantage of Microsoft's WINS and/or DNS services, and so on.

Clients that NetWare and NT can share include MS-DOS, Windows for Workgroups, Windows 95 and 98, NT Workstation 3.51, 4, and 5, and NT Server 3.51, 4, and 5.

NT also integrates well with Microsoft LAN Manager, an older operating system you may be using. You can use LAN Manager servers as member servers on the NT network, supplying files and resources to users from that computer.

directory structure, client software, login scripts or profiles, utilities and applications, and so on. You want to make sure the two systems are compatible and that they will share or compromise on these issues instead of fight you all the way.

Another thing you'll need to think about when introducing a new NOS into an existing system is your network peripherals. Make sure you have appropriate peripheral drivers for the new NOS and that each device is compatible. UPS, backup tape drives, CD-ROM towers, optical disk drives, modems, and print devices are the most common peripherals you may share between two NOS systems. Applications may also be a consideration if you plan to share data or files between the two NOSs; check your applications and plan your strategies before purchasing a second NOS.

Client Considerations

In implementing an integrated NOS, you want to cause the least amount of trouble and modification to the client computers as possible for several reasons; you don't want to disrupt the work or confuse the users, ease of administration, cost-effective implementation, and so on. First, check that you will have client software for each of the client operating systems on your network. For instance, if you have MS-DOS, Windows 95, and Windows NT Workstation client operating systems, check that the new network operating system is going to work with these OSs and that the new NOS supplies clients for these systems.

Other issues to check into with your client computers are login scripts, profiles, home directories, and other personal preferences and requirements you've set for your users. If possible, you should use one username and one password per user, rather than having each user log in to each server with different passwords. The more passwords a user must remember, the more chances for a security problem and administrative hassles.

> **NOTE**
> You might also want to check into upgrading the older client operating systems. For example, MS-DOS or Windows for Workgroups clients may not get full use of security features in new NOS.

Finally, consider training users on the new server and NOS. Provide guidelines for use, information about new services and resources, and any other pertinent data they need to operate on the network successfully.

TERMINOLOGY AND TECHNOLOGY

When planning your network servers, you will need to determine the types of services you want to offer your users. You may want to present simple file storage and print services, or you may want to offer Internet and intranet services and more. Your network operating system will provide many services to your users, but depending on the NOS you choose, you may need more server software to provide the services you want.

This chapter describes various server types and highlights several server suites. In this chapter, you learn about:

- Services provided by file, print, authentication, application servers, and more

- Microsoft BackOffice and Sun's Solaris

- Novell and Netscape server suites

Types of Servers

The term *server* can refer to the machine on which an NOS is installed, or it can refer to the types of services the machine performs. The service can be initiated by the NOS installed to the machine; for example, authentication of users generally only takes place on a server computer configured especially for that purpose. Although there are many services a computer can perform, there are some common server types and uses.

Generally speaking, it's a good idea to use a dedicated server if you have a lot of users accessing the server. Naturally, some servers will generate more traffic than others and at different times of the day; for example, an email server generates more traffic the first thing in the morning and at the end of the day because that's when most people check their mail.

You could always share services on one computer (as seen in the case of the supercomputer). It really depends on the RAM, disk space, the power of the computer, and the type of service you're offering. You may need to evaluate how much a server is used, how often the services are accessed, how much traffic runs to and from the server, and so on, before you can determine each server computer's best use.

Authentication Server

An *authentication*, or *logon*, *server* acts as a sentry to the network. When someone logs on to the network, the authentication server checks the user's name and password with the list of approved users. If the server finds the login, it proceeds to check the permissions and rights of that user and then enables the user to access any resources that he or she is permitted to.

As administrator, you can limit the resources a user can access by using a utility usually contained within the network operating system. Following are some of the types of limits you can put on a user of the network:

- Viewing the server and certain directories and files; opening and modifying specific files and directories; creating and deleting files or directories on the server.

- Access to various peripherals, such as printers, CD-ROM drives, modems, and such.

- Access to the network during specific hours.

- Access to other computers besides the server.

- Access via dial-in as opposed to over the LAN cabling.

- Control over a printer or other peripheral.

- Access to the server such as logging on, shutting down the system, backing up files, changing the system time, loading and unloading device drivers, creating users, modifying and deleting files, and so on.

The rights or permissions assigned to a user depend on that user's job and the access he or she needs to complete the work. For instance, you may grant someone rights to control a printer because that person is familiar with printers and sits near the printer. You may grant rights to an administrative assistant for adding users to the system because that person is head of personnel. The choices you make and enter into the authentication server govern each user's access to that server.

File Server

The *file server* stores files used over the network by one or multiple users. The files may be data, accounting, documents, images, engineering drawings, large data objects, or any other file that can be saved to the computer. The purpose of the file server is to enable file sharing between users who have permission to use that file; however, users often find it handy to back up their hard drives to a server or to store files that are not to be shared there as well.

The file server is a combination of hardware and software that enables users to share computer programs and data. Usually a network operating system is installed to the server; the software accepts incoming requests for files and then send files back to the user who made the request.

When using a file server, users access the file server's physical drive as if it were one of their own local drives. The network operating system takes care of routing traffic across the network and back, between client and server. A file server must be able to find data and get it back to the requesting workstation quickly. Factors governing the speed and efficiency of the file server include the following:

- Type and speed of the network interface card

- Type and length of the cabling between the server and the client

- Efficiency of the network software

- Type of application being run

- Number of users on the network

- Amount of RAM available

For an effective file server, you need a large, fast, hard disk. Also, consider the capacity of the disk (take the amount of space you think you'll need and double it and make sure it's expandable). The controller is also important; an

---

Fault Tolerance

Fault tolerance is a method of designing your system that ensures continued operation in the event of the failure of one component, such as a hard drive crash or failed processor. Fault tolerance can be as simple as attaching a UPS to the server in case of a power failure, or as complex as replicating the entire contents of the server to another machine in a remote location as a backup in case of disaster. Maintaining good backups is another form of fault tolerance, although neither the UPS and backing up should be your only forms of protection.

Other common forms of fault tolerance include the following:

Disk duplexing.   A technique that writes the same information simultaneously onto two different hard disks, each using a different

Continues

> ### Fault Tolerance *(Continued)*
>
> disk controller for improved redundancy. If one disk fails, the other disk can continue operations because it contains the same information. This technique is designed for a single disk system.
>
> **Disk mirroring.** A technique that writes the same information simultaneously onto two different hard disks or partitions, but with each disk using the same disk controller. If one disk or partition fails, the other continues operations. This technique is designed for a single disk system.
>
> **RAID (Redundant Array of Inexpensive Disks).** Multiple disk drives are used in an array to provide fault tolerance in the event one or more of the drives should fail. Different levels of RAID are available, such as mirroring to one drive, or writing data to multiple drives. In general, RAID level 5 or above is the most trusted, effective fault tolerance.
>
> There are other methods of fault tolerance; however, the most effective method is to replicate the server to another exact server located off-site, if possible. By replicating the authentication server, you guarantee continued service to the users in case of a server crash. Also, the expense of a second backup server is well worth the money when you consider the cost of recovering data from a crashed hard drive and the hours spent installing and configuring the NOS, installing software, restoring the tape backup, configuring users and permissions, and so on.

intelligent hard disk controller can add enormous performance improvements. For safety's sake, add fault tolerance to every server.

Application Server

An *application server* is a file server, of sorts, that is optimized for a specific task such as communications or database applications. An application server allows users to share data while security and management services ensure data integrity and security. Applications run on this server might include databases, email or messaging programs, groupware, accounting, or other specialized software that the entire company can use. Most of the time, an application server is a dedicated server.

Generally, an application needs a higher-end hardware than a typical file server, meaning better fault tolerance, more RAM, and more disk space. You'll also want to ensure tighter security on an application server, since files are often of a critical or sensitive nature.

Database Servers

A *database* is a collection of related objects—such as tables, reports, forms, and so on—that are organized by a Database Management System (DBMS). A DBMS is application software that controls the data in the database. A DBMS organizes, stores and retrieves, secures, and maintains the integrity of the data. Many database management systems can also format reports of the data to help you understand the relationships between bits of data.

A *relational database* is one in which the data always appears from the point of view of the user, with the data organized as a set of two-dimensional tables. Presented in rows and columns, the columns represent fields such as names, addresses, cities, and so on; the rows represent records that are collections of information.

A *database server* is an applications server that uses specialized database software built specifically for use with the client/server architecture. The server runs on a central machine and stores and controls the data. The server also protects the data, granting access to multiple users, updating and deleting records on disk, and often communicating with other database servers attached to the network.

The client runs on one or more workstations, provides the user interface, and allows users to request information or modify records in the database. Database clients can run a variety of different front-end programs (customized spreadsheets, query languages, and such) and still retrieve data from the common database.

Web Server

A *web server*, also an application server, lets you publish and transfer information in HTML (Hypertext Markup Language) formatting using the HTTP (Hypertext Transfer Protocol) to the Internet. You also can use those same features to provide effective services to your private LAN users via an intranet. You can create your own web pages, search engines, index pages, reports, FTP and gopher services, and more, depending on the software you use.

When planning your web server, consider whether to use a standalone computer that is attached to the Internet but not your local network, or a proxy server and/or firewall between your web server and local network to protect your data and users from the outside world. If you plan a web server for your LAN's intranet, you should use a server that is not also attached to and providing services to the Internet, for security's sake.

A computer that will be a Web server will need additional disk space and perhaps an extra network interface card, depending on how you connect the server to the network; for example, you may need a network adapter card to connect to your LAN and an ISDN card to connect to the Internet. You may also need a router to help manage traffic to and from the Internet.

Figure 2.1 shows a network configuration using three servers: LAN (application and authentication), proxy, and Web. Notice that, of the three servers, only the LAN server is connected to the workstations. The LAN server is also connected to a proxy server, which protects the private LAN from intruders. The Web server supplies Web pages to the Internet and contains all of the data and information it needs to complete this task without passing through the protective proxy server to the private LAN.

Proxy Server

A *proxy server* is a server you place between the Internet and your LAN to protect your users and data from penetration by unknown or untrustworthy users (refer to Figure 2.1). Some proxy servers also let you control your LAN users' access to the Internet, limiting Web sites and newsgroups, for example. Most proxy servers also enable authentication of users and data protection features.

The proxy server should be installed to a dedicated server. You should remove every file and application from that server that you wouldn't want an outsider to see. You may also need a router to send packets to the correct LAN segment, depending on your network configuration. A proxy server should have two network adapter cards. One card communicates with the internal LAN and the other card communicates with the Internet. Using separate addresses ensures the security of your LAN system; the addresses on the inside of the proxy server are never exposed to the outside.

Figure 2.1 The proxy server protects the LAN from Internet hackers.

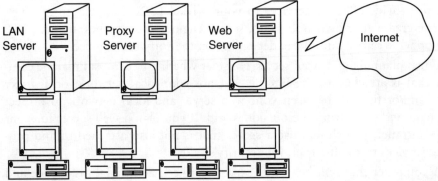

> **NOTE**
>
> A *firewall* is a barrier to the outside world, protecting a LAN from intruders and controlling the traffic between the Internet and the LAN. However, a firewall's function is rudimentary compared to a proxy server because a firewall simply examines packets and either accepts or drops them depending on the source and destination addresses. A proxy server translates requests between the Internet and the LAN, supplying a more sophisticated service than the firewall. Sometimes firewalls and proxy servers are run together to protect the LAN, and some proxy servers act as firewalls.

Groupware Server

Groupware enables users to collaborate, send and receive email, join discussion groups and bulletin boards, and otherwise share data over the network using the groupware client software. The groupware server software manages and distributes the data—mail, images, text, shared folders, scheduling data—and controls the flow of work over the network. The server software also offers security to its clients, so that only those with permission can access the shared data, and sensitive materials remain confidential. Lotus Notes/Domino and Microsoft Exchange are two good examples of groupware server applications.

A groupware application needs special connectivity to communicate with both local and foreign servers; for example, an SMTP (Simple Mail Transfer Protocol) connection for exchange of data over the Internet and a link for remote users are necessary for a groupware application to be useful. Also, the application should have some sort of conversion tools so that various email and user account information from other services can be used.

Depending on the number of users that will access the groupware server, it is best to use a dedicated server since many different services are offered by this server software. Users can connect with email, send comments to a bulletin board or shared folder, create and modify shared documents, and such; this type of collaboration can keep the server busy.

As with most servers, you'll want more than adequate disk space for a groupware server; users' email and public folders will quickly use the extra space. You may want to use multiple physical drives to speed access as well.

Print Servers

A *print server* provides access to one or more centralized printers or a workstation's shared printers. Using a print server, users send their printer output to the server, which stores the job temporarily, and then sends it to the printer of choice. Print servers allow fewer printers to satisfy more users; they're especially useful for expensive laser or other high-speed printers because the cost of these machines is shared by several users.

Depending on the size of your network and the amount of network printing, you may need a dedicated print server or several print servers. Use a dedicated print server if you'll have heavy traffic to multiple printers. If, however, many users have local printers (printers attached to a workstation and not shared with the network), you may not need to offer such extensive print services.

If you choose to use one server as a print and file server, remember that file operations always take first priority over printing transactions, although the impact printing has on file access is insignificant. Another consideration is security. A print server should be available to all users but a file server may need to be isolated.

When configuring the computer for a print server, add extra RAM to help manage the print devices and large document printing. Disk space required for a print server is minimal.

Fax Server

A *fax server* combines a fax board with software that allows access by all users in the system. The fax boards drop into a PC slot and enable the server's users to send faxes to any fax machine or fax board. Sending a computer file is easy and it saves printing and paper.

Fax server software enables all users access to the services of the fax board. While a fax machine or fax board is limited to a single location, a fax server enables any workstation on the LAN to send a fax from any location. It's also faster than a fax machine. One problem with electronic faxes is that the document must be on a computer; therefore, you must type or scan the document in before you can fax it.

If the server is not a dedicated fax server, then only one user at a time can send a fax. Another problem is that the server must be available to send a fax and someone at the server must switch to fax mode; this can cause bottlenecks at the server end. If you use a dedicated fax server, multiple users can send faxes simultaneously. There is still a problem with verification of the messages that have been sent; a fax server can't normally send a message back to the user if there was a problem with delivery. An alternative is to send faxes as if they were regular email to a fax gateway. The gateway strips away email codes and sends the fax on its way; users will be notified by email, and it's easier for users to learn than a new fax client software.

A fax server uses communication software to implement a fax and you should use an intelligent fax board. There are a few features in the software that you should look for:

- Compatibility between the network and fax board

- Compatibility between the fax board and fax software

- Ability of software to handle the appropriate file formats

- Preferable use of logs and notification

- Ease of use

- Operation in the background

- Ability to send faxes within their applications

Server Suites

A *server suite* is an integrated set of server software that runs on a network operating system. A server suite enables you to access information regardless of its platform or location, facilitates communications among coworkers and systems, and enables efficient workflow in the organization. Many companies offer server software, some for application development and others as client services. Following are a few of the more common and popular server suites available currently.

Microsoft BackOffice Server Suite

Microsoft's BackOffice is a collection of server software that you can use to provide various services to your users. Microsoft has several configurations and collections of servers; you can purchase any server separately or you can purchase one of Microsoft's sets of BackOffice servers. Following are the currently available Microsoft servers:

NT Server.   The network operating system that provides the foundation for all BackOffice servers. NT offers file and print management, security and auditing features, user and group management, and more.

Internet Information Server.   A web server integrated into NT that provides a basis for publishing Internet pages, and even intranet possibilities.

SQL (Structured Query Language) Server. A database management system that structures and stores data and permits data manipulation and retrieval.

Exchange Server. An email and groupware server application that includes group scheduling, electronic forms, shared folders, and more.

SNA (Systems Network Architecture) Server. A server that enables a connection between PCs on a LAN to IBM host computers (mainframes and AS/400s). Figure 2.2 shows how an SNA server might work between a mainframe and PCs on a network. The figure illustrates a centralized model for SNA Server management that connects all servers and clients by WAN, using one networking protocol, and connecting to the host through a fast connection type.

Systems Management Server. A server that enables you to manage hardware and software inventories, automated software distribution, remote systems control, and application management.

Proxy Server. A tool for securing the network from Internet intruders and governing your LAN users' use of the Internet.

Transaction Server. A server that provides application developers with the tools they need to deploy scalable server applications.

Site Server. Software for enabling businesses to run an Internet site, gathering site usage information, measuring and analyzing the data, and modifying the site to improve it.

Commerce Server. A server that lets you create and manage Internet stores, process orders, and manage payments.

Commercial Internet System (CIS). A system for telecommunications carriers, ISPs, cable network operators, and so on. MCIS (Microsoft CIS) provides full Internet services for the Internet.

Advantages to using a set of servers that are built to work with each other and compatible with each other are many. Hardware is easier to configure, protocols and data storage formats are compatible, a similar interface means each server is easier to learn, and integrated installation and use mean easier administration.

NOTE

For more information about planning for, installing, and configuring BackOffice servers, see Sue Plumley's book *Documented BackOffice* (John Wiley & Sons, 1998).

Figure 2.2 SNA Server connects PCs to a mainframe.

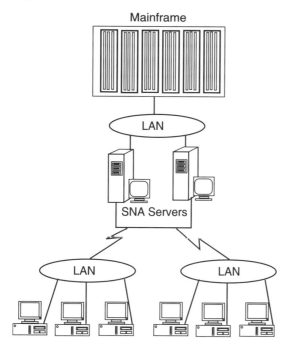

Novell Products

Novell doesn't offer a prepackaged server suite; you can't really load programs onto the NetWare server, only NLMs. There are, however, several server applications you can use with NetWare. NetWare is the foundation server supplying file, print, and authentication services. NetWare offers security features, user and group management, directory organizational features, and multiple network administration utilities.

There are various servers you can add to your NetWare network. Some database servers include Oracle and Sybase. Application services from UNIX will work well with NetWare; NetWare for SAA (Systems Application Architecture) and for Digital Access supply host and UNIX connectivity, as well. Following are some additional servers you can use with NetWare:

GroupWise. Although not technically a server, GroupWise offers calendaring, document management, messaging, and collaboration with dial-up Internet access. Web publishing and web access are also available.

ManageWise. A set of network management services that enable you to control NetWare servers, print queues, and other devices. Analyze network traffic, remotely control workstations, prevent viruses, and inventory network devices.

Netscape Servers for NetWare. Three servers that work on the NetWare platform: Enterprise Server, FastTrack Server, and Messaging Server (see the next section).

Netscape SuiteSpot

Netscape's SuiteSpot provides various servers that help you manage large-scale intranets and enterprises. SuiteSpot offers messaging, virtual servers, user management, bundled clients, and more. SuiteSpot runs on NT server networks and most UNIX-based operating systems. SuiteSpot offers the following services:

Information management. Integration with other products, open standards, HTML and JavaScript, content management, and more.

Collaboration. Messaging, discussion groups, group scheduling, forms, remote user support, and security features are available with SuiteSpot.

Security and administration features. Centralized administration and security certificates enable useful controls over the network.

Netscape also offers some separate servers for use over a network, including:

Application Server. Enables a company to develop and manage business-critical applications.

FastTrack Server. Create, publish, and run applications on the Internet or on your LAN's intranet. An entry-level web server that includes the Netscape browser.

Enterprise Server. A web server that enables web publishing in a variety of formats, automatic messaging, information management, and more. It's an application platform for developers and integrates with Java, HTML, object-oriented applets, and so on.

Solaris Internet Server Suite

Sun Microsystems offers the Solaris Internet Server suite to provide connectivity software, mail servers, and administration tools designed for the Solaris operating system. The Solaris suite is powerful and includes many features; however, it is difficult to set up and to use because much manual configuration is required.

The Solaris Internet Server suite includes some useful features and utilities. Webscout/NW IPX connectivity software includes Netscape browser, news reader, and a set of TCP/IP utilities. Internet Gateway for Solaris (IGS) contains POP2 and POP3 (Post Office Protocol) and Internet Message Access Protocol mail servers. HTML IGS administration tool includes a browser-based interface for administering the connections. Although the interface provides minimal control over the services and no control of the Web, mail, FTP, or other services, it does provide control over password setup and dial-up connections.

Additionally, following are three servers from Solaris x86 Workgroup Server product that you can use to extend the reach of NetWare clients to the commercial Solaris-based MP database applications:

Application Server.   Enables LAN users to engage in enterprise-wide distributed computing by offloading partial mainframe application loads to Pentium servers, bringing database applications to NetWare LAN users, eliminating NLMs (NetWare Loadable Module) with 32-bit scalable applications, and more.

PC Administration Server.   Provides centralized PC administration from a Windows client environment, centralizes backup and host configuration, and removes NLM management.

Internet Gateway Server.   Offers a plug-and-play connection of TCP/IP to the Internet, uses POP3, offers firewall network security and WWW (World Wide Web) publishing optional products.

PLANNING SERVER STRATEGIES

In addition to choosing a network operating system, specialized server software, and planning the services each computer will offer, there are a few other approaches to planning your servers on the network. A common and popular method of setting up servers is by centralizing them for ease of administration and maintenance. Also, consolidation is a practice you may want to use if your current network is made up of several server computers spread out over your site. The strategy you choose depends on your network, number of users, server computer, operating system, and many other factors.

In this chapter, you learn about the following:

- Centralized computing advantages
- Guidelines for consolidation
- Guidelines for setting up a server room
- Planning strategies

Centralized Processing

The mainframe offers centralized control over a network. One host controls all functions, features, and services offered to the client. For ease of administration, physical security, troubleshooting, and maintenance, centralized control is most efficient and effective. Now, multiprocessor computers are offering that control once again. Supercomputers containing more processors and hard drives enable administrators to manage the network from one central location.

Distributed architecture describes the use of multiple smaller server computers that are scattered throughout the network. Distributed architecture places servers closer to the users; however, with processing power constantly growing and the cost of telecommunications dropping, centralizing processing seems to make more sense. Even if you don't use a supercomputer, you can consolidate your server computers to one location and perhaps fewer, more powerful computers.

Why Centralize?

By centralizing your servers to one large server room or at the very least one office, you cut your administration time, cost, and effort considerably. Instead of traveling from site to perform such administrative tasks as monitoring performance or troubleshooting problems, you remain centered in one area with all servers close at hand. You can still delegate tasks to assistants; however, in a centralized server environment, supervising activities is more practical.

Figure 3.1 shows an example of centralized servers. Each server is dedicated to one service yet all servers have been moved to a room so that administration, troubleshooting, and maintenance are easier.

> **NOTE**
>
> You might want to leave a print server in an office closer to the users; a manager or assistant can supervise the print server.

Figure 3.1 Centralized servers place all or most servers in the same area or room.

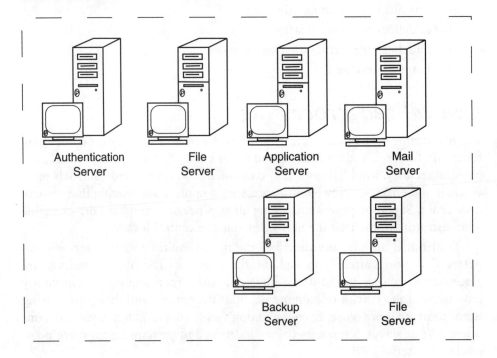

| Authentication Server | File Server | Application Server | Mail Server |

| Backup Server | File Server |

Additionally, consider these points for centralizing your servers:

- Servers are more secure when locked in one room; more eyes can watch the servers when they are centralized.

- Account creation, directory organization, and file modification all become easier and quicker than if you had to connect remotely or travel to other server sites.

- Logs are close at hand in case of a system or application error or a security breach.

- Installation of new applications and upgrades can be completed more quickly.

- Backing up, restoring, and replicating data are faster, which means less of a burden on the network traffic.

- Regularly scheduled maintenance is easier to control and accomplish.

- Troubleshooting is less of a chore because all hardware is in the same area.

- Print and peripheral management, maintenance, and troubleshooting are more precise.

Why Consolidate?

Consolidation of servers is a method of using more than one server on a computer or hard disk. You might, for example, implement a supercomputer to run an authentication, file, and mail server. You could also centralize your server computer(s) by placing your supercomputer and any other servers in a room together.

Figure 3.2 shows an example of consolidated servers. Supercomputers, or at least powerful computers with multiple disks and processors, are used to house two or three services. In addition to being consolidated, these servers are also centralized, or located in one room.

A very good reason to consolidate servers is the total cost of ownership. Consolidation can reduce the total cost of ownership by as much as 30 percent, even though hardware costs may go up. The reduction centers around less management and time spent administering. A distributed system is more labor intensive than consolidation of servers. For each server, costs involve the following:

- Asset management
- Capacity planning
- Support strategies

Figure 3.2 Consolidating computers reduces the number of computers but not the number of services.

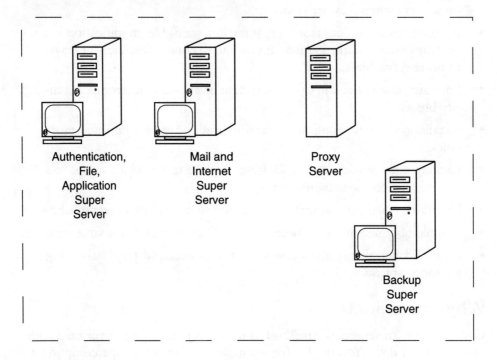

- Training
- Security auditing and control
- Vendor selection
- Migration strategies
- Service agreements

If you reduce the number of servers, you reduce the time and expense needed to perform these tasks. Fewer servers reduces the number of vendors your company works with, forces you to comply with enterprise-wide standards on software, makes the enterprise easier to secure, and allows a company to engage in predictive maintenance, such as detecting a failing disk before it crashes. You can have on-site engineers; with more sites, this is unfeasible.

To find out if you should consolidate servers, ask yourself these questions:

- Does the server crash a lot or the hardware show signs of deterioration?

- Do you know if you're in compliance with your software licensing agreements?

- Do your department managers routinely purchase and install their own servers?

- Is physical security of your servers hard to accomplish because they are so spread out?

- Do you need more and more systems administrators to take care of the servers?

- Are you running more than two operating systems?

> **NOTE**
>
> To get the most from server consolidation, make sure the workload is balanced. Manage the sharing of such resources as tape drives, storage disks, peripherals, and memory so that no one server is overtaxed. Take applications that are now running on several servers and load them onto one large, powerful server.

Setting Up a Server Room

Whether you choose to centralize your servers or not, you should isolate your server(s) whenever possible. Setting up a room or rooms to house your servers ensures security for your data and server configuration. You can lock the room when you're not there to supervise and you can also keep an eye on the room during regular working hours.

Figure 3.3 shows a layout example of a server room. Servers and UPSs are placed in the center of the room for protection from outside walls. The data communications and telecommunications equipment line two inside walls on racks containing a modem server, fax server, switches, and cross-connects. Notice that the documentation is also in the same room as the servers. CD-ROM towers are also located in the same room.

Server Room Contents

The server room holds 1 server or 10 servers or more, CD-ROM towers, jukeboxes, wiring, and any other equipment you want to secure. Additionally, you might locate the system component in which communications circuits are administered between the backbone and the horizontal facilities, telecommuni-

Figure 3.3 A server room houses all of the servers and wiring to protect the equipment and to centralize server management.

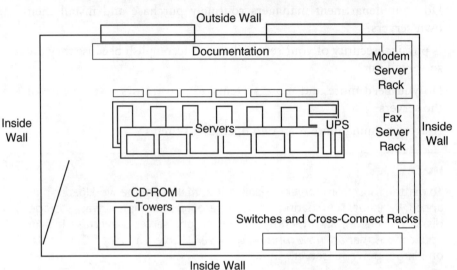

cations equipment, cable terminations, and cross-connect cabling. Often these components are stored in a TCS (Telecommunications Wiring Standard) room; however, you can combine the two rooms, if it is practical.

A TCS, also called telecommunications and/or data communications closet, contains such elements as your key telephone systems, PBX (Private Branch Exchange) systems, hubs, routers, cables, bridges, and other equipment, for security's sake and for easy troubleshooting.

Before designing your server room, check with members of various departments, perhaps form a design team to outline priorities. You should also enlist an outside consultant or technician if you're not sure of the placement and structure of the equipment.

Telecommunications Closet Contents

You may want to store your telecommunications and/or data communications equipment in the server room or, more likely, in a separate room, also called a telecommunications closet. Telecommunications elements include automatic call distribution, key telephone systems, and PBX systems. Data communications components include hubs, routers, jacks, cables, bridges, perhaps server computers, backup and storage equipment, modems, and remote access equipment.

The room must contain equipment like switches and servers and infra-structure-related elements, such as cross-connects and interconnection equipment. Interconnection equipment includes main, intermediate, and horizontal cross-connects, patch panels (devices in which temporary or semipermanent connections can be made between incoming and outgoing lines), cable trays, raceways, and conduits.

Server Room Goals

There are several goals to designing your server room. Probably the most important goal is for improved operations and productivity. As previously mentioned, server administration, maintenance, upgrades, troubleshooting, and such are more efficient when servers are centralized in a room suited to that purpose.

Following are some additional goals to keep in mind as you locate, design, and build your server room:

• Cost-effective space utilization

• Security from power failures and environmental hazards

• Provision for expansion, additions, and modifications to the network

• Reliability

Additionally, the server room must be physically secure. Use audible alarms and visual alarms. Magnetic swipe cards and badges insure only those with permission are allowed to enter the room. You can even use hardware locks and keys to protect the room and the servers. Make sure you do lock the server room door. And make sure your server is in a fire-safe room.

Inside of the server room, servers should be located away from any windows so they are not visible from the outside and to protect them from the weather. Similarly, don't locate servers near the outer walls in case of dampness or damage from outside forces.

When planning and building the server room, keep records of all interconnections, pathways, power sources and connections, and equipment locations for later reference. The logical facilities should also include software for operations, service, and network management.

> **NOTE**
> Consider using email alerts of viruses in unsolicited email messages or attachments to protect your servers, as well.

SERVER PREPARATIONS

The network operating system you choose will outline the minimum server hardware necessary for optimum performance. You should add to those minimum requirements, for future growth of users, applications, and general expansion of server and network use. Also, any specialized server software added to a network server will require minimum hardware equipment for operating; consider these provisions when purchasing your hardware.

In this chapter, you learn about:

- Basic server requirements

- CPU, memory, I/O suggestions for servers

- Hardware equipment guidelines for servers

- Causes of bottlenecks

- Steps to take to alleviate bottlenecks

Hardware Suggestions

You'll need to consider your system and its configuration when choosing your individual approach to building a server. Following are a few thoughts about various hardware components of the server.

In general, your hardware selection will start with the following:

- Intel Pentium or RISC-based (Reduced Instruction Set Computing) processor such as MIPS (Management Information System) R4x00 or PowerPC that is compatible with the network operating system

  - 32-bit processor

  - VGA monitor

  - Minimum 128MB RAM

  - Triple the free disk space you think you'll need

- CD-ROM and a 3.5 floppy drive
- Mouse or pointing device
- At least one network adapter card
- UPS
- RAID
- Tape drive or other type of backup equipment

Although you have an outline of necessary hardware, the following offers some ideas for improved performance.

> **NOTE**
>
> RISC-based designs are more expensive than Intel processor chips, but are enormously faster and more efficient. RISC-based systems require special versions of operating systems and programs and are often used as imaging, CAD, and 3-D modeling servers, because these applications are sensitive to the speed of floating point calculations. RISC processors do floating point calculations about 20 percent faster than CISC (Complex Instruction Set Computing) processors.

Processors

The central processing unit has a big impact on your overall server throughput. Presently there are clock speeds up to 300MHz, but that will soon be more. Pentium and Pentium Pro offer the most speed and efficiency in a processor; Pentium Pro offers improved scalability in SMP (Symmetric Multiprocessing) configurations so you'll see better throughput and significantly faster processing times than with the older Pentium.

Don't use a Pentium MMX or Pentium II as a server, however, these processors are aimed at workstation applications. Also, Alpha 21064 chips aren't much used on servers anymore; the 300–500MHz 21164 is a better processor for server use. Alphas cost more than Intel systems, but Alphas are great for high-load, mission-critical transaction processing environments.

> **NOTE**
>
> You can't use Alphas with Novell's NetWare.

If you plan to use multiple processors, you'll need a system board that supports them. In general, it would be cheaper to upgrade a current uniprocessor server to a single-processor Pentium Pro or Alpha. However, that won't provide much in the way of upward scalability; you would get better speed and a bit more room but not much upward scalability. Also, uniprocessor systems aren't much good for applications like databases, messaging, and/or groupware.

Processor Scalability

Scalability is the ability to upgrade a network or computing platform so it can handle a heavier workload. Processing and I/O functions are two important factors in upgrading server computers.

Processor scalability means faster, more complex processors that allow greater data throughput, larger files, and more addressable memory. Also, larger amounts of RAM (4GB and up) enable servers to manipulate even larger amounts of data and make better use of the memory cache, thus substituting memory accesses for disk accesses. This method is not inexpensive, however.

When using more powerful processors, operating systems and applications must be modified to take advantage of the chip's capabilities. Intel's 64-bit chips (expected in 1999), for example, will be met with a 64-bit version of Microsoft NT that can take full advantage of the processing architecture.

Multiprocessing, in which two or more CPUs work together in one machine, is another way to increase scalability. SMP (Symmetrical Multiprocessing) is a technology used mostly for large databases, data warehousing, and decision support systems. SMP systems are limited because the individual processors share a single memory bus, which becomes less efficient as the number of processors rises. Some high-end SMP machines include a separate high-speed memory cache for each processor; however, the limitations keep the number of processors to 2, 4, or 8 at most. There are other options besides SMP; however, customized code must be written to run them and the price for the architecture is exorbitant.

Clustering is another technology that fosters scalability. Clustering involves running multiple operating systems on integrated processors. UNIX has the most efficient, well-tested, high-end clustering technologies. RISC has also created clustering technology. Microsoft has created a low-end Windows NT-based clustering market that at the time of this writing supports only two clustered machines.

Memory

You've perhaps heard that you can never install enough RAM to your server computer. For the most part, you want as much RAM as you can afford because too little memory can cause problems with system paging and severely impact disk performance. However, too much memory may cause the operating system and the applications to suffer from managing the unused resources.

So what do you do? Go by what the NOS and server software suggests as optimum for their use. In general, never use any less than 64 MB of RAM for the operating system and add more memory if you're using more processors; for example, use 128MB RAM for a quad-processor configuration.

Disk Subsystem Optimization

The I/O may be a limiting factor in a server system. If you can use SCSI instead of IDE, you'll help this problem. IDE isn't good for server applications because it's slow, has no RAID capabilities except through software, has few devices per channel, and limits overall functionality. EIDE is only marginally better; it's faster. SCSI-2 (or new Fibre Channel devices) or UltraWide SCSI-3 offer you maximum transfer rates. SCSI also offers greater bandwidth and upgradability.

Fibre Channel (FCAL) is a switched-fabric standard that offers increased throughput capabilities over Ultra SCSI-3 standards. FCAL supports more drives on a single bus and multiple simultaneous accesses. Fiber optics are capable of extremely high data transfer rates, but throughput is limited because of FCAL's serial nature.

Hard Drives

The more hard drives you have in a server, the more likely a hard drive will crash; eventual failure may bring on downtime. Also, the more drives you have, the more difficult and time-consuming it is to back them up. To help with this problem, you might try consolidating multiple smaller drives into one or more larger drives on one or more servers.

To accomplish this consolidation efficiently, first prioritize data in order to manage it effectively. Good organization of the drive, directories, and files is the key to success. When considering a server-based storage plan of all or multiple drives, you're making administration, backup and replication, and maintenance easier and more effective.

However, some problems will result from consolidating hard drives. For instance, if the server goes down, users can no longer work on the files associated with that server. Also, if users access many small files and these files are loaded frequently, fast random access is necessary. Large files, on the other hand, demand large throughput when they're loaded. You can lessen this problem by buying fast drives to offset the many small files being accessed and then perhaps use a second large hard drive for the large files, since speed isn't as important on these.

Network Interface Cards

When choosing a network interface card you must consider speed, topology, and compatibility with the server and network operating system. Naturally, expense is also an issue. In the server(s), spare no expense with your network card. The better cards will stand up to the heavy traffic and use on a server and will save you time and effort in replacing inexpensive card after inexpensive card.

If you are really pressed for money, try the 10/100Mbit card, which can attach to a 10Mbit network to begin with, and then attach to a 100Mbit network when you can afford to upgrade; use a 10Mbit hub to begin with and move on to a 100Mbit hub later.

Upgrading Servers

If you're planning to upgrade your current server, consider this: You'll need larger hard drives, added RAM, faster CD-ROM drives, and so on. You might want to consider purchasing a new computer that already has this equipment rather than upgrading, depending on cost. If you do choose to upgrade, get your computer and/or parts from a known vendor instead of letting your cousin's friend build the computer for you. Computers built in this way may not have standard, compatible parts and will definitely be difficult to service.

When purchasing parts, check warranties, technical support, full documentation, spare parts availability, and so on. And don't forget to acquire service manuals and diagnostic software.

> **NOTE**
> When upgrading memory, make sure to match the type of RAM chip; match controllers for hard drives and CD-ROMs, and so on.

Redundancy

This can never be said enough: You must provide some sort of fault tolerance to your network server(s). Use hardware-accelerated RAID controllers; RAID brings fault tolerance and improved I/O performance to standard servers. RAID is generally built around SCSI or Fibre Channel controllers and enables the read and write activities across multiple drives simultaneously.

RAID levels range from 0 (simple disk striping) to 5 (disk striping with parity). RAID 5 is the most commonly used currently because it allows multiple simultaneous reads and writes. There are also higher levels of RAID: 6, 10, 30, and even 50. RAID 50 is defined as RAID 0+5—mirrored RAID 5 sets.

You must implement some sort of fault tolerance; check the network operating system to see if it supports one process over another. You can use two hard disks, multiple disk striping, or an entire replicated server to provide the protection against hard drive failure that you need, but you must use something.

Network Maps and Documentation

Whether you're planning a simple LAN or a more complex enterprise network, you need to prepare good documentation of your network. Although you may think you can remember all connections and hardware in a LAN, you should create maps anyway in case you're not always there when someone needs to find a problem bridge, for example.

As for enterprise networking, the more hardware and software you add to a network, the more candidates for failure points. Cabling, hubs, browser software, a network card, and such could each cause a problem; with hundreds of hubs and thousands of network cards, finding the problem point can be difficult in an enterprise network. Many problems such as this can be tracked and solved by the use of good network maps and documentation.

Even though it's time-consuming, even though it is difficult to render, a network map is the only way you can understand and track hardware problems. Create your maps with specialized software, a database, or organizational charts; you can even draw them by hand. Have your administrators in each office or building take care of their own network segments to help you with this huge job.

Following are some things you should consider adding to the network maps:

- Servers and the number and type of clients each serves

- Hubs, switches, and routers

- Cabling and connections

- Server rooms, telecommunications closet numbers, riser cable assignments, wall jack numbers

Tracing every detail about the wiring and networking hardware throughout the system helps you execute changes, moves, and additions more efficiently. Usually, when wiring is originally installed, a diagram is made by the technician. Use this map as a base and then upgrade it as you add or remove equipment in your enterprise.

When adding your own information, use a logical method to describe the physical system of cables and networking equipment. Use a simple cable numbering scheme that's not based on room numbers or names, since those may change. Combine letters and numbers to identify the equipment as well as its location.

Good documentation minimizes the amount of testing, tracing, and installation work your staff, technicians, and vendors must do to support expansions and repairs. In addition to keeping detailed records of your networking equipment, documentation of software and individual machines is also important. Again, each administrator can record his or her own documentation, or even managers of individual departments can implement these records.

Included in the documentation should be all users on the system; include the user's name, department, and his or her rights or permissions, as well as where he or she accesses the network. Also record hardware information, operating system, current software, Mac (machine) addresses, serial numbers, IRQs, I/Os, and so on. In that same vein, keep all software and hardware documentation in a central area of each network segment.

Bottlenecks

A bottleneck is the slowest component in the network; the component causing an abatement of the traffic flow. You must consider the entire network, from one end to the other, to find the bottlenecks. Consider the following: Say the client computers and the network cards can transfer so many packets per second. The LAN, the routers, and the server's CPU can handle even more packets per second than the clients can. But, if the server's hard disk can only transfer one-half of any one amount of packets per second, the server's hard disk becomes the bottleneck, slowing the packet transfer for the rest of the system. So you upgrade the server's disk only to find the next weakest link, which becomes the new bottleneck.

The solution here is to try to find and eliminate all bottlenecks in the system. By building the network so that all parts work at maximum efficiency, you can eliminate the points of diminished capacity. Some of the server components that can be improved upon in this area are the central processor, hard disk, video card, memory, and the network card. Naturally, all attached network equipment can be possibilities for bottlenecks as well.

Causes of Bottlenecks

There are three main areas on a server where bottlenecks occur: memory, processor, and disk. Memory problems occur when more than one program is run in memory and the server doesn't have enough actual memory to complete the process. An operating system that makes use of paging or memory swapping can boost performance considerably and help alleviate bottlenecks.

Disk bottlenecks happen when an application performs a large number of disk accesses quickly. A hard disk must complete one I/O request before starting the next request so when multiple requests are sent to the server, they start to queue, which slows the server considerably. Finally, a processor can cause bottlenecks when multiple concurrent tasks require concentrated processor time. A multitasking operating system increases the likelihood that the CPU will become constrained.

Examples of Bottlenecks

Following are a few devices and areas in which you may find bottlenecks; naturally, you'll need to check with the device's documentation and/or manufacturer for specific information about that device.

Windows NT's Pagefile.sys

Windows NT uses a paging file on its hard disk that acts as a swap file. With NT's virtual memory, some of the program code is kept in RAM while other information is temporarily swapped into virtual memory to supply the RAM with an extra boost. The pagefile works as virtual memory your computer uses when NT demands more of the system memory than it can give.

The pagefile.sys is a contiguous block of disk space that allows NT to bypass the file system and do direct hardware disk read and write. NT enables the file to enlarge when it reaches the specified limit. The file enlarges in small amounts until it finally runs out of space and the computer slows drastically.

Generally, you set a paging file to the amount of RAM on the system plus about 16MB; of course you must also consider the amount of available free disk space on the hard drive. Often you can alleviate problems and get better performance out of a virtual memory system by establishing paging files on more than one local drive.

Software Programs

How a software application is written may cause a microprocessor to slow if the processor is frequently required to stop what it's doing and jump elsewhere in the program. More delays can occur when the processor isn't able to process a new instruction until a current instruction is completed.

Image Bottlenecks

Increased traffic to a server, as when multiple users access image documents to their workstations, can slow the server down. Using higher-bandwidth networks, such as ISDN or ATM for imaging, will not usually increase performance because of the workstation's limited ability to accept and decompress high-speed image data from the network. Problems with traffic may also occur over low-speed modems using telephone lines to access images.

Suggested solutions may be a document management systems application or screen overview files. These solutions will help to insure that the user retrieves the appropriate document before downloading instead of downloading files he or she "thinks" are correct.

Document management systems normally handle image documents as well as other application objects, like spreadsheets, word processing documents, and so on. You might also try an application that enables you to display full-page images in a window as minipages, or thumbnails.

> **NOTE**
>
> Win-Track is a Windows-based document manager that can create, scan, index, delete, and otherwise manage documents. Another application you might check out is Data General's AV Image.

Also, consider using a magnetic disk for image storage and retrieval. Jukeboxes may cost less per megabyte but they are slow devices that must physically load platters into a drive before image access can begin. Magnetic disk caching is a bit faster; however, since there's no way to predict which files will be accessed next, you still can't guarantee a faster access rate. Again, using a third-party application to create compressed minipages that are stored on magnetic disks may help speed the process and prevent bottlenecks.

Bandwidth

Bandwidth bottlenecks could be causing your problems but first consider the speeds of other equipment, such as your desktop and workgroup switches. For example, if you switch your desktops over to 10Mbps and workgroup switches to 100Mbps, your backbones may become overwhelmed. Similarly, applying higher-speed network cards to your workstations may cause the network to become overloaded. Try to limit the available bandwidth by reducing the number of switched 100Mbps ports on the desktop to forestall the need to add expensive switches or wiring.

Alleviating Bottlenecks

You might try using third-party applications, such as performance optimizers or server monitors, to track server usage and locate the bottlenecks. Often you can use additional hardware to alleviate a bottleneck as well. Larger hard drives, extra memory, and more powerful CPUs will help. Additionally, some advances in technology can help to make your system's performance more efficient. Consider the following advances:

- CPU/IO buses are accelerating up to 100MHz.
- SDRAM (synchronous DRAM) is available to match the higher bus frequencies; soon available SLDRAM (SyncLink DRAM) and RDRAM (Rambus DRAM).

- New Intel CPUs address L2 caches over a private bus to keep traffic off the main I/O bus.

- New systems are moving the graphics controller off the PCI bus to a private channel called the AGP (Accelerated Graphics Port) to quadruple the graphics throughput.

Also consider the following when trying to eliminate bottlenecks:

Symmetric Multiprocessing (SMP) servers. You can transparently scale up your servers to multiprocessing servers with no modifications required to the application programs or database management systems currently running on single-processor versions of the same operating system. As you need processing power, add processors up to the physical limit of the server. Unfortunately, there is a potential bottleneck since SMP processors all share the same disk I/O and memory subsystems.

Massively Parallel Processing (MPP) servers. MPP servers consist of multiple independent processors, each with its own memory and disk I/O subsystem. The problem here is that the software developer has to create the software with MPP in mind. There are various sophisticated MPP database server software applications from Oracle (Oracle Parallel Server), Informix Software (Extended Parallel Server), Sybase (Sybase MPP), and IBM (DB2/6000 Parallel Edition). MPP requires proprietary hardware and a highly specialized operating system, and it's very expensive.

Clustered servers. A compromise between SMP and MPP is a cluster of multiple SMP servers. Application software must be designed to take advantage of the parallelism; however, existing nonparallelized software can take advantage of single SMP systems in the cluster with some efficiency loss. The clustering solution is also expensive.

Chapter 5

ADMINISTRATION

Whether you're building a new network or upgrading an existing network, you should carefully plan your approach. Take the deployment in steps; make a list of the tasks you'll need to perform to complete the deployment. Within the many and varied steps to building a network is a set of steps for preparing the server(s).

As administrator of the network, there are many tasks you'll perform or delegate in preparing the server. You must tackle file and directory management, user preparations, outsourcing tasks, software installation, and so much more. This chapter presents an overall list of tasks that can help you get organized for the job ahead—installing and/or upgrading your network server(s). Add to the list any supplementary steps specific to your business.

In this chapter, you learn the steps to complete the following:

- Planning the deployment
- Getting help
- Preparing file and directory structure
- Defining policies
- Ordering NOS and applications
- Ordering the server
- Preparing the site
- Collecting information
- Installing and configuring the server
- Setting up client computers
- Testing the server

Planning the Deployment

Planning the deployment of your new or upgraded server(s), as detailed in Chapters 1 and 2 of this book, include the following tasks:

Analyze your needs.

Choose the network operating system.

Choose the server types and select server software.

Decide on the number of servers you need.

Think about the server hardware.

Consider the networking hardware.

Plan the client computers.

Diagram the placement of the servers in your office.

Getting Help

No one can perform all of the duties it takes to deploy a network. You'll need administrative assistants, technical support, and perhaps even outsourcing help. Your next step should be to enlist and contract the help you'll need for implementing your servers into your network.

Hire additional staff, if necessary and applicable.

Hire outside help for jobs that are outsourced:

- Consultants
- Technical help
- Programmers
- Internet service providers

Assign administrative assistants:

- Inform assistants of everything you do.
- Train assistants in specific jobs you can delegate to them.
- Delegate duties.

Preparing File and Directory Structure

Before you can store anything on the server, before even one user accesses a server, you should have the directory structure prepared and ready. Consider where you will store employee data, accounting and payroll files, customer information, users' home directories, private files, and so on. Create a naming convention for your files and directories so they are well organized and easily recognizable. Think about which files will be stored on the server and which will be kept on individual workstations.

Consider data security and outline a plan.

Create a structure that supports file accessibility for users.

Determine areas for file storage.

Prepare directory structure.

Create and list shared resources, files, and directories.

Defining Policies

Policies are often not a priority when so many other tasks pull you in other directions; however, policies help your network run smoothly, keep your users informed, and support you in case any circumstances arise. You don't have to write the policies yourself but you should review any policies submitted by managers, supervisors, and so on. The policies don't need to be finished before you move on to the next step; however, they should be completed before the network is up and running. And finally, policies should be written down, distributed to every employee, and reviewed with employees.

- Security issues
- Backup schedule
- Disaster recovery
- Assistant and user training
- Naming conventions
- User guidelines
- User accounts

> **NOTE**
>
> Prepare an FAQ (Frequently Asked Question(s)) and/or guidelines to distribute to employees. If you set up a company intranet, you can also post your policies for everyone to see.

Ordering NOS and Applications

Your next step is to decide upon and order the network operating system for your server(s). Check on licensing of servers and users while ordering the software and then go ahead and purchase the appropriate licenses at the same time. You'll also want to order any server applications, such as a database management system or email server software, at this time.

After you choose the NOS and any server applications you will use, you can determine the server hardware required to run these programs.

Order the NOS.

- Check hardware requirements and compatibility.
- Check licensing and order.

Order any server applications you need.

- Check licensing and order.

Order any third-party programs you'll use on the network.

Ordering the Server

When ordering your server, you need to refer to the information you gathered while in the planning stages. Make sure everything you order is compatible with your network operating system and server software. Also make sure your applications will work with the hardware you're about to purchase. Try to order everything you need so as not to delay the deployment later while you wait for a second network card or UPS to arrive. See Chapter 4 of this book, "Server Preparations," for more information about server and networking hardware.

Order the server and/or upgrade equipment.

- Order any network cards or other equipment for server.
- Check peripheral compatibility.

Purchase fault tolerance disks, servers, UPS, backup tape drives, or other equipment you need.

- Purchase new and/or upgrade network equipment.
- Order outside connections and lines for the Internet.

Preparing the Site

In preparing the site for the server(s) placement, you must decide first whether you will centralize your server computers. You may place the servers in one room or divide them among various offices within your building. Within the general location of the server(s), you must decide where to place the other equipment that is needed for server and network use.

For each server, you must consider wiring and cabling, peripheral equipment, monitor and keyboard use, and so on. Do you want to include racks for switches, cross-connections, fax and/or modem servers, and other data and telecommunications equipment within the server room, or do you want to provide rooms, or closets, for this equipment? See Chapter 3 of this book, "Planning Server Strategies," for more information.

Check server location and placement.

- Check the physical security of the server.
- Sketch server placement.

Sketch networking equipment placement.

- Include data communications racks.
- Include telecommunications racks.
- Diagram cabling.

Place peripherals in the same area as server.

Install cabling, phone, or other connection lines.

Add any furniture needed for the server.

Collecting Information

For convenience and organization, you should collect all of your documentation for your server(s) software and hardware and keep it in a central location. Nothing is more frustrating than needing to know about the jumpers on a card, for example, and not being able to find the diagram. You might also want to gather and bind a list of contact names and numbers for consultants, technical support, outsourcing, and even help desk personnel in your own company. Keep this list with the rest of your documentation.

- Application and hardware documentation
- Documentation for drivers, updates, patches, and such
- Contact numbers for technical support, consultants, outsourcing
- Reference materials
- Data, such as Web page content, catalog entries, images, text, and so on
- Map of IP addresses

Installing and Configuring the Server

Installing the network operating system is a matter of following the directions in the documentation. Often, while installing, there are options from which to choose that determine how the server works, such as whether the server authenticates users or simply provides services, or whether the server connects to the Internet, and so on. Carefully check the documentation along with your needs list to see which of these options you need to install.

Configuring the server may not be quite so easy. Usually, there are specific steps and choices to make to prepare the server for your use. For additional help, you may want to check with a network consultant or perhaps purchase a third-party book that can help you set up the server for your needs.

Set server in place and connect to the network.

Load NOS.

- Load drivers, updates, patches, resource kits, and any other suggested operating system modifications.

Configure server.

- Create and configure user and group accounts.
- Set security permissions and rights.
- Create directories for applications, sharing, users, and so on.
- Set any features for optimization, backup, file maintenance, and such.
- Make a system disk.

Install any additional server software or applications needed.

Configure additional applications to suit your system and needs.

Back up the system.

- User accounts.
- Data files.

Setting Up Client Computers

When setting up the client computers, you must consider hardware, software, networking equipment, and so on. Also, you must consider the users' needs. Provide guidelines for network use, a list of contact numbers, training, and support for your users; after all, if they are tentative about using the system, they may avoid it and your network will become nothing more than a group of connected standalones.

Users forget their passwords, lose files, have applications lock up and workstations crash. Often printers won't print and backups don't work. You need to take care of these day-to-day occurrences by delegating tasks to assistants. Create a help desk, perhaps, for users to call on for advice. Even a printed set of guidelines to follow when these common problems pop up would help users to feel comfortable with the system.

Purchase new or upgrade workstation hardware.

- Network cards.
- Peripherals such as CD-ROMs, modems, UPS, and so on.

Install new or upgrade operating systems.

Configure operating systems plus networking software.

- Use profiles or scripts to quickly configure OS.
- Install and configure protocols, clients, adapter drivers.
- Check to make sure each user can attach to the network.

Install software.

- Using CD-ROMs or network installation directories, install any applications needed.

Prepare and train users.

- Provide guidelines for use of network.
- Provide contact names and numbers for support.
- Provide training and/or training material.

Testing the Server

If at all possible, you should test the server with a small number of clients before placing it into action on the entire network. By testing first, you can avoid any problems with configuration, security, or missed components. After testing, you should monitor the server performance carefully to make sure the users are getting the most out of the server.

Test the server (one new server at a time).

- Use a small number of clients.

- Test for at least a week before implementing to the entire network.
- Troubleshoot problems and find solutions.

Open up the entire network.

- Monitor the server carefully.
- Check performance continually.
- Troubleshoot and find solutions.

Optimize network and server performance.

Back up the server on a consistent and reliable schedule.

APPLICATION MANAGEMENT

Introduction to Book Three

A major part of your administrative duties is application management. You need to install and configure applications—both on the network and on individual workstations—maintaining consistency while modifying programs enough so users can get their work done. You also supervise the upgrades, licensing, policies, security, and troubleshooting of those applications.

Applications are the core of any business, whether they are commercial applications like Word, Excel, Lotus 1-2-3, or SmartSuite and Office, or vertical applications created specifically for your business, such as real estate marketing or printing estimation. Your company may use accounting programs, such as Peach Tree, Mas90, QuickBooks/QuickPay or Internet applications like Netscape, FrontPage, or Internet Information Server. Database programs such as Oracle or SQL Server also play an important role in the network.

Managing these applications is a huge job, one not to be tackled alone. Consider hiring extra help for application control, such as consultants, programmers, and such. Additionally, this book offers some advice that can help you in your application management. Following are a few of the topics covered:

- Application types and examples of common programs

- Installation on server or client

- Security information

- Network traffic and applications

- Program licensing and policies

PRELIMINARY GROUNDWORK

When considering the types of applications you'll use in your business, you must first assess your needs. Your business may be product-based and therefore a database application suits your purposes; on the other hand, if you perform mostly graphic arts and desktop publishing, you'll use different applications to complete your work. Most businesses need an accounting or payroll program of sorts, and perhaps a word processing application. You may want to add networking applications such as email and Internet browsers to boost collaboration and sharing within the company.

After you choose the applications necessary to run your business, you can plan their installation and configuration. You want to get the most from any application you add to your network. This chapter will help you decide just how to do that. In this chapter, you learn the following:

- Location of program files

- Application types

- Client/server applications

- Planning for applications

- Questions to ask before purchasing

Location of Program Files

When installing your applications, you'll need to decide whether to install to the server or to the workstation. If you install applications to the server, those applications are distributed for use to users over the network. If an application is installed only to the workstation, it can only be used by the person(s) sitting at that computer. Where you install the applications affects the users, administrators, file storage, program configuration, file naming, security, and so on.

Workstation or Server

Applications for use on an individual computer help the user perform his or her day-to-day chores, such as writing letters, typesetting a newsletter, retouching a photograph, and so on. Workstation installs are not available to anyone unless that person is sitting at the particular computer. Although document and data files can be stored on the network server, generally they are stored on the user's hard drive so the files are available when needed.

Nearly any program that can be loaded to a workstation for use by one person can be loaded to the network for use by many, with the proper licensing and application installation package. Generally, however, the following applications are considered for use on a workstation: word processors, spreadsheets, presentation, drawing/art/paint, desktop publishing, and often office suites.

Applications for network use are those shared among two or more users attached to the network. Users share the data used with the applications so that updates and current data are always available; for example, a database program containing descriptions of all products a company sells would be shared by many different users—sales, customer service, billing, complaints, inventory, manufacturing, and other departments within the company.

Ordinarily, the following programs are used over a network by many people: email, groupware, accounting applications, database applications, and vertical applications. Some of these are client/server applications, meaning there is specific software you install to the server and matching client software that enables the user to request services from the server.

Often programs such as office suites, or any one component of the suite, are used on workstations and/or servers. An office suite is a group of programs, such as a word processor, spreadsheet, database, and presentations or mail or scheduling applications. Use of a suite on a server means more control over program configuration, less expensive and time-consuming upgrades, and easier and sharable file storage.

Client/Server Applications

Applications such as email, groupware, and databases are most often made up of two distinct programs: the server software and the client software. The server software installs onto a server computer that is accessible to the users on the network; client software installs to the workstations on the network.

Figure 1.1 shows the relationships between servers and clients on a client/server network. Various multiple services occur at the same time. Some

---

Figure 1.1 Clients request and servers reply.

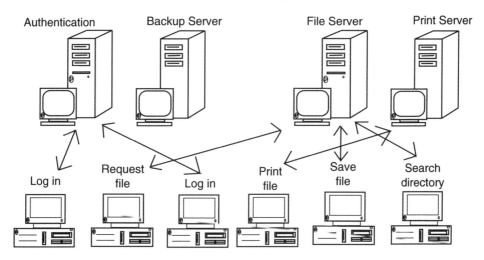

clients log in to the network via the authentication server; others open, save, and request files from a file server; and yet other client computers print through the print server. The arrows in the figure show the server/client connection; however, the actual requests and replies travel over the network cables.

Following are some additional facts about client/server applications:

• The server software supplies security and access, files or data, and a shared directory in which to store the data.

• Client software enables the user to communicate with the server, and to receive services.

• Client/server applications share resources, such as files and/or directories.

• Client/server software is independent of the hardware and the operating system; therefore, various client applications can be mixed with a server platform.

The client/server application is made up of three components: the server, the client, and middleware. The server runs on top of a network operating system. The server software depends on the NOS to interface with the middleware component.

The middleware part runs on both the client and the server sides of the application. Middleware is the distributed software that supports interactions between clients and servers. It doesn't supply the services (server's job) and it doesn't include the user interface or the application's logic (client's jobs). Middleware is the adhesive that lets the client obtain the service from the server.

The client component runs on the client side of the application, on top of the operating system providing the graphical user interface or object-oriented user interface. The client can access distributed services wherever they are offered on the network.

As an example of a client/server application, consider an email program such as Microsoft Exchange. The Exchange server software provides electronic mail functionality for users, good security, integrated system administration, gateways to foreign messaging systems, a distributed directory, public folders, and so on. The server offers user mail boxes, connectors to the Internet, replication services, an address book, and administrative tools for optimizing performance, tracking messages, and logging activities within the system.

The client side of the software enables users to connect to the server, retrieve messages from their mailboxes, send and retrieve mail, join in public discussions, post and read documents to be shared, and more.

Advantages and Disadvantages

There are definite advantages to installing an application to the network, as opposed to installing it to a workstation; there are disadvantages, as well. Consider the type of application, its licensing, and the way you want to use it as you decide where to install it.

The advantages of installing an application to the network are as follows:

- Program files are located on the server and therefore anyone with access can work on the shared files.
- Administrator has control over the application's configuration and users' settings.
- Administrator has control over who can access the application, program directories and files, and who cannot.
- Updated data is most usually available for use.

Disadvantages of installing an application to the server are as follows:

- The program may not always be available for use.
- Network traffic affects the speed of the program. Application use adds to the network traffic, thus slowing other services.

- If the server crashes, work stops.

- Workstation hardware and operating systems may need to be upgraded to run the application from the server.

- Administrator must work harder to keep application and network traffic running smoothly. Also, the administrator must provide security, backup and restore, monitor storage space, move and manage data, and so on.

> **NOTE**
>
> As administrator, you might want to have users install applications to their workstations but save their working files to the server, so the files can be shared and so files can easily be backed up and restored.

Application Issues

Before you purchase and install applications for use over the network, you need to ask a few questions so you'll know how to prepare the server, the network, and the users. There are some facts you'll need to consider as well about licensing, file storage space, and so on. Planning your use of applications before taking action is important for several reasons. Some applications use more bandwidth than others do so you need to prepare the network for optimum performance. Some applications may not work well in conjunction with others. Some may require special hardware or additional software. The requirements for applications are as varied and numerous as the number of applications available.

Planning Considerations

As you plan and prepare to add applications to your network servers, first consider the server hardware you may need to upgrade or add so the applications can run at optimum performance. Check an application's documentation or with sales or customer service for an exact listing of hardware requirements for the servers, the network, and the workstations. Some programs require special or extra hardware to work properly.

Next, check to see that the application doesn't conflict with any of your current applications, drivers, operating systems, and so on. A conflict with the operating system you use on some or all of your workstations could cost you in upgrades, in both OSs and hardware, if the new OS requires it. Also, you may need new or updated device drivers, library files, or other software to make the application work. Find out all you can before you purchase the application so you will be prepared for whatever is next.

Additionally, here are some concerns you should think about before purchasing the application:

For network use.   Make sure the version of software you get is either for network use or not for network use. Some applications that are not for network use will not run on the network or will not let more than one person access the program.

Administration duties.   Realize that server installation may be easy because all options are the same and applications are consistent to all users. However, maintenance and support over the network may be more difficult because of misplaced data, hung workstations that affect the application or data, user-caused problems, and so on. Be prepared to spend more time, especially initially, in maintenance and control.

Loading and access speed.   Applications installed to the server and accessed by more than one person will take a bit longer to load and use. Screen redraw will be slower over the network (depending on your networking hardware). Workstation installation means accelerated response time and more efficient use of the program. Be prepared with the networking, server, and workstation hardware to handle traffic and speed problems.

Network traffic.   Use of a program from server to workstation means more traffic added to existing traffic of users accessing files, printers, and other resources. Remote connections (as in a WAN) are already slowed compared to a direct connection; then add loading large applications over the network. Install applications to a server on the same side as the users so applications don't have to travel so far.

Productivity.   Consider this: If the server goes down, anyone using an application over the network stops work as well. Be prepared for this occurrence by having other work that can be completed on standalones and have a backup method of performing key tasks normally performed on the server. Suppose your hotel billing server crashes. You will need an alternate method of preparing bills until the server can be restored.

Workstation operating systems.   Consider the compatibility between your various workstation operating systems when installing the application to the server. Varied OSs can mean many and various application configurations.

Application control. Do you want all applications to look exactly alike on each workstation? If so, you'll need to control the application settings from the server. Make sure the application can handle this option and that you'll have the time to configure and troubleshoot the application for the users. You might want exact settings for all work-stations, for example, when you're training users or for users who move from workstation to workstation within the office.

Questions to Ask

When preparing to purchase the application you'll install to a server, you must do some research. Check with the manufacturer, salespeople, documentation, or look around on the Internet to get the information you need. Following are some questions that may help you decide what you need.

What type of security does the application provide? Are there any special requirements, configurations, add-ons, or such that make the security more useful to you? Or does the security come from your network operating system?

What happens when the number of locations and users grows? Is the application scalable? Will you need more licenses (for server and/or workstation)? Are there any add-ons, patches, additional software you need to make the application work when you expand your network?

What is the network bandwidth cost allocation? In other words, will you need to upgrade your networking hardware to take care of the extra traffic caused by the application?

What impact do changes in other applications have on this new one and vice versa? Do the applications share libraries, security, files or directories, DLL files if Windows-based, and such? If you install or remove or upgrade one application, will that change affect others on the server or network?

What happens if database and/or applications servers are moved or split? Will the application need to be reinstalled, modified, reconfigured? Will the application continue to operate in the same configuration if it is moved or split?

What type of licensing does the application require? Some applications keep track of how many people are logged on at one time; others don't limit usage in that manner. Make sure you have appropriate licensing for the software, including server(s) and client(s).

How many workstations can use the application? Is there a limit imposed by the application? Are there special client software, driver files, or other modules that should be loaded to the workstations for the application to work?

Does the application track users? Does it log activities, security breaches, application errors? Is there a method of optimizing the application included with the software?

Are there any special installation instructions for the server? Check the various methods of installation—usually called typical, custom, and so on—and examine all of the options to make sure you understand how to install the application.

Before Installation

There are just a couple of questions you need to ask about any application before installing it. Undoubtedly, each application will cover the questions you need to answer in order to complete the installation, such as number and type of licensing, type of connections, and so on. However, here are just a few more points to consider:

How many people will use the application?   Count the number of people who will use the program and have that number handy. Many times you must specify that number so the program can update files, lock records, perform file purges, or compress data. (For example, Access—a database application—can run on the network or on a standalone computer but you must specify to the program the number of people who will use it since it tears down files and rebuilds them periodically.)

How much disk space will you need for the application?   Make sure you have enough disk space on the server(s) to accommodate not only the program files but the data files as well. Design a directory structure for data files (you'll likely use the application's own directory structure for the program files) that makes sense to users and to saving within the program.

Who will help administer the application?   You should certainly assign one or two assistants to the server, the application, and the users of the application for troubleshooting, training, and maintenance. Don't try to do it all yourself.

PLANNING NETWORK STRATEGIES

During the life cycle of your network applications, you will need to upgrade several major and perhaps minor revisions, change configurations, troubleshoot problems, and otherwise monitor and supervise the use of the applications. Depending on the number of applications, servers, and users on your network, performing application management tasks could take up to 50 percent of your time.

The average number of applications per desktop is increasing, operating systems seem to be more and more unstable, and there is more information for the user to learn in order to use his or her computer and the network. Ultimately, the obligation for the network, hardware, operating systems, peripherals, and applications is on you, the administrator. If you can manage applications well and plan your strategies skillfully, you may save yourself some time, effort, and stress in your daily responsibilities.

In this chapter, you learn about the following:

- Network resource planning

- Software licensing

- Informing users

- Security and policies

- Administrative tasks

Network Resource Planning

When any application must be deployed to the clients on a network, you should plan your network resources. Network resource planning is a method of ensuring that applications achieve an acceptable quality of service at a minimum network cost. Especially as your network grows in size and complexity, your quality of service level may waver, especially for business-critical client/server applications. You'll want to plan your network resources for several reasons:

- The capacity and configuration of your network topology directly impact the quality of service to your users. You want the most efficient, practical network setup possible.

- Applications contend for network bandwidth; setting up a new application adds to the problem unless you plan for the additional traffic ahead of time.

- Client/server environments are unpredictable in terms of network utilization. It's difficult to know when users will access applications and how much they will use the resources.

- Many transactions demand consistent uptime; this can be a major problem, especially when your network covers a wide geographic area.

Network and Server Issues

Knowing your network hardware, topology, bandwidth, and other networking factors makes it easier to determine how to deploy your applications. Additionally, you must understand the server configuration and its network parameters in order to effectively serve the clients.

Following is a list of preparations and tasks that can help you get ready for installing and configuring a new application to the network:

Create and maintain accurate and complete documentation of the current physical network configuration. List servers, workstations, and networking hardware such as routers, hubs, switches, cabling, and so on. Figure 2.1 shows a sketch of servers and clients, hubs, routers, switches, and operating systems of both the network and client. This type of map can help you trace problems, quickly identify clients, manage upgrades, and so on.

Create and maintain accurate documentation of network traffic use. Many NOSs contain an applet for traffic tracking and network optimization. Alternatively, you can purchase a third-party program to perform these tasks.

Create an outline of your applications' needs of network resources, such as bandwidth, frequency of transactions, and so on. You can find this information in an application's documentation or by calling the manufacturer.

Keep a record of how the network currently responds to application errors and/or failures, changes in fluctuation of traffic intensity. Where does the network slow? Where are the bottlenecks? Test the network systematically to determine points of failure.

Figure 2.1 Sketch out a network map of hardware and operating systems.

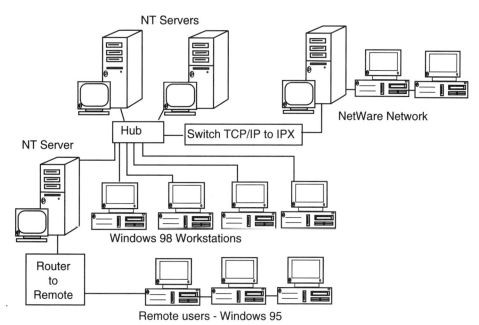

Troubleshoot any current application performance problems and resolve those problems before adding another application to the mix.

Standardize your servers. Try to use only one NOS across the network if possible; make sure server hardware is fairly consistent so network traffic can be easily balanced.

Consider the status of the server to be used by the application. If the server contains too many other applications or services—such as simultaneously supporting bandwidth-intensive browsers and multimedia applications—then you must add power to the server or remove some of its burdens before trying to deploy a new application.

Workstation Issues

In order to supply your users with applications over the network, you must be aware of the performance and configuration of the workstations involved. As

> **NOTE**
>
> When documenting your server, network, and client inventory, identify the general characteristics of the system, location of database and application servers, number of users and their locations, specific application transactions, interfaces to other applications and information systems. Define the topology, LAN media types, protocols, type of routers, and number of sites. Check traffic flow and volume; collect and analyze data so you can identify anomalies and figure out trends.

you plan the implementation of your network applications, ask yourself the following questions:

Are the clients running a compatible operating system? Perhaps there are many diverse operating systems that should be changed or upgraded before deployment of the application server. The fewer client operating systems you must deal with, the easier your job.

Do any workstations contain a program that may conflict with the new application? Check for possible conflicts and remove the offending programs.

Are the workstations performing at the highest level possible? You may want to upgrade hardware or optimize the drives on the client computers, clean old files and TMP files from the drives and run a defragmentation program, delete old programs, check for viruses, and otherwise perform a full maintenance on each drive before adding new applications and new files.

Do the workstations have enough disk space to handle the new application, client software, extra files, or whatever else is needed to deploy the application? Check for disk space, clean the disk of obsolete files and programs, or upgrade the hard drives.

Is there enough money in the budget for upgrading workstations? Estimate the cost for supplying the hardware and then plan a schedule for upgrading workstations. You may need to adjust the application deployment schedule due to financial constraints.

Are your remote computers standardized? If your remote users have varied operating systems and assorted hardware, your job will be easier if you can enforce standards in these computers.

> **NOTE**
>
> Consider, too, that depending on the type of application you're installing, you may be able to let the users install the client software to their own computers from the network. Many client/server applications enable this option. You install the client software to the server in a special, shared directory. Users can then log on to the network and install the software at their convenience. This can save a great deal of administrative time and effort.

Miscellaneous Strategies

There are a few more things you should check into, tasks you should perform and responsibilities to fulfill, before you're ready to install and use your applications. Make sure you understand the licensing procedures for the application(s), create naming conventions and security policies, and so on.

Licensing Software

You should check the application's licensing before purchasing the server and/or client software. Each manufacturer issues software licenses differently so you must make sure you have the proper certification for each application you add to your network. The Software Publishers Association (SPA), a software vendor trade association, is an organization that tracks software licensing abuse. Tips about licensing abuse usually come from disgruntled employees so don't think your company is immune. You could end up paying hundreds of thousands of dollars in court costs and fines for copyright infringement.

Follow these steps to help ensure you have the appropriate licensing for every operating system, NOS, server software, and application on your network:

Appoint a software manager to monitor software installation, usage, and license compliance.

Create an application policy that prohibits employees from installing software on their computers without permission.

Require employees to report unlicensed software that they discover.

Make sure employees understand the risks of illegally copying software.

Audit your company's computers and software periodically and confirm all licensing.

> **NOTE**
>
> You may want to use a software metering program to help keep an eye on licenses. Microsoft's SMS (Systems Management Server) is one such program. Another example is SPA's SPAudit, which is available free from the Net (www.spa.org). Or there's ON Technology Corp.'s SofTrack, Tally Systems' CentaMeter and Cenergy. These types of programs analyze usage patterns, determine the number of licenses needed for each application, and ensure license compliance.

Naming Conventions

After naming your servers, sites, domains, containers, server directories, and other networking entities, you're familiar with the idea of using consistent naming conventions so users can easily find their way around on the network. These naming conventions are extremely important for your applications as well.

Make sure you establish one or more common, shared directories in which users can store communal application files; name and locate the directories so they are easy to find and recognize. Also, institute a file-naming convention that all users follow so the files are easily found in a directory of thousands and easily distinguishable to save time.

Make a list of your naming conventions, the directories, files, and public folders or directories, if applicable, and distribute the list to all application users for future reference.

> **NOTE**
>
> You should also make it a practice to inform your users of changes you make to the system, including adding and retiring applications. Make sure they receive guidelines for using new applications, a list of policies, security information, as well as training.

Security and Policies

Just as you would protect your network and server, you must protect the applications on the server. Using a physically secure server, UPS, fault-tolerant services like RAID, and such will help. Even though the machine on which the application is located is secure, there may still be threats to the applications and data on that machine. A disgruntled user with the rights to access the application can destroy data, templates, configurations, and such. An untrained user can also destroy everything you've worked so hard to establish.

There are certain precautions you can take to limit the effects of this type of problem. First, as always, delegate your administrative tasks. Let others help you with your tasks and responsibilities. By letting others help you supervise and monitor the network, the server, and the applications, you can hopefully head off problems before they become too serious.

Next, back up often and test the backups. Form a backup plan for each application and its data and follow that plan precisely. Also, your backups will be worthless if you don't test them each and every time you make a backup. The few minutes it takes to test a backup will be well worth it if you need it.

Track the application's usage using a built-in monitor from the network operating system or the application itself, or purchase a third-party monitoring device. Survey who uses the application, how often, and other details so you can eliminate problems before they can begin.

Use passwords and security features of the network and the application to protect data and access. Most applications have built-in features that protect the data and settings.

Additionally, you should form a set of policies governing your applications. List who can use them and when the use is permitted, such as only during work hours. Notify the users that data applying to the company, customers, services, and other sensitive issues are strictly for company use; such data cannot be removed from the building (on disks, laptops, and so on). Also, apply limits on copying and moving files to other parts of the network, workstations, diskettes, and such.

After creating your policies, make copies and in an open meeting, review the policies with the users. It's even a good idea to have users sign a paper acknowledging that they understand and agree to your set of guidelines. Although signing an agreement of this sort is perhaps not legally binding, it will make users think twice before violating a written policy.

Installation of Applications

You can install an application to a workstation or to a server. When you install to the server for network use by multiple users, you must follow any special guidelines in the program's documentation that targets network installation. Network installation specifically enables shared directories, data files, multiple users, licensing, and other activities and configurations that enable the program to work properly in a client/server situation.

Following are a few general guidelines to follow when installing an application to the network; however, let the application's documentation override all other rules and guidelines.

Always read documentation, especially installation and configuration instructions.

Use the "install" or "setup" program (EXE), often located on the root directory of the floppy or CD, to install the program.

If given the choice, install the application from the CD-ROMs rather than a floppy, for speed. Furthermore, consider installing from the network to workstations and/or other servers for the quickest installation.

Always read the README files or any other last-minute updates on the disk with the program files before installing the application, in case a network, installation, compatibility, or other problem is listed.

Administrator's Duties

As always, you'll have a list of tasks you must perform to complete the deployment of your network applications. Following is a list that will help you remember the tasks:

Research the market to find out what's available.   Poll your managers and assistants to discover what is needed in the way of applications. Choose which applications you will configure for network use and workstation installation.

Check server and workstation hardware for compatibility.   Upgrade hardware before installing new programs. Also, check the other applications on the server and workstations to make sure there are no conflicts with the new program(s).

Plan a directory and file-naming convention and notify all users of that convention.

Plan your security now.   List users and their probable levels of access.

Write security policies dealing with application and review these policies with all users involved.   Also, add a list of steps, shared directories, file-naming conventions, and common tasks performed in the application to help guide users after their training is complete.

Install and configure the application software on the server.   Train any administrative assistants or managers who will work with the program and help users to complete their work.

Install and configure any client software. Make sure users are trained and understand policies and guidelines.

Test the installation and adjust configuration. Perhaps install software to one server and a limited number of workstations to test it for a week or more. Work out the initial bugs in a limited environment before installing the application to all application servers and workstations on the network. Additionally, install and test upgrades before enabling everyone on the network to use it.

Testing gives you an idea of potential software and/or hardware problems and enables you to develop documentation, like training materials, guidelines for use, instructions for file storage, and so on. Test first so you don't end up with a server failure or other network problem that severely impacts productivity and perhaps puts your data at risk.

Deploy to the entire network when ready by installing the software and configuring it as planned. Document installation in case you run into trouble, or if successful, you can use the steps to deploy the next application to the network.

Monitor the application's performance and adjust the configuration as needed. Check with assistants and users periodically to make sure the application is performing as expected. Also, monitor the network resources to see how the application has affected the traffic, usage, and so on, and adjust configurations and upgrade hardware as necessary.

Back up the application and data. Test the backup thoroughly and make sure you keep accurate and current backups.

NETWORK APPLICATIONS

There are many types of applications you can use over the network by installing them to a server and enabling access to the program and data by clients. Some of these programs require special client software; others open from the server onto the client computer. Many of these programs supply shared directories and enable shared files. Often they also include administration, security, and customized configuration features.

Network applications can be database management systems or Internet email applications. Network applications can be manufactured by the same company that made your NOS or by a different company completely. This chapter introduces you to various types of network applications and gives some examples of each type. In this chapter, you learn about the following:

- Database management programs

- Groupware applications

- Email and scheduling programs

- Accounting applications

- Vertical software

- Suites and their components

Database Management Applications

Databases disseminate relevant information to every person on the network. A database is a collection of information organized for easy access and manipulation—catalogs, address book, listing of products, people, and data—and enables you to get your job done. A database includes a road map, of sorts that helps users find specific data and figure out how the data relates to other information in the file.

A Database Management System (DBMS) controls access to data, protects data from accidents or malicious intent, manipulates data, and provides tools for interpreting the data. The DBMS provides fast, easy access to data. A database management system transfers user inputs into a collection of tables, views, indexes, and other objects the user can quickly read and understand. A database management system enables a user to store and retrieve data, add and remove data, update data and query the database for data retrieval.

> **NOTE**
>
> Many databases, such as Microsoft Access, Lotus Approach, dBase, and so on, also work over a network; these applications are not management systems, however, simply database applications.

You can create a database to suit any business. A database might contain products or services, ceramic bodies and glazes, music CDs and tapes, garden pests, fish and fishing equipment, or any of thousands of other items and topics.

DBMS Components

Many database management systems are relational, meaning the users do not see the technical details associated with manipulating data because the management system takes care of those details. A database management system can also provide data to multiple users simultaneously, while protecting the data and ensuring that each user receives the same data at the same time by locking data until the operation is completed and then unlocking it when it becomes available again.

Additionally, most database management systems include the following common components:

Tools and utilities. Database design and maintenance tools consist of a programming language called Data Definition Language (DDL) that's used to build a database, define the data, and maintain the data.

Data administration and control. Tools that enable various levels of privilege to users and restrict access, such as write, read, and administrative rights or permissions.

Data entry management. Utilities for entering the data into the database, such as prompt/response routines or screen forms.

Data-checking utilities. Tools for verifying the data is correct and error-free.

Report design and generation. Utilities that enable you to design reports that extract certain data from the database in answer to queries. Reports are a method of organizing and displaying data.

Query. A feature the lets users question the database to obtain reports without having to design the reports.

Backup and recovery. Utilities that permit a database to be restored to its original state when it becomes corrupted (transaction rollback and recovery, for example).

Distributed databases, or those with many servers and many users, work transparently with data no matter where the data resides. DDL can write updates to two or more sites as part of one transaction.

Database Management Guidelines

The operation of a database system includes the application's installation and configuration, upgrades, the development of databases, and the use of design packages and their associated tools. You must also consider a security plan to protect the data and a contingency plan for growing system needs. As your database grows, so must your protection of the application and its related data.

Within the database server and application, outline a schedule of backups and a plan for recovery should hardware or software fail. You may be surprised at how much you depend on your databases once you get them up and running.

When preparing a database server, upgrade or purchase a high storage capacity, extra memory, and fast processor speed of the machine for best performance. As with any new or upgraded application, you should test any database management system and its components before actually putting it into use. Correct any problems before the users begin using the system. Provide support and guidance to users of the database or supply resources for users to consult for answers to their questions.

When implementing a database management system, you'll want to keep in mind the following:

Data in a database constantly changes, new users may be added, and servers are often added. In light of the additional processes you should monitor the system and find ways to improve performance. Upgrade hardware as the need arises. You may also want to increase your staff for application development, user support, and operations management. Primarily, however, consider the server and system performance, data integrity, system security, and other factors that make the system worth more when it's working than when it's not.

Depending on the size of your organization, the number of users, the amount of data, and the total of your already-assigned duties, you will likely want one or more assistants who can help with day-to-day administration of the database server. Delegate training and the generation of training materials and support after the program is in use. Backups can also be delegated.

Testing your databases is also important. Write policies on testing— such as checking the quality, consistency, and soundness of the database—allot adequate time for testing, make plans in case you run across some serious errors while testing, and evaluate the testing results.

SCRIPTING

Use a scripting language to execute administrative duties. Automate common setup, configuration, and so forth, using small scripts written in any scripting language (ActiveX, Java) to map network shares, setting default printers, reading, writing, and deleting registry keys, accessing special folders, launching programs, creating shortcuts, writing environment variables, and so on.

SQL Server

Microsoft's SQL Server is a relational database management system. Using the SQL language, this DBMS transfers user inputs into tables, indexes, views, and such so the user can quickly display, read, and understand answers to the queries he or she makes.

SQL Server uses a process of rollback and recovery to protect data and server operations. Each transaction is recorded in a log file, marking completed transactions and replaying (or rolling back) any transaction in which a problem occurs. To warrant against damaged data, SQL Server erases any operations that have not been completed successfully (called *recovery*).

Other features of SQL Server include distributed data management, data protection while accessed by multiple users, and synchronization and replication between multiple SQL Servers. SQL Server also provides numerous administrative utilities and tools that help organize data and manage the server.

> **Database Development System**
>
> A database development system provides developers with language tools, applications, and objects to build interactive database applications. Choose the views and fields and the way they are displayed on screen, determine how queries are executed, optimize object performance, and so on, with a development application. Additionally, many database development systems also enable you to design reports and forms, manage large databases, index fields, query, and so on.
>
> Microsoft's Visual FoxPro is an object-oriented database development system. Using ActiveX, you can increase performance, improve connectivity, and strengthen the development environment. Additionally, FoxPro lets you drive Office and other applications using automation; you can even add third-party ActiveX controls with this development application.

Oracle

Oracle produces several data management systems as well as data servers and various application servers. In addition to supplying query-intensive data services to users over the network, Oracle's system provides administrative tools for the control and support of data management. Oracle provides both client and server open data access, database links, updates and queries, and more.

> **NOTE**
>
> Oracle offers many database systems and servers. Some are directed at mobile users and others focus on database development or workgroups in particular. Before purchasing an Oracle application, research heavily and ask questions; the multitude of choices can be overwhelming.

Oracle8 is a relational DBMS that provides full processing power, scalability, cluster management, and server-managed backup and recovery. Oracle supports customers and users with a variety of query features, report components, and thorough indexing. Replication and online backup and recovery are also included for data protection.

Groupware

Groupware is based on five basic technologies: multimedia document management, email, conferencing, scheduling, and workflow. Most groupware products include one or more of these technologies; the more technologies included in the application, the more useful it will be in allowing your users to collaborate on projects. However, your office may benefit more from just one of the technologies that are the foundation of groupware products.

Most groupware applications include a shared database that's available to all users. Within the database are common documents and/or electronic discussions. While some packages include group schedulers, calendars, and/or email, others have real-time meeting support and public folders for group discussions. Users can work on one document, discuss ideas on-line, maintain records, prioritize and schedule teamwork, and schedule meetings.

Examples of groupware packages are Lotus Notes/Domino, Microsoft Exchange, Novell's GroupWise, Netscape's Collabra Share, and Ventana's GroupSystems. Most of these groupware products require user training and an administrator or manager to keep information current.

Is Groupware for You?

A groupware application can be simply an email program or it can be an entire set of applications. You'll first need to decide exactly what you want in a groupware package. If you need only email, for example, installation, configuration, usage, training, and administration will be much simpler than if you purchase a full-blown groupware package containing email, scheduling, document-sharing, and work flow features. Some groupware packages, such as Lotus Notes/Domino, are extremely difficult to configure and manage; generally a full-time administrator is hired when these applications are to be used.

Consider, too, how much you use any particular groupware component. If, for example, email has become mission critical in your business or scheduling interconnects throughout the enterprise, a groupware package may be more effective than smaller, less robust applications.

For example, you may now use Microsoft Outlook for email and scheduling. Over the network, everyone can send and receive messages and view each other's calendars for scheduling purposes. However, say you've added another office and more users to your original network configuration. As the network expands and more users are added, you will find you need more than an email application to serve everyone's needs; you may want to add Microsoft Exchange Server to this mix to provide faster, more efficient services. After adding a groupware package, you may find use for other features such as document management and shared public folders, for instance.

Another consideration is network traffic. When you put a groupware application into use, network traffic will naturally increase. You may need to upgrade your networking hardware to alleviate this situation, or you can take other steps within your company, such as limiting the number or size of messages sent.

Bandwidth Solutions

Since purchasing and installing networking hardware to increase bandwidth is relatively expensive, there are a few things you might try first to save money. Think about creating some email policies, using a third-party application to monitor usage and control bandwidth, and so on.

Policies can help regulate your users' use of the system and alleviate many bandwidth problems. For example, limit the forwarding of huge presentation files, graphic images, humor messages, and so on. Restrict the size of attachments of multimedia and image files that users can send. Also, since most email messages are sent between 8 A.M. and 9 A.M., around noon, and again between 4 P.M. and 5 P.M., ask users to vary the times they send their messages to help lighten the traffic problems.

You also can use tools to control and prioritize bandwidth based on a proportion of bandwidth allocated to certain email messages. Guarantee a minimum amount of bandwidth for high-priority messages and set a specific bandwidth ceiling for low-priority messages.

If your company is heavily invested in Internet commerce, in particular, you can use a performance-monitoring and bandwidth-control product instead of buying more bandwidth (which is very expensive). These programs analyze and intelligently prioritize messages. Also, there are options in many firewall programs that add control to limit bandwidth among internal users and external customers; Checkpoint and Packeteer are two programs that can perform these tasks.

Groupware Components

Following is a bit more detail about the various components that make up a groupware package. Most components can be purchased separately, although they may not be as efficient as those in a package built specifically for networking.

Email

Email is one of the most popular collaborative tools used in business today. Users can relate ideas, questions, motivation, inspiration, opinions, goals, and such, over the network to coworkers, associates, and customers. Users can send memos, notes, files, images, charts, and other electronic items. Users can use email within the office to set meetings and confirm project ideas; mobile users can communicate with colleagues at the office via email. Users can transfer files over the network as well.

Email is a connection users can make without the time investment of a phone call or office visit. Answering messages is more convenient than taking or making a phone call or office visit.

Individual users use an email application on the workstation to send and receive mail to a central post office (located on a server that collects the mail for the entire company). Depending on the size of the company, you may need to establish a post office for each office, building, or other entity. Email is a perfect complement to other groupware technologies such as document management, scheduling, conferencing and workflow, because email facilitates collaboration via communication.

Email over the Internet opens new routes to business contacts, customers, and vendors. You can research new products and services, order tools and software upgrades, keep up on the news, and check competitors' products and services.

When configuring most email applications, your administrative tasks will include the following:

- Setting permissions and/or rights
- Scheduling backups of the mail system
- Naming mailboxes within a consistent convention
- Creating public directories or folders
- Training users and assistants
- Installing and configuring server software
- Installing, configuring, and troubleshooting client software

Scheduling

Scheduling refers to creating calendars, setting meetings, keeping ongoing to-do lists, and other methods of organizing the work day. A scheduling program enables an individual to list appointments, pencil in meetings, and even set alarms to announce upcoming appointments. Rescheduling is easy and the calendar for weeks and months in advance is readily available for reference.

On the network, a group scheduling application allows each person to see the others' calendars and, with permission, update others' calendars when necessary. Assistants can keep their boss' schedule up to date; partners can pencil in appointments for each other; group meetings can be scheduled after checking everyone's calendar for availability. Group scheduling is especially effective for lawyers, doctors, salespeople, realtors, or anyone whose schedule affects others in the office. The use of scheduling programs improves everyone's organization, time management, and efficiency.

The administrator's tasks for scheduling programs after the initial installation and configuration breaks down to troubleshooting and solving users' problems with the program. A good training course and written guidelines can help alleviate these problems; consider too, implementing a help desk for problems with the scheduling program and others in the groupware application.

Conferencing

Conferencing is an electronic meeting in which users can post messages, questions, and ideas and read replies to their messages from other members of the group. There are two types of conferencing—real-time and anytime—that are supported by various groupware applications. Real-time conferences enable groups to collaborate on a project together, at the same time, for immediate feedback. Anytime conferencing enables people to participate in a group discussion when and where it's convenient for them by collecting messages and answering when they're ready.

Conferencing is particularly useful over long distances—such as between buildings, cities, or countries—but it is even useful within one office or room. Over a long distance, conferencing enables many people to meet and share ideas where otherwise a meeting may not have been possible. Conferences with colleagues, customers, manufacturers, sales or public relations people, publishers, or anyone else who is normally not on-site are possible.

Conferencing within an office is useful for brainstorming ideas. Also, having users meet electronically gives everyone a chance to communicate his or her thoughts completely without interruption. In conferencing of this type, only one person may display his or her comments at a time; each must wait his or her turn to "speak," thus guaranteeing everyone the chance to have a say.

Administration for conferencing is not too difficult. An assistant could easily install and configure this component. Even problems are usually minimal.

Document Management

Document management groupware compiles multiple documents, organizes them into related topics, and stores them on the network so the documents can easily be located and utilized. Users can access documents, contribute new documents, sort, copy, save, and search the documents in the database.

Documents within the management system can be made available to all network users or to only certain groups or individual users. Small workgroups can access the documents they need to complete their work while users of the entire network can access other documents as needed. Most document management systems include reliable security features that make it easy for an administrator to designate user access.

Documents can be created by an administrator, IS manager, department head, or anyone who needs to distribute data to multiple users. Even individual users can create documents to share, if they have permission.

Documents can include text, images, graphics, tables, charts, voice and video clips, and so on. Documents using multimedia technology are generally more interesting and therefore more likely to be used. Depending on the networking hardware and the groupware application, documents extensive in multimedia files may take longer to transfer, open, and view than plain text documents.

A document management server stores documents and makes them available to users. The server can also index and retrieve documents by title, subject, author, or some other identifier.

> **NOTE**
>
> Generally, within the document management portion of the groupware application, a bulletin board or other shared folder module exists. This module lets users "chat" with each other, about accounts, projects, or even personal topics. The user sends messages or documents to this area where others may read them and respond.

Document management presents more administrative tasks than the other groupware components. An administrator must install and configure the component, but must also prepare databases and documents. Following is a general task list for the administrator of the document management component of a groupware application:

Install and configure the program.

Set security for each user and/or group.

Create databases and/or shared folders to hold documents and keep them updated.

Create documents or delegate the job, and keep updated.

Install and configure client software.

Train users.

Manage network traffic to server.

Optimize server performance.

Make backup schedule and delegate backup and restore tasks.

Troubleshoot problems on server and with clients.

Workflow

A workflow program routes work (documents, forms, memos, and such) from one program and/or computer to another. When using workflow applications, you can define the operation at each stop, the value added at any stop, and what needs to be done at the next stop.

Equate workflow with the paper trail at an office, for example. The front office starts the process of running a job through the entire shop by listing the customer's name and address, the order number, product requirements, due date, quantities, and so on. The job form goes to the order department that sends an order to the warehouse and another to the billing department. The warehouse fills the order and passes its form to the truck driver; meanwhile, the billing department double-checks with the warehouse, then enters the form in the system for billing.

The paper trail was created through a workflow model, similar to the way an electronic workflow can be handled. Using a network application and electronic forms to complete these various steps throughout the process means a more orderly and efficient process, more accurate records, less likelihood of lost paperwork, and better documentation of the process. Workflow applications help route information to people who need to supervise, manipulate, or act on it. Each workflow application provides some or all of the following:

- Status reports of work in progress

- Notifications of actions required

- Help on how to proceed at each step

- Routing from one person or stop to the next

- Rules that define what needs to be done and by whom

- Definition of roles of those involved with the process

As with document management programs, workflow applications also require quite a bit of administration. Configuration of the program and problem solving may be the majority of the work for the administrator.

Microsoft Exchange Server

One example of a groupware application is Microsoft Exchange Server. Exchange includes an email program for use over a LAN, WAN, and over the Internet. Users can send and receive messages, forward and store messages, attach various files to messages, and perform other common email tasks. The Exchange client comes with the Windows operating system—Windows 95 and 98, NT, and such—and is fairly easy to configure and use.

Exchange also includes the following:

- An inbox for each client where a user can collect, filter, sort, and reply to messages.

- Public folders to which users can post messages, displayed in a hierarchical configuration so users can see how the messages relate to each other and trace the initial message and all of its replies.

- Internet mail that supports Simple Mail Transfer Protocol (SMTP) and multipurpose Internet mail extensions (MIME).

> **NOTE**
>
> SMTP is used to get and set status information about a host on a TCP/IP network. MIME is a standard utility for specifying the format of messages; MIME enables the exchange of objects, character sets, and multimedia between different computer systems.

- Support for communication over network links at speeds from 9600bps dial-up to 11Mbs FDDI fiber networks.

- Support for workflow with inbox and out-of-office assistants that can automate email.

Lotus Notes/Domino

Probably the most popular and important groupware product on the market today, Notes/Domino easily handles all five of the basic technologies of groupware. Domino is, however, difficult to administer and usually requires a full-time administrator just to handle Notes, Domino, and its processes.

Additionally, these administrators should be trained and certified in Domino/Notes because it is so very complex.

> **NOTE**
>
> Notes is the client portion of the program and Domino is the server software.

Notes enables users to share information, email, plus interact using the following functions:

- A document database server that stores and manages documents that include text, images, audio, and video. Users can share documents with others, add documents to databases, and so on; permissions and security may also limit or grant access to databases to certain users and/or groups.

- Email server that manages multiuser client access to mail, plus email features such as type-ahead addressing, collapsible sections, a prevent copying items feature, and so on.

- A backbone server that supports mail routing and database replication. Notes features synchronous replication between servers and between clients and servers, including mobile users.

- Distributed services, such as electronic signatures security and access control.

- Server-based agents that run when scheduled to distribute mail and perform other workflow operations.

- Internet integration through SMTP support, TCP/IP connectivity, for HTML browsers, and such.

- A bulletin board service for conferencing and a calendar for scheduling.

Additionally, Notes/Domino provides integrated services with the Internet. Domino includes an HTTP server, translates Notes into HTML, and enables access to Notes databases and views via a Web browser. Additionally, Lotus supplies integrated Internet access for Notes with InterNotes Web Publisher and Notes Web Navigator. The Web Navigator is a Web browser built in to Notes 4.5 and later versions that you can use to browse the Web, save a Web page to a Notes document, send Web pages to other Notes users via Notes mail, retrieve previously viewed Web pages without reconnecting to the Internet, and much more.

> **NOTE**
>
> Novell's GroupWise is another groupware product that provides email, calendaring and scheduling, document management, workflow, imaging, threaded discussions, and status tracking. GroupWise is, however, difficult to configure, administer, and use.

The InterNotes Web Publisher is a server application that converts Notes databases into HTML files and copies them to the HTTP server so people browsing the Web can retrieve them. The Web Publisher enables you to convert Notes documents, publish Notes databases as HTML pages, maintain HTML links, extend a full-text Notes search capability to Web users, and more.

Internet Applications

The Internet applications you use on the network are many and varied. If you have an Internet connection for your users' email, for example, all users who connect must have a browser, like Microsoft's Internet Explorer or Netscape. With connections to the Internet, you will likely also use a proxy server of some sort for protection of your data and your users. If you have a Web page on the Internet, you may also have a Web application, a site and/or commerce application, indexing or searching applications, and Web publishing tools.

Client Browsers

Client browsers are those applications installed to users' machines for the purpose of viewing the Internet's Web pages or your own company's intranet pages. A browser offers a window in which the user can switch from page to page and site to site, search and surf the Web, and print and download from various sites. Browsers include tools to simplify the process, including forward and back buttons, bookmarking tools, URL addressing boxes, and more.

Two of the most popular browsers are Microsoft's Internet Explorer and Netscape's Communicator. Internet Explorer comes with the Windows operating system and is also available by download from the Internet. Both browsers offer the tools and features you need to get the most from the Internet; the choice you make will depend on personal preferences, operating systems, user preferences, and so on.

A bit of advice here: Try to get the same browser for all client computers instead of letting users choose their own browser software. Your administrative

Email and Scheduling

There are many smaller applications you can use to provide limited groupware services, such as email programs, calendars, and so on. Two such products you may want to consider are Microsoft Outlook or Lotus Organizer.

Microsoft Outlook is an email program that ships with Microsoft Office. Although it is not a full-fledged groupware product, it does have email and scheduling that are very useful over a network.

Outlook provides email features and tools, mail management and storage, an address book, text formatting and spell checking, file attachment utilities and such. The calendar and scheduling features include appointments, events logging, automatic invitations to meetings, and a contact list. Also, you can use Outlook's task list tool for managing your to-do list and/or journal for recording phone calls, meetings, and other events. Outlook also provides full and useful integration of the various utilities such as email, journal, task list, and calendar, plus Internet services.

Lotus' Organizer works in conjunction with Notes/Domino, cc:Mail, and/or Lotus SmartSuite, although you can also use Organizer by itself on a network to schedule and prepare users' calendars. Organizer lets you schedule appointments on a daily, weekly, or yearly basis, print the calendar, set alarms, easily change appointments, and display appointments in varying views.

Organizer also includes a task list feature in which you can create a to-do list, set alarms for tasks, rearrange tasks, filter and sort tasks, and print the to-do list. A contact/address section in Organizer enables you to enter names, companies, addresses, and phone numbers; then you can use a find feature to locate any number you need quickly and efficiently. You also can record information about your calls and print that information.

duties will be easier, troubleshooting and training will be faster, and by creating a consistent working environment, changes will be more easily effected.

Web Server Applications

A Web server contains Web pages that users from the Internet can attach to and view; documents such as advertising, catalogs, newsletters, job opportunities, and so on can be published to the Web via a Web server application. A Web server application transmits information in HTML format using HTTP protocol over a

TCP/IP network. You also can use a Web server to publish information—such as handbooks, network guidelines, company schedules, and so on—over your own private LAN or WAN via an intranet using Internet technologies.

Many Web server applications are available. Two common applications are Microsoft's Internet Information Server and Netscape's Web Server. Both offer various advantages, but all Web servers present security features, basic Internet protocols and services, and work with various client software for the users' convenience. Netscape's Web Server works on a variety of network operating systems but it is also advertised as an addition to one of Novell's NetWare modules.

> **NOTE**
>
> When creating Web pages for publishing to your Web server, or any Web server, you can use a variety of applications or you can simply use a word processor and enter HTML code. Microsoft's FrontPage is an excellent tool for publishing documents and many Microsoft products offer a command to save in an HTML format. For more information about FrontPage, see *FrontPage 97 Sourcebook* by Wayne F. Brooks (John Wiley & Sons, 1997).

Commercial Applications

Commercial Internet applications vary in their roles. Some might gather site usage information and others may present an online store for Internet shoppers.

An application that gathers usage information generally enables you to personalize sites by targeting specific groups of users and manage the site so you can offer updated information to your regular site visitors. Also, it enables you to view and analyze server logs with information about managed links, site maps, and content. Other components might be administration tools for managing site services and content creation tools for publishing Web content. A good example of this type of application is Microsoft's Site Server.

Another commercial Internet application is a commerce server that lets you create a "store" on-line in which users can purchase your products. You can usually build your store from a supplied template that provides secured credit card use, real-time product pricing, search features, and so on.

Two examples of commerce servers are Microsoft's Commerce Server and I/NET's Commerce Server/400. Both commerce servers offer security enhancements, links to Web servers, mailing lists, on-line support, and other such features for your convenience. I/NET's Commerce Server/400 is especially built for the AS/400 platform, whereas Microsoft's Commerce Server is generally meant for use on NT Server.

Proxy Server Applications

Proxy server applications enable information exchange between a private LAN and the Internet while maintaining security for the computers on the LAN. A proxy application supplies firewall-class security to your LAN. Depending on the application, you can control access to your LAN from the Internet, authenticate users of the proxy service, protect your data on the LAN, and control your users access to the Internet.

Before adding a proxy server to your network, you should first review your security policies, user passwords, guest accounts, and so on. Additionally, make sure you have appropriate bandwidth for your LAN and get a reliable and fast connection to the Internet. Prepare the networking hardware, contact an Internet Service Provider (ISP), and check the compatibility of your NOS.

There are many proxy server applications available. Microsoft Proxy Server supplies a safe connection between your LAN and the Internet, using specific protocols designed for Internet services: HTTP, FTP, Gopher, and so on.

Netscape also has a Proxy Server; Netscape boasts special features that reduce traffic, user wait times, and relieve bottlenecks and bandwidth congestion. Additionally, the Netscape Proxy Server supplies network security features for internal and external access of information, easy administration, and support for Internet protocols. The proxy server application you choose will depend on your clients' Web browsers, your network operating system, and personal preferences.

Vertical Applications

A vertical application, or vertical software, is one that is designed for performing a specific job or for a particular business. For example, one program might enable the user to quote commercial print jobs based on the number of printed pages, size of the page, colors of ink, number of photographs, type of folding, and date of delivery. Other applications have been designed for the following:

- Real estate sales
- Restaurant delivery systems
- Computer solutions
- Retail point-of-sale

- Hotel sales
- Hospitals
- Book and music stores
- Accounting systems
- Theater seating and pricing
- Rental businesses

Accounting verticals are probably among the most common systems written currently. Quotation systems, job costing, work orders, product management, utility billing, sales orders, purchase orders, accounts payable and receivable, and so on are just a few of the needs in the accounting area.

A vertical application makes it possible to store data to the computer and use it in a way necessary for your business to survive. However, vertical applications have many drawbacks. First, a vertical application is generally written for a specific network operating system and all upgrades are written for that same NOS as well. Upgrading your NOS may leave your vertical application crippled or useless.

Another problem is that technical support is not always the best, simply because the errors and problems are many and the support staff is too busy to get to everyone immediately. If you purchase a vertical application, make sure you get a signed contract stating the exact support options you want.

You may find compatibility problems with a vertical application, too. For example, you might have to install new hardware to make the application work properly; this is an important issue to check on before purchasing the application. Also, some of your current software may not be compatible with a vertical application.

Finally, make sure you receive proper training and guidelines for the vertical application. Since it is not a mainstream program, you'll not find many third-party books about it in the bookstores.

Accounting Applications

Accounting applications are often used over a network, for shared data files, use by multiple departments, and examination by supervisors. Accounting programs may contain separate modules for each function or combine several functions in one program. Some of the accounting functions are accounts payable, accounts receivable, payroll, inventory, general ledger, cash manager, order processing, bar coding, travel and expense, contract management, budgeting, and more.

An accounting application contains some of your company's most important information. Make sure you use adequate security precautions, any application passwords, and your network operating system's security features when handling your accounting program.

Many accounting applications are designed for client/server use, but since some are not, make sure you check with the salesperson, manufacturer, or documentation before you purchase the program. Using a network version of the accounting program helps you keep your books up to date by using several data-entry operators.

There are many different accounting programs available, some more difficult to use than others. Your first step is to ask your accountant what he or she recommends. Two of the more elaborate and difficult accounting programs are Solomon and Great Plains. MAS90 and Peachtree are a bit easier to handle; both boast easier and faster accounting and reporting than previous versions. However, QuickBooks is probably the easiest reliable accounting program you can get.

Solomon, which is available for NT or NetWare, offers its applications in the following module series, each purchased separately:

Financial Series: general ledger, financial statement, currency manager, and so on

Distribution Series: order processing, purchasing, inventory, and such

Project Series: project controller, analyzer, timekeeper, and so on

Reporting and Analysis Series: crystal reports

Customization and Development Series: customization manager, basic script language, and such

Web Series: application server, WebAssistant, and so on

QuickBooks presents only one "module," or application really, for much less expense. You don't need to be an accountant to use QuickBooks; actually, QuickBooks doesn't even use accounting terms as many other accounting programs do. Also, QuickBooks provides the following features:

• Instant recall on recurring bills and invoices

• Sales tax calculations

• Customizable invoices and statements

• On-line banking and on-line payment

• Accounts receivable tracking

• Inventory tracking

- Time tracking
- Compatibility with TurboTax

Suites

Application suites, such as Lotus SmartSuite and Microsoft Office, are sets of programs including a word processor, spreadsheet program, presentation applications, and often email and/or scheduling, clip art, and other add-ons. Generally, suites or any of their components are installed to individual workstations instead of to the network; however, some companies prefer to install them to an application server.

Advantages to installing a suite to the network include administrator control over where files are saved, control over each application's user settings, tighter security over documents, saved space on user's workstations, and cheaper application and upgrade investment. Disadvantages to installing the suite to the network include more space used on the server, more network traffic, and more chances for errors since more people are using the programs.

When preparing to install a suite or one of its components to the network, make sure you have adequate licensing and that you choose the network installation option. Read all program documentation first to ensure you select all of the appropriate network options.

MANAGING PRINTERS

Introduction to Book Four

Networks today must be more adaptable and robust, with corporate downsizing, more powerful PCs, increased application workloads, and so on. These factors also impact network printers, adding more print jobs that are increasingly more difficult and complex. Centralized management of printers can help make network printing easier and less complicated for the user and the administrator.

Because today's networks are made up of a variety of printers, network operating systems, client operating systems, and hardware configurations, the use of centralized networking and servers and common vendors and software programs means less administrative duties, easier problem solving, and less complex upgrading. For example, using the same NOS on all servers, whether file, print, application, or other, makes installation, configuration, and other administrative duties easier and more efficient.

The same is true for print servers. If all or nearly all of your hardware, software, and configurations for print servers are the same, your job starts out on an easier level. Unfortunately, many networks are put together piecemeal and budgets change from year to year so therefore purchases are not always the same. Most networks require a variety of printing needs, especially as the network grows and expands.

A single print solution may not be possible for your network. This book offers advice and information about the many possible printing options open to you. In this book, you'll learn about the following:

- Using a print server
- Print server types
- Printer management
- Hardware and protocols
- Configuration guidelines

TERMINOLOGY AND TECHNOLOGY

Networks have changed the way in which offices work. For the most part, network technologies have improved individual productivity by allowing workers to accomplish more than ever. As networks grow, so does the network administrator's job of management and support. Network optimization, server performance, application compatibility, client issues, and more are also added to the network administrator's job. The task of managing network printing alone could keep an administrator busy full time.

Network printing has become more and more important as networking technologies advance. Information is more available to the user than ever before; printing that information requires faster and more sophisticated print devices attached to the network. Consider the following types of printed material that might be generated in one workday:

Text documents: business reports, letters, and such

Envelopes and labels: company, customers, vendors

Graphics and images: within documents, engineering projects, multimedia pictures, and so on

Email: messages and attachments

Company intranet: documents, handbooks, policies, and manuals

Forms: expense, purchase orders, and the like

Faxes: memos, confirmations, requests

Internet: Web pages, gopher and FTP downloaded files

This chapter can help you prepare for adding or upgrading printers to your network by discussing the types of printers available, the job of a print server, and other factors key to your decision-making process. Following are some of the terms and technologies covered in this chapter:

- Printer types and brands
- Printer drivers and data types
- Common printer languages
- Parallel and serial ports
- Protocols

Printer Technologies

Today's market provides many different printer types that you can use on your network. Depending on your needs, you can find a printer that matches your budget and your network configuration. When purchasing a printer, you'll be better off if you buy a better-known brand for several reasons. Brand-name printers (such as Okidata, Hewlett-Packard, IBM, and so on) are usually better built and last longer than unknown, less-expensive brands. Also, brand-name printers are easier to find replacement parts for and easier to repair. The type of printer you purchase depends on your network printing needs.

Selecting Printers

The following printer types are in common use today. Each has its advantages and disadvantages. You will more than likely use a combination of printers with your network; for example, you might use dot matrix printers in your accounting department and laser printers in the sales department.

Dot Matrix

Dot matrix (or impact) printers are generally considered workhorses, especially for network use. Many forms, such as tax forms, carbonless forms, and so on, require a dot matrix printer. Also, certain paper types, such as 11 inches by 17 inches or larger may require a dot matrix printer. Although a dot matrix printer doesn't turn out pages very quickly, it can accommodate certain user and network needs.

Ink Jet

Ink jet or liquid ink jet printers propel droplets of liquid ink toward the paper surface. Ink jets are fairly low-cost printers; however, the ink cartridges and specialty papers make up for any money you save on the printer. The main advantage of an ink jet printer is in the inexpensive color output, as compared to a color laser jet or other color printer's cost.

Ink jet (or bubble jet, paint jet) printers are usually used more as local printers, connected to one computer or department rather than the entire network.

Ink jets are slow, use quite a bit of ink (in cartridge form), and require some drying time where the ink contacts the paper. If you need a color printer and don't want the expense of a color laser printer, the ink jet will work for your network if you limit the number of users who access it.

Plotters

Plotters are printers used mostly for drafting and other fields where the output is line oriented and large formats are necessary. There are pen plotters (most common), ink jet, electrostatic, and thermal plotters. Ink jet plotters have the same disadvantage as ink jet printers: they may be low cost, but they are very messy. Electrostatic output comes out dry, but the electrostatic plotter is expensive and difficult to maintain. Thermal plotters are fast but they require special paper and they're limited to only two colors.

Laser Printers

Laser printers are the most common printers used for business documents, letters, reports, and any other high-quality document you want to print. They are fast, economical, and produce excellent output. Newer laser printers include their own processors for better speed and efficiency and can print 300, 600, and 1200dpi resolution.

Color laser printers produce good-quality, durable, and light-fast output. The color is very nearly photorealistic. Many color laser printers use 256 colors with 300 or 600dpi resolution. Naturally, color laser printers are very expensive.

What to Look for in a Color Laser Printer

When you purchase a color laser printer, you're investing a lot of money; not only in the product, but in maintenance, supplies, cost of ownership, and so on. It's important that you shop around and get the best deal you can for your money. Here are some tips for buying a color laser printer.

When viewing the output of the printer, make sure the colors are vibrant as well as smoothly shaded without color bands. If you see moiré patterns (spots or grids) in the color, that means the printer has a limited color palette and poor image processing.

Check the primary colors—red, yellow, blue, and black—for intensity. The more intense the primary colors are, the more color range the printer has.

Continues

What to Look for in a Color Laser Printer *(Continued)*

You may want to match the colors with a Pantone color swatch book (available from commercial printers and/or paper and ink companies) to make sure the output is true to pure and common colors.

Look closely at any lines in the output, especially diagonal lines, to see if they are jagged; you want clean, sharp lines instead.

Make sure the dots are small, consistent in size and shape for the highest-quality printing. You may want to take a printer's loupe or other magnifying glass to closely examine the dots.

Using your magnifier, check that the registration is accurate. Registration refers to the line between one color and the next. If those lines overlap where they shouldn't, the registration is off. If it is, you'll also see extra bits of color around the edges, which means a poorer quality of printer.

Try to smear the color with your hand to see if the color is permanent. Also, moisten your finger and rub across the color.

Check the small type for consistency and legibility; check the larger type for smooth, clean edges.

As far as print speed goes, it will be difficult to really depend on the spec sheets because various colors, images, and combinations of colors will take varying amounts of time to print. Try printing some of your own color documents and time the printer; you'll at least see how fast it can print those documents common to your usage.

Before purchasing a color laser printer, check the connectivity options. Since you will be connecting to a network, the printer should be able to connect with parallel, serial, Ethernet, NetWare, and AppleTalk. Also, make sure the ports can be simultaneously active.

If possible, you should choose a printer with PostScript 2 and/or HP-GL compatibility.

You may want to get dual paper trays and ask how much paper the tray will hold.

Make sure to check the paper types and weights of paper you can print (24 to 28 lbs., for example).

Find out about how much the toner or inks cost and about how often they need to be replaced.

Thermal-Wax Transfer Printers

Thermal-wax transfer printers are used to produce color overhead transparencies and/or printing on bond paper. Thermal-wax transfer printers print about two pages per minute and the quality is fair. These printers provide reliable, cost-effective color quality. Instead of ink, thermal-wax printers use a transfer roll of colored wax; the printhead is heated to melt pinpoint spots of color onto special paper or transparency film.

Dye Sublimation

Dye sublimation printers produce continuous-tone, photorealistic output. These printers require special paper and are expensive to purchase and to run.

Network Interface Printers

Network interface printers are print devices with built-in network adapter cards that don't have to be physically connected to the print server. Using an interface kit, you can attach a printer directly to your network at any location without affecting performance as long as users and print devices aren't on the opposite sides of a network bridge or gateway. Depending on the memory, size, and types of documents sent to the print server, and the server's processing capability, dozens of network-interface printers may be installed to the network.

There are many advantages to using interface printers; for example, you can locate them anywhere on the network, they eliminate the bottleneck associated with serial or parallel connections so they improve printer performance, they support automatic protocol switching, and so on. These types of printer interface kits are available for Windows, NetWare, and UNIX network operating systems. Hewlett-Packard makes a JetDirect Network Interface, for example, and Lantronix makes a similar device for UNIX networks.

> **NOTE**
>
> If you have trouble with adding multiple print devices, you should add more memory to the server.

Printer Drivers

Although the print device is often and correctly called a printer, sometimes the term *printer* refers to the printer driver or application that enables the device to perform its job. A printer driver is the software that enables applications to communicate with the print device. When data is exchanged between one type of device and another, such as a computer and printer, usually the electrical and mechanical requirements of the two devices are different; it's the software driver that translates the data.

Printer drivers are made up of three files that work to provide printing services: a printer graphics driver, a printer interface driver, and a characterization data file. Together, these files interpret the printer language, provide a user interface, and specify certain characteristics and capabilities about the make of the printer.

Usually, your network operating system provides common printer drivers, such as Hewlett-Packard, Apple, Compaq, Digital, Epson, IBM, Lexmark, NEC, Okidata, and so on. Printer manufacturers also supply drivers for the printers they make. It's extremely important to use the latest updated printer drivers for your printer and operating system to get the best performance and the least printer trouble.

Data Types

A print server receives and prepares jobs by various clients. Generally, the print server assigns print jobs in a data type, which tells the spooler whether and how to modify the print job so it will print correctly. The printer and the type of data being sent to it is one point at which printing bottlenecks may occur.

On nonlaser printers or plain text jobs, the physical printer engine may be the limiting factor. Check the speed at which the printer is rated in pages per minute (laser) or characters per second (nonlaser).

When you use a complex page description language, such as PostScript, the printer's formatter may be the limiting factor. The spec sheets given with printers seldom address this parameter.

Examples of Windows data types are EMF (enhanced metafiles) or RAW. EMF is used if the printer is a PCL printer and is generated by the Graphical Device Interface before spooling. EMF files are portable, can be printed on any print device, and are smaller files than RAW files. Generally, EMF format frees up your program faster.

RAW is used if the printer is Adobe PostScript. Generated by the printer driver, the RAW printer data type tells the spooler not to alter the job at all, that the print job is ready to print as it is. RAW format is specific to the printer and because it's PostScript formatting, it may take longer to convert the printing information.

There is also a TEXT data type that tells the spooler that the job is made up of ANSI text. Using the current print device driver to create the print job, the text is printed in the default font and form. This data type prints the fastest but uses the least formatting.

Printer Languages

Printer languages, the component that converts the print data into dot patterns, fall into two general categories. PCL (Printer Control Language) and HPGL (Hewlett-Packard Graphics Language) are printer languages that use data streams. The data in these streams consists of text bytes, command strings for horizontal and vertical spacing and vector graphics, and strings of bit-image graphics. This type of printer language makes the data easily converted.

Page Description Languages (PDLs) like PostScript (PS) are a subset of the printer languages group but they use more complex data streams. PDLs allow more complex data manipulations than the simpler PCL, HPGL, and others, but PDLs also need more time to convert the data.

PostScript Printing

Adobe Systems Incorporated created the PostScript printer language as a page description language. PostScript enables an application to interface with high-quality printers and produce sharp graphics and intricate fonts.

There are some special requirements for PostScript printing; for example, the printer must be PostScript capable. The printer needs a driver that generates the PostScript code for each file that is sent to the printer; drivers are provided by the applications, if they support PostScript printing. So check your applications for PostScript compatibility before purchasing a PostScript printer. Although most PostScript printers are capable of printing in both PostScript and text mode, they are more expensive so you don't want to pay for the extra language if you can't use it.

Also, some problems can result from the use of PostScript. A PostScript printer will flush the entire print job if there is anything about the job that the printer doesn't understand; and you may not see an error message when this happens.

Network Printing

In nonnetwork printing, the data is simply sent from the computer to a printer cabled directly into the standalone computer. However, in network printing, the process is more complicated. Typically, the application compiles the data and passes it on to a printer driver, which generates actual printer data and passes it on to the LPT1 (default printer port). The printer driver may be part of the application software or may be supplied by the client's operating system or third party. The printer data is now in the format of a printer language, such as PCL or PostScript, as defined by the printer driver. The time it takes to generate the print data depends on the complexity of the character formatting, graphic additions to the text, font size, and so on.

> **NOTE**
>
> A *font* is a text formatting term meaning a complete assortment of printer characters in a particular typeface. Most fonts include letters, numbers, punctuation, and special symbols. An example of a font is Times Roman. The font family includes the complete set of characters, including all type sizes and styles (bold, italic, underlined, and such).

Next, the data is redirected to a file in the network print queue where it's stored until it can be sent to the printer. The printer queue enables the user to resume work without waiting for the printer to complete the print job. A queue also means multiple people can use a single printer and each user can send jobs to printers at different locations.

The data is stored in the print queue until its turn to print. Jobs are taken first-come first-served, unless the administrator has set priorities or limits on the jobs in the queue. For example, large print jobs can be stored until the evening hours for printing so as not to interrupt the printing of other, smaller jobs. When the print server receives information about the status of the printer, saying it is free to print a job, the server sends that data to the printer where the job is formatted and printed.

Since there are so many steps involved with network printing, you'll want to think about printer speed, network connections, and other issues that affect the network as you pick out your new or upgraded printers. Bottlenecks can always appear when you add a new peripheral, hardware, or computer to your system; adding a printer is no different. There are certain things you can look for within the printer and hardware that will help speed things along.

Spooling and Redirection

A print job is the data type that has been sent to the printer from an application on a workstation or server. The print queue is a list of jobs waiting to be printed and it's the print spooler that receives, processes, and schedules the print jobs waiting to be printed. The spooling (Simultaneous Peripheral Operation On Line) process writes the contents of a print job to a file on disk where it remains in the server's memory until the job is sent to the printer, even if the power is lost to the printer.

Additionally, the spooler performs the following functions:

- Prevents multiple users from accessing a printer at the same time by maintaining a queue for each printer.
- Prints header pages so users can easily find their jobs among others.
- Handles communications parameters for printers connected to serial ports.
- Runs special filters to format jobs in various printer languages or capabilities.

Printer redirection is a process where the user tells the network operating system to redirect all output headed for the local LPT1 port over the network to the print server's port. Spooling may occur if the printer is busy or if the printer isn't fast enough to take a whole file at one time. The *buffer*, a storage device that compensates for the differences in the rate of data flow during the data transmission between devices, is used to feed print jobs to the printer at the appropriate pace. The larger the buffer, the faster the printing, since fewer accesses to disk are necessary to pick up the file. Spooling and the buffer improve the performance of printing over the network.

Parallel or Serial Printers

You can choose to add either parallel or serial printers to your network, or you may want a combination of both. Each has its own advantages and disadvantages. For example, both the parallel and serial port speeds vary greatly, but in general, parallel port speeds are better than serial—two to four times faster, as a matter of fact.

Additionally, parallel printers offer a standard maximum distance of 10 feet, although some cables guarantee 150 feet. Parallel printers provide limited error checking but they are relatively error free. Finally, parallel printers are universally compatible.

Serial printers, on the other hand, offer a standard maximum distance of 25 feet, even though some cables guarantee 500 feet. Serial printers also have better error-checking capability and require less-expensive cabling.

Many printers come with both parallel and serial ports; check the number and type of ports before purchasing the printer and make sure you have the correct cables to attach the printer to the network. Use a printer that's appropriate for your needs. For instance, if printing is frequent and time and quality are important, use a fast laser printer. If the mix of your print jobs contains mostly plain text, then the speed of the print engine is most important.

Also, advanced printers, like the thermal transfer printer and even some laser printers, may require complex drivers to handle the printer control information. Make sure these printer drivers are available before purchasing the new printer.

Protocols

Network clients printing to a network printer use the network protocol to get the data to the printer. Various network operating systems support different protocols, and many support multiple protocols and provide services so a variety of clients can print to a printer. For example, Windows NT Server enables printing from UNIX, Macintosh, and NetWare clients if the appropriate protocols and services are installed to the server.

Printer protocols are sets of rules implemented to facilitate communications and to provide an interface between different hardware systems. A protocol governs format, timing, sequencing, and error handling. The network operating system you use will offer various protocols for use on the network and with the printers. Windows clients, for example, commonly use NetBEUI, NWLink, TCP/IP, and AppleTalk. NetWare uses IPX/SPX; and UNIX uses TCP/IP.

TCP/IP is a common and useful protocol to implement in your network, especially if your network includes Windows or UNIX computers, both of which work quite well with TCP/IP. UNIX clients generally use the LPR (Line Printer Remote) client software to add a job to a print queue. The LPD (Line Printer Daemon) service sends data from the queue, or spooling directory, directly to a printer. The UNIX TCP/IP network services are supported by a number of *daemons*, or programs, that run in the background and provide services directly or maintain tables that are used by other network programs.

Network interface printers require the TCP/IP protocol; you usually assign a TCP/IP address to the print device. The AppleTalk protocol is one required by AppleTalk printers. NetWare clients use IPX/SPX to send print jobs over the network.

PLANNING NETWORK STRATEGIES

You want to get the most from your printers while using the network to make your hardware operate efficiently and effectively. One way to successfully manage your network printers is to use print servers. Whether you choose to use a computer or a detachable network device, whether you use the NOS administrative features or purchase a third-party application depends on the size of your network and your usage of the available printers.

This chapter can help you determine the direction you want to pursue. In this chapter, you learn about the following:

- Advantages to using a print server

- Types of print servers

- Organizing network printing

- Print management software

- Taking inventory of current equipment

Using Print Servers

The term *print server* can refer to many different things. A computer running an NOS that controls printers, printer drivers, the print queue, and so on, can be a print server. If this computer services only printers and doesn't handle files, applications, or other services, it is a *dedicated* print server. Novell NetWare and Windows NT both enable you to make a print server from a computer running the server software. Both NOSs supply print queues, various printer drivers, and other features that let you administer a printer.

Another print server is a device that attaches to the network and provides shared network access to printers for a variety of network protocols and operating systems. This device often has several parallel and/or serial ports and may be configured via an attachment to a workstation. The network nodes normally spool print jobs to this device and the print server queues multiple jobs in the order in which they are received.

Some software can be considered a print server, such as Novell's NLM loaded to a file server to handle print jobs. The NLMs are loaded to the file server and can control up to 16 printers attached to the network.

Advantages of Using a Print Server

Although in the past, the combined file/print server was commonly used for network printing, it is impractical today because of more users, larger print jobs, greater draw on both the file and the print server, and so on. Naturally, if your network is small with only one superserver and less than 100 users, combining file and print services may work; but as your network grows, a dedicated print server is the answer.

There are many advantages to using a computer attached to the network as a print server as opposed to attaching printers locally to workstations. For one thing, everyone on the network can share a network printer attached to a print server. Another advantage is in the number of printers you'll need to buy to enable each workstation to print to its own printer. Following are some additional benefits to using a print server.

Print processing requires a great deal of CPU power. If you're using a file/print server, the computer is also processing other types of jobs and serving files to the network, so there may not be enough power left over to adequately process the print jobs. Also, print processing may affect the file server's ability to manage other tasks.

> **NOTE**
>
> Programmed character I/O is the process that causes printing to require a lot of CPU power. When the computer is sending a job to the printer, the CPU gets interrupted once for every character it sends; that demand increases significantly when several printers are being served from the same server computer. A print server that uses the DMA (Direct Memory Access) process interrupts the CPU only once for every data packet (around 1500 characters). Called *offloading*, this process results in a significant improvement over the server's performance as well as provides faster network printing.

Printers attached to a print server may be in a central location so all users can easily retrieve their print jobs, or the printers may be scattered throughout the network and still be controlled by the one print server computer.

Printers attached to a print server can process jobs from many different operating systems or networks, if the print server is configured for a heterogeneous network environment. Macintosh, UNIX workstations, Windows, and NetWare can all print to the same laser or color laser printer, for example, simply by loading a variety of printer drivers to the print server.

A print server is easier to administer and troubleshoot than many local printers would be. One person can check the print server's queue to see if jobs are completed, check problems and status, rearrange the jobs in the queue, and cancel or pause print jobs sent to the server.

Often print server software enables load-balancing, a feature that enables the server to equalize print jobs between two or more printers. If you have multiple laser printers connected to the server, for example, this automatic feature prints jobs to the available printer so jobs are handled more efficiently.

What to Look for in a Print Server

A print server should enable the users to control the printer and the server, to a point, from their own PCs. For example, the user should be able to manipulate his or her own print job in the print queue; deleting the job or changing its position on the queue list should be well within any user's rights. A user should also be able to view other files in the queue, reconfigure the printer for his or her particular job, and perform other necessary tasks without leaving his or her desk.

The administrator must be able to limit access to the print server via passwords and/or rights. This may be a function of the network operating system or of print server software. Primarily, users should only be able to modify (delete and/or move within the queue list) their jobs in the print queue and no others.

Network Printing Methods

There are several ways you can set your printers up in conjunction with your network. You might, for example, connect one or two printers to a computer configured as a print server. Users can then see the printer over the network, specify the printer they want to print to, and send the job. On the other hand, you may want to share multiple printers, each connected to different servers throughout the network. Printers can also be connected to workstations and shared with other users on the network.

Following are some other printing configurations you can use alone or in conjunction with others:

Multiple print servers with multiple printers. This method works well within two or more network segments so that printer traffic doesn't cross segments and slow progress of all network traffic. Figure 2.1 illustrates this network printing configuration; traffic to the printer remains within the network segment.

One printer assigned to multiple print queues. If printing is not a major concern and one printer can handle most jobs, you can assign multiple queues to that printer and configure each queue to perform specific tasks. For instance, one queue could print large jobs at night, when the printer isn't in use.

Multiple printing environments, such as NetWare and UNIX interface printers, attached directly to the network cabling. This enables different network clients to print to the same or to different printers, depending on your configuration.

Multiple printers servicing one queue. Use this method when you have many print jobs that will be printed, for example, to a laser printer. Set up two or more laser printers to take the jobs in order as they arrive at the print queue. This balances the load between multiple printers so jobs are processed more quickly.

Figure 2.1 Two network segments in which printers and print servers each take care of its own clients.

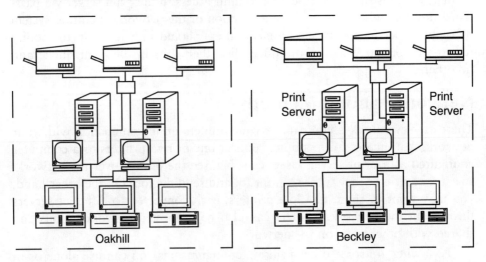

Printing Pools

As previously explained, the term *print server* can refer to a variety of things: server computer, server software, a device attached to the network, and so on. Generally, however, you'll likely use a computer with a network operating system that controls printing by use of a print queue and other administrative tools.

An option for managing multiple users' access to print devices is to form a printing pool. A pool consists of multiple, identical print devices associated with one printer driver (representation on the network). When someone prints to the network printer, the available device takes the job and prints the document. Load balancing is generally handled by the network operating system so that the queue feeds the next job to the next available printer.

All of the print devices in a printing pool are the same hardware model and act as a single unit; therefore, all print settings apply to the entire pool. Ports, however, can be the same type or mixed: parallel, serial, and/or network. If one print device in the pool stops working for some reason—paper jam, out of paper, and so on—it holds the last document sent to it until someone fixes the problem. Other documents sent to the pool continue to print from other devices.

Figure 2.2 illustrates one print server attached to six identical printers in a printing pool. When a client sends a print request to the print server, it holds the request in the queue until the next printer is available.

Figure 2.2 A printing pool balances the workload.

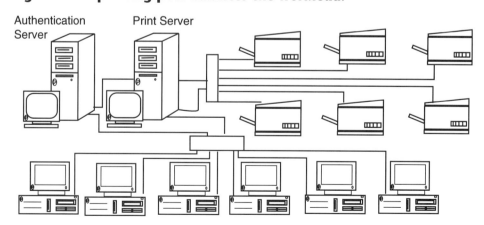

Print Management Software

Your NOS can generally control the print queue, permissions, and other factors determining how and who prints what to the network printers. However, very large networks and enterprise networks may need some additional direction in order to get the most from the printers.

NOS Print Management

Depending on the NOS, you should be able to control the printer security to some extent. Generally, printers should always be available to all users all of the time. However, you may want to control access to special printers, such as color printers or high-resolution laser printers, for example. Following are some of the software printer controls you may receive with an NOS:

Print queue.   Controls over documents to be printed: pause, delete, reorder, and so on.

Scheduling.   Choose whether the printer is always available or available only during certain days and times. This is a handy feature for limiting expensive printing to work hours only or for controlling traffic to certain printers.

Permissions/rights.   Assign specific permissions and revoke certain rights from one or multiple users. This is another good way to regulate traffic to the printer and print server.

Configuration.   Set the amount of memory, specify paper trays and paper sizes, and so on, to designate a printer for specific tasks.

Third-Party Print Management Applications

Third-party print management applications may be of interest to you if your network is very large and/or if your network printers are heavily used. Print management software can provide the following services, among others:

- Status of printers on the network, including remote printers
- Easy installation and configuration of new printers
- Detailed diagnostics of printers on the network
- Web- and browser-based management of printers
- DHCP and SNMP compatibility
- Multiple protocol support
- Automatic negotiation between various network interface cards

Integration with a variety of network operating systems, printers, and client operating systems makes a network management system important for operating, organizing, optimizing, and otherwise administering large networks.

Some printers, such as Xerox printers, are now being shipped with built-in Web servers, enabling these printers to be managed anywhere on the network if a browser is installed. The software makes the printer easy to install and set up.

Also available are multivendor printer management tools that provide a single or group view of all SNMP-based network printers in the system. Users can manage and track printer usage of a broad range of printers from various manufacturers, such as Xerox, Hewlett-Packard, Lexmark, and others. The software is designed to function like a universal remote control for office printers, regardless of brand.

> **NOTE**
>
> Network management platforms such as Hewlett-Packard's OpenView and Novell's ManageWise offer a single view of network nodes and capabilities for managing individual devices, particularly printers. There are also printer applications such as Xerox's CentreWare DP software, Lexmark's MarkVision, and Hewlett-Packard's JetAdmin that offer useful installation and configuration tools; these are limited to being printer-specific and proprietary.

Determining Needs

Whether you're upgrading an existing network or building a new one, you have some decisions to make before you can create an efficient, cost-effective printer network. You may already have printers in your office or you may plan to purchase new and improved printers to add to your network. There are a few organizational chores you should do before you choose and purchase your printers.

Following is a task list to help you determine your needs and organize your thoughts about printers:

List your current print devices, including all local printers as well as network printers.

List the computer(s) you can use as a print server. Add to the list the processor, memory, disk space, operating system, and other pertinent information about the computer.

Consider methods of sharing your printers and configuring them for maximum use. For example, the faster laser printer should be located in the network segment that needs it most; slower ink jet printers might be placed in a segment that needs good quality output but not necessarily the speed.

Determine the importance of speed in the printer. Is it more important to some departments than others?

Determine if you need a few high-volume print devices or multiple less-expensive ones. Remember that fewer printers affect more users if one or more break down.

Ascertain how many pages are printed in each department, each hour. Match the printing volume with the number of pages a printer can print. This will give you fewer maintenance problems.

List special needs, such as graphics support, extra or specialty fonts, halftone printing, and so on. Do some departments need color printing or higher resolution than 300 or 600dpi?

Make note of various print devices' compatibility issues with your network operating system.

Consider fast printers to save time and money and to increase the printer's use. Along this same line, think about how much resolution you really need. Although there are 1200dpi systems out now, would 600dpi or even 300dpi do just as well? If so, you can save quite a bit of speed in the printing processes.

SERVER AND NETWORK PREPARATIONS

Preparing your network for changes and upgrades is difficult, if not impossible. There are many considerations and decisions you must make to ensure you do not slow the system rather than improve it. Servers, ports, software settings, and networking hardware all have an effect on network traffic, speed of printing, and frustration level of both the user and administrator.

This chapter offers some advice for implementing printers into your network. In this chapter, you learn about the following:

- Server plans
- Cabling, protocols, and ports
- Network preparations
- Internet printing
- Printing policies

Server Preparations

As with adding any hardware and/or software to your network, there are some general steps you should follow as well as some specific moves to make. Generally, you'll want to determine your needs, shop around for the hardware and/or software, and purchase the equipment you need. Onsite, you will physically attach the hardware to the network, install hardware and/or software to the network, configure it, test it, and optimize the system before enabling the entire network to use the new additions.

The rest of this section offers some more specific advice for print servers and attaching them to a network.

Print Server Preparations

As you know, you can use a computer or a device as a print server, either of which requires some preparation before users can begin using the attached printers. You'll need to consider, for example, the amount of RAM and processor power a computer server needs to manage the network printers. If you're using a print server device, you may need to make certain hardware adjustments before installing it to the network.

Use the computer or device's documentation when preparing, installing, and configuring it; the manufacturer knows its product best. If you have any questions or problems and the documentation does not help, consider calling the manufacturer instead of beating your head against the wall trying to figure the problems out on your own.

Computer Print Server

For the print server computer, preparation is fairly straightforward. Make sure you use a computer with plenty of processor power and RAM; just as an example, processor speed should be 300MHz or better and RAM should number at least 64MB. Naturally, if you are serving only a few users, you may not need too much power and memory; if you're serving hundreds of users, you'll not only need more power but you may also need more print servers.

If you're using a computer that was once another type of server, make sure you clean any unnecessary files from the disk drive. You might run utilities to check for and fix errors, but you will be better off reformatting the drive and starting from scratch to ensure the computer has no major file allocation problems and such.

To a clean drive, install the network operating system and configure for network use. You may want to include security settings, optimization components, and any other settings that make the NOS suit your needs and your network. While installing the NOS, check for available print drivers and install the ones your clients will need; you might, for example, install drivers for Windows, Macintosh, and UNIX workstations.

Next, install and/or configure print management software. The NOS may include print server software or you may purchase a third-party package. When you're finished installing and configuring, attach the server(s) to the printer(s) and test the system to make sure it behaves as it should. After thorough testing, you can attach the server and printers to the network for general use.

When configuring the print server, follow these tips for the greatest potential:

- Maximize the printer's use by staggering printing times. If traffic is heavy during the day, postpone printing of less-important documents by sending them to a printer that prints only during off-hours.

- Depending on the NOS or print management software, you can assign priority levels to printers so that documents routed to a printer with the highest priority level print first, second-priority printers print jobs second, and so on.

- You can assign more than one type of printer software to a printer; for example, you can assign 300dpi and/or 600dpi resolution to a Hewlett-Packard laser; in this case, 300dpi prints faster than 600dpi and looks nearly as good. You can also assign other print properties, such as adding separator pages, printing only at night, and such.

Print Server Devices

Most print server devices, or multiprotocol print servers, are simple to install but difficult to configure. You'll need to make sure you have all documentation before you start; read the documentation in detail. Following are some tips on things to check when preparing to install a print server device; however, each device is different, so you must check the documentation to be sure of the correct procedures.

You'll likely need a specific network operating system already in place, perhaps print server software, and other possible requirements such as a minimum amount of conventional memory or minimum disk space. In some cases, you'll need to configure some NOS options before you can continue, such as granting permissions or rights to the printer, naming the printer, and so on.

When preparing to install a print server device, make sure you check any cabling restrictions. Cabling may use standard pinouts or you may have to customize or use adapters for the correct configuration. Also, there may be some limits to the length and baud rate of serial cables. The device's documentation should outline any restrictions and requirements.

Next, check for DIP switch settings and make those modifications. Configure the IP address for the print device, if applicable, and follow any other special instructions outlined for your particular device. Depending on the device and your use of it, you may have to configure protocols, addresses, passwords, or other components to make the device work.

If the device requires software, follow installation instructions and configure the software for the printer and protocol you'll be using.

Ports and Cabling

Cabling and ports have certain requirements; read all documentation included with a print server computer or device and the printers to make sure you understand and follow these guidelines to get the most from the equipment. Following are just a few specifications and suggestions to help you with cabling and port assignments.

> **NOTE**
>
> Pinouts, cables, and ports create the majority of the network printing problems.

Parallel cables must be less than 20 feet long; serial cables can be up to 100 feet long. Be careful then when placing printers on the network.

Standard Intel computers support three parallel ports and two serial ports. RISC-based computers usually come with one parallel and two serial ports built in but support as many as there is space for. Print devices usually have at least one parallel and one serial port, but sometimes more.

When configuring parallel ports, you may have to set hardware jumpers or switches. Serial communication requires flow control (handshaking), which defines a method of the print device to tell the NOS its buffer is full. See the print device's documentation for more information on communications settings.

The number of devices you can attach to the print server is dependent on the number of interface card slots, addresses, and interrupt request (IRQ) lines available. Standard devices are assigned to the following IRQs:

COM1   IRQ4

COM2   IRQ3

LPT1   IRQ7

LPT2   IRQ5

On RISC-based systems, LPT1, COM1, and COM2 are built in and don't conflict with IRQ levels on the EISA bus. Some interface cards support sharing of interrupts, meaning that two device addresses can use the same IRQ level. However, some devices require exclusive use of certain interrupts. Check the hardware manuals before configuring ports.

Most print server devices provide at least one serial and one parallel port that network nodes can spool print jobs to. Depending on the type of device you use, ports and cabling will differ. For example, one print server for use with

UNIX networks has an AUI port for connection to an external network transceiver and an RJ45 connector for use with 10baseT. This same unit supports AppleTalk, Digital Equipment Corporation's LAT, NetWare, and TCP/IP protocols. Some devices need no host software or configuration; others do.

Network Preparations

Printing on a network is never easy. For one thing, there are no real printer standards between printer manufacturers. If you can, purchase printers made by the same manufacturer for easier installation, setup, configuration, and troubleshooting. Additionally, purchase the better brand of printers and within any one brand, purchase the better models for network printing. Putting extra money into the equipment up front will save you time and money later on. This section contains advice and guidelines for preparing the network for the addition of printers.

Ports

Serial or parallel ports connected to a computer server are slower than print devices that connect directly to the network using built-in LAN cards. Generally, network links are faster than parallel and serial buses, but it also depends on the amount of network traffic, the network interface card installed, the protocol used, and the type of print device.

When using a computer print server, you should use parallel ports whenever possible. Serial ports are less predictable than parallel ports. They're also more difficult to manipulate and data travels more slowly over a serial port than a parallel port.

You should also avoid purchasing exotic printers that use different cables, different handshaking protocols, and different interfaces. Printing to a standard, common printer can be difficult enough; adding so many dissimilar elements to the network can only cause more problems. If there is a specialty printer you must add to your system, try adding it only to a small portion of the network—such as the art department or engineering segment—and keep it off the main network.

Protocols and Adapter Cards

You likely already have your cabling in place for the network, but you might want to consider some changes to speed traffic and prevent bottlenecks. One suggestion is to use the Fast Ethernet protocol. Ethernet is a popular protocol and cabling scheme with a transfer rate of 10 megabits per second. Network nodes are connected by either thick or thin coaxial cable, fiber optic cable, or by twisted-pair wiring. Ethernet uses CSMA/CD (Carrier Sense Multiple Access/Collision Detection) to prevent network failures or collisions when two devices try to access the network at the same time. Ethernet uses the IEEE 802.3 standard specs. 802.x is a set of communications standards that define the physical and electrical connections in a LAN, as defined by the Institute of Electrical and Electronic Engineers (IEEE).

Fast Ethernet runs 10 times faster than the existing Ethernet standard by running the IEEE 802.3 higher speed. With the need of additional bandwidth due to more users and more demanding applications, standard Ethernet is simply too slow for network printing. Fast Ethernet supports speeds of 10 and/or 100 megabits per second. It also retains the 802.3 frame format, plus meets the same error-detection requirements as 802.3.

Fast Ethernet runs on 100baseT, which uses unshielded twisted-pair cabling, meaning it's easier to manage. Using Category 5 twisted-pair wiring requires two pairs of wire per connection and uses an RJ45 connector with identical pinouts. This is called 100baseTX and is generally used in newer building installations. 100baseT4 is a variation that uses Category 3 twisted-pair wiring (used in older building installations). 100baseT4 requires four pairs of wire per connection, uses an RJ45 connector, but has a different pinout since all eight wires are used.

A 100baseT adapter card also supports a 10baseT network, meaning you can begin to integrate these newer, slightly more expensive cards into your network so that when you're ready to upgrade routers and other equipment, the cards will already be in place; thus deferring some of the expense. The same goes for the print server; if print servers with the 10baseT and 100baseTX capabilities are priced about the same, buy the 100baseTX so your servers won't be obsolete when you're ready to upgrade the rest of the network.

You may not need the 100baseTX technology now for most printing applications, since most printer speeds can't reach the limits of standard Ethernet. However, the incremental cost of a 100baseTX print server is small, it works on existing networks, applications are becoming more graphics-intensive, color graphics will make performance more of an issue, and as newer printers become faster and faster, they will soon be capable of exceeding the performance capabilities of Ethernet.

Internet Printing

IPP (Internet Printing Protocol) is a proposed standard for interoperability over IP-based networks that many vendors are currently working on—Hewlett-

Packard, Adobe Systems, Lexmark, Microsoft, Novell, and Xerox Corporation, to name a few. This standard will hopefully be ready in 1998. Any computer conforming to IPP standards will be able to print to any printer over a network (Internet or LAN), enabling end users to send, monitor, and cancel print jobs to printers as close as the desktop and as far away as several time zones. IPP is meant to totally enable a distributed print environment. A client browser or a desktop client will manage each individual print job.

In these standards, a printer will have its own URL destination; HTTP 1.1 (upgrade of the current protocol) will act as a transport agent; a new MIME type (called application/IPP) will be a part of mapping functions and can act as a container for operations and responses.

IPP will let administrators within a large company manage printers over an entire WAN from a single console. IPP will make it easier to deal with a variety of servers, operating systems, and print drivers.

Clients

Clients should be able to browse the network for available printers and then choose the printer that best serves their needs. Printers should be easy to locate and to use. There are several ways you can prepare client computers and users for the addition of one or more printers; keeping users informed of the changes to come is the first step.

You should also provide a list of printer use guidelines to each user; outline such information as the printer type, paper usage (kind and weight), whom to contact with a printer problem, and specific policies concerning each printer. You might, for example, have set times during which certain printers may be used. Keep the users informed and train them in the use of the network printer, if necessary.

Another step you can take is to install the printer drivers to individual client computers. Some network operating systems supply printer drivers on the print server as each client attaches and sends a job. Other NOSs supply a directory of printer drivers the user can download and install to his or her own computer. Make this process as easy and painless as you can, whether that means sending an assistant around with a disk or letting more proficient users do it themselves.

Keep in mind that clients shouldn't be allowed to administer printers. You may want to enable users to manage their own documents within the print queue so they can pause or delete a job, for example. The administrator or his or her assistant should be the only ones enabled to administer printers, print servers, documents, and printer drivers. Also, make sure you configure the system so you can administer printers remotely as well.

If your network serves various client operating systems, font management may be a problem. There are device fonts, screen fonts, and downloadable fonts your users can use. The easiest way to take care of font problems is to formulate a policy that lists the types of fonts that are supported and monitor client applications so that new fonts meet the set guidelines.

Policies and Security

Policies are necessary evils when it comes to a network. As difficult as they are to formulate and enforce, they are important to your company for several reasons. Protection of your data, hardware and equipment, users, time, money, and legal protection are just a few of the reasons why you'll want to create policies throughout each facet of the network. Security is also important to networks; however, you may not want to put too many restrictions on your printers, since most users need to print.

Policies

Policies make it easier to control users and their activities on the network. You can use policies to save wear and tear on equipment; limit the waste of time, money, and resources; protect data; defend actions; and so on. For policies to be effective, however, you must consider them carefully and define them well. Make sure all policies are in written and printed format, distribute them to all employees, meet with the staff and cover each policy, and make sure everyone understands them. You will also want to periodically review and update your policies.

Following is a list of standard printer policies for your consideration. Modify these and add your own to formulate a set of printer policies that benefit your company.

List the types and weights of papers that each printer can use; list any specialty papers (such as mailing labels or gold foil) that you do not want used in a printer; add to the list where the paper is stored and how it can be obtained. Do not use transparencies on the printer unless it's specifically for transparencies.

List acceptable fonts, font cartridges, and specialty fonts that may be printed from each printer.

Let users know they should not print multiple copies of documents on printers; they should use copy machines instead.

Designate someone to collect printed materials from each printer. Consider what steps you'll take to protect sensitive materials that are printed over the network, like letters of termination or payroll reports.

Determine whether blank pages may be inserted in a group of documents, say for separator pages.

Determine what constitutes wasted paper and set guidelines covering this.

Color printers may require other types of policies:

Do not use the color printer to print multiple copies of color documents; perhaps your company has a color copier or at least access to another establishment that has a color copier.

Users should not attempt to fix perceived problems with a printer; instead, they should report problems to technical support personnel.

Security

Most printers should be available to the users at all times so they can complete their work. However, you may want to limit the use of some printers, such as color laser printers or other printers that use expensive paper or special printing techniques. You can use an NOS or print management software to limit access to printers by password, scheduling print times, and so on.

TROUBLESHOOTING AND OPTIMIZATION

E very network uses printers and every network administrator will have problems with those printers. If you apply a bit of preventative mainte-nance to the printer and exercise caution when purchasing papers, you can save yourself a lot of hassles with your network printers.

Additionally, by applying some optimization techniques, you can provide your users with efficient and practical network printing. This chapter outlines some troubleshooting and optimization steps where your printers are con-cerned. Specifically, this chapter covers the following:

- General troubleshooting techniques
- Laser and dot matrix printer troubleshooting
- Paper specifications for laser printers
- Optimization advice for more efficient printing

Troubleshooting Printer Problems

Since they are used so much by so many, printers will likely cause the majority of problems for users on the network. You should assign one or two assistants to each printer for maintenance and troubleshooting purposes, and make sure the users have the contact information for the assigned assistant to report prob-lems to. You might also consider passing out guidelines for general trou-bleshooting that users can perform from their workstations or that users located close to a printer can check, like paper jams.

General Troubleshooting

Following are some very general things to look for when having trouble with a printer. You should also check the printer's documentation and/or the network operating system's documentation and online help to find solutions. These first ideas are very basic, but you'd be surprised at how many people don't check these options first.

Make sure the printer is turned on.

Check that it is on-line.

Check the paper to be sure the tray has paper, is positioned correctly, and there are no paper jams.

Make sure the toner or ribbon is positioned correctly and ready to use.

Check all power cords to see that they are firmly plugged in to both the printer and the wall outlet.

Turn the printer off and then back on again to reinitialize any internal settings that may be corrupted.

If all of the previous checks are okay and the printer still doesn't work, try running the printer's self-test. If the test fails, the problem is inside of the printer. If it passes, try using Print Screen from DOS; if that fails, the problem is in the relationship between the printer and the computer. Check the cable and cable connections; try replacing the cable. If Print Screen succeeds, the problem may be with the application or its configuration.

> **WARNING**
>
> Never open a printer unless it's turned off and unplugged; some printers do not have shielded power supplies.

If you're still having trouble, try printing from a Windows program and again from DOS to see if the problem is operating system-based. Output is considered to be printer noise, LED indicators blinking, even garbage that's printed on the page. If the printer outputs, then the problem is not the network; therefore, it may be a print driver on the workstation that's configured improperly, or the wrong driver is installed, or it may be the page setup as well. First, clear the print queue, and then look at workstation setup. Check the printer driver in Windows and in DOS and check for proper printer type and port. Check page margins and printer settings and make any adjustment. Try printing again.

If you're still having problems, check the print queue to see if the job is making it there; if your job is not in the queue, make sure the user is logged on to the network. If the user is logged on, check to see if the queue is properly captured (in NetWare). Does the user have sufficient network rights to print? Perhaps the user is not using his or her own machine, for example. If the print job does make it to the queue, check the job status for ideas. If the status is ready, the printing problem isn't related to workstation setup.

Paper Storage

The storage of your printer paper has a lot to do with the final printer output. Paper that is damp or wrinkled cannot only produce defective printer output, but it can damage your printer as well. Follow these guidelines when storing printer paper, envelopes, and/or labels:

- Place cartons or reams of paper on a shelf, or if you store them on the floor, raise slightly using wooden shelves or pallets.

- Be careful when storing reams; make sure the paper is flat so it doesn't curl or warp on the edges.

- Don't stack more than six cartons of paper on top of each other.

- Don't stack other things on top of the paper, such as heavy equipment, books, or boxes of parts.

- Stack each carton upright and squarely on top of the one underneath it.

- Protect stored paper from extreme temperatures and humidity.

- Cover any unused portions of paper by wrapping them in plastic so moisture and light do not damage them.

Troubleshooting Laser Printers

A multitude of problems comes hand in hand with any printer, but especially laser printers. Laser printers are sensitive to paper weights and surfaces; plus there are many sensitive parts to a laser printer that can go bad. The first list in this section describes the common causes to many problems; the rest of the section discusses problems in more detail.

- Fuzzy output could mean a dirty corona wire, or you're running out of toner.

- Horizontal lines or splotches may mean a damaged or dirty print drum or roller.

- If images are disproportionately long or short, check the paper's surface. Too smooth or too heavy paper can cause problems of this sort.

- If the printer doesn't go on-line, you could have a faulty control panel or bad cable. Power the printer without the cable and if it goes on-line, suspect the cable as the problem.

- Speckled print is probably caused by the corona grid, a part of the toner cartridge. Replace the cartridge.

- White streaks on the page may mean the toner isn't equally distributed. Remove the cartridge and rock it gently from side to side and try again.
- If the network printer goes off-line for no reason but works fine when you reinitialize it, your problem could be static generated by specialty papers. Ground the printer properly.

Faint Print

Faint print conditions may indicate the toner cartridge needs to be replaced, naturally, but there are also other problems that can cause the print to be light. The paper finish or moisture content can cause the problem; make sure the paper you use is made for the laser (electro-photographic) printing process.

Two other possible solutions are as follows: If the print density is not set properly, adjusting it transfers more toner to the drum, or the transfer roller may need to be replaced or reseated.

Faulty Registration

Registration describes how the image (text, picture, and such) is placed on the page. In color printers, it describes color placement; in black and white printers, it may indicate the placement of items in accordance to the edges of the paper. If you're having trouble with registration, consider the paper first. The surface of the paper may be too smooth for the roller to move through the paper path. Try a different paper to see if that is the cause.

If the pickup roller or the separation pad is worn, this can also cause registration problems. Alternatively, driver gears may be worn or dirty or the paper tray may be preventing the paper from moving through the printer.

White Streaks

White streaks down the page may be indicative of several printer problems. If you've checked the toner and that yields no success, try cleaning the lenses within the laser/scanning device. If they're blocked with paper pieces or just dirty, that could cause the problem. You may need to replace the lenses if you cannot clear the path. Finally, the laser shutter may also be blocking part of the beam by not lifting at all or by sticking.

Repetitive Defects

If you notice defects at intervals, such as dirty specs or blocked type or images, suspect the toner cartridge is damaged. If the drum and roller in the cartridge have a problem, the printed page will show it every two to four inches on the page. If this is the case, replace the toner cartridge.

A faulty fusing assembly or fusing roller could also cause repetitive defects. You'll need to clean the fusing assembly or perhaps replace it. Dirty rollers along the paper path may also cause this problem. Check and clean all rollers along this path.

Image or Print Distorted

If the print image is distorted—characters are too tall or too short—the paper may not be moving at a uniform speed. This could be caused by a drive mechanism problem. Check the transport rollers for wear, the toner cartridge, drive gear assembly, main motor, and fusing assembly.

If the image is askew, the input sensor may not be sensing the presence of paper. Replace the sensor to alleviate this problem. Alternatively, if drive gears are excessively worn or dirty, erratic paper movement might result. Clean and replace the gears as necessary.

Holes in the Printed Image

If your printed image—text or pictures—has holes, or voids, in it, you might want to check the paper type first. Some paper surfaces are just too smooth for laser printing. Also, wet or damp paper can cause this problem. Try a different paper first to see if the problem continues.

If you still have the voids in the image, check all rollers for dirt, stray paper pieces, and so on.

Other possible causes: The laser shutter may be defective. Check to make sure the shutter has full operation. Fusing could also be the culprit; replace the fusing assembly.

Laser Paper Specifications

A lot of the problems with laser printers are caused by the paper used. Old paper, damp paper, or paper that is too smooth, for example, can cause different types of problems with the printed output. You should always make sure you use the exact paper specified in the printer's documentation—check for recommended paper surface, paper weight, and size.

In addition to paper, envelopes and labels can cause problems with the final output. Cheap envelopes, window envelopes, and uncommon envelope sizes may not feed through the printer as well as those

Continues

Laser Paper Specifications (*Continued*)

specified in the documentation. And printer labels must be of high quality and meet recommended specs to successfully print through a laser printer.

Following are some other possible paper problems:

- Recycled paper with more than 5-percent groundwood or fiber composition
- Coated papers
- Curled, wrinkled, or bent papers
- Heavy textures or glossy smoothness
- Embossed or raised surface paper
- Greasy or dusty papers
- Paper with cutouts or perforations
- Preprinted forms with multiple copies

For printing envelopes, be careful of the following:

- More than double thickness of paper on the leading edge of the envelope
- Heavy weights (over 28 lbs., for example)
- Exposed adhesive that may stick to the rollers
- Nicked or wrinkled envelopes
- Windows, clasps, snaps, or other synthetic materials
- Curved edge on the leading edge

For labels, avoid adhesives that cannot withstand temperatures greater than 400 degrees Fahrenheit. Make sure the top sheet (the label) will accept the toner and provide good adhesion and that the carrier sheet (bottom sheet) is compatible with the temperatures and pressure of the fusing process. Also, never print a label sheet that has one or more of the labels removed from the sheet.

If you print transparencies on your laser printer, the transparency paper must be able to withstand the temperature, usually around 400 degrees Fahrenheit. If you're careful to purchase and use *only* paper, envelopes, and labels made specifically for laser printers, your results will be good and your printers will be safe.

> **NOTE**
> Avoid any media, media coatings, dyes, or inks that produce hazardous emissions or melt when exposed to the fusing temperature specified in your printer's documentation.

Troubleshooting Dot Matrix Printers

Following are some ideas for troubleshooting dot matrix printers:

- If you're having trouble printing jobs from the computer but the printer's self-test is okay, check the dip switch settings, make sure you have the appropriate drivers installed for the application, and/or check the cable.

- If the printer has both a serial and parallel connection and one connection isn't working, change cables to try the other connection. If one works and the other does not, the problem could be with the port.

- When the *thermistor*, the part that keeps the printer from overheating, goes bad, the printer may shut down and recover frequently.

- For double-spaced output when you expect single-spaced, reset the dip switch(es) that control Carriage Return and Line Feed.

- For poor print quality, first check the ribbon. Also check the print head spacing; if the head is too far away from the platen for the paper thickness, you'll need to adjust the spacing. If you still have problems, clean the print head with a cotton swab dipped lightly in alcohol.

Other Print Problems

There are other miscellaneous problems with some printers that may be caused by an application, fonts, or the data being printed. Following are some things to check if the printer doesn't perform properly:

If a job has trouble getting to the print spooler, there may be a conflict between an application and the network. Check to see if the application has its own print spooler. Other possible print buffers include the PC, the printer, and the network; you should only use the network print buffer. Generally, all buffers work together, but sometimes one buffer waits for another and that slows things down. If that happens, use only one buffer.

Multiple users sharing one printer may cause trouble; printing various fonts, images, or using specific settings may slow the printer or lock it up. It's a good idea to include limits for unusual settings, fonts, and large images in your printer policies. You might also designate one network printer to these special circumstances, or you could attach a local printer to the user or department needing to print specialty items.

Applications sometimes enable users to send printer control codes that reset a printer and interfere with network operations or network printer control codes. If the print output is garbled or looks like garbage, you should find the offending application and reconfigure it to not use printer control code commands.

Multiple users have different requirements for paper. The easiest way to handle these needs is to get printers with different paper trays, or specify certain printers to use the specialty papers.

Optimizing Network Printing Performance

Periodic maintenance and care will help your printers perform well and last longer. Also, you can get better printer performance by using certain hardware and upgrading the server and/or client computers. By upgrading hardware in the bottleneck areas, you can speed printers, but remember, there is always another bottleneck. Adding printers may be the answer in some of these cases.

Preventative Maintenance

If you keep your printers clean, you can stop many problems before they even begin. Realize that the inner workings of printers are sometimes delicate, so you must be careful when cleaning. If you prefer, you can outsource or contract a technician to come in periodically (every three months or so) to clean your printers for you.

Vacuum your printer occasionally to clean up spilled toner and loose paper particles. Make sure the vacuum cleaner is capable of filtering toner particles when cleaning laser printers. Toner powder is hazardous to breathe, so you want to be sure the vacuum cleaner is not releasing toner into the air after removing it from the printer.

Also, use a lint-free cloth to gently clean the paper and ribbon paths and/or the corona wires and rollers periodically. It's a good idea to clean these areas each time you insert a new ribbon or toner cartridge. Additionally, maintain the temperature and humidity around the printers, as some printer components may be sensitive to environmental changes.

With laser printers in particular, follow these maintenance procedures:

Check a new toner cartridge carefully before inserting it into a printer to make sure there are no toner leaks or spills.

Clean the corona wire and roller each time you change the cartridge.

Provide proper ventilation around a laser printer since they generate a lot of heat.

Use only address labels intended for laser printers so the glue will hold up during printing.

Never place the printer near water sources, humidifiers, air conditioners, refrigerators, or other major appliances. Don't expose the printer to direct sunlight, open flames, or ammonia fumes.

> **NOTE**
> There are certain consumable laser printer components that will be necessary to replace periodically. Keep an eye on toner cartridges, roller assembly, separation pad, charging rollers, fusing assembly, and the exhaust fan. Check the manufacturer's documentation for more information.

Improving Print Speed

Network print speed is primarily affected by whether the printer is connected by parallel or serial ports. Parallel ports are at least two times faster than serial ports at 9600 baud and up to four times faster than serial ports at 4800 baud. Use parallel ports whenever possible for the best performance.

The application and print driver versions also have a great impact on printing performance. Maintain a record of all versions, configurations, and types of application for each of your installations. Updating to the latest printer drivers will help solve many printing problems.

Files containing graphics affect printer performance, as well as some types of documents. Graphics, drawings, halftones, specialty type, and so on, will always take longer to print than straight text.

Slower computers may also limit printer performance. Use the fastest server computer possible; especially with fast processors and clock speeds. The networking hardware may also affect printer performance, although not as much as the previously mentioned elements. Slow hard drives and not enough RAM may also be causing a bottleneck. Printing speed can be increased, for example, by increasing the speed of the workstation CPU.

Performance may be hampered by too few servers or excess network traffic. Using individual network segments separated by routers and bridges can help localize network traffic and free passage for printing.

CLIENT MANAGEMENT

Introduction to Book Five

Client/server computing enables processing to occur at both the desktop and server, facilitating cooperative computing between the two. Also, the client/server system promotes optimal performance and ease of use of network resources. There are many applications, productivity tools, communication packages, and groupware solutions from many different vendors available for use with the client/server architecture. Yet, with all of the available software and hardware, there are also greater complications with compatibility, connectivity, and administration of a client/server network.

One challenge you will find in administering your network is in the client portion of client/server. Network clients, Internet clients, and remote clients all play an important role in the stability and utility of your network. You must provide useful services, quick access to files and resources, appropriate responses to problems, and security for all users of the network. And the users must help by following certain guidelines and reasonably using the resources.

This book shows you some ways you can manage the users of your network while providing them with the services they need to complete their work. This book offers advice and information about the following:

- Managing network clients: client operating systems, user accounts, security considerations, training, policies, and so on.

- Administering Internet clients: hardware and software, protocols, server and network preparations, providers, policies, and such.

- Directing remote access users: telecommuting, remote control, hardware and software, connections, and configurations.

PRELIMINARY GROUNDWORK

Chapter

1

The PCs you currently use in your workplace may be a single-user system, several standalones, or a network of computers you need to upgrade and reorganize. Perhaps you need to purchase all new hardware to create a useful network or simply upgrade some of the hardware and software.

There are several issues you should consider before you continue; more than likely, you've already planned and perhaps completed the upgrade and purchase of the server computers. If you have not, you should complete that step before concentrating on client computers. You may not need to purchase the server computers beforehand; however, you should know the type of servers, network operating systems, and networking hardware and connections you will implement before purchasing client computers.

You should use the server and NOS to help you determine the type of client operating system you'll need. The client operating system, client/server applications, user needs, and so on will help you determine the client hardware you need to complete the system.

Determining Needs

As you choose to either purchase new or upgrade existing workstations, try to keep ease of installation and maintenance in mind. Consistency in your hardware purchases can mean the difference between administrative ease and administrative nightmares.

The more brands of computers you have, the more different client operating systems employed, the more diversified software configurations, the higher the chance of administration nightmares. Incompatible CPUs and cards, specialized software installations, technical support and troubleshooting all become more difficult when you're dealing with a variety of components, programs, and configurations.

Administration Needs

When deciding on client workstations, you'll need to consider your NOS, client/server applications, existing hardware and software, budget, users' needs, ease of administration, as well as other factors. Make a list of your needs as far as software and operating systems go. If, for example, you're using a NetWare network, you may be able to use some old DOS computers as clients until you can budget money to upgrade workstations. On the other hand, if you plan to use Windows NT Server, you'll likely need to upgrade workstations to at least Windows 95 or 98 to get the most from the network.

The network operating system helps determine the workstation hardware and client operating system you use; although most NOSs today can work with a variety of client operating systems, including Windows 95/98/NT, OS/2, UNIX, Macintosh, and even NetPCs or NCs. Client operating systems have minimum requirements for workstation hardware.

Another factor in choosing the hardware is the applications you plan to use on the workstations. Each application you need for your work—accounting, word processing, databases, office suites, email, and so on—has certain specifications for operating systems and hardware requirements. Be especially mindful of any vertical applications you'll be running on one or more workstations; vertical applications often require a specific operating system and often explicit types of hardware.

User Needs

You'll also want to consider users' needs when planning the purchase or upgrade of workstation computers. Some users may need special programs to complete their work; others may have a special need for security. Some users may need Internet access, whereas others may need specialized peripherals, such as a scanner or digital camera.

As you're making your list, add these special needs to it. Also add specific requirements of groups or departments. The art department, for example, may need a color laser printer or a Macintosh application to set type and design documents. Planning a Macintosh system in the middle of a network of PCs means special networking hardware and software.

Figure 1.1 shows a list of existing users and their current operating systems. As you view this illustration, you can readily see the numbers of client operating system upgrades and the departments that need them.

Figure 1.1 For each network segment, indicate the number of users, operating systems, department, and other information to help you organize your needs.

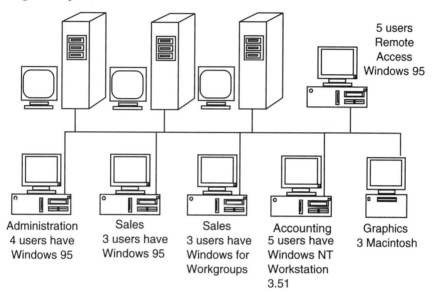

5 users
Remote
Access
Windows 95

Administration
4 users have
Windows 95

Sales
3 users have
Windows 95

Sales
3 users have
Windows for
Workgroups

Accounting
5 users have
Windows NT
Workstation
3.51

Graphics
3 Macintosh

Following are some more considerations:

Group the users as much as you can to help determine numbers. Similar users with related job activities might use like computer systems. While you're at it, list all users and groups and beside their names, make note of the resources, applications, and files they need access to for later reference.

List all existing hardware and determine if you can make use of it. Also, list current operating systems, software, networking cards and cabling, and so on.

Determine whether the NOS supplies any client software you can use. NT Server, for example, includes Windows 95 on CD for installation to workstations, with the purchase of additional licenses. Client/server applications also often include client software.

> **NOTE**
>
> You might want to use existing PCs as standalones and purchase all new workstation computers. A few standalone PCs are good to have around for when the server goes down or is unavailable. A standalone can serve a variety of user and/or company needs; for example, users can use a standalone computer to print an invoice, in a pinch.

Make a list of the applications' requirements, such as memory, disk space, sound cards, and such.   Check to be sure existing workstations have what is needed.

People Needs

You'll likely need to consider some people issues when determining the new or upgraded equipment list. You may need to hire employees to help with the transition and/or to remain after the changes are made. Also, as long as you're making sweeping computer and network changes, consider the type of people changes you might need when you're finished.

Justifying Hiring Additional Staff

If you need to justify hiring more people to the powers that be, try appealing to the profit center of your boss' thinking. A little research will go a long way. Try the following:

Determine the business value of new personnel.

Base the increase on projects you need to complete instead of departmental needs.

Hire consultants to assess specific staffing requirements.

Tie in the request to long-term business goals.

If you hit your bosses with the profitable aspect of hiring more people, you're more likely to get what you want.

Making Moves or Transitions

As long as you're preparing and planning for client computers, you might think about any moves or transitions of employees before continuing. If you have certain departments or even individuals who need to move to another office or building, do it now before installing the cabling and computers.

If you're unsure about whether you'll need to move some of your employees, consider the following. Naturally, you can also enlist the help of department supervisors or managers in the following tasks.

Outline each employee's predominant skill sets.   Make sure the skills are applied in the area of most need and use to the company.

Develop skill sets that are lacking by moving employees to appropriate departments or jobs.   Some skill sets may be more beneficial if users share responsibilities and tasks.

Forecast the needs of the company.   You may want to move users around in preparation for transitions to come.

Make sure you communicate to the employees.   Let them know what you are doing and why so as not to upset them needlessly.

Additionally, ask yourself: How are people doing? If you know of a group of people who work well together, move them together now. Track the flow of talent through the organization and restructure to promote the smooth flow of work. Identify who is going to move in any department and then cover that person's area to promote smooth workflow. Finally, plan now for any promotions, retirements, and other major transitions by adjusting locations to compensate.

Desktop Costs

If you want to lower the total costs of your desktop systems, standardize your workstation configurations by using the same or similar hardware and software. First, you may get a drop in the cost of the original hardware simply because you're ordering multiple computers or application copies; it doesn't hurt to ask the vendor for this favor. Second, replacement parts such as hard and floppy drives, memory, even keyboards, mice, and such, are easier to buy because you're buying the same brand and model. Also, you can keep a small inventory of these parts in case of an emergency and save the cost of downtime. Third, administrator time spent troubleshooting is less because configurations, and likely problems, are the same.

By standardizing the software and operating systems on workstations, you can also rein in the users' implementation of applications, utilities, and tools that you don't support. Simply add a statement to your user policy that you will support only the company-issued software and that users should not download applications from the Internet or load applications brought from home. This may also help you in the fight against viruses.

If you're upgrading your workstations instead of purchasing new, you can still standardize them. Analyze the system and make note of hardware and software. Move, add, and modify each workstation to make them as similar as possible in hardware and configuration. Then install the same operating systems and applications on all PCs that you can.

After initial installations, don't rush to purchase new software upgrades to applications and operating systems. For example, if your standard client operating system is Windows 95, don't install Windows 98 until there is an overwhelming reason to do so, such as a requirement by a vertical application. The same goes for any other software you use. When you wait on software upgrades, you save a great deal of downtime and administrative headaches; and there's no need for the change if the upgrades don't benefit your business.

Also, consider the following:

When purchasing hardware, software, and peripherals, buy late in the vendor's quarterly accounting cycle. If you use this strategy, you may be able to get discounts on the products.

Buy for the future by getting the most powerful and upgradeable hardware, with the most memory and most slots, you can afford. This may seem like a large expense up front, and it is; however, you'll save money in the long run since your computers will stand up to software and network needs longer.

Consider removing disk drives to prevent viruses on workstations. Time, money, and a great deal of effort is spent cleaning viruses from workstations and/or replacing damaged hard drives. If there is no floppy drive, the virus can't get into the system.

An alternative is to set up a virus scanning station. Users are required to use one computer to scan any disk they bring in. After the disk is scanned, users load the disk's contents to the network and then access the files they need via the network. This option will be unpopular with the users but it can save a lot of time and trouble for administrators.

CLIENT OPERATING SYSTEMS

The Client Operating System (COS) resides on a personal computer and handles the interface between the computer hardware and the application software. The COS negotiates the input and output between the computer and the application. A user types data into a word processing program, for example, and the operating system enables the program to save and store the file until the user retrieves it. Users can also print, delete, move, and otherwise manipulate files because of the operating system installed to the PC.

In this chapter, you learn about the following:

- COS terminology

- General requirements for operating systems

- Pros and cons for specific operating systems

Client Operating Systems Introduction

From the earliest DOS-based systems to the faster, graphical 32-bit Windows operating systems, PCs that attach to a network have saved users and administrators time, work, and money. Whether the user is printing to a shared printer or sending email, the advantages to being a client on a network are many. The client operating system used on a workstation attached to the network provides the user with the tools he or she needs to receive the services offered, such as shared printers and files, email, and secure Internet access.

Naturally, there are certain requirements a client operating system must have to work on a network. Additionally, there are many bonuses to some COSs, such as offering faster, more efficient connections or special tools for viewing network resources. The client operating system you choose depends on several conditions; following are some facts to help you decide.

History of the PC Client Operating System

Early PCs used DOS (Disk Operating System), a text-based interface that required users to enter a series of commands to control the system. In order to initiate changes, additions, and deletions, for example, to client-level resources, the user typed cryptic commands into the application. Many DOS-based systems are still in use today despite the limited scope of available applications.

DOS-based systems require very little in the way of PC hardware—processor speed, RAM, and disk space requirements make the DOS computer attractive to people who cannot afford a more powerful and sophisticated machine. Many networks still cater to DOS workstations because of certain vertical, DOS-based applications, many of which are outdated and inappropriate for business use.

Apple Macintosh brought the GUI (Graphical User Interface) to users early in personal computer history and since that time, the Macintosh has evolved into a popular and easy-to-use system. Many schools use the Macintosh. Although not in general circulation in businesses, the Macintosh is typically used in marketing and graphic art departments. The Macintosh's strengths include paint and drawing programs as well as desktop publishing applications.

Windows (3.x, 95, 98, and NT) is the market leader of client operating systems. Sixteen-bit Windows 3.1 and Windows for Workgroups (version 3.11) offer basic functionality for many businesses, depending on software and uses of the computers. Windows 3.x applications are not technically operating systems because they work on top of the DOS operating system. Also, Windows 3.1 is not technically a client operating system, although with the proper client software, it can be used on most networks.

Windows for Workgroups (WFW) is Microsoft's venture into a peer-to-peer networking system. WFW worked very well in enabling users on a small network to share files and resources. Client software has also been created for WFW computers so they can be added to different networking systems. WFW clients, however, do not offer the network security of more sophisticated client operating systems; and WFW clients don't offer as much connectivity or flexibility as other COSs.

> **NOTE**
>
> Not only does the WFW operating system hold a user back on the network by limiting network options, the hardware on which the WFW application is installed limits the user's options on the network as well.

Additional limits for the Windows for Workgroups clients appear when the network uses 32-bit applications such as databases, browsers, and such. Windows 95, Windows 98, and Windows NT are all 32-bit operating systems that are more powerful and reliable than earlier versions of Windows. These more sophisticated operating systems offer improved memory management, preemptive multitasking and access to more Windows resources.

Preemptive multitasking enables a user to perform multiple activities on the PC at the same time, such as simultaneously backing up files while editing a document. Also, the redesigned graphics subsystem offers the file manager—Explorer—and a central repository for configuration data—Registry—to help manage files, configurations, and settings. Additionally, plug-and-play features usually recognize and configure hardware such as sound and video cards, network adapters, and CD-ROM drives. Windows' newer operating systems offer more power and features to the users. Figure 2.1 shows the Windows 95 Registry as represented in the graphical user interface.

Figure 2.1 Use the Windows 95 Registry to modify configurations.

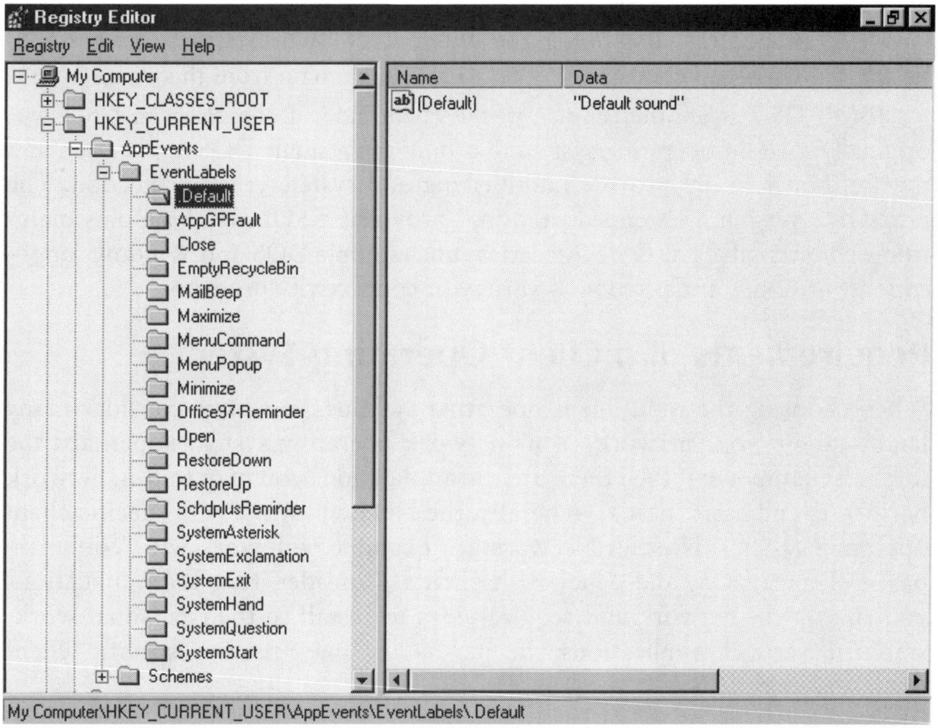

Windows NT Workstation offers even more memory protection and multi-processing than Windows 95/98. Memory protection divides applications and processes in memory so that a failure of one application or process doesn't bring the entire system down. Multiprocessing enables multiple processors to run simultaneously. Multitasking offers compatibility with 16- and 32-bit applications.

> **NOTE**
>
> When preparing to use Windows NT Workstation, check the compatibility of your applications with the operating system first since NT requires quite a substantial hardware investment for upgrading.

The later Windows versions (95, 98, and NT) are built for networking. These clients can take advantage of many and various network operating systems by making use of a network browser (Network Neighborhood), a file and computer search feature, improved security features, client software, and much more as discussed later in this chapter. Figure 2.2 shows the Client for Microsoft Networks Properties dialog box in the Windows NT Workstation Network configuration. Users can choose to log on to an NT domain from this box.

IBM's OS/2 is another choice in the client side of client/server. OS/2 was originally a 16-bit operating system that only ran a single DOS application at a time, although it did provide multitasking and system crash protection. The next OS/2 version, "Extended Edition," provided a SQL database plus mainframe connectivity. The OS/2 2.x series runs multiple DOS and Windows applications, is 32-bit, and provides a variety of connectivity products.

Requirements of a Client Operating System

When choosing the right client operating systems, you must consider many factors about your network. Your network operating system is perhaps the foremost component, then there are the applications you plan to run, network hardware, and users' needs. Generally, the NOS will work with specific client operating systems; Novell's NetWare, for example, will work with Windows-based clients, DOS, and Macintosh clients. Consider, too, the applications you run on the network and require users to install to their personal workstations; vertical applications, in particular, may require specific client operating systems.

Figure 2.2 Built-in networking options and features make configuring the Windows NT client quick and easy.

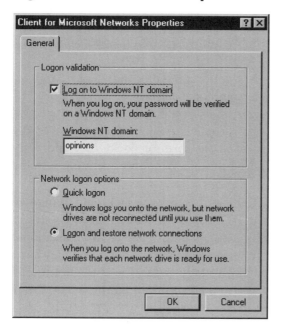

You also want a COS that provides good performance and stability for the user on the network. The better the performance, the fewer problems the user will have, and the fewer problems you will have with the user. Part of the stability issue is memory protection between programs.

> **NOTE**
>
> Without memory protection, one application may overwrite the memory space of another so the data's correctness cannot be guaranteed; this could cause a real problem when the data is saved back to the network for others to share. Make sure the client operating system has memory protection before purchasing and installing it.

Also, consider that all new PCs have 32-bit hardware and many applications are now 32-bit. Make sure your client operating system can also handle 32-bit; Windows NT, Windows 95 and 98, and OS/2 are examples of 32-bit COSs.

Another feature to look for in a COS is that it supports true preemptive multitasking. Preemptive multitasking is especially necessary for client/server networks so the user can work while other processes, such as retrieving data from a database and printing, operate as well. Multitasking enables users to interact with the system. Thirty-two-bit Windows operating systems and OS/2 provide preemptive multitasking.

A good client operating system has good communications and database support, such as for midrange computers and/or mainframes. You may need to access data from a corporate data server; if so, you'll need suitable connectivity. OS/2 has a wide range of connectivity products available (because it's IBM). Microsoft supplies connectivity software in the form of BackOffice and SNA Server to connect to the IBM world, even though Windows operating systems don't provide connectivity directly.

Another important feature of a COS is that it runs DOS and Windows applications efficiently. There are many DOS and Windows applications still in use, and some die-hard users that may never give up their DOS applications. Windows 95 and 98, and OS/2 can run most 16-bit applications; you may have trouble with some programs but you can usually tweak the configuration to make them work. Windows NT imposes some restrictions on the use of 16-bit applications because of its hardware protection. All of the previously mentioned COSs run 32-bit Windows applications.

Finally, make sure the programming interface or API of the operating system is stable and will not need to be replaced within two years or so. DOS or Windows 3.1 run 16-bit applications, have no memory protection, no multitasking capability, and are limited in communications handling. Therefore, these are not a good choice for client/server applications because the programs are becoming more complex and require more and more from the hardware.

> **NOTE**
> Even though Windows 3.1 can run 32-bit apps, it doesn't provide full memory protection or multitasking; even though parts of the application are 32-bit, the operating system is still 16-bit code running on DOS.

Client Operating Systems in Detail

When purchasing client operating systems, you first need to check your network operating system to see what is recommended for the client software.

Next, consider the applications you'll be running, user expertise, hardware costs, and so on. There are many different client operating systems available; however, you should implement one that is common and popular for technical support, ease of administration, and easy upgrades. Following are descriptions of some of the more popular client operating systems.

DOS-Based and Windows 3.x

The only reason you should be running a DOS or Windows 3.x workstation on your network is if you have not yet upgraded the machine. Such antiquated hardware and client operating systems will not add a thing to your network and will likely cost you more money than it's worth to keep them running. If you do have computers running DOS and/or Windows 3.x in your office, you may run them as network clients or even as standalones, if you must. Many network operating systems include the client software necessary to run these older systems; however, the client software cannot provide many of the network services, features and options, and security offered by the network operating system. As standalones, users could run outmoded applications that may be necessary to their work; however, you should upgrade all applications, operating systems, and hardware as soon as you possibly can.

When you run older systems on your network, you increase your administrative workload, technical support headaches, and total cost of operation. The best idea is to ditch these old systems and programs and move at least into the present with 32-bit client operating systems and the corresponding hardware. You may have to beg for more money and/or replace each workstation one at a time, but in the long run, you'll be glad you did.

Windows 32-Bit Operating Systems

A 32-bit operating system offers many advantages over previous 16-bit OSs. Preemptive multitasking and multithreading support for 32-bit applications, for example, enable a computer to perform multiple tasks quickly and to handle separate concurrent processes (threads).

Other advantages to a 32-bit operating system include support for long file names, more efficient memory addressing, and increased system resources. Sixteen-bit Windows 3.x programs share a single address space in the system and it is therefore possible for one 16-bit program to usurp another 16-bit program's memory (RAM). Thirty-two-bit Windows-based applications each have their own address spaces; each address is protected by the hardware so one cannot get hold of another's RAM.

System resources is a part of memory that stores vital parts of the user interface for Windows and its applications. In Windows 3.x, limited system resources restricted the number of applications you could run simultaneously before the system became too taxed to continue. Thirty-two-bit operating systems free those resource limits so that the system can run multiple applications more efficiently.

These advantages serve the network user in many ways. While the user may run a multitude of 16- and 32-bit applications for his or her use on the PC, network applications and client software also run more efficiently and effectively on a 32-bit client operating system.

> **NOTE**
>
> Windows 95, 98, and NT all provide dial-up services for users to attach to the Internet, bulletin boards, and servers offering remote access services. Users dialing up the LAN, for example, can access files, directories, and other resources for which they have permission and/or rights.

Windows 95/98

Windows 95 and Windows 98 offer built-in features that make them the perfect network clients. Microsoft includes various networking components with the operating system, including clients, protocols, and network adapter card drivers. Specifically, Microsoft also includes the following:

- A Novell NetWare client and protocol you can use to attach immediately.
- A Windows client that can be used with peer-to-peer or Windows NT networks.
- The TCP/IP protocol for both Internet communications and LAN networks.
- Single login for multiple networks.
- Network browser for locating servers and other network resources.
- Automatic reconnection to servers upon login.

Windows supplies various versions of network components for your use. The components are adapter drivers, protocols, clients, and services. Adapter drivers refer to the adapter for the network interface card that enables communication between the computer and the network. Microsoft includes drivers for Ethernet, token ring, Arcnet, FDDI, and ATM.

Protocols—the basic language the computer uses to communicate with the network—included with the operating systems are TCP/IP, IPX/SPX, and NetBEUI. Clients are specific to a network operating system; for example, Novell requires a specific client be loaded to a workstation to communicate with the server. Windows 95 and 98 include clients for Novell, Microsoft, Banyan, and others. Finally, services enable the computer to share the hard drive and/or printer with others on the network; Windows includes these services and others. Figure 2.3 shows the Windows 98 TCP/IP Properties dialog box.

Windows NT Workstation

Windows NT Workstation includes most if not all of the features and components that Windows 95 and 98 do. Protocols, clients, and other networking components are included with the operating system. You can actually apply everything in the previous section to Windows NT Workstation.

Figure 2.3 Configure multiple TCP/IP settings in Windows 98.

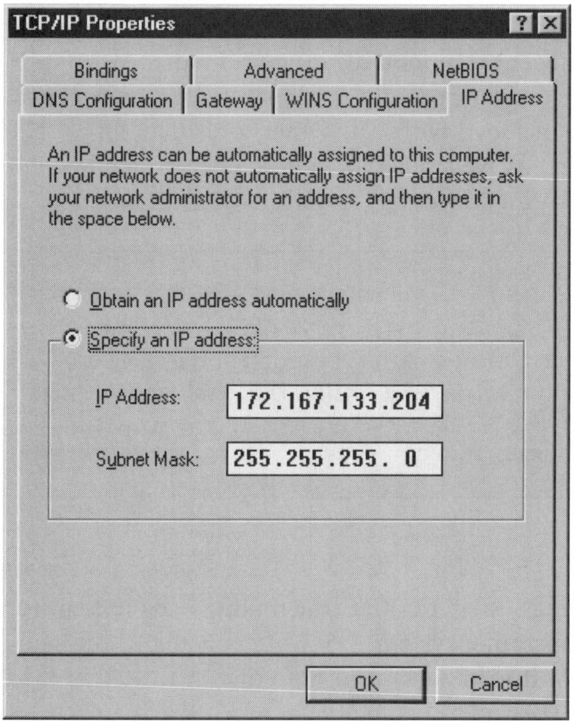

Additionally, NT offers more support and supplementary features not found in Windows 95 or 98. For example, Windows NT offers better security features and control than any other Windows version. NT's user and group accounts enable the workstation user to assign rights and limit access to his or her own machine. Another user, then, cannot access a workstation from the network without the user's permission; similarly, another user cannot delete or change protected files unless he or she has been granted permission.

There are also some limitations to NT that are not present with Windows 95 or 98. Hardware compatibility is a large concern with NT; hardware you use with the operating system is so specific, in fact, that you must confirm brands and models with NT's Hardware Compatibility List before installing the OS. Also, NT requires more power and memory than Windows 95 or 98 to run efficiently. Finally, there are not as many compatible applications written for NT as there are for 95 and/or 98. Although you can use just about any 32-bit application on NT, the operation may be a bit unstable if the program isn't written specifically for Windows NT.

One more note of interest: Windows NT Workstation is compatible with UNIX, especially in the areas of TCP/IP and Internet services. An FTP (File Transfer Protocol) client is installed to NT Workstation with the TCP/IP protocol and rudimentary commands are supported in text mode. Also, RCP (Remote Copy Program), a file transfer program that enables you to exchange files with other systems, is also included with NT. Other tools that enable NT to work with UNIX are included as well, such as NFS (Network File System) for mapping drives and TCP/IP print services.

> **NOTE**
>
> Microsoft has created two NT operating systems: NT Workstation and NT Server. Windows NT Server runs on a powerful computer and usually provides file distribution, printing services, application dispersal, and so on to clients. You can, however, use NT Server as a client in a network situation as well as using it as a server.

OS/2 Warp

OS/2 Warp was the first operating system to offer true multitasking (except for UNIX, of course). As a client operating system, OS/2 offers many of the same features as Windows 95 and 98. It is important to note that at this time, IBM has stated that although it will continue to enhance the OS/2 Warp 5 client, it has no plans to release a version 5; it does however, plan to release new versions of the server product. With no real version upgrades planned, purchasing OS/2 as your client operating system may mean a total client operating system change for your company in the not-too-distant future.

The OS/2 Warp operating system offers the following features:

- Easy-to-use graphical user interface

- Protected memory spaces

- Runs DOS and 16-bit Windows applications, as well as 32-bit applications

- Uses the high-performance file system

- Connectivity options for other IBM servers

- Integrated runtime support for Java applications (so the applications will run on the desktop without a Web browser)

- Integrated IBM VoiceType technology so you can use voice commands, for example, to surf the Web

You can use OS/2 Warp clients with OS/2 Warp servers, Windows NT Server, NetWare, and other popular operating systems.

Macintosh

The Mac OS provides users with a graphical interface, a desktop, and other features for file and application management and productivity. Additionally, Mac OS offers what Apple calls *human interface features*, as opposed to (or in addition to) a user interface. Some of these features include popup windows that minimize to the title bar at the bottom of the screen, nested folders, contextual menus, short menus, live scrolling of window contents, and so on. Other features in Mac OS include Internet assistants and the ability to run Java applets and programs.

The Mac OS is a base, of sorts, for Rhapsody, a second operating system in addition to its Mac OS. Rhapsody is a stable, high-performance system that offers features more suited to Internet and network use, such as full memory protection, preemptive multitasking, multithreading, and symmetric multiprocessor support to make the operating system more useful to networking and current technologies.

Rhapsody also offers the following features:

- Enables a user to run Mac OS software

- Includes the human interface, color management, font, and scripting technologies of the Mac OS

- Uses Internet technologies such as TCP/IP, Java, and so on

Macintosh Open Transport

Apple's Open Transport, a subsystem for the Macintosh operating system, is based on industry standards and enables easy and efficient networking with Macintosh computers. Open Transport protects the network infrastructure and applications, supports cross-platform industry standards, and is easy to set up and use.

Open Transport makes it easy for a user to switch from one network configuration to another, say from various Internet setups, without rebooting. Additionally, Open Transport makes life easier for the administrator by supporting centralized configuration, DHCP, IP multicast, simultaneous TCP connections, and more. Also, Open Transport enables an administrator to detail network connections and configurations in advance, thus giving the administrator more flexibility and control over the network.

Other features include a standards-compliant domain name resolver as well as increased control of domain name resolution. Open Transport/AppleTalk supports the use of static AppleTalk node addresses, which enables the administrator to assign addresses based on a management plan rather than use DHCP. DHCP (Dynamic Host Configuration Protocol) enables administrators to allocate IP addresses from a DHCP server, which is also possible using Open Transport.

Finally, Open Transport is perfect for the software developer in that, among other features, it includes tools that enable applications to send and receive data over an AppleTalk LAN and a TCP/IP-based network using the same programming interfaces. Applications written for Open Transport can support a wide range of networking environments, such as LAN, WAN, dial-up, and so on.

XWindows

There are several types of UNIX operating systems for servers and networks, and UNIX can work with a variety of client operating systems. XWindows is an application that supplies a graphical user interface between the UNIX operating system and the user. Using XWindows, a user can open and run several applications at the same time. You can use XWindows, for example, on a Sun Workstation or X terminal.

XWindows uses a mouse to cut, paste, and copy text within windows; minimize and maximize windows; and otherwise manipulate windows and document contents. An xterm provides a window where you can use a system prompt to enter normal UNIX commands; you can even move the mouse within the xterm window. XWindows provides menus of commands, such as common UNIX commands, window operations, and tools and applications. An intricate Help system also provides information about XWindows and XWindows programming.

PLANNING STRATEGIES

In planning for the purchase of new workstations, or upgrades to those you are currently using, you'll need to consider the type of workstation you want to use as well as some other configuration information. You may want to replace your current PC workstations, for example, with NetPCs or NCs. On the other hand, you may prefer to run only PCs as workstations because of the convenience, needed hardware, or user predilection.

This chapter offers some advice on hardware choices for your workstations and some information about configuration choices you'll need to make. Specifically, this chapter includes information about the following:

- Specific hardware suggestions for Windows 95 and 98, and other client operating systems.

- Information about hardware choices, advantages, and disadvantages of using network computers.

- Advice about client software for workstations.

- Descriptions and definitions of the common networking protocols.

- Suggestions on choosing network interface cards.

Personal Computers

When purchasing or upgrading your hardware for the client computers, you must consider the client operating system and its requirements. You'll also want to think about the applications you plan to use and the network services offered. For instance, using a client computer for engineering or drafting will require different hardware than one you use for word processing. Similarly, clients that use the network with groupware applications need special hardware, as do clients connecting to the Internet, processing large amounts of data, and so on.

> **TIP**
>
> It's always a good idea to use industry-standard hardware and peripherals and to stay away from cheaply made workstations; however, you don't have to spend your entire budget on the finest, most powerful machines either.

In general, purchase more than the minimum required for any client operating system—RAM, disk space, and processor speed, primarily. Also, consider the other hardware on the computer, such as floppy and CD-ROM drives, internal modems, video graphics display, network cards, and so on. Make sure you get what your user will need to operate within the network and try not to skimp on the quality of these items; you'll save yourself money and headaches in the long run.

Windows 95/98

Consider the minimum requirements listed for both Windows 95 and 98 to be inadequate for most network purposes. Although Windows 95 *can* run on a 386 DX with 4MB of RAM and Windows 98 *can* run on a 486 DX2 with 16MB of RAM, your user will be much better off if you use Pentium computers with at least 32MB of RAM for either COS. In addition, add more disk space, RAM, and peripherals to suit the network services and applications that the client computer will access.

When using Windows 95/98 with a network, you'll need to add a 32-bit network interface card (and the software for use with the network), cabling compatible with the network topology, and possibly a modem for communications. You should, of course, consider adding a CD-ROM drive and controller, which is pretty standard in today's workstations.

Windows NT Workstation and OS/2 Warp

These two 32-bit operating systems require more hardware than other client operating systems. The OS is larger and requires more disk space, memory, I/O, and so on. Luckily, most entry-level PCs can now run these operating systems without much problem. And in defense of these operating systems, they offer more speed, stability, and reliability than previous versions and other systems.

When purchasing hardware for NT and/or OS/2, make sure you check for hardware compatibility with the operating system. NT, in particular, specifies

Plug-and-Play Devices

Plug-and-play hardware devices have been a large part of Windows 95/98 marketing. Supposedly, the device dynamically passes its configuration information along to the Windows operating system when Windows boots. In many cases, this process works fine; in others, plug and play can cause problems with the system and setup. When purchasing new or upgrade hardware, don't necessarily limit yourself to plug and play; check prices and quality and buy legacy, if you prefer. If Windows doesn't detect your hardware, you can always manually define and configure it; you may be better off in some cases, such as with network cards.

There are many devices compatible with plug-and-play specs but their compliance varies by type of device. For example, SCSI devices are used in hard drives and CD-ROMs. For a SCSI device to be plug and play, it requires design changes; if those changes are not built in to your particular SCSI devices, you'll need to configure such issues as the SCSI device ID assignment, terminations of the SCSI bus ends, SCSI parity, command sets, and software.

You may notice a problem with your PCI (Peripheral Component Interconnect) bus and plug and play. Most PCI devices use a standard identification scheme and meet most of the requirements for providing plug-and-play functionality. However, PCI cannot automatically transfer its plug-and-play compatibility to another bus in the system. PCI is often the secondary bus and its parent bus may not be plug-and-play compatible. If the parent bus is not compatible, the PCI bus cannot use the plug-and-play functions. Check your documentation or contact the device manufacturer if you have problems.

the processors and peripherals that will work with the COS in a Hardware Compatibility List. Also, with NT, realize that this operating system doesn't always support the same drivers, software, and hardware that previous versions of Windows do. For example, NT doesn't support Windows 95 plug and play.

Here are a few other things to keep in mind about NT Workstation:

NT doesn't support a 386 machine at all and 486 doesn't really work well with the OS. Go for the Pentium in order to get reliable and acceptable performance. NT only supports a 32-bit processor.

Carefully read the footnotes for all equipment but especially for hard drives and adapters. Also, NT doesn't read any compressed drives except those that are NT-compressed.

NT Workstation may not support laptop features.   Features such as power management, PCMCIA hot-swapping, and infrared ports may not be supported. Check the documentation carefully.

Make sure your BIOS is updated.   Check the manufacturer's Web site on the Internet or call the manufacturer. NT can cause many problems if the BIOS version is outdated, such as not recognizing the hard disk.

Macintosh

Macintosh operating systems and hardware are a bit different than PCs because of the way Apple builds the systems. Since other vendors and manufacturers don't build systems to fit the Mac's operating system or produce alternative operating systems for the Mac's hardware, Apple can guarantee compatibility between hardware and software.

You will need to check the network operating system requirements for Macintosh workstations, however, to make sure the client has everything that is needed. Windows NT Server, Novell's NetWare, and other network operating systems can work well with a Macintosh client with the addition of services software and some hardware to encourage communication. For example, the Macintosh operating system may be specific, Apple networking software is often required on the client, and depending on the NOS, the networking technology supported may be specific, such as Ethernet or token ring only. Check the NOS documentation carefully before purchasing and/or upgrading your Macintosh client workstations.

Linux

As important as you may consider the processor in a Linux client, you'll be better off if you put your money into the system bus and disk I/O subsystem. Whereas upgrading your motherboard may show a throughput increase, the changes are also related to improved cache memory and an increase in the system bus' clocking speed.

In a Linux operating system (as well as Windows NT and OS/2), virtual memory is heavily used, the OS keeps a lot of ondisk logs, and so on; thus, trading excess processor clocks for a faster bus and disk subsystem makes more sense.

You should buy a PCI-bus machine, a SCSI controller, and the fastest SCSI disks you can. PCI gives you maximum bus throughput over the old ISA bus. PCI is currently used in high-end Intels, Alphas, and Macintoshes. SCSI runs around 10 to 15 percent faster than EIDE, which is designed over an older system. SCSIs are built to scale up to high speed and deliver high throughput.

As for the processor, you can safely buy one or two levels below the commercial state of the art. For example, buy Pentium 133 or 166 instead of the Pentium Pro. There are a couple of reasons for this: Save your money when you don't really *need* the faster processor, and new and untried system designs can cause you more problems than you want and need. Also, prices for the higher-end systems generally plunge a few months after they're put out new on the market.

> **TIP**
>
> Real-time 3-D graphics and modeling programs do tax your processor so if you plan to use CAD or engineering programs, for example, you'll want to invest more in the processor.

> **TIP**
>
> Stay away from the plug-and-play peripheral cards and any card that doesn't have jumpers. Support and maintenance for this type of card is iffy, at best.

Network Computers

Network computers offer simple, server-based software installation and easy application administration; however, sometimes, the client hardware is expensive. If your users are performing video editing, 3-D modeling, or software development that need the full capabilities of a well-equipped PC, then network computers won't work for them. However, many users spend their time with a small group of common applications. These users could make use of network computers without noticing any functional difference.

> **NOTE**
>
> Currently, there's a lot of controversy over whether to switch to network computers or not. Your best bet may be to run a test program with a limited number of network computers on your network. Getting the users and administrators acquainted with the thin client, user issues, and so on, is a good way to see if network computers work for your company.

Types of Network Computers

There are three types of network computers: NetPCs, Java-based NCs, and Windows terminals. NetPCs process at the server and/or locally and include Windows applications. Java-based NCs process at the server and/or locally. And Windows terminals process everything on the host.

In network operation, the application is generally downloaded from a server and run on the local processor. In the thin-client operation, the application is run on the server and the local machine performs only I/O functions. Most network computers are capable of both modes of operation, depending on the server and the server-based software.

Network computers generally come with a sealed case and with no floppy disk drive or expansion slots. The chassis is sealed to maintain standard configurations. NCs and NetPCs can be updated and managed over the network. Network computers are designed for centralized management. The software is downloaded from a management server and provides end users with the power of local execution and the choice of storing data locally or on servers.

Basically, the thinner the client, the more robust the network needs to be. Consider that even though thin clients can reduce the overall total cost of ownership for PCs, the change on the network and network staff causes increased costs.

Advantages

Network computers offer immense savings by alleviating administrative and hardware costs. Advantages to using network computers include quiet operations, the absence of local drives (although they do come with optional hard drives), built-in Ethernet connectivity, and audio I/O connections. The cost savings is primarily in centralized administration—you can deploy an application to the entire system or to just the server and centralized control is allowed, not required.

Support is another issue for the company running network computers. When there is a support problem, it can be corrected over the server instead of running to the network computer. Also, users cannot bring in their own software and/or viruses to their computer. Users can, however, bring in software and disks to be loaded onto the server and used from there, if necessary; this gives the administrator a chance to check the disks for viruses and to control what goes onto the network.

> **Thin Clients on the Internet**
>
> Network computers are also called *thin clients—thin* meaning there is very little hardware included in the machine itself. One of the more popular uses of the NCs is as an extension of the Internet or in intranet communications. A connection to the Internet means access to applications and services and easy communications through efficient protocols without the errors, configuration nightmares, and other problems often present with PCs.
>
> Also, if your company relies heavily on its own intranet for forms, data, correspondence, collaboration, and such, NCs make the perfect clients. Using server- and host-based applications, NCs can communicate through terminal emulation such as 5250 and 3270 and X server functions, and to the Internet and intranet via a modern browser environment.
>
> Added bonuses include Java applications modeling NCs into intelligent desktops and OLAP (Online Analytical Processing) and OLTP (Online Transaction Processing) available through a server connection and the Internet.

You may want to implement only a few network computers within your company to use with specific applications and/or groups. Call centers, service bureaus, reservations, and point-of-sale are the types of applications that work best with network computers. Use network computers when you have vast numbers of staff doing work that is limited in scope.

Disadvantages

Network computers have met with great resistance in the networking world. One of the problems with network computers is there are no standards as of yet. Another problem is that they're too trimmed down. They have no floppy or hard drives; your power users may resist switching to a network computer.

Other disadvantages and problems with network computers are as follows:

- IT managers may not like this total dependability on the network and servers.

- Network computers don't accommodate mobile workers; if your company is moving more into that area, network computers are just too difficult on which to send data back and forth from server to laptop.

- Some network computers do require proprietary server software to let the network computer boot and initiate its own operating system.

- Some need special server hardware and may require multiple servers in order to offer the desired combinations of user applications.

Add to all of this the steadily decreasing price of PCs, and you see that many companies are staying away from thin clients.

> **NOTE**
>
> Instead of network computers, Wyse is working on the Java Network Terminal (JNT). JNT offers a small client footprint and is less expensive than PCs. Also the computing power and Java elements move completely to server.

Workstation Configuration

Within the planning and preparation of your workstations, you'll want to decide a few workstation configuration issues, such as the client software (drivers) and protocols you'll use for your workstations. More than likely, you'll use the protocol you've selected for the network; however, there are a few exceptions to this rule. Although the network operating system greatly influences the choices you make for client configuration, there are a few options you may want to consider.

Client Software

Client software enables the workstation to communicate with the network operating system. Often, client software is included with the NOS; all you have to do is create installation disks or install the software to the network and share the files so the workstations can access the appropriate files needed to complete the process. Additionally, client software is often included with client operating systems. For example, Windows 98 includes client software for Banyan, Microsoft, and Novell, among others (as shown in Figure 3.1). You also can install other client software files from disk.

When installing and configuring client software, you must be sure you're using the appropriate software version for the network and client operating systems. The wrong version could obstruct network communication between the server and the client. Check the operating systems' documentation for correct

Figure 3.1 You can use a Microsoft client or a manufacturer's client software to access a network operating system.

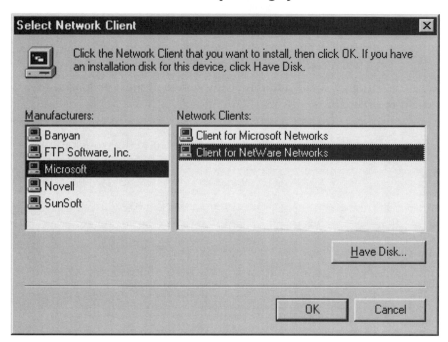

> **TIP**
>
> With server applications, client software often requires licensing; make sure you check the documentation before installing the software on multiple workstations.

versions; you may also try the manufacturer's site on the Internet for the most recent versions of client software.

Try to use only one client software for all workstations, if possible, or at least limit the use of various clients as much as you can. The fewer clients you have, the less support you'll need and the fewer problems you should have. Here are a few more bits of advice:

Check that the server's file system and its options and the client are compatible. For example, using the NTFS file system for an NT Server enables you to partition very large drives, which DOS-based clients cannot read.

Verify that you have enough space on the workstation(s) to install the client software. Check for other requirements as well, such as RAM, processor speed, and video requirements.

Determine any special configurations required and make note of them. You may want to list steps in the configuration so you don't accidentally miss steps when configuring multiple client computers.

Check to see if there is any additional software that must be loaded to the client in order for it to work. Additional software might include drivers, service packs, and the like.

Confirm that the appropriate protocols are installed to the workstation.

> **TIP**
>
> When in doubt of which client to use for your workstations, use the simplest solution, such as Microsoft's client with a Microsoft operating system. Microsoft's Novell NetWare client, for example, works very well with the Windows 95 client on a Novell network, whereas Novell's client for Windows 95 causes quite a bit of trouble in configuration and with connections.

Protocols

The protocol you use for the client(s) will most likely be the same protocol you use for the network. You may additionally use a second and even a third protocol, depending on your network's uses, configurations, and services. For example, if you're running an NT server and a NetWare server side by side, your clients will likely use IPX/SPX to communicate with the NetWare server and perhaps TCP/IP for the NT server. Similarly, you may use the TCP/IP protocol to contact the Internet but use NetBEUI for your internal Windows LAN.

Figure 3.2 shows an example of a network using various protocols inside and outside of the LAN. The NT Server uses TCP/IP to communicate with the Internet and can use either TCP/IP or NetBEUI to communicate with the Windows clients on the LAN. The NT server also uses its built-in NWLink protocol to communicate with a NetWare server. The NetWare server uses IPX/SPX to communicate with its clients.

Protocols define format, timing, sequence, and error checking used on the network. There are three transport protocols normally used in networking LANs: NetBEUI, TCP/IP, and IPX/SPX.

Figure 3.2 Running multiple network operating systems on the same network requires multiple protocols for communications between servers and clients.

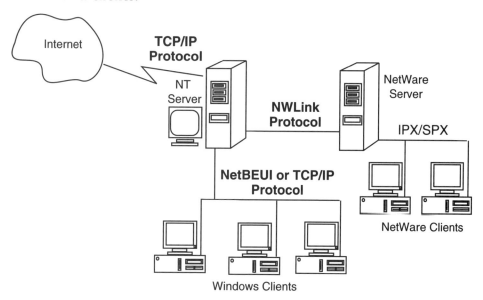

NetBEUI

NetBEUI (NetBIOS Extended User Interface) is an enhanced version of the NetBIOS (Network Basic Input/Output System) protocol. NetBIOS provides an Application Program Interface (API) with a consistent set of commands for requesting lower-level network services to transmit information from node to node. NetBIOS is generally used by network operating systems such as LAN Manager, LAN Server, Windows 95/98 and NT.

NetBEUI is the default protocol used in Windows networks and is a fast protocol for small- to medium-sized LANs. NetBEUI provides high performance over slow links, has good error protection, uses small amounts of memory, and doesn't require much configuring. However, NetBEUI doesn't work well over WANs and it's not routable. A routable protocol enables message packets to be directed from a source node, or computer, to a destination node through the most appropriate path, thus speeding transmissions and making the transmissions more efficient.

NetBIOS

NetBIOS was originally developed by IBM as an Application Program Interface (API) for IBM PC programs to access LAN facilities. Since its inception, NetBIOS has become the basis for other networking programs. NetBIOS is now an industry standard offering applications a way to communicate with the network and across networks.

NetBIOS is supported on Ethernet and token ring. NetBIOS also supports both broadcast and multicast services: Name, Session, and Datagram. The Name service issues names that are used to identify resources. Each process or resource must have a name, which is dynamically assigned and then listed in a table of all names currently owned by that NetBIOS node.

The Session service provides a message service to a user process. One station must have issued a Listen command while another station issues a Call command; the Listen command refers to a name in its NetBIOS name table. If the call is successful, the Send and Receive commands transfer the data.

The Datagram service sends datagrams to a specific name, all members of a group, or to the entire LAN. NetBIOS datagrams are connectionless and unreliable so if all commands are not received correctly, datagrams are discarded.

NetBIOS provides the interface to the network protocol that is used to reach services and manipulate data; NetBEUI is the actual network protocol that performs the service.

TCP/IP

TCP/IP (Transmission Control Protocol/Internet Protocol) is specially designed for use with WANs, and fine for LANs as well. One advantage of TCP/IP is that it provides connectivity across different operating systems and hardware platforms, such as UNIX, Macintosh, Open VMS systems, Windows, NetWare, and printers with network adapters connected directly to the network. Completely routable, TCP/IP not only provides access to the Internet but it supports other Internet protocols, including SNMP (Simple Network Management Protocol), DHCP (Dynamic Host Configuration Protocol), and WINS (Windows Internet Name Service), all of which make communications over the Internet and configuration for the Internet easier.

Since it is the Internet protocol, it has become a standard in the industry today. TCP/IP provides the highest degree of interoperability, encompasses the widest set of vendors' systems, and runs over more network technologies than any other protocol suite.

> **NOTE**
>
> Over the years, UNIX (and Linux) and TCP/IP have become synonymous; however, TCP/IP is now built into all modern operating systems.

TCP/IP is a protocol stack—several layers of software that define the protocol—consisting of many protocols working together. TCP is a connection-oriented protocol that provides reliable stream transport. TCP guarantees the delivery of packets, insures proper sequencing of the data, and provides features to validate the accuracy of the data.

Together with IP, TCP provides a reliable stream delivery for data traffic. The IP protocol regulates packet forwarding by tracking Internet addresses, routing outgoing messages, and recognizing incoming messages.

Some other protocols included in the suite are User Datagram Protocol (UDP), Address Resolution Protocol (ARP), and Internet Control Message Protocol (ICMP). The suite of Internet protocols defines how computers communicate and how networks are interconnected. UDP offers a connectionless service that doesn't guarantee delivery or correct sequencing of packets, so it doesn't necessarily consume network resources or processing time. ARP is a maintenance protocol that supports the TCP/IP suite. ICMP is another maintenance protocol that enables two systems to share status and error information.

IPX/SPX

IPX/SPX (Internet Packet Exchange/Sequenced Packet Exchange) is Novell NetWare's protocol stack that is used to transfer data between the server and workstations on the network. IPX/SPX is a routing protocol that also provides network node addressing and switching of information packets from one location to another on the network.

> **IPX/SPX and UNIX**
>
> Although IPX/SPX is generally used for NetWare networks, some UNIX workstations (Sun, for example) can use the IPX/SPX protocol instead of the common TCP/IP. Managing and maintaining the structure of a
> *Continues*

> ### IPX/SPX and UNIX *(Continued)*
>
> TCP/IP network requires expert knowledge of UNIX and the UNIX file system and structure. IPX/SPX makes that job easier for the network administrator who wants to use Novell NetWare servers in the UNIX environment.
>
> With IPX/SPX, there's no need to set a different address for each client because IPX uses the hardware address of the network interface card; each cable section is assigned an IPX address inside the file server. IPX clients "listen" to the IPX address that is broadcast by a Novell file server and use that address. A TCP/IP client, on the other hand, has to use the TCP/IP protocol to determine the structure, which includes an IP address, or use the Boot Protocol (BOOTP), or the Reverse Address Resolution Protocol (RARP) to get an IP address.

Other Protocols

There are many other protocols used over networks for communications and transportation of data. Following is a brief description of the more common protocols:

AppleTalk. The Macintosh network protocol that includes several other protocols, including AppleTalk Filing Protocol (AFP) that transfers data at a fast and efficient rate and links up to 32 devices.

FTP (File Transfer Protocol). The part of the TCP/IP protocol suite that is used to log in to a network, list files and directories, and transfer files; FTP supports a range of file types and formats, like ASCII and binary files.

Kermit. A file-transfer protocol that's used to transfer files between PCs and mainframe computers over standard telephone lines. Kermit detects transmission errors and initiates repeat transmissions automatically.

PPP (Point-to-Point Protocol). Provides router-to-router and host-to-network connections over synchronous and asynchronous links.

RIP (Routing Information Protocol). Used on TCP/IP networks to maintain a list of reachable networks and calculate the degree of difficulty involved in reaching a specific network from a particular location.

SAP (Service Advertising Protocol). Provides a way for servers to advertise their services on a network, generally associated with NetWare networks.

SLIP (Serial Line Internet Protocol).   Used to run IP over serial lines or telephone connections using modems; SLIP has generally been replaced by the PPP protocol.

SMB (Server Message Block).   A distributed file system network protocol that enables the computer to use files and other resources from the network as if they are local.

SMTP (Simple Mail Transfer Protocol).   A part of TCP/IP used for exchanging electronic mail.

SNA (Systems Network Architecture).   A proprietary terminal-to-mainframe protocol; SNA isn't compatible with the ISO/OSI model.

SNMP (Simple Network Management Protocol).   Another part of the TCP/IP suite that's used to manage and monitor nodes on a network. SNMP enables the setting and monitoring of configuration information and adds increased security, among other things.

TELNET.   A terminal emulation protocol (part of TCP/IP) that provides remote terminal-connection services.

V.*xx* protocols.   Protocols that are generally associated with the transmission of data via modems and telephone lines. V.32, for example, is a standard for 9600bps modems used over two-wire, dial-up, or two- and four-wire leased lines. V.32 bis is another standard that extends V.32 to 7200, 12,000, and 14.400 bits per second.

Network Interface Cards

Network Interface Cards (NICs), also called *network adapters*, enable the client operating system to control the flow of information over the network. The cards you choose for your clients depend on several factors: speed, expense, and the topology of your network.

Basically, there are four types of network cards: 10Mbit (megabit), 100 Mbit, fiber, and wireless. Each works with a specific topology and each has its advantages and disadvantages.

The 10Mbit card is used with a 10BaseT topology and has been around for quite some time. The 10Mbit card is a waning technology, but it is okay for small office use. One definite advantage is that a 10Mbit card is relatively inexpensive; however, it's not very fast, especially for sending large amounts of data or images over the network.

The 100Mbit card is used with 100BaseT topology and is 10 times faster than the 10Mbit card. The 100Mbit card is perfect for using with large data files, video or sound files, images, and such. Although the 100Mbit card is more expensive (both to purchase and install) than the 10Mbit card, the increase in speed is well worth the price.

When using the 100Mbit card, consider that installation of the cable will be more expensive because the cable must be certified. Also, you'll need to make sure the computer you're installing the 100Mbit card to has a PCI (Peripheral Component Interconnect) slot. PCI is an Intel specification that defines a local bus, allowing up to 10 PCI-compliant expansion cards to be plugged into the computer. The PCI controller exchanges information with the computer's processor at either 32 or 64 bits.

If your budget is tight but you want to use the 100Mbit card, purchase the 10/100Mbit cards to begin with. The 10/100Mbit cards can attach to either a 10Mbit or 100Mbit network so that you can start by using a 10Mbit hub and then as your budget allows, add 100Mbit hubs to the system to make it a 100BaseT network.

The fiber card uses FDDI (Fiber Distributed Data Interface) networking, which follows a ring topology. You'll need a PCI slot for the fiber card, as well as fiber cabling. Fiber cards, cabling, and fiber hubs are expensive to purchase and to install.

The wireless card is another choice. Wireless is a method of connecting workstations to the network without using conventional cabling. Infrared is one method of wireless connection; infrared uses high-frequency light waves to transmit data between two computers up to 80 feet apart using an unobstructed path. Another method of wireless connection is through high-frequency radio signals, which can transmit data between computers up to 130 feet apart. Spread-spectrum radio limits distances to 110 feet and data rates are usually less than 1Mbps. Wireless cards are very expensive and slower than the previously mentioned cards. Wireless uses the token ring topology.

NETWORK AND SERVER PREPARATION

You're likely ready for adding clients as far as your network and server go, since you've already set up the hardware and installed the software. There are a few issues, however, that you might want to consider when preparing the network for your clients.

One thing to think about is how much control you want over your clients. You can choose to control every application, desktop, setting, and such, or you can let the users control their own setup themselves. More than likely, you'll want to exert control somewhere in the middle of these two extremes. After all, you must get along with your users and keep them happy; you must also try to lessen your workload and keep the network safe.

This chapter gives you some advantages and disadvantages of several control issues. Also, the following topics are covered in this chapter:

- Information about software distribution and asset management
- Client security issues
- Advice for setting up user accounts

Centralized Control

Generally, users load applications to their systems, change their systems, edit configuration files, and so on. As a result, it takes time to support users when they make mistakes, accidentally delete configuration files, or otherwise make a mess of their systems.

You could create a common desktop and mandate it to all users or to a group of specific users, but it takes time to develop a common desktop. Also, deployment of new applications is slow since the administration has to certify and integrate applications. Users may not like a common desktop, but if you gather input from them in advance and let them pick the look and feel of the desktop, you'll have fewer complaints. You may need to audit applications on the server and on users' desktops to confirm the appropriate use of the common desktop.

Advantages

Often, when you install a new application, it replaces modules on the system, sometimes with newer modules and sometimes with older ones. Conflicts between the newly installed modules often cause conflicts in applications, memory, and other areas of the system. A common desktop can help you maintain a standard list of modules, such as DLL files, and the correct revision that works with all certified applications.

Another problem with allowing users their own individual desktops and settings occurs when a user installs an application that edits configuration files or the user edits the files himself. A common desktop with limits asserted on the users can prevent any installations or configurations other than those set by the administrator.

Disadvantages

Creating a common desktop can be exhausting. You must coordinate the control of desktop changes, deploy new applications carefully, and certify all modules, such as DLLs, that you install. You'll also need to test older applications to make sure they still work after installing newer ones.

Perhaps the biggest problem with creating a common desktop occurs when your users don't like it. If they don't like your new system, they won't use it, and they may even cause problems. Consult with the users to decide which applications should reside on the server and which should reside on the clients. Consider giving users a bit of latitude whenever possible.

Steps to Deployment

If you choose to create a common desktop/configuration and centralize administration, there are a few steps you should take in preparation. First, are you going to use Windows, and if so, will you use networked Windows or Local Windows? Following are some more ideas:

Choose the applications you'll centralize and determine how each application affects each desktop. For example, are there modules or other client software to be loaded, specialized hardware drivers, and so on? What needs to be installed to the server and what goes on the client computers?

Keep track of all version numbers, directory names, overwritten files, and search paths as you install the applications. You may need this information later for troubleshooting.

Consider any user profiles or scripts to add to all PCs first, and then to individual PCs for specialized needs. Write the required software and install it.

Create any specific settings, icons, batch files, and so on that will apply to all users and/or to specific ones. Also, standardize any configuration files and formats if needed.

Apply the common desktop and configurations to a small number of PCs and test thoroughly before implementing to the entire network. Gather users' ideas and comments before implementing to all PCs.

Finally, after deployment, perform periodic compliance checks to make sure your configurations and settings are being used appropriately. There are several tools available for checking versions of software, modules, drivers, and so on, such as Symantec's Norton Administrator for Networks.

Software Distribution

Software distribution is about packaging and sending files to PC desktops, workstations, and servers. It's also about addressing the differences between remote computing environments, as in the enterprise network. Distributed environments are diverse since there are many different types of systems and applications in use today; the more diverse a distributed environment, the more complex the software distribution.

There are several software distribution packages you can use to help standardize your desktops and centralize administration. Software distribution applications use asset management, job scheduling, help desk, production control, auditing features, and such to successfully track and manage the software on your system.

No matter which package you choose, make sure it includes an asset management application for determining software and hardware inventory. Software distribution packages should also include a method of grouping machines so that a piece of software can be sent to a group of clients rather than an individual client; this feature will save you administrative time and money.

Also, software distribution includes installation of applications. Make sure your package includes the following:

• Automated routing

• Authentication of files

- Automated back-out error logic
- Installation scripts
- Transfer scheduling

Asset Management

Asset management software, usually bundled with software distribution packages, helps you track inventory on your client computers. Asset management software should collect hardware and software information, including configuration, on each machine on the network. The software then registers this information in a database that the software distribution package can use when preparing to install an application.

The software distribution package queries the asset management database for specific client profiles, such as needs for particular software. Machines not matching the query are passed over for the software to be installed or upgraded.

Using a product with asset management software can help save network bandwidth, time, and frustration.

Planning Network Access

When preparing for adding users to the network, you need to consider the limits you want to impose on the users. Not all network resources are meant to be accessed; not all users should have the same rights and permissions across the network. Your first step is to make a list of users and the resources each needs access to; for example, applications, files, printers and other peripherals, and so on. Use this list to organize and prepare your entries into the authentication server on the network.

Following are some factors to consider when preparing the list of users:

- How much do you want each user to be able to access?
- What hours will the network be accessible?
- Where will you store files on the server?
- Will you implement account and/or password expiration dates?
- Which servers will be accessible and to whom?

- How much freedom should administrative assistants have within the server; will some have permission to load device drivers, for example, or delete and restore files, create users, and such?

- Will there be a home directory or other default directory for each user on the server?

Think about how much control you want over the network, the server(s), users, and resources. Remember, with control can come order and/or chaos depending on many factors, including the users and your company's philosophy of resource sharing.

User Accounts

It's standard practice to create an account for each user of the network in which you specify the files, directories, and server(s) the user may access. When a user logs on to the system using the account name and password, his or her access is granted to the system, but only to those resources you defined. Authentication to a server involves adding the user's account to the system's Access Control List (ACL) or an equivalent security database. It's the ACL that authenticates users and enables them to access the resources for which they have permission.

In a client/server model network, the system may be a complex collection of many different workstations and servers. Adding servers and dividing computing responsibilities among the servers makes the network scalable but also can cause management and organizational problems. Administration of multiple clients and servers is difficult, especially when it comes to enterprises encompassing thousands of servers and tens of thousands of users. Add the fact that most client/server applications have their own access control schemes and matters become even more complicated.

Users will likely need to log on to several servers, such as the network authentication server, groupware servers, database servers, and so on. If you can synchronize passwords, enable users to log on using one password that is the same for all servers, you reduce the number of passwords the user must remember and cause yourself less administration and troubleshooting later on.

NOTE

Novell NetWare 4.x and NT Server 5.x use directory services to help the administrator synchronize multiple access control lists.

Security

When creating user accounts, make sure you apply all of the security your NOS will allow. Password expiration, account lockouts, limited access hours to the server, and so on, will protect your data and the integrity of the network. Additionally, user rights and/or permissions determine what the user can and cannot do on the network; carefully assign these rights and periodically review them to keep your network secure.

Also, following are some tips for controlling users and access to the network:

Keep a tight control on guest accounts.

Remove inactive user accounts promptly.

Require that users change their passwords periodically.

Display a warning on your system that access is restricted to authorized users and that sessions may be monitored. (It is against the law in some places to monitor user sessions; check with your attorney to make sure the warning enables you to monitor sessions on your network.)

Creating User Accounts

One of the most frequent system administrative activities is adding new user accounts. The user might not necessarily be an individual person, however; users can be any entity that can execute a program or own files, such as other computers or server software. An accounting system may require a user account; you can assign groups of people—the research group, for example—a user account. In general, though, a user is an individual who can log in, edit files, run programs, and otherwise make use of the system.

A user has a username (or login name) to identify him or her; often a password, and an assigned, unique User Identification Number (UID in UNIX; SAM in NT, and so on). The user's ID number is the system's way of identifying the user. A user may also belong to a group or collection of users who share a specific function—say they all work on same project, for instance. Each group may have a group ID number as an identifier for the system.

To add a new user, generally follow these steps:

1. On the authentication server, assign a username, ID number, and optionally, a group.

2. Enter any data necessary to identify the user or define the user, such as password restrictions and expirations, account expiration date, resource limits, and such.

3. Create a home directory for the user and perhaps a login script (a small file that executes the same set of instructions each time the user logs on to the network); initialize and/or share the user's directory; add the user to other facilities, such as a mail system; define any other group accounts and rights.

4. Test the account and make any necessary adjustments.

User Logons

Use logons to protect access to servers and resources on the network. Logon information includes the username and password. The user's account is defined in the authentication server's database and determines whether the user may log on to the network and which resources should be available to the user. Using the operating system's directory services as the reference, authenticated accounts may access server applications, printers, and other network services.

Authentication takes place when the user enters his or her username and password into a computer and submits it to the network operating system. The authentication server on the network first checks the identification of the computer (client) to make sure it has permission to access the network. Next, the server compares the user's name and password to all valid user accounts. If the user account is verified, the user is permitted access to the network and resources, within the definitions of his or her account. If either the computer or the user is not verified, the authentication server may pass the identification request on to another server within the network or refuse to connect the computer and/or user.

Note: You can also create a batch file, located on the user's machine, to automatically log users on to the network; however, even with a batch file, a specific username and password must be used.

Groups

Often, an NOS will let you assign individual users to groups to make administration easier. Whether the group is built in to the NOS or you create the group, you assign group rights and then appoint users to the group that fits their needs. It's easier to revoke or assign rights to a group that encompasses a hundred users than it is to assign those rights to each user individually.

Following are some of the more common user groups:

A Guest group is for people without an actual account on the network. Guests usually don't require a password to log on to a workstation or server only and receive the barest minimum access.

The Users group enables regular members of the network to log on to workstations and use the server to access files and other resources.

Members of the Printer Manager group can create, delete, and manage printers and printer shares for a portion of or the entire network.

Members of the Account or User Manager group modify, add, or delete users to the system; generally, it's a good idea for the members of this group to be the people responsible for hiring new employees.

The Backup Operator group has access to all files on the server and workstations that need to be backed up. Members back up files, test the backup, store the backups, and restore the files when necessary.

Server Operators manage the server, performing such tasks as logging on to the server, shutting down the server when necessary, perhaps creating and modifying printer shares and network shares, and so on.

Members of the Administrators group have the rights to manage the entire network. Be careful when assigning members to this group; too many administrators can wreak havoc on the network.

Control Considerations

Think about how much control you want over the network and how much control you want to appoint to the users. Some users prefer they have no control over their workstation and/or the entire system because then, there's no chance they will accidentally bungle things. Other users want full control over their own system and perhaps even parts of the network.

Consider how much of the system infrastructure you are willing to expose to user access. How might your users' freedom hamper your ability to administer the system and security policies? You'll need to reach a happy medium to prevent a user rebellion and keep your management techniques intact.

You can use the lowest common denominator approach in which you control only the most necessary factors of the network, such as sensitive files, premium printers, and so on. On the other hand, you may want to control most of the networking components by planning file formats, directory contents, server(s) access, users' naming conventions for their own files, and such. Consider the minimal requirements for each group of users across all client platforms and work from there.

Also, you should outline guidelines for the use of the server and network. Include naming conventions, directories for public and private files, and other rules that will help keep the network organized and accessible.

Client Management

Client, or workstation, management software can help you control the workstations on the network. Most client management programs can automatically handle software distribution, hardware and software inventory, desktop configuration, and other management tasks. When choosing a client management application, consider the following as necessary functions of the program:

- Restarts client computer when it has crashed

- Takes remote screen snapshots so you can analyze problems

- Executes tasks on the remote clients

- Synchronizes the client clocks to the server clock

- If Windows, then it lets you manage the registry remotely

- Enables you to display, modify, and add groups and icons to the clients' desktop

- Enables you to add and remove programs to the client computer

- Backs up system files on the clients

- Enables you to edit system files and transfers files to and from the clients

INTEGRATED NETWORKING

Many of today's networks use a mixture of network operating systems, clients, peripherals, and networking hardware. Although this isn't the most efficient method of building a network, sometimes the mix-and-match method is the only option due to budget constraints, distributed management, and other factors.

It's not unheard of for a company's network to include a mainframe, NT servers, and NetWare servers, all cooperating to serve DOS, Windows, and even Macintosh clients. Your eventual goal may (and should) be to standardize your network to one NOS and one or two COSs.

Mixing a network means more work for the administrator and generally more work and often confusion for the users. If a user needs access to multiple NOSs, you need to create two accounts for that user; anytime the user information must be modified, you have to make the changes in two places. Additionally, you must manage servers and services with two different sets of rules and using separate tools. Users who access two systems must log on to each separately, and then remember two passwords, directory structures, naming conventions, and such.

This chapter offers some ideas and advice for modifying and improving upon your integrated networks from the client's point of view. In this chapter, you learn about networking:

- Novell NetWare and Windows NT

- Mainframes or AS/400s and NetWare

- Mainframes or AS/400s and Windows NT

- Macintosh clients and common NOSs

- UNIX and NetWare

- UNIX and Windows NT

NetWare and Windows NT

These are the two most popular PC network operating systems today. Generally, administrators are using one or the other, but often, both a NetWare and an NT server will appear in the same network. Both Microsoft and Novell realize the two operating systems must work together, at least in part, so each provides products that integrate the other NOS.

NetWare Side

Novell provides a package called NDS for NT that actually runs on the NT servers with the NT server acting as the Primary Domain Controller. NDS for NT installs the IntranetWare Client for Windows NT service on the NT server and redirects requests to the NDS database. This product works without installing any software to the NT clients.

> **TIP**
>
> You can also find third-party packages to help synchronize Novell's NDS (Network Directory Services) with NT's authentication database.

Other features of NDS for NT include the following:

- NDS for NT provides a setup program for the NetWare Administrator for NT utility, which you can use to view and manage objects in the NDS directory from the NT server.

- NDS for NT makes it easier for you to manage NT domain users, using NT's trust relationships by applying Domain Access via the NetWare Administrator.

- NDS for NT provides a single login.

- NDS for NT simplifies the deployment of NT applications.

A downside to NDS for NT is that if the NetWare server goes down for any reason, you lose all access to the NT server as well. The NT network is totally reliant on NDS. After installing NDS for NT, you no longer have the option of running the NT servers separately from NDS. The only way you can rectify this problem is to uninstall NDS for NT.

NT Side

In addition to adding Microsoft NetWare clients to Windows 95, 98, and NT for clients to communicate with NetWare servers over the network, Microsoft included several features with NT Server to promote integration between the NT and NetWare operating systems.

NT's Gateway Service provides NT clients access to NetWare print and file resources. The Gateway Service for NetWare would be beneficial to use for any of the following reasons:

- You're thinking of migrating to NT from NetWare but aren't sure if you want to move all of your users and data yet.

- You want to use NT Server with the Internet in addition to using NetWare services.

- You want to set up a Remote Access Server for mobile users.

- You want the advantages of a Windows 32-bit operating system.

- You want the benefits of using domains in the network.

- You need to attach to other NT domains in the corporation.

For your NT clients, access to the NetWare resources is available using the NT server as a gateway. As long as the users have permissions and rights to the NT server and to the NetWare resources, they can use NetWare files, directories, and printers. You'll need to install the IPX/SPX-compatible protocol to each workstation, although you don't need to install the NetWare client.

As for security, the NetWare administrator has complete control over file, directory, and printer access to the NetWare server. The administrator also controls which NT Server computers are gateways and which files, directories, and printers on the NetWare network are available to the gateways. Naturally, the NT administrator has control over the users' access to the NT server.

Figure 5.1 illustrates a network using an NT Server and NetWare Server through the Gateway Service. Using the Gateway Service for NetWare enables shared remote access services and shared backup services for all clients on the network—NT and NetWare. All accounts become integrated so that NT Server handles login validation and permissions for both NT and NetWare clients. Additionally, the NT server computer running the Gateway Service can access files, directories, printers, NetWare utilities, NLMs, and so on, from the NetWare server.

Figure 5.1 The Gateway Service for NetWare enables sharing of resources between the two servers.

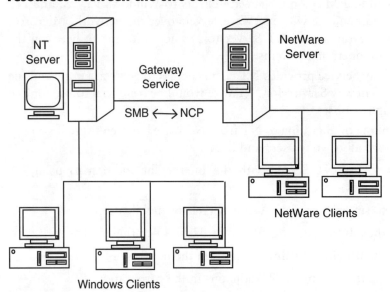

There are, of course, problems with the Gateway Service. Data transfers at a slow rate, so if a lot of users need access to the NetWare server via the Gateway, you may want to install the client software to those workstations instead of using the Gateway Service.

Another possible problem is that if a client's NT password is different from the NetWare password, that user will be denied access unless he or she uses the NetWare SETPASS command to change his or her NetWare password to match NT's.

NT also supplies a migration tool you can use to transfer data from the NetWare server to the Windows NT Server. This tool is very effective in transferring users and data; however, you normally use the migration tool when you plan to leave the NetWare server behind, so technically, this is not integration.

NOSs and IBM Mainframes/AS/400s

Most major network operating systems realize the importance of IBM mainframes and minicomputers in today's networking world. Often, companies have a large quantity of data and mission-critical applications stored on mainframes or AS/400s that must be made available to the PCs on their network. Some sort of host connectivity arrangements must be made in order to access this data. Both Windows NT and Novell NetWare provide methods of connecting to host computers and transferring data to PCs on the network.

Windows NT

If you're using NT Server as your NOS, you can install a BackOffice server—SNA Server—to enable your clients to access data from IBM mainframes and AS/400s. SNA Server uses protocols to enable it to communicate with both the SNA network and your NT network to provide bidirectional communications. PCs use standard LAN protocols to attach to the mainframe or AS/400 computer through the SNA Server's shared link. Figure 5.2 shows how the SNA server could fit into a network.

Figure 5.2 Use SNA Server as a gateway between your LAN and mainframes or AS/400s.

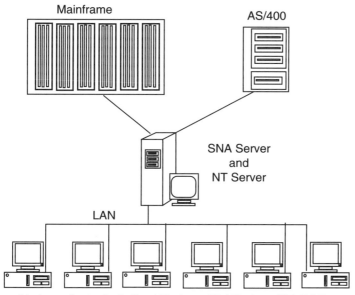

IBM's SNA is a set of communications protocols and message format specifications that work with IBM hardware and software. Microsoft's SNA Server provides a gateway between the PC and the SNA network, enabling PCs on an NT network to access data from IBM S/370 and S/390 mainframes, IBM AS/400s, and even IBM 3287 printers. SNA Server is capable of using high-speed, bidirectional communications providing quick transmission of applications and data from the IBM host.

Novell NetWare

Novell offers a variety of products that enable LAN-to-host connectivity, depending on the type of Novell server product you're using. One typical product is IntranetWare for SAA. Secure and reliable, this product acts as a gateway between the LAN and the IBM hosts (S/390 and AS/400 systems).

Following are some of the features of IntranetWare for SAA:

- Provides comprehensive SNA support
- Works with thin clients, including Java and ActiveX-based emulators
- Supports DOS, Windows, Macintosh, Windows 95 and 98, NT, and OS/2
- Offers multiple server-to-host data-link types and adapters
- Includes load balancing to optimize server utilization

Administration of IntranetWare for SAA is centralized and easy to use with full NDS support to automate administrative tasks. Also, the management utilities are browser enabled, client configuration is simplified, and it includes built-in NetView support.

Macintosh Clients

The Macintosh client still exists on many networks today. Macintosh are excellent computers for art and typesetting applications and thus are used in many graphic and commercial art departments, commercial printers, and other such shops that need the Macintosh's particular strengths. Therefore, many popular network operating systems provide file and print services for Macintosh clients. NT and NetWare are two in particular that can add the Macintosh client to the network with a minimum of configuration and installation. Linux also adds its own services for Macintosh (and Windows clients).

NT

NT Server provides Services for Macintosh to make it possible for PC and Macintosh clients to share files and printers. All that's needed on the Macintosh is the operating system software; no other software is required. NT's Services for Macintosh provides a secure logon, easy-to-use graphical administration tool, non-PostScript printing, and more.

Macintosh clients can share files and printers with the PCs connected to the NT network. A PC client, for example, can open and modify an MS Word file, save it to the network server, and the Macintosh user can then open that same file with MS Word for Macintosh. After the user modifies and saves the file back to the server, the PC client can once again open that file. The Mac user can also send files to a printer attached to the NT server; Services for Macintosh also enables spooling for AppleTalk printers so the user can start another task after sending the job to the printer.

Services for Macintosh provides simplified administration in that you have only one set of users to maintain. Also, file permissions are transferred and translated between the NT server and the Macintosh clients. Finally, the NT server can also provide routing for the Macintosh clients using an AppleTalk router to broadcast routing information.

NetWare

Novell provides various client software files for the Macintosh that you can download from the Internet easily and quickly. Most include server and client software that provides file and print services, administrative utilities, and AppleTalk routing for Macintosh users.

The client software enables the Macintosh user to log on to a NetWare network using the Macintosh Chooser; other elements of the Macintosh desktop remain the same so that the network access is transparent to the user. Mac users can share files with PC clients as well as use the same network services that Windows, OS/2, and other users enjoy. Following are a few more features:

• Mac users see files on the NetWare server as graphical icons, while other users see the files as their operating systems dictate.

   • Macintosh users can send messages to other clients on the network.

   • NetWare users can print to printers connected to AppleTalk networks.

- Network supervisors can assign access rights to the Macintosh user as he or she would any network user.

  - Supervisors can manage print jobs in the NetWare print queue.

  - Supervisors can also set file and folder attributes from a Macintosh workstation.

Linux

Linux Internet Services for Macintosh Users enables a Macintosh client to access the Internet via a Linux operating system. Linux is an operating system that provides services for TCP/IP Internet resources, including IP routing, email, USENET news, and the World Wide Web.

Eudora, a popular email application, works well with the Macintosh client via Linux, as do LeeMail, MailDrop, and POPMail. Macintosh clients may also use Netscape browser as well as other commercial browsers with the Linux server. If you're using TCP/IP, your Macintosh computers can attach to file and print services from Linux systems. With the Macintosh client, simply run the appropriate AppleTalk package on Linux.

> **NOTE**
>
> Linux Internet Services for Macintosh Users also includes Windows users, providing similar services for Windows as it does for Macintosh. Windows clients may also use Eudora, or AtisMail, dMail, WinElm, and others, and Netscape or Mosaic works well as a Windows browser; many other tools and utilities are also available. While running TCP/IP, Windows computers can run a utility named SAMBA, a freeware SMB-protocol server to attach to file and print services from Linux systems.

UNIX

UNIX clients can integrate into LANs with some work and a bit of trouble. Novell provides more help with this task than Microsoft does, for example, but you can always find third-party applications to help you even if your NOS isn't cooperating.

NetWare

NetWare NFS (Network File System) Services is a Novell NetWare Loadable Module (NLM) that adds NFS server capability to an existing NetWare file server. Once loaded, UNIX NFS clients see the NetWare server as another NFS server. There are also multiple versions of NFS for IntranetWare and other Novell systems. NFS provides transparent, bidirectional file and print services to both IntranetWare and UNIX clients.

In addition, NFS offers the following features:

• IntranetWare NFS services uses the TCP/IP suite.

• Centralized software installation; both the NFS server and client services are installed to the IntranetWare server, meaning you don't have to change the client software to access UNIX data over the gateway.

• A print gateway allows UNIX users to access any printer on the IntranetWare network, and other IntranetWare clients can access printers connected to UNIX machines on the network.

• XCONSOLE allows remote management of IntranetWare NFS services from Windows/UNIX environments.

• Administrative controls over user access to files and directories.

• Integration of UNIX host systems with IntranetWare workgroups.

NT

NT uses the TCP/IP protocol and some TCP tools; however, its UNIX connections could be improved upon. You might try some third-party companies that include NFS client software and X Windows Server software to help in UNIX connectivity.

Intergraph DiskShare, for example, provides a way to map UNIX names and passwords to the NT user accounts and passwords, thus providing the same permissions as the NT users to which they are mapped.

USER PREPARATION AND HELP

With all you have to do in getting a new network set up or in upgrading your current network configuration, you may have little time to get your users prepared for the changes that come with networking your company. You must, however, try to find some time or delegate the responsibility in order to save yourself and other administrators time, effort, and money down the road.

Training is always a sore point with administrators because it's difficult to find training that works. Outsourced training may not cover needed technologies and procedures, and inhouse training may take too much time away from those who need to get the work done. This chapter offers some advice for getting your people help with the network and their networking problems.

There are several alternatives besides sending people to a class that may help your users and save your time. A help desk, interactive training, third-party books, and printed procedures are just a few of the things you might consider. This chapter discusses these options as well as the following topics:

- Types of training
- Morale boosters
- Help desk ideas
- Policies for regulating users
- Topics for procedures to help users

Training

Training doesn't normally take priority for corporations because no one has time to be the instructor or the student. Knowledgeable people are spending their time putting out fires and uninformed users are stumbling around on the network starting more fires. It's a vicious circle that could be broken if you can take the time to plan some useful, workable user training.

Training doesn't have to consist of eight hours in a classroom listening to lectures or viewing slides; training can come in any number of forms. You may, for example, simply publish a list of terms and guidelines for users to read on their own time. Or, check into an interactive training program on CD-ROM. You can also try a mentoring type of training in which more experienced users help those less knowledgeable. However you plan to implement training in your corporation, the time and effort spent will be well worth your while.

Getting Started

Imagine fewer questions and problems, less lockups and lost files, fewer fires to put out. Providing users with a basic understanding of their workstations, applications, network, and servers will trim away some of the everyday problems you're seeing now. Following are some suggestions for getting started:

Make sure users understand the terminology related to their hardware and software.

Contract product support staff or vendors or consultants to train your managers; let your managers train the users.

Consider classrooms, videos, computer-based training, environment training (it is most important for users to understand those terms and methods used in your company).

Distribute a set of guidelines that explain common terms and procedures, directory names, names of shared directories, file-naming standards, password procedures, and so on.

Create a list of contact phone numbers, sites on the Net, books, and such for users to refer to when they need help. Make the list available to all users.

Cross-Training

If you'll use the cross-training technique when making out training schedules, you'll save time and money and boost morale, all at the same time. Cross-training is a method of putting both employees and upper management into the same classes or sessions. You can even shuffle jobs around some to make sure everyone gets to participate everywhere in the company. For example, the sales staff might manage the help desk for a few days or weeks; network managers might sit with the end users to see what it is they do with their days. Send some managers and some data entry people to a class about the Internet so they can talk with each other about what they have learned.

Benefits to cross-training include improved network management, stronger employee relationships, more effective problem solving, and a boost in morale. In addition to employees and managers understanding each others' jobs and positions, you'll find it's easier to move employees into other departments as the workflow changes, since everyone has an idea about another job in the company.

Types of Training

There are many types of training available on the market today, whether your users need help running a spreadsheet or accounting program or guidance in saving files to the network. You'll want to consider the cost of training as you choose the type of training; taking people away from the work at hand costs the company money. But think about the money and time saved in the long run when your users work more efficiently and have fewer problems with the technology.

The type of training you choose will depend on the application and your goals. You can, for example, send users to outside sources for training in a particular program or peripheral use. However, these outside sources won't know anything about your network configuration, company policies, specific files and shared directories, and so on, so you can't outsource this type of training.

When you need training for a specific application or peripheral, consider asking the product's vendor for a seminar or training session. You may also want to purchase a video or a computer-based training package that guides individuals step-by-step through the program. If your users are fairly experienced and bright, you can purchase some third-party books to introduce and teach the users how to correctly and efficiently implement the program.

If the training you need is more hardware- or network-specific or if it's related to a vertical application your company uses, you may need to consider alternate types of training. In these cases, the user needs knowledge of how the application or hardware is used in his or her work environment. Only someone else more experienced and knowledgeable in your company can help users with this type of training.

Start a mentoring program in which the experienced employees help less-proficient employees with applications and/or procedures. You don't need to dedicate a worker to this task; simply assign two people together for a couple of hours a week or so to get them used to working together and to share some experience.

You may also want to try some self-learning techniques. Third-party books provide a wealth of information, as do interactive computer training CDs. You may try providing a list of guidelines and procedures to your users to help them navigate email or other network transactions. If your company has an intranet, you can create intranet-based training that each user can take advantage of as the need arises. Finally, check the Internet. Many companies do training, testing, and evaluations on-line.

Morale

As you probably know, huge changes in the workplace may cause problems with your users. If a user doesn't understand what is happening, he may worry about his job security. If a user isn't happy with changes, she may choose to quit instead of discussing problems with management. As you build or upgrade your network, as you strive to better organize the system, you must consider your users' morale, if only to a small degree, to keep peace and a spirit of cooperation.

Developing a Team Attitude

Often the network administrator's job directly conflicts with what the users perceive as their job or situation. Without careful consideration for your users, you may find yourself in an "us versus them" situation, whereas the more effective, beneficial situation would be "all of us versus the problem." Convincing your users to work with you in the deployment of a new or upgraded network makes your job easier and keeps them happy and cooperative.

Following are some ideas for improving relations and attitudes:

Keep the users informed of changes.   Whether you send a memo or gather people together each week or two, you must keep your users informed of changes to the network. Notify users when, for example, a server will be down, printers and other peripherals are added to the system, new directories or applications will be implemented, and especially when a user's own workstation will be upgraded, replaced, or otherwise rendered out of service. Announce and advise users of all activities related to the network.

Listen to all suggestions and input.   You may want to assign assistants or departmental managers to gather requests, complaints, suggestions, questions, and such, within each department. Managers can weed through the suggestions and submit the best ones to the administrative staff. You should also offer some sort of feedback for suggestions; since you won't have time to answer all input, assign that task to an assistant or other trusted employee.

Offer training.   Whether you outsource training or simply make use of the knowledgeable users on your staff, you should offer training to those users who feel a need for help with a new system, application, or procedure. In addition to or in place of training, you may check into the numerous third-party books available for users of network operating systems, applications, and so on.

Form a help desk.   You can set up a help desk within your company and staff that division with people who can answer network- and application-related questions. Depending on the size of your company and the number of users, you can establish a small help desk or multiple larger desks spread out over the enterprise.

NOTE

Use an intranet site to inform users. If you already have a network in place and an intranet in place, you can use that format to inform users of the network upgrades and system status.

Keeping Your People Happy

IS and IT turnover rates are high; watch your people to make sure they're happy with their jobs. There are certain signs that people are about to leave your company and if you recognize those signs, you may be able to head off some departures with cash or other incentives, like flexible work hours. Listening may be the biggest factor to keeping your employees; many employees say that their biggest problem with the company is that their ideas are ignored.

Watch your employees for signs such as the following: Employees who are withdrawn from others or not participating in group activities may be tired, bored, or fed up with their jobs. Less productivity and changing work hours may signal a problem you can correct quickly. Employees who take longer lunches, bring a newspaper to work every day, or start wearing suits, may indicate they have interviews elsewhere. Open whining and complaining, talking about being overworked and underpaid, for example, are other indicators of unhappy employees.

If you cannot pay your overworked, disgruntled employees more money, try to provide other incentives and perks. You might consider vacation time, theater or ball game tickets, company/family picnics, and so on. Also, consider the following: Help employees develop interests outside of their general area of responsibility, outside of their primary scope. This will show an interest and confidence in their capabilities and provide the company with employees who can work in various areas. Also, suggest that employees take classes unrelated to their current field to keep interest and challenge high.

Help Desk

You create a help desk to answer user questions, troubleshoot problems, and guide users through procedures when they need help. Users may ask about printers or modems, file attributes or directory structures, locating a specific server or resource, or any of hundreds of other topics. Even though staffing the help desk seems like an impossible job, it's really not.

The members of the help desk staff should be knowledgeable but do not need to be experts. You can provide them with documentation, books, Web sites, and other information that can help answer users' questions. Also, provide the contact information for technical consultants, vendor technical help, and such, that the staff members can refer to when they cannot find a solution to a problem themselves. They should understand how to use a database and enter problems in the database as they are reported. When the problem is solved, that solution should also be entered in the database for future reference.

In your help desk policies, you'll need to make some decisions. For example, will the help desk staff answer questions related only to the network, clients, and servers, or will they also answer questions about printers, individual applications loaded onto workstations, email, and such. By outlining policies for help desk use and then distributing the policies to your users, you can avoid wasted time and unnecessary calls.

Other policy considerations include the following:

Decide what the staff will do in case of an emergency and outline a list of steps. Include contact numbers and alternative help for the problem.

Establish reasonable hours of operation in accordance with your company size, your network, and your business. A 24-hour-a-day help desk may be reasonable, for instance, if you have three shifts of employees that work around the clock.

Determine who will fix the problems that involve hardware—such as replace a printer toner cartridge or floppy disk drive—and software— like reinstalling an operating system or reconfiguring an Internet browser. You may have help desk staff talk a user through the less-complex tasks, assign certain administrative assistants to the job, or outsource the work, for example.

Establish a policy for the creation of periodic reports. For example, repetitive server problems or network bottlenecks should be quickly reported to the network administrator. Establish a problem hierarchy that describes the problem types and outlines a procedure to follow for reporting those problems.

Establish a policy that forbids the blaming game. Users, administrative assistants, and help desk personnel will want to blame someone for misconfigurations, downed servers, poor network cabling, bottlenecks, and such. If you set a policy that reminds everyone that finger-pointing is counterproductive, everyone can join together to find a solution for the problem without hard feelings and wasted time and effort.

Setting Up a Help Desk

Each help desk is unique to suit the business, administrator, users' level of knowledge, and so on, so it's difficult to outline a format for setting up your help desk. However, there are some common tasks and procedures that may give you a good start.

Answer the users' needs. Check your inventory, documentation, network maps, and so on to find out exactly what type of hardware and software your users are working with, and provide help in those areas. There's no need to establish an accounting expert on the help desk, for example, if only one or two users work with an accounting program; instead, outsource that area to someone who can answer questions as they arise. Make sure you know which technologies need to be supported and supply the documentation and help needed in those areas.

Plan the help desk carefully. Before you set up one lone person in a corner with a computer and a phone, make sure you know the needs of your users and supply enough equipment, software, and staff to supply those needs. You'll likely need an entire office with phones, supercomputers, network connections, databases, and Internet connections to handle the calls from a small network. Outline your needs while referencing the number of users and workstations, the type of network, types of applications, and other factors. Research your needs and then prudently plan for the help desk.

Since the cost of providing a help desk may be high, keep in mind the benefits as you plan for the equipment and staffing of the help desk. First, consider that the help desk will mean you and your assistants will no longer need to deal with minor user problems. Since most of your time is usually applied to putting out fires, a help desk can alleviate many of those worries and problems for you. Second, think about the users; a help desk means their problems can likely be solved faster and with greater efficiency. Once the problems are solved, the users can get back to work and feel better about the company because they didn't have to wait or beg for help.

As difficult as it may be, you'll need to find a way to balance your help desk staff against the needs for its services. You may want to assign a set number of staff members to the desk and supply phone numbers of others in the company who can help if the problems are overwhelming or if there's an emergency.

Alternatively, you could allow the help desk staff to make note of a problem with a promise to call back in an hour, by the end of the day, or within two days, for example. As the staff members take calls, they can prioritize problems and offer solutions within a reasonable amount of time; it's important, however, that users are not put on a waiting list that never seems to get satisfaction. Using this technique also gets users back to work quickly instead of having them wait on the line while the helper finds an answer to the question or problem.

Offer the help desk staff members promotion opportunities. If you implement an on-the-job training program, the staff can help train new people and then advance as a reward for a job well done. You don't want the staff to become stranded at the desk because they're too valuable and therefore feel taken advantage of or bored. Reward your staff.

Make sure all solutions are documented in a database for others to reference when needed. Outline a policy and procedure for documentation so that valuable information won't be lost if one staff member moves on.

NOTE

When staffing a help desk, you must not only choose knowledgeable people, you must choose friendly, patient, and easy-going people as well. And you might want to give staffers a mini-test before putting them into action; make sure each member can explain procedures, reducing tasks to the most basic level or to an intermediate level as needed.

You might use email to answer some of your help desk calls. If a user has asked for the steps to a common procedure, for example, the help desk staff member can simply email those steps if they're documented in the database or in some other file. This will save time and effort for both the user and the helper.

Another idea is to use word processing documents containing steps, procedures, or troubleshooting techniques in the help desk process. Staffers simply refer users to a server, directory, and file to access that contains help for their problem. Think about having assistants produce FAQ lists and/or guidelines as you plan your help desk policies and procedures.

> **NOTE**
>
> If you have an intranet you can place your policies, guidelines, FAQs, and other files there for easy retrieval by users.

Establish a course of action for notifying users when there's a problem with the server, email, network segment, or other problem that concerns them. This could be a responsibility of the help desk personnel since notifying users of planned outages or downtime will reduce the number of calls the help desk receives.

Self-Help Support Systems

If your network is very large with thousands of users, for instance, you may want to consider automated self-help support systems. There are many possibilities from which you can choose; you may even consider using a staffed help desk and a self-help support system in your network.

There are intranet-based applications you can purchase to provide help to users. Many of these applications include text, videos, diagrams, graphics, and so on; however, you may be happier with a text-only system, depending on your users and network configurations.

Another possibility is to create static files of information—step-by-step procedures, for example—and let users locate the file from a help server. In this case, you could then use email alerts and announcements to provide updated information and important alerts. Public folders are another possibility for displaying updated information to users.

Before choosing a self-help support system, consider the following:

Is it cost-effective?   Since the servers are already in place, your costs won't be centered in the hardware area; however, the cost of creating, reviewing, and updating information might be extensive. Also, if users cannot open or retrieve the files they need because of network problems, user frustrations, or other problems, you will still need to answer the users' concerns and problems.

Is it easy to implement? You'll need servers and network components with enough capacity to handle the additional work. Also, your NOS should include features that enable the self-help support system to work with appropriate security and information protection.

Does the system conform to your users' needs? You should evaluate your users to see if they can successfully deal with and use the support system. You may need to assign assistants to train users to make sure they understand how the system works.

Policies and Procedures

You create and enforce policies and procedures for many reasons. For the administrator, providing more cost-effective computing services to the users is easier if the users follow the rules set forth. Time and energy isn't wasted performing menial tasks and rescuing users from problems that should never have come up in the first place, if they followed the rules. Control over the network is easier, planning strategies can take center stage more, and computer downtime can be greatly minimized, if the users follow the rules.

The users also benefit from the enforced policies and procedures. If the user has a list of policies readily available, he can often answer his own questions quickly without wasting time trying to contact an administrator. Also, user confidence is higher with even a little bit of knowledge about the system, the procedures, and the company plan.

You should create written policies and procedures, make sure all users have a copy, go over the policies with the users, and update the policies and procedures periodically. Policies dictate how a user is to proceed under certain circumstances; procedures may list steps or instructions on how to perform common tasks on the network or within the system.

Policy Guidelines

There are hundreds of possible user policies you can formulate; however, try to keep the number to a minimum. Too much control over your users may translate into more problems. Do publish the policies you feel are necessary to the operation of your network, though; the goal is to define and outline steps, directives, and guidelines that will save you headaches and worries in the end.

Following are some ideas for basic user policies; you may want to modify them to suit your company's philosophies.

User Accounts

While you want to control users to make your work easier and to enforce security on the network, you don't want to make it difficult for them to use the system. Too many rules or restrictions may alienate users.

List the types of user accounts available; for example, sales, data entry, accounts, service, and so on, and define the accounts' responsibilities and rights.

Define the components of a user's accounts: unique username, random password, unique email address, home directory, and user information sheet, for instance.

Describe reasons for user account deletions, restrictions, or inactive states.

Outline password regulations, such as words not allowed as passwords (spouse's name, login name, child's name, phone number, and so on).

Define what constitutes account misuse, such as copying and distributing sensitive files, security breaches, advertising or selling something other than company products and services, obscenity use, and so on.

Network Resources

If users follow policies for resource use, all users can have the chance to reasonably use and benefit from the network's resources.

Define resources—printers, modems, CD-ROMs, and such—and outline the proper method of requesting access.

List limits to using others' workstations and/or servers on the network.

Describe dial-in access procedures and guidelines.

Describe limits and rules concerning the Internet and its use.

Responsibilities

Moderate, yet precise, definitions of a user's responsibilities help everyone benefit from the network. If the users understand this, your job will be easier.

Define licensing for software and any limits it includes; also list limits on user installation of software that hasn't been approved by management.

Describe amount of server storage space allotted to each user. You might add some tips on how to reduce disk usage as well.

List printer privileges and limits, such as limits to the number of copies that can be printed, paper types, and so on. Perhaps include some simple printer troubleshooting instructions.

Describe users' responsibilities for backing up files on the workstation or for getting files to the server for backup.

Set forth email policies limiting the size of files, time of day email may be sent, message types, and so on.

List and explain all items that constitute abuse of network resources, such as theft, vandalism, unauthorized use of services, and so on.

Possible Procedures

You can list any procedures in your policy statement that will help the user to understand the steps for performing tasks over the network. You also can include diagrams or illustrations, screen shots, listed steps, explanations, contact numbers, and other information that will help the user. The procedures you list depend on how your company uses the network; you may want to outline steps for using the Internet or an intranet, or simply list the steps to printing a large report.

Here are a few suggestions of procedures you can include:

Outline the procedure for requesting a new password.

Explain the steps for dial-in access.

Describe how to configure a computer for Internet use and the steps to accessing the Net from the LAN.

Tell users how to save files to the network: list naming conventions, appropriate directories, and such.

Explain how users can protect their data stored on the network.

Define steps to adding a network printer to a workstation and the preferred method of printing to a network printer.

Explain the steps for using email.

Add the contact names and numbers of anyone who can help users when they have problems.

List the steps for reporting major problems with a workstation, hardware, or software.

Define the steps to recovering deleted files or files from a backup.

Outline the procedures to follow when the server crashes.

Finally, you may also want to create a document for the user to sign, stating he or she understands your policies and agrees to abide by them. Include in the document such topics as acceptable use of policy, account limitations, resource usage, abuse of services, technical support policies, and so on.

CONFIGURING INTERNET CLIENTS

Book Six

Introduction to Book Six

Understanding the benefits of the Internet in your everyday business will likely encourage you to connect your users despite some of the disadvantages and technical problems you may have. There are many reasons to use the Internet in business today. Your competition is using the Internet; your customers are using the Internet; and naturally, your users want to get on the Internet. To keep up with the new and existing trends in business today, you must provide that access.

Client configuration for the Internet consists of many things; not only must you provide the appropriate hardware and software for each user, you must prepare networking hardware, connections to the Internet, set policies and security for your users, and so much more. This book explains some of the technologies you'll need to know in order to make connection and configuration decisions. In addition, this book covers the following topics:

- Advantages and disadvantages of connecting to the Internet
- Internet technology and terminology
- Business uses of the Internet
- Client hardware and software for use over the Internet
- Outside connections and service providers for the Internet
- Suggested Internet policies for safe and efficient use of the Internet
- Security issues

PRELIMINARY GROUNDWORK

Internet use has exploded in the last few years, not only by the government and individuals, but by business as well. The removal of restrictions to commercial development of the Internet has enabled more and more businesses to expand their customer base, vendor sources, and advertising range. Hundreds of new sites are added to the Web each day. You need to be a part of this growth, for your company's sake and for your users' sake.

The advantages of Internet use to your business and your users are many. You'll notice a quick improvement in productivity, unity, and morale after providing your users with a few weeks of Internet access. Naturally, there are some disadvantages as well; after all, you're opening your business to the world when you employ the Internet on your network. There are some precautions, protections, and other steps you can take, however, to insulate your business data, your network, and your users from the pitfalls of the Internet.

This chapter covers some basic uses of the Internet as well as a few Internet technologies you should consider as you plan your business strategy. Following are the things you learn in this chapter:

- Advantages and disadvantages to using the Internet in business

- Various business uses of the Internet

- Definition and uses of a virtual private network

- Ideas for planning your future use of the Internet

Using the Internet in Business

The Internet is a fast, interactive medium from which you can collect data for a small fraction of the cost of conventional data-collection methods. Data can be accessed or distributed in a variety of ways; sensitive data can be effectively secured; and the methods of data collection are versatile and expedient.

Additionally, Internet access and use are growing at an incredible rate. Sales of goods and services over the Internet are estimated to reach $6.6 billion by the year 2000. You can promote your company and products, enhance customer satisfaction, generate leads from the Web, and stay abreast of the latest developments in your field, all from using the Internet.

In addition to boosting your business by using the Internet, you can help your network users by enabling them to use the Internet. Research products and services, collaborate with colleagues, increase morale, and more, by connecting your users to the Internet.

Nothing this wonderful, however, is not without risks and costs. Security breaches, wasted user time, and so on can also cause problems with Internet access. This section offers some of the advantages and disadvantages of using the Internet.

Advantages

One of the biggest advantages of using the Internet in your business is that Internet technologies build on the current technologies of your network. Most modern network and client operating systems support TCP/IP, HTTP (Hypertext Transfer Protocol), HTML (Hypertext Markup Language), POP3 (Post Office Protocol), and other Internet protocols and standards. Some NOSs and COSs even offer built-in browsers and mail programs.

Also built in to many NOSs are security features you can use to limit access to the Internet, special client software you can extend to your users' computers, monitoring tools for determining bandwidth usage, and more. Additionally, there are many third-party applications you can apply to your network to offer even more Internet features and technologies so you can get the most from your equipment.

Cabling and other networking hardware is already in place for your LAN or WAN, so all you'll need to add is the connection to the Internet, and perhaps some upgrades. You may already have an ISDN or T1 line installed as part of your WAN, so an extension to the Internet is easy. Network cards, modems, and other hardware are most likely in place as well. Therefore, adding to your current network to extend to the Internet should be easier than you think.

There are many other advantages to attaching to the Internet, both for your company and for your users. Following are a few more ideas:

Promotes collaboration and cooperative learning. Users can email and share files over the Internet. Also, users may send links to interesting or useful Web pages to each other. E-zines and newsletters available over the Internet provide a wealth of resources your users can discuss; and user groups and chat rooms are available for discussion of a variety of topics. Figure 1.1 shows that by email, one colleague can quickly notify another of the status of a project.

Encourages global literacy and communications. Users can email and meet people from all over the world in the same or similar line of business to share ideas and opinions.

Advances research. The wealth of information that is available on the Web means users can learn about products, services, procedures, and anything else they need to help them in their work. Also, communicating with others over the Internet means an exchange of data and information.

Provides current information. It's so very easy to keep information up to date with Web technologies that the Internet is often a better source than books and even magazines.

Figure 1.1 Send quick notes, reports, files, and other information over the Internet by email for quick collaboration.

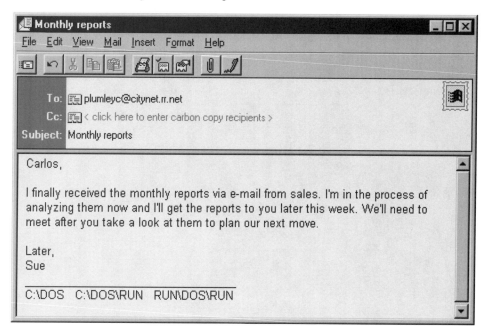

Increases motivation.   The Internet encourages exploration and rewards interest with an abundance of documents, video, music, animation, and more. When faced with the prospect of a dingy library or the Web, most employees will run to the Web.

Increases access to experts.   The Web makes it easy to locate authors, instructors, scientists, doctors, and other experts; almost everyone has a homepage or email address these days. Users can effortlessly contact people in their field to question, discuss, and exchange information.

Promotes the company.   Advertise products and services using audio clips, graphics, and video images. Develop worldwide sales; publish an online catalog or interactive product demonstrations. Offer attractive payment terms to prospective customers and generate leads from audit information you collect. Figure 1.2 shows a company's homepage on the Internet, complete with links to pages that advertise the company's services.

Keeps your customers happy.   Offer new electronic services and support and entice new customers with online clubs, games, quizzes, and such.

Figure 1.2 Advertise your company on the World Wide Web.

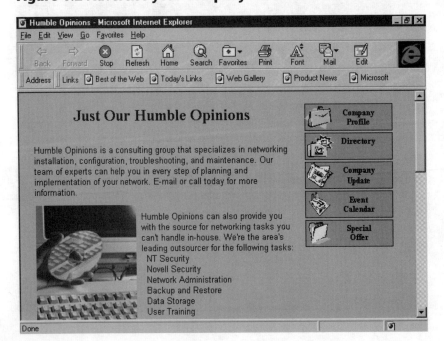

Disadvantages

As with using any technology, product, or service, there can be disadvantages for your business. Hopefully, however, you can find methods of avoiding and/or lessening these obstacles by applying common sense, policies, and additional technologies.

Security is perhaps the biggest worry among network administrators. Hackers slipping into your system to steal information or damage your data are one threat to be wary of; another concern is with users who accidentally or deliberately leak sensitive materials to the outside world.

Following are some other disadvantages to using the Internet connection in your business.

Wasted user time. Users who connect to the Internet to email friends, join user groups that do not relate to the business, or surf the Web for nonbusiness-related information waste their time and the company's. Some surfing and frivolous emailing is to be expected and allowed; however, you can set policies to help curb these activities. There are even some software products you can apply to your network to monitor your users' Internet activity and limit it. Figure 1.3 shows the type of Web site you might want to discourage among your users.

Hardware, software, and peripheral requirements. Even if you build your Internet connections on existing hardware and software, you'll need to add some equipment to complete the connection. Communications lines to the service provider, perhaps a proxy server or firewall, modem pools, and so on are going to cost the company in purchase price, installation, and maintenance.

Tech support. Some of the Internet technologies will require outsourced technical support. An ISDN line, for example, is installed and maintained by phone company employees who are the only ones allowed to work on it. Also, you may need to train some assistants to help users within the LAN to access the Internet.

Upgrade workstation hardware and/or software. If your workstations are older and outdated, you'll need to upgrade or even purchase new equipment to enable Internet access. You may also need to upgrade operating systems and install browsers and email applications.

Reliability of vendor and ISP. Depending on others to supply your connections and services always means the risk of their going out of business or canceling your services for some reason. Also, you must

Figure 1.3 There are thousands of ways your users can waste time online.

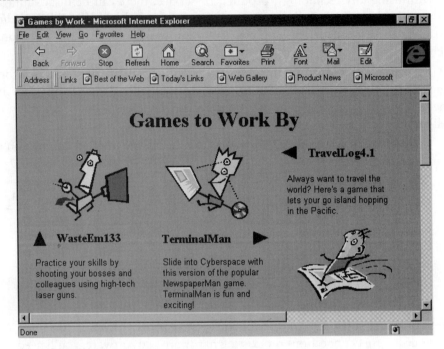

depend on the outsourcers for continuous and qualified service; without it, you're wasting your time and money.

What Can You Do with the Internet?

The list of things you can do with the Internet goes on and on. Connect your network to the Internet and your users will discover more things to do with it than you ever imagined. As far as your business is concerned, you can promote productivity, good will, research capabilities, customer satisfaction, and keep an eye on the competition.

To accomplish these goals, you can use email, real-time conferencing, virtual networking, and surveys and questionnaires. You can publish white papers and other data, disseminate newsletters and other information, and scope out competitors' sites. Advertise, open a store or a mall, or use a Web page to promote one service or product. Following are some detailed ideas for Internet uses.

Email

One of the simplest and most popular uses for the Internet is email. Users can send messages all over the world as well as to the next desk over. In addition to messages, users can attach a variety of files to send to recipients. Email enables the sharing of information and collaboration between users; memos, notes, schedules, documents, and many other types of information can be sent in a matter of minutes, and the recipient can answer any message at his or her convenience.

Email security is one of the worries you may have about the Internet, and so it should be. Internet email isn't necessarily secure or private. Anyone can easily forge a mail message to make it look like it came from someone else. If you understand email headers, you can likely tell when you receive a forged message. Using a digital signature is one way to validate whether the sender is who he or she claims to be.

Another problem with email is that it's relatively easy to intercept messages during transit. Make sure your users understand that email isn't secure or private and so they should be careful of content—both of the message and in any attached files. *Encryption* is a way to scramble a message and/or file so that it's virtually impossible for someone other than the recipient to decrypt the messages. See Chapter 5 of this book, "Configuring Internet Clients," for more information.

Transferring Files

Transferring files over the Internet is much faster than other methods of moving files. Instead of copying a file to a disk or zip cartridge and mailing it to someone, you use the Internet. In addition to attaching a file to an email message, you can transfer files using certain Internet protocols—FTP, Gopher, and so on.

It's possible to send and receive files to and from one person or multiple people, download one or more files from a site without any people contact, and place your own files onto a site for others to download and share. The Internet has made the distribution of files and information simple and effective.

Real-Time Conferences and Meetings

Chat rooms have long been a method of meeting people and talking to them in real time over the Net; however, chat rooms are generally for fun. Business conferencing is currently one of the hottest topics in Internet services. Meet with colleagues around the world to share business ideas, questions, and plans. There are a few methods of conferencing available:

- Applications are currently available for meetings that are similar to chat rooms but targeted to business associates. Members of the meeting can type in their messages, conversing with each other in real time.

- Internet telephony enables people to engage in voice conversations, if they are using similarly equipped computers.

- Videoconferencing builds on telephony by including video cameras at both ends of the conversation.

- Whiteboarding allows people to demonstrate ideas on a shared blank space.

- Application sharing enables two or more people to collaborate on a project in that project's native application, such as a slide presentation.

Web-Based Calendaring

Many corporations use calendaring and scheduling programs to keep the staff informed of all appointments, meetings, days out of the office, and so on. Sharing calendars makes scheduling conflicts a thing of the past. There are many products that enable you to share calendars over your LAN—Lotus Notes/Domino and Microsoft Outlook, for example—but they can be tricky to manage in a large corporation. Web-based calendars make building a common calendar simple and efficient.

Applications that enable you to create a corporate Web-based calendar provide various features and advantages, so compare products before you buy. Some of the features you can expect include the following:

- Capability to set and modify meetings, notes, and task lists

- Forms and time sheets for use by all

- Event tracking and recording so you can view calendars at a glance and are warned of conflicts

- Contact information sheets for email addresses, phone numbers, and such

- Security measures to limit access to certain parts of the calendar

- Multiple levels of control for managers, administrators, and users

- Notifications of changes in schedules or meetings

Internet Telephony

Telephony replaces the traditional telephone with a computer, microphone, sound card, and speakers. Two users exchange IP addresses to use Internet telephony software to call each other over the Internet. The call consists of voice transmissions sent from a microphone to a computer over the Internet and received through the speakers via the sound card on the other end. Telephony calls are free (except for the charges for connecting to the Internet).

Advantages of telephony include the following: low cost for talking across the country or around the world; a good Internet connection makes the call sound like a regular phone call; and users can talk to other users across platforms: PC/Macintosh/UNIX.

One disadvantage of Internet telephony is that it doesn't allow face-to-face contact. Another disadvantage is that both users must have the appropriate equipment and software. Also, audio quality is poor. While telephony may not provide the best quality, most computers come equipped with the hardware that it takes to implement telephony. And many telephony programs are downloadable from the Internet for free. Finally, telephony requires a full duplex hardware and a faster modem for smooth talk and better quality.

Increase Business

Many corporations are using the Internet to increase their visibility in the marketplace; e-zines, online newsletters, advertisements, and online stores and malls are all evidence of the impact of the Internet. You see URLs in newspaper and magazine ads, on commercials, flyers, business cards, and such; nearly everyone has a Web page. Your competitors have a presence on the Web, and so should you.

NOTE

The emergence of secure transactions on the Web means more and more people are doing business over the Internet and doing it in a safe and secure manner.

Your presence on the Web may start with a simple homepage for your company. You can publish a list of accomplishments, products or services, philosophies, and so on, to interest people browsing the Net. You may want to expand on the homepage idea with links to more pages that perhaps show images of products, tables of prices, contact numbers, technical help, white pages of technological information, and so on.

You can add banner advertising and links to other people's pages; for example, advertise in an e-zine that covers your particular business or service. Add your company's page to multiple search engines under many and various topics so as to garner hits from potential customers. Advertising on the Internet presents many opportunities that conventional methods do not.

Your next step could be to publish your catalog of products on the Web. From there, it's only a short distance to opening an online store. Online stores advertise your company and product, enable purchases over the Internet, and provide the opportunity to collect information about your customers and potential customers so you can build and individualize your business.

Following are some of the types of documents and Web pages you can publish on the Internet to support and advertise your business:

- Glossary of technical terms

- Biography page

- Technical support and/or report page

- Technical white papers

- Banner adverting

- Press releases, newsletters, brochures, and flyers

- Download page—documents, files, device drivers, bulletins, bug fixes, archives, and so on

- Forms and surveys

- Search engine

Figure 1.4 shows a company profile page that offers the Internet surfer information about the company and a map to other pages in the site.

Virtual Private Networks

A *Virtual Private Network* (VPN) uses a secure transmission of private IP traffic through the public Internet. Service providers or other carriers can support

Figure 1.4 You can display different types of information about your company on the Net.

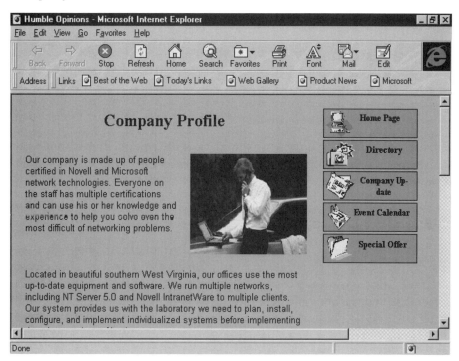

your private network because of bandwidth and performance; and their security safeguards protect your data as well. VPNs limit traffic between specific end points and the traffic is completely encrypted, so that your corporate data is safe and secure.

Corporate users can dial in to a remote access server acting as a gateway to the VPN. The server challenges the caller; information is routed to a Remote Authentication Dial-In User Service (RADIUS) server in the corporate network. The corporate network administrator retains control of the authorization database, updating it when necessary without relying on the service provider.

Managing a VPN is a huge task, however; much of the administration is just making entries into the authentication server and firewall software. Setting up user billing and accounting is also a large job. For these reasons, you may want to outsource your VPN business to a qualified professional service provider. A VPN service consists of a public communication network that uses Internet technologies to deliver information securely to a closed user group.

> **NOTE**
>
> The underlying network can be the Internet, a closed private IP net, frame relay, ATM, X.25, or any combination of network technologies.

Phone companies may provide a VPN service including secure dial-up access, managed firewalls, routers, network-based address protection, user authentication, and packet filtering at the edges of their public IP backbone network. Outsource VPN management and planning to ease support and administration for dial-up users.

Planning Strategies

As you read through the rest of the chapters in this book, think about the overall plan for implementing the Internet for your clients. There are some basic steps to take before you complete the deployment. Many steps have to do with the server side and the networking hardware of your LAN or WAN. Still other steps involve outside sources for communications lines and perhaps other items. Finally, you have steps to take to prepare the client computers and your users.

First, consider your plans for the future. Is your only goal to provide your clients with access to the Internet? Do you want Web access only, or do you want to add email and newsgroups? Other considerations for your future use of the Internet may include a company Web page, an entire site, online advertising, publishing product information and catalogs online, creating an online store, and so on.

Next, examine your method of connecting to the Internet. Will each individual have a modem and line to the Net or will you provide one fast connection line for all users? Will users go through a modem pool, a cable modem, or have a direct connection? Will you set up an Internet server with firewall and/or proxy server protection for your LAN? If you do provide a protective server, will it eventually turn into a Web server that contains company data for distribution over the Internet?

With these plans in mind, you'll need to upgrade and prepare your server(s) for the venture. Next, check network connections and hardware within the LAN to make sure you have enough bandwidth to handle the added traffic.

Upgrade and/or purchase newer network cards, routers, and/or cabling to improve speed and access.

Install and configure any server software necessary for connecting to the Internet, such as proxy services. Make backups of all server configurations you've modified or installed for the project.

Check with service providers in the area and arrange your connection to the Internet, register for a domain name if applicable, and have the equipment necessary for connections between the LAN and the Internet installed and tested. Also, create and print your policies and procedures dealing with Internet access and distribute these policies to your users.

Finally, you can assess your client computers and hardware. Upgrade any client hardware that cannot run the operating system, Internet software, and network and communication software necessary for Internet access. Check network client software, protocols, and network hardware in the workstations and upgrade if necessary.

Install and configure browsers and an email application to client computers. Make backups of all client configurations. Train your users for the programs you've installed. Also, make sure you thoroughly cover all policies and procedures with users at this time.

After you get the Internet connections up and running, you should periodically monitor usage and check for problems, bottlenecks, and so on. Also, provide help to the users in the form of a help desk, technical contacts, troubleshooting tips, books, and such.

TERMINOLOGY AND TECHNOLOGY

Internet access and connection involve many terms and technologies that can be confusing. You'll hear such terms as *dial-up* or *dedicated*, *Internet* or *intranet*, and *ISP*, *IP*, and so on. You may not, for example, realize that once you have the technologies to attach to the Internet available to your LAN, you also have the equipment, protocol, and connections to create a corporate intranet.

IP addressing and its associated terminology can be intimidating; however, with a little explanation, the terms are more easily understood and configuring for the Internet becomes less of a chore. Finally, the task of locating a service provider can be easier with a little guidance and some suggestions for questions to ask the provider.

This chapter defines some terms common to Internet technologies while offering some suggestions to make your choices easier. The following chapters in this book explain the technologies introduced here in more detail. This chapter covers the following:

- Dial-up connections

- Leased lines

- Service providers

- Internet addressing

- Intranet information

Dial-Up or High-Speed Connections?

The methods by which computers or terminals are connected to the Internet are high-speed, dedicated lines and dial-up access. A high-speed, or hard-wired, connection is permanent—the connection is always ready to use. Any client computer with access to your LAN can then have a fast, full-time connection to the Internet. Dial-up access is slow but works well if your users are few and your network is small.

Dial-up access through an ISP can be expensive if you have many users who need access. Since you already have LAN connections, using a dedicated connection from the LAN to the Internet may be a better solution for your company. The dedicated connection goes from your LAN to the ISP; you supply the hosts, router, and TCP/IP applications on your end.

Phone Lines versus High-Speed Lines

The limitations of the phone line (Plain Old Telephone Service, or POTS) are many when it comes to Internet access. First, the phone lines are stretched to their limits as is, with voice use, fax machines, and the like. Also, analog technology was designed for voice; the Internet uses a digital technology designed mainly for data. Bandwidth limitations of the analog transmission just don't serve the needs of newer modem technologies. Also, a high-speed modem can reach its top performance only if the lines on which it's used are efficient and problem-free.

A high-speed Internet link enables users to perform multiple activities simultaneously over the same link; transfer large data files and read the news at the same time, for instance. Similarly, videoconferencing requires more bandwidth than simple text transfers do. With the newer technologies available on the Internet, switched/dedicated 56 K, ISDN, T1, cable TV, fiber optics (T3), and DSL lines speed the transfer of these files and end up costing you less than a modem/telephone line does in the long run. Chapter 3 of this book, "Hardware and Connections," describes the line types in detail.

To connect to the Internet, you need a host (yours or a service provider's) that can run TCP/IP, a software application that can communicate with the Internet hosts, a router to direct traffic from the LAN to the Internet, and a communications line to carry traffic to and from the router.

Dial-Up

Using a dial-up connection over a phone line is flexible. You can easily move users and/or modems to other offices or even buildings. You also can connect multiple computers on your LAN using dial-up connections, and the investment in equipment is less than with dedicated phone lines.

A dial-up connection, however, is much slower than a dedicated connection; transfer rates can cause frustration and noise, or other problems on the phone lines can cut off transmissions unexpectedly. Also, dial-up connections tie up the phone lines unless you use dedicated lines. A dial-up connection won't be efficient if there's a lot of traffic from your LAN to the Internet. However, it may serve the purpose if your company is small and access is intermittent.

> **NOTE**
>
> You can set up a dedicated phone line that is always connected to the Internet using PPP (Point-to-Point) ISDN for an economical way to establish Internet access.

High-Speed Lines

High-speed lines are often leased lines, meaning Internet access is available 24 hours a day, 7 days a week. You can lease lines from local phone companies, long-distance phone companies, and specialized companies. Depending on the type of connection you get, you can transfer data from 56Kbps to 45Mbps.

One problem with a hard-wired connection is that if you want to move your computer or terminal, you must move and reconnect the cables. Another problem is that it's expensive; costs include a high-speed leased line, a DSU/CSU (digital service unit/channel service unit), a router to connect the LAN to the DSU/CSU, and installation charges. You'll need a DSU/CSU to interface between your equipment and the data line. Basically a modem for leased lines, you should buy a unit that will enable you to increase the speed of the data circuit in the future to save the expense of buying another unit later down the road.

The most cost-effective connections for leased lines are digital, frame relay, and SMDS (Switched Multimegabit Digital Service). A digital connection can carry data at speeds from 56Kbps over a switched-56 line to 45Mbps over a T1 line. Frame relay (56Kbps to 512Kbps) and SMDS (56Kbps to 10Mbps) handle faster speeds but are also more expensive. See Chapter 3 of this book, "Hardware and Connections," for more information.

> **NOTE**
>
> You can connect over a leased line and run TCP/IP on PCs on the LAN. You install an IP router that's connected to an ISP over a leased line if you have workstations and network servers but no host computer.

Connecting a NetWare LAN to the Internet

Using a NetWare LAN as an example of a LAN attaching to the Internet over a leased line, you run a TCP/IP client on each workstation. The PCs then have the capability to direct IP datagrams to the Internet through a router on the LAN. A router on the LAN forwards IP datagrams to and from the Internet service provider's access point; you can use an established router in your system to route IP traffic as well as the IPX traffic. The Internet TCP/IP hosts provide the processes needed to honor your clients' requests.

In this scenario, you obtain your official IP network address from the InterNIC and use that address to configure the router, which acts as a gateway for the devices on the LAN. The router port (that's attached to the ISP) is assigned a unique IP address, as are the PCs on the LAN.

The PCs can also use Novell's IPX/SPX protocol to communicate with the NetWare servers and the same router can route IPX traffic to other NetWare LANs. If the network also has UNIX clients on it, TCP/IP can be standardized for use by all clients.

Service Providers

Commercial Online Services (CompuServe, Prodigy, America Online) offer Internet access plus databases, online shopping, games, and file libraries. Connection is generally via a local phone call or 800 number to save on the phone bill. Some BBSs (Bulletin Board Systems) also offer Internet access; however, access is not generally reliable or do not offer complete Internet services.

Service providers are the better choice for professional Internet services. Consider that you may also need to pay for local phone access when purchasing services from an ISP (Internet Service Provider). Ask about access restrictions and appropriate-use policies, required software, storage space on the ISP's server, security, and technical support.

ISP Services

Subscribing to an Internet service provider means you only worry about the configuration details of your site—your LAN's protocols, software, and connection, for example. The ISP takes care of the configurations from its server to the Net. The ISP's host server runs the TCP/IP protocol that communicates with

LAN-Connected Minis

Many Internet host computers are DEC Alphas, Sun systems, HP minis, IBM AS/400s, and the like. UNIX systems include all the tools necessary to be Internet hosts and/or IP routers. TCP/IP is the native protocol and they can create and manage users' mailboxes and run communications protocols necessary for Internet connections.

As another alternative for Internet access, a LAN-connected minicomputer or mainframe may be the appropriate choice for you. The host computer acts as a router and a host running the UNIX operating system as its native device operating system. The TCP/IP protocols, electronic mail process handlers, and FTP and Telnet client and server processes of the UNIX system can be configured for Internet services.

A system administrator must configure the UNIX system kernel to support TCP/IP processes so that it supports networking on a LAN and/or an X.25 serial interface. Kernel configuration binds the TCP and IP protocols to the UNIX kernel; other processes (daemons) must also be started to service other routing and service protocols needed to deliver datagrams. The IP address and subnet mask of each interface must also be configured, one of which should be configured to support PPP or SLIP for a directly connected Internet host.

SLIP and PPP enable hosts on the Internet to communicate over serial lines; both support asynchronous dial-up and synchronous, private-line transmission. SLIP, an older, waning technology, frames datagrams with special characters to signify the beginning and end of a datagram. SLIP does not do error detection or support data compression; it simply transmits IP datagrams. PPP is a standard serial line protocol that includes features to negotiate connection establishment and termination, and to negotiate options. PPP does error detection and thus guarantees reliable data delivery.

your LAN and the Internet. Additionally, the ISP is responsible for connecting to the Internet and routing your traffic, plus other companies' and individuals' traffic, to and from the Internet.

Also, the ISP provides and administers user mailboxes. With a mail server on-site, the ISP can receive mail from your users and transfer that mail to the Internet; the service provider's mail server also receives mail from the Internet, holds it until users call for it, and then releases the mail to the user.

ISPs also maintain or subscribe to news servers that index all news services on the Internet and provide access to them. The service provider also furnishes the basic technologies needed to connect to the Internet: a default gateway, an IP address, and a subnet mask. Service providers furnish these and often additional services such as DNS name resolution, DHCP, and so on.

Finding an ISP

Before signing up for services, survey the providers in your area to make sure they supply the appropriate services for your users. There are local, regional, and national providers available. Local providers are connected to the Internet through larger or regional providers. Regional carriers are often connected to other regional networks through a backbone carrier, such as Sprint or AT&T. You can locate ISPs over the Internet, especially the regional and large providers (see Figure 2.1).

Consider going through the regional or larger providers if your network will have a lot of traffic and require a high-speed line. You can connect directly

Figure 2.1 Find out about service providers over the Internet.

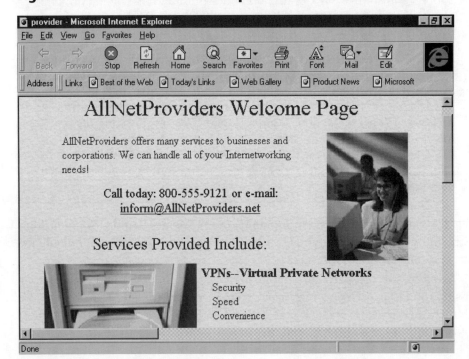

to a regional network, for example; usually the only requirement is that you have a T3 line.

You should ask the ISP for at least three references from companies similar to yours in size and needs. Ask the references, among other things, if they've encountered any problems with the service provider and if so, how fast were the problems corrected. You might also ask about technical support, transfer rates, and so on.

Following are some additional questions you should ask a service provider before signing up for services:

How long have you been in business?

Which services do you provide? What types of access do you offer (ISDN, dial-up, or frame relay, for example)?

What is the backbone connection you use (T1, multiple T1s, or a T3, for example)? To which other networks do you connect and at what speeds?

Do you guarantee a minimum bandwidth? Do you have plans to upgrade the hardware, software, and/or communications circuits?

What type of security is in place?

Which service outages do you normally expect? How long do outages normally last? Do you give a rebate against system outages?

How do we report problems?

What are installation costs and monthly costs? Are there any restrictions on how we can use the Internet connection?

Internet Addressing

When configuring your browsers, Web servers, and routers, you use three common and important configuration components: IP address, subnet mask, and default gateway. An IP address is an identifier for a computer, or other node, on a TCP/IP network. Other nodes include other computers, printers, gateways, routers, and so on. Each node on the network must use a unique IP address. The subnet mask is used in conjunction with an IP address to create subnetworks that enable computers in one segment of a network to communicate with other computers in the same part of the network. The gateway is a device that is connected to two segments of a network and routes messages from one segment to another.

This section explains these three basic items; see Chapter 3 of this book, "Hardware and Connections," for more information about other configuration elements.

IP Address

Directly connected networks require an IP address to identify the system to others on the Internet. IP addresses are unique; to insure uniqueness, IP addresses are assigned by the InterNIC. IP addresses are in the form of four period-delimited octets consisting of up to 12 numerals. An IP address is a binary number expressed as a series of four decimal digits.

The IP address consists of two parts: a network number and a host number. For example, in the address 206.148.33.5, 206.148 is the network address and 33.5 represents the host. Other types of addresses use the first octet for a network number and the last three octets for a host number, or the first three octets as network and the last as host.

Because IP addresses can be difficult to remember, friendly domain names are also used to represent an IP address. When the domain name is used instead of the IP address, a DNS server resolves the domain name to an IP address and then contacts the computer with that address. Domain names must be registered for permanent IP addresses in the Domain Name System before Internet users can see the domain on the Internet. Often a service provider will assign the IP address and can also register the domain name with the Internet Network Information Center (InterNIC).

There are five classes of IP addresses and each has limited and specific uses. Briefly, the following list describes the classes:

Class A is reserved for very large networks. Values of 126 or less in the first octet indicate a Class A address.

Class B is used for medium-sized networks. Values of 128 to 191 in the first octet indicate a Class B address.

Class C is reserved for smaller networks. Values of 192 to 223 in the first octet indicate a Class B address.

Class D is a special multicast address that's not used for networks.

Class E is reserved for experimental purposes. Values greater than 223 indicate a reserved address.

Basically, you can only get Class B or C addresses and there's really little chance you'll get a Class B address. If you ask for more than 16 Class C networks, you'll need to provide a network plan. Also, you'll need at least two domain name servers when you register; an ISP may be willing to provide the primary and/or secondary name service for you.

Subnet Masks

You use a subnet mask when you have multiple segments to a network, such as in a LAN that has two or more offices, and the network is therefore divided into segments, or in connections to the Internet. The subnet mask identifies the network on which the computer is located. Subnet masks modify the IP address by using host address bits as additional network address bits; thus, the line between the host and network addresses is moved to the right to create additional networks and to reduce the number of hosts in each network.

Subnetting offers many advantages. Subnetted IP networks can be routed independently so as to make better use of the bandwidth. Subnetting also minimizes network traffic, maximizes performance, and enhances the ability to secure a network.

Default Gateway

The gateway device can be a server or other computer, a router, or other network node. The gateway acts as a bridge between two network segments enabling communication between hosts, servers, and networks. Gateways must have an IP address to route data between the segments.

Intranets

While you're preparing for connection to the Internet, you may want to consider planning for an intranet. An intranet is a private network that uses Internet technologies to extend information to its users. Through an intranet, you can publish forms, guidelines, policies, and other company documents. You also can provide areas for users to join together and share ideas, questions, projects, and so on.

An intranet can improve communication within a company, but, understandably, from a network manager's point of view, the time, energy, and cost required to create and maintain an intranet may not be justified when more pressing technological concerns are at hand. However, you can easily delegate the responsibilities of the intranet to a committee and just oversee the progress and changes.

Although an intranet is not a critical business need, it is worth the time and effort because users' productivity increases when they are provided easier access to company documents, guidelines, and proposals. Figure 2.2 shows a time sheet published to an intranet, along with many other internal forms, that employees can print and use as needed.

Plan and deploy your intranet over a period of time, like a year, if necessary. You don't have to have it ready to go in any specific amount of time, and by planning ahead, you'll find your content better organized and your costs less.

Requirements for an Intranet

Your client computers can use the same protocol (TCP/IP), browser, email application, network card, and cabling as they use for the Internet. The difference in the client is the configuration. Instead of configuring dial-up networking, for example, you configure TCP/IP for the network and assign each workstation a different IP address.

The other requirement for an intranet is a Web server on your local LAN. You can use nearly any server computer for a Web server, and there are Web server applications you can install to complete the package—such as Microsoft's NT Server with Internet Information Server. The Web server, a file and information

Figure 2.2 Publish internal forms for use by employees on an intranet.

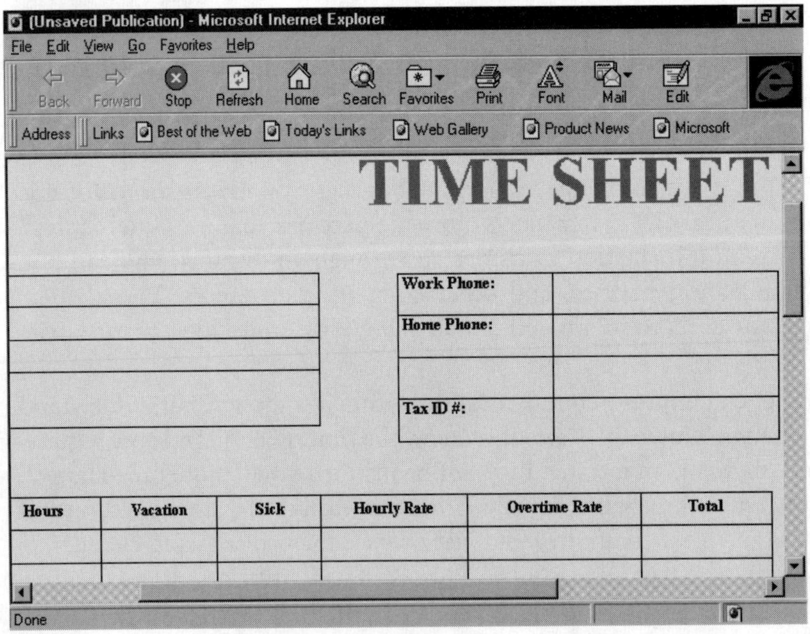

server, enables the transmission of information in HTML using HTTP over a TCP/IP network. Most Web servers also include a Gopher and FTP service. And your intranet Web server can also act as an Internet Web server.

Making the Most of an Intranet

With an intranet, you can publish shared data on your corporate web. Make electronic copies of employee handbooks, phone lists, company forms, guidelines, policies, and so on and make them available on your internal web servers.

At first, creating and updating content for your intranet may seem like a problem; that's one reason you can take your time creating and organizing the information you want to publish to your corporate web. First, you need to establish a common look and feel for the documents across the company; try using templates and assign a team to design the look of your documents.

Next, have the team determine the types of documents and the content. After the initial decisions are made, everyone can contribute to the store of documents. The team then can review and modify documents as needed before publishing them to the web.

Following are some more ideas for planning and implementing an intranet:

Appoint someone to take charge of training users.

Select someone to take charge of statistics reporting and traffic monitoring.

Assign people to handle technical support.

Standardize the messaging, database access, and search engines across departments.

Establish a guideline book for server hardware, acceptable browsers, permissible applications, page design, and so on.

Don't forget scalability; with a growing number of documents, services, and users, the intranet will soon need to grow.

> **TIP**
>
> Lotus Domino is handy for building intranet applications. It includes a document-sharing database, discussion group templates, email, shared folders, and more.

HARDWARE AND CONNECTIONS

The hardware and connections you use for attaching to the Internet from your LAN or WAN directly affect the requirements for your client computers. You may, for example, use modems to connect to the Internet or you may use a direct line. In addition to changing your LAN's networking hardware and configuration, the method of connection changes the client configuration.

The type of Internet access you employ also affects the client computers. Full Web, email, and news services require different software, which in turn requires a different client operating system and hardware than only email services do, for example. Other factors affecting client hardware include budget, user skill and training, and so on.

This chapter covers the common connection choices available to you and offers advice about which to choose for your specific goals. Also, this chapter covers the following:

- Modem and cable modem information

- ISDN, frame relay, and T*x* line information

- Client hardware suggestions

- Client operating system suggestions

Connections

The connections you have to the Internet will depend greatly on the number of users on your network, the amount of use and traffic to the Internet, and other similar factors. If you're connecting one workstation to the Internet, you'll need a modem, dial-in account with a service provider, and the software (browser, email, and such) to connect the client.

You could alternatively run a server on one computer and enable other Internet users to access that server computer. You need a domain name, a permanent IP address, and a more secure and faster connection than a phone line (perhaps ISDN, T1 line, or other connection).

To connect a LAN to the Internet, you need a router of some sort between the LAN and the Internet. IP packets travel from client machines in the network to the router and are then sent to the Internet. If your network contains more than one subnet, you need a router that can automatically maintain a TCP/IP router table.

Figure 3.1 illustrates one possible placement of the hardware involved in an Internet connection. The LAN and its clients attach to a router that routes packets either to the clients on the LAN or to the Web server. The Web server, Opinion.com, then sends packets through a firewall and a router to the leased line that speeds the request to the Internet. In this scenario, Internet clients may also send requests to the Web server; in this case, the firewall protects both the Web server and the private LAN from hackers and illegal requests. Notice that the LAN also contains an intranet for corporate use only; LAN clients access the Web server for shared documents on the intranet.

The modem and router connect to an outside line that carries the packets to the Internet. The modem attaches to a phone line, but the router attaches to other types of communications lines. Table 3.1 is a summary of Internet connection types and the following sections explain these types in more detail.

Figure 3.1 Use routers to direct the traffic to the appropriate network.

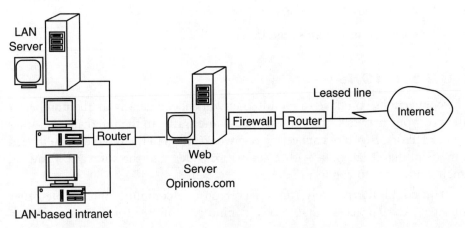

Table 3.1 Internet Connection Types

Connection	Description
PPP (Point-to-Point Protocol)	Dial-in connection at the speed of the modem
SLIP (Serial Line Interface Protocol)	Dial-in connection at modem speed
Dedicated PPP or SLIP	Dial-in connection at modem speed
56K line	Requires special equipment; connects at 56Kbps
DSL/ADSL	Modem that connects at 6 to 8Mbps; availability currently inconsistent
PPP ISDN	Requires special equipment; usage charges; connects at 128Kbps
Fractional T1	Uses part of a T1 line to provide varied speeds, depending on the size of the part
T1	Dedicated line connects at 1.5Mbps; price varies depending on distance
T3	Dedicated line connects at 45Mbps; price varies depending on distance

> **NOTE**
>
> A *router* is an intelligent connecting device that can send *packets*—a block of data sent over a network—to the appropriate network segment. A router can act as a network backbone to connect many LANs together; connect individual LANs to a central router; or connect through a remote connection.

Modems

The CCITT (Comité Consultatif Internationale de Téléphonie et de Télégraphie), a part of the International Telecommunications Union (ITU), has developed world-wide telecommunications standards that govern, in part, the definition of modem speeds and operation. *V.32 bis* is an example of CCITT standards.

A V.32 bis (a CCITT extension of the original V.32) can be used over two-wire dial-up lines or two-wire or four-wire leased lines. V.32 includes error correction and is a standard for 7200, 12,000, and 14,400 bits per second. Whereas V.32 bis is a modem, the V.42 standard is a standard for error correction, rather than a modem. V.42 uses Link Access Procedure-Modem as the primary error-correcting protocol.

More importantly, V.34 modem defines a 28.8Kbps modem for use over dial-up lines. Included error-correction and data-compression techniques boost the effective transfer of data. When V.42 bis compression is added to V.34 modem, data transfer rates soar.

Modem Protocols

SLIP (Serial Line Internet Protocol) and PPP (Point-to-Point Protocol) are protocols used to run the IP protocol over telephone connections via a modem. SLIP establishes a direct connection to the Internet during which the client computer appears as if it were a port on the host's network. SLIP is an older technology that doesn't include error-correction capabilities and is therefore being replaced by PPP. PPP also allows a temporary connection to the Internet using a phone line and modem. However, PPP includes automatic assigning of an IP address for mobile users and error correction. PPP provides router-to-router, host-to-router, and host-to-host connections.

DSL Modems

DSL (Digital Subscriber Lines) is a new technology that doesn't refer to lines but to a pair of modems. The pair of DSL modems creates a digital subscriber line. A DSL modem transmits data in both directions simultaneously (duplex) at 160Kbps over copper lines; a limit of 18,000 feet is set for DSL.

There are several categories of DSL but the one most applicable here is ADSL. ADSL (Asymmetric DSL) converts existing twisted-pair telephone lines into access paths for high-speed (6Mbps) communications. In interactive mode, ADSL can transmit more than 640Kbps in both directions.

ADSL transmits two data streams, with more bandwidth devoted to the downstream leg to the customer than returning. The ADSL targets—Internet access, video on demand, remote LAN access, multimedia, and so on—work very well with a low upstream data rate.

To take advantage of ADSL, you'll need to find a service provider that's willing and ready to offer the service. ADSL is less complex and less expensive than ISDN but currently, the use of ADSL is limited.

ISDN

ISDN is a digital service that can transmit data, voice, and video on the same line. ISDN uses copper twisted-pair cabling from the normal telephone system, so you can contact your phone company for information about ISDN services. ISDN uses a terminal adapter or ISDN modem to interface between your office and the ISDN system.

There are two types of ISDN lines: BRI and PRI. BRI is Basic Rate Interface and consists of two 64Kbps channels (B channels) and one 19.2Kbps signaling channel (D channel). BRI is sometimes referred to as 2B+D. Each B channel can be considered a separate line, which means you can download a file at 64K on one channel and talk to someone on the other B channel at the same time. You also could use both channels at the same time for a combined bandwidth of 128Kbps; using compression, the data rates can soar to 512Kbps.

PRI (Primary Rate Interface) consists of 23 B channels and one 64Kbps D channel (23B+D). Each B channel can be run separately or can be used together to get about 1.5Mbps, or any combination thereof. PRI lines are only used when large amounts of bandwidth or connections are required.

Cable Modems

Cable modems are currently capable of handling downstream speeds up to 30Mbps under perfect conditions. However, when deployed on a shared cable system connected to a standard PC or Mac, the speeds will be lower, but still very fast. Very few models of PCs or Macs can handle the 30Mbps.

The speed of the cable modem is just one factor in the overall speed. You must also consider how fast the PC can handle the IP traffic, how fast the PC-to-cable modem interface is, how fast the cable modem system runs, and how much congestion there is on the cable network. Also, cable modems on the same node share bandwidth, which means that if there are too many people on simultaneously, congestion slows things down. A good example of forced speed limits is the Ethernet cable modem interface standard. The Ethernet 10BaseT, the most popular cable modem interface for the PC, automatically limits speeds to 10Mbps even if the cable modem can handle 30Mbps.

Frame Relay

Whereas phone lines can transmit both data and voice, *frame relay* transmits only data. Bandwidth for frame relay ranges from 56Kbps to 1.544Mbps. Frame relay can transmit packets from multiple protocols, including TCP/IP, IPX/SPX, and so on. To use frame relay, you'll need a router and a line from your office to the carrier's point of entry.

Check to see if your service provider can arrange the installation of a frame relay line for you; you should get a discount by going through the service provider. You can use either frame relay or conventional point-to-point circuits, but generally, frame relay is cheaper (check with the phone company tariffs for prices).

One major advantage of frame relay is that you can increase your line speed simply by notifying the service provider and the phone company; frame relay is a software-defined implementation that can grow with your needs.

Frame relay is a protocol that is based on packet switching, so it allows multiple subscribers to share the same backbone and every subscriber receives its fair share of bandwidth when it needs it. Another major advantage of frame relay is that it handles bursts of data well, improving throughput and making it a good choice for Internet connections.

T1, Fractional T1, and T3 Lines

A T1 line is a high-quality, long-distance communications circuit that you can lease, usually on a monthly basis. T1 provides 24 channels of 64Kbps for a total bandwidth of 1.544Mbps. Although expensive to install and maintain, T1 provides fast, reliable, long-distance links to the Internet.

To connect a T1 line, you need a CSU (Channel Service Unit), a DSU (Data Service Unit), a multiplexor, and a bridge or router. The CSU/DSU prevents faulty equipment from affecting the transmission systems and converts local area network signals to the T1 signaling formats. A multiplexor loads multiple channels of voice or data onto the T1 line, and the bridge or router provides the actual connection points between your LAN and the T1 system.

A Fractional T1 is a subchannel of a T1. You can purchase one or more fractional lines and add to that as your needs increase. Naturally, Fractional T1 lines are a small part of T1, so the speed is less as well.

T3 is equivalent to 28 T1 circuits and provides a bandwidth of 44.736Mbps. The T3 lines carry 672 channels of 64Kbps. Naturally, T3 lines are very expensive to install and maintain.

SMDS and ATM

There are other types of connections than previously listed; however, most of these are very expensive and often targeted at corporations with special needs.

SMDS (Switched Multimegabit Data Service) is a connectionless service that provides high-speed WAN connection rates. Prices for equipment and installation are exorbitant. ATM (Asynchronous Transfer Mode) is a high-speed digital data transmission technology. ATM rates range from 155.52Mbps to 622.08Mbps, even though the capabilities are quite a bit more. ATM is often used as a backbone for WANs.

Which Lines to Use

When trying to decide on the type of connection to the Internet you'll need, consider how many simultaneous users your network will support. For example, if you will have only 2 or 3 users on the connection at the same time, a V32 or V.34 modem will suffice. For 10 to 20 users, try a frame relay, ISDN line, or a Fractional T1 line; DSL may be an alternative to an ISDN line. A Fractional T1 line can support more than 20 users successfully, especially if you add lines as the number of users grows.

As you add more users to this formula, you will need more bandwidth. For instance, if you plan on having 200, 300, or even 500 users on the connection at the same time, a T1 line makes good sense. And if your number of users will be over 4000 or 5000, use a T3 line.

Client Issues

The installation and configuration of the client hardware and operating system depends on the NOS you're using on your LAN and the COS of your choice. What you need to install to the workstation is all dependent on what your operating systems require. Following are a few items you should check for, but generally, follow the operating system instructions.

Client Hardware

The hardware you purchase for your workstations depends a great deal on your client operating system. You must use both the hardware and the software that will make connection to the Internet efficient and effective. Users who must sit and wait for their computers to redraw a screen or display an image from the Internet, for example, become easily frustrated and will therefore stop using the resources.

To make sure your users get the most from the Internet connection, supply them with the equipment they need. Following are minimum recommendations for any workstation that will be attached to the Net for browsing and email. Make sure you check your COS's documentation for a thorough outline of workstation hardware.

Intel: Pentium or later processor with at least 16MB RAM

Apple: 68030 (minimum) or PowerPC with at least 16MB RAM

Digital: Alpha with at least 64MB RAM

IBM: RS/6000 with at least 64MB RAM

Silicon Graphics MIPS with at least 64MB RAM

Client Operating Systems

The main thing to remember is that you need to modernize your older operating systems. DOS and Windows 3.x will not attach to the Internet and provide advantageous access. Following are the recommended COSs for workstations that will connect to the Internet:

Windows 95, 98, and NT 4 or later

Macintosh System 7.5 or later

Digital UNIX 3.2, 4.0 or later

HP-UX 9.05, 10.x or later

AIX 4.x or later

Linux 2.0.x or later

IRX 5.3 or later

Solaris 2.4 or later

Client Network Configuration

Check the client operating system to see what you must do to prepare the workstation for Internet access. You'll need, for example, the TCP/IP protocol, a network client software, and perhaps additional services. Refer to the network and client operating system documentation.

You may need to install a dial-up networking application. Windows 98, for example, uses Dial-Up Networking that comes with the operating system, but depending on the configuration of the computer, it may or may not be installed when you first get the equipment.

You'll need to install TCP/IP to the client computer and configure it with the IP address, subnet mask, and other information you can get from your service provider. See Chapter 4 of this book, "Software and Configuration," for more information. Make sure the modem is installed, if applicable, and configured.

SOFTWARE AND CONFIGURATION

One of the most difficult tasks involved with connecting to the Internet is configuring the network clients. True, clients already have LAN configurations—client software, protocols, and such—but deciphering a service provider's terminology and requirements can be problematic.

There are other configurations you have to consider, too—Internet applications such as browsers and email can be complex, and dial-up installation and configuration can also prove difficult. This chapter presents some suggestions for configuring clients, dial-up access, and TCP/IP information as well as describing some of the popular applications you can use to access the Internet. In this chapter, you learn about the following:

- Information on common browsers and email applications

- Other types of Internet applications your users can implement

- Information on specific client configuration

- Terminology and definitions relating to ISP's Internet setup

Internet Browsers

A browser enables the user to view Web pages, jump to hypertext links listed on pages, keep track of favorite sites, and perform other tasks on the World Wide Web. When choosing a browser, you want to make sure the browser includes certain features, such as reading standard HTML, control over how pages appear, controlling graphic images, and so on.

Common browsers include Microsoft's Internet Explorer, Netscape's Communicator, and Mosaic. There are many other browsers, but most do not offer the advanced tools and utilities that these three do.

Internet Explorer

The Internet Explorer (IE) is a Web browser, email application, and newsreader that comes with Microsoft Windows 95, NT, and is available for Windows 98. The IE lets you navigate the Web while providing tools for viewing and organizing your Web choices. Internet Explorer even includes an Internet Connection Wizard that helps you configure TCP/IP and the program for the Internet. Figure 4.1 shows the IE 4 in a Windows 98 workstation.

Other features available with the IE allow for:

- Bookmarking pages to which you'll return
- Entering addresses in a URL address bar
- Offline browsing
- History list for a quick revisit

Figure 4.1 The IE 4 offers options and features you can use to browse the Internet.

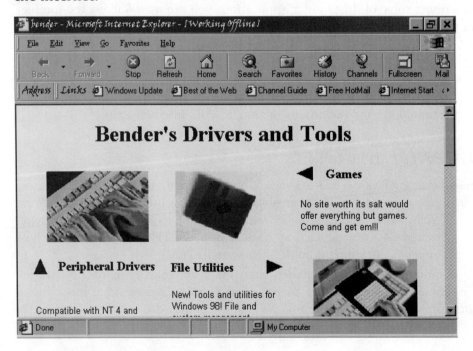

- Channels and subscriptions for receiving notification when your favorite sites change content
- Viewing HTML codes of Web pages
- Printing Web pages in frames
- Email links
- Security features

Netscape Navigator and Communicator

Netscape's browser—Navigator—performs many of the same functions as IE. In addition to enabling frames, security, HTML formatting and so on, Navigator also supports interactive 3-D and provides context-sensitive help. Also, Navigator supports multiple application technologies, including HTML, Java, and JavaScript. Figure 4.2 shows the Netscape Navigator browser.

The Netscape Communicator, an integrated suite, adds other applications to the Navigator browser. Email, groupware, editing, calendaring, and browsing tools

Figure 4.2 Navigator is the basic browser available alone or in the Communicator suite.

are integrated together to enable users to communicate, share, and access information. Communicator is available for Windows, NT, Macintosh, and UNIX.

NCSA Mosaic

NCSA Mosaic is an Internet-based browser that's free for academic, research, and internal commercial use. Mosaic offers a hypertext interface to the Web and common Internet tools such as FTP, Gopher, WAIS, and so on. NCSA Mosaic is available for XWindows, Macintosh, and Microsoft Windows for use over a modem connection that supports TCP/IP.

Mosaic offers basic browser functionality without a lot of the bells and whistles you'll see with IE or Netscape, but Mosaic works very well and is easy to install and configure.

Email Applications

Email provides instantaneous contact with anyone on the Internet for whom you have an address. You can even check the Yellow and White Pages on the Internet to find addresses of people listed there. Email applications provide the tools you need to read and write, receive and send, and organize your email messages. Many programs offer additional utilities to help you with your mail. You can specify a priority status, attach a file, send carbon copies, and so on.

Both Internet Explorer and Netscape include an email program that enables users to send and receive mail messages over the Internet. Following is a brief description of the common email applications.

Internet Mail, Outlook Express

Internet Mail is available with Windows 95 B Internet Explorer, and Outlook Express is available with the later versions of Internet Explorer. Although Outlook Express offers more sophisticated tools and accessories, both programs offer basically the same features. Using either Internet mail program, users can perform the following tasks:

- Send and receive email over the Internet
- Read and write email messages
- Sort, save, move, delete, and archive messages
- Send carbon copies and blind carbon copies

- Set priorities
- Attach files
- Send HTML or plain-text messages
- Use toolbars and icons for shortcuts to most commands

In addition, Microsoft's Internet mail programs enable the user to set options for sending and receiving mail, use fonts, check spelling, add a signature, mark messages, and more. Figure 4.3 shows Windows 98's Outlook Express, which has more features and compatibility than Windows 95 Internet Mail.

Netscape Messenger

Netscape includes an email application with Netscape Communicator called Netscape Messenger. As with Microsoft's Internet mail programs, Messenger provides the tools and features to send and receive mail, organize mail, sort and save messages, attach files, set priorities, and more. Similar to Microsoft's application, Messenger also enables the user to encrypt and digitally sign email, sup-

Figure 4.3 Outlook Express provides options other than email, such as scheduling and a newsreader.

ports HTML email with embedded images, spell checker, hierarchical folders for easy organization of email, and more. Users also can work offline, insert images and tables into a message, and send plain-text mail.

Eudora

Eudora is an older email application that many users still stand by, even though it can sometimes be difficult to configure and maintain. There are Eudora versions for Macintosh and PC users (including a 32-bit version). Just as with other email applications, you can send and receive mail, send carbon and blind carbon copies, organize your folders and messages, and get context-sensitive help. Eudora also offers an address book, IMAP support, file and messaging filtering, drag-and-drop tools, a toolbar, and other features.

Other Applications

There are other applications you can use with the Internet, including file transfer programs. Many come with the client operating system, others are available for free by downloading from the Internet, and still others you can purchase from any applications vendor. Following is a list of common applications you can use with the Internet:

Telnet is a program with which you can log on to Internet sites as a terminal. Telnet is also an Internet protocol. It allows users to log on to remote computers and download and upload files, play games, and so on. Using a Telnet client, you can connect to remote systems on which you have an account.

FTP (File Transfer Protocol) is a command-line program you can use to download and/or upload files to and from remote computers on the Internet. There are also FTP Windows-based programs available. You use FTP with specific FTP servers that offer these file services.

Newsreader enables you to read messages from Usenet newsgroups. There are Windows-based readers that are available from the Internet for free. Most newsreaders identify threads (series of messages on the same topic) and let you sort the messages so you can follow threads that interest you. When you first open a newsreader program, it prompts you to download the current list of newsgroups from a news server (generally your service provider's news server, but you can also specify a news server). Thousands of newsgroups download for your perusal.

File search utility enables you to locate files over the Internet; Gopher, Archie, and Veronica are three such programs. Gopher servers maintain lists of files on multiple computers. With a Gopher client (a menu-based Gopher program you can run on the workstation) you can search Gopher servers. Archie servers, computers that index files available on FTP sites, are one method of locating FTP servers and files if you know the filename. Veronica is another search tool that allows the user to search menu items on Gopher servers. Veronica servers keep databases of Gopher menus and file information. One final common search tool is WAIS (Wide Area Information Server). WAIS has an index of keywords contained in all the documents on servers all over the world. Using keywords to find a file is a lot easier than trying to find a file without knowing the filename.

Common Configuration Details

Each client will have to be configured for the Internet. You'll need to enter an IP address (or mark the IP address as appointed by server), username and ID, POP3 server name, and various other details as given to you by the service provider. Each operating system and/or Internet software is set up differently, but the information is very nearly the same. Each application may call the information by a different name; for example, a Name Server may also be called DNS, or Domain Name Server.

This section lists many of the names for configuration details and briefly explains each. If you have trouble with setting up any client, you should check with your service provider for a complete explanation.

Account Information

Following are some of the most common elements called for under account information:

Access phone number is the local number your computer dials to attach to your service provider's Internet server.

IP address is an identifier for a computer, or other node, on a TCP/IP network; using the TCP/IP protocol enables the routing of messages based on the IP address of the destination. Each IP address on the network must be unique.

Subnet masks (or net masks) are used with IP addresses to create subnets within the IP address space. A subnet mask enables computers in one segment of a network to see and communicate with other computers in the same part of the network, but not with computers in other parts of the network. 255.255.255.0 is an example of a subnet mask.

Gateway (or Default Gateway) is a physical device, usually a router or other computer, that is physically connected to two segments of a network. The gateway routes messages from one segment to another.

Name Server 1 (also DNS, or Domain Name Server) is an Internet server that translates domain names into IP addresses.

Name Server 2 represents a second DNS server that can take care of the extra requests if the first DNS is busy.

Host name (when configuring for a dedicated line) is the name of your computer in your domain.

Domain name (when configuring for a dedicated line) is the domain to which your computer belongs.

Userid is the username that represents the user to the service provider for access to the Internet.

Password is the word assigned by the service provider for access to the Internet.

Interface type (PPP, CSLIP, SLIP) is determined by the server to which you're connecting. PPP, CSLIP, and SLIP are protocols.

Figure 4.4 shows the Windows 95 dial-up networking TCP/IP Settings dialog box. The user specifies the IP address, name servers addresses, and other options as necessary.

Email Account

Following are common sections to fill out for the email account:

Email username is the name assigned by the service provider to represent the user on the email server; this name may or may not be the same as the userid.

Email password is the word assigned by the service provider that provides access to the ISP's email server; this word may or may not be the same as the user account password.

Figure 4.4 The information you specify depends on your operating system and network configuration.

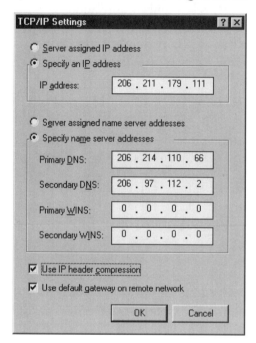

POP email host is the mail server, or the server that holds the email messages for clients on the network. POP or POP3 (Post Office Protocol) is the part of the system that receives incoming mail and moves it to the right mailboxes.

SMTP relay host may also be called the SMTP Server; SMTP (Simple Mail Transfer Protocol) is the part of the system that sends the mail out to other systems on the Internet.

Email address is the username, the @ symbol, and the domain name of the service provider.

News

Following are some of the items you'll need to fill out for the news service:

News server is a remote computer that controls access to the news-groups. It may also be called an NNTP server (Network News Transfer

Protocol), which distributes network news messages to NNTP clients (newsreaders).

Server port (also known as TCP/IP port, port number, port address) is a unique identification number that specifies the path of communication between client and server applications. Port numbers for server applications are preassigned by the Internet Assigned Numbers Authority and do not change.

Common Port Numbers

The IANA assigns processes to port numbers 0 through 1023; these numbers are reserved for services. A client application or process that uses TCP/IP as a transport is assigned a port number greater than 1023 by the operating system. Following are some common port numbers, as assigned by the IANA:

Number	Process	Description
1	TCPMUX	TCP/IP Port Service Multiplexor
5	RJE	Remote Job Entry
20	FTP-DATA	File Transfer Protocol-Data
21	FTP	File Transfer Protocol-Control
23	TELNET	Telnet
25	SMTP	Simple Mail Transfer Protocol
42	NAMESERV	Host name server
49	LOGIN	Login Host Protocol
53	DOMAIN	Domain Name System
70	GOPHER	Gopher
80	HTTP	Hypertext Transfer Protocol
110	POP3	Post Office Protocol version 3

Configuring the Client

Before configuring your clients, you'll need to contact the service provider for the configuration information, such as IP addresses, subnet mask, protocol, and so on. To set up individual workstations, you'll enter the information into a remote access or dial-up utility.

Make sure the workstations have the appropriate hardware—processor speed and RAM as well as a modem or other device—before beginning the project. Next, you'll need to add various software programs and/or utilities to complete the process, such as the TCP/IP protocol, dial-up networking, MacPPP, and so forth. This section covers the general needs for common operating systems.

Windows 95/98

Windows 95 comes with the utilities you need to connect to the Internet. In addition to a browser, you also get a mail program and a news program. With Windows 98, you may need to download the Internet Explorer, mail, and news programs from Microsoft's site on the Internet.

Make sure the Dial-Up Networking, the TCP/IP protocol, and modem are installed, as well as the Internet Explorer, Netscape, or some other browser/mail package. Your next step is to set up the Dial-Up adapter. In the Control Panel (Start, Settings, Control Panel), double-click the Network icon. Open the TCP/IP Properties dialog box and enter the IP address, Gateway, DNS configuration, and WINS resolution, if applicable, according to your ISP's instructions.

Open the Dial-Up Networking program (in My Computer or in the Accessories menu) and create the ISP connection. You'll configure the connection by entering a name, the phone number, and verifying the modem type and other data. Click TCP/IP Settings and enter the IP address, server name, DNS information, and so on. You may need to reboot the computer after configuration, depending on the items you added.

To configure news and mail, you'll need the Outgoing Mail (SMTP) server, Incoming Mail (POP3) server, the POP3 username, and the News (NNTP) server, as supplied by your ISP. You also will enter the username, email address, and other options as required by the specific program.

Windows NT 4.0

NT 4 comes with the tools you need to connect to the Internet; however, you may need to install the utilities if they're not already installed. You'll need Remote Access Service and Dial-Up Networking. Use the NT CD-ROM to install these components, if necessary, before continuing.

Remote Access Service is configured in the Control Panel (Start, Settings, Control Panel). Use the Network icon, Services tab. If you haven't installed a modem, do that first; then configure the modem according to the manufacturer's documentation. Next, choose TCP/IP under the Dial-out Protocols; if TCP/IP isn't there, you'll need to add it.

To configure Dial-Up Networking, you choose Start, Programs, Accessories, and Dial-Up Networking. A wizard guides you to enter the information for your ISP connections: phone number, protocol, and so on. Also, if your ISP requires a script, you can add it in this dialog box.

To configure news and mail, you'll need the Outgoing Mail (SMTP) server, Incoming Mail (POP3) server, the POP3 username, and the News (NNTP) server, as supplied by your ISP. You also will enter the username, email address, and other options as required by the specific program.

NT 3.51

You may have some workstations running NT 3.51. You can install the TCP/IP protocol and RAS to this workstation and use it on the Internet as any other workstation. If the protocol isn't installed, go to the Control Panel, Network icon, and add TCP/IP. To install RAS, go to the Add Software icon in the Control Panel and install the remote access service.

In the RAS screen, you'll need to enter the ISP information: name, phone number, modem type and information about the modem, protocol (PPP, for example), IP address, and other information to configure it for the Internet. You also can set up an automated script by using Notepad to edit the SWITCH.INF file; carefully check the instructions supplied by the ISP.

To configure news and mail, you'll need the Outgoing Mail (SMTP) server, Incoming Mail (POP3) server, the POP3 username, and the News (NNTP) server, as supplied by your ISP. You also will enter the username, email address, and other options as required by the specific program.

Macintosh

To configure a Macintosh for the Internet, you'll need a TCP/IP protocol stack such as MacTCP or Open Transport, and a PPP dialer such as MacPPP or FreePPP. By default, Macintoshes usually come with MacTCP and MacPPP installed, but you may choose to use another program.

Make sure your modem is installed and properly configured. You choose Modem from the Control Panel to set it up. Click Connect Via and choose the Modem Port. Choose the type of modem you'll use from the Modem popup

Login Scripts

Some service providers ask that you use an automated login script to facilitate the login process. You can create the script in any application—Notepad is a handy text editor—as long as you save it as a text file. A login script usually gives the ISP's authentication server such information as your username and password, and perhaps the protocol with which you'll connect.

Following is a sample login script:

```
[ISPNAME]
COMMAND=
OK="login:"
COMMAND=LOGINUSERNAME
OK="word:"
COMMAND=LOGINPASSWORD
CONNECT="PPP"
COMMAND=
```

In the script, you would replace LOGINUSERNAME and LOGINPASS-WORD with the user's name and password.

menu. Set options, such as the modem speaker and dialing options, and then close the Modem Control Panel.

To configure the MacTCP, check in the Apple menu for Control Panels, and then MacTCP. If it isn't there, install it from the operating system disks. From here, you can open the PPP icon and enter the address, DNS information, and routing information supplied by the ISP.

NOTE

Apple's Open Transport, a subsystem for the Macintosh operating system, is based on industry standards and enables easy and efficient networking with Macintosh computers. Open Transport protects the network infrastructure and applications, supports cross-platform industry standards, and is easy to set up and use. Open Transport also makes it easy for a user to switch from one network configuration to another, say, from various Internet setups, without rebooting.

To configure the Open Transport (as opposed to MacTCP), choose TCP/IP in the Control Panels. Again, if the option isn't there, you'll need to install it from the operating system. You'll then enter the PPP server information, IP address, subnet mask, router address, and so on, as supplied from the ISP.

To configure the MacPPP dialer, go to the Control Panels, ConfigPPP icon. Enter the PPP server name, port speed, flow control information, phone number, and other information as supplied by the ISP. Also, click Connect Script, if applicable, to enter any script supplied for the dialer.

You'll also need to configure the email and/or news programs you've added to the Mac. You might use Netscape Navigator, Eudora, or some other package. Follow the directions carefully. You'll need to know your SMTP server and POP3 server, your POP3 username, and the NNTP server for news. You will also enter your name, email address, and any other options called for in the software package.

TRAINING, SECURITY, AND POLICIES

A final area in which you should prepare before attaching users to the Internet is in user training and control. You'll want to train your users to implement the browsers, email applications, and connections to the Internet without endangering their configuration or the network in any way. Training should help user confidence and enhance their skills as well.

Policies regarding security and behavior on the Internet should make this venture safer for your LAN and data. This chapter discusses the following topics:

- Training
- Security and passwords
- Internet policies
- Guidelines for Internet use

Training

There are many types of training available on the market today. Internet training is probably the most common; just go to a bookstore to see how many books are available for beginner Internet users. The type of training you choose for your users will depend on how much use you want them to get from the Internet. If you don't provide training, however, your users may not get the most from the resource and may even cause some network, company, or security problems.

You can send users to outside sources for training or bring a trainer to your office. You can also ask vendors for help, purchase a video or a computer-based training package that guides individuals step-by-step through the program, or buy some books to introduce and teach the users how to correctly and efficiently implement the browser, email programs, and the connections to the Internet.

Outsourcing Training

Using an outside consultant or trainer to show users productive methods of using the Internet will save you money as well as time. List your company's specific needs from the Internet—such as researching, checking the competition, establishing an online presence, and such—to present to the trainer or consultant. Additionally, ask yourself these questions:

Do I need training or consulting services for technical staff, managers, customers, or other specific groups within the company?

What skills do I want my users to get from the training?

What do the users already know?

Security

You can use your LAN security policies to help you formulate some of your Internet security policies and procedures. Keep your sensitive files and data safe and secure, using NOS features and safeguards. You can also put forth extra effort to make sure you protect your users from attacks via the Internet; more applicable, perhaps, you should prevent users from accidentally or purposely distributing company information, offending potential customers, or carrying out any illegal activities over the Internet. This section offers some advice and guidelines to help you reach these goals.

Passwords

The password file is typically the first point of attack on a system's security. The password file on the server contains all usernames, passwords, and other account information; if a hacker get his hands on your password file, he can easily get into your system using any number of names and passwords. That's why it is wise to follow some simple guidelines with passwords:

Assign all accounts a password and an expiration date. Users should pick a new password periodically, say, every two months as opposed to every two years.

You should delete accounts that are no longer in use. A hacker using an old account would be hard to trace through the system.

Carefully monitor guest accounts. It's even a good idea to do away with guest accounts when you're dealing with the Internet; however, if you do keep guest accounts, make sure you use a unique name and password per guest and that you remove each account when it's no longer in use.

Avoid group accounts on the Internet.   It's far more difficult to link responsibility to a group as opposed to a single person.

Although you want to consider users' needs and you want to provide access to the information available on the Internet, you also want to make sure your system and data are safe. Educate users not to blindly contribute to break-ins by opening security holes on your computer. Following are some guidelines specifically for your users:

• Don't use the same word for a username and a password.

• Don't use the same password on multiple machines.

• Don't write your password down.

• Don't use your name or initials as a password.

• Don't use a spouse's name, child's, or pet's name as a password.

• Don't use a password of all the same digit or letter, such as wwwwwww or 222222.

• Don't use your phone number, license number, social security number, address, or other personal information as a password.

• Don't use a word that can be found in the dictionary.

• Make sure the password is at least six characters long.

Email Security

Most email messages are text and so can be read by anyone who captures them. SMTP protocol for electronic mail isn't very secure. Also, there are no safeguards to prevent someone from changing the contents of a message while it's in transit or in storage; email messages can be forged easily. Senders can deny having sent a message since messages can't be bound to a sender. Also, attached files sometimes have viruses included with them; email accounts are often open for spam.

Solutions for the previously mentioned problems are based on a *public key encryption*. Public key technology is one in which the user is assigned a pair of keys that work together. One key is the user's private key and the other is a public key. Both keys can encode and decode data; what one key encodes only the other key can decode. When a user sends a confidential email message, he or she encrypts the email using the second user's public key; the only key that can decode the message is the second user's private key, so no one can read the message except the second user.

For this to work, users must be able to trust that a user's key is valid. CA (Certificate Authority) is the entity that provides verification and assigns each user a unique digital certificate that assures a certain public key belongs to a certain user. Currently, there is no central CA in existence that the general public can use to verify public keys. Some organizations internally act as their own CA for their users. There are also some third-party products that follow this model and use a proprietary CA scheme.

There are also some alternatives: PGP and MOSS. PGP (Pretty Good Privacy) is a secure email program in which each user keeps a list of certificates from other PGP users they trust. When a user receives an email message from someone he or she doesn't know, the user can check the chain of certificates or try to trace a link between certificates.

Another alternative is MOSS (MIME Object Security Services), which enables users to secure multimedia messages. S/MIME, or Secure MIME, leaves the matter of setting up a certificate structure to the implementing organization.

Policies and Guidelines

While planning for Internet connections and access, you want to plan a set of administrative policies to control that access. If you have an intranet in place, you can publish your policies so that all users can access them online. Otherwise, you should print your policies and review them with the users so they completely understand the company's philosophy of Internet use.

You want your users to get the full benefit from the Internet, but you must also limit their enthusiasm. For example, users who save multiple bookmarks, all of their email, and downloaded documents and applications, will soon fill the hard disk to the server or to their workstations. Additionally, users who transmit sensitive company files or obscene language over the Net endanger your business and your company. You must put some limits on the users to protect the network resources and the company. This section provides some ideas for Internet policies as well as some suggestions for help and guidance you can give your users.

Internet Policy Suggestions

Your Internet policies are going to limit users' freedom on the Net and protect your network and your company. From simple limits you set on access times to rules about emailing sensitive files, all policy statements should be reasonable, resolute, and well qualified. Policies for Internet use may very well be among the most important policies you create because the Internet offers more contacts, risks, and exposure to the outside world.

Following are some suggestions for Internet policies; naturally, you will likely add your own policies and perhaps modify these to better suit your business strategies.

Limit disk space usage.

Use the Internet resources for informational, educational, or research purposes only. Recreational use of the Internet during the workday is prohibited.

Users should not use the Internet for illegal or unethical use.

Respect intellectual property rights by making only authorized copies of copyrighted, licensed, or otherwise controlled data, software, and other information on the Internet.

Respect the privacy of coworkers and the company by not misrepresenting oneself to other users; not attempting to gain access to files, passwords, or data of others; and by not seeking to disallow access to any computer system via the Internet.

Refrain from damaging equipment and altering the setup of the computers that access the Internet from the company.

Avoid installing or running personal software on the Internet computer(s).

Do not alter or damage software or data stored on the Internet-accessible computers.

Refrain from transmitting threatening, harassing, or abusive language and images over the Internet.

Respect posted time limits, sign-in procedures, and other guidelines set forth by the company.

Email Policies

You need to create email policies for a variety of reasons. You can let your users know your company's philosophy on certain issues through the policies you set; for instance, sending private email or forwarding jokes with company email may be frowned upon. Policies should also help to save on bandwidth; for example, users shouldn't attach files with video clips or sound clips unless they are directly related to the business at hand. More importantly, email policies should protect the company and the users; a written and distributed policy against sexual harassment, for example, may protect the employer in a lawsuit.

First, make sure your users understand that email is not truly private. Email is forwarded, printed, downloaded, and regularly backed up by the people who receive it. A user needs to be careful about what he sends in a message because it could come back to haunt him. Email is a written record and can be used in a court of law.

Second, make sure users understand your policies by having them read and sign the written policy. Periodically have employees read and sign off on it again. You can also display electronic versions of your policies on your intranet. In covering the policies with users, explain why each policy was developed and why it's important to the company and the employee.

Here are some ideas and issues to consider about email policies:

Be reasonable in setting policy; don't ban personal email use because that's unrealistic. You can, however, state a limit or mention that you frown on personal messages to limit abuse to a degree.

Set a policy on sexual and racial jokes, and rants about corporate practices, bad bosses, or lazy colleagues.

Notify users that email is company property and may be monitored for legitimate reasons. This protects you and the company; there should be no privacy for employees with company email.

Do ban sexually explicit material or other content inappropriate for the business environment.

Make sure to add a policy that says there is to be no dissemination of trade secrets to unauthorized persons inside or outside of the company.

TIP

Failure to prohibit race, sex, and age material can be used by a plaintiff in a discrimination suit to prove you created a hostile work environment.

Security Policies

It's important to let your users know about your security measures because if they understand how serious your security concerns are, then they will be more likely to support your policies and help protect the system. Following are some suggestions for security statements to share with your users:

Don't let users use guest accounts; actually, it would be best if you didn't provide guest accounts for the computer attached to the Internet.

Ask users to use any built-in encryption features on files and email sent over the Internet.

> **TIP**
> Users should encrypt files they plan to send, attach the file to an email message, and then encrypt the message for maximum protection.

Require users to use and monitor virus protection measures on their workstations.

Explain the firewall or proxy service to the users so they understand security measures.

Internet Guidelines and Information

In your policies, you should have a section or two of guidelines and information that will help the user through certain procedures, answer questions, and provide important contact numbers and names if the user needs help. The more help you provide your users with, the less calls you and your staff will get for common questions and problems.

Within the guidelines, present the users with any or all of the following:

FAQ (Frequently Asked Questions) lists with clear and concise answers. You might include the following: how security works, why security is important to the user, definition of terms, descriptions of technologies, explanation on how email or the Web works, and so on.

Contact numbers for administrators, assistants, outsourced or vendor help lines, and so on. This way users can contact someone in case of a problem or emergency with the Internet. Also include email addresses for contacts who can help with technical questions.

Technical information, such as what steps to take when the modem doesn't respond or the router locks up, is good to add as a troubleshooting section. Users can perform simple checks on their system and perhaps fix their own problems before reporting them.

Add steps and guidelines for using the browser and/or email application. If a user gets stuck creating a bookmark or printing a page of frames, he can refer to the guidelines for help.

Add a page or two with Netiquette suggestions for the users. Explaining why a user shouldn't type in all caps in a message or how to properly include parts of a message when responding can help everyone use the Internet more effectively.

Introduction to Book Seven

Remote access enables users to call the office computer from home, for example, to work from home. Remote access enables users to connect to another computer, and then upload and download files—word processing, spreadsheets, databases, forms, video clips, or any kind of document. Users on the road can use their laptop to dial up the office and attach to the network, taking advantage of files, folders, printers, and other network resources. Consultants can provide technical support to customers via remote access, monitoring the user's actions or remotely controlling the user's desktop.

Remote access users, business travelers, and telecommuters require many services from their corporate network, including the following:

*   File and print services

*   Email

*   Internet access

*   Database services

*   Fax services

*   Application

*   Technical support

PRELIMINARY GROUNDWORK

Remote access enables users to attach to a network server or a workstation. Depending on the software and its configuration, the host computer may be able to transfer files, be a gateway between two computers, enable remote networking, provide online services, or remotely control another computer. Any connections and access between a remote computer and another computer are totally dependent on the rights and privileges allotted to the remote user on the host network.

Remote networking is probably the most common method of remote access. The person sitting at the remote computer can connect to the network and access all applications, files, and other resources as if the user were attached to the network locally. This method enables the user to work at home, on the road, or anywhere there's a connection to the network.

Both the host and the remote control computer should be able to transfer files in a remote access session. If the host is acting as a gateway, the remote computer can access another computer (server or workstation) on the network by going through the host. An online service connection to a bulletin board service, an extranet, or the Internet enables the remote computer to act as a member of the remote network by accessing files and resources.

There is a difference between remote control and remote services. In a remote control solution, users share a CPU, screen, keyboard, and mouse control over a WAN connection. Someone sitting at the host, then, can open files, scan the directory structure, and troubleshoot problems on the remote computer. A remote access service is dedicated to communications, not to running applications.

In this chapter, you learn about the different types of remote access services. Following are some other issues covered in this chapter:

- Types of remote users
- Advantages and disadvantages of remote access

- Needs of the remote user
- Tips for the remote user

Defining Remote Networking

In today's business world, there are many new definitions of "going to work" and being "on the job." Many people still work in traditional offices from 9 A.M. to 5 P.M. But many people work irregular hours, telecommute from home, and/or travel in their job rather than remain in the company office all day. These workers need access to network resources—files, applications, printers, and other resources—while they're away from the office.

Mobile sales forces, after-hours workers, and people needing off-site support are just a few of the types of people who take advantage of remote access. Anyone with a home desktop or a traveling laptop computer can attach to the office network, with appropriate rights and permissions, to use the network as if in the same room or office.

Remote Access Solutions

Remote access can refer to a variety of procedures: remote networking or node, file transfer, remote control, and so on. The type of remote access you use in your company depends on your needs and your users' abilities. As you plan your remote access system, you should consider that you may be forced to choose between one technology and another, based on availability or performance. Knowing what is available to you will help you make those choices.

Remote Node

Remote node is the most common and popular of the remote access solutions. A remote user connects to the corporate network and proceeds to work as if he or she were on the network in the same building or office. With remote networking, an out-of-town user can connect to the network to open a customer's file and make changes to it, print a report for a colleague at the office, or pencil in meetings with coworkers on a shared calendar program for a time when he or she returns to the office.

Figure 1.1 illustrates two remote users attaching to a corporate LAN. While one user is accessing his email, the other is downloading files to the corporate file server.

Figure 1.1 Remote users perform network tasks as if they were in the same building as the LAN servers when using remote node.

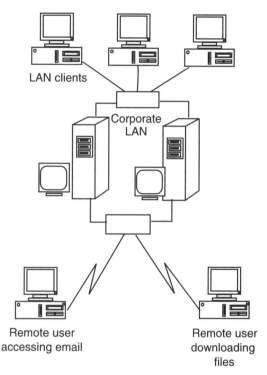

LAN clients

Corporate
LAN

Remote user
accessing email

Remote user
downloading
files

With the remote node, the user can run applications—such as email, terminal emulation, and often word processing or spreadsheet types of applications—from the server on the remote computer, just like normal network clients do. There are many other advantages to remote node access, including better security, easier management of resources, and more scalability. Any number of users can dial in to a host (via a modem pool or leased line) and work simultaneously, as long as the host system has enough modems and bandwidth, and the remote access doesn't tie up the server computer the way it would on remote control.

There are also disadvantages to using remote node access. For one thing, some applications will not work well over the connection, even if you do have high bandwidth. The other problem is the cost—leased lines, RAS servers, and the like are not inexpensive; however, you may find the cost reasonable if it suits your company's and users' needs.

Remote Control

Remote control involves two computers—a host and a remote computer—with one computer controlling the other. A dedicated computer (host) within the LAN can control a remote computer, for example, to perform troubleshooting tasks or to show the remote user how to complete certain procedures. Or the remote computer can control the host, such as with an administrator calling in to the network to perform certain functions. The person at the controlling computer can execute programs and process data on the controlled computer via keystrokes and mouse while viewing the screen of the controlled computer.

> **NOTE**
>
> Usually a remote computer connects to the host via dial-up using a proprietary protocol software like Symantec's pcAnywhere, Stac's ReachOut, Quarterdeck's RapidRemote, Microcom's Carbon Copy, and so on.

Remote control is quickly being replaced by remote node access, but there are still advantages to using it. Troubleshooting and training are perhaps the two most popular uses. Teaching a user how to access network resources, access a script or macro, or other tasks is easier by remote control than going to the site. Also, by looking at a remote computer's configuration files, device setups, directory structures, and so on, a person trying to troubleshoot the user's problems can quickly and efficiently search out the problem without leaving her desk.

Figure 1.2 shows a common use for a corporation to use remote control. The help desk can dial up the remote user and troubleshoot the computer without leaving the office.

Figure 1.2 With remote control, the help desk can manipulate the remote computer to help with problems.

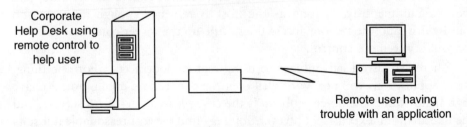

Corporate Help Desk using remote control to help user

Remote user having trouble with an application

There are also disadvantages to remote control. For one thing, a remote computer usually relies on a dedicated host on the other end, which limits the uses of the host on the LAN to just one user—a costly solution. Also, most remote control applications require you use another application for file transfer between the host and remote computer. This can be time-consuming and adds extra steps and tasks to the job of accessing the LAN. Finally, security with remote control isn't the best. The passwords on the host system and the remote control application may or may not synchronize; and callback isn't always secure either.

File Transfer

File transfer is another method of remote access. The remote user connects to a network for the express purpose of uploading or downloading files. When the transfer is complete, the remote user disconnects. Remote users might upload time sheets, expense forms, and equipment requests, for example, and then the remote user could download customer information he needs for his next assignment.

Some file transfer programs that enable users to transfer programs, pictures, sound files, and data include FTP, NCFTP, Kermit, Xmodem, Ymodem, Xferit, Fetch, and Archie.

Gateway

Another method of remote access is where the remote user connects to the host and uses it as a *gateway* to other computers and resources on the network. An example of this solution is a user connecting to the remote access server over the weekend to access his own workstation at the office. While connected, the user may run applications, print documents, create files, and so on.

> **NOTE**
> Online services via remote access are extremely common. Users can send and/or receive email, for example, on a company's extranet. Other online services are bulletin boards and VPNs over the Internet.

Software-Controlled Access

There is also a type of remote access that is application-specific, also called *software-controlled access*. This type of remote access consists of one application and only allows access to that one application, may require a separate host and client software, and may also require a dedicated gateway or a remote control connection.

Generally, software-controlled access employs the authentication through a password and username. The remote user dials in to the server software, is authenticated for that one application only, has rights and permissions for use of the application and data, and so on.

You'll see this type of remote access with mainframes or minis hosts for the most part. Examples of this type of application include Microcom's Carbon Copy, Norton-Lambert's Close-Up and Symantec's pcAnywhere. The PC client can often access these applications using a terminal emulation utility, such as the one available in Windows.

Types of Remote Users

Remote users may come under any of the following headings, as well as others:

Home-based.   Users may be self-employed, conducting business from offices in their home or own office. Users access customers', vendors', or other corporate networks as part of their daily business.

Satellite offices.   Offices opened in another part of town or in another city or state reduce commute time for employees and alleviate traffic and parking congestion problems at the main office. Users can attach remotely to the main network for files, applications, and resources.

Hoteling.   Office space that's designed for use on a shared, as-needed basis. Employees check in and out of one or more offices as needed, leaving behind standard business tools and technologies. From this office, users can attach to the main network in another building, city, or state.

Mobile office.   Workers equipped with tools and technology to perform job duties at home, office, hotel, car, customer's location, and so on, take their technology and work with them. These workers have a traditional office base, but not necessarily an assigned office.

Teleservices.   Remote call-center representatives take routed calls from a home-based office. Teleservices improve access to information and government services in inner cities and rural areas by providing information over the phone.

Remote Access Activities

Following are some of the activities or jobs a remote access user could perform:

- Project management

- Hardware or software evaluation

- Training development

- Online consulting or help

- Documentation creation

- Online meetings and conferences

- License tracking

- Financial analysis

- Referral consulting

- Programming and analysis

- Web content development

- Research

- Remote technical support

Advantages of Remote Access

Remote access enables an employee to produce work outside of the company premises and exchange data with the company via telecommunications links. Early in its conception, the advantages to remote access were different than they are today; easing highway congestion, fuel use, and saving wasted commuting time were the great benefits. Although those benefits still stand strong, so many more advantages have been defined in relation to remote access, for both the employer and the employee.

Business today is heading toward more telecommuting. Employees can work on their own, set their own schedules, and send their work in via remote access. Employers spend less time and money on remote workers yet still get the work they need when they need it.

For the employer, remote access means increased productivity. Employees who work out of the traditional office setting are happier, more well-adjusted, and produce higher-quality work. Also, remote workers don't miss as much work as those who regularly work in an office.

Employers who encourage workers to use remote access also see a large financial savings through a reduced demand for office space, as well as great tax incentives for allowing employees to telecommute. Employers will also notice a savings in the allocation of on-site facilities and resources. Workers who remain in the office have more equipment and resources because of the reduced demand.

There are many advantages to the remote employee as well. Productivity is increased because of less pressure, a more relaxed atmosphere, flexible schedule, and so on. Since the employee is happier, his work is improved; since the work is improved, better work performance evaluations result. Naturally, the remote worker's daily schedule is more flexible, producing a more relaxed attitude as well.

The employee also saves money from working remotely. Reduced commuting and parking costs, lower clothing bills, perhaps no baby-sitting or day care costs, and less money spent on eating out for lunch and/or dinner.

Disadvantages of Remote Access

The biggest disadvantage of remote access is in trusting the remote user to complete his or her work properly in the allotted amount of time. You must first make sure the remote user is well-suited for working away from the office. Choose someone with good organizational and time-management skills who has proven herself with her previous job performance.

Also, keep in touch with the remote worker. Set regular meetings to discuss problems. Encourage the remote worker to keep in contact with the in-office staff as well. Finally, make sure the in-office staff understands the importance of the remote user and the job he or she is doing. Keep communications open between inhouse and remote users so misunderstandings and tensions don't develop.

There is also the fact that the cost of buying and supporting a mobile computer may be more than that of an in-office desktop. First, laptops are more expensive than desktop computers. Second, the wear and tear on a laptop may also factor in to the costs of remote services.

Finally, keeping a remote user's computer upgraded to the applications needed could be a problem. Remote upgrades and updates may be handled by the end users themselves, however, and scheduled for when they are in the office. This may make updates infrequent, but can still serve the purpose.

Providing for Remote Users

Remote employment is any working arrangement where the worker spends a significant portion of work at some location other than the employer's central office. A virtual office is the operational domain of a business whose work force includes a significant portion of remote workers.

If a worker often produces documents, for example, that can be transmitted electronically via modem or fax, or if the employee's main duties are telephone related, he or she might make a good candidate for a remote worker. Examples are business or departmental managers, accountants, bookkeepers, engineers, budget analysts, technical researchers, journalists, estimators, technical writers and illustrators, commercial artists, telemarketers, data-entry staff, and so on.

Generally, a remote employee works on a personal computer, maintains one or more Internet access accounts or a bulletin board service, and uses a dedicated phone line.

Supplying the Virtual Office

As the employer of remote users, you should supply the users with the equipment they need to work and access the network. You may opt for splitting the costs of equipment with the worker, or some other method of meeting the requirements of a virtual office.

Naturally, remote users need a computer. A desktop is fine if the work area will be fixed, like in their home or a branch office; however, remote workers on the road need a portable computer to carry with them. You should also supply a modem, cable modem, or other peripheral plus connection to the corporate LAN. Again, the connection and equipment will depend on whether the user will be mobile or fixed, as well as other factors.

The type of connection you supply to the user should depend somewhat on the frequency and the type of information accessed. There is a tremendous variety in link speeds and costs; you must consider the type of access (file transfer or terminal emulation), the volume of data transferred, how far the worker is from the office, and how long the link will be established each day. The type of access and the volume of data transferred will determine how fast a link is necessary, while the distance from the office and hours of use will determine the most cost-effective technology.

A modem will be required at both the remote location and at the company; make sure you use only reliable hardware. Your most flexible, cost-effective solution for taking care of multiple remote users may be a remote-access server with integrated modems, routers, and application cards. This kind of server can negotiate different line speeds, support different network protocols, locate LAN addresses, and be remotely monitored and managed.

Add local printers and docking stations, if applicable. You may also need to install a business phone line; a pager, palm-top computer, cellular phone, and such are also handy for your remote users. Naturally, you must consider the user's goals, amount of travel, remote office location, and so on, when considering the equipment needed.

Technical support is another important issue. Remote users tend to work hours that aren't necessarily regular working hours to you. You may need to outsource evening and weekend support from a vendor, consultant, or other source.

> **TIP**
>
> If you're supporting mobile users over a VPN, use a national ISP with a toll-free telephone number to save on the phone bills.

Tips for Remote Users

You should meet with your remote users and strongly suggest some common safeguards and guidelines they can implement on their own. Remote users must take more responsibility in protecting their equipment and their work, since they are not at the office regularly.

Perhaps most important are backups. Whereas office workers generally depend on an administrator to back up their systems to the network or to a tape drive, remote users may not have the opportunity to participate in company backups. Make sure the remote user has the necessary equipment—zip drive, floppy disks, tape backup, for example—and keeps a regular schedule of backups. Naturally, a remote user could back up to the network when attached, as well.

Virus protection is another issue to mention to remote users. Notebook users tend to have more virus disasters because they are exposed to more floppy disks. Running a good virus-scanning program, consistently, should be required.

Finally, remote users should keep a survival package with them at all times. Include such items as an extra charged battery, a double-female RJ-11/12 jack, a spare phone cord, a printed list of all support vendors, and a CD-ROM player.

TERMINOLOGY AND TECHNOLOGY

Carrier services you use for remote access can be temporary or full-time, analog or digital. Temporary services include using a modem for dial-up access. The line is switched for the time the user is implementing the line, but when the user is finished, the line becomes available for others again. *Full-time services* refer to leased lines, such as ISDN, T1, and so on.

Analog refers to transmission methods developed to transmit voice signals rather than high-speed digital signals. Analog dial-up services are used in conjunction with a modem and offer typical speeds up to 28.8 or perhaps even 33.6. Data compression makes even faster transfer rates available, up to 112Kbps or more; reduced transfer time means reduced cost. Analog uses standard phone lines, so it's easily accessible and ideal for mobile users requiring a temporary connection.

Digital technology represents values in the form of binary digits. Services such as ISDN lines can offer faster speeds (128Kbps) for dial-up users. Most digital lines can also be used to place analog calls by converting the analog signal into a digital format.

This chapter introduces other terms and technologies you'll need to understand to set up or even outsource your remote access. This chapter covers the following:

- Remote access modems
- Remote access connection lines
- Virtual Private Networks (VPNs)
- Security for remote access

Modems for Remote Access

It's difficult to separate modems and connections because modems depend on some sort of line to transfer information and data. Most modems use telephone lines; however, many use ISDN, frame relay, and even TV cables. Common remote access options include 56Kbps modems, ADSL modems, and cable modems.

Your use of modems for remote access will depend on the number of users, the amount of time spent online, and the tasks the users must perform while remotely connected to the network. Make sure you don't purchase outdated equipment—such as 28.8 modems—when you could easily use a 56Kbps modem and plan ahead for the future at the same time.

28.8 and 33.6 Modems

Under ideal phone connections, 28.8 and 33.6 analog modems (V.34) will transmit 28,800 or 33,600 bits per second; if the modem uses data compression, however, those speeds can achieve higher throughputs. The V.34 standard is pretty mature and stable, so firmware upgrades should be few and far between (unlike the 56K V.90 standard that is new and will likely require a few upgrades).

It's always a good idea to ask the service provider if it supports a 33.6 modem before purchasing; actually, if you're going to upgrade modems, ask the service provider about 56K support and upgrade to the higher speed if possible.

56Kbps Technology

56Kbps analog modems (also called V.90) use the X2 or the K56 protocol. There are two competing standards for 56Kbps modem connections, both of which support downloading at speeds up to 53Kbps (FCC regulations prevent us from getting 56Kbps in the United States) and uploading speeds of up to 33Kbps (see Figure 2.1). The actual speed you get depends on the conditions of the telephone lines and individual connections. However, because of data compression, the 56Kbps modems can achieve throughputs of two or more times the rate on compressible files.

A 56Kbps dial-up connection works well for both mobile and fixed users, also for offices with 10 or less workers. 56Kbps is affordable; it is less expensive than frame relay and ISDN. Also, 56Kbps is easy to use and provides good security. Again, a problem with a 56Kbps connection is that the local infrastructure may not support the speed.

When shopping for 56K technology, make sure you question your service provider about compatible equipment, protocols, and connections.

ISDN Modems

ISDN is considered a digital subscriber line service that shares some of the same technologies as xDSL, including use over existing telephone copper cabling

Figure 2.1 Download speeds are faster because users generally download more often than upload.

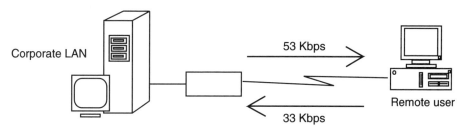

infrastructure, digital quality, low noise, less interference, security, and so on. ISDN is, however, a switched technology as opposed to a point-to-point service. To ensure constant service, ISDN requires external power, such as a backup power system or a redundant POTS line (xDSL carries its own power online).

With ISDN, you need a modem and terminal adapter on your end of the line. ISDN modems provide up to 128Kbps speeds with uncompressed data. The distances for ISDN modems range up to 18,000 feet, although additional equipment can be used to extend the distance. Use ISDN modems for Internet or intranet access, remote LAN access, videoconferencing, frame relay, and so on.

xDSL

DSL (Digital Subscriber Lines) is a new technology that doesn't refer to lines but to a pair of digital modems. The pair of DSL modems creates a digital subscriber line. A DSL modem transmits data in both directions simultaneously (duplex) at 160Kbps over copper lines; a limit of 18,000 feet is set for DSL.

There are several categories of DSL—as in HDSL, ADSL, and so on—and so the entire array is often referred to as xDSL. xDSL is perfect for telecommuters, small businesses in need of more bandwidth, and power users. xDSL is scalable, offers more bandwidth than ISDN, and the cost may become a bit lower than ISDN over time. Also, xDSL is available through existing copper infrastructure. Unfortunately, xDSL is at this time expensive and difficult to find.

The most applicable xDSL here is ADSL. ADSL (Asymmetric DSL) converts existing twisted-pair telephone lines into access paths for high-speed (6Mbps) communications. In interactive mode, ADSL can transmit more than 640Kbps in both directions.

ADSL transmits two data streams, with more bandwidth devoted to the downstream leg to the customer than returning. The ADSL targets—Internet access, video on demand, remote LAN access, multimedia, and so on—work very well with a low upstream data rate.

Figure 2.2 illustrates how ADSL modems work. A modem is placed at both ends of the remote connection and attached by an existing copper twisted-pair telephone line.

To take advantage of ADSL, you'll need to find a service provider that's willing and ready to offer the service. ADSL is less complex and less expensive than ISDN, but currently, the use of ADSL is limited.

Cable Modems

Cable modems connect to the TV cable to provide high-speed Internet access. A small percentage of cable companies are making this service available to their

Types of DSL Service Offerings

xDSL means there are various types of digital subscriber line services. Following is a brief description of the DSL service offerings:

High-bit rate DSL (HDSL). Uses two or three pairs of copper wire to form a T1 or E1 connection; T1 is preferred. E1 is the European basic multiplex rate that carries 30 voice channels transmitted at 2.048Mbps. HDSL is *symmetric,* which means it provides the same bandwidth both upstream and downstream. Its speed is 1.544Mbps over two copper pairs and 2.048Mbps over three copper pairs. HDSL is an alternative to repeater T1/E1 lines. HDSL has a 15,000-foot operating distance but signal repeaters can extend the range. HDSL is ideal for connecting PBX systems, POPs, Internet servers, and campus-based networks.

SDSL (Single-Line Digital Subscriber Line). Also supports symmetrical T1/E1 transmissions using a single copper pair wire with a maximum operating range of 10,000 feet. SDSL is good for videoconferencing or collaborative computing.

ADSL (Asymmetric DSL). Allows more bandwidth downstream than upstream, which makes it ideal for applications such as video on demand, remote LAN access, and Internet access. It supports rates as high as 8Mbit/sec downstream (users typically download more than they send) and up to 16 and 640Kbps upstream. Also, it supports voice and data simultaneously, and carries voice at lower frequency (as does HDSL) so it doesn't impact data throughput. ADSL transmits at distances of up to 18,000 feet over one wire pair and optimal speeds of 6 to 8Mbps are achieved at distances from 10,000 to 12,000 feet using standard 24-gauge wire.

Rate Adaptive DSL (RADSL). These newer versions of ADSL enable the modem to adjust the speed. RADSL operates at the same transmission rates as ADSL but adjusts dynamically to varying lengths and qualities of twisted-pair access lines.

ISDN DSL (ISDSL). The cheapest and slowest DSL provides end-to-end connectivity over the public switched telephone network.

VDSL (Very High Speed DSL). Provides downstream speeds of 13 to 52Mbps and upstream rates of 1.5 to 2.3Mbps over a single copper pair wire. It delivers voice, video, and data for operating distances of 1000 to 4500 feet. VDSL is primarily used for high-definition television program delivery and multimedia Internet access.

Dial-Up Services Example

One university currently offers dial-up services for nearly 4000 users per day. The enterprise-wide MAN (Metropolitan Area Network, which is a city-wide network linking together multiple LANs) connects to the Internet with a T1 trunk. The university provides terminal access, a 24-hour SLIP/PPP dial-up connection, and a remote node dial-up connection with restrictions on time and use.

The dial-up resources consist of five modem pools totaling 400 modems. The modems support 9600 to 28,800bps from telephone lines. While this is serviceable, at the moment, growing needs demand this university upgrade connections and equipment. It is currently planning to upgrade the Internet connection for T3 speeds for 20 times the bandwidth increase.

Figure 2.2 A pair of ADSL modems create a digital subscriber line over phone lines.

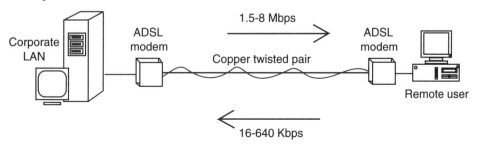

customers, but the number is growing. Cable modems provide high bandwidth at an affordable price. Offices with 25 or less users and even individual telecommuters will find this remote access method useful. Cable modems may be difficult to find, however. Also, security isn't all that it should be for corporate use.

Cable modems present speeds of 10 to 30Mbps downstream and 128Kbps to 10Mbps upstream for a distance of up to 30 miles over coaxial lines. Cable modems are primarily used for Internet access by private consumers for residential use.

Modem Guidelines

What should you look for in a modem? Following are some guidelines:

Buy known brands of modems and steer away from cheap, no-name brands. Cheaper modems will always cost you more in the long run—setup will likely be very difficult, tech support will likely be nonexistent, and driver updates may never be executed.

Check online support of the modem before purchasing one. The Internet is the usual source of updated drivers and often technical support, so make sure the manufacturer is generous with information and help on the Web.

Pay the better price. Popular name brand models are sometimes expensive but well worth the price. Support is better, firmware upgrades are easier to obtain, quality is better, and the manufacturer is likely to stay in business for a long time to come.

Remote Connections

You can connect two computers for remote access by a phone line, dedicated leased line, or through a network connection. A modem connection transmits data over standard telephone lines to another computer with a modem. A dedicated leased line uses an ISDN, frame relay, Fractional T1, or similar line to connect two computers directly. Leased lines provide fast connections, usually carrying data at speeds from 56Kbps to 10Mbps.

Frame Relay

Frame relay is good for tying larger branch offices to a corporate net, as opposed to a leased line or modem connection. Cost and performance are the

> **NOTE**
>
> Lines can be dedicated for a permanent connection, or switched for a connection on an as-needed basis.

main reasons to use frame relay. Frame relay supports speeds of 56Kbps; public frame relay is less expensive than private dedicated frame relay. Other advantages: frame relay is highly scalable, it's not distance-sensitive, and voice as well as data can be carried over it.

Disadvantages of frame relay: the equipment is a bit more expensive than analog dial-up and some ISDN equipment, and the quality of the voice transmission is not the best. Hopefully, these conditions will improve over time.

ISDN

Small businesses and telecommuters can make good use of an ISDN BRI line. ISDN provides good digital quality and it is available almost everywhere. Bandwidth for BRI is limited to 128Kbps, however, and that is at a relatively high cost; but bandwidth and performance are greatly increased.

ISDN PRI (Primary Rate Interface) gives you 23 B channel (64Kbps) connections, equivalent to a T1 or E1 circuit. Naturally, PRI is more expensive than BRI but also provides higher bandwidth, up to 1.536Mbps.

In the case of ISDN, you'll need to find a third-party provider with an ISDN network infrastructure from whom you get a circuit that's terminated at your server or router location. You supply an interface card to support the connection. Then your remote users dial the provider and the call is switched to your host site.

X.25 Technology

X.25 is a packet-switching technology that is available just about everywhere and designed for WAN connectivity. X.25 enables you to multiplex multiple inbound calls into virtual ports on the server. You use an interface card for the remote access server to interface with an X.25 connection. The remote node software (such as NT RAS or NetWare Connect) has drivers that work with the card and control the available virtual ports.

You must also make sure that X.25 is compatible with your NOS, and the COS, and that the service provider you use supports X.25.

Fractional T1, T1

A T1 line is a high-quality communications circuit that you can lease. It provides 24 channels of 64Kbps for a total bandwidth of 1.544Mbps. Although expensive to install and maintain, T1 provides a fast and reliable link to the Internet. Corporate offices can use this connection method successfully for connecting a large number of remote users. T1 is ideal for a virtual private network connection because it does support multiple protocols (including PPP and frame relay). Security is also good.

To connect a T1 line, you need a CSU (Channel Service Unit), a DSU (Data Service Unit), a multiplexor, and a bridge or router. The CSU/DSU prevents faulty equipment from affecting the transmission systems and converts local area network signals to the T1 signaling formats. A multiplexor loads multiple channels of voice or data onto the T1 line, and the bridge or router provides the actual connection points between your LAN and the T1 system.

> **NOTE**
>
> A Fractional T1 is a subchannel of a T1. You can purchase one or more fractional lines and add to that as your needs increase. Naturally, Fractional T1 lines are a small part of T1 so the speed is less, but they may be just what you need for connecting remote users.

Understanding Virtual Private Networks

Virtual Private Networks (VPNs) are becoming more and more popular because they save a company money, an administrator time and effort, and the user frustrations. A virtual private network is a connection between remote users and a corporation's LAN, using a private and secure path across a public network system, such as the Internet. Using an already established connection line and compatible protocols, a remote user can access his company's network resources quickly and with little corporate investment in equipment, administration, and/or technical support. This section defines VPNs; for more information about planning to use a VPN, see Chapter 3 of this book, "Planning Strategies."

Remote Access Protocols

When connecting remotely to a VPN by modem, or dial-up, you connect using a remote access protocol. SLIP, PPP, and PPTP are just a few of the remote access protocols you can use. SLIP (Serial Line Internet Protocol) is an older communications protocol used in UNIX environments and it doesn't provide automatic negotiation of network configuration and encrypted authentication that PPP can provide.

PPP (Point-to-Point Protocol) is a set of protocols that are used by dial-up connections, often in relation to remote access and Internet access. If the server complies with the PPP standard, remote computers running PPP can connect to those servers for network access. The PPP architecture enables clients to load other protocols such as TCP/IP, IPX, and NetBEUI as well.

PPTP (Point-to-Point Tunneling Protocol) supports virtual private networks to enable remote users secure access to corporate networks across the Internet. Virtual Private Networks are also called *tunneling* or *extranets*. The VPN enables an organization to use a public data network for some or all of the WAN communication needs.

Advantages of the VPN

A VPN requires less equipment and fewer lines than a private network because the service provider furnishes much of the equipment. Also, the service provider maintains and repairs the connection lines, modems, and other equipment on its end so you have less expense there as well.

VPNs require less administration. All you have to do is prepare the remote users and the equipment on your end. Keep your remote server going and let someone else worry about troubleshooting the connections to the Internet. VPNs are also extremely flexible in that you can choose from a variety of technologies, depending on what your service provider offers. You can tie into an ISP's connections, for example, with different lines and devices. VPNs also provide worldwide reach to remote users, whether they travel to the next town, state, or even to another country.

Outsourcing the management of a VPN to an ISP saves a company the expensive of private dial-up configurations such as modem pools, unending reconfiguration, long distance phone bills, and so on. Figure 2.3 shows the possibilities for communication over a VPN by using the Internet as the network backbone.

VPNs use security methods that make it safe for your company network to exchange information with your remote users. Authentication methods—such as RADIUS and tokens—mean your data is encrypted and therefore well-protected from hackers on the Internet. The next section explains more about security methods involved with remote access and with virtual private networks.

Figure 2.3 A mobile user can communicate with anyone on the corporate virtual private network.

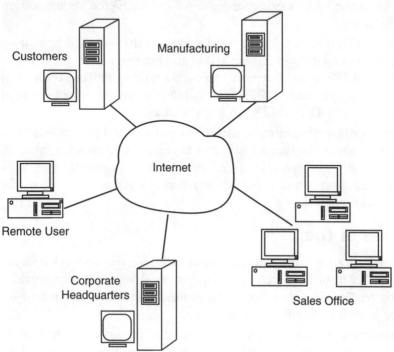

Security

Anytime you open your network to outside influences, whether it's the Internet, an extranet, or remote access, you must take precautions to protect your valuable data and resources, and your users. At the same time, you don't want to make it difficult for your remote users to access the network resources. Simple passwording is almost always supported in remote access software; however, clear text passwords are easily sniffed out by hackers and thus provide a serious threat to your network.

Callback systems can help with your security. With callback, the remote user dials the server and checks in. The server then hangs up and calls the user back at a predetermined number. The problem with this type of system, however, is that the user must be at that location, so mobile users are left out of the loop. Another problem is that someone else could break in and use the remote computer to call the network without proper authentication.

There are other security options you can employ with remote access, though. Authentication services provide the best security for your system.

Authentication

Authentication requires remote users to enter a username and password upon connecting to the remote access server. For remote access, there are password protection options that can help guard the system: PAP (Password Authentication Protocol) and CHAP (Challenge-Handshake Authentication Protocol).

PAP is a basic authentication in which the user enters a name and password and that information is compared to a database on the server for authentication. Passwords are encrypted on the server, but the user transmits the word to the server in clear text that is readable by hackers.

CHAP takes care of this limitation by allowing users to send encrypted passwords to the server. CHAP uses a challenge-response mechanism to authenticate the user on the network. Each user's system calculates a value using some algorithm and then passes that value to the server. The server compares the value to its record for that user and if it matches, the user is allowed access to the network. With CHAP, no passwords are sent across the wire.

There are variations of CHAP, such as running tokens across the network and RADIUS.

RADIUS

RADIUS (Remote Authentication Dial-In User Service) is a method of consolidating and centralizing the authentication, authorization, and accounting (AAA) of remote users. A RADIUS database of VPN user profiles includes data about the user's access privileges, passwords, tunneling parameters, and so on. RADIUS provides for a central point of control that enables better network security and less administrative overhead.

Additionally, RADIUS provides the following:

- Token-card security

- High-performance scalability

- Database storage interfaces

- Fault tolerance

- Policy-based controls

Some available RADIUS server products support several modes of authentication; for example, the server could compare login information against a local database that contains user information. Or if you use Novell Directory

Services or Microsoft's NT, RADIUS servers can pass login data to these servers to authenticate the user. This way, you would only have to maintain one database of user information.

Tokens

Another type of authentication for remote users employs *tokens*. These tokens display a randomly generated number in specific time intervals. The tokens are synchronized to a server in the company so that the user makes the connection and enters his or her username and the number displayed on the token at that moment. The number must agree with that of the server at that time or the user is denied access.

> **NOTE**
>
> *Payload security* is how the data carried over the line is protected. You can use a third-party application to encrypt data, but this uses more processing power on both the server and the client.

Miscellaneous Security Issues

It's important to remember that telecommuting users have locally stored company information on disk and may receive sensitive information about the company, customers, or coworkers via remote access. You'll want to plan some policies for the protection of this material and compile them in a telecommuting agreement. The remote user must take responsibility for security issues, more so than when working at the office.

Limit remote users' access to the network resources. You might, for example, limit remote users to email or give them read-only rights to some resources. You don't need to give remote users access to everything; that's why authentication is important with dial-up and Internet access.

Planning Strategies

In addition to understanding the technologies for remote access, you need to ask yourself some questions about what you need now and in the future, how your users will implement the remote access, what management techniques you will employ, and so on. Are you connecting one user or a branch office? Can you handle the management of your remote access network or should you outsource it? Will the equipment you currently have in place be of any use for remote access?

After you answer these questions and a few more, you should have an idea of the direction you want to take with remote access. Planning ahead means assessing current needs and planning for the future. This chapter offers some questions and advice to help you outline your remote accessing needs. This chapter covers the following:

*   Questions to ask about user needs, network and connection issues, and management considerations

*   Information about virtual private networks and outsourcing remote access

*   Security concerns for VPNs and dial-up access

Planning for Remote Access

When planning remote access, you want to consider purchasing more hardware, faster connections, and configuring for more users than you think you'll need. Whenever you add mobile users, the internal users decide they need at least occasional remote access; when you add occasional remote access, more users want even more access. You can figure that almost all of your employees will require at least intermittent remote access at some point, thus making it difficult to accurately calculate the hardware you'll need, but necessary to consider for the future.

Additionally, Web browsing has become a legitimate business application. If you're not currently using the Internet, you may soon need to add Internet access to your remote network. Remote-node-to-LAN connection ports, high-speed lines for Internet and intranet links, routing, and firewall protection should also be in a plan for the future.

> **TIP**
>
> Larger internetworking suppliers—like Cisco Systems or 3Com—have excellent products, solutions, and technical help; they are also very expensive. You may want to check into some of the smaller vendors for internetworking solutions before choosing the one best suited to your company's needs.

As file sizes increase and business needs expand, your users will always need more speed. Whereas you previously could get by with a 28.8Kbps modem for a couple of users, growing needs demand an ADSL modem and ISDN line to serve your users now and in the near future.

As your number of users and their needs grow, so will your need for more bandwidth, available ports, and such. As you add more equipment to your remote access network, you add more expense and administrative time. Eventually, you'll want to consider outsourcing your remote access. While outsourcing is expensive, it is well worth the cost in the long run. Consider the equipment prices, installation and support, and ongoing management of remote access; if a service provider furnishes the services and equipment you need and manages the remote access, outsourcing may be the answer you're looking for.

Don't plan for the minimum in remote access. Plan for the maximum, plan for the future. You'll be surprised at how quickly you'll use that remote access technology.

User Considerations

Think about your users when you're planning remote access and choosing technologies. You want to make connection easy on remote users, but you also want to optimize the connections and equipment. Consider the following when planning remote access:

Will users be implementing applications remotely? If so, what are the requirements of those applications for bandwidth, speed, and so on?

Are your remote users PC literate? If not, you'll need to make sure you have the easiest connection software, the server is easy to navigate, and so on. If the users are fairly experienced with computer, network, and remote access use, you have a lot more options for connections, equipment, and procedures.

How much user support and training will you need to provide, both for the remote user and any inhouse user who will assist the remote user? Support of untrained, nontechnical users can be time-consuming and costly.

Outline the steps the user must go through for logging in to see if the process is reasonable or long and difficult.

Check connection time to make sure it is quick and stable.

Network and Connection Issues

Think about your network, servers, and the connections between the office and the remote user and try to plan ahead for any choices you'll need to make. Following are some suggestions to think about:

How many connections will there be at the same time, on average? If only one or two users connect at the same time, bandwidth, connection lines, server equipment, and software requirements will be less than if 20 or 200 users connect at the same time.

Can you arrange for bandwidth only when it's required or would it be better to purchase a set amount of bandwidth and only use it part-time? Examine your users and their general needs for help with this question.

Check all protocols, platforms, and software applications to make sure they are compatible and supported.

Does your remote access server and other equipment integrate into your existing network?

Make sure the remote access solution is scalable for substantial increases in user numbers and traffic.

Can you combine technologies and connectivity solutions to make a more effective and efficient remote access service?

Make sure you consider security of your network, sensitive files, and other resources whenever you think about your remote access solutions.

Are data types going to be text or graphical?

Will there be several users connected from the same location (as in a branch office)?

Installation and Management Considerations

In planning the remote access for your network, you want to implement a system that doesn't take all of your administrative time. Remote access is important, but it's also a small part of the overall network and you have plenty of other duties to perform. Find a solution that is easy to install and manage. Following are some more things to think about:

Make sure the local and remote equipment is easy to configure and maintain.

Will you need additional drivers and/or modem scripts? Will they be simple to configure and maintain?

Can you use login scripts or executable modules to configure local or remote equipment?

Ask your vendor(s) about any diagnostic equipment and applications he provides. You'll need management, monitoring, and reporting applications as well.

Also, find out how much control you have over the equipment, routers, and servers. Can you reboot remotely, for example, or reset ports?

Avoiding Bottlenecks

Your network traffic will increase with the addition of remote access users, so you must consider planning for this change. If you're currently using 10Mbps Ethernet technology, you'll want to upgrade to Fast Ethernet or FDDI (Fiber Distributed Data Interface). Following are some elements that affect the rate of data transfer across the network:

- 10Mbps Ethernet connections
- Connecting multiple remote offices
- Bandwidth associated with each connection
- Not enough connections

The Ethernet connection receives all streams of data from remote sites and directs them into one gateway; if there's too much data, traffic backs up. Ethernet has a transport rate of 10Mbps (actual throughput is about 6Mbps).

With T1, ISDN, and other lines streaming data in at speeds up to 1.544, current Ethernet connections can't handle the bandwidth demand.

Fast Ethernet and FDDI can help handle the large capacity load. Fast Ethernet is 100Mbps and so can open the gateway for multiple, simultaneous remote users. FDDI also offers 100Mbps throughput; however, because of FDDI's features and design, it makes a better choice if you can afford it. FDDI isn't collision-based, like Fast Ethernet; rather FDDI supplies bandwidth on an as-needed basis as the bandwidth increases. You might consider using FDDI as your corporate network backbone, now or at some point in the future.

> **NOTE**
>
> You can add 10/100 10BaseT cards to your network nodes in preparation for a switchover to Fast Ethernet, especially if you cannot afford to switch all at once.

VPNs—Internet Remote Access

Depending on your needs, basing your remote access system on the Internet, as in a virtual private network, may be the best strategy for you. A VPN is easier to manage and build than most other remote systems, mainly because your service provider can take a lot of the responsibilities for administration and the initial creation of the system. For more information about VPNs, see Chapter 2 of this book, "Terminology and Technology."

Using a VPN over the Internet means the user can connect to any place, anyone, and at any time, inexpensively. Also, the network can utilize a greater variety of remote applications and leave the management to someone else.

Following are some more advantages of using a VPN:

- No long-distance phone calls; charges for local calls and ISP access fees are all the corporation pay.

- Reduction of network complexity, administration, and support for the network administrator.

- Lower demand for remote access technical help; help calls are transferred to the ISP help desk.

- Provides a consistent architecture for all remote users, no matter where they are.

- Reduced cost of technology upgrades since ISP is providing much of the technologies.

Of course, there are disadvantages to using the Internet. Security is always a concern, even when there are multiple encryption methods for use. Secure remote access over a VPN is only possible if several security technologies are combined to authenticate users and encrypt data traveling over the Internet. Also, performance over the Internet is unpredictable for the most part. Heavy traffic may slow the connection for the VPN user as well. Finally, there is no guarantee of the bandwidth over the Internet; connections are dependent on many things, all of which you have no control over.

Defining a VPN

VPNs use dedicated, secure paths, or tunnels, that ease the transmission of data between the local POP and the corporate network. A VPN doesn't make economic sense for local telecommuters since they're making calls associated with a flat tariff; the public-switch telephone network is most cost-effective in this case. But for users on business trips, long-distance calls make connection to the network more expensive. In this case, VPN technology is more economical.

Tunneling

Tunnels are containers that condense packets, and thus turn into a new IP packet header that contains the destination address. *Tunneling* provides a method of transmitting private IP and non-IP applications (like IPX) over the Internet and enables controlled access.

Tunneling guarantees authentication via encryption. Popular tunneling protocols include PPTP, L2TP (Layer 2 Tunneling Protocol), ATMP (Ascend Tunnel Management Protocol), and Mobile IP for tunneling SNA packets in IP. IPSec (IP Security) offers digital certificate authentication and encryption and is considered to be perfect for financial applications on the Net, such as the safe transport of credit card information.

Outsourced VPNs usually use the gateway mode of tunneling, which requires that the edge device provide IP routing and firewall protection. This means that since no other features are required, you can probably fully outsource for a VPN; the ISP carries all of the responsibility for the configuration and running of the VPN.

> **NOTE**
>
> When you select PPTP filtering, you disable the network interface card for all other protocols, thus ensuring secure access. In addition to enhanced security, PPTP offers lower transmission costs and administrative overhead. PPTP uses Password Authentication Protocol (PAP) and the Challenge Handshake Authentication Protocol (CHAP) encryption algorithms.

A bona fide VPN network consists of authenticated and encrypted tunnels over a shared data network; typically, IP networks and the Internet. The network access point encapsulates packets sent by the mobile user so that the data travels securely over the shared network.

Security and Authentication

User authentication and data security are always a concern when your corporate data is at stake. User authentication is best performed at your LAN or WAN so the user database need not be exported to a service provider. Most basic authentication validates passwords using various methods of encryption such as PAP (Password Authentication Protocol) or CHAP (Challenge Handshake Authentication Protocol), and token cards and keys or digital certificate technologies. For more information about these encryption methods, see Chapter 2 of this book, "Terminology and Technology."

RADIUS is another method of protecting data and the network. With RADIUS, corporate users dial in to a remote access server acting as a gateway to the VPN; the server challenges the caller; information is routed to a Remote Authentication Dial-in User Service (RADIUS) server in the corporate network for authentication, authorization, and accounting. The corporate customer retains control of the authorization database, updating when necessary without relying on the service provider. See Chapter 2 of this book, "Terminology and Technology," for a full description of RADIUS.

Tokens are also used as a method of protection during authentication. See Chapter 2 of this book, "Terminology and Technology," for more information. Digital certificates are yet another method of providing security for information traveling over the Internet. Digit certificates identify users to ensure the successful transfer of encrypted communication using an X.509 standard. IPSEC (Internet Protocol Security) provides network layer encryption and authentication and is slated to be a part of IP version 6.

> **TIP**
>
> Firewall use is common in implementing VPNs. Firewalls provide encryption on the servers and within routers. Implement firewalls in both the central and remote site for the most effective protection.

VPN Management

Managing a VPN is a huge task, much of which is just making entries into the authentication server and firewall software and setting up user billing and accounting. Outsourcing your VPN may be the most beneficial move you can make, depending on your network, users, and setup. VPN technology enables you to cut telecommunications costs, increase mobile worker productivity, and ensure continued scalability of the company's remote access offering.

> **TIP**
>
> In addition to ISPs, phone companies often provide a VPN service that provides secure dial-up access, managed firewalls, routers, network-based address protection, user authentication, and packet filtering. The phone company sets up the VPN at the edges of its public IP backbone network. Outsource VPN management and planning to ease help desk management, support and administration for dial-up numbers, and equipment.

In planning the management of the VPN, you'll need to consider your user training and help base. You might expand telephone support for remote users so they can call in to the company when they need help. Phone support is another task you can outsource or confer to the service provider; however, the service provider will only support the technologies directly related to its connections and such.

You can also provide CD-ROM–based training, books, or guidelines on the subject, or inhouse training or inservices periodically for remote users. Add a page or two of tips and techniques to your company's Web page for remote users to access.

Dial-Up or VPN?

When you're trying to decide whether to use a dial-up and modem connection or a virtual private network, you'll have to consider your users, the applications and tasks the users will perform, your time constraints, the networking environment, and so on. Following are a few things to think about as you make your decision:

User needs. How many users will connect? How much access time will each need? Will users connect simultaneously? How computer literate are your users? Which applications and data will be accessed and how often?

Ease of implementation. Which method makes more sense when you think about your current technology and equipment? What is the availability of connection lines and equipment in your area? Talk to other companies in your area, service providers, and so on, to see what is available and what is working for others.

Complexity of administration. Do you, or any of your network assistants, have the time and training to completely manage the remote access service? Can you configure the equipment and software, maintain it, monitor the service, and troubleshoot problems? Would it be easier and more cost-effective to outsource by VPN?

Security. How much sensitive material will be accessed remotely? If you were to use a VPN, can you trim the sensitive material away so there isn't as much risk? Are you comfortable with the security features, or can you enhance them?

Performance. Will modems and the speeds of dial-up connections be enough to transport the applications, data, and other information remote users will need?

Adequate technical support. Can you, or someone in your company, support the technology? If you can't support it but you can manage and problem-solve the connection choice, can you outsource the technical support for remote users?

Cost of ownership. What is your current inventory of remote access equipment? Can you upgrade and get satisfactory performance more cheaply than by purchasing new equipment? How much will the equipment for each technology cost? How much time investment for each technology will be involved?

Security

Remote access software anywhere on the network presents the potential for a break-in; the remote access server could be at risk as well as any other server attached to the RAS server. You must use safeguards within the network in addition to training users to employ the appropriate security measures. Passwords, encryption, callback, and other security measures can protect your network; some can even lead to a false sense of security when hackers try to break in to your system.

Miscellaneous Issues

The password is the most common safeguard, and the easiest to break. With just some knowledge about the user, a hacker can guess a password or even run a dictionary program against the password prompt. Make sure users change their passwords often, use a combination of numbers and letters for their password, and never give their password to anyone. Even with all of the precautions you might take, passwords should only be considered the first line of defense.

Using a separate login and password for the host computer's network connection can also be helpful. If a hacker breaks in to the host system, this may keep him or her confined to the files on a single computer. Only the administrators should know the login, but then you would have to supply everything the remote user needs on the host computer.

Using firewalls on both sides of the remote access computer is another method of protecting your network. A firewall sits on the edge of the network to protect the private LAN from unauthorized individuals while allowing trusted external parties to access network resources. Firewalls can filter data by protocol, data stream, source, and destination, providing flexibility with protection.

You can implement routers (acting as firewalls) to facilitate transparent access to and from the network and to restrict access through the router from specific facilities. All traffic must travel through a router, so it makes sense to let a router perform some of your security at the same time. For example, you can instruct a router to restrict incoming communications to a single network server or to specific services on the server.

Encryption is a method of scrambling data so that hackers cannot easily determine the contents. Encrypted authentication of the remote user protects the network and the user. You might also consider encrypting all data files on a computer connected with a dedicated remote access link. Use Symantec's Norton For Your Eyes Only, for example, to automatically encrypt files when they're closed from the application.

Callback capability is a handy security feature. Remote users call in and request a callback; the server can then verify the phone number and call the computer back. A similar system for Internet-based remote-access configuration is for the remote user to have a fixed IP address. The server must then confirm that the remote system has the correct IP address during the login process.

As extra precautions, the administrator should also log all accesses on the host systems to help determine which files were accessed and help track down a hacker in case of a break-in.

More on Passwords

Passwords are the least effective method of security. Many users write their passwords down and leave them in an obvious place, like on the back of their keyboards. Anyone with office access, then, can find a user's password and get into the system without detection.

A static password—one password that is used continuously over time—is the best target for a hacker to break your first line of defense. Outsiders may randomly guess the password, use a dictionary program to discover the password, or use programs called *sniffers* to find the password that is often hardcoded in the system. You could implement token or RADIUS authentication to make it harder for someone to break in to the system.

Also, *Challenge/Response* is the strongest implementation of password technology. Challenge/Response improves security, streamlines security management, and reduces the costs of safeguarding remote access. The user enters a PIN (Personal Identification Number) to unlock the token. The user ID is sent to the secure server. The secure server sends a random number (challenge) to the software token. The token encrypts the challenge and sends the response to the secure server. The server verifies the correct response and then gives the user access to the network resources.

There are also hardware tokens that look like calculators; they are expensive and easy to lose. Also, hardware tokens take several steps to log on with and are difficult for nontechnical employees to use. They are platform independent, though, and very portable. Software tokens streamline security management and are easier for the user, are less expensive and don't wear out, and are less likely to be lost.

CLIENT, SERVER, AND NETWORK PREPARATIONS

Chapter

4

In preparing for implementing remote access services on your network, there are several steps to take to complete the process. The following task list briefly describes these steps:

Allocate a server or router as the remote node host. Consider having a redundant host available for high-traffic relief or in case of a downed server. Attach the host to your network on one side and the communications line on the other side.

Acquire asynchronous or synchronous connections to the phone network; connect modems to your host or install a leased line with DSU, for example. If using a VPN, contact a service provider, then order equipment and services.

Set policies and guidelines for remote access.

Configure remote clients. Train users, prepare a help desk or similar technical source of help for users. Review policies and guidelines with users.

Set up host security (authentication). Enter remote users' information, check rights and permissions, make sure all sensitive files are protected. Set up a firewall.

This chapter offers information about the hardware you'll need to make remote access possible, plus some advice about connections, modems, client computers, RAS servers, and such. In this chapter, you learn about the following:

- Remote servers
- Modems and remote devices
- Routers and bridges
- Client computers and remote access
- Client operating systems

Network Equipment

After you decide on the connection type you'll use for remote access, you'll have to decide on the equipment that must be added to your network in order to connect and efficiently access remote users. The connection type governs the equipment you use; see Chapter 2 of this book, "Terminology and Technology," for more information.

Before purchasing any equipment, check with your service provider, phone company, and vendors, to see if anyone supplies equipment—modems, terminal adapters, routers, and so on—for your use if you subscribe to their services or buy certain other equipment from them. Many ISPs, for example, supply routers when you subscribe to a connection for use as a VPN.

Figure 4.1 illustrates how you might connect various remote clients and offices. Within the corporate office is a remote access server that directs all remote access requests. Analog links attach a remote PC and its modem to a switch, which then attaches to the remote access server. Connected to the remote access server are clients using an analog modem, ISDN lines, and a 56K modem. Two remote clients use a 56Kbps connection to the LAN via a router and a CSU/DSU. Note another CSU/DSU must terminate the line at the other end before sending the messages to the remote access server. The same is true for the ISDN connections, whether they are attached by ISDN router or by ISDN-TAs (Terminal Adapters).

RAS Servers and Equipment

There are many solutions to a RAS server, from a very basic PC set up as a modem server to a high-performance RISD processor with multiple ports and interfaces. Following are some ideas for RAS servers.

You can set up a dedicated PC as a modem server that would house a modem(s) or a multiport serial card. The multiport serial card is usually bundled with management software, enables at least 28,800bps with little error, and requires only one interrupt for all channels. Instead of a multiport card, you could use a port switch, which is simpler technology and less expensive. The switch allows a modem to be connected to a master port in the switch, which connects to one of four data terminal ports.

An alternative is to use a third-party modem-server software that supports your operating system and various protocols, and manages either multiple modems or multiport serial cards. In the case of multiple modems, the modems tend to share ports and/or modems.

Figure 4.1 Many solutions for remote access exist.

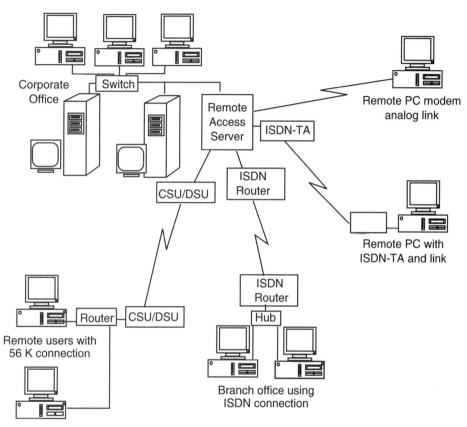

Depending on the size of your remote user network, you may want to use a server built for and dedicated to remote access. You can find any number of computer servers for RAS, from a Pentium 300 Intel processor to a 200 MIPS processor. The size and strength of the server depends on your needs.

Digital communications servers are becoming popular now. Many include support for both digital and analog calls with support for multiple PRI/T1/E1 links, high-performance RISC or MIPS processors, multiple-channel modem cards, TCP/IP LAN interfaces for 10/100BaseT Ethernet connections, and more.

Server Operating System—Windows NT Server

Windows NT Server is a great NOS for extending your company's network to remote users. NT enables users to access your corporate network securely and work, print, and run applications remotely.

A RAS server is a Windows NT computer configured to use the RAS server software included with the NOS that enables remote users to connect to a network over modems. Microsoft operating systems provide either a Remote Access Service client or a Dial-Up Networking client to allow users to connect to remote systems.

Windows NT's Remote Access Services (RAS) presents many features and utilities that make the administration and management of the service effective, including the following:

- Includes RAS as a built-in dial-up service for remote clients.
- Supports up to 255 concurrent RAS connections via multiport serial devices in the server (like Digiboard) connecting to an external modem pool.
- Supports multiple transport protocols over standard PPP facilities: TCP/IP, IPX/SPX, and NetBEUI. Windows 95 and 98 dial-in clients can connect as well.
- Security is handled by NT: PAP and CHAP mean remote users must be authenticated by NT before they can access the network.

The Windows NT RAS Server supports only PPP connections, not SLIP. Serial Line Internet Protocol (SLIP) only supports one network protocol, TCP/IP, and provides no error checking or compression; SLIP is however still used in UNIX environments. PPP provides fast and reliable remote communication using multiple network protocols. Unlike SLIP, PPP provides both error correction and data compression.

Modem Pools

Modem pooling, or *nesting*, is a method of providing multiple modems to remote access users. Generally stored in a rack, a device holding multiple modems and/or modem cards enables multiple users simultaneous access. Each modem pool has a defined set of data transmission characteristics (speed, lines, and such). Some perform digital-to-analog and analog-to-digital conversions, automatic answering, and so on.

When looking for a modem nest, look for hot swapping of cards and power supplies, separate power supplies for redundancy, and support for a variety of modem card types.

ISDN Modems

An ISDN modem, or *terminal adapter*, is built to utilize the high speed available with ISDN BRI (Basic Rate Interface) connections. BRI consists of two 64Kbps channels (B channels) and one 19.2Kbps signaling channel (D channel). Each B channel can be considered a separate line, meaning you can download a file at 64K on one channel and talk to someone on the other B channel at the same time. You can also use both channels at the same time for a combined bandwidth of 128Kbps and even more with integral compression.

xDSL

xDSL modems can be used over existing copper telephone wires, meaning reduced costs for remote access in addition to the high bandwidth offered by DSL technologies. Over clean telephone lines, xDSL can blast data at high speeds from site to site. On lines that are noisy, performance drops off some. Distance limitation inherent in DSL devices is about 12,000 to 15,000 feet; although addition of a repeater may double a modem's maximum reach. A *repeater* is a hardware device that moves all packets from one network to another by regenerating, retiming, and amplifying the electrical signals; the purpose of the repeater is to extend the length of the transmission beyond the normal maximum cable lengths.

When considering xDSL, you must realize that in addition to the limited distances, communications are often hampered by line impairments, such as white noise and near-end crosstalk generated by the presence of other ADSL, HDSL, ISDN, or T1 signals. If you can check with others using the technology in your area, you may be able to find out just how stable and reliable the lines are.

When searching for xDSL modems, be concerned with consistency as well as speed and distance. You might check for lab tests involving several modems to find one that delivers constant, dependable upstream and downstream speeds. *Latency*, or delay that the modem introduces before relaying the data, is another important factor. If latency is high, problems with streaming applications (such as video, interactive data, telephony, and so on) are more likely; when the stream is interrupted, the program can crash. Again, you'll need to check lab and benchmark tests in popular computer magazines to find out about these statistics.

xDSL modems are considerably larger than analog modems or ISDN transceivers, so you must consider this when you're planning. Also, if you've set a power budget for the equipment you install and use, take into account DSL modems consume 8 to 12 watts of power; increased power consumption factors into increased heat dissipation, too.

Currently, the cost of xDSL modems is high; remember, you must buy two modems to form the digital subscriber line. Prices may come down as their popularity increases and the technologies advance; and distances will surely improve as well.

When looking for an xDSL modem, make sure it offers a graphical user interface for management applications, reports, configuration, and diagnostics. Also, check for standard protocol support (PPP and IP), easy upgrades, rate adaptivity (so it adjusts the data transfer rates to the highest speed possible), and a POTS splitter for voice-band support.

CSU/DSU

A CSU/DSU (Channel Service Unit/Data Service Unit) is a digital circuit modem of sorts. Other names for a CSU/DSU device include digital sharing device, digital bridge, multiple-access unit, and modem sharing device. A CSU/DSU provides the termination of a communications circuit from the telephone company into the users' equipment; generally, the circuit is carried over copper twisted pairs. The CSU terminates a digital circuit by performing line conditioning and equalization. The DSU converts the signaling protocol to and from the format used by the user's terminal equipment and the format used by a digital circuit or channel.

When buying a CSU/DSU device, purchase any diagnostic tools and indicators that come with the device. Examples of indicators include methods of reading loopback mode, transmitting and receiving data, control signaling indicators, and so on.

There are many types of CSU/DSU devices and each provides different services. You can buy a CSU/DSU that provides full SNMP management, or works over T1 or frame relay, or supports speeds of 2400 and 56,000, or maintains analog or digital; this is another list that goes on and on. Be careful if you must purchase the device; get some technical help and planning advice.

Routers and Bridges

Although you can use either bridges or routers with your remote access network, routers provide the best value for your dollar. Bridges may, however, fit

Data Compression

The purpose of *data compression* is to reduce the number of bytes of data that are stored or sent without changing or losing any data. Data compression programs can reduce data to the smallest number of bytes, compress quickly, decompress quickly, or any combination of the three; some programs can even perform all three tasks.

There are basically two types of data compression algorithms: *dynamic* and *static*. The compression ratio is the data's original size divided by its compressed size (X:1 format). The larger the compression ratio, the greater the amount of compression.

Dynamic, or *adaptive*, compression algorithms are usually used in bridges and routers. Dynamic algorithms maximize data throughput of all kinds of traffic, for all applications and all user data. The data stream is constantly monitored for repetitive characters and then the most effective method of compression is used.

Static, or *fixed*, compression algorithms vary with different types of data; for example, the compression ratio may be 4:1 for text but 1.2:1 for executable files.

NOTE

Mobile computing often means slow throughput, dropped connections, and clumsy equipment. You may want to try wireless connectivity for connections to mobile users, say those who stay at hotels or must connect from road sites. Wireless radii for the most part is about 100 miles.

better in your budget; just make sure you understand that security isn't nearly as tight with bridges and your bandwidth will suffer.

Bridges are devices that can connect LANs or networks, using different wiring or protocols by managing the flow of traffic. A bridge reads the address of every data packet. If the address isn't on its local address table, the bridge transports the packet across the bridge. If the destination address is on the bridge's local table, the packet is dropped on the LAN segment where it originated. Bridges cannot, however, make forwarding decisions like routers can, so bridges broadcast packets throughout the LAN, causing noise and using up bandwidth.

A *router* is an intelligent device that sends packets to their destination on the correct LAN segment. A remote router connects beyond its device driver limitations, through a modem or other remote connection. Routers enable many common interfaces that are used in remote access, including ISDN basic rate, FDDI, asynchronous serial PPP and SLIP, and so on. Also, routers support various dial-up interfaces, such as parity, start/stop bits, flow control, transport protocols, terminal characteristics, and such. There are Ethernet-to-Internet routers, high-speed multiport routers, multiport Ethernet switching routers, and the list goes on and on.

Routers are particularly useful for remote access linked by analog or ISDN connections. In addition to the intelligent directing of packets, routers ensure better network security. Anyone with the phone number of your remote access connection can dial a bridge using a matching bridge; however, a router can be configured to filter out certain users, applications, and other traffic.

You can buy routers that handle the common LAN and network protocols—IP, IPX/SPX, PPP, ISDN, and so on. There are routers that are built specifically for T1, 56K support, ISDN, frame relay, and such. Check for appropriate security features, such as password protection, PAP, CHAP, callback, and firewall filtering as needed. You'll also want a menu-driven user interface for network management.

> **NOTE**
>
> If you are using fully integrated ISDN, make sure your router provides the appropriate number of channels, simultaneous voice and data transmission, and supports two simultaneous connections to two different locations. For ISDN with a V.34 modem, you'll need PPP support to 128Kbps, bandwidth on demand, and support of the V.34 protocol for connecting to 128Kbps modems.

Routers are expensive and they're very difficult to set up and configure, no matter what the dealer or documentation says. You'll want to enlist some technical help before purchasing a router. Make sure the manufacturer supplies a toll-free help line, for example, or hire a consultant to help you if you have no router experience.

Although each router requires different hardware, operating systems, and such, generally, you'll need to have a leased line, a CSU/DSU, cable to the LAN, and a PC to set up and run a router.

Multiplexors and Multichannels

Multiplexors and multichannels are two additional equipment types you may need. A *multiplexor* (also called *mux*), is a device that merges several lower-speed transmission channels into one high-speed channel at the end of the link. Another multiplexor reverses the process at the other end of the link to reproduce the low-speed channels.

A *multichannel* interface enables you to concentrate many remote sites at a central site by multiplexing 24, 48, or more channels onto a single T1 line. You add a multichannel interface to a compatible router for transmission and hardware cost savings.

Client Computers

Hardware for remote access client computers can be simple or complex. For remote access computers, you want to purchase hardware that suits the user and the applications. There are some options, however, that you might consider. Hand-held computers, for example offer a variety of options for remote access and computing, depending on the users' needs and skill level. Following are a few suggestions and guidelines for client hardware.

Hand-Helds

Perhaps the simplest method of keeping touch with the office is for the remote user to carry a hand-held, or palm, PC. These small PCs have become very powerful over the last year or two, sporting the Windows CE operating system, supporting a variety of software, and such. Most hand-held computers can perform scheduling, word processing, emailing tasks, and others that are common and necessary in our everyday work life. Additionally, many of these computers offer additional features and utilities, including the following:

- Integrated modem and phone jack

- Integrated speaker and microphone

- Easy-to-use keyboard and stylus

- Synchronization with a desktop or server

- Encrypted multilevel password protection

- Pocket versions of popular desktop applications

Notebooks and Desktops

Generally, the only requirement for a remote user's notebook or desktop computer will be a modem for dial-up services. If you plan to use xDSL, ISDN, or other technology, you'll need to supply the remote user or branch office with the necessary equipment to complete the connection, of course.

As for hardware requirements for the computer, let the applications the user plans to implement be your guide for the amount of CPU, RAM, type of monitor, and so on. Computers with greater memory and faster processors will facilitate the use of remote access, naturally; however, following are some very basic, minimum recommendations for remote access computers.

PC and compatible

> 80486/66 MHz or Pentium processor
>
> 16MB RAM
>
> VGA color monitor
>
> Windows 95, 98, or NT or OS/2
>
> 28.8Kbps or faster modem

Macintosh

> 030 processor or higher
>
> 16MB RAM
>
> Color monitor
>
> System 7.5 or higher
>
> 28.8Kbps or faster

Client Operating Systems

Many modern client operating systems include the utilities needed to connect remotely to a host; if your COS doesn't include that feature, you can likely buy an add-on from the operating system vendor or from a third party. When configuring for remote access, you'll need to know the protocol, network client, and any connection information, such as modem speed, and so on.

> **TIP**
>
> Consider migrating your COSs to one operating system to cut down on the administration of maintaining multiple operating systems and remote access configurations.

Portable Computers and PCMCIA

The PCMCIA (Personal Computer Memory Card International Association) standard is for credit card-sized, plug-in adapters designed for portable computers. There are several versions of the card. Type I card is the thinnest PC card and is used for memory enhancements such as dynamic RAM; Type II is used for modems or LAN adapters; Type III is used for mini hard disks and other devices, including wireless LANs. The majority of PCMCIA devices are modems, Ethernet and token ring network adapters, dynamic RAM, and flash memory cards. The most important characteristics of PCMCIA modems are as follows:

- PCMCIA modems can exist as wireless, or "normal," cable-needed types.

- Either variety of PCMCIA modem operates without relying on the UAR/T chip on the motherboard.

- The "wired" type of PCMCIA modem can run at speeds up to 14,400bps.

- Wireless modems in this group can run as full V.34 devices.

Windows 95/98

Windows 95 and 98 workstations are perfect as remote access clients because of their built-in connection features. Both operating systems include Dial-Up Networking as well as Remote Network Access (RNA) to enable the user to connect to a LAN and use the resources as if he were physically connected rather than remotely through a modem.

Before you configure Dial-up Networking, you must first set up the network client on the workstation, if it is not already configured. Client software is required—the Microsoft client or NetWare client, for example—for the workstation to communicate with the network server. Using the Network dialog box, you can configure the client, the computer name, and domain or workgroup name that are also necessary for network use. Naturally, the user must have permissions and rights on the network server to connect and use the resources.

Configuring Dial-Up Networking includes installing and configuring a modem; you'll need to know modem speed, dial-up access number, connection protocol (PPP for example), compression and encryption information, and so on.

The configuration also includes the type of protocol to use: IPX/SPX, NetBEUI, or TCP/IP. If you choose TCP/IP, there are more options to configure, such as whether the IP address is server assigned, DNS addresses, and so on.

There is also an option for adding scripting to the configuration. A script can automatically log the client on to the network or perform other tasks during the connection.

> **TIP**
>
> Encourage remote users to use IMAP (Internet Message Access Protocol) to reduce the time the user spends retrieving email. IMAP enables the email client software to view headers of messages so the user can decide whether mail with attachments should be downloaded or skipped.

Windows NT Workstation

NT's remote access is similar to Windows 95/98 in setup and configuration. You must, however, enable the remote access service in the Network dialog box (Services tab) as well as configure the client and computer identification.

Dial-Up Networking (DUN) works similarly to Windows 95 in that you need a network adapter card, modem, or X.22 or ISDN adapter card. Configuring DUN means selecting port usage (dial-out or receive calls) and configuring the protocol(s). TCP/IP configuration enables you to use either a DHCP (Dynamic Host Configuration Protocol) host or to manually enter the IP address, subnet mask, and gateway yourself.

A wizard helps you set up the rest of the Dial-Up Networking requirements, including how you will call, encryption information, and so on. You also can use scripts with NT's Dial-Up Networking to automate the login to a host. The script provides the username, password, and any other information you might need.

NT's RAS provides both client and server remote node functionality. NT Workstation includes a RAS server service that supports one inbound connection using IP, IPX, or NetBEUI.

Novell NetWare

NetWare Connect is an add-on package designed to provide dial-in and dial-out capabilities on a Novell network. NetWare Connect supports IPX, IP, and AppleTalk ARAP (AppleTalk Remote Access Protocol) clients. NetWare Connect servers can support up to 128 simultaneous connections, provide authentication using NDS, and provide auditing and management of port usage.

A common solution for remote user dial-up access is to use NetWare Connect with a bank of analog modems and an asynchronous adapter in the NetWare Connect server. These ports can support speeds up to 115.2Kbps.

Login Scripts

A *login script* is a text file that provides specific information the host needs for the client computer to connect, as well as commands, parameters, and expressions that retrieve information from the remote computer. Scripts usually include the following parts: a section header (name of the script), comment lines (notes), commands (orders and responses sent to the host), responses (expected replies to the commands you expect from the host), response keywords (words that specify what to do when a response is received), and macros (special functions or tasks—insert a carriage return, for example).

Following is a sample script for NT:

```
[Responses]
;This section is temporary
;CONNECT:= connection completed ok
;ERROR_DIAGNOSTICS:=connection attempt fails (X-25)
;DIAGNOSTIC:=information will be extracted from the response and
sent to; the user
;ERROR_NO_CARRIER:=remote modem hung up
;ERROR:=responses for general failure
ERROR="BUSY"
OK=
COMMAND=
OK=
;Send userid/password
COMMAND=USERNAME
ERROR_NO_CARRIER="NO CARRIER"
OK="Password:"
COMMAND=PASSWORD
ERROR_NO_CARRIER="NO CARRIER"
OK="granted"
```

The adapter is intelligent and enables high-speed data transfer without high server utilization.

Apple Remote Access

ARA (Apple Remote Access) presents a Personal Server for use with remote access that's easy to use, uses TCP/IP protocols, supports a variety of modems and network types (LocalTalk, Ethernet, and token ring), and enables various levels of security. Additionally, ARA Personal Server provides flexible client capabilities, such as supporting a variety of connections and a variety of client software (PPP for Mac OS and Apple Remote Access Client) and operating systems (Windows and UNIX).

The ARA client is an easy way to connect a Mac OS desktop or notebook to a network from a remote location. The client software enables quick access, onscreen assistance, and lets you work with familiar Mac features like the Chooser and Finder. Also, the client supports AppleTalk and TCP/IP over a single PPP dial-up connection. Flexibility means the client can work with a small workgroup or a large corporation for connections via modems and ISDN terminal adapters.

There are also options for configuring remote access for a Macintosh client and an NT network or NetWare network. As previously mentioned, NetWare Connect supports AppleTalk ARAP (AppleTalk Remote Access Protocol) clients. NT Server supports Macintosh via the PPP client as well.

POLICIES AND PROCEDURES

E ven though the hardware and connection areas of remote access can be daunting, dealing with your users is going to be a major part of remote access administration. Once the connections and equipment are in place, you have less to worry about than you will with ongoing support, technical difficulties, people politics, and other matters that have to do with both the remote access user and the inhouse users left behind.

You can prepare for some problems by forming a procedure and policy document that outlines how you want to handle the situation. List how things will be done, explain how users will behave during work hours, limit accesses, and set forth security rules and guidelines. The better organized you are about your policies now, the easier administration will be in the long run.

This chapter covers the following:

- Administrator and user task lists
- Remote access user policies
- Security policies

Task Lists

There are a multitude of tasks or chores you should perform before sending users out on the road or to their homes to work. Purchasing hardware, contracting connections, installing and configuring software are all major parts of an administrator's to-do list. There are also some tasks for administrators to perform that will help remote users, inhouse users, managers, and others to adjust to remote access networking.

In addition to chores for the administrator, this section includes some advice for the user to make telecommuting a successful and beneficial experience for everyone concerned.

Administrator's To-Do List

You must make sure the person you choose for telecommuting is well-suited to working remotely. Check his or her personal work style. Is he organized? Does she complete jobs on time? Is she self-motivated? Previous job performance will help you determine how well-suited a user might be. Check his or her time management skills as well. Following are some more points to consider:

Make participation in telecommuting voluntary.

Train managers and employees; telecommuting requires initiative from employees and direction from managers.

Write explicit agreements between employees and managers in which you define expected output levels, reporting requirements, time spent in the office, and so on. Review with employees and then have the employees sign them.

Plan the program well; leave no room for doubt in the user's mind as to his or her duties, responsibilities, and job performance.

Promote good communication between managers and remote users, and coworkers and remote users.

Develop a telecommuting policy in which you set measurable objectives and regularly evaluate the results.

Determine remote access policies toward the equipment. Determine, for example, who supplies which equipment, who pays for damaged equipment signed out to a remote user, and so on.

Let inhouse employees know about the policies for remote users.

Meet with remote users to discuss problems periodically.

Evaluate employee performance periodically.

Keep telecommuters in the loop when they're out of the office.

Provide a booklet or instructions on how to solve common problems (or things that can go wrong) and how to fix them, such as replacing a battery, what to do when the modem fails, dialing information, connection data, security concerns, instructions on making and using an emergency boot disk, and other troubleshooting techniques.

Remote User's To-Do List

The remote users have a lot of responsibilities, especially in following your policies and procedures. Following are some extra suggestions to help the user keep in touch and perform his or her job.

Use phones and email to keep in touch with the office and your coworkers.

Be accessible in order to maintain good working relationships with all. Let them know where you will be and how to reach you quickly if necessary.

Manage your time wisely, especially at home; keep a regular schedule.

Establish physical and mental boundaries in your home. Separate office space from home space and work time from personal time. Work in a separate room; set boundaries on the others in your home as well—roommates, children, spouses, and others should respect your work time.

If traveling, protect your equipment by doing the following:

Use hotel safes to store your notebook, routers, and other expensive equipment.

Conceal expensive equipment by not using manufacturer's bags—a travel bag with Cisco Systems imprinted on it announces to technology-aware thieves that you're carrying a valuable router.

Carry your costly equipment with you on the plane, through luggage pickups, and everywhere you go so you can keep your eye on it.

Remote Access Policies

Just as with other facets of network administration and management, you'll need to create policies and guidelines related to remote access and your users. Naturally, the types of limits and controls you assert will depend on your company philosophy, network, security concerns, and other factors. The following are some ideas you may want to include in your policy statement:

Define telecommuting as it refers to your company's needs and your users.

Issue guidelines for the purchase and use of equipment, office furniture, telephone lines, and so on: who owns what, how often are printers cleaned, and so on.

Define your stance on insurance of the remote user, of the equipment, and other resources.

Include a statement about worker's compensation.

Add procedures and recommendations for safety on the job.

List the methods of evaluation for the telecommuting structure.

Define the job duties and tasks for the telecommuter.

Determine how installation and configuration of software and upgrades will be handled.

Make sure you print the guidelines and policies and distribute them to remote users. You should also review the printed material with the employee and then ask the employee to sign a written agreement about your policies and guidelines, to protect yourself legally.

Defining Remote Access Users

Define who can use remote access and who will pay for equipment: The cost of providing remote access services should be paid by the company or shared with staff members depending on the requirements of specific job descriptions. If, for example, employees must be away from the office because of the specific job description, the company will pay the costs; similar considerations may apply to staff who travel extensively. However, if the employee works at home because of preferences, then that employee must share at least some of the cost of equipment and connection.

You probably will want to grant remote access services to technical operations employees who require access to parts of the system for repair or monitoring purposes. The network operations staff, for example, will need remote access to routers and servers. Asking them to come to work at odd hours is inconvenient and stressful and delays repairs; granting remote access and remote control makes better sense. You may need to set policies distinguishing between mission-critical and noncritical problems.

Remote access can also be granted to administrators and/or managers, as well as other groups, for convenience rather than necessity. Email access is useful in such cases.

Legal Issues

Many, many legal issues can be related to employees working away from the office. It's important that you protect your company by considering these issues and forming a policy of some sort. Following are a few things to think about concerning the legal considerations:

What are the legal aspects of employees who injure themselves while working at home? Will you be responsible for work-related injuries or damages to equipment occurring at home or on the road?

How will you deal with overtime? Since the law requires you pay overtime compensation, for example, you may want to limit telecommuters to 40 hours per week.

If applicable, research the Americans with Disabilities Act when facing the prospect of providing accommodations for individuals with disabilities at that person's home.

It's a good idea to check with a lawyer if you have any legal questions or problems with remote access services.

Other Issues

It's perfectly reasonable for you to request the user be available to the office staff during the time the office is running, either by email or telephone. Remote users shouldn't, however, be on call 24 hours a day, 7 days a week.

You should provide training and technical support for your remote users. You may want to send users to a class, provide books or interactive CD-ROM training, or provide a help desk for your users. You can also print a set of general procedures and troubleshooting techniques that will help the users when they cannot get help, on weekends or at night, for example.

Consider developing a printed procedure document for how to obtain data or information from the network, corporate communications guidelines, methods to protect equipment, responsibilities for theft or damage of company equipment, and so on.

Following are some more suggestions:

Make sure you require virus scanning of some sort.

Set procedures for disposition of critical company data (faxes, files, and such) at remote sites.

Require physical security at remote sites.

Require an inventory of company equipment at the remote site. Make sure you have the vendor name and model numbers of all equipment at remote sites.

Verify backups are kept off-site.

Record a process for the return of equipment and proprietary data upon termination of employment.

Users should not use more than one modem line at a time.

Security Policies for Telecommuters

When determining your security policies, you must understand that there will be some trade-off between user productivity and security measures. Your goal is to provide maximum security with minimum impact on user access and productivity—a fine line.

Whereas some security measures such as data encryption do not restrict users' productivity, excess or redundant authorization systems can frustrate users and perhaps even prevent access to the network resources. You must be flexible with the policies, yet strict enough to protect your business. You must be willing to update and revise your policies to reflect technological changes and resource allocations.

Developing a Policy

When developing a security policy for remote access, there are a few things you can do to organize your thoughts and make the task a bit easier. Many of the things you need to do are from within the system—guarantee physical security, limit access, identify the network assets to protect, and so on. But there are also a few user-related steps you can take when developing your security policy.

Determine the points of risk.   Check user rights and permissions on the network, check passwords and expiration dates, limit access to sensitive materials on the network, and so on.

Limit the user's scope of access.   Use firewalls and proxy servers, hide files and directories, and maintain a high level of security for the entire network.

Monitor remote users.   If your security measures are interfering with the use of the system, your users may discover methods of circumventing them.

Make sure your users understand the security procedures and policies. Things such as never tell anyone your password and don't write your password down must be emphasized so users don't unwittingly give their access to the network away.

Sample Policies

Following are a few general suggestions for security policies:

- Remote access may be used for business purposes only.

- Users may not share passwords or access devices. Users other than company employees are not allowed on to the corporate network.

- Users may not download sensitive corporate information for long-term storage on home PCs.

- Users agree to corporation monitoring of systems and networks for security violations.

- The corporation controls all data links to the network.

- All inbound connections must be protected with authentication and encryption.

EXPANDING THE NETWORK

THE INTERNET, INTRANETS, AND EXTRANETS

Book Eight

Introduction to Book Eight

Today's global workplace includes worldwide offices and projects. With team members spread out over different states and even countries, collaboration would be difficult without the Internet. The Internet enables your employees, customers, vendors, technical help, and others to work together efficiently and cheaply.

In addition to using the Internet, intranets and extranets support the sharing of information by allowing you to publish your own information for only those people you want to receive it. You can extend a private intranet or extranet through a virtual private network over the Internet to reach far and wide, all over the world.

Collaboration, information-sharing, virtual meetings, and email contact are all-important in business today, and the Internet helps to make these activities possible. Further, the Internet provides opportunities for expanding your business, advertising your products, and reaching people who would normally never know your company existed. E-commerce, e-malls, online storefronts, banner advertising—the reach of the Internet can help you to promote your business and your company.

The Internet is great, no doubt about it. But how do you plan for it? How do you sort through the technical information? How do you really know what's available as far as Internet services go? This book will help you in all of these areas. In this book, you'll learn the advantages and disadvantages of using the Internet, the difference between intranets and extranets, how to secure your LAN when using the Internet, and more.

This book provides information about protocols, hardware, common terms and uses, as well as advice on how to efficiently incorporate Internet technology into your company. Along with policies, administrative guidelines, suggestions for Web content, and so on, you'll find information about IP addressing and ISP services. This book will give you a head start on planning and organizing your Internet strategies.

PRELIMINARY GROUNDWORK

Almost everyone has a Web site these days. Corporations advertise their sites on TV commercials, in newspaper ads, even on their product packaging. Advertising on the Web reaches a set of potential customers not accessible 10 years ago. Selling over the Web is big business; anyone can reach across the United States or the world to sell their books, software, baseball cards, vitamins, and other products.

Email, mailing lists, newsgroups, and such offer immediate communications with people all over the world. Cheaper and easier than a phone call, email provides an efficient way to contact anyone with an email address at your convenience. Discussion groups, prescheduled meetings, and real-time conferences make the telephone nearly obsolete for those with Internet access.

Research, buying and selling, collaboration and information sharing; the possibilities for Internet use are endless. In this chapter, you learn some of the advantages and disadvantages to using the Internet with your business.

In this chapter, you learn about the following:

- Legal issues
- Internet etiquette
- Future of the Internet
- Advantages and disadvantages of using the Internet

About the Internet

The Internet is made up of multiple networks—including federal, regional, campus, and some foreign networks—that cooperate together to form a larger network for all of their collective users. Using both IP- and even some non-IP-based networks, users can send email, browse the Web, transfer files, and otherwise share information with other connected users all over the world.

The Internet means new ways of doing business, more commercialized use of the information highway, changes in our relationships with other countries and peoples, and so much more. Each day new systems, equipment, software, and such are created to speed up our access, secure our networks, and sell more over the Internet. The technologies are becoming more complex rather than easier to deal with, as some would have you believe.

Where do you and your business fit in? Is it a necessary evil? Will you lose business, customers, and even employees if you don't jump on the bandwagon? Most likely. The Internet is here to stay, so it's time to make your presence known.

Legal Issues

Since the Internet is a global network as opposed to one that's confined to one state or even the United States, you must consider some of the legal issues that affect your company if you choose to do business over the Net. If you're in doubt about any legal issues, you should check with a lawyer before embarking on your business ventures over the Internet.

For one thing, consider exporting goods to other countries. If you're selling products over the Internet to anyone outside of the United States, then you're subject to the same export laws as other corporations. For example, you cannot export anything without a license. Also, there is a list of restricted items that cannot be exported; some encryption codes, for example.

Copyright and patent laws are another consideration. You should carefully research these laws and be careful to get permission before sending, shipping, emailing, or otherwise transporting any literature, books, or writings to another country.

Ethics and Netiquette

Naturally, there are many personal ethics you should hold to for your communications over the Internet, such as no hateful or harassing behavior, no obscenities, and so on. There are also business ethics you should adhere to. Although there is no governing body of the Internet, no Internet police so to speak, the Internet community seems to police itself.

One of the major rules of the Internet is to limit commercialization. Ads, banners, Web pages devoted to businesses are okay because a user can come to your pages, or not; however, spamming is *not* okay. Sending an advertising email to a large group of people over the Internet will more than likely lose business for you than increase business.

Web Site Legalities

If you plan to create a Web site, there are other legal considerations. Say you hire someone to create your Web site for you. You must then form a legal agreement, in writing, that clearly defines rights and obligations of the parties.

The agreement should include the following issues:

Timing. Include a timetable for the site development and any penalties for failure to meet the deadlines. Make sure you list the deliverables with a clear definition of each.

Ownership. If you want to maintain the uniqueness of your site, include in the agreement "work for hire." Otherwise, the developer owns the site, in which case the usage rights should be clearly defined.

Warranties. Make warranties of quality, material, workmanship, and so on, part of the agreement.

Escape clause. Add to the agreement an "out" in case the developer takes too long or the site is not what you wanted. Adding a line about retaining the right to terminate the contract at any time is also a good idea.

Confidentiality. Include a statement to the effect that the developer and his or her employees are required to keep all information confidential.

Maintenance. Include a definition of who will update the site, correct missing links, register with search engines, and other tasks for maintaining the site.

Following are some other considerations, or Netiquette guidelines, to consider when you're doing business on the Internet.

Provide fast and easy access to information for the convenience of the customer.

Don't use large graphics, multiple video or audio files, and other bandwidth consumers unless necessary (see Figure 1.1).

Organize material logically from the viewer's point of view.

Offer a text-only option for your site for users with older systems.

Give something back to the Internet. In addition to advertising your product or services, include helpful information, steps or procedures to useful tasks, or some sort of information that your readers can use.

Figure 1.1 Large graphics take a long time to load and they don't add much to the page.

Never send unsolicited email to a list of users.

Because it's difficult in a text-based message to express humor, sarcasm, surprise, anger, and so on, *communicons* (communication icons) have become popular. Advise your users to use communicons in their email messages to help the recipient to better understand the intent of the message. Following are some common communicons: :) ;) : (:-O and so on.

The Future of the Internet

The Internet is big. Businesses are already scrambling to create a presence on the Internet, to accumulate new customers, keep up with competitors, to train employees, connect with partners, to make money, and more. Clearly, as a growing, thriving business, you need to connect to the Internet if you're not already there. At the very least, email will help your company move into the millennium, but so much more is available to you that you should at least research the possibilities.

Technology is the basis of all things on the Internet. New technologies are being developed every day and old technologies are being improved upon. Java, a multiplatform language developed by Sun Microsystems, is one of the Internet technologies that is taking over. Most programming languages must be compiled for a specific platform—UNIX, Windows, Macintosh, and such—but Java enables communications across platforms. Using Java, a developer can create interactive programs that can communicate with anyone using any type of computer operating system.

NOTE

JavaScript is Netscape's own scripting language. JavaScript enables the development of basic programs within HTML code and serves as an interface to Java applets, among other things.

In addition to new technologies and new business, the Internet provides a rich foundation for new and improved education techniques. Interactive sites, research online, and information of any kind provide students with a wealth of knowledge. Science, too, can benefit from the Internet. Medical research, NASA, astronomy, can all benefit from information-sharing, interactive research labs, and other resources that are available.

Virtual communities already exist on the Internet. Mailing lists, UseNet groups, chat rooms, and such provide people with forums for discussion of their favorite topics, hobbies, and other activities. Virtual workplaces are also becoming more popular as corporations use the Internet to expand their businesses.

Extranets—semi-private networks that corporations share with business partners, vendors, customers, and such—run on Virtual Private Networks (VPNs). Corporations also use the Internet to connect remote users to their private LANs via VPNs. VPNs provide secure channels for businesses to publish catalogs, white papers, and documents of all types to locations all over the world.

Benefits of using the Internet to extend corporations' networks are many: fewer hardware and maintenance costs, less administration time, and perhaps the most important advantage is happier workers and increased productivity. Experts say that the growth of the Internet has added momentum to the telecommuting movement, which will continue to grow well into the millennium.

Figure 1.2 shows a technical support page a business partner might see over a corporate extranet. The company's logo and name appear on every page of the site, so it's easily identifiable. Also, the layout, fonts, graphic lines, and such are similar on all pages of the extranet. For more information about extranets, see Chapter 6 of this book, "Intranets and Extranets."

Advantages and Disadvantages of Using the Internet

Whether you're using the Internet for personal or business reasons, you'll soon find there are a great many activities you can accomplish over the Internet. There are advantages to using the Internet, including entertainment, education, technical knowledge, meeting people, and so on. Of course, there are also many disadvantages to using the Internet, such as credit card security, personal safety, and information risks.

When using the Internet for business purposes, you'll soon learn ways of taking advantage of its services while using technologies and common sense to

Figure 1.2 Provide technical support to customers, business partners, and others who attach to your corporate extranet.

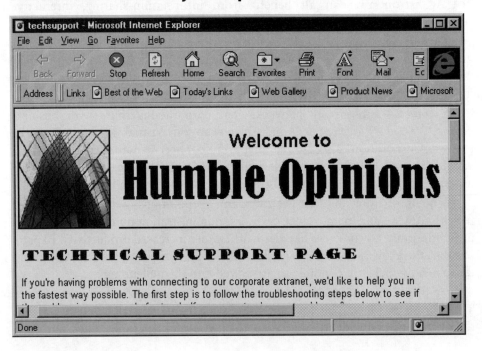

protect you and your company from the hazards and exposure possible from Internet use.

Advantages

The biggest advantage of the Internet is what you can do with it. There are numerous tasks you can perform with email alone; add to that the World Wide Web and the possibilities are endless. As a start to this section, here are some of the things you can do over the Internet:

- Send and receive email
- Transfer files
- Download software programs
- Chat with others in real time
- Read newspapers, magazines, and books online
- Research anything
- Find anything
- Locate people and companies
- Discuss your favorite hobbies, TV shows, technologies, and so on with others
- Play games
- Shop for anything
- Buy anything
- Sell anything
- Watch TV
- Listen to radio shows from all over the world
- Take classes
- Reserve plane tickets, buy opera tickets
- View a weather map

    And the list literally goes on and on and on.

    As far as your business is concerned, there are many more advantages to using the Internet. Your users can stay in contact with colleagues, collaborate, take classes, and research new techniques or technologies. Email enables you to stay in contact with customers, associates, and partners. Advertise your prod-

The Internet and Your Business

Why use the Internet?

- The majority of people on the Internet are educated and come from middle-income families.
- The majority of Internet users use the Web every day.
- Over 1/4 of the total U.S. population now uses the Internet.
- By the year 2000, it is predicted that over 80 percent of businesses will be on the Internet.

The Internet offers instant access to the global marketplace. Your message can be heard 24 hours a day, 7 days a week, meaning the information can be updated easily. Distribute information worldwide in text format, images, video, or audio. Clearly, the Internet is the most cost-effective way to grow your business. After you establish your Internet presence, it will cost nearly the same to contact 10 people as it will to access a million.

ucts and/or services on the Internet. Following are more advantages to getting on the Internet:

- Generate sales leads, access new markets, and reach new customers with the Internet.
  - Stay competitive by researching your competitors, learning new technologies, and keeping informed about the marketplace.
  - Strengthen your corporate image by displaying your technological ingenuity.
- Reach more people with Internet advertisement than with ads in magazines, newspapers, or snail mail.
- Obtain the latest information about sales, promotions, projects, and so on, to pass on to your customers or sales department.
  - Bolster customer service by responding immediately to concerns, requests, and problems.
  - Conduct business with vendors, consultants, and other businesses.
  - Reduce advertising costs and technical support costs.

- Present a constant image of your company on the Web; send newsletters, brochures, announcements, and such by email to your customers.

    - Get customer feedback via surveys, questionnaires, and other methods.

Disadvantages

The major disadvantage of using the Internet in your business is the security problem. You open your company data up to all sorts of risks when you get on the Internet. Fraud, theft, and other crimes run rampant on the Internet. Someone could steal sensitive company information if he or she can get into your system. Some advertisers on the Internet, just as in any business, are not trustworthy and may try to swindle you. Hackers could break into your system or viruses could infect your system and damage data and/or equipment.

Luckily, there are steps you can take to protect your system and your users from unscrupulous people; technological devices and safeguards can protect your data and policies, and outlined procedures can help to protect your users as well as your system.

Expense is another disadvantage of the Internet. You must install various hardware and software to enable users to attach; and there is even more equipment to purchase if you plan a Web site or other Internet presence. You have to contract connection lines, services from a provider, and perhaps server space for your Internet dealings, as well.

There are other disadvantages to the Internet, such as wasted user time, tremendous amounts of disk space and resource usage, and so on. But again, most disadvantages can be canceled out by the precautions and guidelines you set forth. The good more than outweighs the bad.

The three most powerful features of the Web include the capacity to incorporate a variety of media objects into a single document, utilization of hypertext in a document, and the ability to span a variety of client/server platforms. New standards and technologies over the last few years have produced a plethora of new terms related to the Internet—services, hardware, software, and so on. Many of these terms you are familiar with but there are a few definitions that need clarification.

This chapter presents some common Internet technologies and terms and their definitions and use. In this chapter, you learn about the following:

- Internet protocols and services
- TCP/IP terminology
- IP addressing and related technologies

Basic Terminology

The Web is basically a client/server network. Clients, or users who attach to the Net, request information, files, definitions, directions, and other services from servers on the Internet. The servers respond by providing the resource requested; basically, a client/server model for distributed computing.

Using a browser, the client can move from Web server to server and from page to page, viewing the content and moving on to other topics at will. By the adoption of certain standards, the Internet has become accessible to more people and thus more and more popular for personal and business use.

HTML and HTTP

HTML (Hypertext Markup Language) is for formatting documents. You use hypertext to present information within a browser. Using links, the document highlights certain terms or phrases and those enable you to jump to information that is related to the link you just came from.

Hypertext is text with links; instead of referring to a document, you can use a link and the reader can jump to the actual document by clicking the link. You can also create hypertext links to images, sounds, movies, databases, and so on.

HTTP (Hypertext Transfer Protocol) is for transmitting documents from one computer to another. HTTP is the standard protocol that enables a browser or other HTTP client program to retrieve HTML documents from an HTTP server.

Secure Protocols

Secure protocols make communications between clients and servers over the Internet safe by using encryption methods to scramble the data. Secure Hypertext Transfer protocol (S-HTTP) and Secure Sockets Layer (SSL) are two popular protocols that provide security and encryption.

S-HTTP is a protocol for insuring security and encryption over the Web. S-HTTP supports both public-key technology and password technology. S-HTTP is able to authenticate clients and servers, secure communications through corporate firewalls, and support differing layers of security.

SSL negotiates security between a client and a server program before sending or receiving any data, so all data is sent securely. SSL is easy to use, hides the entire communication session so as to increase security, and provides better server authentication than S-HTTP. Also, since SSL is part of the underlying communications layer, it provides more reliable client/server communications.

URL

A *URL* (Universal Resource Locator) is an HTML element that points to another document that is linked to the original. The URL is the linked document's address; a sample URL would be http://www.humbleopinions.com/services/network/index.html (see Figure 2.1). Following is a breakdown of what the parts of the sample URL stand for:

http://   Type of server software that handles the resource; could also be ftp://, gopher://, and so on.

www   World Wide Web.

humbleopinions.com   The domain name, or computer name where the resource is located.

Figure 2.1 Enter the URL in the Address box of the site and page you want to view.

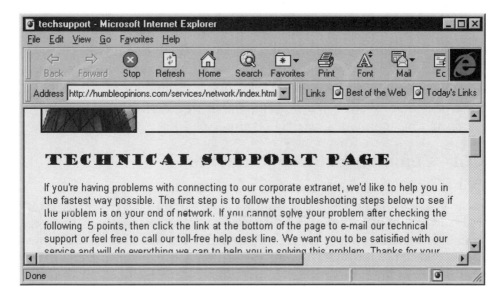

services/network   The directories on the server in which the data is stored.

index.html   The document you want to view.

Internet Services

The Internet offers many services you can use to communicate and exchange information with others. Most operating systems include tools and utilities that enable you to take advantage of these services; or you can purchase third party applications for the services you need. Following are the Internet services you may use in your business.

Anonymous FTP (File Transfer Protocol) is an Internet service that gives any user access to data files and applications on an FTP server. The user doesn't need a password or even a username to retrieve files; the files are available to the public for logging on as "anonymous."

Archie is a software tool that makes finding files stored on an FTP site easier if you know the exact filename or a substring of it.

Finger is a software tool that enables you to locate people on other Internet sites.

Gopher is a method of making menus from the available material on a server. Gopher requires both a client and a server program.

Telnet is a terminal emulation program for TCP/IP networks, such as the Internet. Telnet enables a PC to connect to a server and then enter commands through the terminal emulation program.

World Wide Web is a system of Internet servers that supports HTML documents transported over HTTP protocol.

CGI—Common Gateway Interface

CGI is a set of rules that describes how a Web server communicates with other machines using CGI. CGI shuttles information between Web servers and backend applications, such as databases and email systems. A CGI program takes standard input from the Web server and extracts the data, then passes that data on to the backend application and vice versa. Examples of CGI programs are turning collected data into a database query or changing its form into an email message. CGI provides greater interactivity for Web clients. A CGI program is executed in real time so that it can output dynamic information.

TCP/IP Basics

TCP/IP (Transmission Control Protocol/Internet Protocol) is the protocol suite that is the language of the Internet. TCP/IP was developed by the Department of Defense specifically to enable various network types designed by different vendors to communicate with each other via the Internet. The initial services provided included file transfer, electronic mail, and remote logon. Additionally, TCP/IP is standardized to ensure that all types of systems from all vendors can communicate.

Many network operating systems enable the use of the TCP/IP protocol for LAN and WAN use. Because TCP/IP is standardized, any network using TCP/IP can communicate with other TCP/IP networks.

TCP and IP

TCP/IP is made up of many different protocols, each performing a job to promote communications; however, the two primary protocols are TCP and IP.

IP is a protocol that's responsible for addressing and routing packets between hosts. It's connectionless because it doesn't establish a session before exchanging data. It doesn't guarantee delivery but makes a best-effort attempt to deliver a packet; unfortunately, the packet may be lost, delivered out of sequence, or delayed on the way. IP doesn't require acknowledgment when data is delivered, so if a packet is lost or sent out of sequence, no notification or acknowledgment of that is generated (TCP is responsible for that task).

IP identifies a destination address as either *local* or *remote*. For local, IP transmits the packet directly to the host. For remote, IP checks the local routing table for a route to the remote host. If it finds the route, it sends the packet on; if it doesn't find the route, is sends the packet to the source host's default gateway (or router).

TCP is responsible for verifying the correct delivery of data from client to server. TCP adds support to detect errors or lost data and to initiate retransmission of the packet until the data is completely received.

TCP is a connection-oriented delivery service. TCP transmits data in segments using byte-stream communications, meaning the data is treated as a sequence of bytes. Sequence numbers are assigned to each segment so the host will know when all pieces have been received. The host does send acknowledgments for each segment it receives.

IP Addressing

All network types have their own convention for transmitting messages between machines. The *MAC address* is a unique identifier used in many LANs to distinguish various machines; *Logical Units* identify each machine in an SNA network. Each technology has its own scheme for identifying its member computers. TCP/IP works on top of these specific network addresses by assigning a unique number to each workstation: an IP number.

The IP address has two parts: *network ID* and a *host ID*. The network ID identifies a physical network and all hosts on the same network require the same network ID. The host ID identifies the workstation, server, router, or other TCP/IP host within a network. A unique IP address is required for all hosts and network components that communicate using TCP/IP.

There are two formats for referencing IP address: *binary* and *dotted decimal*. An IP address is 32 bits long and composed of four 8-bit fields called *octets*. Octets are separated by periods and represent a decimal number in the range of 0–255. If the binary format is something like 10000011 01101011

00000011 0001 1000, the translated dotted decimal notation would be 172.16.124.23, for example.

Binary Format

Each bit in an octet has an assigned decimal value. When each bit is converted to decimal format, the highest value in the octet is 255. Each octet is converted separately. A bit set to 0 is always a zero value. A bit set to 1 can be converted to decimal value. Low-order bit represents a decimal value of 1; high-order bit represents a decimal value of 128. The highest decimal value of an octet is 255, when all bits are set to 1.

The following table shows how the bits in one octet are converted from binary code to decimal value:

Binary code	Bit Values	Decimal Value
00000000	0	0
00000001	1	1
00000011	1+2	3
00000111	1+2+4	7
00001111	1+2+4+8	15
00011111	1+2+4+8+16	31
00111111	1+2+4+8+16+32	63
01111111	1+2+4+8+16+32+64	127
11111111	1+2+4+8+16+32+64+128	255

There are five classes of IP addresses and each has limited and specific uses. Briefly, the following list describes the classes:

Class A is reserved for very large networks.   Values of 126 or less in the first octet indicate a Class A address.

Class B is used for medium-sized networks.   Values of 128 to 191 in the first octet indicate a Class B address.

Class C is reserved for smaller networks.   Values of 192 to 223 in the first octet indicate a Class B address.

Class D is a special multicast address that's not used for networks.

Class E is reserved for experimental purposes. Values greater than 223 indicate a reserved address.

Basically, you can only get Class B or C addresses and there's really little chance you'll get a Class B address. If you ask for more than 16 Class C networks, you'll need to provide a network plan. Also, you'll need at least two domain name servers when you register; an ISP may be willing to provide the primary and/or secondary name service for you.

Assigning Network IDs

For each network and wide area connection, you must assign a unique network ID. If you connect to the Internet, you must obtain a network ID from the Internet Network Information Center (InterNIC). Otherwise, you can use any valid network ID. If routers connect your network, a unique network ID is required for each wide area connection.

Components to configuring TCP/IP include the *IP address*, *subnet mask*, and the *default gateway*. The IP address is a logical 32-bit address identifying a TCP/IP host. The subnet mask blocks out a portion of the IP address so that TCP/IP can distinguish the network ID from the host ID. The subnet mask is used to determine whether the destination host is on a local or remote network. The default gateway enables you to communicate with a host on another network. Assign the gateway an IP address to enable it to communicate across two networks or segments. Without the default gateway, communication is limited to the local network.

When assigning host IDs, remember the following:

- The host ID must be unique to the local network ID.

- All TCP/IP hosts, including interfaces to routers, must have a unique host ID. The host ID of the router is the IP address configured as a workstation's default gateway.

  - Host IDs should be assigned in groups based on host or server type.

  - Routers must be designated by their IP addresses.

- Each host on a TCP/IP network must have a subnet mask, either a default mask (used when the network isn't divided into subnets) or a custom mask (used when the network is divided into subnets).

NOTE

IPv6, the updated version of IP4 created in the 1970s, was created to solve the current network addressing problems and provide a solution to the address space depletion problem. IPv6, a new version of IP addressing, uses 16 octets. IPv6 can be easily extended as needed.

Subnets

The *subnet* defines a physical segment in a TCP/IP environment that uses IP addresses derived from a single network ID. You can divide a network into subnets, but each segment must use a different network ID, or subnet ID. Create a unique subnet ID for each segment by partitioning the bits in the host ID into two parts: one part identifies the segment as a unique network; the other part identifies the hosts. Subnetting is not necessary if your network is private.

You subnet to apply one network across multiple physical segments. You can mix different technologies, like Ethernet and token ring; overcome the limitations of our current technologies (like exceeding the maximum number of hosts per segment); and reduce network congestion by redirecting traffic, all by subnetting the network.

Implementing Subnetting

You may want to use subnetting on your own TCP/IP network. To implement subnetting, follow these steps:

Determine the number of physical segments on the network and the number of required host addresses for each segment (each TCP/IP host requires at least one IP address).

Define one subnet mask for the entire network; a unique subnet ID for each physical segment; and a range of host IDs for each subnet. Also, consider your future requirements for the number of segments and hosts per segment. When you use more bits for the subnet mask, more subnets are available but fewer hosts are available per subnet.

If you divide your network into subnets, you must define a subnet mask. Determine the number of physical segments and convert that number to a binary format. Count the number of bits required to represent the number of physical segments in binary. Convert the required number of bits to decimal format in high order (from left to right).

IP Routing

When messages travel across a TCP/IP network, IP routers direct the traffic to its destination. Routers choose the path a packet takes by deciding which path is the most efficient. A router may also be called a *gateway*.

With TCP/IP, routing occurs when the TCP/IP host sends IP packets and again when the IP router sends it on to the next network. In order to make the routing decisions, the IP layer consults a routing table that contains entries with the IP addresses of router interfaces to other networks. IP determines first whether a destination host is local or remote. If the host is local, the local routing table is checked and the packet is delivered to the destination.

If the host is remote, IP checks the routing table for the root to the remote network; if no route is found, IP uses its default gateway address to deliver the packet to a router at the end of the gateway. That router's routing table is then consulted for a path to the remote network or host. The packet continues to be forwarded to another router's default gateway address until the remote host is found. If the route is never found, an error message is sent to the source host.

Java and ActiveX

Java is a programming language used on the Internet; Java programs, or *applets*, are usually embedded in World Wide Web documents to add motion and interactivity to Web pages. Java is a serious language that can be used to write full-scale applications, but its strength lies in the fact that you can write small programs to create dynamic Web page content.

Java was created and developed by Sun Microsystems. *JavaScript* is being developed by Netscape Communications Corporation for use with Navigator and Web server products.

ActiveX, developed by Microsoft, also enables interactive content on the Web. A programming language, ActiveX supports a number of platforms and industry standards. ActiveX also works with Java applications to extend and link the two programming languages.

PLANNING NETWORK STRATEGIES

When planning your Internet access, consider capacity, scalability, costs, performance, reliability, and manageability. You want to provide access to your users, perhaps set up a Web site, and even add a Web server at some point. Plan for the future as well as for the present.

Do a cost analysis to see how much the modifications, upgrades, and new equipment might cost. Consider the capital outlays for hardware, media, software, installation and configuration costs, maintenance, and technical support. Think about outsourcing some or all of the planning, installation, configuration, and/or maintenance of the Internet connection. Compare costs, your time and expertise, and other factors before you choose the direction of your Internet connection.

In this chapter, you learn about the following:

- Business advantages

- Internet services

- Service providers

Planning Internet Uses

The Internet has made it possible for even small, capital-tight enterprises to expand and realize its benefits and value. If you make appropriate use of the Internet, your business can soar as well. The Internet offers many services you can use to improve life for your users, customers, vendors, and business partners. All you have to do is carefully plan your approach and take advantage of the opportunities.

Business Advantages of the Internet

As you're planning for your Internet connections, hardware, and so on, you'll want to consider what advantages your business can derive from getting online.

No matter if your business is large or small, every user online can gain something from the Internet.

The Internet has dramatically changed how businesses communicate. For a fraction of the cost of traditional means, the Internet provides a way to send messages and information to anyone in the world, quickly and efficiently. Newsgroups, email, and file transfer methods provide opportunities for your users to network with others; collaboration and communication offer convenience and leverage in today's business world.

Your marketing efforts and customer support can also benefit from Internet use. Even if your direct sales from the Internet don't soar, you'll make potential customers and create a good relationship with your customers. Providing better customer support, an online Web site can ask customers to fill out reports, surveys, email for technical help, and more.

You can also disseminate information over the Internet and access research. Publish data that's helpful to your customers and colleagues to bolster your company image as experts in the field (see Figure 3.1). Alternatively, locate any kind of information you want—market research reports, community and business trends, references, competitive intelligence, news, and more.

As you plan your Internet strategies, you should first decide what it is you want to accomplish with your Internet connection; then work from there to accomplish your goals.

Internet Services

Many Internet services are provided by client/server applications that offer Internet resources, including formatted HTML documents, file transfer, email, and so on. Whether you're planning to provide access to your users or establish a presence on the Web, these services can change the way you and your users do business.

Following is a list of common Internet services:

World Wide Web (WWW) uses hypertext to organize and distribute information on the Internet. The WWW service is easy to use, uses industry standards, and offers a multitude of data. Using a browser, a user can view HTML pages and images, listen to sound files, watch video clips, and so much more. Mosaic, Netscape, Lynx, and Microsoft make popular browsers.

Email over the Internet enables users to send messages to one or more users easily and quickly, receive messages from all over the world, attach files and receive them, and so on. With email, users can col-

Figure 3.1 Publish useful information in addition to advertising.

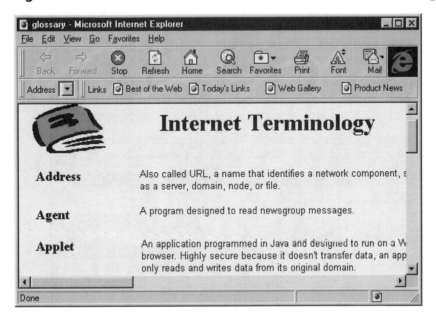

laborate and share information with other users they normally wouldn't contact. Most browsers, including Netscape and Internet Explorer, have built-in mail programs. Also, Eudora, Elm, and Pine are mail programs available for use. Figure 3.2 shows the Internet Mail program on Windows 95; the current message contains an attached link for office products.

Gopher enables the sharing of files on the Internet. Gopher represents these files and resources in a menu-based system so the user doesn't have to worry about IP addresses. Gopher also performs other functions—such as transferring FTP files, conducting searches, logging off, and so on—without the user's knowledge. Both text-based and graphical Gopher clients are available for Windows, DOS, NT OS/2, UNIX, and the Macintosh. WS-Gopher, Netscape, and Lynx are some Gopher applications.

Newsgroups are electronic bulletin boards on the Internet that enable the sharing of messages with other users. UseNet newsgroups are usually devoted to a single topic; subscribers to the service post messages and all other subscribers can read the articles.

Figure 3.2 Send messages next door, across the state, or to other countries.

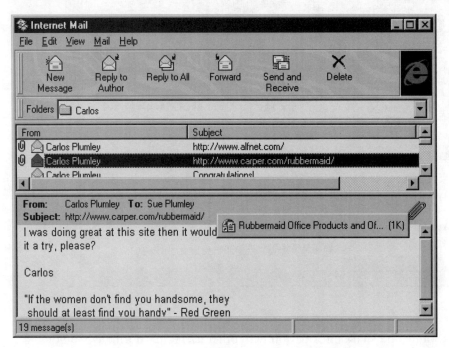

Telnet enables the access of files and other resources on the Internet. Telnet is a terminal emulation protocol that makes it easy to log on to an available server and access its resources. Popular Telnet client programs include WS-Telnet, QVTNET, and the telnet command.

FTP (File Transfer Protocol) enables you to transfer files and programs between computers. Users can log on to a computer, list files and directories, and transfer files. FTP supports a number of file-transfer types and formats, including ASCII and binary. Popular FTP clients include WS-FTP, QVTNET, Netscape, and the ftp command.

Three other common services are Internet Chat and Talk, and CU See Me. Internet Chat provides interactive text message exchange, and Internet Talk provides full audio communications between users. CU See Me provides full audio/video communications between users.

Internet Service Providers

Before choosing a service provider, you'll want to find out a few things about the service, the hardware, costs, and so on. You'll need to make a few decisions before talking to the provider and then ask some pertinent questions before making any decisions.

Which Services Do You Want?

You'll need to decide the types of services you want from the provider. You might, for example, want only email and UseNet services, or you might want to add Web browsing as well. Also, think about your needs for the future, such as server space for a homepage or an entire Web site, and/or space for a commercial store or other large commerce site.

Determine how many users you'll attach to the Net and how many connections will be simultaneous. Decide the number of mailboxes you'll need; not only will you want a mailbox for each user but you may want mailboxes for sales queries, customer complaints, or other such topics. You will eventually need to list the names for the mailboxes as well.

If you plan to fax over the Internet, download large files such as image or multimedia files, and perform other large-bandwidth consumers, the connection line and method will be important to your configuration as well. Discuss your plans with the service provider to get suggestions.

Questions to Ask

You want to make sure your ISP's setup is the best possible for your needs. Before contracting with any service provider, you should find out as much as you can about its hardware, connections to the Internet, backbone, and so on. Also, ask the ISP for a couple of references from companies with similar needs as yours. Make sure you call the references and ask how their service is.

Following are some additional issues and questions to ask an ISP when searching for Internet services:

What is the provider's backbone?   If you're paying for a T3 connection, for example, the backbone must be strong enough to provide the bandwidth you need.

What does the provider's network diagram look like?   Ask to see a map of its backbone. Ask about the network's architecture and scalability.

Does the provider have backup and redundancy so service is continuous? Even in the event of a downed server?

What type of support is available? Do they have technical expertise on-site? What size is the staff in the local office?

Do they have peering partners, where they share lines to distribute an equal amount of traffic across their network? Peering partners help to avoid bottlenecks.

How many Internet Exchange Points does the ISP's backbone include? Your connection will be stronger, faster, and more reliable depending on that number.

When was the backbone last upgraded? If the backbone is outdated or in need of repair, your connection will be slower and unreliable.

Is the local ISP located near its Network Operating Center? If you're near it, you may receive higher bandwidth.

What type of routers, servers, and switches are used at the NOC and throughout the backbone? You can determine whether the service provider is dedicated to efficient and reliable service by the number and type of networking equipment they use; look for modern equipment as well as knowledgeable technicians.

Where are the Points of Presence (POP), the locations where you can connect to the ISP's network? The more POPs, the better. Ask about the connections at the POP. For example, if you're connecting to the POP with a T3 line but the POP uses a T1 line to connect to the backbone, you're losing bandwidth, not gaining it.

Web Server Questions

If you're planning to start a Web server, you'll need a little more information from your service provider. Following are a few more things to learn before you contract for services:

- Obtain at least two domain name servers when you register for your domain name. Ask if the ISP is willing to provide the primary and/or secondary name service for you.

- Get your IP address from the ISP if possible. For more efficient routing on the backbones, get the provider to assign adjacent blocks of addresses if you need more than one. There's little, if any, chance you'll get a Class B address; most likely, you'll get a Class C.

- If you ask for more than 16 Class C networks, you'll need to provide a network plan.

- If you can't get an address through your Internet provider, look for a subnet registration form on rs.internic.net.

Internet Access Task List

Following is a list of things you'll need to do to prepare for your Internet connection:

Define the reasons why you want your business on the Internet—email, research, Web page or site, and so on.

Determine the applications you'll need on both the workstations and the server.

Ascertain which users will need access, how often and how long connect time might be for each user; then list user's names for mailboxes.

Decide which existing equipment you can use and which needs to be replaced and/or upgraded.

Choose a connection method (56K, fractional T1, full T1, or other) based on initial and future bandwidth requirements.

Obtain costs and timelines for delivery of needed hardware and software.

Obtain costs, figures, and timelines for installing a circuit from the phone company. Check with ISPs; often they can arrange for installation of the line and get you a discount.

Ask the ISP if it requires you to use a certain kind of router (so the ISP can make fine-tuning adjustments or apply microcode updates to the router without visiting your site). Ask if the ISP supplies the router or other equipment; it's worth a chance.

Buy a DSU/CSU (Digital Service Unit/Channel Service Unit)—only if you need one—to interface between your equipment and the data line. Buy a unit that will enable you to increase the speed of the data circuit in the future to save the expense of buying another unit later down the road. You can, for example, buy a unit that lets you configure for a 56K line, a full T1 line, and anywhere in between.

Purchase modems—analog, DSL, ISDN terminal adapters, or other equipment—that you'll need to complete the connection.

Purchase firewall and/or proxy server and install and configure.

Install browsers and mail programs to users' computers, if they are not already installed.

Review your Internet and email policies and distribute to users.

PREPARATIONS AND HARDWARE

Deciding upon the types of connections and other hardware you'll use for Internet access is difficult because there are so many technologies available. Your final decision should not only be based on your current needs, but on your future needs as well. Also, consider the number of users you're connecting and try to estimate the amount of use each will require from the Internet—downloading files, email, Web browsing, and so on. Try to think of it in terms of bandwidth, time connected, and simultaneous connections.

If, for example, you never plan to set up a Web site and/or server for your small company, then you can probably use a 56Kbps modem over the phone lines and provide your users with all they need to access the Internet. Now, add to that mix the fact that you have many, many users needing to access the Internet; a 56Kbps modem won't be enough. You might want to add a modem pool or go to frame relay.

The more users you add to the mix, the more bandwidth and speed you'll need from your connection, and the more equipment you'll need to accommodate those users. In this chapter, you learn about the connection and hardware options available. This chapter covers the following:

- Dedicated and dial-up connections

- Various types of modems—analog, 56Kbps, ISDN, and xDSL

- Different connection services—frame relay, T1, ATM, and so on

- Security devices

Connections and Access Devices

There are many types of connections between your LAN and the Internet and the one you choose depends on the number of users to connect, whether you need simultaneous connections, the type of work that the users will perform on the Internet, and your budget. You might choose to use a modem and a 56Kbps leased line, T1 links, T3 links, or some other connection or backbone.

In addition to the connections you get to the Internet, you'll need a device that attaches the connection to your LAN. These devices help to translate the protocols and transfer messages back and forth to the Internet.

> **Internet Gateways**
>
> For very small networks—two to four PCs on a LAN—you can use a software product to attach to the Net and share one or more modems or ISDN adapters. Internet gateways use dynamic IP addressing, require little administrative overhead, and use no routers or hardware gateways to attach to the Internet.
>
> Also called *proxy server gateways,* some products offer management features that let you restrict user access. These products can supply page caching, remote administration, and scheduled downloading of selected pages from the Web. Some products even let you share two or more ISDN B-channel connections to balance the load and speed transmissions. A single connection, however, is limited by the maximum speed of each modem.

Dedicated or Dial-Up?

The methods by which computers or terminals are connected to the Internet are through dedicated lines or dial-up access. A high-speed, dedicated connection is permanent—clients have a fast, full-time connection to the Internet. Dial-up access is slow and intermittent; clients connect only when they need to be on the Internet.

Dial-up access through an ISP can be expensive if you have many users who need access. Also, analog technology was designed for voice, so digital use isn't at its optimum. The bandwidth limitations of phone lines don't serve high-speed modems well, either.

Dedicated, high-speed links enable users to perform multiple activities simultaneously, supply more bandwidth, and end up costing less than a modem/telephone link does. 56Kbps, ISDN, T1, fiber optics (T3), and xDSL are all high-speed connections to the Internet.

Modems and Phone Lines

Modems are the most common device used to connect to the Internet; however, 28.8 and 33.6 modems are best for home or remote user situations. Faster modems, such as the 56Kbps may suit your company but for the most part, you'll likely want a dedicated line instead of dial-up access.

You could use a 56Kbps modem with a dial-up connection, but using a dedicated line makes more sense. A dedicated line maintains a permanent connection to the Internet so users can always attach. 56Kbps modem connections support downloading speeds up to 53Kbps and uploading speeds up to 33Kbps, depending on the line traffic, noise, individual connections, and hardware capabilities. With data compression, 56Kbps modems can achieve throughputs of two or more times those rates on compressible files.

56Kbps is less expensive than frame relay and ISDN. Also, 56Kbps is easy to use and provides good security. The only possible problem with a 56Kbps connection is that the local infrastructure may not support the speed. When shopping for 56K technology, make sure you question your service provider about compatible equipment, protocols, and connections.

> **NOTE**
>
> A *terminal adapter* is a device that converts the data it receives over ISDN to a form your computer can use (often called an *ISDN modem* or a *digital modem*). The terminal adapter handles data digitally rather than as an analog signal.

ISDN Modems and Lines

ISDN (Integrated Services Digital Network) is a digital subscriber line service that works over the existing telephone copper cabling infrastructure. ISDN supplies digital quality, low noise, less interference, and high security.

With ISDN, you need a modem (actually, the modem is a terminal adapter) on your end of the line and the ISP must have a similar device on its end. ISDN modems provide up to 128Kbps speeds with uncompressed data. The distances for ISDN modems range up to 18,000 feet, although additional equipment can be used to extend the distance. Use ISDN modems for Internet or intranet access, remote LAN access, videoconferencing, frame relay, and so on.

ISDN modems are difficult to configure; before you buy one you should ask some questions. First, make sure ISDN is available in your area and find out just what the monthly costs will be; ask your phone company for this information. Next, ask your service provider if it supports ISDN connections and if so, which ISDN modems are supported.

xDSL

DSL (Digital Subscriber Lines) is a new technology that doesn't refer to lines but to a pair of digital modems. The pair of DSL modems creates a digital subscriber line. A DSL modem transmits data in both directions simultaneously (duplex) at 160Kbps over copper lines; a limit of 18,000 feet is set for DSL.

There are several categories of DSL—as in HDSL, ADSL, and so on—and so the entire array is often referred to as xDSL. *ADSL* (Asymmetric DSL) allows more bandwidth downstream than upstream, which makes it ideal for applications such as video on demand, remote LAN access, and Internet access. It supports rates as high as 8Mbit/sec downstream and up to 16 and 640Kbps upstream. ADSL transmits at distances of up to 18,000 feet over one wire pair, and optimal speeds of 6 to 8Mbps are achieved at distances from 10,000 to 12,000 feet using standard 24-gauge wire.

VDSL (very high speed DSL) provides downstream speeds of 13 to 52Mbps and upstream rates of 1.5 to 2.3Mbps over a single copper wire pair. It delivers voice, video, and data for operating distances of 1000 to 4500 feet. VDSL is primarily used for high-definition television program delivery and multimedia Internet access.

To take advantage of ADSL, you'll need to find a service provider that's willing and ready to offer the service. ADSL is less complex and less expensive than ISDN, but currently, the use of ADSL is limited. It's difficult to find and that sometimes makes it more expensive.

X.25

Many ISPs are looking to upgrade their internal support networks by replacing X.25 technology with IP applications running across frame relay, ATM, or Sonet. The X.25 protocol runs at 64Kbps, much slower than many newer technologies available today. As an older protocol, X.25 can't keep up with increased demands for voice and data switches, routers, multiplexors, and so on.

Frame Relay

Frame relay is used in LANs and some WANs but can also be used for connection to the Internet. Bandwidth is 56Kbps to 1.544Mbps. Frame relay cannot transmit voice or video, however—only data. With frame relay, you can increase your line speed simply by notifying the ISP and phone company; frame relay is a software-defined implementation that can grow with your needs. To connect to frame relay, you'll need a router and a line.

Fractional T1, T1

A T1 line is a high-quality communications circuit that you can lease. It provides 24 channels of 64Kbps for a total bandwidth of 1.544Mbps. Although expensive to install and maintain, T1 provides a fast and reliable link to the Internet. T1 is ideal for a virtual private network connection because it does support multiple protocols (including PPP and frame relay). Security is good as well.

To connect a T1 line, you need a CSU/DSU (Channel Service Unit/Data Service Unit), and a bridge or router. The CSU/DSU prevents faulty equipment from affecting the transmission systems and converts local area network signals to the T1 signaling formats. An optional multiplexor loads multiple channels of voice or data onto the T1 line; and the bridge or router provides the actual connection points between your LAN and the CSU/DSU and onto the T1 circuit.

Figure 4.1 illustrates a connection between a LAN and the Internet. T1 circuits connect the LAN and ISP and the ISP and the Internet. CSU/DSUs work between the LAN and the ISP to convert signals.

A Fractional T1 is a subchannel of a full T1 channel for a lower price. A full T1 line contains 24 fractional T1 lines so for Fractional T1 lines, you can purchase 6, 8, or 12 Fractional T1 lines to provide fast access at a fraction of the cost.

T3

T3 is made available over high-speed fiber-optic cable. It is the same as 28 T1 circuits and provides a bandwidth of 44.736Mbps. Telephone companies use T3 almost exclusively, but Fractional T3 lines are also available.

ATM

Asynchronous Transfer Mode (ATM) technology packages all data into predictable byte-sized packets in a hardware solution that offers higher possible speeds. Hardware can deal with data-switching and routing faster than software can. ATM evens the field a bit.

Figure 4.1 Simplified, the connection between the LAN and the Internet utilizes several devices and circuits.

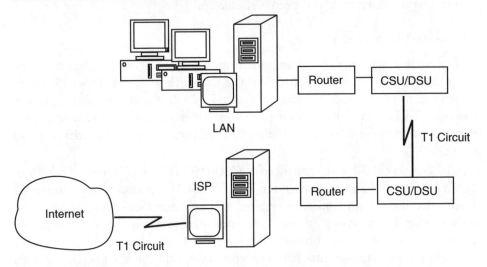

Broadband Access

Broadband usually refers to data transmission technologies that operate at T1 rates or higher. Broadband lines or circuits are usually dedicated, and access can be 100 to 1000 times faster than dial-up or BRI ISDN access.

Medium- to large-sized businesses using the Internet and connected via T1 lines may soon discover the speed is not enough. Adding multiple T1 lines helps but is quite a bit more expensive than broadband and doesn't offer the traffic management capabilities of broadband.

With broadband access, you get more bandwidth than T1, so it's more expensive; but usually as you buy more bandwidth, the price-per-unit of bandwidth goes down. Available products enable the network administrator to manage the size and type of bandwidth consumed by IP traffic.

ATM is a switched, connection-oriented networking technology that provides dedicated, high-speed connections to an unlimited number of users. Dedicated media connections running in parallel allow ATM switches to simultaneously support multiple transmissions, eliminating the bandwidth connection and data bottlenecks found on shared-media networks. The maximum bandwidth and the average bandwidth per connection in an ATM network are the same: 155Mb/s scalable to 622 Mb/s and beyond in the future. Adding more users won't necessarily decrease the bandwidth that's available.

Security Devices

If you connect to the Internet for email, research, easy access to applications and documentation, advertising, or for any of a thousand other reasons, you'll want to protect your network against unnecessary risks from the outside world. Without protection, your data, resources, users, and even your entire LAN are vulnerable to exploitation.

Although security devices can help to protect your LAN resources, you must also take some steps to reinforce these safeguards. For example, you should write and distribute a set of guidelines and policies governing how your users use the Internet and the LAN. Make sure password assignments are enforced, add expiration dates to user accounts, restrict users from endless connections, and so on. For more information on security policies, see Chapter 5 of this book, "Security and Policies."

Proxy Servers

Proxy servers offer an effective barrier between your network and outside networks, such as the Internet. A proxy server enables information exchange between a private LAN and the Internet, for example, while maintaining security for the computers on the LAN. A proxy server gives you security and control of communications through your network, while providing a high-performance gateway to the Internet.

Usually installed to a dedicated computer, a proxy server enables you to control which Internet users can access your resources and which resources your users can access, as well. Most proxy servers offer caching abilities to reduce bandwidth consumption; agree with the Internet standards of HTTP, FTP, IRC, SMTP, and so on; and include system management and monitoring tools.

Figure 4.2 shows how a proxy server sits outside of the LAN and connects to the ISP via an ISDN line.

A proxy server communicates with external resources on behalf of the internal user. The client application makes a request for an object on the Internet, and the proxy server responds by translating the request and passing it on to the Internet. When the proxy server receives a response from the Internet, it passes it back to the client application on the computer making the request.

Proxy servers perform the following tasks:

- User authentication
- Data protection
- Controlling user access to the Internet
- Controlling Internet users' access to the LAN

Firewalls

Firewalls protect the company with IP connections outside the confines of its own environment. A firewall is at the edge of the network and prevents unauthorized individuals from accessing your network resources. You must remember, however, that if internal users and trusted external parties can access network resources, you could still have a breach of your system.

Figure 4.2 The proxy server protects the LAN from Internet intruders.

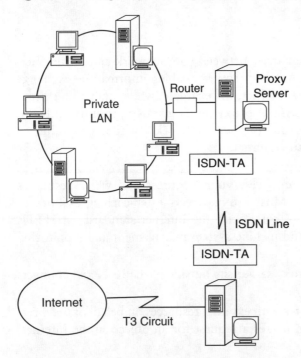

Firewall Requirements

When looking for a firewall to protect your system, make sure the device meets the following requirements:

- Hides the structure of the internal network from the outside network.
- Must not provide dynamic routing, only static routing should be provided by the administrator.
- Has a strong user authentication scheme that doesn't rely on user IDs.
- Rejects protocols that are security risks, such as rexec, rlogin, rsh, rwho, and tftp.
- Rejects unknown protocols.
- Acts as an SMTP mail gateway; all outgoing mail appears to come from the firewall and outgoing mail header fields should be translated to protect the senders.
- Creates an audit trail of system activity, logging both successful and unsuccessful login attempts.

A good firewall should include logging and notification of firewall events, monitor bandwidth usage and network activity, and enable you to create reports and summaries with the information gathered. It should also be easy to configure, provide encrypted sessions, protect internal addresses, and control FTP privileges.

In addition to hardware firewalls, software firewalls are also available. Application firewalls are a secure form of protection. Designed to deny services except for the ones that are explicitly allowed, an application firewall should control secure access to a full range of Internet protocols, provide auditing and reporting tools, and maintain high performance levels.

SECURITY AND POLICIES

An internal network opens a security hole that can cost your company time and money. Users may damage files accidentally, sensitive data may be compromised, or users can sabotage data intentionally. When you connect your internal network to the Internet, the size of that security hole increases radically. Hackers who have no interest in your company may break in to expose equipment weaknesses, steal sensitive information, or destroy hardware and software.

Your basic line of defense is within the company itself. Security depends on how well you inform your users of certain safeguards and operations. This chapter discusses the following:

- Security

- Passwords

- Policies

- Procedures

Internet security problems come from two sources: hackers who are increasingly sophisticated and system administrators who are woefully under-equipped to handle security problems. If you educate yourself to the possible threats from the Internet, and arm your network against these threats, your network and resources will be more secure than if you blindly add safety devices and software to the system.

Crackers (people who hack into systems) use various methods to attack systems via the Internet. Finding security loopholes in common system utilities is the simplest method; using advanced applications is another more complex method. Some programs, such as Trojan Horses, mimic existing system functions while capturing user IDs and passwords as users log on to the Internet. Following are some other threats to your security:

Web server safety is threatened by programs that exploit the system's CGI-BIN scripts. These programs obtains copies of the password files, send fake email, attain root privileges, and so on.

Using Java and ActiveX scripts, intruders can bypass controls, run scripts without a user's knowledge, and execute arbitrary machine code. Scripts are harder to separate from an HTML transmission than applets and run before a user's browser can refuse.

Web spoofing and hijacking attacks involve a malicious Web server that forces access to all other sites to pass through it. Crackers can then tamper with transactions, steal user account information, and even insert offensive material for the user to read.

Security for Your LAN

It's important you check over all of your user accounts, password expirations, old or modified accounts, and other security on your LAN before you ever get on the Internet. If your LAN is secure, you'll have a better chance that your Internet connections will be secure as well. Holes in your LAN security make it easier for intruders who break in from the Internet to get to your data and resources.

Passwords are your first line of defense. Following are some suggestions for making sure the passwords you use both inside and outside of the LAN are safe and secure.

> **NOTE**
>
> Firewalls and proxy servers are another method of protecting your LAN. See Chapter 4 of this book, "Preparations and Hardware," for more information about those devices.

LAN Passwords

Usernames and passwords enable a client to log on to application, file, and database servers, and often email and groupware applications. It's important that you keep security tight within the LAN as well as outside of it. If someone hacks into your system, for example, you don't want everything to be easy to access within the LAN. Keep the following in mind:

Keep a tight control on guest accounts.

Remove inactive user accounts promptly.

Require that users change their passwords periodically.

Display a warning on your system that access is restricted to authorized users and that sessions may be monitored (it is against the law in some places to monitor user sessions; check with your attorney to make sure the warning enables you to monitor sessions on your network).

Implementing a single sign-on for your network is another safety measure you can take. When LAN users begin to accumulate numerous passwords—for login, database access, email accounts, and so on—they start to write the passwords down and that can cause problems. Also, multiple passwords and multiple user accounts mean the administrator has more work to do with creating users, modifying them, deleting accounts when the user leaves, and such. User time is wasted logging in to each server. Migrate your system to the single sign on to save time and effort, and to help secure your system.

Outside Passwords

After you open your LAN to the Internet, you'll find more reasons to enable users to access the LAN from outside of work. Using a virtual private network to supply users with remote access is only one possibility for expanding your network over the Internet; you might also allow outside partners, customers, vendors, or colleagues to use your network over an extranet or VPN. As your network opens up more to users outside of the LAN, make sure you follow security procedures to verify passwords and authenticate those users.

Passwords used over the Internet can be hacked, sniffed, or stolen. You can try any of several methods of authentication to help keep these passwords safe. Using a two-factor token authentication system, an outside user can access the network by typing a username; the system then carries a token to the server instead of a password. The token, a dynamic string of numerals that change with each login and is encrypted each time, ensures a unique password for each login. Tokens are usually used for remote users dialing in to a network, not local users.

Public Key Infrastructure (PKI) is a system of key pairs and certificates, like those used in e-commerce applications. Larger companies have implemented the PKI to safeguard their intranets and extranets. Digital certificates are associated with a public key to provide a way to verify that the key is from a specific individual. Public key uses a mathematically related pair of keys that are nearly impossible to violate. The sender obtains the recipient's public key directly from the recipient; the sender applies that public key to the text, which encrypts it. Only the recipient has possession of the matching private key.

Policies and Procedures

Establishing your corporate policies and procedures will help you protect your company, data and other resources, and your employees, when you decide to attach to the Internet. While you want to encourage and support employee use of the system as a means of improving productivity, you must apply certain restrictions to avoid improprieties, ensure that standards are met, and maintain appropriate security of your system.

Security Policies

Your first goal for security should be within your own network. Enforce password assignments and user policies, add expiration dates to user accounts, delete expired accounts, and so on. Review your user and group accounts to make sure rights, logon times, profiles, and other properties are appropriate. Check to see how many administrators' accounts you have and if all are necessary. Next, you can concentrate on setting procedures, guidelines, and policies for Internet usage.

One procedure you should follow is monitoring Internet connections. You should also inform your users that you will be monitoring the Internet connections all of the time. Monitoring hasn't been tested in the courts as illegal but the Federal Electronic Communications Privacy Act assures employers the right to keep tabs on what is done with employer-owned property, including computers and telephone lines. Make your phone system and Internet system policies similar. Don't limit outside calls, for example, but limit excess.

Following are some additional policy suggestions:

Think about limiting access to time-wasting Web sites, such as sports or soap opera sites, that are distractions in the workplace. You'll need to decide how you feel about restricting your employees from using such sites. Many corporations take a "Let's all be adults here" attitude, offering few or no restrictions. Depending on your users, this may work, or it may result in a large amount of network traffic for non-business surfing. Use the phone bill to see if there is much download or surfing time logged and then decide, if you don't feel comfortable making the policies without provable justification.

Ban sex, gambling, hate speeches, criminal skills, and drugs from your company's Internet use.   Also, consider banning sports, leisure, investing during working hours (unless your business is sports, leisure, or investing).

Require that all text and messages be sent as encrypted over the Internet.   Clear text provides no protection.

Don't use guest accounts.   Limit services to only those for whom it's necessary, and establish a lock-out mechanism for too many bad password attempts.

Provide security training for all administrative assistants and administrators.   Administrators can help the users learn security procedures as well as keep an eye out for possible problems within the system.

Create and enforce an email policy.   Email policies can help control bandwidth, server disk space, and your company's security.

Email Policies

Email has been the focus of lawsuits involving breach of contract and the disclosure of critical corporate trade secrets, sexual harassment, and liability for copyright infringement. Moreover, a corporation that fails to implement appropriate policies for handling and retaining email may increase the likelihood of litigation and corporate liability.

Establish an email retention policy; you might recommend that users save only essential email or you may require they save all email, depending on your corporate philosophy. Tell users not to forward email without the sender's permission, and even with permission, caution users against freely forwarding emails outside of the company.

Following are some more ideas for email policies:

Add a signature line to messages about accidental transmission to unintended third parties.

Bar the use of obscenities and derogatory remarks about customers, employees, and competitors.

Adopt procedures for dealing with complaints about inappropriate or offensive email.

Encrypt sensitive email that travels outside of the company.

Instruct users to check email daily and keep the messages remaining in the electronic mailbox to a minimum.

Web Policies

You may need to categorize your policies for easier presentation. If you plan to allow users free use of browsers on the Web, you should set some restrictions. Also, if users or specific team members are in charge of creating content for a Web page, you should limit them via Web policies as well. Following are some suggestions:

Ask users to turn off or delay inline images, especially if they can do without such images. Graphics are high-bandwidth consumers and by turning them off, the speed of the session will be improved.

Mention that certain sites on the Internet may contain information inappropriate for company use and those sites should not be knowingly accessed. You may want to define examples of such sites.

Ask users to download files to their local PC drive and not to the server hard drive. Also, make it the responsibility of the user to maintain adequate storage space and delete old data from his or her local drive.

Require that users use newsgroups, UseNets, and listservs with restraint. These forums can place unusually heavy demands on disk space.

Limit users from taking advantage of the company's Internet access. Do not allow users to post messages to promote their own personal business, products, or services.

Ask content developers not to include very large graphic images in the HTML documents; using postage-sized images that users can click on to enlarge is a better way to save time on a Web site. Also, content developers should be asked to follow these guidelines:

Include the file size in text alongside the representative icon when using video or sound clips. This way, the user has an option of opening the file.

Keep URL naming standards simple; limit case sensitivity.

Use a trademark (TM) or copyright symbol (c) and date in any original HTML documents; also include an email address and the date of last revision.

Be aware that violation of copyright laws, obscene or harassing materials, and such on Web sites can be subject to litigation and may be a violation of state, national, or even international laws. Content developers should ultimately be responsible for the documents they publish to the Web.

Procedures

By establishing certain procedures for Internet use, you can promote security, safety, and the work ethic. Write a clear set of procedures and then publish them on your intranet with your security policies for all to see. You should also print policies and procedures, distribute a copy to each user, review the content, and then ask each user to sign a page acknowledging the receipt and understanding of the document.

To insure compatibility with your system and to ease administration and support of users, establish a standard software and hardware for Internet applications on user workstations. Use just one browser, one email program, and one news program; and support only these programs. You can prohibit the installation of any software or hardware that is not standard; this may seem harsh but it can save you a lot of time and trouble.

Establish ownership of all hardware, software, programs, applications, templates, data, and files on the server and on the workstation. You do this so that you have the right to access, modify, delete, or alter any data or equipment in your workplace. You also want to prohibit the copying of programs and software and of files, especially the unlawful use of any files or programs taken from the Internet. Be careful of copyright laws.

Chapter
6

INTRANETS AND EXTRANETS

Both intranets and extranets enable you to extend the use of your LAN to serve more people. With intranets, you serve your network users by supplying more information in a format that's easier to use than traditional means. With extranets, you serve people outside of your LAN; but you choose who those people will be.

Intranets enable you to publish policies, guidelines, commonly used forms, technical support, and the list goes on and on. Since an intranet is a private IP network, security within the LAN is maintained while providing supplementary services to your users.

Extranets enable you to publish information to customers, colleagues, business partners, vendors, and such, while maintaining a fairly secure connection over a wide area. Extranets can help you improve relationships with customers, promote collaboration among multiple parties, and in general, keep informed so as to stay ahead of your competition.

An extranet is a selective extension of an intranet. You grant selective access to a controlled group of customers and business partners. Many ISPs have strategies for enabling customers to open up their intranets into extranets by using, for example, virtual private networks.

In this chapter, you learn about the following:

- Advantages and disadvantages of using an intranet
- Preparations for using an intranet
- Common intranet content
- Advantages and disadvantages of using an extranet
- Security problems and solutions of the extranet
- Virtual private networks as an extranet vehicle

Intranets

Whereas a network provides files, directories, and resources such as printers and modems that users may access, an intranet improves upon that model to make files easier to find, access, and use. An intranet is basically a network that uses Internet technologies—software, protocols, and tools—to present information over the network. Files are displayed as HTML-formatted documents, with links and images and icons that enable a user to jump to related documents quickly and efficiently.

Users view documents on an intranet with a Web browser and use the browser's features to move from document to document. Users can use a search engine to quickly locate topics and text. And users can print, copy, and otherwise use intranet documents as they do other documents on the network.

Advantages and Disadvantages of Intranets

Developing an intranet involves many steps, but basically you're developing a network of documents using Internet technologies. However, Web servers made available on the internal network are not available to users on the Internet, which means your LAN security remains intact.

The leading argument for creating an intranet is to improve communication within the company. Electronic publishing enables you to present information to your users quickly and update that information in a timely manner, thereby promoting your users' productivity. If the users have the forms, facts, documentation, guidelines, and other information they need when they need it, they can complete their work more quickly.

Since Internet technology—HTML, HTTP, TCP/IP, and so on—is scalable, so then is your intranet. The technology works well with small-, medium-, and large-sized networks; it can grow with your network as you add more users, workstations, servers, and documents.

Another advantage of the intranet is that you already have most of what you need in place. An intranet runs on a LAN, WAN, or VPN, for example, and if you're using TCP/IP as your network protocol, you're ahead of the game. Users make use of the browsers on their workstations to view the HTML documents over the network. You can use an existing server for your web server for the time being (depending of course on the number of users and amount of traffic your intranet will encompass) and upgrade later if you see the need. So all you need is web server software and the content.

> **NOTE**
>
> See Chapter 7 of this book, "Running a Web Server," for information about Web server software.

Naturally there are disadvantages to creating an intranet for your users. From a network administrator's point of view, the time, energy, and cost required may not be justified when there are other more pressing technological concerns at stake. An intranet is not a critical business need, although the increase in users' productivity may prove very advantageous.

You may have a problem with implementing an intranet because of outdated equipment. If you must upgrade workstations and server hardware, install and configure a new network operating system, and rework your network connections, then an intranet isn't going to be worth the time and money. However, if you're planning to implement the Internet into your users' lives, you'll likely need to perform many upgrades on hardware and software anyway; so the case for an intranet may not be that far off.

As for creating and updating content, someone has to maintain the documents and the links; with interactive applications, bigger files, more pages, and new users, this could be a problem. You can, however, outsource the maintenance or select one or more of your knowledgeable users to provide those services.

Preparing for the Intranet

Before you can successfully set up your intranet, you may want to establish links with legacy applications, increase network bandwidth, upgrade the network, and so on. You may also need to upgrade workstation software and perhaps install and configure Web server software.

In addition, following are some issues you should consider while preparing and planning:

Train administrators, content developers, and users as necessary.

Consider who will perform statistics reporting and traffic monitoring; perhaps invest time and training in two administrative assistants who can then perform these tasks when the intranet is complete.

Hire or train someone for technical support of the intranet.

Enlist managers to help you standardize messaging procedures, database access, and other network activities across departments.

Establish a rule or guideline book for designing the intranet: servers, browsers, applications, pages, and so on. Detail if, how, and where the company logo is placed, for example, or how frames should be set up, use of images, headings, links, and so on.

> **NOTE**
>
> If you already use groupware products—Lotus Domino, Microsoft Exchange, and such—you can integrate those applications very well into an intranet to provide your users with even more data-sharing and collaborative techniques.

Managing an Intranet

As network administrator, you most likely already have enough to do and the thought of adding an intranet is not very inviting. You can, however, make use of the technology and provide for your users by assigning a team to perform content development and upgrade and perhaps another team to perform the management tasks. Plan and deploy your intranet over a period of time; a year of planning and preparation is reasonable, especially if you have many other duties and pressures in your job. Don't rush the task.

You'll want to prepare for the increased traffic on the network. Initially, traffic will be extremely heavy while users discover all of the documents in store for them. Also, email will increase as collaboration and information sharing become routine.

You will also receive email messages about the site—suggestions, complaints, requests, and so on. Assign one assistant to email and publish that assistant's email address on the intranet as the contact person.

Following are some more suggestions for managing an intranet:

Publish data on the Web but also make hard copies of employee handbooks, phone lists, forms, and so on, just in case you need them. Don't totally depend on the intranet for all company documents.

Centralize IP address management; use DHCP so clients can request addresses from a common repository.

Consolidate directories on the intranet and file servers; put all user information, printer and file systems, configuration files, and application-specific attributes each into a common directory.

Issue digital IDs for all employees or use cryptography keys for access control so security is maintained within the LAN.

> **NOTE**
>
> For more information, see *Building Intranets on NT, NetWare, Solaris: An Administrator's Guide* by Morgan Stern and Tom Rasmussen (Sybex, 1997).

Creating Content

The first step to creating content is to establish a common look and feel for the intranet documents across the company. Keep the number of people who develop content down to avoid a "too many cooks spoil the broth" type of thing.

You can use any of a variety of applications to create content. You can format your own documents in HTML; use Microsoft's Internet Assistants in Word, Excel, PowerPoint, and/or Access; or try the web formatting features in FrontPage, Corel Presentations, WordPro, and so on. FrontPage is specifically designed for creating and organizing web documents and sites.

When formatting your documents, keep the following design points in mind:

Don't use large graphics. Try smaller, postage-stamp–sized graphics for quicker loading.

Don't fill the page with too much text or too many pictures, icons, and graphics. You might distract the reader instead of getting your point across (see Figure 6.1).

Keep your formatting consistent. Use the same size body text and headlines, colors and layouts for each page on the site.

Use one major heading on each page. Letting users know where they are helps them navigate more easily.

Create a template for your pages so all pages have a similar look. Consistency makes the documents look more professional.

Use lists or tables to present text instead of long paragraphs. Lists are easier and quicker to read than plain text.

Figure 6.1 An example of what not to do to a web page is filling the page with many different fonts and icons.

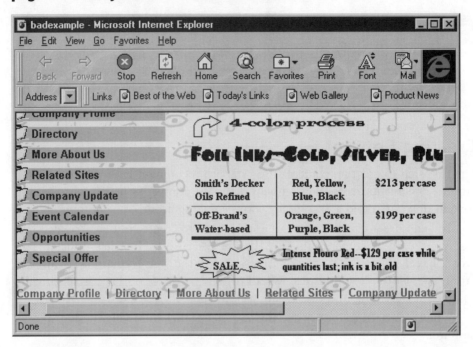

FrontPage

FrontPage is Microsoft's web site management software. FrontPage includes tools for creating a site, formatting pages, managing links, editing pages, and organizing and maintaining the entire site.

FrontPage contains four applets, or components: Personal Web Server, FrontPage Explorer, Editor, and To Do List. The components work separately to perform various tasks in the creation and maintenance of a web site as well as integrate and work together.

The Personal Web Server is useful for creating a web site on a standalone desktop or notebook computer. After you've created the site, you can transfer it to the web server for testing and implementation.

The Explorer is similar to the Windows Explorer in that it enables you to view the files in the site, and copy or delete files, view the pages in the site, and organize the files.

The Editor is the applet in which you create and format HTML documents. Easy to use, the Editor is similar to a word processor and includes page formatting and layout features.

Finally, the To Do List is perfect for keeping track of the tasks you need to complete. You can even link entries in the To Do List to the actual web pages for easy reminders.

NOTE

For more information about implementing an intranet with NT Server, see *Building Your Intranet with Windows NT 4.0* by Stephen A. Thomas and Sue Plumley (John Wiley & Sons, 1997).

Intranet Technology

In using TCP/IP, you might use a DHCP (Dynamic Host Configuration Protocol) server rather than manually configuring IP addresses to every desktop. With DHCP, the server automatically assigns a workstation an IP address when the user logs on to the network and thus centralizes administration. With DHCP, a range of IP addresses are designated for the distribution to clients; a single DHCP server keeps the list of available addresses and assigns them when client machines are rebooted. DHCP can also assign DNS servers, gateways, subnet masks, and so on.

The *DNS* (Domain Name Service) is a distributed database that translates IP addresses of Web servers into their alphanumeric name; DNS works for both host and domain names and addresses. Name resolution is when DNS translates the name of the Web server into the IP address. The IP address for your Web server is assigned to you and the domain name is one that you choose.

Using DNS with an intranet is optional. You can use the DNS with your intranet if, for example, you have several Web servers; users can then use your server's name instead of entering the IP address. For the Internet, you'll need a DNS-registered name and IP address from the InterNIC. Although the DNS-registered name isn't required, it makes it a lot easier for your visitors to get to your site.

In addition to publishing newsletters, company handbooks, and such, you may want to take advantage of the two-way, interactive applications and line-of-business applications technology out there. In that case, application development may be an issue. If you have application developers, either on staff or outsourced, establish guidelines for how applications for the intranet are written, who may rewrite your corporate applications, and so on.

Intranet applications with the highest projected return on investment include database access, inventory management, customer service, commerce, collaboration, order management, and publishing. However, monitor new applications closely until they're proven; new applications can cause traffic problems, operating system glitches, peripheral problems, and so on. Test new applications before releasing to the entire intranet.

> **NOTE**
>
> There are applications available for tracking links within intranet documents. Use something like Linkbot from Tetranet Software for optimizing system resources and finding broken links.

Extranets

An extranet (extended intranet) uses Internet technologies—such as TCP/IP and HTTP—to create a network dedicated to business-to-business, business-to-consumer, or consumer-to-consumer use instead of strictly internal corporate use. You might, for example, create an extranet for your business partners to visit and catch up on new projects, access white papers, fill out surveys, and so on. Another use for extranets is for customers to access information, technical help, question salespeople, and otherwise take advantage of close contact with your company.

Extranets provide online, real-time access to information for external parties who need it; order tracking, product information, product development, marketing planning, and so on, can be quickly and easily executed over an extranet. Updated information is available through a secure network between the corporate LAN and outside entities.

Extranets as an Extended Intranet

Generally, the extranet connects the corporation's intranet to selected users via the Internet. If you can plan your intranet well and use security features and firewalls to protect your sensitive data, then you can safely and efficiently set up an extranet that can save your corporation time and money.

First, you won't have to modify or update existing equipment. Your web server and network connections should be sufficient to handle the extra traffic and users, as long as you planned ahead for your intranet. Also, you already have the security features—such as a proxy server and/or firewall—in place if you're connecting to the Internet.

Next, your intranet documents are already in a central location. Adding extranet documents and files won't take as much planning and preparation as the original documents did; although you will need to add documents more relevant to outside partners than to your inside employees.

Finally, when you start with an intranet and gradually grow into an extranet, you garner the administrative and managerial experience, troubleshooting techniques, and other skills you need to make extranet administration a bit easier.

Advantages and Disadvantages

There are certain advantages and disadvantages to extending your LAN and intranet into an extranet. The biggest advantage is the immediate contact you have with your customers, business partners, or others who access your network. You can promptly receive comments and feedback, supply order and shipping information, collaborate on important projects, and so on, with the use of an extranet; the distance between you and your colleagues is reduced in time and range.

Other advantages to using an extranet include the following:

- Use existing software, hardware, and content if you have an intranet in place.

- Present an opportunity for building and modifying applications between companies.

- Can help increase revenue and sales.

- Reduce costs within the business and between the business and its partners.

- Offer competitive advantages in marketing and distribution.

- Reduce the amount of paperwork and the transaction time for most sales and activities.

- Save time by using email and electronic communications rather than by telephone or traveling to the business meetings.

Of course, there are disadvantages to using extranets in your business. You want to be careful about who you include and who you don't include as an extranet business partner; for example, some colleagues or suppliers may feel you're playing favorites if they aren't included in your extranet. Also, certain extranet technologies may exclude some businesses.

Other disadvantages include:

- Some of your employees will no longer be needed when your extranet is set up. Electronically automating business activities such as billing, tracking orders, customer service, sales, and so on, could reduce the number of employees you need.

- Security is always a risk when doing business over public networks or the Internet. Additionally, you open your network up to even more problems when you extend it to other companies and more people over whom you have no control.

- Check the legalities and responsibilities in case of any loss of business to your extranet users should your extranet go down.

Security and Extranets

When you plan to do business over the Internet, you are naturally going to worry about the security of your transactions. With extranets, your security concerns expand because you're opening your network to more people and possible breaches in security.

Part of the security of extranets is the fact that you decide who you want to allow into your extranet. Naturally, since these people are not members of your organization, you can't control what they do with your passwords and such; however, you can control how they are recognized on your extranet.

Authentication and encryption are part of the security features you'll use with your extranet. Following are a few of the technologies you can consider:

S/MIME (Secure MIME) is a certificate-based encryption and authentication standard for email.

X.509 certificates are digital certificates that provide authentication of the user and encryption of the messages.

Signed objects guarantee that downloaded Java programs are legitimate and not designed to steal credit card numbers and other sensitive information.

Security Goals for Extranets

There are certain objectives that when reached, ensure your extranet is safe and secure. Following is a brief description of each:

Confidentiality. Information sent over the extranet must be private; verify through the use of protocols that use encryption.

Authentication. Identify the individual or the computer, verifying that the party is a member of the appropriate group or access list.

Nonrepudiation. You must ensure that people cannot deny their electronic actions, whether you do so with logs, security tracking, monitoring, or other means.

Integrity. Verify that the information received has been entered by the originator.

Access control. Verify that the person accessing the LAN has authority to do so.

Availability. Ensure that the data and server resources are up and running.

Either you or the ISP must guarantee these goals are met, using various means of security and devices. Talk to your ISP to see what it offers in the way of security and protection.

> **NOTE**
>
> Internet TCP/IP filter technology protects against hackers and intruders. Using public key and standards-based encryption, there are products that can encrypt all data between corporate sites and guarantee privacy and protection against the alteration of data.

Virtual Private Networks

A virtual private network is a connection between remote users and a corporation's LAN using a private and secure path across a public network system, such as the Internet. Using an already-established connection line and compatible protocols, remote users can also attach to a company's extranet.

Although an extranet and a virtual private network are nearly the same thing, they aren't exactly the same. Extranets use the same type of tunneling protocol as VPNs. A VPN can support and carry an extranet. But a VPN can also carry a company's mobile users, for example, to the LAN for remote access; no extranet is necessary for the two to connect. Figure 6.2 illustrates how a VPN works to securely transfer data over an extranet; the VPN tunneling protocol provides secure lines.

Some remote access protocols are SLIP, PPP, and PPTP, to name just a few.

SLIP (Serial Line Internet Protocol) is an older communications protocol used in UNIX environments and it doesn't provide automatic negotiation of network configuration and encrypted authentication that PPP can provide.

PPP (Point-to-Point Protocol) is a set of protocols that are used by dial-up connections, often in relation to remote access and Internet access. If the server complies with the PPP standard, remote computers running PPP can connect to those servers for network access. The PPP architec-

---

NOTE

Some ISPs offer data VPNs in which a business' regional or branch offices are connected to the ISP backbone through frame relay permanent virtual circuits (PVCs). The business' IP traffic then doesn't run with other Internet traffic because it never leaves the backbone.

Figure 6.2 Secure lines carry the extranet via the Internet.

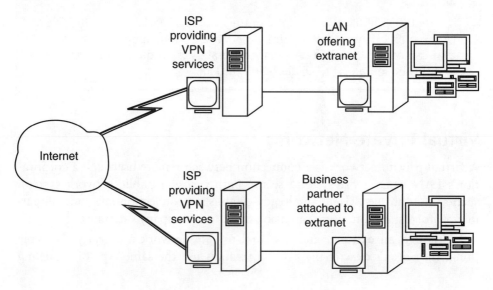

ture enables clients to load other protocols—TCP/IP, IPX, and NetBEUI—as well.

PPTP (Point-to-Point Tunneling Protocol) supports virtual private networks to enable the remote user secure access to corporate networks across the Internet. Virtual Private Networks are also called *tunneling* or *extranets*. The VPN enables an organization to use a public data network for some or all of the WAN communication needs.

Tunneling is more appropriate than SSL when a company wants all communications between two endpoints to be confidential. A tunnel is the creation of a private data stream via a public network (Internet). By placing one packet inside of another and encrypting it, the packet is more secure.

L2TP (Layer 2 Tunneling Protocol) is a derivative of PPTP. The advantage of L2TP over PPTP is that it's easier for firewalls to digest. Firewalls map an internal IP address into the firewall's external address plus a unique port number. L2TP uses UDP (User Datagram Protocol) in a way most firewall designs can handle and it's easier to use with network translation boxes as well. There is a problem with L2TP: It has more information in the header than PPTP and that slows performance.

IPSec (IP Security) is a superior protocol for encryption. It offers an integrity check; ensures that the data stream sent is the data stream received; and supports a variety of more powerful encryption algorithms. There is one downside, however. IPSec is tied to the IP protocol; it's not an independent protocol like PPTP and L2TP.

TIP

A *VPDN*—Virtual Private Data Network—is a service that makes its backbone available to corporations for internal and external secured networks. Check in your area for companies offering VPDN services as an alternative to VPNs.

Secure Sockets Layer

Extranet standards are important since one company doesn't dictate what another will use nor the technologies that are adapted. If two companies don't use the same protocols and technologies, no communications occur. There are not yet any extranet standards, but there are protocols useful to extranets.

SSL (Secure Sockets Layer), created by Netscape Communications to secure credit card transactions, is also useful for extranets. SSL encrypts traffic on the Internet so that people can access sensitive documents via the Internet, attend virtual meetings, monitor data and route information to a workgroup, and so on.

SSL is an encryption known as *public/private key*. This encryption uses separate but mathematically linked algorithms for encrypting and decrypting. The algorithm that encrypts is called a *public key* and the one that decrypts is a *private key*. The public key is distributed freely and only the recipient holds the private key.

SSL enables channel security, which provides three basic advantages: a constantly secure communications channel; the channel is always authenticated between client and server; and TCP/IP provides reliability—messages reach their intended destination.

> **NOTE**
> Adding certificates adds a layer of management. They must be issued, paid for, updated, deleted when an employee leaves, and so on.

ISP Security

Many ISPs are using encryption technology to extend VPNs beyond corporate sites. Encryption is the application of mathematical algorithms to data before it's sent across the network. Without the encryption key, the data can't be deciphered. Typically, VPNs require a rigorous authentication in the form of token-based schemes; but some ISPs are trying different options to secure their VPN offerings.

ISPs can place their own routers with built-in encryption software at the corporation's site and in the backbone. The ISP manages the software and the encryption. Another option is to rely on encrypting firewalls. The corporation then would install and administer a UNIX or NT Server for the purpose of encrypting data. A final option is to use a standalone encryptor at either the ISP's points of presence (ISP managed encryption) or at the corporation's premises (corporation managed).

If the ISP manages the encryption, that saves the corporation administrator's time and effort, but it also takes the security control away from the corporation. If the corporation manages the encryption, that means special training for configuration and maintenance of the equipment. You should check into these options to see if your ISP offers similar solutions; you'll have to decide how much control you want over the extranet security.

There are some disadvantages to using router-based encryption. Some manufacturers' router encryption techniques may not meet industry standards and therefore be difficult to configure; Cisco's encryption technique, for example, is proprietary.

Another problem with router-based encryption is its effect on network performance. Since encryption is such a computationally intensive process, you should expect slower packet throughput. ISPs are dealing with this problem by deploying larger routers and/or adding separate processors for encryption and decryption.

Managed firewalls, software running on a UNIX or NT workstation, for example, separate the corporate LAN from the Internet. Firewalls can also encrypt and decrypt the traffic to and from the Net. The corporation, in most cases, decides who will access the network, sets security policy, and maintains passwords.

There are disadvantages to firewalls as encryption/decryption devices. One is that firewalls are installed to UNIX and NT machines, which are not completely secure from hackers, so security is a problem. Another problem is that the ISP can't configure, monitor, and audit the firewall from a centralized location without linked management consoles, so their use is more expensive.

Standalone encryption devices are placed in front of the router at each corporation site or between routers on the ISP's POPs, making them either corporate network or ISP based. Standalone encryption devices are difficult to hack into and they don't impede network performance; however, the ISP must buy and manage yet another piece of hardware, so that solution may cost you more in the end, as well.

RUNNING A WEB SERVER

Running a Web server has become the norm for many businesses and individuals. The increasing speed of data transfer over telephone lines; the reduced cost of ISDN, frame relay, and other technologies; the multitude of software to help publish documents, monitor and optimize sites, and manage sites—all have made it easy to use the Internet for business purposes.

Why run your own Web server? There are several reasons to run your server as opposed to using available space from an ISP or other service provider. For one thing, you have unlimited storage space for your documents, images, video clips, and other files when you run your own server. You also have instant access; no more uploading files. Running your own Web server gives you the freedom to publish what you want, when you want. You don't have to adhere to anyone else's policies. And finally, it gives you control. You can control who gets in and who doesn't; moreover, you control the configuration of the Web server.

Unfortunately, there are disadvantages to running your own Web server. You're responsible, for example, for keeping the site accessible to the Internet, say if a hacker breaches security or the server fails. Also, the machine must run 24 hours a day, 7 days a week, so that makes maintenance more difficult and puts more expense on hardware. Finally, you must pay for a dedicated line when you run your own server; however, if you already have a dedicated line for your business, this won't be such a large expense.

This chapter offers suggestions for preparing and running your own Web server. In this chapter you learn about the following:

- Planning for a Web server

- Managing an extranet

- Web server security

- Web server requirements

- Web server certificates

Getting Ready for the Commercial Web

After you run an extranet for a period of time, you're more likely to want to move your network to the commercial Web. Prepare slowly, interview managers, and find out all you can about your company's business processes before jumping into the Internet and e-commerce. E-commerce is a means to expand and augment in-place sales systems. It should not be separate from your commerce-related systems, but a part of them. Starting with an extranet gives you a good basis on which you can build.

An e-commerce application includes a Web interface and an e-commerce component, such as a catalog with descriptions, a shopping cart, a payment system, and so on. Microsoft, IBM, Lotus Development Corporation, and others supply off-the-shelf e-commerce servers that integrate with backend systems you may already be using. An e-commerce application provides electronic connections to customer service, joint inventory, sales tracking, and such. You must offer users an easy, reliable, and efficient method of transacting business over the Web as opposed to in-person, telephone, or mail sales.

Planning and Preparation

E-commerce enables quick submission, verification, and tracking of orders and claims. Customers believe they save money and transactions are more quickly processed via electronic ordering. To make your Web site more efficient and effective, make sure each site page or component is specific to each business unit within your corporation. For example, the IT department owns the extranet and controls content. The marketing department runs the WWW site. Sales helps develop content for products, and so on.

Extranets that are not well-planned and organized may be filled with content that is often hard to locate and update. You need to organize the extranet before trying to use it for e-commerce. First, assign one person or a group of like-minded people to control each Web server. Each server should be configured and operated similarly in such areas as logon access, file and directory naming and organization, and so on. Make sure you document the extranet structure listing for future reference.

Second, list the intended audience and troubleshooting information (such as who to call if a problem develops). You'll need to set guidelines for standards so that all content will use similar technologies, such as application development tools and approaches. For example, will everyone use pure HTML or a vendor-specific extension? Will JavaBeans or ActiveX Controls be used? No matter what technologies you choose, make their use consistent; using a variety of applications and standards will make revisions and upgrades of the content pages difficult.

Make sure those who develop content for your extranet understand your business goals. The focus should be to disseminate information. And if you plan to expand to e-commerce, focus on generating new business opportunities, not on saving money.

Extranet Management

Operate the extranet as a mission-critical service. Support the extranet desktops, servers, and applications with a help desk or via the extranet. Assign one group or team to be responsible for end-to-end service delivery; publish information—contact list names, phone numbers, and/or email addresses—that lists this team for technical support. Centralize your extranet support for both browsers and applications.

When you're ready to expand your extranet to the Internet, make sure you check the following list. Here are some suggestions for what you'll need:

- Backend systems: databases, data management and report generation applications, transaction applications, activity reporting and tracking.
- Web Servers that offer user authentication, authorization, and account management.
- Web page generation and data formatting programs.
- User query, transaction, and purchasing interfaces.
- Firewalls that filter by protocol, data stream, source, and destination.

Commerce Servers

Before buying commerce server software, make sure it has a common database connectivity, a reporting and analysis tool, a shopping cart, secure connections, and support for taxation software. IBM's Net.Commerce, Microsoft's Site Server, Lotus Development Corporation's Domino.Merchant are some ideas for a commerce server.

Site Server has the best documentation and is the easiest to install. It requires 600M of disk space plus the space required for content. It uses ODBC (Open Database Connectivity) and comes with Microsoft SQL Server for use as the database. Site Server supplies four sample shops from which you can build your site, or you can use one sample shop as your template and change it to suit your needs.

Net.Commerce is the next-best commerce server. Its documentation is a bit sketchy and cryptic. Net.Commerce supports DB2 and ODBC databases and it works with CyberCash. The program comes with a Site Manager, a Store Manager, and a Template Designer so you can create and then customize your store. Net.Commerce also includes helpful demonstration stores.

Domino.Merchant is based on Notes and uses a Notes database as a store for documents. If you've ever used Notes, you already know how complicated these Lotus products are to install, configure, and administer; Domino.Merchant is no different. It is, however, the perfect commerce server if you're familiar with Notes and Domino.

Domino.Merchant is compatible with DB2, CICS, and ODBC. It also works with CyberCash and taxation software. It's also important to note that Microsoft Internet Explorer 4.0 won't communicate with Domino.Merchant's SSL service under some circumstances (if the products are configured with self-signed certificates) so that can cut the number of public users who can access your site.

Preparing to Secure a Web Site

When running a Web site, you must know your systems to appropriately secure them. You should understand how the backend system is connected to the Web server and you'll need to audit all accesses to your server. It's also a good idea to assign a security team to review policies, audit logs, and carry out general Web site administration and procedures. The team can keep an eye out for problems, report periodically on any breaches or updated security actions, and gather information and suggestions for improved security.

Here are some additional security suggestions:

Use firewalls and routers to protect your LAN and data; filter protocols are not generally required for business operations.

Evaluate CGI (Common Gateway Interface) scripts and programs periodically to make sure they're performing at optimum level and upgrade these programs and utilities when necessary.

Use a cryptographic authentication system to protect your site from DNS corruption.

Change your administrative passwords once a month or so.

Document all services running on the site, such as FTP, telnet, SMTP, and so on, and keep running logs of activities on these sites for evaluation.

Make sure you have a backup and a disaster recovery plan.

E-Commerce

Electronic commerce (e-commerce) and *iMalls* (Internet shopping centers) enable a business to reach millions of potential customers and increase sales through electronic marketing. They also provide low-cost advertising, enable customer feedback, and make it easier for customers to get in touch with you. Conventional marketing methods no longer limit the business world today.

There are a couple of disadvantages to Web marketing. Exposure over the Internet isn't the same as running a commercial in prime-time TV. There is no guaranteed audience on the Internet and the effectiveness of your Web site is hard to measure. Additionally, many people have limited access to the Internet and/or limited knowledge about the technology. By advertising only on the Internet, you'll lose a certain sector of the public that doesn't even own a computer.

However, if you maintain a good Web site, you'll usually benefit from it. An interesting site, for example, is passed from user to user for good word-of-mouth advertising. You might want to provide technical support, product information, useful tips, or some other "hook" that makes people want to visit your site.

The Business of Running a Web Server

As you consider what type of site you'll run, which products to sell, and what information you want to place on the site, you'll need to think about your Web site as an extension of your business. How will users pay for their transactions? What are some common mistakes you should avoid? How will you manage the server with everything else you have to do? This section offers some suggestions.

Credit on the Net

Will you accept credit cards for purchases over the Internet? If so, you should process all orders using SSL (Secure Sockets Layer) session encryption technology. SSL leaves the card information decrypted on the server so it's not exposed to unscrupulous employees or hackers.

SET (Secure Electronic Transaction) is a standard used in merchant servers that requires credit card users to receive digital certificates to authenticate buyers and sellers. Upgrades are expensive to any merchant server that is SET compliant; but VISA and MasterCard will make it worthwhile by reducing the rates charged to you. SET lowers the risk of bad credit transactions because of end-to-end encrypted authentication between consumer, merchant, bank, and card.

Common Internet Business Mistakes

Before you go online with your commerce server and Web site, consider some common mistakes businesses make where Internet commerce is concerned:

Legal issues.   Find out about sales taxes and watch copyright violations. Be careful of using encryption as it is regulated (regarded as a military weapon); you cannot take encryption software to some foreign countries (on your laptop for example), so sending it in email messages may also be illegal.

Don't spam.   Spamming gives you a bad reputation; and some ISPs will kick you off of their network if you're caught spamming.

Don't ask visitors to your sites so you can gather information from them, such as name, phone number, and so on.   If you do ask for information from visitors, disclose your plans for use of that information. Also, give the visitor a chance to not give you the information. The Federal Trade Commission is voicing fierce opposition to certain data collection practices—about children, for example. Publish a privacy policy to display on your site.

Keep your content up to date.   Respond to customer inquiries, troubleshoot their problems.

Continue to improve your site.   Add chat, video, push technologies for greater efficiency and to reach customers more effectively.

Check out the competition, consistently.

Don't overdesign the Web site.   Large graphics take a long time to download and you'll likely lose the customer before your page appears.

Web Site Management

Your Web site should reflect the philosophy and attitude of the entire company. Check with colleagues, users, and coworkers to see what they feel is important to add to the Web site. Balance your ideas for the site with those of everyone else in the organization.

Assign a team to content creation and Web site management so you don't have to manage everything. The members of the team should possess the skill set for graphic design, simple programming, visual layout, technical writing skills, computer system management, networking configuration, maintenance, and troubleshooting. Someone should know the OS of the server as well as the ins and outs of the server itself. Someone else can produce the basic traffic reports from the Web server and interpret the data; then use it to improve the Web site. And yet another team member can troubleshoot problems with the site.

PINGing as Troubleshooting

PING is a utility or diagnostic tool (Packet Internet Grouper) you use to test connectivity. PING tests TCP/IP configurations and connections failures by using the Internet Control Message Protocol ICMP echo request and echo reply messages to determine whether a particular TCP/IP host is available and functional. You can use PING to test your connection to the ISP's router or server, to your own router, and to other servers on the Internet. All you need to know is the IP address of the node you want to check.

Type ping *IP_address* to test an Internet connection. If the ping is successful and the connection is good, a message will read something similar to the following:

Pinging IP_address with 32 bytes of data:

Reply from IP address: bytes- x time<10ms TTL- x

Reply from IP address: bytes- x time<10ms TTL- x

Reply from IP address: bytes- x time<10ms TTL- x

Reply from IP address: bytes- x time<10ms TTL- x

TTL (Time To Live) number of seconds a datagram is allowed to stay on the wire before it's discarded.

If the PING does not return the preceding reply, then that particular node, router, or server is not working.

Preparing to Run a Web Server

Your commercial Web may flood you with 5000, 10,000, or more queries each week. Plan ahead to handle the load. If you don't know how you will distribute the incoming mail and requests, you'll likely be overwhelmed and perhaps even lose business due to your lack of response.

To prepare for publishing a Web site, you should set up an intranet that extends throughout your entire organization. Assign duties to each employee;

some could gather information, others disseminate it, and still others can respond to messages and requests.

Include on your intranet procedures for handling situations, such as customer complaints, information requests, problems, and such. Also include the information needed to make responses: product sheets, service outlines, contact numbers, and so on. You also can use the intranet to complete your business by creating product information and marketing materials on it, receiving orders and inquiries, and performing shipping and billing paperwork.

Web Server Requirements

To determine the exact requirements for your Web server, refer to the documentation for the server program and operating system you'll be running. There are some basic recommendations, however, that are based on the job the computer must do to perform as a Web server.

You'll want a fast processor—Pentium or RISC system, for example—for quick processing of requests and responses. RAM is another important item. Don't skimp on memory. Disk space is important for the Web content. In addition to text files, video and sound clips, images, and multimedia files require a lot of disk space. SCSI drives are best for performance and reliability for this type of server. Additionally, consider a second, mirrored drive for redundancy, if you don't choose to get a second exact copy of the first server as a backup.

You'll also want a CD-ROM drive, a tape drive for backing up files, and communications equipment—modem, ISDN TA assembly, or other equipment you need for the Internet connection.

As part of the requirements for a Web server, don't forget about the device drivers, operating system, Web server software, content publishing software, proxy services, and so on.

Domain Name

A domain name has two parts: the name and the extension that identifies the type of organization. The domain name must be unique, so you'll want to think of alternative names in case your first choice is taken. The extension is the top-level domain. Following are the most common top-level domain extensions:

COM	Commercial
ORG	Not-for-profit or noncommercial
EDU	Educational institution
GOV	Government organization

MIL	Military institution
NET	Larger network
US	Geographic location. Also UK (United Kingdom), JP (Japan), and so on

Next, register your domain name with the InterNIC. First, try your ISP to see if it registers names for customers. The InterNIC Web site is http://rs.internic.net. You may need additional information when you register the name, such as a contact name in your organization, your organization's technical contact name and information, and facts about your ISP's server (machine names and IP addresses for the primary and backup name servers).

Content

Your next step is to set up a homepage and other HTML documents in which your content will be presented to the public. You can either learn the HTML language or you can use an application to help you easily set up your Web pages. Microsoft Word and other Windows programs offer HTML conversion for your documents, but they are simplistic pages at best. Microsoft Publisher offers templates for setting up a Web site with some very good designs—links, icons, and formatting included. There are also other programs, like Microsoft's FrontPage, that let you create, publish, and organize entire sites on the Web.

Figure 7.1 shows an HTML document in text format, with codes keyed in as the document is being designed. Figure 7.2 shows the HTML document as it looks in the Web browser.

Web Certification and Training

Training programs are available for download from the Internet; you also can find training programs on video or cassette tapes, in classes, books, and so on. Certification programs are offered by various organizations as well. At this time, there are no standards for Web certification training, so it's difficult to gauge the expertise gained from the training, but it won't hurt and will likely offer much needed information about managing a Web site.

Check training and certification programs carefully. There are many different meanings for the term *webmaster*; for example, one type of training may be related only to the Internet or only to an intranet; other certifications may only be specific to one NOS or designed only for marketing, finance, or public relations.

Figure 7.1 HTML tags describe the size of text and the location of images.

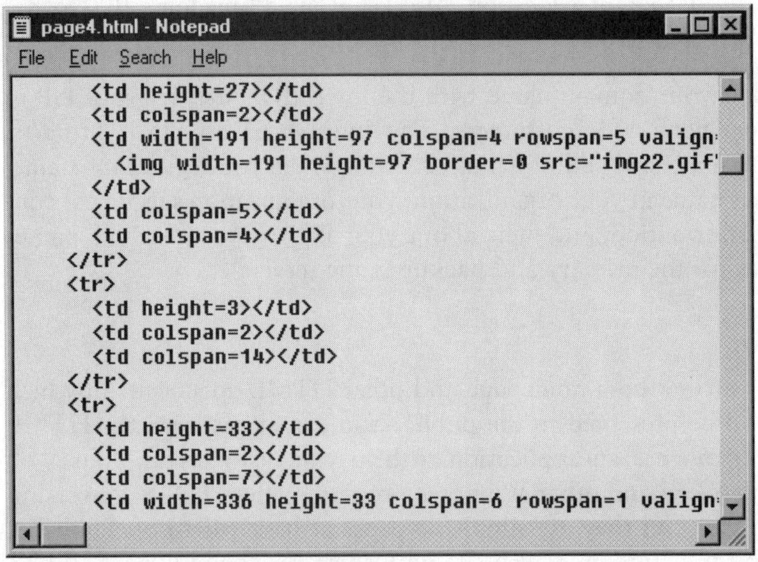

```
page4.html - Notepad
File  Edit  Search  Help
      <td height=27></td>
      <td colspan=2></td>
      <td width=191 height=97 colspan=4 rowspan=5 valign
        <img width=191 height=97 border=0 src="img22.gif'
      </td>
      <td colspan=5></td>
      <td colspan=4></td>
   </tr>
   <tr>
      <td height=3></td>
      <td colspan=2></td>
      <td colspan=14></td>
   </tr>
   <tr>
      <td height=33></td>
      <td colspan=2></td>
      <td colspan=7></td>
      <td width=336 height=33 colspan=6 rowspan=1 valign
```

HTML Language

HTML is fairly simple. Using a text editor or saving the file in a text-only format, you can enter the HTML codes that create a nice-looking Web page. You can view your page in progress and upon completion with your Web browser, to see how the formatting is going.

To work in HTML, you enter the text as you would with any document. Then you can come back and enter the codes. Codes such as <TITLE>, <H1>, <I>, and so on, represent title, heading, and italics. You enter the code at the beginning of the text you want to be a title, for example, and enter the same code plus a forward slash at the end of the text, as in the following:

<TITLE>Humble Opinions Company</TITLE>

Other codes enable you to insert images:

<IMG SRC="http://www.bender.net/computer.gif"> and links: <A HREF="http://www.bender.net">.

Figure 7.2 The HTML page displays photos, logos, and colored text in a Web browser.

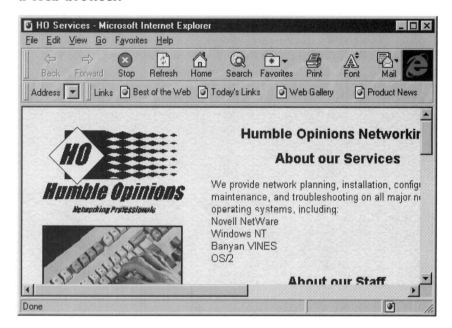

> **NOTE**
>
> With an FTP server, you set up user accounts for those you want to log on to your server. You can receive files from users and you can provide files to others. To set up an FTP server, you need a permanent connection to the Net and FTP server software compatible with your operating system. You must be careful with FTP servers. They are a possible point of failure where your Internet security is concerned. Anonymous FTP users are the hazard.

Webmaster

Web technologies are changing so quickly that it's hard to agree on the definition of a webmaster's responsibilities. Generally the term *webmaster* encompasses everything from a beginning programmer to management-level marketing professional, managing all Web work, HTML and technical work, and acting as an overall project manager.

Major Web Certifications

Web development is a hot career in IT and Web certification may help you get the training needed to get your Web site up and running. Naturally, Microsoft and Novell are offering Web and Internet training and certification, but other companies are coming into the picture and many are providing certification in nonsoftware-specific fields.

Following are just a few of the available certifications. Since there are no standards for Web certification, definitions, requirements, and skills vary from company to company and from test to test.

Intranet

Internet

System Security

Web Administration

Web Development

Windows NT Web Administration

Windows NT Web Development

Java Programming

Certified Systems Engineer+Internet (Microsoft)

Certified Internet Business Strategist (Novell)

Certified Web Designer (Novell)

Certified Internet Architect (Novell)

Certified Internet Webmaster

Certified Internet Webmaster Administrator

Certified Internet Webmaster E-Commerce Professional

Prices for certification range between $600 and $8000 with the average cost being around $2500.

If your company or Web site is small, you can likely handle it by yourself or with the help of several assistants. However, as your Web site grows and becomes more complex, you will want to hire people to manage the site or even outsource the job. Following are some skills a Webmaster needs to know:

• Graphics and multimedia techniques

• Web development tools like HTML, Java and JavaScript, CGI scripts, and such

- Applications programming in UNIX, NT, Perl, C, C++, Java, HTML, CGI scripts
- Relational databases familiarity
- Network engineering in UNIX or NT administration
- Router installation and configuration
- Network monitoring and performance measurements
- Network security and protocols (TCP/IP, HTTP, FTP)

Also, a Webmaster will need a mix of communications, marketing, and technical skills to work on e-commerce projects and consumer-oriented retail sites.

Web Site Engineer

A *Web site engineer* is a technical person who maintains the link between the Internet provider and the Web site. Naturally, this person may also perform other duties, but connectivity between Internet and LAN/WAN sites within the company is the majority of his or her responsibilities. The Web site engineer must keep abreast of new technologies, create and maintain the connections between the Internet and email, insure the firewall mechanisms are working, and perhaps oversee security as well.

Web Site Programmer

A *Web site programmer* designs programs and coding for the site. He or she would also perform testing and debugging. A programmer may also modify procedures to solve problems with equipment, capacity, and limitations of the hardware. Technical knowledge in application software used to develop and maintain the Web site is a definite requirement.

Web Site Performance

It's difficult to create a Web site that balances between cutting-edge content and high performance. Too much data, graphics, sounds, or video, for example, can cut down on the performance of your site, but too little content can prove boring to your site visitors. A cost-saving approach is to deliver cutting-edge content quickly, without planning ahead, and investing in support resources.

Users cannot enjoy a site that doesn't perform well, and thus they don't return. Keep an eye on performance (using a performance monitor). Plus, there are organizations that can test your site for you at various times of day and provide reports about the performance seen by users. Alternatively, you can get a product (such as Site Technologies' SiteSweeper) to calculate the size of files and the time it takes a user to download pages.

Network Performance

Bottlenecks in the network connection to the Internet, which handles the Web site traffic, email, requests, and other activities, can cause a slowdown in network performance. If your ISP is three or four hops away from a major backbone, that could be causing performance problems; ask your service provider about the connections. You might consider getting a major provider closer to a backbone, which will probably be more expensive but will give you better performance and provide fewer possible points of failure. If you are close to a major backbone, you can upgrade your Internet connection, which may prove to be costly.

Machine Performance

Check your computer; your Web server may be slow. You can upgrade to a faster processor or to multiple processors if this is the case. Check the speed of the server by monitoring the load on your current machine during peak hours of access on the Net—say 8 A.M., noon, 5 P.M., 7 P.M., and 10 P.M. If the load rises significantly for long periods of time, you should get a faster machine.

You should also watch for memory swapping. When your RAM becomes full, it begins memory swapping, which can slow access time and create performance bottlenecks. Increasing RAM will help.

Another problem with performance is a Web server that's not a dedicated machine. You can move databases, ad rotations, usage analysis tools, and content generators to another machine to get the best performance from your Web server. Each of these programs use RAM and CPU cycles and so they hamper performance and speed.

Server Performance

Spot-check your server periodically by opening a browser and accessing server pages; make sure they load quickly. Try to do this from a network segment other

> **NOTE**
>
> If your Web server is UNIX-based, increase the maximum number of processes, as well as the maximum number of open connections on the system. If your machine handles more than a few hits per second, these steps will help. Also, apply all available patches for the UNIX operating system you're running to possibly increase performance.

than the one on which the Web server resides and it's best if you can use a dial-up connection rather than network connection; this gives you the most accurate test. You can also use testing tools, such as SQA LoadTest (Rational Software).

If a Web server is a bottleneck, try balancing the Web site across multiple servers that mirror site content; this distributes incoming requests. Another method to relieve a bottleneck is in dynamic URL redirection: the main Web server handles all incoming requests but it redirects the browser to another URL that fulfills the requests and balances the traffic.

Content Optimization

The size of the content affects the server's performance. Use usage analysis software to understand how the Web site is performing and how the site is being used. By studying the click-stream path of users, you can optimize the content they see. Java applets and modules that force the browser to load a plug-in slow the site; keep this type of content on the homepage so that pages off the main path load quickly.

Also, don't make multimedia effects the default for viewing your site; you can offer these effects as special features instead and let the user decide. Banner ads can slow a site, especially when new banners are from servers that are not local to the Web server. Don't refer to banner ad generators on another site; store banners locally if at all possible. Keep images as small as possible and in JPEG format instead of the larger GIF format. Use several small images instead of one large and include a text alternative for every image.

> **TIP**
>
> Consider compatibilities. If your shop uses UNIX and NT, use Netscape servers and browsers. Microsoft Internet Explorer doesn't run UNIX. Using Netscape means it runs on UNIX and NT and you only have one product to support.

Web Server Search Engines

To make your corporate Web site a success, make sure you have a good search engine. A search engine is vital since information can become buried in mounds and mounds of content. A search engine lets users find keywords appearing in your documents within your site. You need an application that can maintain indexes of the site, searchable database, and display results.

Each search engine uses a different way of performing searches, which is why your results vary so much. Some search engines search for a keyword in the URL; others search for a title on the page; and still other search engines search the full text of pages and display results depending on how many times the text was found in any given page. So realize that the search engine you use will follow its own rules for listing search results; make sure the engine you use is the best candidate for your Web site.

Web Server Packages

There are many Web server packages you can use to help develop your site. Microsoft, Netscape, and other companies make it easy for you by providing templates, samples, and the foundation for sites. You also can purchase software programs that are just email servers or FTP servers; you can find an application for just about any purpose. This section outlines the most common Web server packages.

Netscape SuiteSpot

SuiteSpot is a server suite that provides everything you need for Web publishing, content management, messaging, and so on. Netscape SuiteSpot comes in Standard and Professional Editions. The Standard edition includes the following:

- Calendar Server for scheduling and calendaring

- Collabra Server as a discussion and collaboration server

- Enterprise server for Web management

- Messaging Server for the distribution of email

The Professional edition of SuiteSpot includes the previously mentioned servers plus the following:

- Compass Server to manage your Web documents

- Certificate Server to enable the creation and management of public key certificates

- Proxy Server for replication and filtering of content

Netscape's SuiteSpot can work with UNIX, HP-UX, SIX, and Solaris operating systems as well as with NT Server.

Robots, Spiders, and Ants

Web *robots* are programs that automatically cover the Web to retrieve documents that have specific references or terms in them. When you request a term or topic from a search engine, for example, robots go out and look for that term or topic. Robots are also called *bots*, *spiders*, and *ants*; basically, they all refer to the same process.

Each type of robot uses different search strategies. They generally start from a list of URLs. An indexing robot may also file or list HTML titles—as in the <title> code—or other special hidden tags. When you create your own Web page, you should register it with multiple search engines, or robots. Check the search engine's page for a submission form or a URL address you can use to notify it of your new page.

If you're a Web server administrator, robots may cause you some consternation, although they likely will cause no harm to your site. To find out if a robot has visitied your site, check your server logs for sites that retrieve multiple documents in a short period of time. You might also keep an eye out for any sites checking for the file /robots.txt, which is a list of special instructions you may create for visiting robots.

If you notice problems with your site when you're monitoring or analyzing an access log file, that could be caused by a robot. Called *rapid-fire*, a robot may be trying to access your entire site very quickly and this could cause performance problems. If you have a low-performance server, you may see refused connections, performance slowdowns, or even a system crash.

If you run into a problem such as this, try to find out the IP address of the robot. If you can identify the site, you can email the responsible party and ask them about the robots.

You also can keep robots off of your server. A basic method is to create a text file, called robots.txt, and in it put the following:

    User-agent:
    Disallow: /

Fill in the name of the search engine, such as yahoo or webcrawler, after User-agent:; the disallow statement as is means no robots are allowed on your server.

You can be even more specific in your robots.txt file. After Disallow: / list the directories on your server you don't want the robot to access. You can list multiple directories, one on each line of the file.

UNIX Web Servers

There are many Web servers for UNIX because it has been around for so very long. UNIX and Linux are extremely stable operating systems that provide functionality and speed. Any Web server you create on UNIX is going to be powerful, but not necessarily easy to use. Following are only three of the many available Web server applications.

CERN httpd is a hypertext server that can be used as an HTTP server. CERN httpd can act as a proxy server for HTTP, FTP, Gopher, WAIS, news, and others. It performs caching, runs server-side executable scripts, and includes an index search interface. CERN httpd also handles multiple file formats.

The Apache Web server is an HTTP server for UNIX. It provides virtual servers, server-side push, and CGI.

The AOL Server for UNIX provides server caching, server-side includes, and vendor-specific database accessing API and CGI.

Microsoft's BackOffice

Microsoft's BackOffice provides many server systems for making and managing a Web site. NT Server is the foundation of the BackOffice Suite. NT's security features, performance monitoring, communication tools, and other features make it the perfect base for other server applications.

Also included in NT Server are the Microsoft Internet Information Server (IIS) and FrontPage. FrontPage is a Web publishing application capable of creating, managing, storing, and updating Web pages and links. IIS is a Web server program that provides various services to visitors, including WWW, FTP, and Gopher.

BackOffice offers a Proxy Server, Exchange Server, Index Server, and SQL Server that you can use to help develop and organize your Web site. Use SQL Server to manage the databases needed not only in a network LAN but to organize and supply a Web server with data and information. Exchange Server can deliver email services for the LAN and the Internet. Index Server is a search engine you can use on your Web site. Proxy Server creates a safe barrier between your LAN and the Internet.

In addition to the BackOffice servers, Microsoft has a Site Server for helping you gather information about your Web site and then analyze that information. You can target groups of visitors with your ads on the site and use Site Analyst to view and update links, trace specific files, and more.

Microsoft's Commercial Internet System and Merchant Server provide the tools and utilities to run your own online storefront, mail server, news server, and more.

Microsoft Internet Information Server

Microsoft's Internet Information Server (IIS) is a part of NT Server. It's also a part of BackOffice, but you don't have to use it with the other BackOffice server applications. IIS is a network file and information server. It also includes a Gopher and FTP service. But mainly, IIS is an Internet and/or intranet Web server.

IIS is compatible with SSL, TCP/IP, and other Internet standards. Since IIS is integrated with NT Server, that NOS's security features work well with the Web server. Additionally, NT includes FrontPage, a Web content program that you can use to create and format your Web pages and organize your Web site.

IIS includes views and utilities that enable you to administer and manage your Web site, from links to email, to troubleshooting problems with configuration and access.

Claris Internet Solutions

Although not a Web server by any means, Claris does offer some Internet applications for the Macintosh computer, including the following:

- Claris Home Page is a Web authoring tool for creating Web pages.
- ClarisWorks—a word-processing, spreadsheet, and database application—provides for HTML formatting so you can also format documents in ClarisWorks to publish to the Web.

Claris also includes a database application, FileMaker Pro, for enabling database solutions on a Web site.

Claris OfficeM@il is an email package for Internet use.

OUTSOURCING

Introduction to Book Nine

O*utsourcing* is using outside resources to perform jobs within your company. Outsourcing is also a management strategy; you choose what functions you want to outsource based on your company's resources, priorities, staff experience, administrator's time, and so on. Businesses have always hired consultants and contractors to perform noncore jobs; to share access to resources and technologies; or to help when workload is extreme. Using outsourcing simply means the company will restructure around these outside relationships now to change the look and feel of the company.

Outsourcing not only saves you money, but also enables you to partner with organizations that have expertise in certain fields instead of dealing with those fields inhouse. Generally, you outsource those functions that are not core competencies; but what you outsource depends on what business you want to be in—you may need to outsource mission-critical operations as well.

Outsourcing provides you with access to specialized skills and technical expertise—someone with specialized knowledge and skills. View outsourcing as another management tool that supplies the growing demands for expertise that's difficult and expensive to develop internally.

Following are some reasons to outsource:

- To get jobs done that are difficult to manage or technologically complex
- To improve the administrator's focus on other networking functions
- To provide resources not internally available
- To reduce operating costs
- To free resources and staff for other purposes
- To access experts and skilled help

PRELIMINARY GROUNDWORK

Outsourcing is using outside companies or individuals to perform services for your company. You might want to outsource training or administrator testing, application development or Internet services. By outsourcing some of your company's network activities, you receive the knowledge and expertise of professionals at a fraction of the cost it would take for you or someone in your company to learn and perform the same functions.

Suppose you want your company to have a presence on the Internet. To set up and run a Web server and site means hours and hours of work—choosing and contracting connections to the Internet, purchasing hardware, configuring hardware and software, creating and formatting content, installing and configuring Web software, and creating, managing, maintaining, updating, and troubleshooting the site. All of this on top of your current duties is just not possible. And to try and hire someone with the expertise means interviewing, possible training, constant supervision, and so on. What can you do? Outsource.

There is an outsourcer available for just about every network job you can think of: software support, technical expertise, server administration, and so on. Just about anything to do with the Internet is made up of one large outsource function; ISP's outsource their fast connections, mail and news servers, Web services, and so on, to companies and individuals all the time. Also, following are just a few services an outsourcer might offer. See Chapter 3 of this book, "Types of Outsourcers," for more detailed information.

Training: network, application, administration, hardware repair and maintenance, and so on.

Mail and messaging: both LAN and Internet.

Groupware: document collaboration, bulletin board services, shared information folders, and so on.

Remote access services: virtual private networks, private accesses, remote server management, and such.

Security: policies, procedures, network configuration, and such.

In this chapter, you learn the following:

- Advantages and disadvantages of outsourcing

- What's hot in outsourcing

- The future of outsourcing

Advantages and Disadvantages

For every advantage of outsourcing, you'll find a disadvantage. For instance, while you're saving money by removing capital items from your traditional budget and reducing personnel costs, you're also increasing telecommunications costs and vendor overhead. While improving system reliability and availability, you may also decrease service levels resulting from poorly defined requirements.

There is no doubt that outsourcing offers many advantages, say, for your human resources. Improved services without adding positions, new services without expensive staff retraining, and more budget flexibility are a few of the benefits. Detriments may include restaffing once the outsourcing relationship ends, loss of critical knowledge in-house, staff morale may be adversely impacted, and so on.

Clearly, you'll need to judge for yourself and your business whether to outsource or not. This section outlines a few of the advantages and disadvantages for your convenience.

Advantages of Outsourcing

Most outsourcers offer services that can be individualized to fit your company's needs. Whether you require a monthly service or random assistance, minor help or significant work, a few tasks or many, you'll likely find an outsourcer who can help you.

Outsourcing can be a reliable and cost-effective option for most modern companies. Outsourcing enables you to save time in training administrators and/or managers in new technologies as well as save time performing administrative responsibilities. Problems can usually be solved quickly when outsourcers are involved and therefore you save on downtime or wasted users' time.

The dynamic nature of the technology and products makes it nearly impossible for you to keep up with everything. Ever-changing requirements mean dedicated attention must be paid to the technologies. When you outsource to a professional who works with one or two technologies, you gain benefits from that person's skill and expertise.

- Outsourcing can improve the likelihood that you'll be able to manage the mission-critical network tasks while someone else takes care of the details.

- If your network is spread out over several locations, outsourcing some of the responsibilities can save in downtime, maintenance tasks, response time, travel, and so on.

- If your management staff is already overburdened or if you have an ineffective management structure, an outsourcer may provide better overall service for your network.

- Outsourcers often provide support when the regular staff cannot, such as after hours. Also, you can let the outsourcer take the monotonous jobs, leaving the more exciting tasks to your staff.

- If you use outsourcers to perform some of the many administrative tasks that must be accomplished, you have more time to concentrate on network development, planning, and monitoring.

- Outsourcing eliminates the tasks of hiring temporary or perhaps non-skilled people, dividing the workforce into shifts, finding enough resources to cover new staff, and dealing with obsolete equipment.

- Outsourcing also means a savings in salaries and training; the out-sourced, contracted labor can replace new employees you might need to hire otherwise.

- Often outsourcers provide an instantaneous response to issues by a team of experts.

- Outsourcing can also offer you competitive advantages, since you'll have more time to concentrate on business.

Disadvantages of Outsourcing

Naturally, there are problems with outsourcing. Most administrators hate to relinquish control over the network and business. Letting someone else into your system means you no longer hold the reins. You don't know if the out-sourcer has real-world experience with the kinds of problems you encounter, or if that outsourcer has the technology available to diagnose and fix your problems quickly and accurately.

Security is another disadvantage. Any time you let someone from the outside into your network or system, you risk a security breach.

Sometimes, the suggested cost savings or improved service of outsourcing never materializes, which is why you must be very careful when contracting with an outsourcer—get and check references, state your requirements, get a contract, and so on. For more information, see Chapter 2 of this book, "Planning and Preparations."

Another possible problem is that the quality of support may not be what you thought it would be. Again, the answer is in your contract. If your contract states that you have the right to cancel the contract at any time, you can try to rectify the problem and then get out before you lose time, effort, and money.

Following are a few more disadvantages of outsourcing:

- Losing control of the outsourcer.

- Losing personnel to either the outsourcer or to another company because of improved training.

- Outsourcing for the wrong reasons and therefore not getting the most from the experience.

Outsourcing Now and in the Future

The popularity of outsourcing has grown considerably in the past 10 years, considering how quickly technology has developed. In the future, some enterprises may well outsource their entire network to integrators, consultants, and service providers. But for now, there seem to be many varied consultants and outsourcers out there, each offering a different service and some that may fill your needs.

What's Hot in Outsourcing

Although many network tasks can be outsourced, the hot fields now are network management, enterprise and wide area networking, Internet Web services, remote access, and client/server migration. The demand is so huge, outsourcing providers proliferate. Large vendors, such as IBM, Digital Equipment, and so on, now offer various network consulting and system integration services. Consulting corporations, value-added resellers, telephone companies, and others are also willing and eager to help you with your outsourcing needs.

Network management outsourcing can include anything from total network administration to simply backing up the system. Most outsourcing jobs, however, will fall somewhere in between. Outsourcers offer to monitor; optimize; update servers and workstations; install, configure, and maintain connections and routers; analyze and improve bandwidth; train users; and so on. If the network administrator must perform a task, that task can also be outsourced.

Enterprise networking outsourcing is hot now, not so much the management of the network but the planning, organizing, and building of the network. When a network must stretch across a city or the country, there are many factors to consider in building an efficient and effective network. Outsourcing the overall design and engineering of that network makes sense; outsourcing provides the expertise and knowledge to get the job done well.

Internet strategies are even more involved than setting up an enterprise network. The number of Internet technologies is staggering; the importance of an Internet presence is mammoth. Web design, Web site hosting, content creation and organization, e-commerce—all of these responsibilities can weigh down the network administrator. Outsourcing to the experts is a smart solution.

Remote access has become more and more important in recent years because there are more salespeople, business travelers, and telecommuters working out of the traditional office setting. The corporation saves money and the remote user can often accomplish more when remote access is used. Mobile computing is a growing practice with developing technologies to support it.

Remote access outsourcing is hot now for many reasons. Primarily, however, is the advent of virtual private networks. By using secure connections that travel over the Internet between the corporate LAN and the mobile user, the LAN administrator doesn't have to install, configure, maintain, or manage any of the hardware or technology, thereby saving time, energy, and money.

Client/server computing has become more and more popular in the last few years. Migrations from mainframes and minicomputers mean more flexibility for corporations: remote user support, more easily managed data and applications, and so on. This major migration also means hardware and software must be modified or installed, new applications must be developed, strategies formulated, users and administrators trained, and the list goes on and on. Depending on the business of the company, the switch to client/server computing can be intimidating. Outsourcing the migration can help the IT or MIS department tremendously.

What the Future Holds

With the current popularity of outsourcing, there is no doubt the business will continue to grow and services will tend to improve as the technologies expand and multiply.

Predicted as future strategies for outsourcing are general "contractors" who gather different vendors, suppliers, consultants, and other outsourcers to consolidate and manage their services for the customer. With each outsourcer comes a different expertise; when a company requires more outsourcing, more sources will be called upon. Rather than you managing multiple outsourcers, the general contractor's job is to plan, manage, and implement the various outsourcers.

Outsourcers will also invest heavily in technology to drive down their cost of labor on specific services. This will make the technological advances push forward at remarkable rates and thus provide better services for everyone involved.

PLANNING AND PREPARATIONS

Outsourcing can reduce costs; introduce cash; increase satisfaction among users, customers, and administrative staff; and benefit your company in many other ways. However, when planning outsourcing arrangements, you'll need to make sure you've considered every option.

Enlist the help of your colleagues and coworkers by forming a committee to review the needs and requirements. Have everyone work separately and then come together to work out the following issues:

- Identify your objectives for outsourcing.

- Determine the corporation's core and support functions.

- List the expectations from outsourcing.

- What are the service levels you expect?

- Consider the future goals of the company and the outsourcing.

- What factors are influencing you to outsource?

- What are the cost expectations for initial services and maintenance of services?

- Select the services to be outsourced and define the manner in which the services should be provided.

- Figure out baseline service-level requirements, financial information, a measurement system, and evaluation criteria for vendor proposals.

Outsourcing any or all of your networking duties is not an easy job. You must consider the reputation of the outsourcer, fees, responsibilities of your staff, and more. This chapter offers some advice. In this chapter you learn about the following:

- Deciding when you should outsource

- Finding a reliable outsourcer

- Using contracts and legal service agreements
- Renegotiating a contract

When to Outsource

Network administration and management is more than a full-time job. It's tempting to outsource some or even all of your tasks to someone else, so you can get on with your core business duties. The network is, however, critical to your business and the flow of information; you can't get on with your business without it. So, as integral as your network is, can you really trust the entire network or any part of it to someone else?

You might find it necessary to do so. With technologies advancing every day, new applications and procedures necessary for a successful network to run, more users with varying needs added to the system, and so on, you can't do it all. So how do you decide when and what to outsource? It's not easy, but perhaps these guidelines will help.

First, consider if you have any network tasks that are not currently being managed efficiently. For whatever reason—lack of knowledge, time, support, or such—these tasks are being forsaken or inadequately supervised. Also, do you have any network resources or tasks that are out of control? Perhaps the technology is more than you can deal with, or the needs of the users are more than you can handle. These are the types of projects or tasks that you should consider outsourcing.

Here are some examples of the previous criteria:

- Backups that have not been regularly kept up or checked are going to cause you a large problem at some point; it's guaranteed.

- Security has always been good but with the move to the Internet, you realize your system can likely be breached.

- You've been adding more and more mobile users since the corporation declared a telecommuting directive.

- You want to connect multiple LAN segments but the installation and configuration of the routers is beyond your capabilities.

These are the types of jobs you might outsource.

Second, consider what jobs you have that require expertise you and your staff do not have. Could you hire a full-time expert or train an existing employee to perform this job? If not, then you might want to outsource. Consider setting up a Web site, for example. You need to set goals, create an overall design for the site, gather data for content and enter that data, format the content pages, manage links, optimize the site and constantly update it, just to name a few things. Now what if you want to extend your Web site to an online store, capable of taking online orders and processing transactions? Can you and your staff deal with these tasks?

Depending on your job, your network, your data, your budget, and other factors, you'll have to decide whether it's worth it to you to outsource some or all of your networking functions. It's definitely worth the consideration.

Finding an Outsourcer

Generally, outsourcers are trained in one specific area, product, or procedure; however, usually they are better trained and more knowledgeable than the average person is. Outsourcers are particularly motivated to stay on top of the emerging technologies that will benefit you so they will remain valuable to you. The most important thing you want in an outsourcer is to be able to trust him or her in handling your system.

A good price is important, of course; however, you also need someone who can offer the required services with experience and effectiveness. In addition to pricing, look for confidence, dependability, competence, and quality of service.

How much outsourcing you need will depend on your business, your priorities, your duties, what you need to get done in a day. Try to find an outsourcer who can grow with your needs. Establish a relationship with a company so that you can learn to trust the work and the people involved. Don't look for short-term solutions when outsourcing; the more familiar you are with them, the more work you can trust them to do.

Also, consider these points:

Do a lot of up-front research before signing a contract, measure and evaluate performance. Ask for references and check the references thoroughly.

Make sure the outsourcer has enough financial stability to compete and succeed.

The outsourcer should know about the latest technologies and use state-of-the-art equipment and tools.

The outsourcer should be able to provide a series of reports—both standard and custom-made—that enable you to review and monitor their work.

Ask the outsourcer if he or she has a help desk or other support line.

As you work with the outsourcer, you should try to determine if he or she can meet the following requirements:

The outsourcer should be able to easily identify problems and quickly dispatch of them and be able to see problem areas before there is an actual problem.

The outsourcer's staff should all be skilled and experienced.

The outsourcer should have a commitment to research and development of new technologies.

NOTE

Consultants, vendors, manufacturers, service providers, and other specialists in their fields offer services that can be considered outsourcers to a network administrator.

Working with the Outsourcer

When you have an outline of your requirements and objectives for the outsourced job(s), you're ready to sit down with an outsourcer and discuss your outline. First, if possible, hire the outsourcer to do a small or simple job to begin with so you can see how he or she does. Then you can hire him or her for larger jobs if you're happy with the work.

Next, you should assign a key liaison to work with the outsourcer and have that person attend all meetings with the outsourcer. The liaison should be informed of all contract negotiations, guarantees and promises made by the outsourcer, and your reservations and expectations. Also, have your staff member turn in periodic reports about the outsourcing, detailing progress, standards, quality of work, and so on.

When working with an outsourcer, try to develop an approach that is cooperative rather than argumentative, and tactical rather than strategic. Try to come up with a shared vision for the outsourcing and reflect this vision in your contract. If you both agree on what needs to be done, the best way of performing the task, and your future goals, the outcome should be accurate.

Include performance measures to motivate the outsourcer. Specify your requirements in terms of outcomes rather than facts. And then, include the outsourcer in the rewards—for meeting deadlines, for example, or doing quality work.

Make sure you determine an explicit plan for communications. The more complex a job is, the more important communication becomes. Regular reports, meetings, and evaluations must be a part of the cooperative effort.

Following are some more ideas:

Form an explicit contingency plan in case the relationship breaks down.

Make sure the outsourcer understands your goals and your expectations.

Make sure you discuss and define both the outsourcer's role and your own role.

Set up milestones for the initiation of the project to be carried out in phases. A schedule will help you both in completing your tasks.

For the contract, ask the outsourcer to provide a detailed statement of the work he or she will do. A list should include each step in a process, and an itemized set of procedures should be added as well.

Hold regularly scheduled status meetings with the outsourcer to make sure things are going as planned. Also, ask for regular status updates in writing.

Ask the outsourcer to orient staff in changes in operation and/or any new techniques adopted.

Employee Support

As always, you must consider your employees in any outsourcing arrangements. First, keep your people informed. Make sure they understand what is going to happen well before the outsourcers come into your company. As a situation changes, notify them of the change; if possible and beneficial, involve them in the changes. Have the outsourcer meet with everyone, or at least key personnel, to explain the process and procedures.

You can keep the lines of communication open via company-wide meetings, newsletters, and announcements on the intranet, emails, and other methods. Provide your users with contacts to call on in case of problems. You might appoint one or more people as specific contacts or liaisons between your users and the outsourcers.

Actually, you should assign at least one person in your organization to work with the outsourcers; but assigning a team of two or more people is also a possibility. The team should be in on the earliest meetings possible so they

Service Level Agreements

A Service Level Agreement (SLA) can be used to monitor the outsourcer's performance but also to assess penalties to the outsourcer, if needed. The agreement must be contractual, explicit, and well-defined.

An SLA ensures the optimal performance of outsourcers and enables the network administrator to evaluate the effectiveness of the outsourcer. Some administrators are also employing SLAs to demonstrate their own ability to outperform outsourcers who may take their jobs away. And some administrators are establishing SLAs with their end users to demonstrate the administrator's promise of reliable, high-quality network access to the users.

Generally, you would add an SLA to your contract with an outsourcer or service provider. The service level agreement commits the outsourcer to a predetermined level of performance. You set exact criteria for the service and call for penalties if the commitments are not met.

When forming an SLA, be careful not to set unrealistic goals. Without the experience of writing SLAs, often the performance criteria level is set wrong. Speak to your lawyer about the SLA if you're not sure of the goals to set.

Another problem with SLAs is that the network administrator doesn't have a baseline of data that indicates prior performance. For example, if you already have a network in place, the outsourcer's function is to improve upon it; you might use one of the many network performance management tools available to test the current situation and compare it to the completed product.

No matter what you do, however, it will be difficult to set a baseline from which you can judge your outsourcer. Your best bet is to gather as much data as you can in the area your outsourcer will be working; collect data several times over a period of six months, for example, so you'll have something to compare when the changes are complete.

It's compelling to add an SLA to your contracts with outsourcers; however, make sure you outline appropriate goals, levels of service, and penalties to make it valuable for you and the outsourcer. If you're not careful, an SLA can turn outsourcers away from doing business with you.

understand the circumstances involved in the outsourcing decision. The people you choose for this team depends on what you are outsourcing; you want people familiar with the technology as well as the fundamentals of the job to assist the outsourcers in any way possible.

The assigned team can work to smooth the people politics between the outsourcer and the company. Many misunderstandings can be arrested through calm discussion and awareness. Members of the team can also effectively assess the work and submit periodic reports.

The team doesn't need to be a full-time assignment; frequent monitoring and guidance of the outsourcers should be sufficient. Let the size of the job determine the time involved.

Contracts

No matter the type of outsourcing, you should make sure you get the agreement in writing. Contracts for outsourcing may be fairly standard, in the case of Internet access or web publishing, for example; however, newer areas of outsourcing may not have a regular contract to offer. You might even want to write your own agreement, with the help of your lawyer, of course.

When outsourcing, use only a few vendors or outsourcers, or use a general contractor who can coordinate the activities of other outsourcers. Also, you want to hire an attorney to help you review the contract; make sure the attorney is experienced with outsourcing agreements. Both during the negotiations and after you hire an outsourcer, you should document all discussions and decisions.

Items to Check or Add

One important item to add to the contract is that either you or the outsourcer can cancel the contract at any time, with a reasonable amount of notice. Don't sign up for an extended period in which you must pay for services, as you would with leasing equipment or a building. You want to make sure you have a way out if the service is not up to your standards.

Another important clause to be wary of is one stating that the outsourcer has the right to assign your agreement and their obligations to another party. The outsourcer may turn your work over to someone who is not as capable, not certified or skilled, not known by you, or a party you wouldn't normally do business with. If this clause is in your contract, you need either to delete it or modify it to state "with approval" from you or your representative.

Other important details to look for include the following:

- Exactly which services will be supplied? The outsourcer should define those services clearly and in detail.

- What tools, utilities, software, documentation, and/or hardware are supplied by the outsourcer? What will you need to supply? Are you responsible for any specific services, procedures, and such?

- How are fees to be paid, how often, how much? Is there a retainer, and do regular fees come out of the retainer?

- Is there a minimum charge, time limit, amount of services you must purchase?

- What additional charges may be added? How are they determined?

- What guarantees does the outsourcer give?

- Is there any penalty for canceling the contract? Will you receive a refund if you or they cancel the contract?

- Are there any exclusions to the contract?

- What provisions are made for confidentiality of your systems, data, site, and so on?

- If the outsourcer generates any data or information, who owns that data?

- What is the outsourcer liable for? How will damages caused by the outsourcer to equipment, data, or software be handled?

- In your agreement, specify a shorter-term renewal option, such as two to five years. Also stipulate that a renewal of the contract occurs only if renewal notice is sent.

> **TIP**
> If any exhibits are included in the contracts, especially in the first drafts, read them very carefully; exhibits are often incomplete.

Consider adding incentives to the contract, such as shared benefits/risks, profitability index, or cross-marketing opportunities.

Provide for both good and bad times in the contract for services. If your company becomes smaller, for example, you could be paying prices based on conditions that no longer exist.

Before Signing

There are just a few more issues to discuss before you sign the contract. You want to make sure to develop a transition plan with the outsourcer. In writing, address contingencies for potential problem areas, a schedule of the transition, and an outline of tasks both you and the outsourcer will need to perform.

Also, make sure your team or liaison person is informed of the contract and understands the transition plan. With the team's help, determine what impact the outsourcing will have on the company and come up with a plan to address any issues now, before the outsourcing begins. Once again, make sure you communicate with the outsourcer during all phases of the project. Document everything.

Additionally, avoid the following traps:

* If the outsourcer is reluctant to give you references, find someone else.

* Be careful with a company that's been in business a long time and is overly reliant on its reputation. The outsourcer must use and understand new technologies, as well as understand your business.

* Make sure the outsourcer's solution for your needs is customized to suit your situation; you might ask the outsourcer's references about their experience and the solutions offered them.

Ask a lot of questions to make sure the outsourcer is experienced and knowledgeable. Make sure the outsourcer is not presenting a flashy show with lots of buzzwords. Also, make sure the outsourcer explains terms and procedures so that you understand them clearly; communication is key.

Renegotiating Outsourcing Contracts

As your business changes, or if your outsourcer's performance isn't quite what you expected, you'll need to renegotiate your outsourcing contract. Ask your outsourcer to sit down with you and set new goals. Renegotiating the contract and making contract amendments strengthens the relationship and maintains customer satisfaction, so the outsourcer should be happy to comply.

There are always risks to renegotiating a contract. If you have to change outsourcers because an agreement can't be reached, you want to consider what impact that will have on your company.

Prepare a list of issues before you sit down with the outsourcer. Do you want lower prices, better performance, or do you want to get out of the contract? List any points of dissatisfaction as well as those accomplishments you're happy with. Try to include a detailed description of your wants and/or requirements. However, try not to make the list long; rather, list the few issues that are principal points of tension and limit it to five or six issues. Leave out the little things don't need to be addressed in the contract.

Involve upper management, both of your company and the outsourcer's. Make sure you know what your bosses want and what you're authorized to offer. It's also a good idea to bring in the outsourcer's bosses so you know your complaints and concerns will be heard.

Know what the contract says and know your rights and responsibilities before going to the table. Be willing to compromise. Make sure the contract is easy to understand and that all parties understand their responsibilities.

TYPES OF OUTSOURCERS

You can get outsourcing help for just about any service you need—networking or otherwise. It's important to find out what types of services are available in your area. You use outsourcers to augment your existing staff, manage large projects, deploy new technologies, maintain multiple platforms, and so on.

Some specialized services you may want to outsource include the following:

Disaster recovery: providing alternative operating sites or replacement equipment in case of disaster.

Backups: backing up your data and systems periodically, on a preset schedule.

Data entry: providing routine processing of documents and data.

Application development: writing specialized applications for corporate use.

Equipment installation and maintenance: installing new hardware or software, configuring for use, and maintaining it.

Strategic planning: assisting with planning of long-term operational plans, application development project plans, and so on.

Equipment procurement: furnishing desktop workstations, printers, and/or other peripherals needed in the company.

Internet services: providing dial-up services and modem pools or high-quality connections and the appropriate hardware.

Help desk: providing end-user assistance for technical problems.

End-user training: providing training either on-site or off-site.

Legacy systems migration: maintaining and/or redesigning mainframe applications systems to operate with the client/server platform.

Mainframe operations: operating your mainframe system, either on-site or off-site.

> **NOTE**
>
> There are many computer and network consultants you can hire to help you install, configure, manage, maintain, and/or troubleshoot your system. Consultation services for operating systems, software applications, hardware and peripherals, training, organization and planning, and so on, are now found in every major city.

With so many administrative duties, you might wonder what type of outsourcing you can use in your situation. This chapter covers various types of activities and procedures that are commonly outsourced. In this chapter you learn about the following:

- Network services
- Internet services
- Remote access
- Intranet services
- Enterprise and WAN services
- Migration services

Network Services

You can outsource a part of or all of your networking services, from the most basic dial-up applications to multisite private wide area networks using the latest router and bandwidth solutions. Many outsourcers simply supply the connection lines and various devices needed for a WAN; other outsourcers provide full security and protection from hackers. Following are some more services you might contract for in the network area:

- Network evaluation, design, and implementation
- Network planning and organization
- Troubleshooting/problem solving
- Help desk and other user support
- Internet access, applications, performance analysis
- Custom private WANs

- Network security analysis and testing
- Firewall planning and deployment
- Application development
- Application installation, configuration, and troubleshooting
- Equipment evaluation and upgrade advice
- Telecommuting
- Network installation and configuration
- Inventory control
- Strategic planning
- Virus protection
- Backup of data
- Router, switches, and hub installation and configuration
- Hardware maintenance, upgrade, and repair
- Workstations and servers installation and configuration

Internet Services

Whether you decide to outsource your Internet services—from simple user online access to full-blown e-commerce sites—depends on how important the use of the Internet is to your business and how much you and your staff know about Internet technologies. The more integral the Internet is to your business, the less likely you will outsource.

Many Web services currently exist because the Web is such big business. Since there are so many services, you can be careful to choose the outsourcer that provides just the right services for the right price. You may need only consulting and advice, or you may want someone to run your entire e-commerce storefront. Following are some of the services an outsourcer may supply:

- Page layout
- Content creation and/or analysis
- Web site hosting on shared servers
- Internet access provider
- Forms development
- CGI script development

- Performance analysis
- Security and firewall design and review
- Credit-card transaction processing
- Full-text searching of contents of your Web site
- Debugging and analysis of Web sites
- HTML consulting

Most Internet projects have narrow time frames, so the strategy for planning and implementing must be flexible. Unexpected delays, cost overruns, or technical obstacles lose business when you're talking the Internet, in particular. Often, Internet outsourcing contracts can be limiting because Internet outsourcing is one of the most difficult to achieve successfully. Typically, the amount of change required to establish and maintain an Internet presence is greater than that of traditional outsourcing tasks. Flexibility is key to successful Internet outsourcing.

When searching for an outsourcer for your Internet work, consider the following items:

- The outsourcer must be flexible, since new technologies are always being developed.
- Automate as much of the e-commerce system as possible to save time and ensure accuracy.
- Be careful of commercial Internet applications; they must deliver information quickly and efficiently and not all are designed with that in mind.
- Establish your standards first—TCP/IP, SSL, and so on—and then find the technology that allows you to use these technologies.
- Try to limit the design and implementation time frame to no more than three months; more time than this has a greater chance of failure.
- Use a phased approach to Internet implementation; build operational and architectural aspects slowly and refine in the later phases of development.

Finally, if your business still maintains legacy systems on which your Internet system will depend for data via file transfers, you must address the possible problems caused by this implementation before anything else. Do you want to duplicate data on the Internet servers? This really isn't a long-term solution. Your Internet applications must be able to access backend legacy systems directly and seamlessly. Also, access should be secure; an access control mechanism should be in place to enable layers of access to the system. Make sure you discuss your legacy system and the possibilities with the outsourcer before signing the contracts.

Remote Access

When using an ISP or value-added network for remote access, you widen the reach for your mobile users. Although monthly charges can be quite expensive, the benefits are many. Virtual private networks (VPNs) are an excellent way of outsourcing remote access. A virtual private network is a connection between remote users and a corporation's LAN using a private and secure path across a public network system, such as the Internet. Using an already-established connection line and compatible protocols, a remote user can access his company's network resources quickly and with little corporate investment in equipment, administration, and/or technical support.

VPNs benefit your company in many ways. Following are a few:

- You forego the costs of purchasing and supporting an enterprise remote access infrastructure.

- You can provide seamless and secure connectivity to employees and to business partners using the same, single service.

- Administration from your point of view is easy.

- Users have a dial-up access to your LAN no matter where they travel.

When outsourcing for remote access by using a VPN, there are some questions and conditions you should specify. Ask for a guarantee of a given level of uptime and impose penalties for nonperformance of the system. Ask if the provider has a comprehensive plan to deal with errors and equipment problems. Ideally, fixes should be implemented without disabling any equipment or keeping remote users from attaching to the LAN.

Following are some more things to consider before contracting for a VPN:

Is the provider equipped to grow with your company? If you add more users, for example, will the connection lines handle the added bandwidth? Will the equipment be easy to upgrade?

What type of security is offered? Are Layer 2 and/or Layer 3 tunneling used?

What provisions are made for monitoring and troubleshooting the VPN? The outsourcer should have the ability to look at the state of the connection and the number of packets traversing the port and analyze the data quickly to provide the best service.

What type of accounting and billing options are offered?   Flat rates are the best for you; however, to enable the provider to diversify his or her service offerings, usage-based accounting may be all that's offered.

Layer 2 and/or 3 Tunneling

Tunneling supports virtual private networks to enable remote users secure access to corporate networks across the Internet. Virtual Private Networks are also called *tunneling* or *extranets*. The VPN enables an organization to use a public data network for some or all of the WAN communication needs.

With tunneling, the remote access server places the user data inside of IP packets and then routes the packets through the network to the endpoint. At the endpoint, the packet is unwrapped and then forwarded in its original form. Tunneling prevents unauthorized access to your corporate network.

Point-to-Point Tunneling Protocol (PPTP), Layer 2 Forwarding (L2F), Layer 2 Tunneling Protocol (L2TP), Virtual Tunneling Protocol (VTP), and Mobile IP (Layer 3) are current protocols under consideration as standards for VPNs. Each is supported by different groups of networking vendors, accommodates different types of payloads, and has different advantages and disadvantages.

Layer 2 tunneling is simple, provides end-to-end compression and encryption, and is bidirectional in initiation. However, Layer 2 tunneling presents some scalability, security, and reliability questions.

Layer 3 tunneling, on the other hand, provides scalability, security, and reliability. Unfortunately, Layer 3 is also difficult to develop so there is, at this time, limited vendor participation.

Outsourcing Your Intranet

Implementing an intranet in your company can serve many purposes. It builds morale, promotes communication and collaboration, and prepares your network for expansion in the form of an extranet and perhaps the Internet for commercial purposes.

An intranet is basically a network that uses Internet technologies—software, protocols, and tools—to present information over the network. Files are displayed as HTML-formatted documents, with links and images and icons that enable a user to jump to related documents quickly and efficiently.

Users view documents on an intranet with a web browser and use the browser's features to move from document to document. Users can use a search engine to quickly locate topics and text. And users can print, copy, and otherwise use intranet documents as they do other documents on the network.

The problem with implementing an intranet in your company is that it takes time to create content, train users, administer a web server, maintain the web pages, and so on, time you simply don't have. But if you outsource your intranet, you get all of the benefits without taking the time from your mission-critical functions.

You might want to outsource the entire job or only parts of it; for example, outsource the design and innovative application development only. What you outsource depends on inhouse capabilities. You may have people experienced with creating and formatting contact, configuring and maintaining the server, tracking the web site activity, and so on.

Similar to the reasons for outsourcing any networking service, the reasons you outsource your intranet might be lack of expertise in content development or web server configuration, lack of internal resources to complete the job, to reduce operating costs, for cash infusion, to free resources for other functions, to share risks, to access expert services, and so on.

Following are some intranet tasks that you can outsource:

- Design and planning
- Networking the flow of traffic, bandwidth considerations, routers, and so on
- Site and application development
- Web client training, installation, configuration, and such
- Web server installation, configuration, and maintenance
- Load balancing on multiple servers
- Web-database integration
- Maintenance of site
- CGI forms development and/or Java scripting
- Original sound or video file creation
- Content optimization

Enterprise WAN Outsourcing

If you're thinking about expanding your LAN to an enterprise or WAN network, you might well consider outsourcing the job to experts in network design, implementation, and management. Wide area networks are becoming more complex and more business critical. Interconnecting geographically dispersed networks means you need experts in WAN connectivity infrastructure, installation of remote routing equipment, deployment of the transport connections, and ongoing management from a network operations center.

The connected networks may run email, document-sharing and groupware applications, inventory, finance, product development, and so on. Complete end-to-end services most likely will need to be outsourced to keep the flow of information going and optimize network availability and performance.

When considering enterprise network outsourcers, consider asking the following:

- Do they include performance and optimization management?

- What provisions are made for fault management?

- Will they take care of software and firmware version control?

- How do they avoid downtime? What are the contingency plans for outages, disrupted connections, downed servers, and so on?

- Are the technologies industry standards?

- What types of reports on network utilization and performance are made, and how often? Do they include trend reports?

- What type of performance guarantees are made?

- What are the security provisions, technologies, and procedures?

- What special arrangements are made for problem-solving and resolution?

Migration Outsourcing

When you're planning to migrate from one network operating system to another or from a legacy system, such as a mainframe or minicomputer, to a PC-based network, you might want to consider outsourcing the project. The planning phase of the migration alone is a monumental job: You must assess your needs, upgrade or purchase new hardware and applications, analyze networking connections and hardware, and so on. Then you have to order and situate the hardware, software, networking equipment; install and configure the

NOS and applications; train administrators and users; set up security, printers, directories, and such; and the list goes on.

Outsourcing the job may be the way you'll want to go. If you do plan to outsource some or all of the migration, consider the following issues to discuss with the outsourcer:

Disaster recovery plans: What are your plans for the duration of the project as well as after the new network is in place?

Security issues: How will you handle issues of authentication, encryption, user and administrative accounts, and so on?

Server organization: Think about the number of servers you'll need and each server's function within the network.

Planning for the future: How much should you safely add to the new system to make it last a while?

Data transfer: Is it reasonable to transfer data or would a lasting connection to the old server be of use?

Schedule of deployment: Don't speed through the deployment; planning and phasing are very important to a successful migration.

Licensing of network and client operating systems and of applications: Does the outsourcer know about licensing and is he or she prepared to cover all bases?

Creation of vertical market software: Will you need specialized software? Can the outsourcer provide it?

What about backups, network optimization, and similar factors? Will the outsourcer be available for help after the migration? How much of the outsourcer's time after the migration does your contract guarantee you?

NETWORK MAINTENANCE

Book Ten

BACKING UP THE SYSTEM

Introduction to Book Ten

As you know, backing up your system is the one thing you can do to help in case of a disaster. Part of your file management routine should be to back up your data regularly. You make backups in case of a hardware failure; say your hard disk fails, the backup can restore all of your valuable data onto a new, freshly formatted hard drive. But you also make backups in case of human failure. When a user or an administrator makes a mistake, a backup can help restore the system to its previous status and save everyone a lot of worry and time.

You can also use hardware-based solutions, such as RAID or mirroring. You might try other recovery mechanisms or clusters to recover from system failures, in which all services of the primary server are assumed by a backup computer system in case something goes wrong. But backups are important because they can help when a user, system administrator, or programmer causes an error that these hardware-based solutions copy instead of catch.

As you consider your backups, scheduling, and the overall importance of your data, you should also consider the following questions:

How many single points of failure can you tolerate in your enterprise? Can a backup of some sort subsidize those points of failure—hardware or people?

What fault tolerance methods should you implement? RAID, disk mirroring and such methods can help in case of hardware failure; but what other concessions should you make?

Which data on the servers needs to be backed up? Which data on the workstations should be backed up? What is the strategy for backing up?

What types of records should you maintain to recover from failures? How much documentation is necessary? How much documentation would you really use?

Where do you store backups and records?   How many backups and copies of records do you have?

Have you ever tested your backups?   Have you made sure your backups will help you in case of a disaster?

PRELIMINARY GROUNDWORK

Data may be your most valuable asset. Consider this: How much business would you lose, how much time is invested in your network and the data stored there? If the data in your company were lost today and you had no backup, how long would it take to recreate that data? So, how much is it worth to you to keep your data safe from disaster, sabotage, and other calamities?

Lost data costs are calculated in terms of time, labor, lost billings, lost customers, and so on. With larger disk drives, more users, more data being saved to servers, the price of backing up your server(s) is small in comparison. Older, more traditional backup devices are no longer practical with today's large capacity drives and LAN needs. New devices and software are now available, at reasonable prices, so there is no longer a reason for failing to back up your system.

In this chapter, you learn about the following:

- General information about backing up

- Advantages of backing up

- Problems of not backing up

General Backup Information

A typical backup plan backs up some information (usually information that has changed) partially every day and all data once a week. Also, extra backups are usually made in case of problems with the backup media.

The data considered valuable on your servers and system could be estimated at about 50 percent of the disk storage capacity. Multiply the average hard disk capacity of your servers by the number of servers on your network. You can safely surmise that 50 percent of that number is the total you need to back up. The rest of the space is taken up by either empty space that is not backed up or by program and application files.

You do not necessarily need to back up program or application files. Since you have the original program disks, you can easily install operating systems and applications at any time, if necessary. However, some companies back up operating systems and applications because of specialized configurations. You'll have to decide how important these files are as compared to the time it will take to back up multiple program files.

Local or Centralized?

You can back up data locally, so that each server has its own tape drive, for example. Or you can perform centralized backups, in which one or more computers back up to a central location using a single storage device (see Figure 1.1). Centralized backups usually are more reliable, efficient, and secure. You can run backups at the least busy network times, the administrator decides how much to back up, and by using only a single storage device, hardware is used efficiently and economically. Using the software and backup device for such a large operation may, however, take more training for the backup operators. Setup and administration times are required, so the administrator must have a hand in this method of backup.

Figure 1.1 One server attached to a backup device runs backups for all computers attached to the network segment.

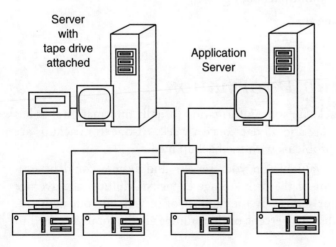

Local backups must be supervised or checked periodically to make sure the user or assistant is backing up properly, according to schedule, and is testing backups for accuracy. If you have several servers and several backup assistants, this job can be time consuming. You reduce administrative overhead in setup and implementation when you use local backups; but most users simply won't perform the backups, or will not back up as often as they should, or will perform the backup wrong. Figure 1.2 illustrates a network segment that depends on local backups.

You could, alternatively, make space available on the server and require that users periodically save files to a home directory or backup directory. This method is easy to administer and you can check quite easily to make sure that it's done. There are even third-party applications that can automate this strategy by running on each user's computer and pushing the data to the server.

If you let users perform their own backups in this manner, they usually only copy a few of the important files, if they remember to copy the files. It's still likely the user will forget, procrastinate, or simply not perform the backups. Also, the network can get congested at peak times while everyone is copying their files to the server.

Figure 1.2 Each server has its own backup device and workstations must fend for themselves.

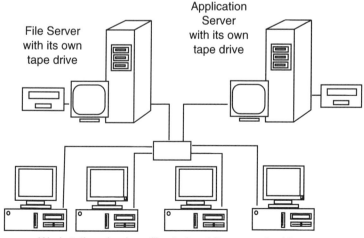

Workstations back up files to local floppy or zip drives

Time and Resources

With all you have to do, it's no surprise that you don't have the time or the resources to carry out time-consuming backup programs on a regular schedule. Smaller staffs and increased responsibilities make the chore of organizing and managing backup tapes nearly impossible. So you're risking disaster and playing the odds. Not a good idea.

You can find an easy-to-use, reliable data backup and restoration system that can work for your network. You must. The search may take your valuable time, but consider how much of your time it will take to recover from a devastating server crash or data loss.

When looking for backup software, look first for a system that is compatible with your network operating system and your application programs. If you plan to use more than one backup device, such as a tape drive, get the same brand and model of tape devices for each location or server so there will be no compatibility issues.

Look for an automated backup, comprehensive data management, and an easy-to-use data recovery scheme. Many programs offer simple protection that isn't enough to really serve your needs. Automated backup is the best way to ensure consistent data protection.

Also, make sure the program alerts you to files that can't be copied during backups and that it skips files that have not been altered since they were last backed up. Get a program with a librarian function that keeps track of the backed up files; you can use this information to quickly track and locate individual files.

Many programs also come with their own tape rotation scheme that plans your tape rotation, Monday through Thursday for partial backups and Fridays for full backups, for example.

The more work you can let the backup program do, the less work you have to do. Find a program and backup device that automates functions and provides the tools you need to quickly and reliably get your backups done.

Advantages and Disasters

When it comes to backups of system, server, application, and user data, there are no disadvantages, only advantages and disasters. If you do not use a backup of some sort, then you will lose data by some disaster or other: user error, hardware failure, hackers, viruses, computer theft, or environmental damage (fire, flood, and so on).

Most people spend more time backing up their personal lives—keeping an extra car key, reminder notes on the fridge, and so on—than they spend backing up their critical work files and data. Isn't it time to take action at work, too?

Advantages of Backing Up

The advantages of backing up your data on a regular basis include time, money, and peace of mind. Consider how much time and effort it would take to recreate the data that is lost. Restoring the data can require hours and hours of unprofitable and frustrating work.

Say your system's hard disk crashes. You install a new hard drive; install and configure the operating system; and then reinstall applications, drivers, and other software. Getting the system to this point will take at least eight hours. Now, you're faced with the nearly impossible task of reconstructing your document, image, and data files. If you can successfully reconstruct these files, it could take months to accomplish.

The cost of all of this time and effort depends on the amount of data you have, but any cost is too much when you could have backed up your files. Consider that the cost of a 250MB quarter-inch tape is less than $100; the cost of losing 1MB of data is anywhere from $2,000 to $3,500, depending on the data.

> **NOTE**
> It's important to realize that only a fraction of the data that's lost can be attributed to natural disasters; most data loss—perhaps as much as 80 to 90 percent—is due to human error. Backups are specifically designed to protect and restore data lost through human error.

More and more businesses depend on the computer network to survive. Systems are larger; more data is input to the network than ever before. Lost data costs in time, labor, lost customers, and such, could shut down your business. Having reliable backups could save your business.

Disasters

Any administrator you talk to can tell you about a disaster or near-catastrophe involving backups. No one checked or verified the backup. The server crashed just before the mirrored server was delivered. The tape drive messed up last week and the new one hasn't arrived. There are no disadvantages to backing up your files and data; there are only disasters as a result of not backing up.

Whether you've lost a file while you were working on it or you've lost entire servers, you know that feeling in the pit of your stomach. You know as well as anyone, even better, that daily backups are important; yet somehow, a backup was neglected.

There are many companies in the business of recovering data from crashed server hard disks. Tens of thousands of dollars are spent to retrieve scrambled user accounts, configuration files, data that would take months and months to recreate from just one hard drive. If only the administrator had used preventative fault tolerance and/or backed those files up.

Here are some other disasters waiting to happen:

- Your company has a backup policy but you haven't read it, passed it around, enforced it, or updated it in more than a year.

- The files on your hard disk drives are critical to your personal success, yet you haven't backed them up in two or more weeks.

- Your company has no formal policy on how often data should be backed up.

- Your application and network operating system CDs are "around here somewhere."

- You have good backups, but all are located in the server room; no backups are kept off-site.

- Backups are made faithfully but no one has ever checked the backups for accuracy.

- You have no fault tolerance options in place for preventative purposes.

TERMINOLOGY AND TECHNOLOGY

Backups are the second line of defense in case there are problems with your system. A backup contains your operating system, applications, user information, configurations, and important data that you need to operate your network and your business. Generally, you use a backup in case of human error—someone accidentally deletes a directory of accounting data or someone breaks into your system and destroys your password files.

Backups can also help if your hardware fails, by supplying the content of a failed drive, for example. Realistically though, you should use preventative measures—such as hardware redundancy or other fault tolerance methods—for your first line of defense against problems with the system. If you have an exact replica of your server, for instance, when the primary server fails, you can start the replica to serve your users while you correct the problems in the original server.

Preventative measures for hardware troubles are just as important as backing up your data. You need to keep your system both safe and protected. This chapter discusses some of the terminology and technology involved with both backing up files and data and redundancy methods for your network.

In this chapter, you learn about the following:

- Basic fault tolerance protections
- RAID levels
- Clustered servers
- Types of backups

Fault Tolerance and Redundancy

Fault tolerance is a method of ensuring continued system operation in case of the failure of a system element. Redundant chips and circuits enable the system to bypass faults automatically when a processor or large disk drive fails. A UPS

(Uninterruptible Power Supply) is a simple method of providing fault tolerance by providing power during a power outage or failure. A more complex method of fault tolerance is duplicating the entire system in a remote location in case of a disaster.

System fault tolerance is a method of duplicating data on several hard disks so that if one disk fails, the data is still available from another disk. This is also called *redundancy*. Hardware redundancy can come in many forms. RAID (Redundant Array of Inexpensive/Independent Disks) is a method of using multiple hard drives to provide for larger volume size, fault tolerance, and increased performance. Disk mirroring and disk duplexing are other methods. This section describes various types of fault tolerance and redundancy.

Basic Protection

There are a few things you should do as preventatives before you even consider network backups. Since your servers are the hearts of your system, you need to protect against downtime in every way possible. Implement antivirus software, firewalls, and UPSs. Monitor your system to prevent problems, to govern the flow of data, and to prevent disasters before they occur.

A UPS is one of the most important basic protections you can buy. A UPS is an alternative power source that usually consists of a set of batteries and is used to power a computer system if the normal power service is interrupted or falls below acceptable levels. All servers, routers, gateways, and independent hard disks on your network should have a UPS. UPSs are expensive; however, the service they provide is well worth the cost.

As for using a UPS for workstations, evaluate the operation and function of each machine; for example, if the workstation runs software that interfaces with the server, data corrupted at the workstation could overwrite good data on a server. Then you should use a UPS.

Also, different kinds of memory (RAM) supply different levels of performance and fault tolerance. Most memories are 60 nanoseconds; higher speeds aren't as critical when you can interleave them for greater bandwidth. ECC RAM provides error-correcting circuitry. ECC and Parity memory won't help or hurt system performance but they will protect you from memory faults, including module failure.

Multihoming—a feature in UNIX, NetWare, and NT—means to run multiple network cards in a server to improve throughput and load balancing.

Additionally, multihoming provides fault tolerance since it spreads the client load over multiple cards and provides for the possibility of one card failing.

RAID

RAID technology brings incredible amounts of storage capacity, excellent performance, and numerous levels of fault tolerance. RAID used to stand for "Redundant Array of Inexpensive Disks," but now the industry uses "independent" to replace "inexpensive" since there are no inexpensive disks anymore. With the huge applications, larger operating systems, and enormous databases comes the need for more and more storage space as well as data protection, none of which come inexpensively.

RAID Levels

RAID improves the speed and security of a system. Some typical examples of RAID installations and configurations include:

RAID 0—disk striping. Disk striping combines a set of disk partitions, located on different hard disks, into a single volume. Disk striping allows multiple disk accesses and thereby improves performance but doesn't provide fault tolerance.

RAID 1—disk mirroring. Disk mirroring is used just for fault tolerance. Mirroring writes the same information simultaneously onto two different hard disks or partitions. If one disk or partition fails, the other can continue working. Most network operating systems offer disk mirroring. Disk mirroring won't improve write performance but may help read performance.

RAID 3—disk striping with parity. Parity is a simple form of error checking. One physical drive is dedicated to the parity information and the data word is striped across multiple drives as in RAID 0. This type of RAID is good for workstation applications with large files, but not so good for networked servers dealing with numerous small files or small disk I/O operations because it ties up every drive in the stripe set for every I/O operation.

RAID 4—disk striping with parity. One physical drive is dedicated to the parity info. The striping algorithm differs from RAID 3, however; the entire data word is written to a single drive, next word to next drive. RAID 4 allows only single-threaded write operations but allows multiple simultaneous reads since each drive holds an entire word. Good for more I/O operations per second.

RAID 5—disk striping with parity. Parity information is distributed across all drives in the volume. Data is written in an algorithm that sends data to drives in the stripe set, one after another. The most commonly used RAID, RAID 5 allows multiple simultaneous reads and writes. You will need at least three drives to set up RAID 5, but it provides complete fault tolerance for single-drive failure and improves read performance.

RAID 6—disk striping plus distributed parity. RAID 6 is RAID 5 enhanced. Two drives in the stripe set can fail, since the distributed parity information has parity information of its own. It has excellent fault tolerance.

RAID 10 (also called RAID 0+1)—mirrored stripe sets. RAID 10 is built directly through the RAID controller with a combination of software mirroring and controller striping. RAID 10 provides a good combination of fault tolerance and performance, but it's expensive. No parity is used in RAID 10; fault tolerance is achieved through the mirror. Some high-end controllers support RAID 10 directly.

Combining RAID 10 with *hot-swap drives* (drives not used actively for data; rather, remain in waiting for other drive(s) to fail) creates a very high-performing, reliable, and fault-tolerant system.

RAID 30 (RAID 0+3)—mirrored RAID 3 sets and RAID 50 (RAID 0+5) mirrored RAID 5 sets. Each provide a multiple fault-tolerant disk subsystem using software and hardware options. Both are extremely expensive.

RAID Advice

On the fault tolerance front, RAID 10 provides a mirrored set of striped disks, so that one-half of the drives could fail without losing any data. RAID 30 and RAID 50 provide mirrored sets of drives that are protected by RAID 3 or 5, respectively. Running RAID results in speed tradeoff. Standard RAID 5 is up to 65 percent slower than RAID 0.

You can choose hardware and/or software RAID. Software RAID, built into the operating system, distinguishes between a master and slave drive. Only the master drive has the boot code information so if the hard drive fails, the system continues to run but booting is often no longer possible. Also, since mirroring on the OS works with standard SCSI host adapters, repair functions like the support of spare hard drives are not implemented.

Hardware RAID enables 100 percent mirroring. RAID controllers are designed to support many different repair functions. Also, a hardware RAID controller can substantially improve performance of the system caching ability.

A hardware-accelerated RAID controller is much better than software RAID; but it does cost more. With software RAID, a system's CPU has to calculate the data distribution and parity information if you're using level 5, in addition to everything else it's doing for the computer. To take full advantage of RAID, you need to employ multichannel controllers or separate I/O across multiple controllers. The more drives you have on a single SCSI channel, the closer you get to the maximum throughput capabilities of the controller. Types of I/O activity your system spends most of its time doing have an impact on overall performance.

Mirrored Server(s)

Another method of protecting your servers is to use a *mirrored server* for each. A secondary server is usually in standby mode, waiting to take over and perform services only when and if the primary server fails. The secondary server can perform file or printing services, authentication, and any other services the primary server can perform. A mirrored server would be better located in a site other than the primary server, in case of fire or other environmental hazard.

Figure 2.1 illustrates a LAN segment with two servers: an authentication server and a file/print server. Both servers attach to a virtual private network through the Internet to another location: building, city, or country. In the second location are two servers, one mirroring the authentication server and another mirroring the file and print server.

Clustered servers, another type of backup support, maintain an active configuration in which all servers in the cluster do useful work and provide failover services for one another. Clusters can also provide load balancing to help tweak performance. Clustered servers are usually located in the same place for centralized administration.

Although expensive, using mirrored or clustered servers can provide your network with complete fault tolerance in case of hardware failure. Figure 2.2 illustrates a network using clustered servers. All servers provide the same services to provide fault tolerance in case of any problems.

Figure 2.1 Mirrored servers at a remote location provide the safest method of fault tolerance.

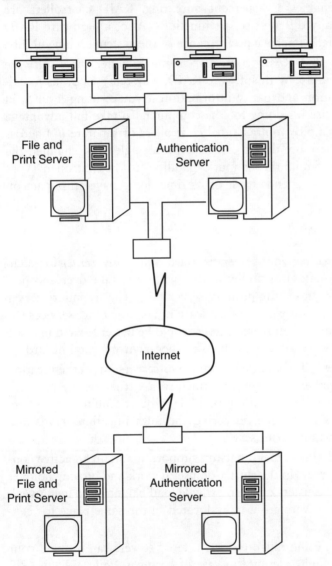

Figure 2.2 Clustered servers balance the load between servers for better performance.

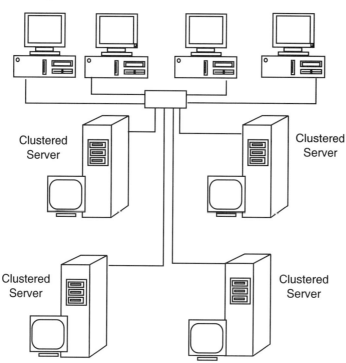

Types of Backups

Your backup schedule must fit the type of data you use, the amount of data, the way you work, and so on; but basically, you should back up your data on a full system backup schedule followed by partial or differential backups spread out over time. The backup enables you to rebuild your system completely, in case your server(s) fail.

There are three types of backups generally used, and the type you choose depends on your data and methods of working. *Full* (or *normal*), *incremental*, and *differential* are three types of backups. You could also do a *copy* backup.

You'll have to decide first of all, how important your data is to you and second, how much time you want to put into the safety of your data.

Full Backups

A *full backup* is a complete copy of all selected files, backing up every file selected one at a time, regardless of when it was last modified. The full backup is the cornerstone of a backup strategy. With a full backup, you have one single backup that can be used to restore the entire system, including applications.

A full or normal backup marks each file as being backed up. This type of marking is also called *archiving*; the backup program keeps a record, or archive, of when each file is backed up. Of course, full backups can take a long time and use a lot of tape or other media.

Incremental Backups

An *incremental* is a backup of only the files that have changed since the last full backup; and it marks those files as being backed up. An incremental backup is a time-saver for backing up but takes longer to restore. When you restore the backed up files, you must first restore the last full backup you made, and then restore each incremental backup made since the full backup was made.

Also, incremental backups use more media because you must keep each incremental backup to build on. More media means there are more chances of media failure. Remember, tapes can and do fail, so keep extra copies of all backups. If you choose to use incremental backups, don't use them for more than 10 days because too many tapes will be involved and something will surely go wrong.

Also, consider that many incremental backup systems don't keep track of which files have been deleted since the last full backup, so restoring from a full backup and one or two incremental backups results in restored deleted files.

> **TIP**
> If most of your data changes daily, you should do a full backup instead of incrementals.

Note that sometimes people will make one or two full backups and then continue to make incremental backups for weeks, months, and even years without ever performing a full backup again. What that means is that when these files must be restored, the full backup must be restored, and then *each and every* incremental backup made since that time must be restored in sequence. Performing an incremental backup daily saves time in backing up but it can also cause nightmares when you have to restore them.

Differential Backups

Differential backups are similar to incremental. Differential backs up everything since the last full backup. A differential is faster than an incremental and easier to restore. A differential backup, however, takes longer than incremental backup because it's backing up more data. The major difference is that with a differential backup, you restore the full backup and then only one differential backup; differential backups do not mark files as being backed up.

Differential backups don't require that each backup tape since the last full backup be restored; therefore, you can continue to run on differential backups longer than incremental backups. Since you're backing up everything that's changed since the last full backup, it's best if you do full backups frequently; the more time elapsed between full backups, the more data the differential backup backs up and the more time it takes.

Copying Files

If you use the Copy command to back up, you copy files but those files aren't marked as having been backed up. You'd use Copy to back up files between normal and incremental; since the files aren't marked, they will be backed up again at the normal, incremental, or full backup.

For very large amounts of data or for backing up files that are needed 24 hours a day, you can copy the data from the directory to a target network drive or disk on the same computer for the fastest copy. After you copy the data, back up the copied file so the original data is still available for use. Make sure you verify the copy, which will take longer than the copy process took. You could, alternatively, use a third-party utility to mirror the data across the network while the files are in use.

Online Services and Backup Security

Backup security can come in various forms. Storing a set of backups off-site will help you secure your data from physical damage and loss, for example. There are other security questions: With Online Backup Services, will prying eyes or hackers break into your data or will the online service lose your data?

> **NOTE**
>
> Some applications may have open files during your regular backup times. To work around this problem, you can skip the open file and hope to catch it on the next backup. Another solution is to wait until the file is available; this could prolong the backup time but at least you know no files will be skipped. You also could choose to delay a certain amount of time and then skip, but this also slows the backup process.
>
> Some databases must be running all of the time so at least some data files are also open all the time, making backup difficult. In SQL Server, for example, you can dump the database—a process that takes all of the data that is in the database and copies it to a file for storage—creating a backup copy of the database on disk.

An Online Backup Service is a business that enables your company to attach to its server(s) and back up your data to store on its site(s). Online services use the Internet, an extranet, virtual private networks, or other connection configuration to attach to your LAN or WAN. The initial backup of your data is time consuming because the service backs up all of your data and files; thereafter, the service only backs up files that have changed. Online services provide automated backup services, off-site copies of your data, and generally save your data to two separate servers in two separate sites for extra security. Figure 2.3 illustrates how an online service might work with a private LAN for backup purposes.

Advantages of online backup services include:

- Online services are generally reliable and backup is automated. These services take the responsibilities and work for regular backups off of the network administrator and place them in the hands of professionals.

- The services back up only incremental portions of large files, after the initial backup, and copy only the portions of the files that have changed. This saves the time it takes to back up database files, for example, that change daily, as well as others.

- The services can save only data files or files you deem as essential, leaving out clip art files and such.

- Most services enable access to backup files from any computer on your LAN at any time.

Now, how safe is that data you send and store on an online service?

Figure 2.3 The online backup service computers are in different locations to provide extra safety for your data.

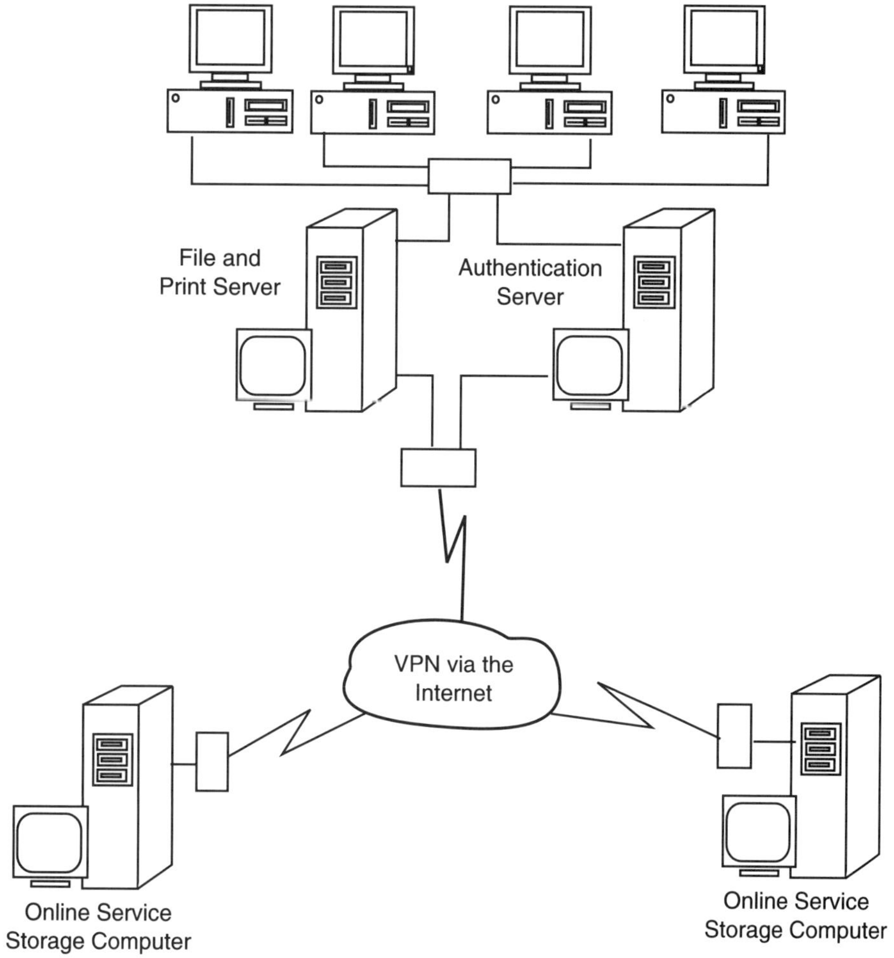

Data Encryption

When using an online backup service, your data will be encrypted before it leaves your network, thus protecting it through the transmission and storage process. Since online backup services are only storage repositories, there is no need for them to decrypt the data.

> **NOTE**
>
> Files are also compressed before they leave your LAN.

Encryption is a scrambling of data that is based on a key, or password. If you have the key, you can decrypt the data; without the key, you cannot decrypt it. The online backup services do not have access to your encryption key. DES (Data Encryption Standard) is one decryption standard; DES is used in many electronic bank transfers, for example.

Additional Security

Most online services also provide additional safeguards. *Transmission checking* is an extensive error-checking function that detects any problems during the transmission of the data and signals that data must be sent a second time if errors were detected.

Most online services also maintain two complete facilities so that your data is stored in two separate locations for protection. Generally, the computers on which your data is stored serve no other purpose than data storage. They aren't accessible over data networks and therefore have no connections for hackers to connect over a network.

PLANNING STRATEGIES

Your first step in planning your backups is to reduce the likelihood of failure in the first place. Add redundancy to the server and network. Don't be dependent on a single drive or machine. Mirror servers or use other techniques to guarantee the safety of your system and your data. If you can prevent an interruption in service, then you can replace failed equipment and components in an orderly and calm environment. See Chapter 2 of this book, "Terminology and Technology," for more information about redundancy and prevention.

You use backups when hardware fails; however, you also need backups when human error (accidentally or intentionally) destroys files, merges the wrong database files, powers off a machine, and so on. It's best to have three full copies of data to protect against media loss or backup device failure. The frequency with which you create backups depends on how often your data changes and its value to you. Remember that backups are also a protection against viruses; since some viruses take weeks to appear, you might want to keep a normal backup copy for a month.

Additionally, always make backups before you make a change to your system, such as adding new applications, installing hardware to the server, creating or modifying sets of users, configuring new peripherals, and so on.

In this chapter, you learn about the following:

- Creating a record book for every server
- Creating system disks
- Configuration files important to include in backups
- Forming a backup strategy
- Scheduling backups

Backup Information and Requirements

Keeping written logs of information about your system is as important as backing up data. In case of a disaster, the hardware and operating system information, network configuration and application setup will be just as important to you as any data you've got on tape or other media. Quick recovery from a disaster is the goal and you can recover faster if you have information at your fingertips.

In addition, a system disk with certain files for rebooting a downed server can be helpful. Making a system disk takes only minutes but can save hours of frustration. Finally, there are certain files you should be sure to include on every server backup—files you can use to get the server back in working order quickly and efficiently.

Backup Log Information

You should keep a log, or record, book for each server and for each workstation that lists the model and type of computer, its uses, hardware, IRQ addresses, peripherals, drivers, and other pertinent information. As you add any computer to the system, add it to the log book and fill in the information you need. You can also designate this chore to each workstation user, department managers, or administrative assistants. But having this list will make upgrades, troubleshooting, repairs, and so on, much easier and more efficient.

This may sound like a lot of work and it is, especially if you have a thousand computers you've never documented before. But you can send out a memo of what you want to everyone in charge of a computer and in one or two days have the logs and disks created for you. Periodically, send a memo out asking everyone to update his or her logs and system disks. This system can work and the information will be invaluable.

> **NOTE**
>
> There are also software applications, like Microsoft's Systems Management Server, that can automatically inventory workstations and servers on your system. You might look into such an application if you have many computers on your network or if your staff is unsuited for completing the task.

Following are some suggestions for entering into the written log. This information will come in handy when you need to configure network clients and protocols, add hardware, update equipment, and so on. The system disk is useful for rebooting the computer after a system crash, providing drivers when the originals are damaged, and recovering from various system errors.

- Computer's manufacturer, model, serial number, location, monitor brand and specs, keyboard type, and mouse type.

- Computer's internal configuration: motherboard, processor speed, amount and type of RAM, number and type and size of hard disks and controllers, floppy drives and sizes, CMOS information, and so on.

- Cabling and external connections, computer BIOS manufacture and revision numbers.

- Firmware information on RISC-based computers.

- Disk subsystem information: makes, models, and serial numbers of disks and controllers.

- Map of SCSI subsystem: SCSI configuration information, which devices are terminated and how, SCSI ID and physical location of SCSI devices.

- Operating system installed applications, users' names, any special additions or custom-made applications or equipment.

- Sound card, video card, network adapter cards: manufacturer and model, IRQ addresses, jumper and/or DIP switch settings, DMA, I/O ports, and such.

- Zip and/or CD-ROM drives types and speeds, manufacturer and model, location, drivers, port connections, and such.

- Modem: manufacturer and model, location, speed, drivers, port connections, and so on.

- Other attached peripherals: printers—manufacturer and model, specifications on memory, font cartridges, printer fonts, ports and cables, and so on. UPS specifications, tape drives, and any other add-ons.

- Insurance policies.

- Kits, tools, and add-on information you've installed.

- Internal documentation like policies, procedures, training guides, and so forth.

- Troubleshooting history (time, date of problem, error messages, events logged, and outcome).
- Phone list of who to call for specific emergencies: administrators, vendors, management, and critical users.

> **NOTE**
> Naturally, keep all manuals, receipts, warranties, and vendor documentation for all computers and peripherals as well as hardware in your network.

System Disk

In addition to the log, keep a *system disk* for each computer in your company. The system disk enables you to boot a computer that won't start on its own. On that bootable disk should be system files, CD-ROM drivers, and so on. If the configuration of the computer changes in any way, the system disk should also be updated and those changes should be kept in the log.

The system disk made automatically with Windows 95, 98, and NT machines is a perfect boot disk; however, make sure you add CD-ROM drivers and any other commands (format, fdisk, and copy, and such). Those operating systems do not automatically add these necessary files to the emergency repair disk.

Following are the files that should be on a system disk:

Command.com: From the root directory of the computer or you can format the disk as a system disk.

Configuration files: Autoexec.bat, config.sys, registry (DAT files), and any initialization (INI) files.

Network startup files: VLMs from NetWare workstations and DOS disks for servers with server.exe and startup.ncf, so if the DOS partition is damaged, you can still get into the NetWare partitions.

CD-ROM drivers: Copy the files to the same directory on the backup disk as is listed in the config.sys file, for example. The statement in the config.sys file that refers to your CD-ROM drive might be devicehigh=c:\qulogic\q151dos.sys, for example. Create the qlogic directory on your floppy and then copy everything in your qlogic directory from C to the floppy as well.

It's important that you use the same computer for making the system disk that you will use the disk on. Do not, for example, make a system disk with a Windows 95 machine to use on a Windows 98 computer; it won't work right. Also, when an NT computer creates an emergency repair disk, it records the hardware, configuration, and other information about that specific computer on the disk; that disk should only be used on the computer you used to make it.

Application Disks

This may be obvious but it's still necessary to mention. All of your commercial software—applications and operating systems—comes on diskette or CD-ROM and these disks are your application backups. All application disks should be stored in a safe, controlled environment, preferably off-site. Applications are expensive and if you plan to back up only your data, you want to make sure you have the backup to reinstall applications and operating systems.

Files to Back Up

In addition to important data files, there are certain other files you should include in your backups. Naturally, a full backup should include the entire contents of the hard drive: operating system, all system files, application files, user information, drivers, configuration files, as well as data files. Following are some of the files you may want to add to incremental or differential backups also.

- System registry (DAT files), initialization (INI) files, and any other configuration files

- User and group accounts

- Login scripts, password files

- Config.sys and autoexec.bat plus any files referenced in these files

- Software drivers: CD-ROM, printer, and any others you may not have copies of

- All data: database, word processing, web pages, accounting files, customer information, spreadsheets, and such

Windows NT Server Registry

Windows NT Server backs up the Registry automatically each time Windows starts successfully. The backup is copied into an SAV file and recorded to a corresponding LOG file.

You cannot import or export NT Server's Registry or copy the Registry files; however, you can update the repair information (stored in C:\WINNT\REPAIR) in case of a major problem with the operating system. This system is only capable of recovering a bootable system if you have a major configuration problem; it's not meant as a backup tool for the system or configuration.

You can copy the Registry files in another operating system, such as MS-DOS, but only if you're using FAT partitions and not NTFS partitions. If you try to copy the Registry files in Windows NT, NT gives you a sharing violation.

To copy the Registry files in MS-DOS, format a system disk at the MS-DOS prompt on the NT Server and then copy all of the files in C:\WINNT\SYSTEM32\CONFIG to a backup folder. You might want to use the xcopy command with the /h and /r swtiches to copy system and hidden files as well.

You can, alternatively, use REGBACK, a Microsoft utility provided with the NT Server Resource kit, to back up the Registry from a DOS prompt.Read the directions with the Resource kit for more information.

Backup Strategy

The strategy you choose depends on your data and how it is stored. You may want to locate a tape drive at each server; you may want to back up client machines to the network. You'll need to decide the best location for your tape drive. You'll also need to answer the following questions:

- Will you run a server backup only or will you need a complete network backup?
- Will the backup device be available to users or just for the server backup?
- Who's responsible for the backing up of individual workstations?
- Will one person be responsible for the entire network backup? Or will one person be responsible for all server backups?

Server and/or Client Backups?

If applications and data are stored centrally on servers, you should back up your servers on a strict schedule. You can attach backup devices directly to each server and schedule the backups at regular intervals. If the data on one server is more than a tape, for example, can hold, you may need to assign someone to change tapes, or add a second or third tape drive to accommodate the server.

Performing only server backups means you need fewer tape drives or other devices and there are fewer tapes or other media to deal with; thus, server backup may be less expensive than backing up each workstation. However, some workstations may contain important files that must be backed up. You can back up these files to a backup device through the network, but this is slow and cumbersome. You could back up to the server from workstations, and then back up from the server to the tape or other backup device.

You could attach tape drives or other devices to the workstations that need backing up. This solution means fewer network resources are committed to the backup procedure and file recovery; however, it also uses more tape drives and is more expensive.

It is important to consider backing up your client workstations. Key data may be resident on a network desktop. Storage management solutions must reach across a variety of platforms—UNIX, DOS, NetWare, NT, Windows 95 and Windows 98, for example. When looking to purchase a backup device and software, make sure it can serve various operating systems, platforms, and architectures.

Creating Your Own Strategy

You'll have to create your own backup strategy, one that suits your data and storage methods. Following are a few ideas for backup strategies:

Make one department responsible for planning and coordinating the backing up of all departments. This department can schedule backups, choose important files, and even set policies. However, the people in charge must understand how each department's data relates to the overall business.

An alternative strategy is to let each department or location develop its own backup plans and implement them. Each department is responsible for the computers it uses. The theory here is that the department's management can better understand the data it uses and the impact of the loss of data. This approach will likely cost more than other approaches because each department has to have its own backup devices, personnel, and so on.

Figure 3.1 illustrates a strategy whereby each location plans its own backups. The Oakhill location uses a tape library (multiple tape backup machines) to back up the entire network—servers and clients. The Beckley location uses one tape backup per server; clients save all critical files to a server for backup.

Another strategy is to let one group develop the backup plans and guidelines but make each department responsible for developing its own procedures and for implementing those procedures. This establishes a company-wide policy while giving departments flexibility and control.

Other Backup Issues

The backup technology you use must keep pace with storage requirements. Today's hard drives hold more data and therefore require larger-capacity backup devices. Make sure you know your storage requirements before purchasing backup devices and media.

Nightly backups will take longer to complete, depending on the amount of data you must back up. You may need to get faster, higher-capacity drives and products. You might gang multiple tape drives together through software support for multiple separate drives. You could also use hardware striping or tape drive arrays to adapt to the larger drive capacities.

Also, finding the right balance between full and incremental backups can be tricky. If you perform a full backup every night, for example, restoring files will be easy, but the nightly backup may take too long and the impact on network traffic may be excessive. If you perform incremental backups with occasional full backups, you reduce the amount of time required for nightly backups and keep network traffic under control; but restoring a file or a subdirectory is a long and involved process.

Scheduling

There are many various scheduling options for your backups. The most common option is to use four tapes for incremental or differential backups on Monday through Thursday of each week and then perform a full backup on each Friday on a fifth tape. You should keep at least three sets of backup tapes before you start rotating and overwriting tapes.

Figure 3.1 You'll have to find a backup strategy that works for your network and data.

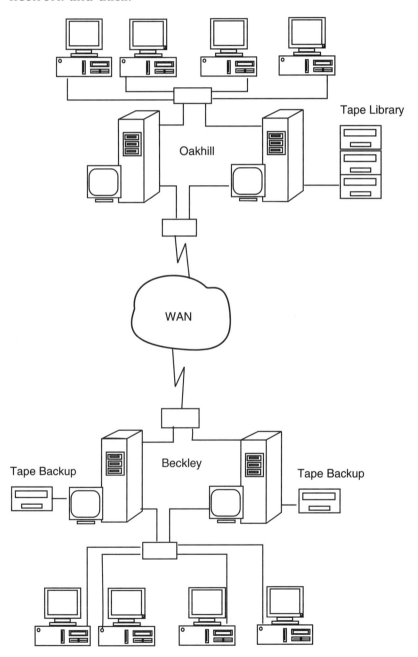

Before purchasing a backup device, you want to make sure you get a device that can handle the amount of data in the required time. You can estimate the amount of data you have to back up and the amount of time you have to perform the task, and then find a backup device to fit your needs.

If, for example, you have 5GB of data for backup, convert that number to megabytes—5000MB. Estimate the amount of time you have to back up that data—say, 120 minutes. Divide the number of megabytes to be backed up by

---

Rotation and Scheduling Examples

Following are some sample scenarios for backing up; you should have at least three full sets of backups and it wouldn't hurt a thing to have four or even five sets. Always have extra sets of backups, in case one set of tapes or other media fails. Tapes break; tapes also have a recommended life span, so you should stop using them after the specified period of time. Damaged or worn-out tapes can cause problems when you need to restore your backups.

You might want to do a full system backup weekly, and then do a differential backup daily. At the end of the week, store these tapes and start again with new tapes at the beginning of the week. Use new tapes for three or four weeks and then you can start overwriting the first set.

You could do a full system backup daily and at the end of the week, store the tapes off-site and start the new week with a new set of tapes. Again, use new tapes for three or four weeks and then overwrite the first set. Use this method if the majority of your data changes daily.

Lower backup costs by alternating tapes. Following are two examples.

On a 12-week schedule, use a different backup tape each day for 2 weeks and then start the first tape again at the beginning of each third week. Incremental backups are performed Monday through Thursday after an initial normal backup; normal backups on Fridays. Normal backup of the preceding week is stored off-site and the most recent normal backup is stored on-site. At the end of 12 weeks, start the cycle over with a new set of tapes.

With a yearly backup, use 19 tapes over the course of one year. Use 4 tapes Monday through Thursday for incremental or differential backups. Use 3 tapes for weekly normal backups, one each for the first three Fridays of the month. The 12 remaining tapes are used for monthly normal backups on the fourth Friday of the month and are stored off-site.

the number of minutes: 5000 divided by 120, which equals 41.5 MB per minute.

You'll need to add time for the verification pass, which ensures that the data was written to the tape correctly and is readable. Generally, you double the number to allow enough time for verification, so in the example, the time is up to 83MB per minute. The disk drive(s) you use must also support this transfer rate.

You can use this formula to select a backup media that suits your needs. You'll want to add some room for growth; for the example, you might want a backup device that runs in the 15GB range with a backup speed of around 240M/minute.

> **NOTE**
> Tapes last longer in a cool, humidity-controlled location. The storage area should be free of magnetic fields (do not store tapes near the back of a computer terminal or near analog telephones, for example).

Documenting Backups

Keep accurate backup records so you can find data quickly and easily. Keep a log book if you have several high-volume tapes. Label tapes with a date, type of backup, and information on tape contents. Make sure you note the type (normal, incremental, or differential) so you won't have trouble finding the right tapes if you need to restore.

Most backup software includes a method of cataloging backup files. Print the catalog or save it to disk for future reference. If the option is offered to log backup operations, use that option. Logs can help you discover problems with the process.

Also recorded in any backup documentation must be a report of the backup test. Each and every backup must be tested to ensure that it will work.

Preparations, Hardware, and Software

Y   ou can prevent hardware problems by performing routine, planned maintenance checks on your system as part of your fault-tolerance plans. Examine system logs daily, perform routine disk maintenance procedures as supplied by the network operating system, such as scandisk or defrag. Create a log book for every server and include in it information about any problems or errors that you may be receiving as well as the measures you take to correct those errors.

Always perform a system and data backup before doing any hardware or software upgrades on a server. Back up system files, make a system disk if you haven't already, and record configurations of the server—such as IRQs, jumper and DIP switch settings, and such. See Chapter 3 of this book, "Planning Strategies," for more information.

Protecting your servers and system is the biggest preparation you can make for securing and preserving the system. Next, you'll need to consider the types of backup hardware available and find the ones that work best for your system and your situation.

In this chapter, you learn about the following:

- Various backup devices

- Tape backups

- Testing backups

- Restoring backups

Backup Devices

There are many types of backup devices and media available. You must consider the amount of data you need to back up, location of the device, ease of use, cost of device, cost of media for that particular device, and other factors when purchasing backup hardware.

Following are the common backup devices you might use for network and/or client backups. The more popular devices are discussed in more detail.

Floppy disks are affordable and readily accessible. They are great for smaller projects or for special files. Users might use floppies to back up certain files and /or directories on their workstations; however, floppies are time consuming and usually limited to 1.4MB. Using a compression program, such as PKZip, does enable one to copy larger files over multiple diskettes.

Zip drives, or removable drives, provide another method of backing up for small- to medium-sized projects. Zip cartridges, or disks, usually hold around 100MB of data, and like floppies, are easy to transport and use. Network users can use a zip drive to back up projects, directories, and other information from their workstation. Naturally, you could use a zip drive with server backup, but you cannot fit very much data on the disk, so it's not very advantageous.

Tape drives are inexpensive, safe, and often fairly easy to use; tape units aren't always compatible with some hardware types and/or NOSs. You should check the tape hardware before you buy to make sure it uses common standards. Tape drives are appropriate for server and network backups; however, since it is difficult to retrieve specific files from a tape, you want to use tapes for full and partial backups.

You might use an additional hard disk as a backup. A second hard disk enables you to mirror the contents of a hard disk and provides an exact replica in case the first disk becomes damaged. Using a second hard disk is a perfect method of backing up important servers, applications, and data.

Removable drives like SyQuest and Iomega Jazz models provide infinite storage possibilities. They furnish a large storage capacity and are especially handy for huge sound or image files. Since these drives are removable, they also enable the easy transport of files. If you want to share data, however, compatibility may be an issue.

Optical devices are more expensive than tape but provide faster access and transfer rates. WORM (Write-Once-Read-Many), rewritable or erasable, and CD-R and CD-writable are three forms in which optical devices are available. WORM and rewritable optical devices come in a variety of sizes—1.3GB or 2.6GB of storage space per platter. Optical devices are random access storage devices so data can be accessed quickly. Generally, optical backups are used when extremely long shelf life—15 years or more—is required or when fast access is needed, as in libraries.

CD-recorders are another possibility for backing up information. You can save quite a bit of information to a CD and may want to back up applications that are configured in a certain way, set up files for client computers, and that sort of data. The media cost is high, however, and there is a lack of support by the market currently. Also, you can only use a CD-ROM once as a backup. 650MB is the usual size. Generally, CD-recorders are expensive and not a good idea for servers.

> **NOTE**
> ZIP, JAZ, Magneto-Optical are not really applicable to server environments. They're fast, but few backup programs support using removable media.

Some companies offer backups online or over the Internet. The backup would be easily accessible as long as the communications lines and the company's servers were in working order. Some companies offer data storage for a monthly fee, for example. Over the Internet, storage is also possible. Both methods are inexpensive and your data is stored off-site. See Chapter 2 of this book, "Terminology and Technology," for more information.

You may not feel comfortable trusting a third party with your company's data; however, you can use an encryption software for which only you have the key. The software encrypts your data before it leaves your company and it remains encrypted at the storage facility. Online backup is slow initially, but after the first backup, it backs up only the files that have changed.

Solid-State Disks (SDDs) hold data in electronic circuits and provide extremely fast backup. Since SDDs are electronic and not mechanical, they are reliable and safe with very fast access times. SDD is a very expensive backup option.

Mainframe backups are becoming more popular as a means of secure LAN data protection. Since network attachments and speed of backing up on a mainframe are limiting, it's good to have another backup for all practical purposes; leave the mainframe backup in reserve in case all else fails.

> **NOTE**
>
> HSM (Hierarchical Storage Management) is a mainframe technology that is just entering the client/server field. HSM automatically frees disk space by migrating files that haven't been used in a period of time to a storage device, such as an optical device. HSM is not, however, a method of backing up files; rather, it is a method of archiving.

Tape Drives

Tape drives are the most popular backup devices in use today. Capacity, speed, and price are the most important factors when purchasing tape drives for backup purposes. Tape offers great capacity at a low cost. SCSI controllers offer high-capacity, high-performance tape drives. Also, consider the cost of tapes and of cleaning cartridges in addition to the cost of the tape drive.

Following are some of the more popular tape drive types. You'll need to research the speed and media cost, reliability, and capacity before making any decisions for your situation.

QIC.   Quarter-inch cartridge tapes come in varied formats. The technology is older. Capacities range from 60MB to 4GB and speed ranges are 25–35MB per minute.

4MM.   Tapes used on UNIX systems for years. The tape is not durable, however; tapes wear out quickly. Capacities range from 1.3GB to 4GB with speeds of 10–30MB per minute. Not really recommended for server environment.

8MM.   Tapes are durable and last well. Store 20GB of data at 3MB per second (180MB per minute).

DLT (Digital Linear Tape).   Drive has capacities to 35GB with transfer rates of up to 5MB per second (300MB per minute). You'll need a very fast disk subsystem with a dedicated SCSI channel or a SCSI wide channel to make good use of DLT.

DAT (Digital Audio Tapes).   4mm and 8mm helical scan tape systems provide more space for data to be recorded on a given length of tape because of the technology. Versatile and compact, DAT systems are portable and easy to use. DAT uses the digital data storage recording format that allows up to 2GB to be stored on a single cartridge (4GB with compression). Also available in cartridge libraries, or autoloaders, which enable multiple cartridges to be used to boost storage capacities to 20GB or more.

> **TIP**
>
> Some DLT manufacturers offer DLT libraries with capacities ranging from 2 to 45 drives and from 16 to over 1300 cartridges to support a wide range of backup needs.

Tape Information and Advice

Tapes are inexpensive and with increased data capacities of tapes and cartridges, storing data on tapes is faster and even less expensive than ever before. There are disadvantages, however, to using tape backups. Organizing the policies, scheduling, and backup types is time consuming and complex. Finding a file from a tape is difficult. However, automated tape backup and rotation schemes are now available to help you through the management of your tape backup procedures.

Here are a few things about using tape devices and tapes for backup purposes:

Most backup technologies use software-based compression. With data compression, you'll get about twice as much data on a tape as is listed; often the backup speed nearly doubles as well.

The quality of the tapes you buy will affect the success of your backup/recovery system. You should use tapes of high quality—such as Verbatim or 3M—because these tapes are quality controlled as opposed to inexpensive, no-name tapes.

You should periodically clean your tape heads, especially during the first few weeks of using new tapes. Excess oxide from the tapes flakes off and builds up on the tape heads. You can use a commercial tape cleaner or you can wipe off the tape heads with a little isopropyl alcohol on a cotton swab. Make sure you wait at least 10 minutes after cleaning before inserting a tape cartridge. Dirty tape heads can cause odd read/write errors.

Internal tape drives versus external drives is a matter of your own preferences. External drives are usually more expensive and take up more desk space than internal; however, they are also portable.

Data Compression

Using data compresion during network backups nearly doubles the amount of data you can fit onto your backup media. A 2GB tape, then, might hold nearly 4GB of data.

Data compression also reduces network traffic. Compression does, however, increase CPU usage and may hamper the performance of lesser processors. If you can purchase a compressing device or drive, as opposed to compression software, the data will generally compress faster and without the excess load on the CPU.

Any generic compressing algorithm typically achieves 2:1 compression (including tape drives); sometimes you get more compression, sometimes less. Use compression during backup to minimize network bandwidth, if you have the available CPU power, and to get more data on the tape or backup media.

It is important to note that compressing already-compressed data has no effect and may even expand the data.

Backup Standards

When planning your tape systems, find out whether the tape storage system uses standardized recording formats, such as QIC-40, QIC-80 (or Quick-80), QIC-3010, DDS-1, and DDS-2. Keeping your formats the same during hardware changes provides full compatibility with previous-generation tapes. Major manufacturers commonly use these formats.

Nonstandardization of tapes and/or backup devices makes it difficult for administrators to exchange tapes within an enterprise unless the same software and hardware are used throughout. Two standards have emerged, however: SMS (Storage Management Services) and SIDF (System Independent Data Format).

SMS, designed by Novell, provides a consistent interface through a set of open instructions sets—APIs and TSAs (Target Service Agents)—to provide a consistent interface into the network's file system. The API provides a consistent software mechanism for retrieving data and the TSAs provide cross-platform compatibility.

SIDF is a tape format that enables data interchange among various vendors and operating systems. SIDF supports high-performance backup and quick file access. It also furnishes quick restores.

It is important to make sure all of your tape devices are either the same make and model or adhere to these standards. If you have a tape device that fails and no other device like it, your backup tapes are worthless.

Backup Software

There are many types of backup software you can use. Many network operating systems include software for backing up in the OS; however, these are not always the most powerful or flexible backup applications available. There are also many third-party backup programs you can buy for every operating system. You'll have to study what's available before you can decide which to use.

Make sure you match the peripheral devices with the software. Compatibility is key between the two, as well as between the device and the network operating system and the backup software and the NOS.

Generally, you probably want a graphical user interface that can be used on both client and server machines. If your company uses a variety of operating systems, make sure your software supports the various systems and syntax. If you use an operating system that utilizes long filenames, consider how the backup software treats those filenames; some programs will truncate the name and not restore it to its original value. You should also make sure the software assigns specific attributes to the files—such as name, length, owner, group, and so on—if possible.

Look for optimization features when searching for tape backup software. Generally, if data placement is set in natural groupings, backup and restore speeds are optimum. Also check error restart procedures, monitoring features, results from connection failures, and so on.

Administrative features are also important. Can the backup administrator manage backup servers both on the LAN and a WAN? How does bandwidth affect the process if backups are made over the network? What are the scheduling options? Can you customize the schedule? Are there possibilities for conditional commands and execution? Can the user define the criteria for backup levels and reference points?

Does the software catalog files? What type of integrity check does it perform? What type of end-of-job reports, backup logs, and progress reports are displayed and saved?

If you plan to back up client machines, check the software for client features, such as client control for excluding specific files, client's rights for restore, and such.

Testing and Restoring Backups

Making backups will only work for you if you periodically test them. Many people make backups regularly but never test them. When it becomes necessary to restore the backups, the administrator finds set after set of worthless backups, caused by data errors, undetected hardware problems, damaged tape, or other disaster. Testing the backups periodically is the *only* way you can be sure the data is retrievable.

Restoring the backup is also important. Hopefully, you'll not have to experience restoration in a panic situation; however, you should know the general steps for restoring.

Testing Backups

You're busy. Your teams are busy. With so much work to do, how do you find time to test backups? It doesn't matter how you find the time, you must perform tests. Many administrators have felt comfortable with their backups, only to find they were worthless because no one bothered to test them.

Some backup software performs error and accuracy testing. Take advantage of all software features that provide these services, no matter how much time it adds to your backup process. Backups are no good if you can't restore them.

Another idea for testing backups actually serves two purposes. You can assign the people on your backup team to practice restoring backups on spare drives. You might, for instance, set an older computer aside and use it for practice purposes only. Make sure they don't practice on a drive currently in use or they will overwrite recent data. The practice drive or computer *must not* be a drive in current use (see Figure 4.1).

Each team member can take a turn (a week's worth of backups, say, once a month) at testing the backups. The practice for restoring the backups guarantees each team member will know what to do if a disaster occurs and the backups need to be restored. The practice also enables the team member to check through some of the applications, data, and configuration to make sure the backup is accurate and works.

These periodic restorations also can uncover hardware problems that don't show up with the backup software; sometimes a controller or backup device will have a problem and cause the backup to be unrecoverable, but no errors appear during the backup process. The team members doing the practice restorations should keep a log of the backups, restores, and, especially, error messages.

Figure 4.1 Test restores on a spare computer, not on a server that contains active data.

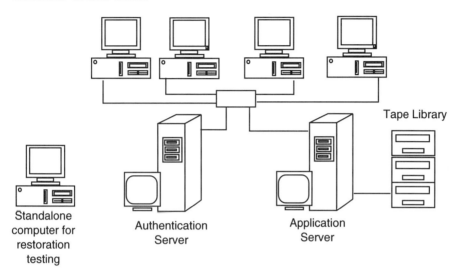

Tape Library

Standalone
computer for
restoration
testing

Authentication
Server

Application
Server

Restoring Backups

When backing up and restoring data, have someone work with you to be trained as well as to help you avoid mistakes. A backup team may be the best bet; a team can form guidelines as well as keep a check on activities and troubleshoot problems together. You should create restoration policies for everyday maintenance as well as for emergency recovery.

Following are some general suggestions to help if you run into problems:

Write-protect the backup media before you start the restore. You don't want to accidentally choose backup in the software and ruin a good set of data on the tape.

After a complete drive failure, you'll first need to reinstall the operating system and any database servers, applications, patches or fixes, and so on. Then install the backup software. Reload any special or updated drivers for the tape drive, or other backup device—SCSI controller, motherboard, or other critical components.

Restore the full backup first. Make sure you watch the restore in case there's a problem. A restore will take about the same amount of time it took to perform the full backup. Next, restore incremental or differential backups. You must restore every incremental backup since the full backup in order, or the last differential backup since the full backup.

After restoring backups, pull your restoration media out of circulation for a few days. Do this in case you didn't get everything restored or need to go back to the tapes for some reason.

POLICIES AND DISASTER RECOVERY

If something should happen to your system and you lose a hard drive, server, or an entire site, what would you do? What's the first step in recovering from the disaster? What's the next step? How long will it take your people to get back to work? How do you get your backups installed to the new server? Do you even have reliable backups?

These are all "what if" questions and you may never need the answers. But more than likely, you will encounter a situation in which you need to restore a backup or confront an emergency situation. At the least, a disaster recovery plan will guarantee your peace of mind; at the most, it will provide a comprehensive set of steps to follow in the middle of a catastrophe that stops your business.

In this chapter, you learn about the following:

- Backup policies
- Disaster recovery plans

Backup Policies

You or your backup team should set backup policies and follow them strictly. Within your policy, you must decide who will determine the computers and files to be backed up, whether to back up servers and clients, how often to back up, and so on.

Policies should be carefully formed and reviewed. When your policies are exactly as you want them, you should put them in writing and pass them around to managers and administrators for review and comments. After you receive input and approval, print out copies of the policies for everyone in your company. It's a good idea to review the policies so that everyone understands them.

Also, don't put the policies away in a drawer and forget them. Especially with backups, it's important to review your policies periodically and update them. You may also want to run frequent checks on those responsible for the backups to make sure they are following the company's backup policy.

Start with Questions

When determining your policies, ask the following questions to help you form statements that outline your philosophy and requirements for backup policies.

- Who will form the policies?

- Will backups include servers and/or clients?

- Which computers and files will be backed up?

- How often will the backups be made—full, incremental, and/or differential?

- Who will perform the backups and who will keep the logs?

- Who will be the alternate for backing up files?

- Who will test the backups and report on the status?

- Who receives reports of successful or failed backups?

- Who should the backup personnel notify in case of problems?

- What are the procedures for backup hardware or software failure?

- Where will backups be stored?

Policy Statements

After you gather the information and answers from the previous questions, you're ready to put your policies into statement format. It's important that you thoroughly cover topics such as scheduling, media rotation, off-site storage, and so on.

Your polices must reflect the decisions you've made for backup devices and media, whether you back up client and/or server, where backup devices are stored, and other such individualized choices you've made. Following are some general backup policy statements you may adopt or use as a basis for your own statements.

- A log listing each server's and/or workstation's hardware and software specifications will be stored by the computer; the log will be updated once a month or when configuration changes.

- A system disk for every computer on the network will be created and stored with the spec log for that computer.

- Application and operating system disks will be handled with care and stored in a central location to be designated.

- Backups will be performed every day.

- Backup media will be clearly dated and labeled.

- One set of backups will be stored in a cool, dry place on premises.

- Backup logs will be completed during each and every backup.

- Nightly backups are performed on a rotation set of tapes, as follows...

- Used tapes will be removed from the set and replaced with new tapes every four to six months.

- Monthly backups will never be recycled so we'll always have a backup of the server.

- A complete set of backups will be kept off-site and updated every two weeks.

- Everything stored in /directory on the server(s) and/or workstation(s) will be backed up.

- A test restore will be completed once a month and a log will be kept to record errors and successes.

- Monthly maintenance checks on all backup devices will be performed.

Disaster Recovery

You may already have a disaster recovery plan in effect, but if all you're doing is backing up files as your plan, you need to consider some other issues. Fault tolerance is the first step to recovering from a disaster. If you have a mirrored server or a RAID drive that can take over in case your server crashes, you can get back on track pretty quickly. If you don't have a fault tolerance plan of action, it's time to get one.

Having a good and current backup of your system means you won't lose information, only time. But how many people actually back up their systems regularly, or even at all? When was the last time you checked your backup to make sure it worked?

Even if you do perform regular backups, what do you do about the downtime? How do you prepare for the time lost while you're replacing hardware, installing and configuring applications, and restoring the backups? You must prepare by creating a disaster recovery plan.

Disasters come in many forms—fire or flood, sabotage, tornadoes, hard drive failure, corrupted files, viruses, and so on. If you lose all of your data today, can your business recover? If so, how quickly?

Problems with Making a Plan

A collapse of your system leads to a loss of service and data. A good disaster recovery plan includes measures for setting up special buildings or hot sites ready to assume operations in case the primary location fails; backing up data regularly and storing it in a fire-safe, off-site location; establishing procedures to restore key personnel and services first, and so on.

It's easy to come up with many problems to planning and implementing a disaster recovery plan. These problems are valid, but they shouldn't stop you from doing your best to get a plan down on paper. Following are a few of the problems you may run into and some suggestions for overcoming them.

A lack of information about which systems are vital to business is an area of concern when drafting a disaster recovery plan. No one administrator can possibly know everything about the network. You need help. Gather a team of knowledgeable people—managers, administrators, users, and so on—to help you form your disaster recovery plan.

This also helps with a problem every network administrator will experience: a lack of corporate support, staff, and money to form a disaster recovery plan. It's a difficult task to accomplish but a plan can help you and your company get through a time of panic and frenzy, save money and time in the long run, and assuage frustrations and tempers when a disaster occurs.

Your network could be made up of widely dispersed systems, for example. The larger the network, the more difficult it will be to form a disaster recovery plan and to implement one if necessary. One way to alleviate this problem is to have each WAN location create its own recovery plan. Local managers and administrators know their systems better than anyone does. Send them some general guidelines and let them come up with their own plan. For consistency's sake, one team could collect all plans and update and amend them; then redistribute the plans for use.

Another problem with formulating a plan is that your network may be made up of many and various systems or platforms. Mainframes, UNIX systems, PC servers running NetWare, and a variety of clients all in one network can be overwhelming to the administrator who needs to form a disaster recovery plan.

One solution might be to assign the administrator or department managers the task of writing their own steps for a plan. A centralized team can then gather the steps and combine them into one plan covering all platforms and systems.

A lack of knowledge about the kind of applications running on various platforms and how critical any of them are is another problem. If you've instituted a policy for creating a log of every computer's hardware, configuration, and software, then this problem is solved. See Chapter 3 of this book, "Planning Strategies," for more information.

In general, you'll need to plan a fundamental recovery procedure that covers many, but not all, circumstances. Take a prioritized approach to your plan. Planning a hot site is your best line of defense. A hot site is a site fully equipped with a server and all backup data that can jump in and take the place of a downed server or other disaster in the original site. You can alternatively contract with a local vendor to provide a basic shell building in case of emergency; the building would include power, networking services, and other items you need to keep your business going while you recover from the disaster.

Forming a Plan

First, gather a team of your most experienced managers, users, and administrators. Make note of the potential disasters that could affect your business. You don't have to think of every disaster, but try to think about a variety of possibilities and the downtime each could produce. For instance, a disk crash can be a simple corruption of the files that can be quickly and easily repaired, or it could be a totally impaired disk from which your data cannot be recovered. Each situation requires different amounts of time, money, and effort to correct.

Consider, too, the other parts of your system that can cause problems: network cards, cabling, memory, and so on. Some problems can cause damage to other files or system components. Other problems can make your system inoperative for an hour, a day, or more.

Next, prioritize your applications. Which are necessary to the operation of the business after a disaster, and which applications can wait a while before becoming operational? Make sure to consult with department managers and others to find out which applications are important to them and why.

Next, prioritize your business functions. Which operations are most essential for your business to continue? Which can you do without for a few days? Rank your operations from most vital to routine. Is order processing more important than billing? Shipping more important than ordering raw materials? Perhaps some functions must continue but can take place only periodically, while other services may only be necessary for secondary business operations.

Writing the Plan

Your next step is to list your recovery instructions. Outline what will be done in case of a disaster, step-by-step. Make sure you list the names of department heads or managers and their phone numbers as a part of the disaster recovery plan; also include any information about vendors or consultants you may need to contact after a catastrophe.

Also, consider doing the following:

Define how to retrieve and restore backups.

Outline information about the server and system components—list drivers, special applications, and any unusual information that may be needed when installing programs or configuring servers.

Detail information about setting up client and server computers. List the configurations, operating systems, and other individual information to make setting up the servers easy when the time comes.

Detail all hardware information about each server that may cause problems or need special configuration or care when installing.

Determine the replacement costs for servers—file, mail, print, Internet or intranet, application servers, gateway servers, and so on.

Determine costs for workstation replacement, individual computer components replacement, network components, and such.

Make a list of lost revenues in sales, customer good will, employee productivity, missed contractual obligations, and so on, and try to figure the best way to handle each problem.

Keep a list of past failures to study; list the failure, effect, total downtime, costs, possible resolutions or workarounds, and actual or expected cost of resolution.

After you create a disaster recovery plan, make sure you review it carefully and make the instructions easy to follow and complete. Test the plan and pass a copy around the office to make sure others can understand it as well. Finally, review the plan periodically, update configurations, and amend it as necessary when your system changes. Let's hope you never need it, but if you do, you'll be thankful you've taken the time to write a disaster recovery plan.

Disaster Recovery Policies

You should form a set of policies you can enforce before a disaster occurs. These policies outline safeguards that will help in case of a catastrophe. As with all policies, review them often and update as necessary.

Following are some sample policy statements for disaster recovery:

Store copies of the backup on-site in case of a problem; store media in a fireproof safe or cabinet under lock and key.

Store copies of the application disks or CDs you'll need to restore as well as a copy of the NOS and client operating systems in a fireproof safe.

Store off-site a full backup performed weekly or biweekly plus original application and operating system disks.

Gather all network maps, logs, and documentation in a centralized place; store copies off-site as well.

Administrators will complete training (or required reading) in preparation for an emergency.

Protecting Hardware Components

Since the following components may fail at some point, it's a good idea to have spare parts or at least the name and number of a vendor from whom you can obtain the part quickly.

Also, you can provide protection for many components and devices to save from problems later. For example, you should use UPS protection for all servers, but especially for routers, bridges, hubs, and switches; these devices are expensive, so protect them as much as possible.

There are two types of UPSs: *online* and *standby*. An online UPS connects between the main power and the computer so your computer system has constant power. It also removes spikes, surges, sags, and noise. A standby UPS connects to the main power directly to the computer and monitors the main power voltage level. Make sure the UPS has enough power to run whatever you're protecting, or supply one UPS per computer.

The server or computer motherboard and CPU are the most reliable computer components, but there are some parts that commonly fail from damage, extended use, poor quality, or other reasons. Following are some components that commonly fail and a few hints on how to identify the problem:

Continues

> **Protecting Hardware Components** *(Continued)*
>
> RAM may cause computer crashes or cause the operating system to display memory error warnings.
>
> Video cards that fail cause application page faults, screen redraw problems, and so on. Make sure you're using the appropriate and updated driver for the video card to minimize problems.
>
> Network cards with dual-channel connections (FDDI, CDDI, and ATM) provide their own fault tolerance—if one channel goes down and the other takes over. However, Ethernet and token ring cards don't have dual-channel capability; you can use the manufacturer's or a third-party diagnostic program to keep an eye on these cards. With sniffers, you can evaluate network segments; sniffers are network packet trace programs that check for corrupted packets, bandwidth saturation, and such.
>
> Network cabling may fail or need upgrading for newer technologies like ATM, 100BaseT, and so on.

Sample Topics for the Plan

Following are some sample topics you might include in your plan or modify to suit your business situation. Use the topics to give you an idea of what you might need and then fill in steps to accomplish the procedure or process.

Procedures for:

- Restoring hardware/software systems
- Rewiring the facility
- Restoring original LAN configurations
- Testing hardware and software
- Training personnel on new equipment
- Restoring backups
- Contacting key staff

Outline and define the following:

- Contact names for vendors, consultants, recovery teams, and management
- Team member responsibilities

- Hardware and software lists, serial numbers, license numbers, and so on
- Wiring schematics, equipment room layout
- Contracts and maintenance agreements

Introduction to Book Eleven

When securing your network, your first step is to minimize the vulnerability of the LAN or WAN. There are certain precautions you can take to protect your data, users, hardware, configurations, and so on, from the inside and from the outside of the network.

Physical security to servers, equipment, and workstations should be top on your list for inside protection. You also want your users to utilize passwords, login scripts, and user accounts. The network must be secure from the inside before you can successfully secure it from the outside. Also, make sure your users understand security risks and protect their passwords and other information from outsiders.

You'll want to secure information systems from outside threats. Someone from your corporation's switchboard or help desk, for example, may be giving out information that he or she shouldn't. An easy way to infiltrate any system is for a person to misrepresent his identity or role to the company. *Spoofing*, email address concealment, is another method of breaching your company's security. Crimes related to spoofing include copyright violations, extortion, forgery, fraud, network identity theft, industrial espionage, sabotage, and other unauthorized system uses.

So what can you do? Following are some ideas; this book outlines many solutions and suggestions for possible security problems:

- Train your users to be wary; they should question the source of all emails, phone calls, and outside contacts.

- Your policies should provide a definitive statement of management intentions, outline procedures for network and data protection, include guidelines and references for new staff, and so on.

- Make sure all employees know what information should not be released to the public, such as employees names, home addresses, phone numbers and other personal information as well as confidential company data.

- Check the backgrounds of new employees, consultants, contractors, and such; for example, criminal record checks, credit history, department of motor vehicles, and prior employment references.

PRELIMINARY GROUNDWORK

If your network has never been breached, you should consider yourself lucky, but don't think the security threat is minor. It may be hard for you to justify spending time and money on security-related work, but there are more holes in your system than can reasonably be plugged.

If you have trouble convincing the powers that be to invest in some safeguards and precautions, then you should breach your own system and write a report outlining how you did it and what needs to be done to implement better security. There are even companies and consultants who will hack into your system for you and provide reports about your network's weaknesses and strengths.

You also might point your bosses to recent security breaches at other companies; cite security studies. Companies will normally spend money on physical security, such as locks, card keys, surveillance, and guards; but you need to protect your network resources as well.

Tell management about competitive losses as a result of break-ins; for example, the cost in customer relations will be high when you notify your customers that their credit card numbers have been stolen. You can talk about recovering from an attack and the effects on your company, users, and customers, as well.

In this chapter, you learn more facts and arguments to help you convince your bosses of the importance of network and data security. In this chapter, you learn about the following:

- Advantages of protecting your network and data

- Disadvantages of lax security

- Risk assessment

- Security hotspots

Advantages and Disadvantages of Network Security

You measure the amount of security you provide for your network in direct proportion to the importance of your data and your network. If your network merely exists as a means of email and collaborative efforts between coworkers, you may not worry about security; however, if you do all of your business—payroll, customer billing, inventory, correspondence, and so on—on your network, you'll want to protect it as much as you can.

Luckily, today's network operating systems and third-party products provide many security features to help you protect your data; there are also several procedures you can perform to keep your network safe from intrusion and sabotage.

Security measures take time and money to implement, but you'll be more than willing to expend the effort when you realize just how easy it is to lose data due to lax security. Whether your security problems stem from uninformed users accidentally damaging files or from deliberate sabotage by outside crackers, there are always steps you can take to protect your data and equipment. Again, it depends on how important your network is to your business.

Following are some of the advantages and disadvantages of implementing security on your network.

Advantages

There are a multitude of reasons for securing your network and your data. If you've never seen a security breach or its results, you may not feel that it is as important as it is. However, if you've ever found an email from an unknown party floating around your system, lost an important database file because a user accidentally got into the directory, or been notified of customers' credit card numbers that were stolen from your company, you know the importance of good security.

Appropriate security measures can save your company time and money. Sure, the initial time spent on setting up the system and the money spent on new equipment, software, training, and so on, seems like a lot to pay out. But think of the time your users will spend recreating lost data, or the time it takes to notify 1000 customers that their credit card numbers were stolen from your computer. How much will it cost you in man-hours to rectify a problem caused by a security breach? What will the cost be for your company's reputation?

Another important advantage, even a necessity, to network security is in the legal ramifications. If you don't properly protect your customer's sensitive information, you and your company could be held legally responsible. Consider, too, your users' part in security. What if a user commits fraud or theft over your company's Internet connection? What part does the company play in charges or lawsuits? The legal concerns may be enough to convince your bosses that security is important.

Network policies are also of primary importance in keeping your company legally safe. If you distribute and enforce good policies, you can avoid a lot of legal problems from employees, managers, business partners, and perhaps even customers. Policies also help you control your network—resource control, access limits, and so on, mean you can save money and effort in managing the network and resources.

There are many advantages to implementing security within your network. You surely won't need or want to implement every security option discussed here, but you should consider adopting a few methods and procedures presented in this book.

Disadvantages

The same disadvantages apply to security precautions as apply to any network improvement you make: basically, time and money. The time you must invest in studying the situation, proposing ideas, polishing solutions, purchasing equipment, installing and configuring hardware and software, testing, optimizing, and supporting security options will be enormous. You already have a lot to do; adding more duties means either hiring new staff, delegating some of the tasks, or simply making more time.

You'll also have to invest money in equipment, administrative and employee time, and perhaps outsourced help. Perhaps you'll need more money than is budgeted for the network systems. You also may want to hire staff or consultants and add training your users to that list of expenses.

Definitely, preparing and implementing security measures for your network won't be simple or inexpensive; however, the consequences of a lax security system can be far more devastating.

Assessing Your Risks

Whether you call it risk management, disaster planning, or something else, you must evaluate the dangers that threaten your network security and then manage those risks to eliminate, or at least minimize, them. Usually, your major risks will come from people. Hackers and crackers might break into your network to steal data or corrupt your system. Your own users may be angry with you and delete important files; or perhaps by mistake, a user destroys data or equipment.

You want to consider all possibilities, but then take action on only the most probable or the most harmful of risks. Following are some ideas for evaluating your risks and some help on finding solutions.

Risk Categories

Start by listing typical areas, or categories, of concern, such as scheduling, financial, technology, communications, and so on. Following are some examples of concerns in each of these categories:

Scheduling: Problems may include night shifts, workers clocking in over the weekend, any staff with odd working hours or little supervision.

Financial: Might include payroll files on the server, or any banking, credit card use, money transfers, and such that are performed electronically or over public communications lines.

Technology: Passwords, security certification or keys, encryption methods, email, Internet access, firewalls and routers, and so on.

Communications: Email, voice mail, bulletin boards, groupware projects, extranet or intranets, and such.

Evaluate your risks and then rank them in order of importance. How likely is a problem to occur and how much is at stake if it does happen? Choose only the most common or likely risks; you don't have to fill every hole, only the biggest and scariest ones.

Finding Solutions

For each risk, plan a response or initiate a solution, depending on the size of the risk and its implications. You can monitor the lesser risks and implement a response if necessary. But this means you must monitor the risks or have an administrative assistant do it for you. Make sure you document everything: your lists, plans, responses and solutions, and the outcome.

Following are some possible solutions and responses that may help in your situation:

Document and verify software licensing and usage policies.

Don't allow users to install software without permission.

Require encryption of all email messages and attached files.

Use and monitor passwords, user rights policies, directory and file permissions, account lockout options, and so on.

Check the physical security of the facility: trash, janitors, locks and building access, even selling used equipment.

Use intrusion detection applications for Internet Web servers.

Implement firewalls, filtering routers, proxy servers, and the like.

Monitor FTP security.

Security Hotspots

You must have excellent internal network security before your external security will ever be effective. There are certain areas of your network that are security *hotspots*, or points of failure. The number of hotspots increases as you add more users, servers, LAN segments, and especially outside connections, such as to the Internet or an extranet.

Your data may be the most important resource you have to protect on your network. In addition to keeping your company data secret, you must protect the integrity and accessibility of your data. You don't want someone to change or delete your data without your permission or knowledge, and you must not let someone prevent you from accessing your data.

To get an idea of the hotspots on your network, you'll need to analyze network configuration, operating systems, network connections, policies, user behavior, and other factors. This section explains a few common hotspots for both internal and external network security.

Internal Network Security

There are many methods of protecting your network from internal threats; a network operating system provides features, for example, like user accounts, auditing features, permissions on files, and so on. There are also third-party applications you can use and even hardware devices that can help you protect company data.

Following are a few ideas for protecting your network from the inside:

Unsecured communications. Emails, bulletin board posts, shared documents, and memos circulated within the company may breach security by revealing passwords, locations of data, and so on.

Software bugs or viruses. When introduced to your system, a virus can rapidly destroy data. Also, some software bugs may enable a user to breach the security of the system.

Improperly configured software. If you improperly configure some network operating systems, you could open some security holes; there are third-party applications that can scan your network to find vulnerable access points.

Vendors' back doors. Many software vendors build in back doors to their software that enable them to access the system for maintenance purposes. Make sure you ask the vendor about the existence of any back doors and take steps to block them.

System files. Users could purposely or accidentally read and/or destroy system files. Hide and lock all system files to be safe.

User Accounts

Each NOS provides different rights, permissions, and authorizations to the system and its resources. Additionally, each NOS enables you to mark these limits for your users differently. Implement these security features to protect your network and your users.

Also, use Read, Write, Access, Execute, and Change permissions; assign permissions to files and/or directories to limit access to those who have been granted permissions for those files/directories.

Most NOSs enable you to define rights for groups of people, such as administrators, backup operators, print managers, and so on. Carefully check the groups you've assigned to make sure everyone included has the appropriate rights. Limit the number of people you include in these groups, especially the administrators group.

Members of an administrators group generally have permissions and rights to make any and all changes to the server. An administrator may try to sabotage the system but more than likely, he or she will accidentally delete, modify, or add something to the server that proves devastating to business.

User accounts provide a basic line of defense in terms of internal network security. You need to maintain user accounts by deleting usernames that are no longer at your company, updating passwords and permissions, setting profiles, and so on. Maintaining accounts keeps the network and data secure by establishing who may or may not access certain resources.

Additionally, you will want to train users in proper procedures for using the network to avoid costly mistakes; sometimes security breaches aren't necessarily intentional. Prepare, for instance, user guidelines governing resources, directories, files, printers, and the like. Ask that users notify an administrator immediately if they find a suspicious event or user on the network, notice problems with their own passwords or rights, or discover unusual problems with files, applications, or directories.

Passwords

Also consider such issues as passwords, account disqualification and expiration, and such. If you want complete control over your users, you can assign passwords. It is easier, however, to assign everyone the same password and require that each person change the password upon login.

Consider the following password and account policies to provide the best network security:

Require a password to be a certain minimum length, such as five letters, so that it is more difficult to guess.

Limit the use of the same password over and over, for security's sake.

Set password expiration dates so users must change their passwords periodically, say, every two or three months.

Lock out a user after a certain number of failed logon attempts, say four or five, to keep hackers out.

Set auditing on logons so that you have a log of attempts at security breaches.

Make sure users understand they should not give their password to anyone, at any time. They also should not write their password down anywhere at work.

Routers

You can protect your internal system with routers and router filtering. An intelligent router can send packets to the appropriate LAN segment. The router can screen packets within your network by using the source and destination addresses contained in the header information on the packet. You set up filters, or rules, in the router to permit or deny access to packets entering the router.

Strategically placing routers within your network segments, LANs, and WANs can help you keep data and resources secure.

C2 Security Compliance

C2 is a level of security that serves as a baseline measurement of a secure operating system. The U.S. Department of Defense defines C2 certification. Certification applies to a particular installation—including hardware, software, and system environment—not to an operating system or particular server brand. Individual sites can become C2 certified, not individual NOSs.

C2 is known as Discretionary Access Control (DAC). Access control is the main difference between C-level and B-level of security. In C2, owners have the choice about whether or not others can access their objects. In B-level (Mandatory Access Control—MAC), security levels are defined for objects without the user's input.

Some requirements of C2 are:

- The owner of a resource or file must be able to control access to the resource or file.

- Users are accountable for all of their access-related actions.

- The operating system must protect objects against reuse by other processes.

- Users must identify themselves through a unique login ID and password, which is then used to track the users' activities.

- Administrators must be able to audit security-related events and even logs must be protected from unauthorized access.

- The operating system must protect data stored in memory for one process so that it's not randomly reused by other processes; the operating system must be able to protect itself against tampering.

External Security

Securing your LAN from the outside world is easier when you have no network connections to the outside. There are still risks of course—theft, breakins, and such—but the risks really magnify when you connect your LAN to the Internet, to a corporate WAN, or use another outside connection. Your data is vulnerable to various dangers from which you need protection.

As with internal security, there are several hotspots you should keep your eye on. Unsecured communications outside of the network, viruses, and software bugs are threats from the outside as well as from the inside. Following are a few more.

Hubs and Routers

Hub security may not be something you're aware of, but it can help you protect your network. A hub modifies transmission signals so that the network can be extended to accommodate extra workstations and more hubs. 3Com makes a series of hubs that also scramble packets on all ports but the destination, thus keeping unauthorized users from accessing packets.

Another hub approach to security is the *switching hub,* as opposed to a repeating hub. The switching hub keeps the network secure by not allowing anyone to receive anyone else's packets. It also boosts bandwidth and network speed. Figure 1.1 illustrates a switching hub between network segments; the hub makes sure each workstation gets the correct packets.

You might use a *router,* an intelligent device that routes data packets to the correct LAN segment, to add extra safeguards to your network. You can run Telnet and/or SNMP standard services on a router for management purposes; however, you can also cause security problems. If you run Telnet, make sure you specify trusted hosts only and that SNMP is configured to use private community names only. Some routers can also be configured as firewalls.

Figure 1.1 A switching hub helps secure the network.

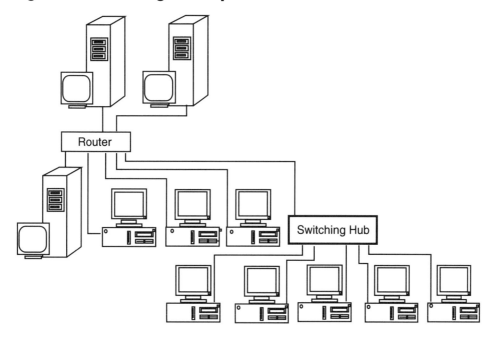

Firewalls

You can configure firewalls in various ways to meet your security needs. A firewall may be implemented on one machine or on multiple machines and routers. There are four methods of configuring firewalls:

Packet filtering is a simple method of configuring a firewall. The packet filter examines packet header information—source and destination addresses and the port numbers—to allow or drop each packet it screens.

Screened host allows only trusted services to pass through the gateway between an outside host and the protected host attached to the internal LAN. Screened host enables only specific types of connections and/or direct connections for select services. Screened host provides strong security but also a single point of failure.

Screened subnet is more secure than a screened host because the protected host is attached to a perimeter network instead of the internal LAN. The perimeter network is connected to the internal LAN and to an external network through two screening routers, creating no single point of failure.

Dual-homed host is the most secure firewall. A dual-homed host is a single computer with two (or more) network cards. One card communicates to the internal LAN and the other communicates to the external network; there can be no communication between the inside and the outside of the firewall. Packets can move from one network to another only after being proxied.

Figure 1.2 shows a computer acting as a dual-homed firewall. The computer contains two network cards—one that uses the TCP/IP protocol to communicate over the Internet and another one that uses IPX/SPX to communicate with the Novell LAN.

Figure 1.2 Using a firewall protects your network from Internet intruders.

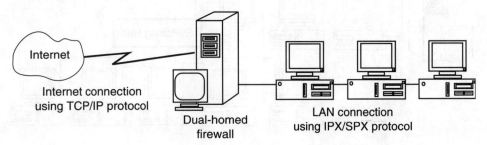

Packet Sniffing, IP Spoofing, and Cryptography

Packet sniffing is a common technique network attackers use to read messages. There are sniffer programs that enable them to intercept, read, and possibly modify your email messages. *IP spoofing* is a technique attackers use to fabricate messages. A firewall or filtering router will look at a TCP/IP header to determine the source or destination address. If you use only packet filtering as your firewall protection, IP spoofing attacks can fool the packet filters by forging IP headers.

Using *cryptography* is one way to prevent packet sniffing and IP spoofing. Cryptography describes various methods of ensuring the protection of messages as they are sent over the Internet. Public/private key, encryption, and digital signatures are all forms of cryptography and work together to protect messages and data sent over the Internet.

Secure Sockets Layer is a form of public/private keys used to encrypt data sent over the Internet. A user encrypts the data in a message and locks the message with a private key. Only a matching private key can unlock that message and decrypt it.

See Book Eleven, Chapter 4, "Internet Security," for more information.

Similarly, *digital signatures* act as a lock of sorts. A user can compute a digital signature for a given message using his or her private key; the digital signature ensures that a user is who he says he is.

PLANNING NETWORK STRATEGIES

In preparation for planning and implementing security procedures, you must consider your goals for security. You might want to prevent some users' access to sensitive customer files or protect your product database from prying competitor's eyes; you might want your users to keep their passwords private or physically protect your servers from access and possible weather damage. You must first outline your security goals, and then decide the best way to implement security to attain those goals.

List the security goals for your network and then list the procedures you must follow to implement the security. For example, do you need to enforce user password policies or make a change in user account options? Perhaps adding routers and firewalls would help you reach your goal for protection from hackers. Relocating your servers and other equipment may better protect them.

This chapter suggests some methods for protecting your equipment and data. In this chapter, you learn the following:

- Physical protection for your network

- Good system administration for security

- Network auditing as a security solution

System Administration

Before you can really protect your system, you must organize your tasks and perform them efficiently and effectively. Good security starts with good system administration. You must check permissions for all files and directories, keep user accounts up to date, monitor server and network use, and perform a multitude of other administrative duties to keep your network and data safe.

One problem you may see in this good system administration is that you have no time as it is to manage the network properly. The solutions to this problem include delegation of duties to other administrators and administrative assistants and software applications that help you perform these duties. There are programs for monitoring the network, limiting user access, governing Internet connections, and more. There are security features built in to most network operating systems. You must take the time to organize and implement the security of your network—to protect your users, your data, your company, your customers, and yourself.

User Administration

You will need to maintain user accounts by adding new usernames, deleting usernames that are no longer at your company, updating passwords and permissions, setting profiles, and so on. Maintaining accounts keeps the network and data secure by establishing who may or may not access certain resources.

Additionally, you will want to train users in proper procedures of using the network; this saves time and effort later in having to correct mistakes and disasters. Prepare, for instance, user guidelines governing resources, directories, files, printers, and the like. Supply users with a list of contacts, or a help desk, they can call for help.

Also consider such issues as passwords, account disqualification and expiration, and such. If you want complete control over your users, you can assign passwords. It is, however, easier to assign everyone the same password and require that each person change the password upon login.

Server Administration

Centralizing your network provides more security as well as easier administration. Servers are more secure when they are centralized because administrators are usually monitoring one or another server at all times during the workday. Also, you're more likely to physically secure a group of servers in a room than one server in a larger office.

Figure 2.1 illustrates a server room and its connections to an open office filled with workstations and printers. The server, routers, cabling, and so on, are located in the server room, which can be locked and monitored. The open office provides hubs for connection to the network plus free use of printers.

It's easier to monitor applications, security, and other event logs on servers located in the same area than to travel from office to office or building to building. Monitoring system events helps you locate security breaches, identify problem areas, and keep your data safe. Following are some more benefits of centralized administration:

Figure 2.1 Centralize control over the servers for better security.

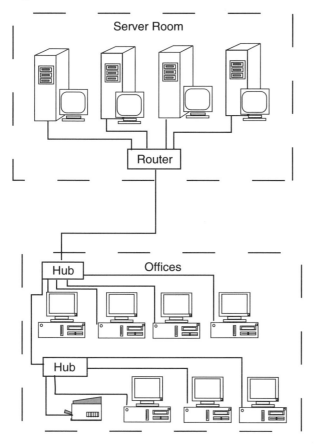

- One important element to your system security is backing up your data. Backups are easier to complete when servers are centralized.

- Regularly scheduled maintenance is easier on servers located centrally. Keeping your servers in working order means better security for your system.

- Troubleshooting is also easier because all hardware is in the same area. You can troubleshoot and solve problems more quickly and thus keep the system secure.

Resource Administration

Most applications and operating systems utilize protection techniques. Passwords, permissions, and so on, help you insulate you resources from attack. Implement passwords for applications on the server; make sure only those users who need to access the program can access it. Also, apply permissions to files and directories on the server. If your user accounts are up to date and accurate, then adding users to a group and applying permissions to that group won't take much time, but it will save you headaches and worries.

You may want to physically secure equipment and peripherals to protect those resources. It's your job to see that resources are made available to the user but that abuse of the equipment doesn't occur.

Physical Security

The physical security of your network is probably the one thing the corporation will always budget with no qualms whatsoever. After all, physical security helps deter break-ins, internal theft, accidental access, and so on, and these types of threats are often considered more indisputable than electronic access to your data and equipment.

Physical security is important for office equipment, phone systems, cash and company checks, networking hardware, software, data, and so on. Doors and locks are the most commonly used safeguards, but there are some other possibilities.

General Protection

In addition to locks and such, you might want to provide a card key access to some or all of the rooms in your office or building. Rooms with accounting information, safes, wiring closets, server rooms, and such shouldn't be easily accessible to everyone in the company. You also can provide card key access to your office or building to protect it from outsiders wandering in.

You should also check the ceiling tiles in rooms that should be secure. Many drop ceilings provide access from one room to the next by simply removing a few tiles and crawling over a wall or two. Following are some more general protection ideas:

Motion sensors are excellent for night, weekend, and holiday protection in some or all rooms and offices.

Video surveillance of entryways and secure areas are another option.

You should also discuss security with your housekeeping staff; make sure they understand the importance of using any safeguards that are in place.

Depending on the work you do and the data you produce, you might want to consider incorporating a shredder for documents you throw away. Also, check the trash for anything you wouldn't want the general public or, especially, competitors to get a hold of.

Be careful about selling used equipment, like computers or hard drives. The data may not be completely or properly deleted. (Run fdisk on any drive and reformat to make sure the data is gone.)

Server Room Security

A server room holds 1 server or 10 servers or more, CD-ROM towers, juke-boxes, wiring, and any other equipment you want to secure. Additionally, you might locate the system component in which communications circuits are administered between the backbone and the horizontal facilities, telecommunications equipment, cable terminations, and cross-connect cabling. Often these components are stored in a TCS (Telecommunications Wiring Standard) room; however, you should combine the two rooms, if it is practical.

Figure 2.2 shows a possible layout for a server room. All expensive equipment is stored in a room with a locking door, secure ceiling, and a video camera for surveillance.

A TCS, also called *telecommunications and/or data communications closet*, contains such elements as your key telephone systems, PBX (Private Branch Exchange) systems, hubs, routers, cables, bridges, and other equipment, for security's sake and for easy troubleshooting.

The server room must be physically secure as well as secure from power failures and electronic breaches. Use audible alarms and visual alarms. Magnetic swipe cards and badges ensure only those with permission are allowed to enter the room. You can even use hardware locks and keys to protect the room and the servers. Make sure you do lock the server room door.

Following are some more ideas to protect your equipment:

Make sure your server is in a fire-safe room.

Use UPSs for battery backups in case of power failures.

Use some sort of surge protectors to guard against damage from brown-outs or lightning.

Implement static protection, such as mats on the floor and proper grounding.

Figure 2.2 Set up a server room to house computers, UPSs, switches, and other expensive equipment.

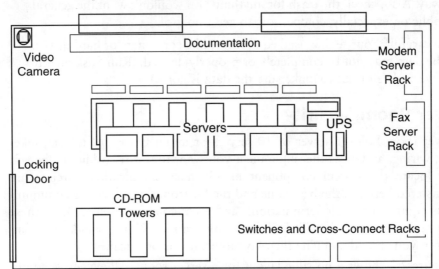

Locate servers away from windows so they are not visible from the outside and to protect them from the weather.

Don't locate servers near the outer walls, in case of dampness or damage from outside forces.

IBM Legacy Systems Security

IBM's OS/400 systems provide excellent security and auditing of every file and resource on the system. Security controls include password limitations, user profiles, and limits to the user's accessibility to libraries and files. Also, integrated auditing provides a detailed review of all system activity as well as user activity.

C2-compliant security is implemented for the AS/400 and AIX for RS/6000. The IBM S/390 model goes beyond C2 to B1-level security. Advanced security functions include user identification, journaling, auditing, encryption, and public-key certificates.

There is a security problem stemming from TCP/IP; systems running TCP/IP are more vulnerable to attack. IBM's TCP/IP applications—Telnet, and HTTP—do use Resource Access Control Facility (RACF) to provide added B1 security to the system and security authorization for these risks.

Network Auditing

Auditing the network can expose the weaknesses in your configuration and security. Many network operating systems support auditing, including NT Server, NetWare, and Banyan VINES. You also can purchase third-party applications and tools for performing specific network auditing. Following are a few of the processes you can audit on the network and/or servers:

Resource auditing. Examine hard disk usage. Many applications enable you to limit the amount of disk space on a server per user and allow you to monitor large amounts of used disk space. Resource auditing can help you discover abuse of the components and control the server's disk space usage.

Print usage. Some printers keep track of such information as the number of printed pages. If someone is printing unusually large files, you can locate the printer in question and monitor its use.

Software metering and licensing. Software metering tools enable you to track users who implement applications. Some go further and track how long users are connected to an application. You can watch for suspicious use of accounting programs, for example, or secure database usage.

Server hardware. Auditing keeps track of the hardware being used and the various BIOS and firmware versions used by the hardware. Supervise use of the hardware to make sure there is no sabotage or damage.

Performance monitoring. The application checks the server's display or console periodically in case there's a warning or error listed. Checking the performance of a machine can help to alert you to unusual situations.

Preparing to Audit

Prevention is the key to keeping your network up and running safely. If you can plan downtime and maintenance, monitor network segments, and solve problems before they begin, you'll have a network that runs smoothly, at least most of the time. Auditing helps you identify security problems.

Preventative maintenance begins with a well-documented network. You should have, for example, network maps and plans that you can use when

> **NOS Auditing**
>
> Various network operating systems provide auditing services that you can take advantage of. Following are the most popular NOSs and the most common auditing services they provide:
>
> **Microsoft NT Server:** DHCP configuration, user accounts, scripts, DNS configuration, and WINS setup.
>
> **Novell NetWare 3.x and up:** System configuration, user scripts, volume information, user accounts, and time synchronization roles.
>
> **Banyan VINES:** Serial communication configuration and communication buffering.

there's a problem with bandwidth, bottlenecks, security breaches, and so on. As a preliminary step to auditing the network, you should prepare and/or update the following:

- Drawings of your network topology
- An outline or diagram of your network's hardware configuration
- Detailed information about the software on each server
- A list of NOS patches or service packs on all servers
- Documented network card settings and the protocols and bindings
- Routing tables and a list of IP addresses including every machine on the network

Knowing your network will help you anticipate problems and perhaps ward them off before they become unruly.

Network Analysis Tools

Using network analysis tools can help you identify points of failure, problem areas, and places in which a security breach is likely, in addition to managing network performance. Many third-party analysis and auditing programs are available; when purchasing a network analysis tool, look for the following features:

- Centralized management
- The ability to monitor various LAN and WAN protocols and technologies

- Traffic analysis
- Possible bottleneck location
- Comprehensive reports via maps, graphs, and statistics
- Event auditing
- Security logs or documentation of events
- File and object auditing
- Logon monitoring
- Process tracking

PREPARATIONS THROUGH POLICIES

Your policies define network asset protection as well as the implementation of certain technologies and processes. You must protect your network from intrusion and destruction, and effective security policies can help. However, no matter how many policies you have written or how good they are, they're worthless if they aren't enforced.

To effectively develop a security policy, follow these steps:

Identify the network equipment and resources that you need to protect, including servers, routers, applications, and data.

Determine where points of risk are within your network—misconfigured servers or hosts, network connections, and so on.

Limit access to the network—protect the areas with sensitive or confidential data.

Determine the cost of security and then weigh the costs with the possible benefits.

Determine a schedule for implementing policies. Be reasonable yet expeditious.

Factor in the users of the network; don't hamper their work with your security efforts.

Your policies will reflect the special needs of your company, network, users, and data. However, there are some general policies that all administrators should consider. This chapter discusses some common policies you can change to suit your needs. In this chapter, you learn the following:

- Server room policies

- Administrative policies

- Application policies

- User policies

- Internet policies
- Procedures

Policies

You can write policies about every process, piece of equipment, task, and activity relating to the network; however, policies are only effective if they are worthwhile and have been read by the users. Writing policies for the sake of having them on record isn't going to do you much good. Distributing policies on every little aspect of your network isn't going to be taken seriously by your users. You must be selective in your policy writing and use only what truly benefits your system and situation.

Following are some policy ideas covering many different aspects of networking. You most likely won't need all of these and you'll likely think of many to add to suit your system.

Server Room

The server room is the most important room for your network. Centralized administration can save the administrator time and effort. More importantly, centralizing servers and equipment in one room can make security easier and more effective. Following are a few ideas for server room policies:

- No individuals are allowed in the operations or server room area without permission.
- Smoking is not permitted in the server room.
- Telephones are for use by administrators only.
- Automatic logoff will occur in 30 minutes if no entries are made within that time.
- Login information will not be furnished to anyone without proper identification. Login information will not be given over the phone or in response to a written request.
- The door to the server room may be unlocked while someone is in the room but must be locked if no one is present.

Administrators' Policies

Members of the administrative staff are the most trusted of your employees. To protect them, the network, and the data, you should have some policies outlining general procedures specific to your company. Additionally, there are some specific policies administrators should follow when creating other policies, for example, password usage.

General Administrative Policies

Following are some general policies to apply to administrators:

Don't make any changes to configuration to a machine that you are not directly responsible for. If changes need to be made, notify the person responsible for that machine.

Don't change any password without approval.

Never leave a computer with an administrative login; always log out before leaving the desk.

Always log, or document, everything.

Consult another administrator before making any sweeping changes to the system.

Protect the privacy of all users and staff, as well as that of the company.

Respect other administrators' privacy. Treat sensitive information with care and consideration.

Password Policies

The password file is typically the first point of attack on a system's security. That's why it is wise to follow some simple guidelines with passwords:

Assign all accounts a password and an expiration date. Users should pick a new password periodically, say, every two months as opposed to every two years.

Delete accounts that are no longer in use. A hacker using an old account would be hard to trace through the system.

Carefully monitor guest accounts. It's even a good idea to do away with guest accounts when you're dealing with the Internet; however, if you do keep guest accounts, make sure you use a unique name and password per guest and that you remove each account when it's no longer in use.

Avoid group accounts on the Internet. It's difficult to link responsibility to a group as opposed to a single person.

Record Keeping

Any time a modification is made to a machine, or a significant event occurs, a record must be kept. You might build a set of mailboxes in or near the server room to dedicate to specific system information. Logs, notifications, packing slips, and such, should be dated and signed and then entered into the appropriate box. Assign an assistant to clean the boxes periodically and record in a log or journal.

Downtime Policy

There are two types of downtime, planned and unplanned. You may need to down one or more servers, printers, CD-ROM towers, networking hardware, or other equipment for repair or maintenance; this type of downtime can usually be planned so that the network and its users suffer the least amount of inconvenience. There's also unplanned, or emergency, downtime in which a power outage, disk corruption, equipment failure, locked up server, or some other event causes one server, one segment, or perhaps the entire network to go down.

Although not specifically a security issue, you should still create policies for both event types and make sure users understand the problem. Uninformed users could possibly damage equipment or software. Here are some ideas:

For planned downtime: Notify users well in advance of the planned downtime; the lead time should be proportional to the amount of projected downtime. In your memo or announcement specify which machines and services (printers, software, and such) will be affected and suggested alternatives for these services; when downtime will occur and how long it will last; when the machines will be available again; and give a brief explanation for the planned downtime. Informing users will save on panicky calls and messages and give the users a sense of being a part of the team.

> **TIP**
> Downtimes that must be done on short notice could be scheduled on weekends, overnight, and on holidays, as well.

For unplanned downtime resulting from a crash or hardware failure: Inform the administration or managers immediately and give an estimate of recovery time. If you have to reboot because of software failure, for example, try to broadcast across the network first if possible. If not, you'll simply have to reboot and then notify users by broadcast when the system is ready.

Routine Preventative Maintenance

Check supplies—toner cartridges, printer ribbons, line-printer paper, spare terminals, network cards, cables, and so on—and keep spares in store in case of emergencies. If you use a lot of hubs, you might keep one or two extras on hand as well. Here are some more ideas:

Vacuum all workstations, terminals, PCs in the server room and in offices.

Clean printers regularly.

Clean screens and keyboards weekly.

Backups

Backups protect your system from user errors, like accidental deletions and corruption of data. With backups, you can restore a file, a directory, or entire databases and other server data. Conscientious backup policies can ensure good and complete backups. Following are some possible backup policies:

Schedule time and dates for backups and adhere to your backup schedules.

Make available a list of when and how restores are done; include guidelines, rules, or tips.

Store backups off-site.

Keep a log listing each server's and workstation's hardware and software specifications by the computer; update the log once a month or when configuration changes.

Create and store a system disk for every computer on the network with the spec log for that computer.

Handle application and operating system disks with care and store in a central location to be designated.

Clearly date and label backup media.

Store one set of backups in a cool, dry place on premises.

Remove used tapes from the set and replace with new tapes every four to six months.

Perform a test restore once a month and keep a log to record errors and successes.

Fault Tolerance

Fault tolerance refers to methods of protecting your data from loss and your equipment from damage. A UPS provides fault tolerance as does RAID (Redundant Array of Inexpensive/Independent Disks) mirroring. *Mirroring* duplicates data on one or more hard disks so that if one disk fails, the data is still available from another disk. RAID also uses multiple hard drives to provide for larger volume and increased performance. Server mirroring and disk duplexing are other methods of providing fault tolerance to your system. Fault tolerance can help protect and safeguard your system; consider implementing an appropriate form immediately.

Disaster Recovery

Disaster recovery refers to what you will do in case of a system catastrophe, such as fire or flood, multiple server damage, one hard drive crash, or other event that stops one or more people from continuing their work. Forming a disaster recovery plan for your company can help you recover your system quickly after a disaster. Following are some precautions and policy statements you should consider:

Store copies of the backup on-site in case of a problem; store media in a fireproof safe or cabinet under lock and key.

Store copies of the application disks or CDs you'll need to restore as well as a copy of the NOS and client operating systems in a fireproof safe.

Gather all network maps, logs, and documentation in a centralized place; store copies off-site as well.

Application Security

Even though the machine on which the application is located is secure, there may still be threats to the applications and data on that machine. A disgruntled user with the rights to access the application can destroy data, templates, configurations, and such. An untrained user can also destroy everything you've worked so hard to establish.

There are certain precautions you can take to limit the effects of this type of problem:

Delegate your administrative tasks. By letting others help you supervise and monitor the network, the server, and the applications, you can hopefully head off problems before they become too serious.

Back up often and test the backups.

Track the application's usage using a built-in monitor from the network operating system or the application itself; or purchase a third-party monitoring device. Survey who uses the application, how often, and other details so you can eliminate problems before they can begin.

Use the passwords and security features of the NOS and the application to protect data and access. Most applications have built-in features that protect the data and settings.

Form a set of policies governing your applications.

Application Policies

Define your policy on software support based on the application's general use, the number of people who use it, its stablility, whether it's supported by all platforms or operating systems in use on your network, and so on. You should also support any software that is appropriate to install on all systems, such as programming tools, mail readers, editors, and such.

Also, make sure you specify upgrade options. Some companies use the latest upgrade for some applications or operating systems; other companies hold off upgrading until necessary for the majority.

You should create a policy for unsupported software. You might name specific programs or make a general statement about support. You can state that no support will be given unless the tech has spare time, or no support will be given at all. It's best to refuse support on shareware utilities and such because of the time and effort it takes.

You might also want to list who can use the applications and when that use is permitted, such as only during work hours. Notify the users that data applying to the company, customers, services, and other sensitive issues are strictly for company use; such data cannot be removed from the building (on disks, laptops, and so on). Also, apply limits on copying and moving files to other parts of the network, workstations, diskettes, and such.

> **TIP**
>
> Each computer within a department should have similar or the same software installed to prevent confusion for the user population and administration. It's best to adopt the same operating systems and as many applications as you can for the entire company, but this isn't always possible.

Software Change Policies

You should write policies that will help secure the network from accidental deletions, configurations, and such. When users don't know about changes, they can accidentally cause problems. Here are a few suggestions:

Test software on an isolated machine before installing it to the network.

Test software again, after installation to the server.

Notify the entire user community of changes to heavily used pieces of software.

If you make a software change, be available the next day to help with any problems that may arise.

Keep the old versions of the software in case a problem comes up with the new version.

User Policies

Accounts left logged in pose a real danger. Someone finding that open account can send mail, destroy files, change settings, and so on. Make sure your users understand the danger and log off when they're not at their computers. You should also include the following in your user policies and distribute the policies for all users to read:

List the types of user accounts available—for example, sales, data entry, accounts, service, and so on—and define the accounts' responsibilities and rights.

Define the components of a user's accounts—unique username, random password, unique email address, home directory, and user information sheet, for instance.

Describe reasons for user account deletions, restrictions, or inactive states.

Outline password regulations.

Define what constitutes account misuse, such as copying and distributing sensitive files, security breaches, and so on.

Define resources—printers, CD-ROMs, and such—and outline the proper method of requesting access.

List limits to using others' workstations and/or servers on the network.

Describe limits and rules concerning the Internet and its usage.

Define licensing for software and any limits it includes; also list limits on user installation of software that hasn't been approved by management.

Describe the amount of server storage space allotted to each user.

List printer privileges and limits, such as limiting the number of copies that can be printed, paper types, and so on. Perhaps include some simple printer troubleshooting instructions.

Describe users' responsibilities for backing up files on the workstation or for getting files to the server for backup.

Set forth email policies limiting the size of files, time of day email may be sent, message types, and so on.

List and explain all items that constitute abuse of network resources, such as theft, vandalism, unauthorized use of services, and so on.

Specify an amount of hard disk space each user is allowed for storage.

Make sure the users understand that their computers are not theirs exclusively. They should not lock the screen but they must log off if leaving their desk. Remaining logged in means the login may be used by another member of the staff.

Remote Access

When enabling mobile or telecommuters access to your network via remote access, you must be careful to follow strict security procedures. Opening your network up to the outside world can expose your data to many threats, even though the users are your own employees.

Assign remote users a separate login and password for the host computer's network connection so if a hacker gets a hold of the password information, he's confined to only that computer.

Use firewalls or routers on both sides of the remote access computer.

Use encrypted authentication to protect the network and the user. Also consider encrypting all data files on a computer connected with a dedicated remote access link.

Employ callback capabilities. The server must confirm the remote system has the correct IP address during the login process.

Check user rights and permissions on the network, check passwords and expiration dates, limit access to sensitive materials on the network, and so on.

Hide sensitive files and directories from a remote user's view.

Monitor remote users.

Internet Policies

You want your users to get the full benefit from the Internet, but you must also limit their enthusiasm. For example, users who save multiple bookmarks, all of their email, and downloaded documents and applications will soon fill the hard disk to the server or to their workstations. You must put some limits on the users to protect the network resources and the company.

Following are some suggestions for Internet policies:

Limit disk space usage.

Use the Internet resources for informational, educational, or research purposes only.

Users should not use the Internet for illegal or unethical purposes.

Respect intellectual property rights by making only authorized copies of copyrighted, licensed, or otherwise controlled data, software, and other information on the Internet.

Respect the privacy of coworkers and the company by not misrepresenting oneself to other users, not attempting to gain access to files, passwords, or data of others, and by not seeking to disallow access to any computer system via the Internet.

Email Policies

You need to create email policies for a variety of reasons. You can let your users know your company's philosophy on certain issues through the policies you set. Policies should help to save on bandwidth; but more importantly, email policies should protect the company and the users.

Here are some ideas and issues to consider about email policies:

Set a policy on sexual and racial jokes, and rants about corporate practices, bad bosses, or lazy colleagues.

Notify users that email is company property and may be monitored for legitimate reasons. This protects you and the company; there should be no privacy for employees with company email.

Make sure to add a policy that says there is to be no dissemination of trade secrets to unauthorized persons inside or outside of the company.

Add a signature line to messages about accidental transmission to unintended third parties.

Adopt procedures for dealing with complaints about inappropriate or offensive email.

Encrypt sensitive email messages that travel outside of the company.

Security Policies

It's important to let your users know about your security measures because if they understand how serious your security concerns are, then they will be more likely to support your policies and help protect the system. Following are some suggestions for security statements to share with your users:

Don't let users use guest accounts; actually, it would be best if you didn't provide guest accounts for the computer attached to the Internet.

Ask users to use any built-in encryption features on files and email sent over the Internet.

Require users to use and monitor virus protection measures on their workstations.

Explain the firewall or proxy service to the users so they understand security measures.

Inappropriate Usage

You should probably add a list of infringements or inappropriate usages for users; but do be careful that all of your policies aren't phrased negatively. These can outline behavior, use of company equipment, and such. Following are some statements you can add to protect your network and resources:

Inappropriate uses of the network include but are not limited to:

Unauthorized access to proprietary information, seeking access to gain information for inappropriate purposes.

Unauthorized use of another's password.

Infringement on any copyrights, license agreements, or contracts, including the illegal installation of copyrighted software.

Improper copying, modifying, distributing, transmitting, or displaying files belonging to the company.

Processing, distributing, or transmitting inappropriate stored electronic media, such as libelous or defamatory material.

Using the company's LAN or WAN for personal profit, personal business, or other commercial purposes.

Do not share your User ID with another person.

Do not delete, examine, copy, or modify files or data belonging to others without their consent.

No email forgery, harassment, or junk mail is to be sent from a company workstation.

Do not willfully introduce computer viruses to the network or into external networks from the company's LAN.

Procedures

You can list any procedures in your policy statement that will help the user to understand the steps to performing tasks over the network. You also can include diagrams or illustrations, screen shots, listed steps, explanations, contact numbers, and other information that will help the user. The procedures you list depend on how your company uses the network; you may want to outline steps for using the Internet or an intranet, or simply list the steps to printing a large report.

Here are a few suggestions of procedures you can include:

Outline the procedure for requesting a new password.

Explain steps for dial-in access from remote computers.

Describe how to configure a computer for Internet use and the steps to accessing the Net from the LAN.

Tell users how to save files to the network—list naming conventions, appropriate directories, and such.

Explain how users can protect their data stored on the network.

Define steps to adding a network printer to a workstation and the preferred method of printing to a network printer.

Explain the steps to using email.

Add the contact names and numbers of anyone who can help users when they have problems.

List the steps to reporting major problems with a workstation, hardware, or software.

Define the steps to recovering deleted files or files from a backup.

Outline the procedures to follow when the server crashes.

Provide an FAQ (Frequently Asked Questions) list with clear and concise answers; include such topics as terms, technologies, and so on.

Provide contact numbers and email addresses for administrators, assistants, outsourced or vendor help lines, and so on.

Provide technical information, such as steps to take when a modem or printer doesn't respond.

Add steps and guidelines for using a browser or other common application.

INTERNET SECURITY

The Internet puts technology and information directly into the hands of users, customers, business partners, and anyone else who is attached to it. Your control over Internet access shouldn't prevent the flow of information, but you must protect sensitive information and business projects.

You can balance this technology and manage your business risks. First, delegate some power to business managers; they must have the freedom to obtain and use the data within the range of tolerable business risks. Your job is to provide clear procedures for limiting security exposure when the Internet is in use.

You can't control every user, test every application, or monitor every incoming and outgoing call from the Internet. But you can let business managers and administrative assistants take on some of that responsibility. Make sure your users understand they are to use the Internet in a professional manner—be careful of posting sensitive content, limit risks, and so on. And use any and all hardware and software technology you can to help secure your LAN and data.

This chapter includes information about the following:

- Threats to your system
- Plans for protecting your system
- Routers, firewalls, and proxy servers
- Web server security

Threats to Your System

When you attach your LAN to the outside world, specifically the Internet, you open your network to a multitude of security risks. Users who accidentally cause a problem, hackers breaking into systems for fun, and crackers who plan to steal anything they can via the Internet are threats to your system when you connect to the Internet. Following is a list of crimes commonly committed via the Internet:

- Unlawful copying of copyrighted or licensed software
- Credit-card fraud
- Unauthorized access to computer files
- Hate email, stalking, harassment, and other personal offenses

Hackers/Crackers

Hackers and *crackers* (criminal hackers) make bold efforts to get into systems that are supposedly unbreakable—hackers for the fun of it or the reputation, and crackers for the money, business information, or data they can steal. Writing and enforcing good security policies, using security devices and software, and educating your users are the keys to keeping your system safe from crackers.

Following are a few more suggestions to help protect your network and your users:

Do background checks on all employees, including cleaning crews, temp secretaries, contract workers, and even consultants and outsourcers.

Warn help desk staff never to give passwords or assist someone in recovering their passwords over the phone. Or, help desk personnel can ask two or three identifying questions before proceeding.

Be careful of the trash you throw away. Shred all paperwork that contains usernames, identification, network configuration information, and so on.

Warn receptionists never to answer any security questions over the phone, such as "How often are your passwords changed?"

Be careful about using DHCP servers or other applications that automatically assign an IP address to any computer or laptop that plugs in to the network. If you use software such as this, make sure you can set your server to trust only certain recognizable machines.

Store your backups in a safe and secure place. Lock them up with your server, for instance.

Internal Users

Internal hits on your network don't get as much publicity as outside hits, but your users sometimes pose a threat to your data. A disgruntled employee, a well-intentioned secretary, uninformed users, and so on, can wreak havoc with your files, programs, hardware, and connections. Infractions range from employees using the company computer equipment for personal reasons to embezzlement.

When protecting your data and your business, don't forget to monitor contract workers, business partners, vendors, temps, and anyone else who has access to corporate data. Many times, administrators give these workers the same rights and permissions they give regular employees, but without the requisite background and security checks. Crackers are getting into corporate systems by signing on as temporary employees.

More than half of the damage caused by internal users, however, is usually caused by errors or omissions on the part of employees. Mistakes are not malicious; users are just untrained. You must take responsibility for training users in the proper procedures using the Internet, intranet, or extranet; in the proper use of passwords; administering access to the system; virus protection; and provisions for making and auditing backups.

You must hold employees responsible for following guidelines and documenting procedures; explain the policies and procedures to everyone. Be concise; list do's and don'ts; revise guidelines regularly.

Protecting Your System

Before you can protect your system, you'll need to identify security threats. Think about the areas of the company's information that are vulnerable to theft, lost, or damage and the impact of losing that information. Is there information on the Web server database, for example, that is confidential? Then it shouldn't be on the Web server. Are you running an FTP server and allowing anonymous users to log on? Then there could be a security breach into your LAN by an FTP user.

Consider the cost of a breach in security or a loss of data. For example, how much is your customers' credit-card information or your products' spec sheets worth on the open market? What is the probable cost of replacing the lost or damaged information within the company?

What are your legal risks? If you handle legal or medical data for your customers, losing it to a hacker could put your business in jeopardy as well. If your network is unguarded, you are liable. If your confidential documents are stolen, you may not have legal recourse if the documents weren't adequately protected in the first place.

Making a Plan

Next, determine what action it will take to reduce the dangers. Do you need to install firewalls and/or proxy servers, protect your sensitive data more appropriately, or terminate some of the services you offer in favor of a safer LAN environment?

Get input from managers and others within the company to help you best protect your system. Consider hiring an external auditor to assess your security infrastructure. Have a consultant help you design a plan if you don't feel qualified.

While considering how to protect your LAN from outside intruders or hackers, don't forget about your employees' responsibilities. Create a plan that covers employee access, authorization, and responsibility. And don't forget to include temporary personnel, consultants, contractors, and customers in your plan.

Decide how much freedom you will allow your users. Can they download shareware, install games and applications from home or the Net, save all their files or just some to the network, use personal email, and so on?

Implementing the Plan

After you formulate your plan, you need to formulate some policies that will reinforce it. Policies about password usage, encrypted email, and so on, will help protect your system by relating your needs to the users. See Chapter 3 of this book, "Preparations through Policies," for more information about policies.

Next, make sure upper management signs off on the plan and policies. You need the support of the powers that be to enforce the policies, make budgetary requests, hire consultants, and so on. If your bosses don't want to cooperate with your plans for protecting your data and network, explain to them their legal responsibilities to customers and the costs of replacing damaged data.

Distribute the policy to your employees, managers, administrators, and so on; maintain security awareness within the company through training, reviews, memos, and such. You should delegate the responsibility for department security to the department managers or heads.

Following are some more things to consider:

Monitor and keep records of all logons to the system.

Identify unauthorized logon attempts.

Remove access and authorization for departing employees.

Add any necessary hardware and/or software for protecting the LAN and monitoring access.

Define hardware, software, and configuration standards to make administration of the network easier on you and therefore more easily controlled.

From Routers to Firewalls

If you connect to the Internet for email, research, easy access to applications and documentation, advertising, or for any of a thousand other reasons, you'll want to protect your network against unnecessary risks from the outside world. Without protection, your data, resources, users, and even your entire LAN are vulnerable to exploitation.

> **NOTE**
>
> For more information, see *Internet Firewalls and Network Security* by Siyan Karanjit, Ph.D., and Chris Hare (Specialized Systems Consultants, Inc., 1996).

Routers

Routers are flexible directors of network traffic that operate by examining the destination address of every packet received and forwarding each packet to the next stop toward the destination. The router drops packets for which it has no address and sends an ICMP (Internet Control Message Protocol) message to the sending system to discourage any more packets from being sent.

A router can screen packets coming in to your network by using the source and destination addresses contained in the header information on the packet. You set up filters, or rules, in the router to permit or deny access to packets entering the router.

Routers execute rules in order. When a packet enters the router, the router checks to find the first rule that governs the packet; if the rule is not entered in the correct order, the router may not execute it. It's difficult to enter rules through a cryptic command line interface; it's easy to mistype a rule. Routers are also extremely difficult to configure, and they are easily fooled.

Additionally, with each rule you add to a router, you decrease throughput performance; a router's job is really to forward packets through a network as quickly as possible. Rules degrade throughput. Another problem with using routers is that hackers can send fake ICMP (Internet Control Message Protocol) packets that tell your router to change its default routing. IP *spoofing* (packets sent with a source address originating from a trusted host on your own network) can also fool routers. Some routers can detect these attacks, but not all routers can.

Routing Tables and Stateful Inspection

Routers use tables to maintain the information about the current state; routing tables determine how the router will deal with packets. Each packet is treated individually instead of as a part of the whole, as if no other similar packets have passed this way before. This function can cause security as well as performance problems. Performance is reduced because the same filtering decisions are made over and over and over again, the router doesn't learn from previous packets. Also, routers have no record or log of past transactions or events.

The *stateful inspection* strategy is a technique for packet filtering that overcomes many of the weaknesses in using routers. A stateful inspection module is loaded into the OS at a point in the IP stack where it can preview packets before they reach the Internet layer where the routing takes place. The module keeps track of all packets in previous traffic and all decisions to permit or deny the packet are stored as state information. Subsequent packets can then be permitted or denied based upon their state (instead of using the rule-based decision-making process that routers normally use).

There are many applications that improve upon router packet filtering, but generally, routers aren't used much as firewalls today; they are used for limiting access between different portions of a LAN or WAN. Application gateways provide better control and logging, while a router using stateful inspection provides better performance and flexibility.

Proxy Servers/Application Gateways

An *application gateway* filters traffic by using a special code for each application. It examines and interprets the data within the packet, not just within the packet header as a router does. A physical application gateway uses proxy servers, codes that represent both client and server. Often, the terms *proxy server* and *application gateway* are used to refer to the same thing.

Proxy servers control traffic entering or leaving the network; the proxy acts as a negotiator between your LAN and the Internet. When a request comes from one side or the other of the server, it uses a proxy application to perform the requested network service instead of letting the internal and external machines connect. A proxy server has critical control over what a client can and cannot do, controlling both the LAN user's access to the Internet and/or the Internet user's access to the LAN.

A proxy server provides accurate logging of events because it recognizes user activity. It will log commands used, filenames accessed, the number of bytes transferred in and out, and so on. It also recognizes patterns in packet headers to speed up process. A proxy server runs outside of the operating system so that the NOS provides security, preventing the gateway from affecting other programs or parts of the system.

There are problems with using a proxy server. It is a program, for example, so you have to start it and run it. Also, network data must be copied from system memory to program memory and then back again. Also, each proxy server product supports only a limited set of applications.

Before adding a proxy server to your network, you should first review your security policies, user passwords, guest accounts, and so on. Additionally, make sure you have appropriate bandwidth for your LAN and get a reliable and fast connection to the Internet. Prepare the networking hardware, contact an Internet Service Provider (ISP), and check the compatibility of your NOS.

There are many gateway or proxy server applications available. Microsoft Proxy Server supplies a safe connection between your LAN and the Internet, using specific protocols designed for Internet services: HTTP, FTP, Gopher, and so on.

Netscape also has a proxy server; Netscape boasts special features that reduce traffic, user wait times, and relieve bottlenecks and bandwidth congestion. Additionally, the Netscape Proxy Server supplies network security features for internal and external access of information, easy administration, and support for Internet protocols. The proxy server application you choose will depend on your clients' Web browsers, your network operating system, and personal preferences.

Firewalls

There are two kinds of firewalls: hardware and software, or application firewalls. A firewall protects the company with IP connections outside the confines of its own environment. A firewall is at the edge of the network and prevents unauthorized individuals from accessing your network resources.

Hardware Firewalls

A good firewall should include logging and notification of firewall events, monitor bandwidth usage and network activity, and enable you to create reports and summaries with the information gathered. It should also be easy to configure, provide encrypted sessions, protect internal addresses, and control FTP privileges.

When you're looking for a firewall device, make sure it meets the following guidelines:

- Hides the structure of the internal network from the outside network.

- Does not provide dynamic routing; only static routing should be provided by the administrator.

- Has a strong user authentication scheme that doesn't rely on user IDs.

- Rejects protocols that are security risks, such as rexec, rlogin, rsh, rwho, and tftp and rejects unknown protocols.

- Acts as an SMTP mail gateway; all outgoing mail appears to come from the firewall and outgoing mail header fields should be translated to protect the senders.

- Creates an audit trail of system activity—logging both successful and unsuccessful login attempts.

Application Firewalls

In addition to hardware firewalls, software firewalls are also available. Application firewalls are a secure form of protection. Designed to deny services except for the ones that are explicitly allowed, an application firewall should control secure access to a full range of Internet protocols, provide auditing and reporting tools, and maintain high performance levels.

An application firewall interfaces two separate networks—your LAN and the Internet, for example—using the network addressing information contained in the packet and higher-level protocol layers that analyze the packets. Typically, an application firewall is a software package that runs on a high-powered platform, such as UNIX or NT Server. Firewalls are more expensive than a gateway or router.

When you're considering an application firewall, research the firewall company first. Larger companies with research and development resources and a longtime standing in the business are your best buy. Look for the following features in an application firewall:

Easy to configure.   A firewall that's easy to configure means there is less chance of making an error that will cause a security problem.

Clear, detailed logs.   If the firewall creates reports and attack details, you save time in analyzing the rules and settings.

Control over your users.   A firewall should offer you control over what your users can and cannot do on the Internet. Some firewalls may enable or disable FTP or Telnet; others let a user FTP to some sites but not others. You should be able to determine exactly what Web sites your users can visit and when.

Breach alert.   Make sure the firewall indicates security breaches, perhaps by paging, email, or alarms.

Centralized administration.   If you have multiple sites, you want a firewall you can configure remotely. You should be able to set security policies from a central site and then pass those policies through the network to other firewalls.

Miscellaneous Security Issues

There are so many uses for the Internet in business today that it's difficult to cover all possibilities. If you're running a business over the Internet, for example, you'll likely have problems with secure transactions. Crackers try to break security codes so they can obtain your customers' credit-card numbers; hackers use sniffers to obtain your users' passwords to gain LAN access past the firewall.

You can use a variety of tools to help secure your network and data. Secure protocols, encryption, firewalls and/or proxy servers—all of these elements can help protect you from intruders and security risks. It's probably best if you implement a variety of intrusion safeguards, from requiring your users to use passwords to using several security devices for network protection.

E-Commerce Security

Will you accept credit cards from strangers? To do business over the Internet, you'll have to. You could guarantee better customer service and more security for your business, however, by creating registered accounts for all first-time customers. After you verify basic background information on the customers, you can process their orders.

How do you make sure the credit card and other account information travels safely and securely over the Internet? Use a secure protocol or encryption technology. SSL (Secure Sockets Layer) was created by Netscape Communications to secure credit-card transactions and has become an Internet standard.

SSL is an encryption known as *public/private key*. This encryption uses separate, but mathematically linked, algorithms for encrypting and decrypting. The algorithm that encrypts is called a *public key* and the one that decrypts is a *private key*. The public key is distributed freely and only the recipient holds the private key.

SSL enables channel security, which provides three basic advantages: a constantly secure communications channel; the channel is always authenticated between client and server; and TCP/IP provides reliability—messages reach their intended destination.

SET (Secure Electronic Transaction) is a standard implemented in merchant servers and browsers. Merchant servers are applications that sell products over the Web using credit-card transactions. SET requires merchants, banks, and credit-card users to receive digital certificates to authenticate buyers and sellers.

Merchant servers that are SET-compliant are expensive; but VISA and MasterCard will make it worthwhile by reducing the rates charged to merchants. SET lowers the risk of bad credit transactions because of end-to-end encrypted authentication between consumer, merchant, bank, and card.

Spam and Cookies

Spam and cookies are two more annoyances you'll have to endure if you allow your users to email and surf the Internet. *Spam* is unsolicited commercial email. Spamming is not a good way to sell products because most people don't like receiving it any more than they like receiving junk snail mail. Still, there are programs that enable unscrupulous people to send advertising email to multiple recipients.

You can't send a reply to a spam message because the addresses are automated and a return message would never be seen. However, you can generally go to the bottom of a commercial email and find an address you can write back to, requesting they take your name off of the list.

Cookies are identifiers placed on a user's hard drive after a visit to a Web site. The cookie collects information, such as your name, email address, password for a particular site, and so on. It logs the information as a file on the user's drive; the next time the user visits that Web site, it recalls the cookie so it knows who you are. Most cookies are harmless; however, you can set options governing cookies in most browsers and/or operating systems.

Email Security

Solutions to all intruder-related problems are based on a public key encryption. Public key technology assigns a user a pair of keys that work together. One key is the user's private key and the other is a public key. Both keys can encode and decode data—what one key encodes, only the other key can decode.

When a user sends a confidential email message, he or she encrypts the email using the second user's public key; the only key that can decode the message is the second user's private key. No one can read the message except the second user.

For this to work, users must be able to trust that a user's key is valid. CA (Certificate Authority) is the entity that provides the needed verification. CA assigns each user a unique digital certificate that assures a certain public key belongs to a certain user.

Currently, there is no central CA in existence that the general public can use to verify public keys. Many organizations internally act as their own CA for their users, though. There are also some third-party products that follow this model and use a proprietary CA scheme.

An alternative is PGP (Pretty Good Privacy). PGP is a secure email program that uses a web of trust; each user keeps a list of certificates from other PGP users they trust. When a user receives an email message from someone he or she doesn't know, the user can check the chain of certificates or try to trace a link between certificates. PGP is also available as an add-on for Internet Mail, Outlook, and other email applications.

Another alternative is MOSS (MIME Object Security Services), which enables users to secure multimedia messages. Another is S/MIME, or Secure MIME, but it leaves the matter of setting up a certificate structure to the implementing organization.

Web Server Placement

You can place your Web server, firewall, router, and other equipment in various configurations for the protection of your LAN. Following are three configurations for setting up the security devices.

The first placement strategy is illustrated in Figure 4.1. The Web server is located within the LAN and separated from the Internet by a firewall and a router. This method provides easy administration because the Web server is directly attached to the LAN; however, it also affords poor security.

Hackers can gain access through blocked services on the LAN by creating a tunnel that enables them to attack internal systems. Also, users treat the Web server like any other internal server, using its resources, saving files to it, and so on, thus placing data in even more danger. The Web server needs to be treated as a part of the security of your LAN. If you use this method, be very careful.

A second approach is illustrated in Figure 4.2. The Web administration appears on the LAN side of the firewall and the Web server is located on the Internet side. A hacker breaking into the Web server has no access to the LAN or the Web administration. The router between the Web server and the Internet protects the server with packet filters.

Administration of this approach is a bit more difficult than the first strategy outlined. Web server access isn't convenient because the firewall is in the way. However, in this configuration, you can keep your databases and authentication inside the LAN to protect from any intruders. The Web administration server authenticates requests and provides a limited view of the data it contains. The Web server outside of the LAN acts as a database client to the Web admin-

Figure 4.1 Hackers could break into the LAN after you let them past the firewall.

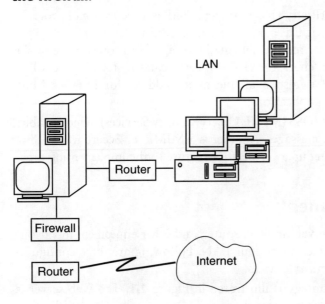

Figure 4.2 The Web administration server contains the product databases and authentication for the Web server.

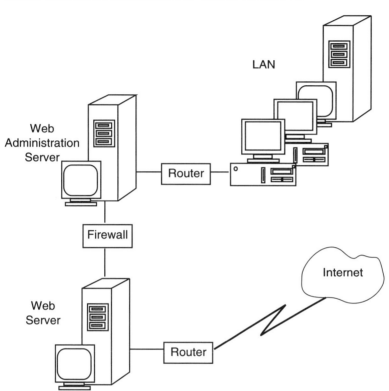

istration server; then it shares the requested information with the Internet visitor.

The third tactic, or some variation, is probably the best. You put the Web server on its own network, separate from your private LAN and from the Web administration server, thus creating a screened subnet. As shown in Figure 4.3, you can place a screening router (firewall) between the Web server and the second network. The second network contains a Web administration server and a mirrored copy of the Web server.

The administrator works on the mirrored Web server and then sends modifications to the Web pages to the Web server attached to the Internet. You can either attach the second network to the private LAN or, for maximum protection, keep the two separate.

Figure 4.3 The protection you enforce depends on the importance of your data.

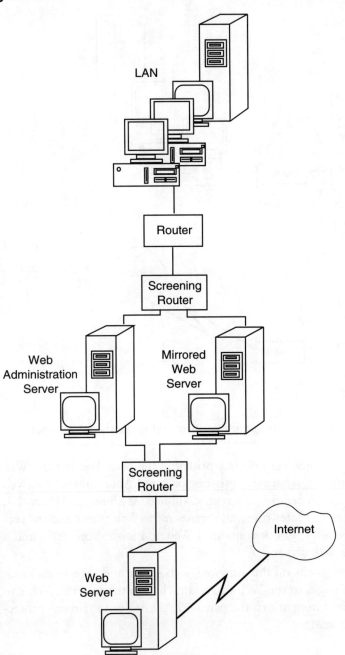

> **NOTE**
>
> In a screened subnet, the protected host is attached to a perimeter network instead of the internal LAN. The perimeter network may be connected to an internal LAN and to an external network through two screening routers, creating no single point of failure.

The firewall permits passage of only HTTP traffic to the Web server from the Internet; the firewall also controls the Web server's access to the internal network. The obvious problem with this method is how to administer the Web server from the internal network. Since the entire network is a target for hackers, administration must be secure.

One solution is to enable the Web server for remote administration. Use an encrypted link—such as Telnet or SSH (Secure Shell software)—for the administrative connection. When configuring a Web server, treat it like a host with only the barest essentials; you cannot treat a Web server like an intranet server. It should contain only the required software and nothing more. A UNIX server, for example, can be configured as a host with fewer than 100 files on it. Reduce the number of user accounts to a bare minimum; the best bet is to include only the system manager and Web administrator accounts.

Alternatively, you could automate the administration of the Web server. The Web administrator would work on an internal Web server that contains data for the public Web server. Then migrate the changes to the external, public server. You can migrate by using file sharing protocols like Microsoft Server Message Block or UNIX Network File System. These are not truly secure protocols or recommended for most data; however, you could use them in this case since the data is intended for the public anyway.

Or you could use a mirroring software that updates the Web server to reflect changes made to the internal server. Mirroring requires no user accounts and provides a complete live backup.

Detecting Network Intruders

When running a Web server off of your LAN or WAN, you'll want to monitor your network to ensure it's safe from intruders. You can always purchase a third-party application to monitor and check; and following are a few methods you can try on your own:

Watch for failed logon attempts in any records or logs on your authentication server. When a hacker is guessing passwords, you'll see multiple failed logon attempts.

Check periodically for loose packets with external source addresses behind the firewall.

Look for any attempts to write a critical file on the host system.

Execution of privileged programs is another clue.

Check for spoofed source addresses from packets that appear to initiate new connections from a server.

Be wary of the PING of Death. This is a common scheme in which ICMP packets of excessively long data length are sent to a network to crash it.

Introduction to Book Twelve

When building a new network or upgrading your current one, you must first study the design. You want to make sure the network fits your objectives, such as secure data, Internet access, collaboration through shared files and directories, and so on. You should discuss the network design with users and managers so that you have a clear idea of what's important to them, of what they feel is lacking in the network. If the network isn't serving your users' needs, then you'll want to re-evaluate the design and modify it.

Next, you must examine the services the network provides to measure the impact on networking equipment. Do you have enough servers? Are the servers and connections fast enough to supply users with what they need? What are the traffic patterns? Where does data slow down? Determine which applications, which servers or segments, are causing the congestion.

Discover the bottlenecks of the network. Ascertain the times of the day or the days of the month that are the busiest on the network. Pinpoint the points of slowdown and document the problems. Document the networking hardware for that area, the server hardware, applications, and other factors that might contribute to the bottlenecks. It is with this documentation that you can analyze your network design and work to improve the situation.

Every network is different and to include all possibilities for network optimization here would be impossible. Instead, this book gives you an idea of things to watch for, general steps to take to prevent problems, and some advice for optimizing basic networking hardware. For a more inclusive view of your networking needs, you may need to hire a consultant who can set a benchmark for your network and make recommendations more specific to your needs.

Following is a general list of things you'll need to consider when optimizing your network:

Document everything—hardware, software, network connections, user needs, problems and their solutions, heavy traffic areas, and so on.

Map out the network to place resource locations—servers, printers, Internet access, and such—and add the types of connections used between LAN segments—routers, cabling, network cards, and so on. This map will come in handy when you're examining bottlenecks and upgrade possibilities.

Poll your users and managers to find out what is important to them and where they perceive a problem with the network; after all, the users are the most familiar with slowdowns and traffic congestion.

Calculate bandwidth requirements, peak and average traffic times, capacity and throughput. Again, if this is beyond your capabilities or available time, hire a consultant.

Select the best LAN/WAN technologies for your networking situation, based on your users needs and the applications and services you offer.

Consider network growth when making any plans for modifications or additions.

PRELIMINARY GROUNDWORK

The foundation of your network is planning and organization. You must start with clear objectives, factor in network growth possibilities, and design a network that will meet your company's and users' needs. Not as easy as it sounds. Planning a good network is one of the most difficult tasks for a network administrator; most of the time, a network just comes together, piece by piece, without much planning or structure. Optimizing a network such as this is even more difficult because its design wasn't clearly charted from the start.

But there are some things you can do to optimize your network without replacing all of your hardware or starting over from the beginning. This chapter covers some basic operations that you should perform, if you haven't already. In this chapter, you learn the following:

- Methods of preventative maintenance

- Using management software

- Planning for optimization

- Forming an optimization team

Preventative Maintenance

To keep your network working at its peak, you must make sure to do anything you can to keep a component from failing. Whether it's cleaning a printer or tracing each cable and connector in your network, preventative maintenance will help keep the network working at its optimum.

You may or may not have the time it takes or the expertise to perform various tasks on the network components—cabling, servers, workstations, peripherals, routers, and so on—so your best bet is to delegate the tasks. You can use knowledgeable people from within your company or you can outsource the work to one or more consultants or technical people. Either way, you need to make sure you take care of the equipment and periodically check configurations and performance.

First Steps

Your first step in taking care of your network is to make sure you have a high-quality system. If your hardware is cheap, if your servers are old, if your cabling is constantly trampled upon, if your programs are installed and configured differently to each computer, you will spend more time putting out fires than anything. Keeping the network well-maintained, organized, and systematic will help with optimization in the long run.

Your next step is to upgrade any hardware or equipment that is outdated or not properly working. Try to use the same or similar brands, configurations, and methods of installation. Document everything and use the documentation to walk you through the steps for the next piece of equipment you install or configure. Using the same steps means it's easier to complete the procedure; all machines are tested in the same manner; and when you have a problem on one, you'll be able to solve it on all machines. Upgrades will also be easier to install.

In your documentation, you should keep records of computer brands and model numbers, peripheral devices and software attached to each server and workstation, details of network cards and IRQ addresses, IP addresses, protocols used, and other such information. You should keep a log for every computer and other piece of equipment. The next time you need to make a change or fix a problem on that piece of equipment, you already have a head start because of the records you've kept.

Final Steps

Following are some preventative maintenance issues to make sure you implement for the safety of your network:

UPS (Uninterruptible Power Source). Make sure you attach a UPS to every server and router, plus every other piece of equipment that needs protection from brownouts, power surges, and power failures. You should also have backup UPS batteries on hand.

Cabling. Make sure you install reliable, certified, quality cabling throughout your network. Check all connectors, patch panels, hubs, and jacks for similar ratings; make sure connections are secure and correct and all cables are connected; and get a cabling map of your system so you can easily find problem areas when necessary.

Backups. You should back up your data consistently and following a schedule. Make sure you periodically test the backups and that you store at least one copy of the backup off-site. Keep good logs or records of your backups so that if there's a problem, you'll be able to trace it.

Computers. Document each computer and prepare a system disk for each one. Within the documents should be make and model, amount of RAM, size of hard drive, types of cards and configurations, software, peripheral details, and so on.

Printers. Cleaning laser and inkjet printers periodically will help keep them working in peak condition. Also, make sure your users understand the proper methods of clearing the paper path, setting the printer menu, and otherwise handling a printer. Many problems with printers come from either intentional or accidental printer abuse.

Routers. Routers are difficult devices to configure, so if you do not have certification or training in the use of your routers, you should outsource or hire someone to take care of them. The same goes for gateways. Reconfiguring or puttering with one of these expensive pieces of equipment is not something you want to do.

Network Resource Planning

It is the network administrator's goal to provide quality service and network resources to the users while supporting the business. Network resource planning can help the administrator in today's more complex and elaborate network environment. There are five management techniques involved with network resource planning:

Fault management is a technique used in the detection, isolation, and correction of faults on the network. Fault management helps you keep the network up and running. Using network monitoring tools and utilities, you can detect and diagnose potential problems on the network.

Configuration management is configuring, or setting up, network devices. By using proper configurations for memory usage, ports and addresses, and so on, you can insure a smooth-running network and server.

Security management is the procedure of controlling users and their access to the network. If your users have access to sensitive files or organizational directories, for example, they could accidentally or purposefully damage all or part of the system.

Performance management involves analyzing network resources and ensuring their efficient and effective use. When you regularly monitor the network for problems or bottlenecks, you can often correct problems before they get out of hand.

Accounting management explains, or accounts for, the problems and successes within your system. If one LAN segment is operating at peak performance, for example, try to examine the success to duplicate it in other segments. If a server is creating a bottleneck, study the situation to help resolve this problem and hopefully similar problems in the future.

Performance Management Software

There are tools you can use to help optimize your network. Performance management software can help you get a baseline on your network, analyze network trends, and recognize bottlenecks. When preparing to purchase a management tool, you should look for the following features or processes in the package:

- Provides bandwidth statistics that tell you how the network is being used

- Supports centralized and multiple monitoring stations over your WAN or enterprise

- Automatically records node names, addresses, connections, and protocols

- Provides extensive reports about network history, trends, peak performance, and so on

- Integrates with your existing management system

> **TIP**
>
> Realize that although network performance software can give you a great idea of how your network is working, it can also impede your efforts at optimizing for speed and efficiency. If the software isn't configured or used correctly, it could send out wasted additional packets that slow or clog traffic. Be careful.

Planning Network Optimization

In planning network optimization, your first step is to understand the network's normal behavior. You need to know the normal usage of the network. When are the busiest times of the day, week, month, and year? How many users are normally on simultaneously? Which servers are used the most? Which applications? Are there some users that you can consider power users? Are there any performance bottlenecks?

You should gather the answers to these questions over a month or so. Ask your managers, administrators, and your users what their problems and successes are. Where do they most perceive problems on the network? Are there specific servers or services that are slower than others? Are there areas or times that are faster than others? The information you gather over this month is the baseline for your network.

Use your baseline to establish a performance threshold. You want to define the average network performance so that if any one component of the network varies too much, then you'll be notified of the problem. If you can, for instance, determine a performance drop in a server before it breaks down or causes major difficulties, you can determine the exact problem and correct it before it gets any worse.

If you can get this far with your planning, you'll be far ahead of the game because you can predict some of the problems and fix them before they bring the network down. If you can take it a step further, you can plan for the future by predicting trends of network use. For example, if you can measure historical trends in the use of the network and data, you can plan capacity use in the future. Considering user behavior, new applications, traffic patterns, server placement, and so on, you should be able to predict some of the future requirements of your network.

Implementation

An important step between planning and implementation is testing. Before you deploy any new system, application, or technology, you should test the effect on the network. You might set up a small network segment using the same protocols, hardware, applications, and so on. Apply any optimization techniques to this segment and test them for a week or so before implementing the changes to the entire network.

Within your testing, look for multiple read/writes, improper packet size, or poor configurations. There are tools you can use to test application designs, new technologies, varied networking hardware implementation, and so on. The more testing you can perform before full-scale use, the better for you, for the users, and for the network.

Often, time and money demand an administrator skip testing and go straight into implementation. If at all possible, you should test first. If you cannot test, you should at least apply the changes to a small segment of the network. Another suggestion is to implement only one change at a time, whenever possible.

No implementation will ever go smoothly and successfully on the first try. When you introduce any changes to the network, you'll likely need to isolate problems and solve them quickly. You should try to anticipate problems in the planning stage and have a good idea of some solutions before you ever implement your network changes.

If you do notice problems after you implement a change in your network, consider first that you may need to upgrade equipment or add bandwidth. Add switched hubs throughout the network, balance client and server networking hardware, locate bottlenecks and provide relief.

Consider using network management and analyzing software to help you locate problem areas. If you still have problems, you might try outsourcing the work to experts in optimization. There are firms that can perform network benchmarks on your system to identify peak traffic times, heavily used routes, quiet times, and less-traveled network paths. If you're tied up with the day-to-day management of your network, outsourcing the job may be the least expensive timesaving step you could take to improving and optimizing your network.

Steps to Optimization

The more you use the network, the more you'll want to boost the performance of your servers, applications, and networking equipment. Today's applications and larger files require more from the equipment than ever before; today's users expect more, too—more speed, fewer problems, enhanced bells and whistles.

The end users use the server every day, so they have some expertise on the performance of the server. Listen to their complaints; have them document what they were doing at the time performance problems took place. You'll be amazed at what you can learn from your users. And if you're going to ask them about network and server performance, make sure you look into their problems and quickly report back to them.

Optimization Team

If you cannot perform the process yourself, you should delegate a team of administrative assistants who can poll the users and follow up on their complaints. If you use a group of knowledgeable people to head up your optimization team, you'll be creating a structured method of problem reporting. Let the team decide how and when to gather information from the users, and the team should be the ones who get back to the user when a solution is discovered. The team should create reports summarizing the complaints, research, and resolution and store all of the data on a system for future analysis.

The team must know the business—When are shipments usually received? When do most customers tend to order? What are the busiest days or times? They should ask managers of different departments for help on these issues. Additionally, the team should regularly perform the following tasks:

Routinely monitor and track the performance of processors, disks, memory, and network utilization.

Be aware that workload changes during the day, the week, and the year.

Monitor server use—when and where it is most used, workload changes, and so on.

Track all network problems and keep a history of time, date, problem, resolution, and other factors.

Implementing Solutions

After the team, or you, isolates the problem(s), decide how to address it. Then implement the selected solution. It's best to change only one factor at a time, whether upgrading hardware or changing server configuration to improve performance.

Slowly testing each solution with all facets of the network is the best way to avoid problems. If you change several things all at once, how will you know which caused the problem? If that same problem occurs later, you won't know exactly what to do to stop it. Also, changing several things at once can cause new problems; and thus you go back to the beginning of the process and start over. Logically, change one item at a time, whether swapping network cards, adding a processor or memory, or whatever.

When you find the problem, you should test extensively (if possible on a nonproduction machine) to make sure the steps continuously improve performance or fix the problem. When changing configuration or upgrading on a nonproduction system, you can test the process itself, making sure you've met all the prerequisites, that you have all the hardware and software you need, and so on. You can readily see what effects the change produces without bringing down the entire system. When you're satisfied with the results, then you can implement the process to the system.

PLANNING STRATEGIES

There are many types of networks, all with varying hardware, applications, combinations of operating systems, and configurations. Each network presents its own services; each network administrator has his or her own goals. Optimizing a network isn't an easy job and isn't something you can do without much planning, preparation, and knowledge. Optimizing just the network connections could be a full-time job and is for many consultants and technical outsourcers.

There are several steps you can take, however, to ensure that your network is operating dependably and efficiently. You can make sure the hardware—server, networking, and so on—is appropriate for your usage, for example. Also, you can check your bandwidth usages to locate and correct areas of congestion. This chapter describes a few common steps you can take to optimize your network, including the following:

- Adding or upgrading a processor

- Adding memory

- Using RAID to boost performance

- Choosing SCSI versus IDE

- Choosing network cards

- Bandwidth implementation

System Improvement Advice

There are many things you can do to improve the performance of your network: add bandwidth, change processors, use two or three network cards in the server, and so on. More than likely, you'll want the most effective method as well as the least-expensive way to optimize performance.

Following are some ideas for optimizing your network components. If you feel you need more help with the process, you should outsource the job to an expert in the field. A consultant or technical person can evaluate your network to find the areas of congestion and make the best suggestions for your situation.

Processors and Boards

Start with the CPU (Central Processing Unit) of your server(s) when you want to improve system performance. The speed and efficiency of your system's processor(s) has a big impact on overall server throughput. Clock speeds exceed 333MHz now, with strides made to increase speeds every day.

Pentium or Pentium Pros are the best bet for server processors; Pentium Pro offers improved scalability in SMP (Symmetric Multiprocessing) configurations, better throughput, and significantly faster processing times than the older Pentium.

> **NOTE**
> RISC (Reduced Instruction Set Computing)-based designs are more expensive than Intel processor chips, but are enormously faster and more efficient. RISC-based systems require special versions of operating systems and programs and are often used as imaging, CAD, and 3-D modeling servers because these applications are sensitive to the speed of floating point calculations. RISC processors do floating point calculations about 20 percent faster than CISC (Complex Instruction Set Computing) processors.

Don't use Pentium MMX or Pentium II as server material because these processors are aimed at workstation applications and multimedia capabilities that you don't need for server performance. Alpha 21064 chips aren't much used on servers anymore; now the 300–500MHz 21164 is more in use. Alphas cost more than Intel-based systems but are great for high-load, mission-critical transaction processing environments. (You can't use Alphas with NetWare).

When adding another processor, you must first make sure the hardware supports multiple processors; next, check that the operating system supports it as well. Check the NOS documentation carefully to see if there are operating system files that need to be modified before you add a processor.

Application software must also be compatible with multiple processors. The application must be multithreaded; if it's single-threaded you won't notice much of an advantage. *Threading* is a process whereby a program divides what it needs to do into separate processing units; for example, a database may start a thread for each user of the database. If resources are available, each thread can do something for a different user. Most applications are multithreaded, but make sure you find out about your own applications before adding a processor.

You must also have a system board that can support multiple processors. It would be cheaper to upgrade a current uniprocessor server to a single-processor Pentium Pro or Alpha, but it won't provide much in the way of upward scalability. You'll get better speed, a bit more room for new users, but generally, uniprocessor systems aren't good for applications like databases or messaging/groupware. And when upgrading processors, or anything, always remember to allow room for the network and/or server(s) to grow.

Memory

Too little memory causes problems with system paging and severely impacts disk performance on a server. Too much memory, however, may cause the NOS and applications to suffer because the system must manage the unused resources. Generally, use 64MB of RAM at least for the NOS and then adjust the amount for applications or processes added to the server's load. Also, add more memory if you plan to use more processors; for example, in a quad-processor configuration, use 128MB RAM.

Different kinds of memory supply different levels of performance and fault tolerance. Most memory is measured at 60 nanoseconds; higher speeds aren't as critical when you can interleave them for greater bandwidth. The following memory types yield incremental differences in performance even if used on the same memory bus; but you generally can't mix them together.

EDO (Enhanced Data Output)

ECC (Error Correcting Circuitry)

Parity

DRAM (Dynamic RAM)

SDRAM (Synchronous Dynamic RAM)

DRAM is a common type of memory that uses capacitors and transistors storing electrical charges to represent memory states. The capacitors lose their electrical charge, so they are refreshed every millisecond, during which time they cannot be read by the processor. DRAM chips are small, cheap, and hold four times as much information as SRAM (Static RAM) chips.

SDRAM is a variation on timing of normal DRAM but generally, SDRAM won't improve performance. ECC and Parity memory won't help or hurt system performance, but they will protect you from memory faults, including module failure.

Disk Subsystem Optimization

I/O (Input/Output) may be the limiting factor in a server system. I/O is the transfer of data between the computer and its peripheral devices, disk drives, terminals, printers, and so on. Following are a few ideas for optimizing system I/O.

SCSI (Small Computer System Interface) is a high-speed parallel interface used to connect a PC with multiple devices using just one port. SCSI is often used to connect hard disks, tape drives, CD-ROM drives, and other mass storage media, as well as scanners and printers. For any server, you should use a SCSI bus instead of IDE (Integrated Drive Electronics).

IDE isn't good for server applications because it is slow, has no RAID capabilities except through software, uses few devices per channel, and has limited overall functionality. EIDE (Enhanced IDE) is marginally better, a bit faster. But the fast and wide SCSI-2 (or new Fibre Channel devices) or UltraWide SCSI-3 offers maximum transfer rates for your network. SCSI offers greater bandwidth and upgradability.

Fibre Channel (FCAL) is the switched-fabric standard, or point-to-point connections, which offers increased throughput capabilities over Ultra SCSI-3 standards. FCAL also supports more drives on a single bus and provides multiple simultaneous accesses. A fiber optic technology, FCAL enables all I/O to go over a single strand of fiber optic cable instead of multiple parallel copper wires. Fiber optics are capable of extremely high data transfer rates, but throughput is limited because of FCAL's serial nature. FCAL is also more expensive than SCSI, but it offers greater flexibility in cabling and configuration.

Additionally, for improved I/O performance on standard servers, upgrade to hardware-accelerated RAID controllers. RAID controllers are built around SCSI or Fibre Channel; RAID lets you spread out read and write activity across multiple drives simultaneously, so it provides fault tolerance as well as better performance.

RAID

RAID (Redundant Array of Inexpensive/Independent Disks) is a method of using multiple hard disks to provide fault tolerance in case one drive fails. RAID uses multiple disk drives, special disk controllers, and software to protect your data and improve disk subsystem performance.

Your data is protected because RAID spreads your data among multiple disks; data exists on several disks so that if one disk fails, another disk can provide the data until the bad disk is replaced. Performance is improved because read tasks are also distributed among several disks—the same data can be retrieved from different locations.

RAID Levels

Most NOSs—such as NT and NetWare—provide native support for one or more RAID levels. RAID levels are optimized for different data storage requirements. Following are descriptions of the RAID levels:

RAID 0

RAID 0—disk striping. Disk striping combines a set of disk partitions, located on different hard disks, into a single volume. Disk striping allows multiple disk accesses and thereby improves performance but doesn't provide fault tolerance. If one disk fails in a level-0 array, then the data on all drives in the array is inaccessible.

RAID 0 is inexpensive and does offer high performance. It doesn't use any disk space to store parity information, so you don't need more or larger disk drives. And RAID 0 uses simple algorithms that require very little from the processor. Optimization issues to keep in mind with RAID 0 include the following:

- You should make sure you have a reliable method of backup for data stored on a RAID 0 array; RAID 0 does not protect your data.

- Chunk size impacts performance; the size of the block (chunk size) determines how much data is written to the disk in an operation. Too small a chunk size (8KB) means reduced performance; chunk sizes of 16KB or 32KB can offer increased performance.

RAID 1

RAID 1—disk mirroring. Disk mirroring is used just for fault tolerance. Mirroring writes the same information simultaneously onto two different hard disks or partitions. If one disk or partition fails, the other can continue working. Most network operating systems offer disk mirroring.

RAID 1 offers complete redundancy and fault tolerance; however, there are a few disadvantages to using disk mirroring. One is that you must buy double the drives so you can create the copy or mirror of the original drive. The second disadvantage is that since there is writing to two drives, the disk writes are slower and performance may be hampered somewhat. The good news is that reads are significantly improved because there are two sources from which to read.

NOTE

Disk duplexing is like mirroring but it adds a second host adapter to control the second disk. Disk duplexing reduces the chance of a single point of failure.

Optimization issues to keep in mind with RAID 1 include the following:

- It can be very expensive to duplicate every drive in a multiple-server environment.

- The hardware solution for RAID 1—such as one supplied with a SCSI adapter—provides better performance than the RAID offered by an NOS. Choose the hardware option if you have a choice.

- RAID writes take significant time and reads are normally very fast. Since the number of reads in most servers outnumbers the writes, overall performance will be increased with the use of RAID 1.

RAID 2

RAID 2—disk striping with parity. RAID 2 is seldom used in a PC or LAN environment, but some hardware RAID devices do offer level 2. RAID 2 requires many disk drives because it uses multiple dedicated disks to store parity information. While good for imaging applications that use sequential access, RAID 2 is not good for random-access applications.

RAID 3

RAID 3—disk striping with parity. Parity is a simple form of error checking. One physical drive is dedicated to the parity information and the data word is striped across multiple drives as in RAID 0. This type of RAID is good for workstation applications with large files, but not so good for networked servers dealing with numerous small files or small disk I/O operations because it ties up every drive in the stripe set for every I/O operation.

RAID 3 is useful for sequential data transfers but the random-access common to PC LANs doesn't work well with this level of RAID. The parity drive is overused; writes wait in queue and take a long time to complete. Consider RAID 3 only if you use very specialized applications that depend on sequential reads, as in an imaging server, for example.

RAID 4

RAID 4—disk striping with parity.   One physical drive is dedicated to the parity information. The striping algorithm differs from RAID 3, however; the entire data word is written to a single drive, next word to next drive. RAID 4 allows only single-threaded write operations but allows multiple simultaneous reads, since each drive holds an entire word.

RAID 4 is good for more I/O operations per second, but level 4 is seldom used in PC and LAN environments because of that single dedicated parity drive. The only way to reasonably use RAID 4 is with a disk that is used with only small random reads, which isn't in accord with a PC LAN.

RAID 5

RAID 5—disk striping with parity. Parity info is distributed across all drives in the volume.   Data is written in an algorithm that sends data to drives in the stripe set, one after another. The most commonly used RAID, RAID 5 allows multiple simultaneous reads and writes. You'll need at least three drives to set up RAID 5, but it provides complete fault tolerance for single-drive failure and improves read performance.

RAID 5 stripes the parity information onto all disks in the array, thus eliminating the bottleneck created by writing the parity information to a single disk. RAID 5 is perfect for the PC LAN environment. When optimizing your system, consider that RAID 5 uses a special method of writing data to ensure its safety and correctness (called *two-phase commit*). This means that RAID 5 writes a bit more slowly but it's also a better guarantee for your data integrity.

RAID 6

RAID 6—disk striping plus distributed parity. RAID 6 is RAID 5 enhanced.   Two drives in the stripe set can fail, since the distributed parity information has parity information of its own. There are various methods of providing RAID 6: a redundant power supply may be added to a RAID 5 array or an additional disk might be added to the array. When purchasing RAID 6, ask the vendor exactly how it works to make sure you're getting your money's worth. RAID 6 does, however, provide excellent fault tolerance.

RAID 7

RAID 7—disk striping.   RAID 7 is based primarily in the UNIX environment and is still fairly new. Level 7 uses a dedicated controller and operating system, fast SCSI-2 multichannel adapters, and such. It can simultaneously connect to more than one host, such as a mainframe and PC LAN server. Be very careful with this level, since it's new and not really proven yet.

Stacked RAID

Stacked arrays refer to multiple RAID levels being used together to gain the benefits of each while compensating for the disadvantages of others. For example, RAID 10 (also called RAID 0+1) combines RAID 0 and RAID 1, providing striping with redundancy.

RAID 10 is built directly through the RAID controller with a combination of software mirroring and controller striping. RAID 10 provides a good combination of fault tolerance and performance, but it's expensive. No parity is used in RAID 10; fault tolerance is achieved through the mirror. Some high-end controllers support RAID 10 directly. Combining RAID 10 with hot-swap drives (drives not used actively for data but rather remaining in wait for other drive(s) to fail) creates a very high-performing, reliable, and fault-tolerant system.

RAID is also stacked into RAID 53—Raid 5 array with subsidiary RAID 3 arrays; RAID 30 (RAID 0+3) as mirrored RAID 3 sets; and RAID 50 (RAID 0+5) mirrored RAID 5 sets that provide a multiple fault-tolerant disk subsystem using software and hardware options.

Implementing RAID

A hardware-accelerated RAID controller is much better than software RAID, but it does cost more. With software RAID at level 5, the system's CPU has to calculate the data distribution and parity information in addition to everything else that it's doing for the computer. To take full advantage of RAID, you need to employ multichannel controllers or separate I/O across multiple controllers. The more drives you have on a single SCSI channel, the closer you get to the maximum throughput capabilities of the controller.

The types of I/O activity your system spends most of its time doing have a big impact on overall performance. Sequential I/O is not as fast as random I/O. If possible, keep random and sequential I/Os on separate volumes.

Also, consider the following before purchasing a RAID solution for your network:

Be careful of proprietary RAID array designs that may limit your choices of compatible drives (say, in the next year when you must replace a disk).

Be wary of any design that makes the chassis an essential part of the drive assembly; replacement drives may be difficult to find.

Watch third-party RAID controllers that say they support various standard SCSI disk drives; check the compatibility list to make sure your drives are included.

Be careful of external RAID arrays that supply a dedicated power supply for each disk drive; individual power supplies tend to increase the number of points of failure. Look for dual load-sharing power supplies instead.

Make sure the RAID management software is intuitive, provides for both static and dynamic rebuild options, and monitors the array's performance.

Multichannel RAID Cards

Most SCSI cards don't have multiple channels; *multiple channels* refer to independent buses that function separately but operate over a single interrupt. Most RAID cards do have multiple channels. Find a RAID card with at least two channels, but three or four channels would be better.

A multichannel card is a good option for optimizing disk I/O on a single RAID volume. You can separate different types of I/O activity, break RAID volumes across high-speed data paths, and then have room to add more disk drives. Multichannel controllers multiply your capacity. Also, you'll find some improvement using the extra channels to separate the sequential and random I/O activity onto completely separate SCSI buses instead of just separate physical drives.

Multiple Network Cards on the Server

Multihoming—available with UNIX, NetWare, and NT NOSs—enables you to run multiple network cards in a server to improve throughput, load balancing, and fault tolerance. Multihoming spreads out client load over multiple subnets instead of filling up even one 100Mbit line with too many packets and collisions.

The network operating system must enable you to run more than one network card with the protocol on the same subnet. For example, Windows NT Server won't let you unless you use either IP subnetting or multiple Class-C address ranges, one for each card.

Multiple network cards add extra overhead for I/O processing, interrupt handling, and so on. For each PCI NIC you add, another interrupt is added to

> **NOTE**
>
> *Dual-homing* is a method of attaching network devices—such as hubs, servers, internetworking devices with redundant links, and so on—to ensure network operability by eliminating any single point of failure. If one link becomes inoperative, then the secondary link automatically becomes active and thus the network's availability is preserved. Dual-homing is generally applied to FDDI networks but can also be applied to collapsed and distributed backbones. On Ethernet or token ring networks, dual-homing is generally referred to as a *redundant link*.

the CPU's load. Also, the CPU must deal with the added amount of data transferred due to the extra card; and more memory is needed when you add extra network cards. If you're not careful, adding multiple network cards could slow down the server instead of speeding it up.

> **TIP**
>
> You also could alternatively try a physical network segmentation using routers and/or switches instead of hubs to minimize collisions and help throughput.

Miscellaneous Optimizing Options

There are many ways to optimize your network. Most importantly, you must observe the network and its components to understand where bottlenecks and problem areas are occurring. Following are just a few miscellaneous ideas for further optimizing components on your network.

Tune Applications

Search engines often cause excess traffic because they provide a lot of information but not necessarily what the user wanted, so they are used over and over again in a small amount of time. If you can better identify the data by using more descriptive keywords, or tags, you will reduce the unnecessary replicated data traversing the network.

No matter what the application, try to break up large files (video clips, for example) to help reduce network traffic. Replicating data for multiple servers also causes extra traffic; you can use mirrored servers or move servers closer to the users to help reduce network traffic.

Architectural Design

Consider the network's architectural design. Is there any place you can use routing switches, for example, to reduce network overhead? By moving the switches to the edge of the network, you may reduce traffic and free the multiprotocol routers for other applications, like routing legacy protocols.

Client And Server Hardware

Sometimes bottlenecks are caused by desktop systems that can't compute quickly enough to keep up with the network. Match your desktop systems with servers to enhance overall performance of the system. Client systems should be less powerful than the servers on the network links appropriate to their systems.

Bandwidth Issues

If you find you're having trouble with bandwidth, you might first try prioritizing traffic so the most important jobs go first. Designate the levels of importance to types of traffic, groups, or individuals with the NOS or a third-party application, such as Check Point's FloodGate-1 or Packeteer's PacketShaper, for example. You must determine the type of traffic or users that will receive priority across the network.

> **NOTE**
> These tools cannot extend the Internet's available bandwidth, only the bandwidth in your LAN or WAN.

Bridges

A *bridge* is a device used to connect two LANs across different wiring or network protocols. Not only does a bridge extend the network, it can also improve performance and make fault isolation possible by dividing the LAN into smaller subnets or segments.

The bridge reads the address of every packet of data so that it can manage the flow of traffic between the LAN segments. Only packets with matching addresses are allowed to pass over the bridge; therefore, the bridge prevents unnecessary traffic from traveling over certain LAN segments.

Bridges can help boost bandwidth performance by dividing the LAN into smaller segments and managing network traffic; however, the routing capabilities of bridges are limited. Consider that bridges cannot route around congested links or redistribute traffic over multiple paths. Depending on your bandwidth problems and your network, you may want to use routers instead.

NICs

A *network interface*, or *adapter*, *card* must support the network architecture (such as Ethernet or token ring) and cabling. You also want to think about card

> **NOTE**
>
> *Gateways* enable LAN workstations to access a WAN or other host environment, no matter the protocol or the platform. Gateways, however, slow throughput and often cause bottlenecks in the network. Make sure you optimize the network when using a gateway; if there are many users who need to use the gateway, for example, you need to find another method of accessing the disparate networks, such as emulation, translation, or encapsulation.

> **Boosting Web Server Bandwidth**
>
> You can maximize your network environment with *proxy cache* technology (also know as *World Wide Web server acceleration*). Proxy caching reduces the load on Web servers, saves bandwidth on the network, and increases the speed of Web requests.
>
> A proxy cache server is placed in front of a Web server to handle the majority of requests coming from the Internet. The proxy cache server can quickly serve most HTML pages, FTP files, and graphics requests; and the Web server takes care of the noncacheable objects. This arrangement increases performance of the Web server and provides greater security for the LAN behind the server.
>
> Proxy cache services use protocol filtering and hide domain names and addresses by sending requests through one gateway. Proxy cache solutions are available for UNIX, NT, and NetWare. Novell's BorderManager includes a proxy cache component you can use on IntranetWare and NetWare 4.11 servers.

performance when deciding which to use in your network. NIC performance depends mostly on bus width and onboard memory. Try to get a card with a bus width that matches the internal bus width of the computer for higher data transfer rates and best performance. Also, onboard memory enables the card to buffer frames to and from the network; a card with the most memory isn't always the best option. Other network components may limit the performance gains of onboard memory.

> **TIP**
> You should definitely buy extra cards to replace any that fail, as well as extra cables, hubs, repeaters, and so on.

Network interface cards greatly affect bandwidth on the network. A 10Mbps Ethernet card is okay when users spend most of their connect time retrieving or sending email, accessing text files, or doing other non-data-intensive work. But when users who need huge databases or run applications remotely are added to the network, you'll need something more than 10Mbps network cards.

100Mbps Fast Ethernet is a smart option. Replace only the NIC at first, if you're using Cat 5 cabling. See if the cards make any difference before you replace cabling. 1000Mbps Ethernet or Gigabit Ethernet using fiber optic are also options, but expensive. Fast Ethernet is the most reasonable and affordable solution, however.

Optimizing Bandwidth

If possible, you should move to an IP-only environment for your network for best network performance. Using various platforms, operating systems, and protocols can hamper performance. By limiting the equipment, software, and protocols you use with your system, you can improve network performance and eliminate many bottlenecks.

Changing multiple protocols to IP should be the first step to optimizing your bandwidth. In preparation for changing over to an IP system, conduct a complete network audit to determine the architecture, protocols, and OSs used throughout. You may need to replace or add routers, switches, and other networking equipment.

As you prepare for changing to the IP environment, list and identify network segments for each desktop OS, network OS, and protocol used.

Determine where legacy protocols and applications reside on the network and find out where legacy multiprotocol routers are required.

The backbone should be gigabit Ethernet or ATM. ATM is specifically for voice, video, and data; gigabit Ethernet is not a mainstream backbone technology yet, but it soon will be. FDDI is also a backbone possibility. What you choose depends on the technology you will feed into the backbone from the workgroup-level routers and switches.

Finding Bandwidth Bottlenecks

Increasing your network speed by throwing more bandwidth at it may only fix the symptom. More bottlenecks are likely to appear as you change your system and try to improve performance. For example, as you switch more desktops to 10Mbps and workgroups to 100Mbps links, the backbone may be overwhelmed, thus causing a bottleneck. To alleviate the problem before it occurs, consider carefully whether all your desktops need the higher speed. Some could make use of slower speeds without noticing the difference in performance and without overpowering the network.

High-speed NICs could also cause the network to become overloaded, depending on the applications being used. Limiting available bandwidth by reducing the number of switched 100Mbps ports on desktops could forestall the need to add expensive switches or wiring.

AFTERWORD

To get the most from your company's network, you will need to invest a great deal of time. Planning and organizing a serviceable network means hours of determination, adversity, labor, and eventually gratification. Just as your users begin to benefit from your hard work, you'll need upgraded software, faster servers, and more networking hardware.

Administering a network is an incessant job. Luckily, it is also one that will become easier with experience. This book offers information based on real-life experiences and solutions to common and some uncommon networking problems.

Whether your title is network administrator, systems administrator, IT manager, or some other designation, this book advises you about many topics and procedures you are likely to tackle in your job. Following are just a few of the chores that are discussed:

- Supervising the creation and management of network users and groups
- Managing printer installation and maintenance
- Planning system backups
- Installing and configuring operating systems and applications
- Supporting the network environment
- Providing user and system support for engineering workstations, servers, and terminals
- Planning hardware and software upgrades
- Troubleshooting client and server problems
- Planning disaster recovery and security
- Performing or delegating user training
- Installing servers and workstations
- Installing and configuring disks and disk arrays

- Maintaining switches, routers, dial-up services, and Internet facilities
- Providing implementation of Internet/intranet projects and networks

This collection of small, specialized books provides various aspects of a network administrator's job. You might use it as a reference book to look up specific hardware, terminology, or procedures. On the other hand, you may read the chapters within any one of the 12 books to learn more about that topic, such as printing or configuring Internet clients. Finally, you may read the book from start to finish to get a better idea of how to manage and organize your network. No matter how you use the book, you'll learn about the various roles a network administrator must play.

Whether you're upgrading a network or building a new network, you can use this book to plan your approach and organize your procedures. Topics such as planning the installation of your servers, configuring remote clients, and outsourcing the more difficult of your jobs, are the focus of this book. Advice about writing policies, delegating tasks, and efficiently building a network that benefits your company helps you perform your job.

As you know, no one operating system is featured in this book; however, many various network and client operating systems are discussed. You should invest in at least one book that is specific to your network operating system for help in configuring and managing that system.

The purpose of this book is to help new and experienced network administrators perform their jobs with optimum efficiency and with the least headaches and hassle. I hope it has helped you and that your job is easier because of this book.

REFERENCE MATERIAL

NETWORK MAPS AND MODELS

Track all details about wiring, hardware, and software used throughout your system. Documenting your system will help your staff quickly execute simple moves, changes, and additions, and pave the way to integration of telephony and computer systems.

Usually cable installers draw a diagram that maps cabling as it was originally installed. You should make sure you update diagrams as changes are made. You can use off-the-shelf documentation programs or you can tailor your network documentation and maps to your needs. Develop an identification scheme that fits your physical environment. Multiple buildings, for example, use a naming scheme that uses separate spreadsheets or database files for each building.

Devise a logical way to describe the physical system. Your maps and documentation should present a view that's clear enough for anyone to quickly locate any device or cable termination. Following are some guidelines to follow as you document your network:

Enlist the help of managers, users, and administrative assistants. Let people document their own section of the network and then you can collect and check the information later.

Organize the information as you prepare it so you won't be overwhelmed later by a mound of paperwork.

Keep numbering schemes simple. Be careful not to base a cable identification system, for example, on room numbers (when changes or additions are made, that numbering system will break down). Also, keep ID numbers short and identify the closet or room where each item belongs.

Avoid different numbering schemes for data and voice cables; rather, number them in different ranges of the same numbering scheme according to where they terminate in the wiring closet.

Good documentation minimizes the amount of testing, tracing, and new installation work your staff and vendors must do to support expansions and repairs.

Know Your Network

Enlist the help of managers, supervisors, and users while determining your needs, since they will be the ones working with the network resources. Here is a general list of the information you should collect; the following sections outline these questions in more detail.

- What equipment is currently in place?

- What equipment is needed to complete the network?

- How many people will use the network and how many network services will you offer?

- What applications are in place and which applications are needed?

- What are the goals of your company and what is expected from the network?

- What growth potential exists?

Take Inventory

Take inventory of your existing system. Examine the equipment, applications, users, space, location, and budget of the current arrangement, and determine the expectations for the new and improved system. Ask the following questions and document the answers:

- Is the company located in one office, one building, over several buildings or cities, or around the world? What types of connections are between these locations?

- What is the current configuration of computers—servers and workstations—in the company?

- What are the peripherals currently in use—CD-ROM drives, modem pools, printers, and so on? Are there UPS devices connected to the servers and/or workstations? Is there at least one tape drive or other device for making backups? Where exactly is each piece of equipment located?

- What are the networking hardware configurations? What type of cabling, network cards, hubs, and other equipment is used to attach and operate the network? If you're unsure about this information, find someone within the company or outside of the company, who can tell you about the networking equipment and help you draw a network map of the cables, hubs, and such.

- How many users are networked? What are the printing requirements, Internet access, and other components in current use?

- What type of applications are now in use—accounting, email, groupware, or specific vertical applications? Does the current configuration require special cabling, servers, or peripherals?

Organizing an Inventory

After you have answered all of the previous questions, you'll have a large amount of information to organize. Divide the information into smaller pieces so it's easier to organize and manage; enter it into a word processing, spreadsheet, or database program. You want to make sure you can rearrange, edit, add to, and delete records and data as you build your inventory through the years.

Divide the information you've gathered into categories, such as Hardware, Software, Users, Location, Peripherals, and so on. You might further organize each category into more topics; for example, Hardware could be divided into Servers, Clients, Networking, and so on. Within each topic, you don't need to write a book; all you need to list is pertinent information. Be specific and identify each entry as clearly as possible.

Next, you should add IRQs and DMAs for cards and devices, list protocols, note the client software, and otherwise document your network. As your system grows and changes, you can easily add to or delete from the list to keep the records up to date. This information assists you when you plan upgrades to hardware and software, in troubleshooting problems with the system, and in case you have to replace part of your system because of a disaster.

You will also want to document your network with drawn layouts. You can, of course, use an art program to record these drawings, or purchase a program specifically for mapping networks, or you can simply sketch the arrangement of computers, buildings, networking hardware, and such, in a notebook. These drawings can help you locate machines or other equipment, trace wiring, or troubleshoot points of failure. There's no specific guide to go by in creating a layout, or map, of your network; you just want to make sure the drawing is easy to follow.

Figure A.1 shows a simple example of a network segment layout that identifies the server and clients. By identifying each server's job and each workstation's

Figure A.1 Sketch out each network segment.

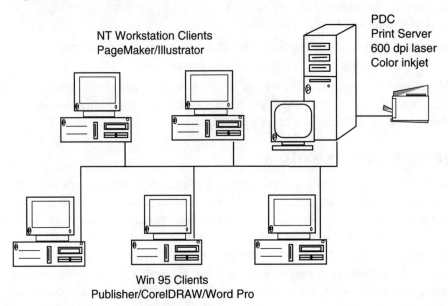

NT Workstation Clients
PageMaker/Illustrator

PDC
Print Server
600 dpi laser
Color inkjet

Win 95 Clients
Publisher/CorelDRAW/Word Pro

**Oak Hill Domain
Art Dept.**

operating system, you make it easy to see the data at a glance. Other information, such as domain and department, helps identify the location of the networking segment; and listing applications, users, and other information may be useful as well.

Figure A.2 shows a network map that describes connections to the servers, locations of switches, routers and hubs, and network connections. Network maps are particularly useful when tracing equipment problems, checking connections, and upgrading network hardware.

You should also keep a record of all applications on the network. You'll need to list the version number, licensing information, upgrade data, and such.

In your many lists of equipment and other networking facts, don't forget to include information about the following:

Peripherals.   Note all peripherals—printers, modems, CD-ROM, and such—attached to servers and/or workstations.

ISP and Internet settings and connections.   List your ISP's or other service provider's phone number, tech support, URL, and such, as well as any Internet settings for IP addresses, gateways, subnet masks, domain name servers, and so on.

Figure A.2 Map out the network connections and hardware for your network.

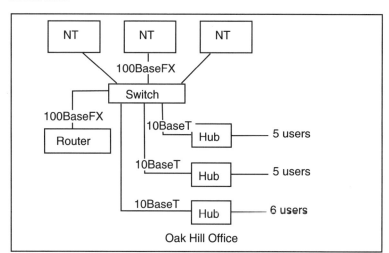

Oak Hill Office

Networking protocols and connections. Record information about all protocols used throughout the network. For example, with TCP/IP you'll list all addresses (IP, subnet, and gateway) for each network segment, each device (including hubs and routers), and each computer on the network.

Outsourcing and technical support contacts. List all outsourcing personnel and companies, consultants, vendors, and others who work on your system in any capacity. Make sure you include the company's name and address, contact's name and phone number, specific details of what the company did for you, guarantees, limitations, and such.

Documentation. Gather the documentation for all computers and networking hardware and store it in a central place for easy access.

Backups. Sort out the information about current backups of the system. Find out about the hardware devices, scheduling, storage location, and so on.

Documenting the Server Room

Document the server room and all equipment it contains. Figure A.3 shows an example layout of a server room. Servers and UPSs are placed in the center of the room for protection from outside walls. The data communications and telecommunications equipment line two inside walls on racks containing a

Figure A.3 Document the servers, wiring, and other equipment of your server room.

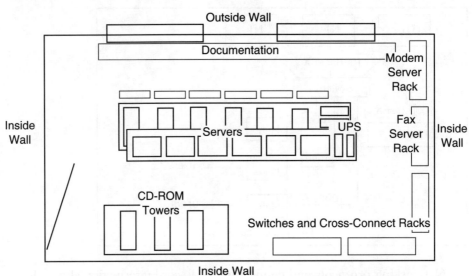

modem server, fax server, switches, and cross-connects. Notice the documentation is also in the same room as the servers. CD-ROM towers are also located in the same room.

Server Room

The server room contains multiple servers, CD-ROM towers, jukeboxes, wiring, and any other equipment you want to secure. Additionally, you might locate the system component in which communications circuits are administered between the backbone and the horizontal facilities, telecommunications equipment, cable terminations, and cross-connect cabling. Often these components are stored in a TCS (Telecommunications wiring Standard) room; but you can combine the two rooms if it is practical. A TCS contains your key telephone systems, PBX (Private Branch Exchange) systems, hubs, routers, cables, bridges, and other equipment for security's sake and for easy troubleshooting.

Telecommunications Closet

You may want to store your telecommunications and/or data communications equipment in the server room or more likely, in a separate room, also called a *telecommunications closet*. Telecommunications elements include automatic call distribution, key telephone systems, and PBX systems. Data communications components include hubs, routers, jacks, cables, bridges, perhaps server computers, backup and storage equipment, modems, and remote access equipment.

The room must contain equipment like switches, servers, and infrastructure-related elements, such as cross-connects and interconnection equipment. Interconnection equipment includes main, intermediate, and horizontal cross-connects, patch panels (devices in which temporary or semipermanent connections can be made between incoming and outgoing lines), cable trays, raceways, and conduits.

Documentation in the telecommunications room is mostly a matter of labeling cables and devices. Make sure you label devices with their IP address, MAC address, circuit IDs, and such. You'll need the circuit ID if communications go down and you need to report the problem area to the phone company, for example.

Mapping Local Area Networks

When mapping out your network, you can draw or sketch out your equipment by hand, use a computer art program, a word processor or spreadsheet, or you can use an application specifically for mapping networks. It all depends on how much time, experience, and energy you have. The main thing is that you do it. Whether it's a list of equipment and connections in each network segment or elaborate drawings of servers, routers, computers, and cabling, it's important that you know the layout and contents of your network.

You can include any of various information in the map. You might want to list backbones, servers, routers and hubs, cabling, and topology. You could also sketch out various LAN segments and their connections. Sometimes you may include operating systems, shared computers, resources, and so on.

NOTE

Don't forget, you should also keep a log book within each LAN segment that clearly describes the hardware, software, and other pertinent information about each device within the segment. See Appendix C, "Task Lists," for more information; the section title is *Keeping Logs and Records*.

Following are some solutions for various network configurations. The maps merely offer some ideas for putting together your LANs.

Network Segments

A network segment is a group of workstations, with or without servers, printers, and other peripherals. Switches are used for segmenting networks to maintain separate areas of bandwidth for these segments, or small groups of workstations.

You use hubs to connect multiple cables from the workstations. A hub modifies transmission signals and allows the network to be extended to accommodate additional workstations. A hub also modifies transmission signals so that the network can be extended to accommodate extra workstations and more hubs. Another use of a hub is for security. The switching hub, as opposed to a repeating hub, keeps the network secure by not allowing anyone to receive anyone else's packets. It also boosts bandwidth and network speed.

Ethernet switching is a packet switching technology that provides a high performance connection between multiple Ethernet networks. Ethernet switching is inexpensive, easy to operate, offers high performance, and extends the throughput of the conventional Ethernet LANs. Use Ethernet switches to divide an Ethernet network into multiple parallel segments. Figure A.4 illustrates an Ethernet network using switches and hubs to segment a network.

Ethernet LANs

Fast Ethernet hardware includes network interface cards, switches, routers, and so on. There are also Fast Ethernet hubs and switches that work with 100BaseT or 100BaseTX. Hubs supply 100BaseT ports for connections to various nodes. Switches also provide multiple 100Mbps ports, as well as other features to improve bandwidth and promote easy network segmentation. Naturally, there are also stacked hubs and switches available that provide multiple ports in various configurations (such as fiber and UTP ports) for use with larger networks.

Gigabit Ethernet operates at 1000Mbps and is often used for a backbone for networks and to connect Fast Ethernet switches. Gigabit Ethernet supports full-duplex for frame-based flow control, supports star-wired topologies, and provides simple forwarding between 10Mbps, 100Mbps, and 1000Mbps Ethernet. Figure A.5 shows an example Ethernet network map.

Token Ring

Using the ring topology, token ring computers take turns sending data via a token that's passed between computers, one at a time. Removal of a node or cabling problems can keep the tokens from passing through the network unless

Figure A.4 Hubs extend the network, and switching hubs and switches segment the network to improve performance.

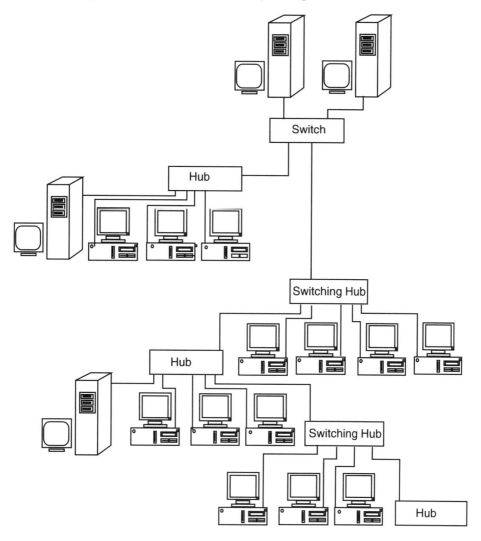

the ring is maintained. In order to protect the connections against cabling problems, stackable hubs can be used.

The workstations in Figure A.6 connect to stacked hubs, called *Multistation Access Units* (MAUs), and then multiple hubs are connected together to create

Figure A.5 Gigabit Ethernet provides the backbone for the LAN.

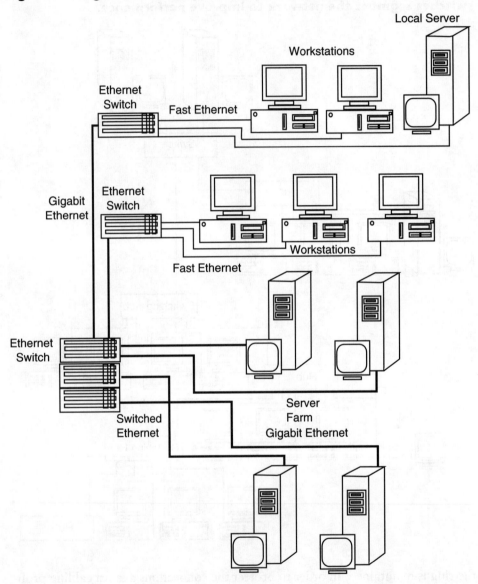

the network. If a workstation fails, the MAU bypasses that station to continue passing the token around the ring. Notice that with the AS/400 server, terminals can also be used within the ring.

Figure A.6 A token ring network attaches each workstation to a hub as a type of fault tolerance.

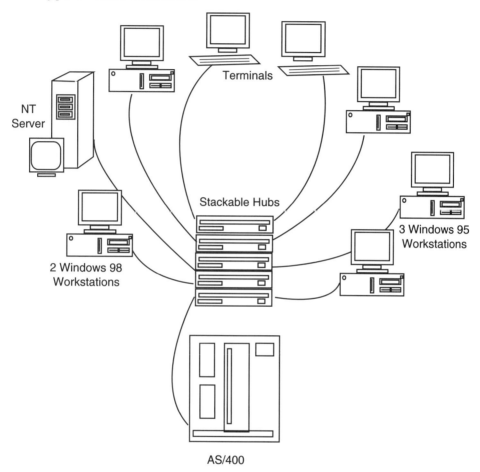

The network map in this figure also describes a few of the resources to help jog the administrator's memory when surveying the network segment.

FDDI

The FDDI standard is a dual ring that offers fault tolerance. A typical FDDI network has one pair of counterrotating rings; it may also have at least one tree of connections. The FDDI network doesn't have to include a dual ring; you can customize the topology to suit your situation.

Figure A.7 shows the dual rings of an FDDI network. A dual ring provides dual connections to other devices. If there's a failure on the ring, the token flow does an about-face and moves the other way. With a tree configuration, devices receive a single connection. This is cost effective, but a single failure fragments the ring so that segments cannot communicate.

Integrated Networks

Naturally, most networks will be a combination of technologies—FDDI and token ring, Ethernet and ATM, and so on—perhaps because of the evolution of the network or because of the needs of the company. You should still fully document your network so you can easily locate problem areas and possible bottlenecks. Generally, integration of networks will occur when a backbone is upgraded for speed.

The backbone is the part of the network that manages the majority of the traffic. Usually, a backbone connects several buildings and networks by using a high-speed protocol and more applicable cabling from that used on the LAN segments.

FDDI and Ethernet

Synchronous FDDI uses priority mechanisms to deliver tokens in a time-efficient method for use as a backbone. Operating speed is 100Mbps half-duplex and 200Mbps full-duplex. FDDI can be shared or switched; it uses star and ring topologies and UTP Cat 5, STP, or fiber cabling. There are FDDI adapters, routers, hubs, and switches available.

If you plan to use an FDDI as your network backbone, make sure you use concentrators to make the backbone stable and reliable. Concentrators protect the backbone from a multitude of problems by giving the administrator access to the logical data stream without requiring access to the physical connectors and cables of the backbone. Figure A.8 illustrates an FDDI backbone that also uses Fast Ethernet to some workgroup servers and Ethernet to the workstations.

ATM and Ethernet

ATM and Fast Ethernet can coexist in a network environment. Figure A.9 illustrates the use of ATM as a backbone with Ethernet switching and Fast Ethernet switches added for certain workstations. The ATM backbone guarantees appropriate bandwidth to the servers. ATM also provides more bandwidth to some workstations that need it for image and multimedia work, for example.

Figure A.7 This FDDI network design utilizes dual rings in each network segment.

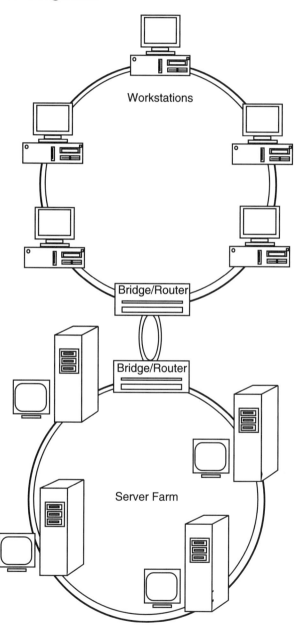

Figure A.8 FDDI backbone and switched FDDI work well with Ethernet and Fast Ethernet.

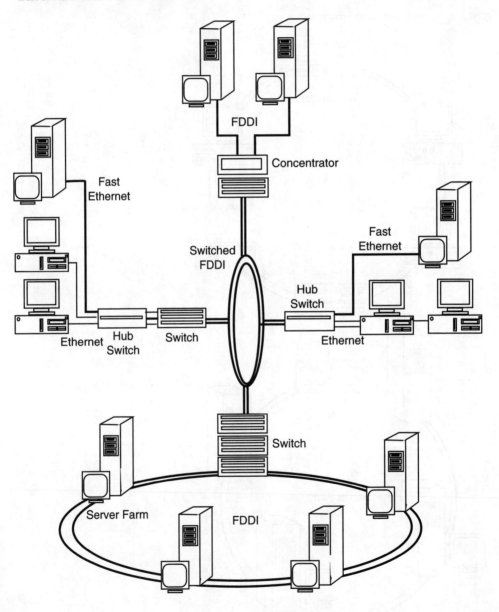

Remote Networking

When you have either remote offices or individual telecommuters who need access to your company files and your network resources, you can choose from many ways to connect those users to your office. A digital modem can be a CSU/DSU, ISDN terminal adapter or a modem that can use both digital input and output. A regular modem takes analog signals in one side and outputs a digital bitstream on the other side. A true digital modem has both digital input and output with a brief analog modulation and demodulation being performed internally.

Under ideal phone connections, 28.8 and 33.6 analog modems (V.34) will transmit 28,800 or 33,600 bits per second; if the modem uses data compression, however, those speeds can achieve higher throughputs. 56Kbps analog modems support downloading speeds up to 53Kbps and uploading speeds of up to 33Kbps. If you use data compression, the 56Kbps modems can achieve throughputs of two or more times the rate on compressible files. 56Kbps is affordable, easy to use, and provides good security. A problem with a 56Kbps connection is the local infrastructure may not support the speed.

Figure A.10 illustrates a remote office connected to a main office using a 56K line with CSU/DSU devices and two modem connections for individual telecommuters. This might be how you would map your remote access network.

A CSU/DSU (Channel Service Unit/Digital Service Unit) is a device that powers the line to run faster than an analog modem. There are many types of CSU/DSU devices and each provides different services. You can buy a CSU/DSU that provides full SNMP management or works over T1 or frame relay or supports speeds of 2400 and 56,000 or maintains analog or digital.

An ISDN terminal adapter is built in to utilize the high speed available with ISDN BRI (Basic Rate Interface) connections. Each B channel can be considered a separate line, but you also could use both channels at the same time for a combined bandwidth of 128Kbps and even more with data compression. Figure A.11 illustrates a remote office connected to the main office by an ISDN line and terminal adapters.

Wide Area Networks

As your company grows, so grows your network. Your LAN may include multiple segments and remote users and offices. If you expand your company or make new acquisitions that span one or more buildings, cities, states, or countries, your network will also expand.

Figure A.9 Notice some switches can switch both ATM and Fast Ethernet or ATM and Ethernet.

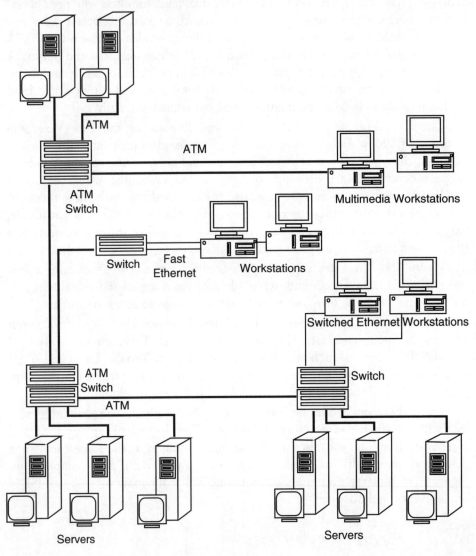

You may call your network a WAN (Wide Area Network), which usually spans over large geographical areas; or you may call your network a MAN (Metropolitan Area Network), which is a bit smaller than a WAN and usually a public high-speed network. Your network could also be named an *enterprise* or

Figure A.10 Map your remote offices and users by detailing their connections and hardware.

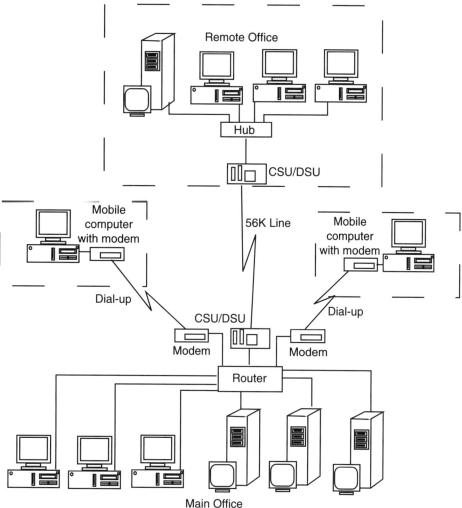

campus network. No matter what you name the network, its purpose is to connect your company so your users can share information efficiently and effectively.

It's especially important to map out a network that spans more than one or two LAN segments; each part depends on the whole. Servers in one city, for example, may hold the information needed for the users in another city to com-

Figure A.11 ISDN lines provide fast throughput for the remote office.

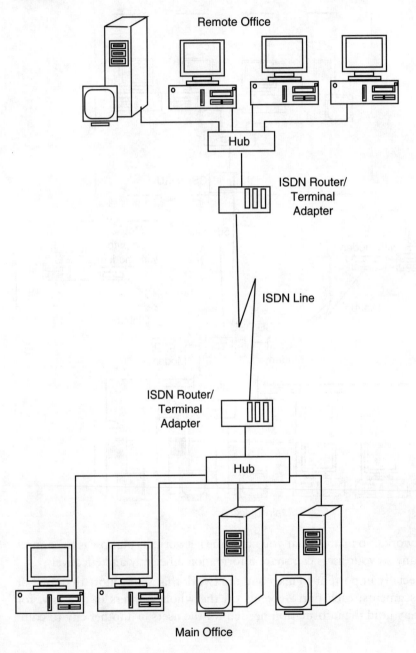

plete their daily reports; a file attached to an email message from one country may hold the data needed in another country to complete a merger or transaction. If one section of the network goes down, you'll need to know where the point of failure is and who is responsible for that area.

More than likely, each network within the wide area network has its own administrator. Each administrator should diagram, or map, his or her own LAN. Then you should have someone knowledgeable about the wide area connections to map the network for you or at least help in the process. When the entire map is complete, every LAN within the WAN should receive a copy of the map with any text or written documentation necessary for total understanding of the network.

This section presents some examples of WAN maps. As with LAN maps, you can include as much information as you want on the map and you can draw it in any way that is convenient, as long as it's precise and easy to understand.

Figure A.12 illustrates a wide area network connecting two networks. The larger of the two is primarily an FDDI network with some Fast Ethernet and Ethernet connections. The smaller of the two networks is made up of Fast Ethernet and Ethernet. This map details server uses plus hubs, routers, and switches within the networks.

Figure A.13, on the other hand, doesn't detail the individual servers and workstations. Showing three networks attached to the WAN, the figure describes topology and connections. Representative servers and workstations aren't really necessary; more notes could describe the individual LAN contents as well as sketches.

Figure A.14 illustrates a wide area network using a mainframe, minicomputer, the Internet, and an NT network. The data stored in the mainframe in Virginia and on the AS/400 in West Virginia is accessed via an NT Server 4.0 computer with Microsoft's SNA (Systems Network Architecture) Server installed.

Today, many PC-based, client/server systems must depend on the traditional legacy systems for data; SNA Server makes it possible. SNA Server accesses mainframes and minicomputers, using proprietary SNA protocols from a desktop PC on the LAN or WAN.

When you're mapping out a very large network, you may want to illustrate each segment or LAN on a page by itself. Using arrows, you can indicate connections between illustrations.

Figure A.12 You can add as much detail to the map as necessary.

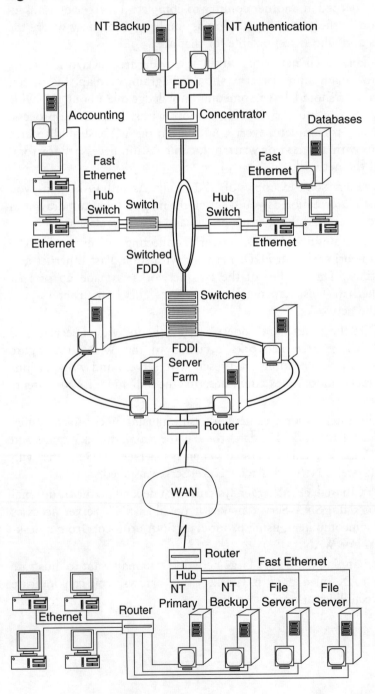

Figure A.13 Different amounts of detail serve different purposes in each map.

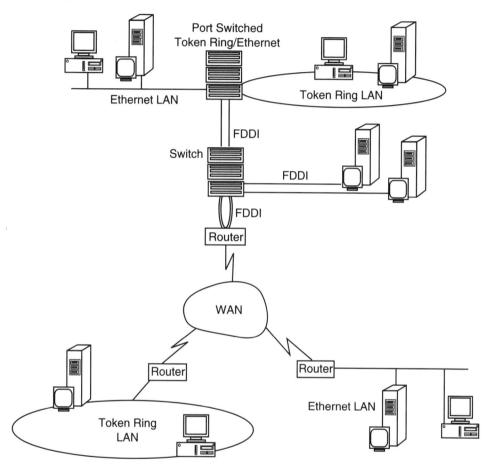

Figure A.14 Hardware, servers, and connections of the WAN are illus-trated here.

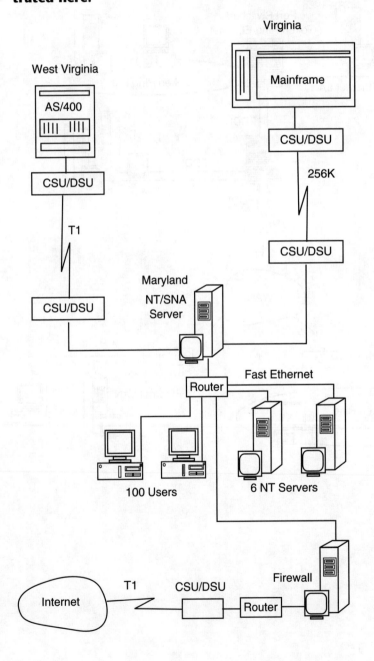

Also, you may want to map only the hardware devices and pertinent information about connections in one of your network maps. In Figure A.15, the map consists more of notes and details than of illustrations. Notice IP addresses are added for each device—switch, router, and CSU/DSU.

Figure A.16 illustrates another page as it would relate to the map shown in Figure A.15.

Figure A.15 Only connections, devices, and addresses in this map.

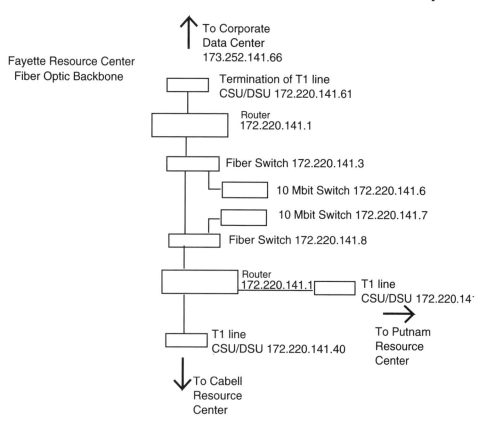

Figure A.16 Listing IP addresses makes PINGing quick and easy.

Putnam Resource Center

Fiber Optic Backbone

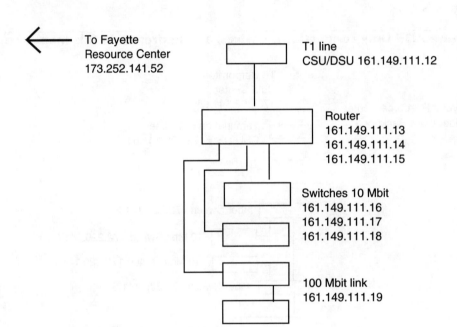

To Fayette
Resource Center
173.252.141.52

T1 line
CSU/DSU 161.149.111.12

Router
161.149.111.13
161.149.111.14
161.149.111.15

Switches 10 Mbit
161.149.111.16
161.149.111.17
161.149.111.18

100 Mbit link
161.149.111.19

TROUBLESHOOTING

This appendix describes common networking problems and some methods of troubleshooting those problems. Also presented here are some solutions to prevalent questions and problems. Generally, when you're troubleshooting any network or computer problem, you should try to isolate the problem. Narrow down the symptoms and the source by identifying whether a component works in other situations. Has it ever worked? Did it work before you changed hardware or installed new software? Did you make any other changes that affected the component? Identify any variable that could be causing the problem by changing one variable at a time until you locate the problem.

Creating a Baseline

You should conduct a baseline evaluation of your network so that you'll have an idea what is normal for your network. A baseline records the measurement of the network's state of operation over a period of time. It involves recording the typical operation so you can use it for comparison and control.

See if you can answer these questions about your network:

How many users are on the network?

What is your greatest network expense?

What is the peak utilization of your network for and when does it occur?

What is the normal utilization?

Which application impacts your network the most?

If you cannot answer these questions, then your first steps are to find out about your network. You can't troubleshoot a network effectively without a basic knowledge of the network. Also, realize that networks are constantly changing; users, hardware, technologies, applications, and such, may change monthly or yearly, depending on your business and your use of the network.

You must continuously monitor the network and build a baseline periodically to maintain control and make troubleshooting easier and more efficient.

> **NOTE**
>
> Bandwidth is a major concern for most network administrators. But consider, bandwidth is expensive and adding bandwidth may only mask the real problems of the network. Before you increase your bandwidth, consider your network evaluation first to see if you can improve the network in other ways.

Documentation

Document your network, users, servers, applications, network hardware, and other components first so that you know all there is to know about how the network works. Make sure you know your network's topology and cabling. You should understand the placement and configuration of all hubs, routers, bridges, and switches. You should also update your documentation every time you upgrade or modify your network.

Identify server and gateway locations, LAN segments, WAN connections, protocols, server operating systems, and so on. You should even know your client operating systems, connections, hardware, and such. You can have each manager document the hardware and applications in her department, if you want; or have assistants perform the documentation for you. But for many reasons, especially troubleshooting, you need to know about every piece of equipment in the network.

If you haven't toured the network and facilities in a while, take the time to do that. You should know the layout of the network. You may want to take a few pictures or sketch some of the physical features of server rooms or offices as you go. You should, by the way, have a detailed design of all server rooms, telecommunications closets, and cabling throughout the network. This is a job you may want to outsource.

Following is a detailed list of the information you should inventory and document in your network:

Company sites and locations.

Servers' and workstations' manufacturer, model, serial number; computers' location, monitor brand and specs, keyboard type, and mouse type.

MAC addresses of servers and IP addresses of all hosts and nodes.

All computers' internal configuration: motherboard, processor speed, amount and type of RAM, number and type and size of hard disks and controllers, floppy drives and sizes, CMOS information, computer BIOS manufacture and revision numbers, and so on.

Cabling and external connections.

Firmware information on RISC-based computers.

Disk subsystem information: makes, models, and serial numbers of disks and controllers.

Map of SCSI subsystem: SCSI configuration information, which devices are terminated and how, SCSI ID and physical location of SCSI devices.

Operating system, installed applications, users' names, any special additions or custom-made applications or equipment.

Sound card, video card, network adapter cards: manufacturer and model, IRQ addresses, jumper and/or DIP switch settings, DMA, I/O ports, and such.

Zip, and/or CD-ROM drives types and speeds, manufacturer and model, location, drivers, port connections, and such.

Modem: manufacturer and model, location, speed, drivers, port connections, and so on.

Other attached peripherals: printers—manufacturer and model, specifications on memory, font cartridges, printer fonts, ports and cables, and so on. UPS specifications, tape drives, and any other add-ons.

Existing network connections and hardware: cabling, NICs, hubs, and such.

Networking protocols and configuration settings.

Peripheral information, including UPS, CD-ROMs, printers, modems, and so on.

User information: needs, skills, security data, and such.

Applications: server installed, limits and sensitivity, licensing, shared possibilities.

Internet connection information: IP addresses, gateways, name servers, and so on.

Outsourcing and technical support contacts: contact's name and phone number.

Documentation for all hardware and networking equipment.

Backup information: devices, scheduling, storage area.

Insurance policies.

Information on kits, tools, and add-ons you've installed.

Internal documentation like policies, procedures, training guides, etc.

Troubleshooting history (time, date of problem, error messages, events logged, and outcome).

Phone list of who to call for specific emergencies: administrators, vendors, management, and critical users.

Building a Baseline

Next, create a baseline evaluation. To create a baseline evaluation, you'll need to determine how efficiently your network is running. You might begin by asking users, managers, and administrators what they think of the network in general. Then you'll want to perform some diagnostic tests to determine the following:

How well does the network support additional traffic loads?

Assess traffic loads, protocols, and flow patterns.

How stable and efficient is the network infrastructure—cables, routers, switches, and such?

What components—hardware, software, or activities—are obstructing the network's performance? Where are the bottlenecks?

You'll want to conduct the baseline evaluation over three to four weeks to get an accurate idea of how things are running. Consider other objectives you have for the network as you analyze its current status. Include your determinations for future growth and equipment scalability.

You'll need to evaluate each network segment for the baseline. Evaluation may occur over the course of 24 hours or longer if you need more information. You can use a network analyzer to capture history and statistics; 24 hours gives you a total view of the environment, including the busiest times and the least busy. You evaluate each segment separately and then analyze them as a whole. Following are the characteristics you'll want to assess:

Utilization level: Peaks and averages for the network, server, and node.

Number of users: Average and in peak.

Protocols used: Check the number of different protocols used and in which segments they appear.

Error statistics: Collisions, fragments, noise, and so on, for the network and nodes.

Reporting on the Baseline

After you collect your baseline information, you'll want to create a report from the statistics so you can better analyze the current network status. In the report, include information about the evaluations you performed, the method, and the reasoning. Clearly establish your objectives for creating a baseline—you might want to locate problem areas before they bring the network down or learn the reasons some segments perform a great deal better than others do, for example. Include a logical network diagram with the report and any general observations you've made, such as conclusions made from what you've learned.

Next, you should include individual segment reports on such topics as bandwidth utilization, frame rate and size, errors, protocol distribution, and so on. Then apply the information to the entire network and show how it affects performance.

Finally, list your overall recommendations for the network. Which segments should be upgraded? What should be done about bottlenecks? What are the most desirable changes you can make and then, what are the most critical changes that must be made?

Network Tools

You should have a set of tools to use for diagnosing various network problems. Hand-held cable testers, network or protocol analyzers, and so on, can provide a wealth of information quickly and easily. Even a basic tool kit—long-nose pliers, wire strippers, crimping tool, electric screwdriver, flashlight, and such—is important for every network administrator. And don't forget the importance of documentation and reference materials, commercial online services, and Internet sites for the latest network documentation.

Following are some other tools you should consider:

SNMP and RMON let you gauge the status of network resources—routers and bridges. There are also network management applications you can use to help you track, inventory, and manage your network and its resources.

A business-frequency FM walkie-talkie or transceiver. These can help your staff carry on conversations as they work at the site.

A digital multimeter measures voltage, current, and resistance. Using a pair of multimeters, you can perform simple continuity and cable mapping.

A tone tracer locates a cable by using an audible tone. Place the signal generator at one end of the cable and then pass the tone tracer over cables at the other end until the tracer beeps; the beeping cable is the one you want.

LAN analysts trace paths of affected LAN traffic with the use of measurements and maps. They sample network frames and enter test frames to find the problems with the network.

Protocol analyzers help determine how much of a protocol flows through the network. Filtering out unnecessary protocols will help improve network performance.

Specialized test equipment—for an Ethernet hub or token ring multistation access unit, for example—may be necessary in your company. Special Ethernet or token ring problems require test equipment designed specifically for those technologies.

A TDR (Time Domain Reflectometer) transmits short pulses of known amplitude down a cable to measure the parallel amplitude and time delay. TDRs are available for all types of LANs; an optical TDR is available for fiber cable.

Optical Power Source and Meter is a device for checking fiber cable. It's also called a *light meter* and is a cost-effective alternative to an optical TDR.

Oscilloscopes measure voltages on EIA-232 and EIA-422 interfaces. Spikes and lows in your voltage can cause severe equipment damage.

SNMP

Simple Network Management Protocol (SNMP) provides a mechanism that enables network administrators to collect data from network components and develop an overall picture of network conditions. SNMP is most often implemented over TCP/IP. UDP (User Datagram Protocol) port numbers 161 and 162 identify SNMP agents and traps, respectively. But SNMP messages can also be delivered with TCP, HTTP, or non-Internet protocols like IPX or AppleTalk.

> **NOTE**
>
> Because of the nature of UDP (connectionless), it doesn't clog the network with management traffic by reissuing a failed SNMP packet; it simply retransmits the request at the next interval.

SNMP-based management platforms are probes/agents you can use for troubleshooting tools; they alert you to problems like excessive packet errors or bandwidth overload on a segment. SNMP standards are associated with MIBs: Management Information Base-I and -II standards. MIBs define the contents of the agent software; they store information about devices in a network.

MIB (the agent) runs on a managed device, and SNMP transfers the information between the MIB and the Network Manager. SNMP gets the value from the agent, gets the next value from the agent, sets a value in the agent, and allows the agent to send a trap to the network manager. The values represent information about the device's functions, such as bandwidth utilization. What this arrangement does is enable the Network Manager to query the MIB agent for configuration or status, make changes on the agent, and acquire reports from the agent when there's a problem (trap). Examples of traps include a device reinitializing itself with or without the possibility of a configuration change or a failure in a device's interface.

SNMP is available on most NOSs, including the SNMP daemon in UNIX, the SNMP Service in Windows NT, and the SNMP NLM in Novell over IPX or IP. Each NOS also includes a subset of the MIB specification as part of its SNMP agent.

RMON

RMON (Remote network MONitoring) uses probes and agents to gather data and store that data in RMON tables. The probes (hardware RMON) and agents (software RMON) can produce statistics, graphs, and perform trend analysis. You can use these probes and agents to troubleshoot problems as well. RMON components run all the time and so they collect the data leading up to a network event; you can use these components to find out when and where problems first occurred.

RMON hardware probes can collect a month or so of data, depending on the configuration. You can use this data to create a baseline for your network. Some of the types of data RMON can collect include statistics such as packet size, history and periodic samples, alarm generation, MAC addresses, a list of the most active devices, and so on.

You configure RMON probes or agents to collect the specific information you want, for instance, collision or utilization statistics. You then can use a third-party application to graph the information. You can also configure the RMON alarms to report when certain thresholds are reached.

Before implementing RMON, make sure your device—hub, router, bridge, or other—is compatible with RMON; if it is not, the RMON will use more resources than intended. Also, don't implement all RMON services at one time or on all segments, for the same reason. Finally, when you purchase RMONs, make sure you also obtain enough memory to store sufficient data amounts.

General Network Troubleshooting

Your first step to finding and solving a network problem is to verify that there is a problem. Often, users report problems that are the result of an error on the user's part or the user's misunderstanding of how an application or process works. Asking the users for a complete explanation may seem to be the way to go, but as you most likely know, the explanation may not be helpful or accurate. You might try asking the user questions to verify there is really a problem. You might want to form a help desk or help team to verify network problems before you get involved.

LAN segment problems can be grouped into three categories: physical layer faults caused by electronic linking devices, network loading faults caused by a device that can't keep up with the demand, and network protocol faults caused by devices that cannot communicate or pass traffic on.

When troubleshooting your network, you'll figure out your own way of working and steps to take to locate the problem. For network configuration problems, you might first check all physical network connections; make sure all adapters and drivers are configured correctly; check for hardware-specific conflicts; and check with any network operating system monitors or third-party add-ons to make sure you haven't caused the problem yourself.

When you have trouble with connectivity, you might try checking cable connections, NIC installation, resource conflicts, device driver installation, protocol configuration, and shared access. This appendix offers ideas and hints for troubleshooting your network and devices quickly and efficiently.

First Steps

No matter what a user tells you about a problem, you or an assistant should physically check the device before going too far in your diagnosis. Users are notorious for saying they have checked that the computer was plugged in; then after hours of checking network connections, an administrator discovers the computer's plug was loose. So the first step to take with any device—computer, printer, router, monitor, and so on—problem is to try a physical check of the machine, printer, peripheral, or other device.

1. Make sure the machine is plugged in and the power is on.

2. Check the network cable and connector to make sure they are firmly connected to each other. Do the lines physically connect to the computer at one end and to a wall jack at the other?

3. If you're using Ethernet (10BaseT transceiver), make sure the link light is on. If it is not on, check the following:

   The cord connecting the machine to the wall is okay; replace it to see.

   The Ethernet cables or transceiver might be bad, loose, or not turned on.

   The jack isn't wired correctly or not activated.

4. Restart the machine. Often that will fix a problem. If the problem reoccurs after rebooting, then you need to check further.

   Next, try swapping parts. You might swap a keyboard, for example, with another to see if a computer's keyboard is bad. To determine whether it's the network or a computer (or other device), try these things:

1. Try a new cable or patch cable.

2. Swap network jacks if possible (if the machine is close enough to another jack).

3. Try a second, near-by machine by testing its connection to the network.

IP Network Problems

If you're running an IP network, problems can arise from misconfiguration of the target or source computers. Other problems might result from the Domain Name Services as well. Following are some steps to take to locate problems on a TCP/IP network.

1. If connection isn't possible to any machine by name—such as humbleopinions.com—try using the IP address (172.16.11.103, for example) instead. You might try it in a Web browser or use Telnet. If you can connect using the IP address, the problem is with the Domain Name Server.

PING

PING is a simple program that makes very basic connections over an IP network. If the target machine responds, PING alerts you that the machine is live; otherwise, PING returns a message saying the machine is unreachable. If you can PING a machine, it indicates the network path, including routers between you and the machine, are up and functioning; PINGing doesn't mean that the machine is fully functional. PING is supported by AppleTalk, TCP/IP, ISO CLNS, Novell IPX, and Banyan VINES.

The syntax is as follows: PING *(optionalparameters) ipaddress* or PING *(optionalparameters) hostname.* Following are the parameters you can use with PING:

-a   Resolves IP addresses of destination systems into host names.

-n *count*   Transmits the number of Echo Request packets specified by the *count.*

-l *length*   Sends Echo Request packets containing the specified *length.* The default is 64 bytes; the maximum is 8192 bytes.

-t   Causes PING to send continuous Echo Request packets until interrupted.

-f   Prevents the Echo packets from being fragmented by gateways.

-w *timeout*   Sets the timeout interval in milliseconds.

You also can test a TCP/IP installation with PING, even if you're not connected to a network. The reserved address 127 is used for a loopback address. Any transmission sent to the IP address 127.0.0.1 is returned to the address that sent it.

NOTE

Trace (and Tracert) enables you to determine the specific path taken to a destination and where packets are stopping. Trace is supported with TCP/IP, ISO CLNS, and Banyan VINES.

2. Try to connect to the same address from a different machine, to determine whether the server is the source of the problem.

    If the server is the problem:

1. Verify the address and name are correct for the server.

2. Check to make sure the server is up and running.

3. Check the router on the server's subnet to make sure it is up and running. Use PING.

    If the problem is on the user side:

1. PING or Telnet the local router from the user's machine. If the PING is successful, the user's network configuration is likely correct (do check the gateway setting) so it's likely a network problem.

    If it's a network problem, PING the server's router. If the PING is successful, it's probably local to the server's network. If the PING is not successful, verify the user's gateway configuration.

2. If you cannot PING the local router, check to see if the router is up, check the local cables, jack, hubs, bridges, and such.

3. Try pinging the user's local router from a different location. If you can't PING the router, then the router is down or its path is blocked. If you can connect to the router, then PING the user's machine from this other location.

    If you can PING the user's machine, then it's likely a configuration or hardware problem on the user's machine.

    If you cannot PING the user's machine, then check the path between the router and the user's machine.

AppleTalk

AppleTalk is the Macintosh networking protocol. Generally, AppleTalk networks are segmented into several zones. A zone is a partition that is associated with one or more network segments. Users access the AppleTalk services through the Chooser. Every AppleTalk network segment has an AppleTalk network number to make it easier to identify the subnet and the network transport used by the AppleTalk devices.

In UNIX, you can use the utility Atlook to query devices within an AppleTalk zone. Atlook identifies the AppleTalk network number, service name, and service type on the network. The syntax for the command is:

    Atlook <zonename>

atpinger is the AppleTalk equivalent of the UNIX PING command. To use atpinger, follow this syntax:

    atpinger "device name:devicetype@zonename"

Use quotes to enclose embedded spaces between names, for example.

InterPoll, a Macintosh program, enables you to perform similar diagnostics to atlook and atpinger by identifying a zone of interest on the AppleTalk network. You can then select the device to PING from a list.

UNIX

nslookup is a UNIX command that queries a DNS server for the machine name and address information. The command syntax is:

nslookup ipaddress

nslookup machinename

If you're trying to improve system performance, you could disable the remote who, name, route, or time daemons. If you disable rwhod, then the rwho and ruptime commands won't work. If you disable named, the /etc/hosts must list all the hosts on the network that connect with TCP/IP.

You can run the netstat command to verify the presence of TCP/IP interfaces and activity. It provides basic information about how much and what kind of network activity is going on. Without arguments, netstat lists all active network connections for the local host. Use the netstat -i command to see which interfaces are currently configured. You should see the loopback interface plus one interface for each network card or serial line interface on the system. If you do not see the loopback interface, reconfigure TCP/IP with the Network Configuration Manager. If you do not see a network card that you know is there, reconfigure the card.

Windows NT

NT also includes the netstat command. When you install TCP/IP to Windows NT, you also install Microsoft's UNIX integration tools, which include FTP, Telnet, rexec, rsh, PING, netstat, route, ipconfig, and others. The netstat service is a command-line utility that works the same way as the UNIX command, from the NT DOS prompt.

NetWare

When you need to diagnose network communications problems with NetWare, follow these basic steps:

Check the configuration settings and network numbering on the server and workstations to see that they are correct.

Check network numbering on the network; you must use a unique IPX external network number. Also, on a network segment, each node must have the same IPX external network number and a unique node number.

Make sure servers and workstations are using the same packet frame type (Ethernet 802.2 or 802.3).

> **NOTE**
>
> Keep an error log; add a screen dump when an error occurs so you can document problems for the next time.

Bottlenecks

A bottleneck is the slowest component in the network, the component causing an abatement of the traffic flow. You must consider the entire network, from one end to the other, to find the bottlenecks. You must find and eliminate all bottlenecks in the system; however, fixing one bottleneck usually uncovers another, so this may be a difficult job.

By building the network so that all parts work at maximum efficiency, you can eliminate many points of diminished capacity. Some of the server components that can be improved upon in this area are the central processor, hard disk, video card, memory, and the network card. Naturally, all attached network equipment can be possibilities for bottlenecks as well.

Following are a few devices and areas in which you may find bottlenecks; naturally, you'll need to check with the device's documentation and/or manufacturer for specific information about that device.

Servers

In a server, there are three main areas where bottlenecks occur: memory, processor, and disk. Memory problems occur when more than one program is run in memory and the server doesn't have enough actual memory to complete the process. An operating system that makes use of paging or memory swapping can boost performance considerably and help alleviate bottlenecks.

Disk bottlenecks happen when an application performs a large number of disk accesses quickly. A hard disk must complete one I/O request before starting the next request, so when multiple requests are sent to the server, they start to queue, which slows the server considerably. Finally, a processor can cause bottlenecks when multiple concurrent tasks require concentrated processor time. A multitasking operating system increases the likelihood that the CPU will become constrained.

Software Programs

How a software application is written may cause a microprocessor to slow if the processor is frequently required to stop what it's doing and jump elsewhere in the program. More delays can occur when the processor isn't able to process a new instruction until a current instruction is completed.

Image Bottlenecks

Increased traffic to a server, as when multiple users access image documents to their workstations, can slow the server down. Using higher-bandwidth networks, such as ISDN or ATM for imaging, will not usually increase performance because of the workstation's limited ability to accept and decompress high-speed image data from the network. Problems with traffic may also occur over low-speed modems using telephone lines to access images.

Suggested solutions may be a document management systems application or screen overview files. These solutions will help to ensure that the user retrieves the appropriate document before downloading instead of downloading files he or she "thinks" are correct.

Document management systems normally handle image documents as well as other application objects, like spreadsheets, word processing documents, and so on. You might also try an application that enables you to display full-page images in a window as minipages, or thumbnails.

Also, consider using a magnetic disk for image storage and retrieval. Jukeboxes may cost less per megabyte, but they are slow devices that must physically load platters into a drive before image access can begin. Magnetic disk caching is a bit faster; however, since there's no way to predict which files will be accessed next, you still can't guarantee a faster access rate. Again, using a third-party application to create compressed minipages that are stored on magnetic disks may help speed the process and prevent bottlenecks.

Bandwidth

Bandwidth bottlenecks could be causing your problems, but first consider the speeds of other equipment, such as your desktop and workgroup switches. For example, if you switch your desktops over to 10Mbps and workgroup switches to 100Mbps, your backbones may become overwhelmed. Similarly, applying higher-speed network cards to your workstations may cause the network to become overloaded. Try to limit the available bandwidth by reducing the number of switched 100Mbps ports on the desktop to forestall the need to add expensive switches or wiring.

> **NOTE**
>
> Policies can help regulate your users' use of the system and alleviate many bandwidth problems. For example, limit the forwarding of huge presentation files, graphic images, humor messages, and so on. Restrict the size of attachments of multimedia and image files that users can send. Also, since most email messages are sent between 8 A.M. and 9 A.M., around noon, and again between 4 P.M. and 5 P.M., ask users to vary the times they send their messages to help lighten the traffic problems.

Alleviating Bottlenecks

You might try using third-party applications, such as performance optimizers or server monitors, to track server usage and locate the bottlenecks. Often you can use additional hardware to alleviate a bottleneck as well. Larger hard drives, extra memory, more powerful CPUs will help. Additionally, some advances in technology can help to make your system's performance more efficient. Consider the following advances:

- CPU/IO buses are accelerating up to 100MHz.
- SDRAM (Synchronous DRAM) is available to match the higher bus frequencies; soon available are SLDRAM (SyncLink DRAM) and RDRAM (Rambus DRAM).
- New Intel CPUs address L2 caches over a private bus to keep traffic off the main I/O bus.
- New systems are moving the graphics controller off the PCI bus to a private channel called the AGP (Accelerated Graphics Port) to quadruple the graphics throughput.

  Also consider the following when trying to eliminate bottlenecks:

- Symmetric multiprocessing (SMP) servers
- Massively parallel processing (MPP) servers
- Clustered servers

Computer Problems

There are many methods of troubleshooting equipment. Trial and error is one way to find the causes for problems, for example. Switch out a network card, change the configuration, and try something else until you see what works. This approach works well in some cases—say, when you have traced the problem to a specific machine and you know it is likely the network card that is bad; but this approach is not purely trial and error because you first traced the problem to the network card.

Pure trial and error is not a good approach to troubleshooting your network because you may never locate the problem. Networks are so complex, there are so many things that could go wrong that experimenting with parts and pieces won't work well for long.

Instead, you must use your knowledge to apply a methodological approach to identifying the source of a problem. As you gain more experience about your network, this approach will become second nature to you. With this approach, you might try defining the parameters of a problem. Ask, for example, does the problem affect workstations, servers, routers, bandwidth, and such, and how often or how long? Use this as a way to narrow the scope of the problem.

Booting and Start-Up Problems

If a device fails during POST, it could be a configuration problem. If you've made changes to the disk configuration and you're using SCSI devices, make sure the devices are terminated properly. Also, check that the bios is enabled on only the first SCSI controller, if at all. Then check for IRQ conflicts.

If you haven't made changes to the disk configuration, check to see the controller cards are seated properly, the cables are properly connected, and the disks are all powered up.

Following are some NOS-specific ideas.

UNIX

If you have a problem with booting the server, you might try power-cycling the affected device or the system to clear disk or controller problems. Turn the device off and count to 10 before restarting to give the internal capacitors time to discharge.

When you have trouble with terminals, here are a few things you can try: See if you can undo the last thing the user did, if he can remember what it was.

Press Ctrl-Q, then press Ctrl-S, the pause key, the screen key, or other keys to see if the user accidentally hit a key that temporarily stopped output.

Check the baud rate in the terminal settings (Setup menu).

Try entering the reset command; if that doesn't work, enter Ctrl-JresetCtrl-J.

Windows NT

You can always reinstall NT if you have a problem; choosing the fix installation option almost always corrects the problem. However, reinstalling takes time and you may have to reconfigure users, groups, print servers, or other important settings. Before you reinstall, try the following:

As your computer boots, it displays the message "Press spacebar now to Evoke the Last Known Good Configuration." Press the spacebar and choose to start the computer, using the configuration that was used the last time you successfully booted the machine. From the list of choices, choose Switch to the Last Known Good Configuration. If you shut down normally after this, the configuration is saved.

If this didn't work, try using the emergency repair disk you created during installation. Reboot the computer, using the floppy disk and follow the directions onscreen. The repair disk has information based on your initial setup; now users, permissions, or other changes you've made to the system will be applied.

If you've changed video drivers and cannot view the screen because of it, restart the system. When the computer displays the boot loader screen, choose the option NT Server (VGA drivers). The system will boot with generic video drivers; go to the Control Panel and double-click the Display icon. Choose the appropriate driver.

Finally, if you think the system has corrupted files, you can use the repair process in the NT Setup program. Insert the original Setup boot diskette in the floppy drive and the NT CD in the CD drive and restart the computer. When the text-based screen appears asking if you want to reinstall NT or repair the files, choose to repair files. Follow the directions on the screen.

NetWare

When you're having server hardware problems with NetWare, you can run diagnostics on the server to check for conflicts in interrupts, memory addresses, I/O ports, DMAs, and such, if you've added new hardware. Otherwise, you may want to use LANalyzer, MONITOR.NLM, SERVMAN.NLM, or another diagnostic program to check the system board, memory board, memory chips, and so on.

Serious problems with the operating system usually result in an abend (abnormal end) message. Abend messages may be caused by consistency check errors, insufficient memory, DMA conflicts, or hardware and software interrupts.

Consistency check errors, the primary cause of an abend message, might be caused by a corrupted operating system file, corrupted drivers or NLM program, or a hardware failure. Also, the errors could be caused by static discharges, power surges, and so on. When you get an abend message, try rebooting the server first. Check the memory, then the system board, power supplies, and other hardware you may need to replace. Make sure all drivers and NLMs are the most current versions.

You can also try unloading individual NLM programs, rebooting, and repeating the steps that led to the abend message to eliminate the NLM causing the trouble. If you still have the abend problem, you might try reinstalling the operating system from the master disk.

VREPAIR.NLM is another option for checking the integrity of data on the volume, directory, and file levels. Use this NLM to fix problems on volumes that won't mount. If volumes do mount but you still think there is a disk error, you can dismount each volume one at a time, and run VREPAIR on each. To run VREPAIR, follow these steps:

1. Disable logins and remove all users from the system. Volume must be dismounted.

2. Load VREPAIR using the syntax:

    load c:\directory/vrepair

3. Choose number 1, to repair a volume. Choose the appropriate volume if prompted. Make sure you make notes as VREPAIR reports errors.

4. Run VREPAIR on the same volume as many times as it takes to clean up all errors on the volume.

5. Mount the volume and re-enable logins.

SCSI Troubleshooting

Common disk faults may be caused by various physical problems. A connecting cable between a controller and drive may be loose or split. Connecting cables shouldn't be pinched or stretched. Check for matching pins; the cable orientation should match pin 1 on the controller with pin 1 on the drive. You might even check for slight oxidation of the bus slot connectors, which would decrease conductivity; clean the contacts and reseat it if necessary.

Make sure controller boards are properly seated in their slots; check power connectors for each drive. Make sure your SCSI devices each have unique IDs, including the controller. And always check your drivers; corrupted or out-of-date drivers can also cause problems.

When having trouble with SCSI devices, it's important to check the termination of the device. Terminators are used to provide the correct impedance at the end of a cable. Too-high or too-low impedance causes noise on the cable that can corrupt signals. Passive terminators are resistors with the right resistance value for the cable; active terminators are more sophisticated and maintain better impedance. Use active terminators whenever possible. Check SCSI cables to make sure they're not longer than they need to be. Check I/O and Interrupt conflicts.

Memory Problems

Memory problems cause a computer to crash randomly and inconsistently. You must make sure you're using at the least the recommended amount of RAM for your server computers. Also check that the memory is well-seated in the memory slots. Loose memory will cause problems. Here are some tips:

Make sure the actual memory speeds match the timing settings in the BIOS.

Check all jumpers; check documentation to make sure it's the right type of memory and that there isn't a limitation to how much memory the motherboard or CPU can handle.

IRQ Address

When your system experiences a conflict of resource usage, the result is usually that all adapters and devices involved stop functioning. You can identify which devices on the system have overlapping resources, then change the configuration of one or more of the devices until the conflict is eliminated.

The IRQ (Interrupt Request) is one likely culprit when a device doesn't work. This problem will only pop up when you install a new device or change the configuration on an existing device.

There are a limited number of available IRQs, and no two devices can share an IRQ. An IRQ conflict stops the device from working until the conflict is resolved. Following is a list of IRQs for common devices, although any computer may use different IRQs than those listed. Ideally, you should have written documentation of each computer's IRQ settings, along with other pertinent information like computer brand, memory, operating system, and so on.

IRQ	Device
0	System timer
1	Keyboard controller
2	Second IRQ controller or floppy disk controller
3	COM 2 (serial port)
4	COM 1 (serial port)
5	Hard disk controller
6	Floppy disk controller
7	LPT 1 (parallel port)
8	System clock
9	Available (network)
10–12	Unused
13	Math coprocessor
14	Hard disk controller
15	Unused

An unused IRQ can be used for sound cards, network cards, or other added devices. Generally, the operating system will assign an unused IRQ to a new device, but sometimes conflicts arise.

Performance Problems

Prevent performance problems by planning for capacity. If you know you will be adding more users in the near future, plan for that possibility now instead of waiting. You must implement a robust network design that can support applications and fault tolerance. This may mean you'll need to divide LAN segments with switches for better performance or simply upgrade network interface cards. Consider other methods of boosting performance, such as a more powerful server or clustered servers. Using RAID devices can also help; in addition to making your system more efficient, RAID can also help make it fault tolerant.

Monitor and tune the performance of the network infrastructure, using measurement tools. You must continually monitor the network. Any time a change is made—new server, new router, new users added, for example—

monitor and then tune the performance. Using LAN analyzers and other network management tools can help.

Locating a Problem

Is the problem static or dynamic? Does it occur all the time (static) or only during some peak busy period (dynamic)? Meet with users and discover the exact nature of the problem.

Look for the possible cause. Dynamic problems usually point to resource problems (shared network bandwidth or host CPU cycles); dynamic problems are typically found in the shared parts of the infrastructure, such as the network or servers.

Network problems occur within the network segments—interconnecting routers, switches, or gateways. Server problems involve memory, CPU, or disk I/O resources. A dynamic problem arises when the requested resources exceed the available resources.

Static problems are harder to solve because there is no obvious resource limitation as with dynamic. Static problems can generally be linked to network or system design problems—such as insufficient bandwidth, insufficient memory on clients or servers, inadequate CPU processing power, or internal bus and disk I/O problems. Also the excessive size of data elements or executables can cause a static problem. When you find the problem, decide whether you need to redesign the application or if hardware upgrades will help. Using third-party tools to monitor clients and servers may help with analyzing the area of concern.

Power Problems

Common problems that are power related include line noise, power surges, spikes, brownouts, and blackouts. Line noise is caused by random electrical impulses that ride on top of the standard power waveform. Electromagnetic interference and radio frequency interference can cause line noise. Line noise can produce defective data transfers from the CPU to disk, printing errors, power supply damage, and static on monitors.

Power surges (increases in voltage greater than 100 percent of the normal level) can overstress power supplies and lead to damaged PCs. Spikes are power surges with large increases in voltage of a very short duration and usually caused by lightning or utility switching. Spikes can damage hardware; large increases in voltage can cause a dramatic increase in the current that overheats sensitive computer components.

Brownouts occur when voltage levels decrease to under 80 percent of the nominal level for more than one AC cycle; a brownout usually lasts less than five seconds. A blackout, or extended power loss, shuts a network down completely. Either could corrupt the server's RAM or hard drive head.

Power Protection

You'll need to appraise your network before buying the hardware you need to meet the network's power protection requirements. Don't forget to check the power outside of the facility as well. In an inventory of all network components, log the type, number, and location of all components and whether they're attached to modem lines.

Where would the likely problems arise? Telephone lines may take lightning hits, for example. Determine the likely problems for all areas of the network. Next, estimate the component replacement costs, risks for data loss, and so on. Now you can decide which components need protection.

Network equipment such as your servers, desktops, modems, CSU/DSUs, terminal adapters, routers, switches, printers, CD-ROM towers, and so on, should at the very least be shielded by surge protectors. Any component that plugs in to the wall should have surge protection and voltage regulation.

As for using UPSs, you need full battery backup on your most important equipment, at the very least. When deciding which network components require a UPS, remember that advanced protection minimizes the risk of disruption and possibly hardware damage, but it can also be expensive. You'll need to weigh the costs.

Don't forget to provide internal protection against line noise coupled onto the data lines. Install dedicated line noise filters to remove line noise from the data lines.

UPS Defense

Since the most risky server operation is when data is written to a disk, a power disruption at this point could severely damage the hard drive. Naturally, any files stored in the cache will be lost if the power fails, but it's the component damage you should be most concerned with. Use a minimum of 5 minutes UPS runtime at full load (to cover most power disturbances). Then, enable data-saving mechanisms to take over before the UPS runs out of battery power. Make sure your UPSs have sufficient capacity to support your heaviest loads.

As for UPS for desktops, evaluate the operation and function of each machine; for example, if the desktop runs software that interfaces with the server, data corrupted at the workstation could overwrite good data on a server. In this case, perhaps you should use a UPS.

If the network must continue to run after the 30 or so minutes that can be supplied by a UPS, consider installing a Standby Power System (SPS). An SPS generates electricity via a diesel-powered engine. When the power fails, a UPS takes over for a few minutes. If power is still out after 5 minutes, the UPS software automatically activates the SPS. When power is regained, software automatically switches back to conventional power.

Purchasing a UPS

When purchasing a UPS, you must consider the type of system, load size, and battery life of the UPS. There are basically three kinds of UPSs—offline, line interactive, and online. An offline UPS protects the system only when a power-related problem switches the system to battery power. It provides reasonably good protection for power spikes but doesn't provide the necessary isolation for complete input protection. An offline UPS isn't suitable for servers, but it is okay for desktop systems.

A line-interactive UPS offers higher performance than the offline model because it has added voltage-regulation features. This UPS switches to battery operation if there's a significant power surge or outage. It provides adequate protection as long as the power brownouts aren't continuously fluctuating.

An online UPS provides the highest level of protection. An online UPS regenerates the electrical current's waveform and thus includes line conditioning and voltage regulation. The online UPS continuously recharges its battery, so it's always ready. Use it for mission-critical network components.

> **TIP**
> A UPS battery won't last forever. Perform regular maintenance checks.

Also, it's important to remember that even a UPS or a backup generator can fail. You should have a contingency plan within your overall disaster recovery plan that takes up where the power protection leaves off.

Cabling

There are cable testers you can use to monitor the performance of your network cables. Hand-held tools may cost a bit up front, but diagnostic tools can help you pinpoint problems such as redundant paths, poor or inconsistent cabling, and so on. Also, there are some guidelines to follow when dealing with cabling.

Problem Prevention

Wiring closets need to be well-structured and documented so that troubleshooting the network is quick and easy. Otherwise, you or a technician will have to trace cables from end to end during a crisis, which will only extend user downtime and multiply frustrations.

Since wiring isn't really a network administrator's direct responsibility, often the job of documenting and organizing the cabling closet doesn't get done. If necessary, delegate the job but make sure the cables are well organized, labeled, and mapped. It's expensive to locate cables in a crisis, to make any changes without a wiring diagram, and it slows down the IT department's responsiveness to changes within the organization; the wiring closet becomes a bottleneck.

You can use a CAD-oriented approach to diagramming the cable layout; a cable management application, though, is difficult to learn and to set into place. You must get all of the data into the cable management applications for it to work properly, and there are potentially hundreds of thousands of pieces of data between the users, backbone pairs, data ports, jacks, and horizontal cables.

You or the installers should have made up a cabling diagram during installation; that's when cable pairs are tested. If for some reason, you didn't get a diagram with your installation, you may want to consider this a job for outsourcing.

Avoiding Cabling Problems

Follow these guidelines to avoid cabling problems:

Use the best wire you can afford (UTP, Cat 5, for example). Use wiring blocks, modular connectors, and such, that exceed the quality of the cable.

Keep wire twisted for all pairs to within one half of the termination for Cat 5 installations. Strip cable sheaths to no more than one-half inch back.

Don't run voice and data on the same cable. Terminate voice and data to separate punch down blocks and racks and label the racks.

Keep the minimum bend radius for cables to 10 times the cable diameter. Don't overtighten cables.

Be careful with terminations; provide a tight twist up to the termination point at the punch blocks, wire plates, and connectors.

Don't route cables near motors, fluorescent lights, or power lines.

Use short patch cables for more Near End Cross Talk.

Never use untwisted cables or flat telephone cables from the wall plate to the PC's NIC.

With UTP, some common problems include reversed, crossed, or split pairs and shortened and open conductors. Keep an eye out for poor-quality cable connectors, too many terminations, and/or too long a cable. Also watch that your outsourcer is not using poor-quality cable, mismatched cable types, or the wrong types of cables.

Network Technologies

Each network technology has its own problems and inefficiencies. These technologies are so complex and so sensitive to changes in the system that you could actually be slowing your system down when you think you're improving it. If you are having trouble with your Ethernet, token ring, FDDI, or other network, you might try some of the suggestions that follow, but do consider an outsourcing expert to help you optimize performance and troubleshoot your problems.

Ethernet

There are a few rules you should adhere to when you're designing, upgrading, or servicing a network. When using Ethernet, make sure you keep in mind its distance limitations: 385 feet per run. Also, a common problem with using Ethernet is to overload a segment. As network traffic increases, the network starts to suffer. Overloading the number of users on a segment can mean longer response times and even corruption of large files during saves. Sometimes users' connections are also dropped.

Traffic above 30 to 40 percent of the maximum causes performance on the segment to degrade. As more traffic appears on a segment, the likelihood of collisions is increased. When packets collide on an Ethernet network, it retransmits them. The more collisions, the more retransmissions, the more traffic, the less throughput. A good rule to follow is to limit the number of users per segment to 12 for maximum efficiency.

Another likely problem on an Ethernet network is overlayering, whereby you use more than four layered hubs and/or switches. You must carefully plan your layering, since it can cause bottlenecks in the connecting links between hubs and switches.

Additionally, watch for redundant paths on your network. Ethernet doesn't support multiple data paths; Ethernet will transmit the data over two or three paths, even if they are the same. Redundant paths might be caused by a jumper cable connecting two hubs together that were already connected via a separate hub or router.

Certain errors tend to center around different types of Ethernet networks. Following are a few things you might run into:

Link errors occur on 10BaseT networks when there's a bad connection between the hub and the NIC; check the adapter, the hub, and the cable.

CRC (Cyclic Redundancy Check) errors happen when data frames have collided and data becomes corrupted. Again, check the adapter, hub, and cable.

The wrong size of network frames can cause long or short frame errors and cause collisions on the network. Check for the wrong network drivers or a poorly configured network card.

Constant collision errors may occur when a terminating resistor is damaged or missing (10Base2 and 10Base5 networks).

Late collision errors sometimes occur when a LAN cable is too long—check your cable lengths.

If you find errors or noise on your Ethernet, use a TDR to find unterminated cables; check host cables and transceiver cables for damage or termination problems; or look for a noisy transceiver attached to a host.

If there is excessive noise on the network, check cables for damage.

When you have no link integrity on 10BaseT, 100BaseT4, or 100BaseTX, make sure you have four pairs of wires available for the 100BaseT4 instead of only two pairs; check for any differences between the hub and the card; and check for the cross-connect cables.

Token Ring

In order for a node on a token ring network to communicate, it must be in possession of the token. Frames can be transmitted by a node once it obtains the token. Nodes receive the frame and examine it for a destination. If the frame belongs to the node, it copies the data into its buffers; if not, it passes the frame on.

Token ring is highly fault tolerant because it uses two twisted-pair wires; one pair is a backup path. Token ring also uses a number of special-purpose frames for control and error detection. For instance, a soft error report frame is generated when an error condition exists, such as when a connection is temporarily broken or when an NIC is failing.

When a node doesn't detect network traffic—as happens when the cabling is bad or an NIC has gone bad—it emits a beacon error frame. If your token ring has more than one ring, you should isolate the ring containing the beaconing station. Then disconnect the beaconing station to see if the problem goes away or if the next node sends a beacon. Check the upstream stations and their physical connections until you locate the fault.

Following are some more problems to keep an eye out for:

If a node doesn't have the buffers to process data coming in from the network, it generates a receive congestion error. Bridges' or routers' reporting this error consistently means you should divide the ring into two or more rings to relieve the congestion.

If a server emits congestion error frames, it could be because of a poorly configured network card or because the server is too heavily used. First, try a higher throughput network card, such as a bus master or LAN streaming token ring card; if that doesn't help, add a server.

Token ring jitter—when incoming signals have shifted frequency outside of acceptable limits—generates a frequency error frame. This could be caused by bad cabling, failing NICs, radio frequency interference, or a long cable run.

If the token ring is nonfunctional, determine the status of the interface; if the interface and protocol are not up, check the cable from the router to the MAU. If the number indicates the interface/line protocols are up, use PING between the routers to check the connectivity. If the router doesn't respond, check the ring specification on all nodes on the backbone to make sure the ring speed is the same on all.

If the ring speed is mismatched, check all nodes attached to the backbone; they should all be configured the same (4 or 16Mbps).

For a duplicate MAC address, use a network analyzer to check the Duplicate Address test frames from a booting station. If the station gets a response, then another station is already configured with the MAC address of the booting station. You'll have to change one of the MAC addresses and reinitialize the node.

For a congested ring, insert the router during an off-peak period; if it's successful during off-peak but unsuccessful during peak load, you need to segment the network to distribute traffic.

Be Careful When You Troubleshoot

When you troubleshoot token ring, you must be careful; some paths can lead to a system failure. If you're unsure of the path to take, get technical help for troubleshooting and/or providing solutions. Although many of the following symptoms may be due to hardware component failure, others are system failure symptoms that you should take seriously.

A ring station, group of ring stations, or the entire network is hanging.

A ring station cannot access ring resources, such as the file server.

The entire network is operating slowly or network logon failures are occurring.

A particular set of network operating system features on the network file server is not working.

Access to a database, fax, communication, or print server is not available.

A host connection connected by means of a gateway on the local ring is not accessible.

FDDI

If you have a nonfunctional FDDI ring, determine the status of the interface. If the interface and line protocol are up, use the PING command between the routers to check connectivity. Also, check the MAC addresses of upstream and downstream nodes to make sure they are correct. If all zeros appear in any of the address fields for these nodes, a physical connection is most likely the problem. Check connections at the patch panel using a TDR or light meter.

If an upstream node has failed and a bypass switch is installed, the signal may be degraded because bypass switches don't repeat as normal transceivers do. Check the upstream node to see if it's working.

Printer Problems

If you're having printer problems, first try the general troubleshooting steps as follows:

1. Physically check the printer:

Make sure the printer is turned on.

Check that it is online.

Check the paper to be sure the tray has paper, is positioned correctly, and there are no paper jams.

Make sure the toner or ribbon is positioned correctly and ready to use.

Check all power cords to see that they are firmly plugged in to both the printer and the wall outlet.

Turn the printer off and then back on again to reinitialize any internal settings that may be corrupted.

If all of the previous checks are okay and the printer still doesn't work, try running the printer's self-test. If the test fails, the problem is inside of the printer. If it passes, try using Print Screen from DOS; if that fails, the problem is in the relationship between the printer and the computer. Check the cable and cable connections; try replacing the cable. If Print Screen succeeded, the problem may be with the application or its configuration.

If you're still having trouble, try printing from a Windows program and again from DOS to see if the problem is operating system-based. If the printer outputs, then the problem is not the network; therefore, it may be a print driver on the workstation that's configured improperly or even the wrong driver installed or it could be the page setup as well. First, clear the print queue, and then look at workstation setup. Check the printer driver in Windows and in DOS and check for proper printer type and port. Check page margins and printer settings and make any adjustment. Try printing again.

If you're still having problems, check the print queue to see if the job is making it there; if your job is not in the queue, make sure the user is logged on to the network. If the user is logged on, check to see if the queue is properly captured (in NetWare). Does the user have sufficient network rights to print? Perhaps the user is not using his own machine, for example. If the print job does make it to the queue, check the job status for ideas. If the status is ready, the printing problem isn't related to workstation setup.

2. Macintosh: Check to see if the user can see AppleTalk zones. If not, physically check the user's machine and then try a network component swap on the user's machine. Then perform a general AppleTalk network check.

   PC: Novell or Windows NT—Verify the user can connect to the server; check user's account information; perform a physical check of the user's machine and a network component swap.

3. If the problem is with the printer, try the following:

   Print another document to see if the original document was corrupted.

   Print the original document to another printer to see if the problem is with the printer, connection, or document.

Print the original document from another machine to the same printer. If the printer is not the problem, you may have a bad network connection for the first machine or the first machine may be misconfigured or have corrupted software.

4. If there's still a problem, you might try an IP network check or follow some of the guidelines that follow.

Troubleshooting Laser Printers

The first list in this section describes the common causes to many problems; the rest of the section discusses problems in more detail.

Fuzzy output could mean a dirty corona wire or you're running out of toner.

Horizontal lines or splotches may mean a damaged or dirty print drum or roller.

If images are disproportionately long or short, check the paper's surface. Too smooth or too heavy paper can cause problems of this sort.

If the printer doesn't go online, you could have a faulty control panel or bad cable. Power the printer without the cable and if it goes online, suspect the cable as the problem.

Speckled print is probably caused by the corona grid, a part of the toner cartridge. Replace the cartridge.

White streaks on the page may mean the toner isn't equally distributed. Remove the cartridge and rock it gently from side to side and try again.

If the network printer goes offline for no reason but works fine when you reinitialize it, your problem could be static generated by specialty papers. Ground the printer properly.

Faint Print

Faint print conditions may indicate the toner cartridge needs to be replaced, naturally; but there are also other problems that can cause the print to be light. The paper finish or moisture content could cause the problem; make sure the paper you use is made for the laser (electrophotographic) printing process.

Two other possible solutions are as follows. If the print density is not set properly, adjusting it transfers more toner to the drum. The transfer roller may need to be replaced or reseated.

Faulty Registration

Registration describes how the image (text, picture, and such) is placed on the page. In color printers, it describes color placement; in black-and-white printers, it may indicate the placement of items in accordance with the edges of the paper. If you're having trouble with registration, consider the paper first. The surface of the paper may be too smooth for the roller to move through the paper path. Try a different paper to see if that is the cause.

If the pickup roller or the separation pad is worn, this could also cause registration problems. Alternatively, driver gears may be worn or dirty or the paper tray may be preventing the paper from moving through the printer.

White Streaks

White streaks down the page may be indicative of several printer problems. If you've checked the toner and that yields no success, try cleaning the lenses within the laser/scanning device. If they're blocked with paper pieces or just dirty, that could cause the problem. You may need to replace the lenses if you cannot clear the path. Finally, the laser shutter may also be blocking part of the beam by not lifting at all or by sticking.

Repetitive Defects

If you notice defects at intervals, such as dirty specks or blocked type or images, suspect the toner cartridge is damaged. If the drum and roller in the cartridge have a problem, the printed page will show it every 2 to 4 inches on the page. If this is the case, replace the toner cartridge.

A faulty fusing assembly or fusing roller could also cause repetitive defects. You'll need to clean the fusing assembly or perhaps replace it. Dirty rollers along the paper path may also cause this problem. Check and clean all rollers along this path.

Image or Print Distorted

If the print image is distorted—characters are too tall or too short—the paper may not be moving at a uniform speed. This could be caused by a drive mechanism problem. Check the transport rollers for wear, the toner cartridge, drive gear assembly, main motor, and fusing assembly.

If the image is askew, the input sensor may not be sensing the presence of paper. Replace the sensor to alleviate this problem. Alternatively, if drive gears are excessively worn or dirty, erratic paper movement might result. Clean and replace the gears as necessary.

Holes in the Printed Image

If your printed image—text or pictures—has holes, or voids, in it, you might want to check the paper type first. Some paper surfaces are just too smooth for laser printing. Also, wet or damp paper can cause this problem Try a different paper first to see if the problem continues.

If you still have voids in the image, check all rollers for dirt, stray paper pieces, and so on.

Other possible cause: The laser shutter may be defective. Check to make sure the shutter has full operation. Or fusing could also be the culprit; replace the fusing assembly.

Troubleshooting Dot Matrix Printers

Following are some ideas for troubleshooting dot matrix printers:

If you're having trouble printing jobs from the computer but the printer's self-test is okay, check the dip switch settings, make sure you have the appropriate drivers installed for the application, and/or check the cable.

If the printer has both a serial and parallel connection and one connection isn't working, change cables to try the other connection. If one works and the other does not, the problem could be with the port.

When the thermistor, the part that keeps the printer from overheating, goes bad, the printer may shut down and recover frequently.

For double-spaced output when you expect single-spaced, reset the dip switch(es) that control Carriage Return and Line Feed.

For poor print quality, first check the ribbon. Also check the print head spacing; if the head is too far away from the platen for the paper thickness, you'll need to adjust the spacing. If you still have problems, clean the print head with a cotton swab dipped lightly in alcohol.

Troubleshooting UNIX Printers

If you've installed a printer but nothing prints, check the printer's documentation to make sure you're using the right cable. Naturally, check all connections; but also make sure you've specified the right port in the configuration file or commands. If the line is serial, it should be deactivated in /etc/ttys or /etc/inittab.

Make sure the queue is properly configured by sending a file to it and making sure something appears in the spool directory. If you see nothing in the queue, you may have the protection on the spooling directories wrong.

You might try removing and reading the queue. Sometimes an invisible character can thwart printing, and this cleans out the queue. Also, aborting the current job may clear things up and power-cycling the printer will usually clear most device hangups, even though you'll lose the job that was printing at the time.

Other Print Problems

There are other miscellaneous problems with some printers that may be caused by an application, fonts, or the data being printed. Following are some things to check if the printer doesn't perform properly.

If a job has trouble getting to the print spooler, there may be a conflict between an application and the network. Check to see if the application has its own print spooler. Other possible print buffers include the PC, the printer, and the network; you should only use the network print buffer. Generally, all buffers work together, but sometimes one buffer waits for another and that slows things down. If that happens, use only one buffer.

Multiple users sharing one printer may cause trouble; printing various fonts, images, or using specific settings may slow the printer or lock it up. It's a good idea to include limits for unusual settings, fonts, and large images in your printer policies. You might also designate one network printer to these special circumstances; or you could attach a local printer to the user or department needing to print specialty items.

Applications sometimes enable users to send printer control codes that reset a printer and interfere with network operations or network printer control codes. If the print output is garbled or looks like garbage, you should find the offending application and reconfigure it not to use printer control code commands.

Finally, multiple users have different requirements for paper. The easiest way to handle these needs is to get printers with different paper trays, or specify certain printers to use the specialty papers.

Client Problems

Problems with clients can be many and varied. Often users like to change the configuration of their computers, add software or shareware without first asking permission, delete files without thinking, and so on. Also, if the client computers are not secured, there may be many different users on each computer. Each user might configure his or her own settings, add viruses or corrupted files to the computer, or intentionally damage hardware or files.

It's important to establish limits on your client support. If you form a clear set of policies that outline what users may and may not do, what software they are not allowed to install, the guidelines for using the network, and so on, you can limit your responsibilities to troubleshooting workstations. However, if you want your users to be able to work, you'll have to support them even when they go against policy; but maybe the policies will curtail their enthusiasm and lessen your work somewhat.

Depending on your network operating system, there are many ways to solve those problems. Following are a few ideas for common issues; check your documentation for more detailed and diverse solutions to specific problems.

Inhouse Clients

Network client computers may experience a variety of problems, as will any other device on your network. You can use the operating system's help and documentation, however, to help troubleshoot general computer problems.

The first step is to make sure the workstation functions as a standalone computer. It should boot, run programs, print, and so on, without attaching to the network. Only after you confirm the computer can boot and operate on its own should you tackle network problems with the workstation.

As the computer boots, make sure you watch for error messages, especially as it loads network drivers. Also, make sure you check the application software on the workstation. Many times, an application causes a problem by trying to write files to a directory that it shouldn't—on the network, for example, or to a directory to which it has no access.

Windows 95/98

To troubleshoot a Windows computer, boot it into Safe Mode by pressing the F8 key during the boot sequence. Select Safe Mode with Network from the Boot menu. You might also bypass startup files to further troubleshoot the system.

NICs

If you have trouble with your network adapter card, check the Plug-and-Play mode. Some NICs won't work with Plug-and-Play so you must disable PnP for that card and enable the jumpers on the card to get it to work. And Windows cannot modify the resource settings of non-PnP hardware. Symptoms include boot problems, connection problems, and shutdown problems.

Booting problems could occur if your NIC is in conflict with another device. Check IRQs in the Device Manager. If you can't locate an unconflicting value for an NIC setting, you may have to modify the configuration of another device to free up a resource for the card. Remove the adapter from the computer and then boot up; check the device manager and reassign the other device. Make sure it works before you install the NIC and try again.

Windows NT Server

When you create drive mappings in a Windows 95 DOS session, they carry over to the rest of the Windows environment but newly created search drives do not. As soon as the DOS session is terminated, the search drives are lost. Global search drives can be created in a login script.

Drivers that conform to the NDIS 2.x and 3.1 versions work fine with Windows 95; however, NDIS 3.0 drivers do not.

Windows will not bind a protocol to a client that it can't use, but all compatible components are cross-bound. Don't bind protocols to clients or adapters to protocols unnecessarily; it will consume system resources.

NetWare

When installing a client for Novell NetWare, use the Microsoft-supplied client if possible. The Novell client can cause problems with Windows 95; but Microsoft's works very well. If you plan to use NetWare/IP, however, you'll have to use the Novell client since Microsoft's client for NetWare Networks doesn't support it. NETX and VLM client files do not ship as part of the Windows product.

If you have trouble communicating with a NetWare network, check the Frame Type auto-detection mechanism. Auto-detect can choose 802.2, 802.3, Ethernet II, token ring, and so on. This setting must match your NetWare operating system configuration. Locate the setting in the Network dialog box, IPX/SPX Protocol Properties dialog box.

Using SAP advertising feature in the File and Printer Sharing for NetWare services can cause huge increases in the overall SAP traffic on a network. More traffic will naturally slow the network speed and use more precious bandwidth.

When using the NDS service to connect to a NetWare 4.x NDS tree, you must enter the full context names. Without the full context, the service cannot locate the appropriate server.

Verify that IPXODI.COM, LSL.COM and the MLID are all loading properly when the computer boots. If not, check the NET.CFG file for errors. You might try updating the MLID for the adapter.

Windows NT Workstation

If you have trouble with an NT Workstation on an NT Server network, check the documentation. Here are just a few problems you might run into:

Don't let RAS clients specify their own IPX addresses because of security risks.

The FTP, Telnet, and rexec utilities all use unencrypted passwords sent to remote systems; each can be the source of a security risk.

If the client has trouble connecting to the DHCP server on the network, check the TCP/IP Properties dialog box on the client; any parameters, even those that are grayed out, can keep the client from using DHCP.

A multihomed computer can only use one Scope ID, no matter how many NICs are installed. Using WINS doesn't change when a different adapter is selected; but using DHCP makes it possible for the IP addresses of different adapters to include different Scope IDs.

UNIX

FTP transfers usernames and passwords over the network as unencrypted cleartext. Hackers attached to the network could sniff and capture FTP logins.

If the client has trouble using FTP to go through a firewall to the Internet, check ports 20 and 21 to see if they are enabled.

If NFS (Network File System) is misconfigured, it can allow any user on any system access to the entire UNIX file system. Be careful.

X program error message "cannot connect display" may mean several things. First, try to run the application locally; if that works, the XServer is working correctly and the problem is likely in the remote X application. If it doesn't work, then the XServer software may be misconfigured.

NetWare

If you have trouble with the Microsoft Client for NetWare, make sure the NWLink protocol is enabled (Control Panel, Services icon).   If it is started, check the Event Viewer, System log, for information related to any errors or problems.

If you cannot get authentication on your preferred server, make sure you have permission from the system administrator; next go to the User Manager on the client (Start, Programs, Administrative Tools, User Manager).   Choose the user's name and select User, Rename. Change the Windows NT username to the NetWare username and close the dialog box.

If users specify None as a preferred server, NT logs on to the nearest available server. If you notice servers are crowded and connections to a particular server are slow, check to make sure users are logging on to a preferred server to balance out the traffic and to keep from overloading any one NetWare server.

If a print job isn't showing up in the Print Manager when the network printer is captured, the NT username and password aren't matching the username and password for the preferred server. Use SETPASS from a DOS prompt to change the user's name and password on the NetWare server.

Remote Access Problems

If you have many telecommuters, mobile users, or remote offices, you may discover bottlenecks at the LAN connection. If you're using 10Mbps Ethernet technology on these connections, that is your first problem. With heavy remote access usage, you'll need Fast Ethernet or FDDI to best serve your users' interests.

Other factors can contribute to network bottlenecks:

- An inadequate number of connections for use by remote users

- The bandwidth amount assigned to each connection

- Multiple remote offices

- Poor performance from the connection

For WAN connections, you should use ISDN, T1, or other similar service for fast connections and fewer bottlenecks. Naturally, the connection you get depends on the number of remote users and the type of transfers they will normally be making; but it's important to acquire the appropriate services and connections to avoid network bottlenecks.

LAN connections can also be slowed for office users if you do not have the appropriate connections for remote users. A bottleneck may form, for example, when remote users connect from a T1 or ISDN line to a 10Mbps Ethernet connection on your LAN. You must add bandwidth to take care of these areas.

Internet Troubleshooting

Many of the TCP/IP troubleshooting methods mentioned previously can be used to troubleshoot an Internet connection. PING, trace, and so on, can help you locate the source of problems. If you have trouble with routers, firewalls, CSU/DSUs, or other such equipment, you should check the device documentation and/or call the vendor's technical help line. Similarly, problems with connections, ISP servers, and such, are the service provider's responsibility. This section covers some general problems your clients may encounter and solutions for those problems.

In general, you check the computer's configuration, check for conflicting software, and make sure the modem or other device is in working order. Make sure everything is plugged in and turned on; check cables connecting your LAN or users to the Internet.

Modem Check

If you and the client are using a modem, check the following things:

The modem is on and the cables are working.

You can hear a dial tone, the modem dialing, a phone ringing, and the handshake.

The modem works with other programs.

The modem works with a different number.

> If you can't get the modem to dial, then it may be a bad modem or cable, loose plug, or bad modem initialization string. Make sure a phone number is entered into the software configuration.

Can you log in or have you been logged in automatically?

Can you connect?

> If not, you should verify the correct username and password are being used. If your password and username are accepted, you have connected. Start up a browser to test the connection. Enter specific addresses to make sure the connection is working.

Does the connection run for a few minutes and then die?

> Check the modem initialization string, make sure there is enough disk space and memory on the computer, try running the modem at a lower speed, try a different modem, and make sure the connection isn't just timing out from inactivity.

General Connection Problems

Following are some general solutions:

Make sure you have the area code correct. Also, check your TCP/IP configuration—IP address, default gateway, DNS servers, and so on.

If there is excessive traffic and multiple packet collisions, use a protocol analyzer to examine the traffic. Determine bandwidth utilization.

If you have trouble accessing the Internet, try pinging routers, firewalls, and the Web server to determine which device, if any, is down.

If there is a problem connecting to an Internet server using a domain name, try the IP address to see if it's the DNS that's not working.

Try disabling software compression; sometimes it can cause problems with communicating over the Internet.

Macintosh Client

Following are some things to check on a Macintosh client trying to connect to the Internet using MacPPP or FreePPP:

Make sure the correct protocol is highlighted.

Check that PPP is in the Extensions folder.

Check the Connect Script folder to verify there is nothing in the connect script.

Check the Config, ICP Options, and LPCP Options to make sure the timeout settings are not too short.

Trash the PPP preferences file and reconfigure ConfigPPP.

Check the baud rate for appropriate settings.

If the modem isn't initializing, change the initialization string to AT&F or AT&F1 first; then to ATZ if necessary.

If the client is using MacTCP, try the following:

Check the PPP extensions and ConfigPPP in the control panel to make sure they are installed.

Try dialing through the ConfigPPP instead of letting the Internet application bring up the dialer.

Check the MacTCP configuration.

The MacTCP or TCP/IP files may be corrupt. Trash the MacTCP control panel, MacTCP DNR, and the MacTCP Prep files and then reinstall MacTCP; you'll have to reenter all of the configuration information.

Windows 95/98 Client

After checking the modem, disabling call waiting, the com ports, and such, you can check the following:

Make sure the Connect to the Internet as Needed option is checked in the Internet Properties dialog box.

Try dialing the connection using the icon in the Dial-Up networking box instead of automatic dialing.

You might need to download the Kernel32 patch from Microsoft if you consistently but intermittently receive a "Can't negotiate compatible set of network protocols..." error. This problem is caused by Windows 95 memory leak.

Check to make sure there is only one occurrence of Winsock.dll on the hard drive. Find any extras by first using Start, Find, Files, or Folders. You want only one copy of the winsock.dll in your C:\Windows directory and another copy in the C:\Windows\System\Backup directory. Rename all others something like winsock.old.

Check that there is only one TCP/IP installed for dial-up networking and that it is configured correctly. You can have one TCP/IP for dial-up and one for network card, but you can't have two for dial-up.

Reboot the computer to see if that helps.

You might try, if all else fails, uninstalling the dial-up adapter and the TCP/IP protocol and then rebooting the computer. Then try reinstalling them again.

Windows NT Workstation

If you're using a digital modem, you may need to dial the connection manually for it to work. You should also apply Service Pack 2 or later from Microsoft and apply the fix for digital numbers. To apply the Post Service Pack Hotfix, ras-fix, download it from Microsoft's site. Check the Readme.txt to find out which version you need to download and apply the fix according to directions.

Web Troubleshooting

Following are a few of the common errors your users might get when using the Web:

"404 Not Found"   This error appears when the page doesn't exist. The cause may be a typo in the address or that the actual page setup or address has changed. Generally, you can work your way back from the page designation in the address and get to the Web site; perhaps from there you can find something similar to the original request.

Say the page address is http://www.humbleopinions.com/index.html and you get a 404. In the URL, remove the /index.html and try again. This will take you to the Web site if it still exists.

"Forbidden"   Often means the page you're seeking isn't properly configured to be readable by everyone. There's very little you can do about it, since it's the owner's responsibility.

"No DNS entry for..."   May mean the DNS service is down or the server has changed addresses. If you know the IP address for the page, type it in place of the name address. Other reasons may be the TCP/IP stack isn't present or is malfunctioning, temporary network problems such as accessing the Internet through the firewall, or the requested site may no longer exist. If the user can reach another remote site without a problem, the TCP/IP stack is probably working; if not, reboot the computer and try again. You can also try pinging the host to see if the name really exists.

Email Problems

First, try to send problem emails at least twice before you try to troubleshoot. The problem could be low disk space, network lag, or other temporary situations that will clear up within an hour or two. Next, verify the recipient's address; sometimes a simple typo can cause the problem. And always read the entire error message when it is returned to you. Following are some common email errors and tips for troubleshooting them:

Error	Possible Solution
Undeliverable mail	Use Finger or Whois, for example, to verify the recipient's address.
Local configuration error	Find an alternate address; or try emailing the recipient's mail administrator.
Looping message detected	Verify the recipient's address.
System timeout during mail transfer	The recipient's server or network may not be functioning; try PINGing it.
Bad host name	Try PINGing the host name to see if you can reach the system; you might try Fingering to verify the host name.

Commands

There are various methods of verifying accounts or checking remote addresses. PING, Finger, Whois, Telnet, and so on, are all possibilities, depending on your operating system and that of the remote system.

Finger   Finger (UNIX) can help verify email addresses by looking into an address book on remote systems to locate the user's ID, UNIX shell, last time mail was checked, and so on. Not all sites permit fingering but most ISPs do. Most corporate sites do not. To use Finger, this is the syntax:

Finger (options) users

Options include such parameters as the following (all are not listed):

Option	Description
-b	Omit user's home directory and shell from display.
-f	Used with -s to omit the heading.
-l	Force long format (default).
-q	Show quick format (requires an exact match of the username).
-s	Show short format.

When you install TCP/IP to Windows NT, you also install the client-side Finger utility (part of Microsoft's UNIX integration tools along with FTP, Telnet, rexec, rsh, PING, netstat, route, and ipconfig). The finger service is a command-line utility that works the same way as the UNIX command from the NT DOS prompt. The syntax is nearly the same:

Finger (options) users@computer

Whois   Whois (UNIX) enables you to search an Internet directory for a person, login, handle, or host machine. Enter:

Whois (option) name

Whois (option) host

The option precedes the name with a modifier such as an exclamation point (!), period (.), or an asterisk (*) to limit the search to the name of the person, the handle, or an organization.

Headers

Learn to read your standard Internet message headers on email. Headers can help you diagnose all sorts of email problems, such as mail bombing, spamming, and messages sent to the wrong address. The key to the header is the Received area. Received headers are appended to the top by each host that relays the message. If a sending machine gives its real domain name to the next machine in the chain, the name outside of the parentheses and the name inside should match. If they do not, then perhaps a spammer obtained a throw-away trial account and sent a single copy of the message with a large number of blind carbon copy addresses.

The Received headers should go back to the source and stop; sometimes though, you'll get extra lines in which the actual domain name and claimed domain name disagree. This is a diversionary tactic to disguise the true origin of the message. Don't trust any Received header after the first one with a name discrepancy.

The From header includes the address that the sender claims the message is from. No checking is done, though, to see if the address is valid. Most bulk emailing programs forge this field. The address could be from an innocent victim drawn at random for the spam. The To header may not bear the recipient's address, especially if you're a receiver of one of many blind carbon copies. The Comments header usually states that the sender's identity has been authenticated, but can also be forged.

TASK LISTS

Administrator's Task List

The administrator's list of tasks is long so you may want to divide tasks among different assistants in your company. Following are tasks divided into different categories to help you.

Administrators in General

Keep apprised of new products and technologies—read trade magazines, get to know vendors, value-added resellers, and such.

Have backup help—like a help desk or consultant—for times when there are problems you can't solve inhouse.

Keep users informed via email, intranet, newsletter, memo, or other method of changes and additions to the network, policies, software, or any other matter affecting them.

Have users notify you when they need training.

Centralize support and administration staff to cut down on paperwork, superfluous work, and so on.

Listen to your people about problems, support, hardware, and ask their ideas for solutions.

Make sure support for remote users is as good as it is for inhouse users.

Outsource support for suites software, remote access, cabling, or any other task(s) you don't have the time or expertise to perform inhouse.

Design and build the network for growth, scalability. Think about fault tolerance, load balancing, and so on.

Use license metering tools to ensure you're purchasing the amount of software that you need.

Keeping Logs and Records

You should keep a running record of all past failures and their causes. You can use the information in planning your next deployment or modification and for preventative measures. Often, solutions are forgotten unless a record is kept.

List failures as:

- Hardware
  - Server
  - Client
  - Network component
- Software
  - Server OS
  - Client OS
  - Application
- Administrative error
- User error
- Accidental error
- Sabotage
- Virus

Inventory and Organization

In order to organize your network—for security, easier troubleshooting and upgrades, backing up, and for a host of other reasons—you should keep an inventory, or logbook, of information about the following components of your network:

Company sites and locations.

Servers' and workstations' manufacturer, model, serial number; computer's location, monitor brand and specs, keyboard type, and mouse type.

All computers' internal configuration: motherboard, processor speed, amount and type of RAM, number and type and size of hard disks and controllers, floppy drives and sizes, CMOS information, computer BIOS manufacturer and revision numbers, and so on.

Cabling and external connections.

Firmware information on RISC-based computers.

Disk subsystem information: makes, models, and serial numbers of disks and controllers.

Map of SCSI subsystem: SCSI configuration information, which devices are terminated and how, SCSI ID and physical location of SCSI devices.

Operating system installed applications, users' names, any special additions or custom-made applications or equipment.

Sound card, video card, network adapter cards: manufacturer and model, IRQ addresses, jumper and/or DIP switch settings, DMA, I/O ports, and such.

Zip and/or CD-ROM drives types and speeds, manufacturer and model, location, drivers, port connections, and such.

Modem: manufacturer and model, location, speed, drivers, port connections, and so on.

Other attached peripherals: printers—manufacturer and model, specifications on memory, font cartridges, printer fonts, ports and cables, and so on. UPS specifications, tape drives, and any other add-ons.

Existing network connections and hardware: cabling, NICs, hubs, and such.

Networking protocols and configuration settings.

Peripheral information, including UPS, CD-ROMs, printers, modems, and so on.

User information: needs, skills, security data, and such.

Applications: server installed, limits and sensitivity, licensing, shared possibilities.

Internet connection information: IP addresses, gateways, name servers, and so on.

Outsourcing and technical support contacts: contact's name and phone number.

Documentation for all hardware and networking equipment.

Backup information: devices, scheduling, storage area.

Insurance policies.

Information on kits, tools, and add-ons you've installed.

Internal documentation like policies, procedures, training guides, and so forth.

Troubleshooting history (time, date of problem, error messages, events logged, and outcome).

Phone list of who to call for specific emergencies: administrators, vendors, management, and critical users.

System Disk

In addition to the log, keep a system disk for each computer in your company. The system disk enables you to boot a computer that won't start on its own. On that bootable disk should be system files, CD-ROM drivers, and so on. If the configuration of the computer changes in any way, the system disk should also be updated and those changes should be kept in the log.

The system disk made automatically with Windows 95, 98, and NT machines is a perfect boot disk; however, make sure you add CD-ROM drivers and any other commands (format, fdisk, and copy, and such). Those operating systems do not automatically add these necessary files to the emergency repair disk.

Following are the files that should be on a system disk:

Command.com.   From the root directory of the computer or you can format the disk as a system disk.

Configuration files.   Autoexec.bat, config.sys, registry (DAT files), and any ini files.

Network startup files.   VLMs from NetWare workstations and DOS disks for servers with server.exe and startup.ncf, so if the DOS partition is damaged, you can still get into the NetWare partitions.

CD-ROM drivers.   Copy the files to the same directory on the backup disk as is listed in the config.sys file, for example. The statement in the config.sys file that refers to your CD-ROM drive might be device-high=c:\qulogic\q151dos.sys, for example. Create the qlogic directory on your floppy and then copy everything in your qlogic directory from C to the floppy as well.

It's important that you use the same computer for making the system disk that you will use the disk on. Do not, for example, make a system disk with a Windows 95 machine to use on a Windows 98 computer; it won't work right. Also, when an NT computer creates an emergency repair disk, it records the hardware, configuration, and other information about that specific computer on the disk; that disk should only be used on the computer you used to make it.

User Guidelines

You should create sets of user guidelines for various procedures and processes, depending on your network and the work you do. Following are some examples:

Set up virus checking procedures.

List standard software and hardware for company use.

Explain the process for deploying new software or upgrades.

Outline the procedure for user support, help desks, or other technical information.

Define hardware, software, and configuration standards.

Create a list of contact phone numbers, sites on the Net, books, and such, for users.

List procedures for Internet, intranet, or extranet use.

Outline the proper use of passwords.

Also, for administrative assistants and/or managers, list guidelines for administering access to the system, antivirus procedures, and provisions for auditing backups. Create a set of procedures for users and a more technical set for managers, assistants, and so on.

Deploying a Network

When you're preparing to build or upgrade a network, you should follow certain steps to make sure you don't forget anything. Following are some steps to take; you may need to add some steps of your own.

Order the server and/or hardware needed to prepare the system.

Contact and contract with any support personnel needed for deployment: network consultants, technical support contracts, outsource contacts for ISDN or channel lines, Internet support, and so on.

Collect applications and data for use on the server: make backups if necessary, create new data if necessary. Set teams to the task of gathering any other data or information you'll need, for example, online catalogs, web pages, and such.

Identify all groups and users that will use data on the server. List users, departments, applications, and resources they need.

Prepare a list of managers, administrative assistants, and/or interns to help you deploy or otherwise complete preparations. Assign leaders for preparing and implementing any training that users will need.

Notify users of the changes that will take place; a staff that is kept informed of impending changes will less likely panic when all is said and done.

Prepare documentation for deployment, including technical specifications, troubleshooting tips, contact information, and other pertinent data.

Plan networking connections (LAN, WAN, Internet) and steps to complete the task.

Plan any transitions from your current system, migration of applications, and so forth.

Design and build the network for growth, scalability. Think about fault tolerance, load balancing, and such.

Use license metering tools to ensure you're purchasing the amount of software that you need.

Client Preparation

As you prepare the network, you'll want to check workstations for possible upgrades or modifications. Also, prepare the users for the changes in the network.

Make sure the client hardware is worth connecting to the network.

Make sure workstations have an available slot for the network card.

Make sure you have necessary software for workstations: drivers for backup tape drives, sound cards, CD-ROM drives, printers, modems or modem server, optical disk drives, and such.

Check on training for users.

Distribute any policies for user review; include procedures for using and navigating the network.

Preparing and Deploying Servers

Plan the deployment.

Analyze your needs

Choose server types and NOS

Decide on the number of servers you need

Consider the networking hardware

Plan the client computers

Hire additional staff.

Hire outside help.

  Consultants

  Technical help

  Programmers

  Internet service providers

Assign administrative assistants.

  Inform

  Train

  Delegate

Define policies.

  Security issues

  Backup scheduling

  Disaster recovery

  Assistant and user training

  Prepare an FAQ and/or guidelines and distribute

  Naming conventions

Order the NOS.

  Check hardware requirements and compatibility

Order the server and/or upgrade hardware.

  Order any server applications you need

  Check licensing

  Check peripheral compatibility

  Check and upgrade network equipment

  Purchase fault tolerance disks, servers, or other

  Order outside connections and lines for the Internet

Prepare the site.

  Check physical security and server placement

  Sketch server placement

  Sketch networking equipment

       Install cabling, phone, or other connection lines

Collect information.

       Application and hardware documentation

       Drivers

       Contact numbers for technical support

       Reference materials

       Collect data, including Web page content

       Map IP addresses

Load NOS.

       Load any drivers and other needed software

Configure server.

       Create and configure user and group accounts

       Set security permissions and rights

       Create directories for applications, sharing, users, and so on

       Back up the system

Install any additional server software or applications needed.

       Back up the system

Upgrade client computers.

       Purchase new or upgrade hardware

       Upgrade operating systems

       Check network cards

Install client software.

Prepare and train users.

Test the server with a small number of clients.

Check performance.

       Optimize network and server performance

Application Deployment

Poll your managers and assistants to discover what is needed in the way of applications.

Research the market to find out what's available.

Choose which applications you will configure for network use and workstation installation.

Check the server and workstation hardware for compatibility. Upgrade hardware before installing new program.

Check other applications on the server and workstations to make sure there are no conflicts with the new program(s).

Plan a directory and file naming convention and notify all users of that convention.

Plan your security now. List users and their probable levels of access.

Write security policies dealing with applications and review these policies with all users involved.

Add a list of steps, shared directories, file naming conventions, and common tasks performed in the application to help guide users after their training is complete.

Install and configure the application software on the server.

Train any administrative assistants or managers who will work with the program and help users to complete their work.

Install and configure any client software.

Make sure users are trained and understand policies and guidelines.

Test the installation and adjust configuration. Perhaps install software to one server and a limited number of workstations to test it for a week or more.

Work out the initial bugs in a limited environment before installing the application to all application servers and workstations on the network.

Deploy to the entire network when ready by installing the software and configuring it as planned.

Monitor the application's performance and adjust the configuration as needed.

Back up the application and data.

Remote Access Administrator

You must make sure the person you choose for telecommuting is well-suited to working remotely.

Make participation in telecommuting voluntary.

Train managers and employees—telecommuting requires initiative from employees and direction from managers.

Write explicit agreements between employees and managers in which you define expected output levels, reporting requirements, time spent in the office, and so on. Review with employees and then have the employees sign them.

Plan the program well; leave no room for doubt in the user's mind as to his or her duties, responsibilities, and job performance.

Develop a telecommuting policy in which you set measurable objectives and regularly evaluate the results.

Determine remote access policies toward the equipment.

Let inhouse employees know about the policies for remote users.

Meet with remote users to discuss problems periodically.

Evaluate employee performance periodically.

Keep telecommuters in the loop when they're out of the office.

Provide a booklet or instructions on common problems and how to fix them, such as replacing a battery, what to do when the modem fails, dialing information, connection data, security concerns, instructions on making and using an emergency boot disk, and other troubleshooting techniques.

Internet Access Task List

When preparing to contract Internet access, following is a set of steps you should take:

Define the reasons you want your business on the Internet: email, research, Web page or site, and so on.

Determine the applications you'll need on both the workstations and the server.

Ascertain which users will need access, how often, and how long connect time might be for each user; then list users' names for mailboxes.

Decide which existing equipment you can use and which needs to be replaced and upgraded.

Based on initial and future bandwidth requirements, choose a connection method (56K, fractional T1, full T1, or other).

Obtain costs and timelines for delivery of needed hardware and software.

Obtain cost, figures, and timelines for installing circuit from the phone company. Check with ISPs; often they can arrange for installation of the line and get you a discount.

Ask the ISP if they require you to use a certain kind of router (so they can make fine-tuning adjustments or apply microcode updates to the router without visiting your site). Ask if the ISP supplies the router or other equipment; it's worth a try.

If you need a DSU/CSU (Digital Service Unit/Channel Service Unit) to interface between your equipment and the data line, go ahead and buy a unit that will enable you to increase the speed of the data circuit in the future to save the expense of buying another unit later down the road. You can, for example, buy a unit that lets you configure for a 56K line, a full T1 line, and anywhere in between.

Alternatively, purchase modems—analog, DSL, ISDN terminal adapters, or other equipment—that you'll need to complete the connection.

Purchase firewall and/or proxy server and install and configure.

Install browsers and mail programs to users' computers if they are not already installed.

Review your Internet and email policies and distribute to users.

Intranet Planning

Establish links with legacy applications and servers.

Increase network bandwidth.

Upgrade the network connections.

Upgrade workstation software.

Install and configure Web server software.

Prepare security safeguards.

Train administrators, content developers, and users.

Consider who will perform statistics reporting and traffic monitoring; perhaps invest time and training in two administrative assistants who can then perform these tasks when the intranet is complete.

Hire or train someone for technical support of the intranet.

Enlist managers to help you standardize messaging procedures, database access, and other network activities across departments.

Establish a rule or guideline book for designing the intranet: servers, browsers, applications, pages, and so on. Detail if, how, and where the company logo is placed, for example, or how frames should be set up, use of images, headings, links, and so on.

Publish data on the Web but also make hard copies of employee handbooks, phone lists, forms, and so on, just in case you need them. Don't totally depend on the intranet for all company documents.

Centralize IP address management; use DHCP so clients can request addresses from a common repository.

Consolidate directories on the intranet and file servers; put all user information, printer and files systems, configuration files, and application-specific attributes into a common directory.

Issue digital IDs for all employees or use cryptography keys for access control so security is maintained within the LAN.

Establish a common look and feel for the content.

Standardize servers and tools across the company.

Get commercially supported products.

Anticipate bandwidth requirements; upgrade switches; get T1 lines.

Upgrade hardware and router software.

Add servers if necessary.

Use pure intranet applications (strictly HTML or Java) only when necessary, such as for real-time collaboration. Otherwise, use existing legacy and client/server applications.

Don't forget to add management and monitoring tools.

Deploying a Web Server

Establish domain name.

Prepare content.

Contact ISP or other provider for prices, scheduling, and so on.

Prepare backend systems: databases, data management and report generation applications, transaction applications, activity reporting and tracking.

Set up a Web Server that offers user authentication, authorization, and account management.

Set up a program for Web page generation and data formatting.

Install and configure user query, transaction, and purchasing programs and/or interfaces.

Install firewalls that filter by protocol, data stream, source, and destination.

Create CGI (Common Gateway Interface) scripts and programs; evaluate periodically to make sure they're performing at optimum and upgrade these programs and utilities when necessary.

Use a cryptographic authentication system to protect your site from DNS corruption.

Change your administrative passwords once a month or so.

Document all services running on the site, such as FTP, Telnet, SMTP, and so on, and keep running logs of activities on these sites for evaluation.

Make sure you have a backup and a disaster recovery plan.

Outsourcing

Do a lot of upfront research before signing a contract; measure and evaluate performance.

Ask for references and check the references thoroughly.

Make sure the outsourcer has enough financial stability to compete and succeed.

The outsourcer should know about the latest technologies and use state-of-the-art equipment and tools.

The outsourcer should be able to provide a series of reports—both standard and custom-made—that enable you to review and monitor his or her work.

Ask the outsourcer if he or she has a help desk or other support line.

As you work with the outsourcer, you should try to determine if he or she can meet the following requirements:

Be able to easily identify problems and quickly dispatch of them and be able to see problem areas before there is an actual problem.

Be skilled and experienced.

Make a commitment to research and development of new technologies.

Form an explicit contingency plan in case the relationship breaks down.

Make sure the outsourcer understands your goals and your expectations.

Make sure you discuss and define both the outsourcer's role and your own role.

Set up milestones for the initiation of the project to be carried out in phases. A schedule will help you both in completing your tasks.

For the contract, ask the outsourcer to provide a detailed statement of the work he or she will do. A list should include each step in a process, and an itemized set of procedures should be added as well.

Hold regularly scheduled status meetings with the outsourcer to make sure things are going as planned. Also, ask for regular status updates in writing.

Ask the outsourcer to orient staff about changes in operation and/or any new techniques adopted.

Optimization

Document everything—hardware, software, network connections, user needs, problems and their solutions, heavy traffic areas, and so on.

Map out the network to document resource locations—servers, printers, Internet access, and such—and add the types of connections used between LAN segments—routers, cabling, network cards, and so on. This map will come in handy when you're examining bottlenecks and upgrade possibilities.

Poll your users and managers to find out what is important to them and where they perceive a problem with the network; after all, the users are the most familiar with slowdowns and traffic congestion.

Calculate bandwidth requirements, peak and average traffic times, capacity and throughput. Again, if this is beyond your capabilities or available time, hire a consultant.

Select the best LAN/WAN technologies for your networking situation based on your users' needs and the applications and services you offer.

Consider network growth when making any plans for modifications or additions.

Predict the behavior of the network under specific conditions. Start with the current network configuration, traffic utilization, resource requirements, and so on, and then test routing, utilization, and response times for any proposed changes.

Test the network systematically to determine how it responds to failure and change over time.

Resolve application performance or reliability problems to support current and future needs.

Prevent problems before they occur.

Standardize remote computing environments.

Identify bandwidth bottlenecks and single-points-of-failure and resolve the problems first, before rolling out a new application.

Provide detailed information about application and network behavior—time-of-the-day behavior and performance.

User's Task List

You may want to outline the use of various network peripherals and resources to users, such as printers, the Internet, storing files on the server, and so on. Also, detail the importance of passwords and virus protection; have users report problems with the network or programs immediately to their supervisor. Users should notify an administrator or manager when they need training or help with a process. Finally, users should follow outlined policies and procedures for server use, network use, backing up, printing, and other network processes.

Remote Users

Use phones and email to keep in touch with the office and your coworkers.

Be accessible in order to maintain good working relationships with all. Let others know where you will be and how to reach you quickly if necessary.

Manage your time wisely, especially at home; keep a regular schedule.

Establish physical and mental boundaries in your home. Separate office space from home space and work time from personal time. Work in a separate room; set boundaries on the others in your home as well—roommates, children, spouses, and others should respect your work time.

If traveling, protect your equipment by doing the following:

Use hotel safes to store your notebook, routers, and other expensive equipment.

Conceal expensive equipment by not using manufacturer's bags—a travel bag with Cisco Systems imprinted on it announces to technology-aware thieves that you're carrying a valuable router.

Carry your costly equipment with you on the plane, through luggage pickups, and everywhere you go so you can keep your eye on it.

Never give your password to anyone.

IP ADDRESSING

TCP/IP is great for connecting your LAN to the Internet or for inter-connection of your corporate network. TCP/IP enables you to use Internet technologies with your own intranet and extranet, for example. But more than that, TCP/IP is supported by a large number of hardware and software vendors; it's also available on many different computers—from PCs to mainframes. Most corporations, universities, and government agencies also use TCP/IP.

TCP/IP

TCP/IP (Transmission Control Protocol/Internet Protocol) was originally designed by the U.S. Department of Defense Advanced Research Projects Agency (DARPA) in the late 1960s. Because of TCP/IP's ability to connect dissimilar systems, it's become today's standard for the Internet, enterprise networks, WANs, and many LANs. Other standards have grown from TCP/IP, such as FTP and Telnet. Many vendors, such as Microsoft, even developed their own set of TCP/IP protocols for use with their operating systems and products.

Internetworking

An *internet* (with a lowercase i) represents internetwork, meaning two or more networks using different networking protocols and connected by a router. The users on an internetwork can access the resources of all connected networks. The Internet (with an uppercase I) is an internetwork consisting of more than 2 million computers and nearly 20 million users. The Internet uses the TCP/IP protocols.

TCP/IP is the standard for open system interconnection in the computer industry. It's used in government, academic, private, and public networks

> **NDIS (Network Driver Interface Specification)**
>
> NDIS provides a common shareable device interface for a number of pro-
> tocol stacks, including TCP/IP. NDIS enables multiple protocol stacks to
> work over the same network interface card by sorting incoming packets
> between the different stacks, also called *protocol multiplexing*. NDIS is
> independent of both the underlying network interface card hardware
> and the protocol used.
>
> NDIS drivers are usually available from card manufacturers. NDIS drivers
> must also use a protocol manager module that coordinates communica-
> tion between the card and various levels of drivers. The protocol man-
> ager reads packets, sorts them, and directs them to the appropriate
> stack. Check your NOS; a protocol manager may be included.

because it's compatible with various vendors, platforms, and network technologies and provides a high degree of interoperability.

The most common hardware connection for TCP/IP is Ethernet, but it will
also run on token ring, AT&T StarLAN, microwave, spread spectrum systems,
LocalTalk with a gateway, and serial lines, among others.

You need a hardware driver to run TCP/IP. Some systems have hardware
drivers built in to the system or system board. You can also get third-party drivers from Microsoft's Network Device Interface Specification (NDIS) and
Novell's ODI (Open Datalink Interface), as well as others. You also need a
TCP/IP stack, which usually comes with operating systems; check the operating
system for a compatible hardware driver before using a third-party brand.
Macintosh, for example, uses the MacTCP stack, available from Apple, and a
hardware driver built in to the system.

TCP/IP Protocols

TCP/IP is a set, or suite, of communication protocols that encompass media
access, packet transport, session communications, file transfer, electronic mail,
and terminal emulation. TCP/IP standards actually refer to over a thousand different communication protocols. Following are the more traditional services
provided by TCP/IP and some of its protocols:

File transfer.   FTP, the file transfer protocol, enables a user on any computer to send or receive files to and from another computer. Security is
enforced by requiring the user to specify a name and password; FTP
works over a modem and a phone line or over a network. It divides

information into smaller units and processes each unit in sequence. FTP also handles error detection and correction.

Electronic mail.   Using SMTP, the exchange of electronic mail between diverse systems is possible.

Management services.   SNMP provides a method of monitoring and communicating status information among a variety of hosts, such as NT, LAN Manager, routers and gateways, terminal servers, minicomputers, and mainframe computers.

Terminal emulation.   Telnet is a terminal emulation protocol that enables a PC to attach to a mainframe or other host by providing remote terminal connection services.

Printer services.   Using LPD (Line Printer Daemon) and LPR (Line Printer Remote), requests for print jobs to a specific device are granted and print status is reported. If LPD is run by a host, LPR can then print a file. LPQ (Line Printer Queue) can then obtain the status of the print queue on the host.

Figure D.1 illustrates some of the more common and useful protocols in the suite and Table D.1 describes the various protocols included in the TCP/IP suite.

Figure D.1 TCP/IP structure incorporates multiple protocols.

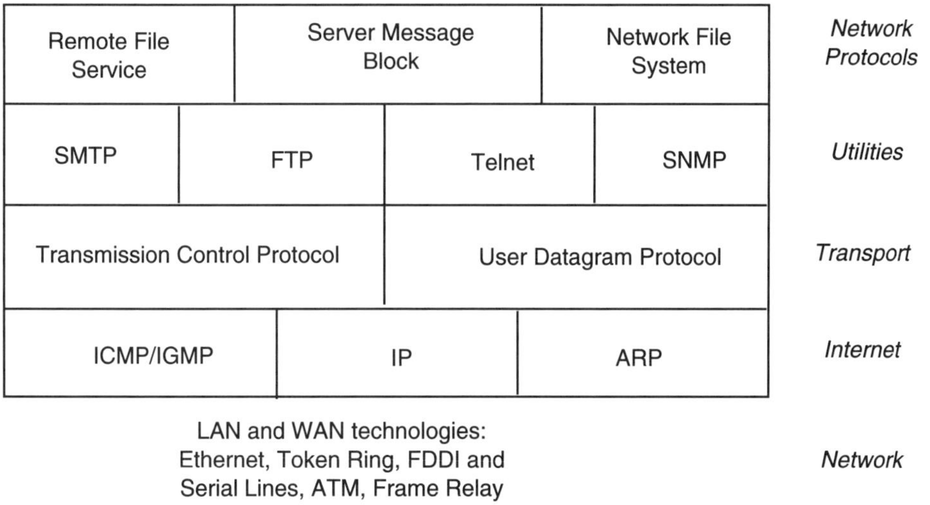

Remote File Service	Server Message Block	Network File System	*Network Protocols*
SMTP	FTP	Telnet	SNMP	*Utilities*
Transmission Control Protocol	User Datagram Protocol	*Transport*
ICMP/IGMP	IP	ARP	*Internet*

LAN and WAN technologies: Ethernet, Token Ring, FDDI and Serial Lines, ATM, Frame Relay   *Network*

Table D.1 TCP/IP

Protocol	Description
Remote File Service (RFS)	Distributed file system network protocol that enables programs to use network resources as if they were local.
Server Message Block (SMB)	Distributed file system network protocol that enables the computer to use the files and resources of another computer as if they were local.
Network File System (NFS)	Distributed file-sharing system that enables a computer to use files and peripheral devices of another computer as if they were local. NFS can run on mainframes, RISC, diskless, and PCs.
Simple Mail Transfer Protocol (SMTP)	Protocol for the exchange of email.
File Transfer Protocol (FTP)	Transfer protocol that divides information into smaller units so information can be conveyed from one computer to another over a modem and phone line or over a network; FTP also handles error detection and correction.
Telnet	Terminal emulation protocol that provides remote terminal-connection services.
Simple Network Management Protocol (SNMP)	Protocol used to manage and monitor network nodes.
Transmission Control Protocol (TCP)	Connection-oriented, transport-level protocol.
User Datagram Protocol (UDP)	Connectionless, transport-level protocol usually bundled with IP-layer software.
Internet Control Message Protocol (ICMP)	Protocol that provides functions used for the network layer management and control.
Internet Protocol (IP)	Session layer protocol that regulates packet forwarding by tracking addresses and routing and recognizing messages.

Table D.1 *Continued*

Protocol	Description
Address Resolution Protocol (ARP)	Protocol that enables the host to find the node's physical address on the same network when it only knows the local address. The NIC, using ARP, contains a table that maps logical addresses to hardware addresses.

The transmission media is the physical cabling used to carry the network information, such as fiber optic, STP, UTP, or coaxial. Also included are network LAN and WAN technologies, such as Ethernet, token ring, FDDI, serial lines, ATM, or frame relay.

NFS

NFS is a file system that consists of a client and server system. An NFS server can export local directories for remote NFS clients to use. NFS runs over IP, using UDP or TCP in some implementations. NFS is a standard for file services on TCP/IP networks on the Internet.

ARP

ARP obtains hardware addresses of TCP/IP hosts on broadcast-based networks. ARP broadcasts the destination IP address locally to discover the hardware address of the destination host or gateway. When ARP gets the hardware address, it stores it and the corresponding IP address in an ARP cache that provides address mapping and resolution.

Most entries last a very short time—10 minutes, usually—unless you add a static ARP entry to the ARP cache, thus decreasing the number of broadcasts and requests. Even at that, a static ARP address lasts only until the computer restarts, it is manually deleted, or a new broadcast indicates a different hardware address.

TCP

TCP is a connection-oriented transport protocol that works with IP. TCP provides the application layer with the ability to reliably transmit a bytestream (in a sequence of bytes) to the destination. Before data transmission can begin, a session must be established. The receiving host monitors the transmission and knows whether all pieces have been received; the host must return an acknowledgment for each segment received. If an acknowledgment isn't received, the data is retransmitted.

UDP

UDP is a connectionless, transport-level protocol that usually bundles with the IP-layer software. UDP's primary functions are error detection and multiplexing. UDP offers unreliable delivery; it doesn't guarantee delivery, so UDP is used by applications that don't require acknowledgment of data receipt. But, if the packet is ever delivered in error, the error will be detected by the use of checksum. UDP provides transport between local or remote hosts. UDP doesn't add overhead and so is sometimes used with SNMP applications.

ICMP and IGMP

IP regulates packet forwarding by tracking addresses, routing outgoing messages, and recognizing incoming messages. ICMP reports errors and controls messages for IP. ICMP provides feedback only for IP. ICMP uses checksum to check errors and verify a packet's arrival at the destination.

IGMP informs routers that hosts of a specific group are available on the network. IGMP also uses checksum. Both ICMP and IGMP packets are carried by IP datagrams and are, therefore, unreliable.

> **NOTE**
>
> IGMP is also the key to IP multicasting; it enables users to sign up for multicast sessions and enables the groups to be managed dynamically.

TCP/IP and OSI

The TCP/IP protocols correspond to the OSI Reference model. TCP/IP specifically works with the Application, Transport, and Network layers. The Network layer defines the protocols for routing the data to the workstations or other node and then moves the information across the network segments. The Network layer performs switching and routing and sends and receives frames over the network.

The Transport layer defines the transport protocols and converts the data into a format for transmission; it also performs error checking. The Transport layer ensures reliable data delivery; the Transport protocols provide communication sessions between computers. TCP/IP's two Transport protocols are TCP and UDP. TCP provides for reliable communications for applications delivering large amounts of data. UDP provides connectionless communications for applications transferring small amounts of data at one time.

Application layer defines how an application interacts with the network and other applications, including file transfer, database management, and network control. TCP/IP provides many utilities that work at the Application layer, including FTP, Telnet, SNMP, and DNS.

TCP/IP also works on an Internet layer using four protocols: IP, ARP, ICMP, and IGMP.

TCP/IP and Network Technologies

TCP/IP works with a variety of cabling schemes and technologies. TCP/IP uses each technology's frame format in a different way to transmit messages, perform error checking, and complete other functions. Following is a brief description of these technologies.

Since Ethernet is one of the most common and popular cabling schemes in use, it makes sense to talk about it with TCP/IP. Ethernet, Fast Ethernet, and Gigabit Ethernet are quickly becoming the technology of choice for LANs, WANs, enterprise networks, and so on.

Ethernet has its own method of addressing to make sure no two machines end up with the same address. Each Ethernet controller comes with an address built in from the factory. An Ethernet address is 48 bits. Additionally, Ethernet is a broadcast medium; when you send a packet on Ethernet, every machine on the network receives the packet.

Ethernet follows the Institute of Electrical and Electronics Engineers standards for Ethernet: IEEE 802.3. The standard specifies a frame structure for protocols. A frame is the basic unit of information that Ethernet transfers. The Ethernet protocol provides a specific design for the frame, including a preamble, destination and source addresses, type, and frame check.

There is no connection between the Ethernet address and an IP address. Each machine has to have a table of what Ethernet address corresponds to what IP address. There is also a type code in every header that allows for several different protocol families to be used on the same network. And there is a checksum, which provides an error checking service to determine if packets were successfully transmitted. TCP/IP uses the original Ethernet framing. In TCP/IP frames, the type field has the same function as it does for Ethernet frames; it distinguishes different protocol types.

Ethernet is a hardware and Data Link layer specification. Other software network protocols can run above this, such as IP, IPX, AppleTalk, NetBEUI, and so on. In turn, other protocols can run over those, such as TCP and UDP over IP, SPX over IPX, and so on.

TCP/IP also works on a token ring network as well. Token Ring "frames" are called *tokens*. The format of a token makes it possible for TCP/IP frames to travel over the network. The fields at the beginning and end of the frame, or token, control the token and enable the token passing. Fiber Distributed Data Interface (FDDI) networks also can use TCP/IP because the FDDI protocol is much like token ring.

Integrated Services Digital Networks (ISDN) is another technology that is increasingly common and useful. ISDN uses high-speed digital connections over telephone lines. With ISDN, PPP makes it possible for TCP/IP to exchange messages across an ISDN link. Generally, only ISDN B channels carry TCP/IP traffic; the D channel usually controls and manages the B channel.

SLIP and PPP are two Internet standards for communications over serial lines. SLIP (Serial Line Internet Protocol) allows any one client to connect to a SLIP server to provide connectivity between different IP hosts. Both systems run TCP/IP stacks for SLIP to work. PPP works similarly to SLIP but gives better throughput. PPP governs an ISDN link when it's part of a TCP/IP network.

AppleTalk provides networking to Macintosh systems and consists of both hardware and software protocols. LocalTalk is the simplest of the protocols; it provides direct connections between Macintoshes with a cable. AppleTalk can run over Ethernet (known as *EtherTalk*), FDDITalk, TokenTalk, and so on.

Other AppleTalk software protocols include Datagram Delivery Protocol, Name Binding Protocol, Routing Table Management Protocol, AppleTalk Transaction Protocol, and so on. MacTCP is a component that allows TCP and UDP applications to run over a Macintosh. MacTCP is required for most Macintosh TCP/IP applications.

ATM (Asynchronous Transfer Mode) is used for high-speed wide area networks and supports TCP/IP. ATM, however, proves to be a problem when using TCP/IP protocols. ATM is a connection-oriented technology, whereas TCP/IP is connectionless. Most of the TCP/IP standards and implementations are designed for use with connectionless LANs, such as Ethernet and token ring. It's difficult to modify those implementations for use with ATM. Additionally, ATM doesn't support true broadcasts and multicasts. Although plans are under way to make ATM more compatible with TCP/IP, it may be best to stick with traditional technologies for now.

TCP/IP and Windows

The Windows Sockets specification provides a single API (Application Program Interface) for programmers and vendors. An API defines the functions available to an application—such as managing files and displaying information on the screen—and how the application uses those functions. When Windows is involved, an API also defines functions that support icons, menus, windows, and other features of a graphical user interface.

Traditional network APIs don't meet Windows requirements, and so Windows Sockets were created. Winsock (Windows Sockets) is an industry-standard transport layer for TCP/IP in Windows environments. Winsock is available in both 16- and 32-bit versions. Winsock bridges the gap between network applications and Windows through the use of Windows-supported DLLs (Dynamic Link Libraries). DLLs are libraries of functions that link with a network application at runtime, rather than when the application is created. DLLs provide a standard application binary interface that makes it possible to create a single version of an application that will run over any DLL.

Sockets function as an endpoint for network communication. An application creates a socket by specifying a host IP address, a TCP or UDP services, and the port the application is using. Protocol port numbers enable a socket application to identify itself within a computer. Certain TCP or UDP ports must be used for other applications to communicate with the application. When a client application requests a service, the operating system dynamically assigns a port; server-side applications are preassigned ports and do not change.

Common TCP ports include FTP-21, Telnet-23, and DNS-53. Common UDP ports include DNS-53, SNMP network monitor-161, and Trivial FTP-69.

Internet Protocol

IP is a connectionless protocol that addresses and routes packets between hosts. *Connectionless* describes a model in which the source and destination addresses are included in each packet, so direct connection between the nodes isn't required; IP can then forward a packet through routers, gateways, and other hosts to get it to its destination.

Additionally, IP isn't a reliable protocol because it doesn't guarantee the delivery of a packet; nor does it require acknowledgment when data is received. Lost packets aren't reported to the sender or receiver. This is where TCP comes in. TCP is responsible for acknowledging and tracking the packets.

IP Addresses

An IP address identifies a node's location on the network. IP addresses must be unique on the network. Each address has two parts: a network ID and a host ID. A network ID names the physical network and a host ID names the server.

TCP/IP Packages

Following are some TCP/IP packages currently available.

For DOS systems:

AIR by SPRY

ChameleonNFS by NetManage

LAN Workplace by Novell

NCSA Telnet by NCSA

PC/TCP by FTP Corp.

For Windows systems:

AIR by SPRY

ChameleonNFS by NetManage

Distinct TCP by Distinct Corp.

LAN Workplace by Novell

Reflection2 by WRQ, Inc.

SuperTCP by Frontier Tech.

For OS/2 Systems:

PathWay by Wollongong

PC/TCP by OS/2

Workplace by Novell

Vantage/IP by Ipswitch

There are two formats for referencing an IP address: *binary* and *dotted decimal*. An IP address is 32 bits long and composed of four 8-bit fields called *octets*. Octets are separated by periods and represent a decimal number in the range of 0–255. If the binary format is something like 10000011 01101011 00000011 0001 1000, the translated dotted decimal notation would be 172.16.124.23, for example.

Each bit in an octet has an assigned decimal value. When each bit is converted to decimal format, the highest value in the octet is 255. Each octet is converted separately. A bit set to 0 is always a zero value. A bit set to 1 can be converted to decimal value. Low-order bit represents a decimal value of 1; high-order bit represents a decimal value of 128. The highest decimal value of an octet is 255, when all bits are set to 1.

The following table shows how the bits in one octet are converted from binary code to decimal value:

Binary Code	Bit Values	Decimal Value
00000000	0	0
00000001	1	1
00000011	1+2	3
00000111	1+2+4	7
00001111	1+2+4+8	15
00011111	1+2+4+8+16	31
00111111	1+2+4+8+16+32	63
01111111	1+2+4+8+16+32+64	127
11111111	1+2+4+8+16+32+64+128	255

IP Address Classes

An IP address is 32 bits in length and divided into two or three parts—the network address and the host address are required, the subnet address may or may not be present. Subnet addresses are only present if the network has been divided into subnetworks. The length of the network address, subnet, and host address are all variable.

For an IP address that consists of two parts—a network address and a host address—an example might be 206.148.33.5. The 206.148 is the network address and 33.5 represents the host. Other types of addresses use the first octet for a network number and the last three octets for a host number, or the first three octets as network and the last as host.

There are five classes of IP addresses and each has limited and specific uses. Briefly, the following list describes the classes:

Class A is reserved for very large networks. Values of 126 or less in the first octet indicate a Class A address.

Class B is used for medium-sized networks. Values of 128 to 191 in the first octet indicate a Class B address.

Class C is reserved for smaller networks. Values of 192 to 223 in the first octet indicate a Class B address.

Class D is a special multicast address that's not used for networks.

Class E is reserved for experimental purposes. Values greater than 223 indicate a reserved address.

Basically, you can only get Class B or C addresses, and there's really little chance you'll get a Class B address. If you ask for more than 16 Class C networks, you'll need to provide a network plan.

IP addresses use Class A, Class B, and Class C addresses. Each consists of four octets separated by decimals: 172.161.123.100, for example. Each number is called an *octet* because it's represented in binary form with eight bits. These eight 1s and 0s can be arranged in a total of 256 different ways. Each octet in an IP address can be a number ranging from 0 to 255.

The first number represents the class of the address. The other octets define something different in each class. For example, in Class A addresses, the first octet is used to define the network address; but the other three octets are used to create unique addresses for network nodes, or hosts. The fewer octets used to specify the network address, the fewer possible addresses. Class A addresses are limited to only 127, and they belong to universities and corporations.

With Class B addresses, the first two octets are used for the network address and the last two octets indicate the host addresses. Class B addresses are reserved for companies and institutions with a minimum of 4000 hosts who need at least 32 subnets. There are over 65,000 Class B addresses but they are hard to obtain.

In Class C addresses, the first three octets are for the network address; the first octet denotes the host address. Because the first three octets are used to specify network addresses, there are nearly 17 million address combinations, each of which can support 254 IP addressable nodes. This means in a Class C address, you control only the last octet, so you can assign the numbers 1 through 254 to the nodes on your network. The numbers 0 and 255 are reserved addresses.

When Class C users need more addresses because of network growth, they apply for more Class C addresses, or they can use a Class A or Class B scheme within the network. If they use Class A or B within the network, they use a translation device for communicating with the outside world because of limits put on the addresses you can use on the Internet. You cannot use a Class A or Class B address on the Internet.

Assigning Addresses

For each network and wide area connection, you must assign a unique network ID; for a class C address, the network ID would be the first three octets and the host ID would be the fourth octet, for example. If you connect to the Internet, you must obtain a network ID from the Internet Network Information Center (InterNIC). Otherwise, you can use any valid network ID. If routers connect your network, a unique network ID is required for each wide area connection.

When assigning host IDs, remember the following:

- The host ID must be unique to the local network ID.

- All TCP/IP hosts, including interfaces to routers, must have a unique host ID. The host ID of the router is the IP address configured as a workstation's default gateway.

- The network ID can't be 127, as it's reserved for diagnostics.

- The host ID and the network ID bits cannot be all 1s or all 0s.

You can assign host IDs consecutively, so they're easy to identify.

Subnetting

Subnetting the network is a way to reduce packet congestion on the wire. It's easier to subnet with Class A or B licenses because they provide such address flexibility. Subnetting is difficult with Class C addresses. Segmenting provides more total networks but fewer nodes per network.

Subnetting offers many advantages. Subnetted IP networks can be routed independently so as to make better use of the bandwidth. Subnetting also minimizes network traffic, maximizes performance, and enhances the ability to secure a network.

Each host on a TCP/IP network must use a subnet mask. A subnet mask is a 32-bit address that is used to block a section of the IP address to distinguish the network ID from the host ID. The subnet mask might be a *default* mask (used when the network isn't divided into subnets) or a *custom* mask (used when the network is divided into subnets).

You use a subnet mask when you have multiple segments to a network, such as in a LAN that has two or more offices, and therefore the network is divided into segments, or connections to the Internet. The subnet mask identifies the network on which the computer is located. Subnet masks modify the IP address by using host address bits as additional network address bits; thus, the line between the host and network addresses is moved to the right to create additional networks and to reduce the number of hosts in each network.

In a subnet mask, all bits that correspond to the network ID are set to 1; all bits corresponding to the host ID are set to 0. Splitting a Class C address into two subnetworks steals two bits from the last octet and adds them to the bits used for network addressing. That leaves only six bits to define host addresses. The universal subnet mask number used in a Class C network split into two is 255.255.255.192. Class C has 24 network address bits; Class B has 16; and Class A has 8.

Determine the number of physical segments on the network and the number of required host addresses for each segment (each TCP/IP host requires at least one IP address). Define one subnet mask for the entire network; a unique subnet ID for each physical segment; and a range of host IDs for each subnet. Also, consider your future requirements for the number of segments and hosts per segment. When you use more bits for the subnet mask, more subnets are available, but fewer hosts are available per subnet.

Default Gateway

The gateway device can be a server or other computer, a router, or other network node. The gateway acts as a bridge between two network segments enabling communication between hosts, servers, and networks. Gateways must have an IP address to route data between the segments.

IP Routing

When messages travel across a TCP/IP network, IP routers direct the traffic to its destination. Routers choose the path a packet takes by deciding which path is the most efficient. With TCP/IP, routing occurs when the TCP/IP host sends IP packets and again when the IP router sends them on to the next network. In order to make the routing decisions, a routing table is used. The routing table contains entries with the IP addresses of router interfaces to other networks.

IP determines first whether a destination host is local or remote. If the destination is local, the local routing table is checked and the packet is delivered to the destination. If the host is remote, IP checks the routing table for the route to the remote network. If IP cannot find a route, then it uses a default gateway address to deliver the packet to the next router down the line.

The next router's routing table is checked for a path to the remote network or host. The packet continues to be forwarded to another router's default gateway address until the remote host is found. If the route is never found, IP sends an error message to the source host.

IP Address Management

IP networks include the Internet and any corporate intranet and/or extranet organizations. You may also run TCP/IP on your network so it can communicate with various hardware platforms and operating systems. You must keep track of IP addresses within the corporation or enterprise. The number of IP addresses a company can allocate depends on the class of IP (see previous sections).

RIP

RIP (Routing Information Protocol) enables the exchange of routing information over an IP network. Routers using RIP exchange the network IDs of the network and the distance to the network, in hop counts. A *hop count* is the number of routers a packet will cross to get to the destination network ID. You can specify hop counts to help relieve congested links and thus direct the router to another path.

DNS

DNS (Domain Naming System) can help you manage IP addresses. DNS is a database of domain and computer names and their corresponding IP addresses. DNS works by using resolvers, name servers, and the domain name space. A resolver sends queries to the name server and the server returns the requested information (or an error message or pointer to another server); a resolver is the client. The name server is the server that contains the database of names. The name server resolves, or translates, the computer or domain name to an IP address.

The domain name space is a hierarchical grouping of names that helps to identify organizations, domains, servers, and so on. Root-level domains are the top of the hierarchy and represented by a period (.). Top-level domains include designations such as com (commercial organization), edu (educational institution), org (nonprofit organization), and so on. Top-level domains may contain second-level domains, or subdomains, that represent various computers within that domain—such as an FTP server.

DHCP

DHCP (Dynamic Host Configuration Protocol) can help you manage your IP addresses as well. DHCP automatically assigns IP addresses to computers that are configured to use DHCP services. Using DHCP means you don't have to manually configure TCP/IP on a computer; when a client requests an IP address, DHCP assigns the address, subnet mask, and any optional values to configure it to, such as a default gateway.

DHCP uses a pool of valid addresses from its database. DHCP can make configuration easier and eliminates problems from users configuring their own computers or using random IP addresses. You can define a scope of IP addresses the DHCP server can use; you can even define multiple scopes. You can also configure a DHCP server always to assign the same IP address to a client; this is called *client reservation*.

IP Multicasting

Real-time audio/video and push technologies cause the rapid consumption of bandwidth in today's networks. You can add more bandwidth and upgrade to faster networks, such as Gigabit Ethernet; but this is an expensive step to take. If you have to make do with your current resources, IP multicasting might work for you.

Traditionally, broadcast and unicast methods are used to send information to IP addresses on the network. *Unicast* is a point-to-point messaging system in which the sender's message or file goes to one recipient at a time, even if it's the same exact message or file. Unicast is good for one-on-one communications, such as email or Web browsing; it does waste bandwidth if the same packets are sent to numerous nodes, however.

Broadcasting is another method of sending messages to workstations; but with a broadcast transmission, the sender dispatches the message to all end nodes, whether they asked for the information or not. Broadcasting is inefficient because it uses up bandwidth for packets that may not be used.

IP multicasting is a one-to-many transmission technology and is therefore more efficient than unicast and broadcast. The sender transmits the message only once; the transmission is replicated and delivered to only the nodes that have been configured as members of the multicast group. IP multicasting conserves bandwidth on your network.

How It Works

In order to use IP multicasting, the sending and receiving nodes and the routers must support IGMP (Internet Group Management Protocol). IGMP comes with TCP/IP stacks; it lets the client tell multicast-enabled routers which sessions he or she wants to participate in. Transmissions are passed from router to router and then to the end nodes that are attached to the router.

IP multicasting protocols use the spanning tree topology that connects all of the nodes in a multicast group. The protocols include Distance Vector Multicast Routing Protocol (DVMRP), Multicast Open Shortest Path First (MOSPF), and Protocol Independent Multicast (PIM). The sending and receiving nodes must also support several IP multicast-enabled components, including network drivers, the TCP/IP stack, and a network interface.

If you're using IP multicasting over a VPN or through a service provider, that service provider must also support IP multicast. If the service provider doesn't support IP multicast, you may be able to use *tunneling*. Tunneling encapsulates multicast packets in unicast packets to route them through parts of the Internet that don't support multicast routing.

The members of an IP multicast group can join or leave a group at any time; they can be members of more than one group at one time; and they are assigned IP addresses from a pool of Class D addresses, which are reserved specifically for multicasting. Class D addresses occupy the space from 224.0.0.0 to 239.255.255.255 and identify host groups. Using Class D addresses means the individual members aren't tracked; IP packets are sent to the group address and so any IP multicast-enabled node has access to the transmission.

> **NOTE**
>
> Novell's IntranetWare, NT, and most UNIX operating systems (HP-UX and AIX) support the multicast technology. Routers from major vendors—Cisco and 3Com, for example—support IP multicast as well.

How to Use IP Multicasting

To make the most of IP multicasting, you shouldn't use it for messaging that is point-to-point or one-to-one, such as IP telephony, Web browsing, or email. However, many types of applications could benefit from IP multicast—audio/video streaming, push applications, and electronic software distribution, for example. The defining characteristic: Use IP multicasting when you want to transmit a large amount of the same information to many users via the existing network infrastructure.

> **NOTE**
>
> Audio/video streaming includes applications like distance learning, telemedicine, corporate training sessions, and so on.

Mobile IP

With more and more users taking to the road, telecommuting, and otherwise working outside of the office, corporate intranets and the Internet have become more important to companies. Mobile workers need to connect to IP-based networks seamlessly and independent of location. With its support of both wireless and wired technologies, Mobile IP may be the answer for mobile users.

Current Solutions

A computer with a fixed IP address cannot connect to a different subnet. Instead of assigning fixed IP addresses, a corporation can use DHCP to assign IP addresses dynamically. Unfortunately, DHCP-assigned addresses are temporary, and temporary addresses have limitations.

First, other nodes can't easily locate the mobile node because the mobile computer receives a new address each time it connects. Second, temporary addresses don't provide for roaming from one subnet to another, which is necessary for wireless LANs.

Mobile IP

Mobile IP is an extension of IP that consists of three components: the mobile node, a home agent, and a foreign agent. The mobile node is built into a TCP/IP stack; the home agent operates on the router or a workstation on the mobile node's home subnet; and the foreign agent operates on a router or workstation on the network the mobile node is visiting. The foreign agent can also operate on the mobile node under certain conditions.

The mobile node first determines, through broadcasting, whether it is on its home network or a foreign network. If the mobile node is on its home network, IP addressing and datagram delivery work normally. But if the mobile node connects to a foreign network, it uses the foreign agent's IP address and notifies the home agent of its current status. If DHCP is available on the foreign network, the mobile node can use it instead.

Traffic to the mobile node first goes to the home agent, where it is encapsulated into another IP datagram and is tunneled to the foreign agent, which sends the datagram on to the mobile node. The mobile node can send datagrams directly to their destination instead of going through the home agent. Also, when the mobile node changes location, the old foreign agent is lost until the node registers its location again with the home agent.

Troubleshooting TCP/IP

The most common problems with TCP/IP include configuration, IP addressing, subnetting, address resolution, and host name resolution. There are many diagnostic utilities you can use to troubleshoot TCP/IP-related problems.

TCP/IP and Heterogeneous Environments

TCP/IP is particularly well-suited for working across different types of hosts and different hardware platforms because it's a protocol that can be used by so many different systems. You can communicate with UNIX, OS/2, Windows NT, NetWare, mainframes, miniframes, and others, using TCP/IP. When communicating across diverse systems, an application, usually a client/server program, must be present at both ends of the communication.

Following are some common TCP/IP utilities that work in this way:

Utility	Description
REXEC	Runs a process on a remote host with password protection security. Syntax is **rexed *host command***.
RSH (remote shell)	Runs commands on a remote server without logging on; therefore, there is no password protection. Syntax is **rsh *host command***.
RCP (remote copy)	Copies files between hosts; no user authentication security. Syntax is **rcp *host.user:source host.user:destination***.
Telnet	Enables terminal emulation with user and password security.
FTP	Provides bidirectional file transfer capabilities with user and password security. Syntax is **ftp *(options) host command***.
TFTP	Provides bidirectional file transfers with no user authentication.
LPD	Submits print jobs to a printer device with user and password authentication.
LPR	Enables a user to send a print job to a printer connected to a server, with user and password security.

Your first step is to check the configuration, since this is the most common TCP/IP problem. Check the IP address, subnet mask, and default gateway of the nodes involved. Next, you might try PINGing or tracing addresses to determine whether the nodes are active and working. Start with a local router or server and PING out from there to other nodes on the network.

Diagnostic Utilities

Following are the most common utilities and a description of each.

Utility	Function
PING (Packet Internet Groper)	Lets you verify connections and configurations.
Trace	Lets you verify the packet's path.
Show	Provides information about interface conditions, protocol status, and so on.
Finger	Retrieves system information from a remote computer.
NETSTAT	Lists statistics and the state of connections.
Route	Lets you view the local routing table.
ARP	Displays the ARP cache of IP addresses and MAC addresses.
SNMP	Supplies statistical information.
Dig	Provides information about the name service.
Ripquery	Provides information about the contents of the RIP update packets on your system.
Etherfind	Analyzes the packets exchanged between hosts on the network.

PING

PING is a simple program that makes very basic connections over an IP network. If the target machine responds, PING alerts you that the machine is live; otherwise, PING returns a message saying the machine is unreachable. If you can PING a machine, it indicates the network path, including routers between you and the machine, are up and functioning; PINGing doesn't mean that the machine is fully functional. PING is supported by AppleTalk, TCP/IP, ISO CLNS, Novell IPX, and Banyan VINES.

The syntax is as follows: PING *(optionalparameters) ipaddress* or PING *(optionalparameters) hostname*. Following are the parameters you can use with PING.

Parameter	Description
-a	Resolves IP addresses of destination systems into host names.
-n *count*	Transmits the number of Echo Request packets specified by the *count*.
-l *length*	Sends Echo Request packets containing the specified *length*. The default is 64 bytes; the maximum is 8192 bytes.
-t	Causes PING to send continuous Echo Request packets until interrupted.
-f	Prevents the Echo packets from being fragmented by gateways.
-w *timeout*	Sets the timeout interval in milliseconds.

You also can test a TCP/IP installation with PING, even if you're not connected to a network. The reserved address 127 is used for a loopback address. Any transmission sent to the IP address 127.0.0.1 is returned to the address that sent it.

Trace

Trace (and Tracert, Traceroute) enables you to determine the specific path taken to a destination and where packets are stopping (the hops). Trace is supported with TCP/IP, ISO CLNS, and Banyan VINES.

Show

The *Show* command displays information about the interface conditions, protocol status, neighbor reachability, router configuration, level of traffic, errors, and more.

Debug

Debug provides information about the router and network status, but you must be careful when using debug because it can make the system performance worse instead of better. Enabling debugging can disrupt the operation of a router; consult a technical expert if you're in doubt.

IPCONFIG

IPCONFIG reports information about the basic configuration of the interface. Use this utility for detecting bad IP addresses, incorrect subnet masks, the wrong broadcast addresses, and so on. To verify a computer's configuration, type ipconfig at a command prompt.

You can use the /all switch to provide even more information, such as the host name assigned to the local computer, the NetBIOS scope ID, whether or not IP routing is enabled, and so on. Using the same switch also provides more information about the network adapter IP configuration, such as the physical address of the adapter card, description of the card, default gateway of the local computer, and so on.

ARP

ARP will provide information about Ethernet/IP address translation. Use ARP to detect systems on the local network that are misconfigured.

Netstat

Netstat provides varied information, including statistics about the network interface, sockets, and the routing table.

Analyzing Problems

If you have a large network, you'll likely want to use a network analyzer and/or a hardware tester, such as a TDR (Time Domain Reflectometer). You can also find some free diagnostic software for testing or purchase third-party software. In addition, you can ask some questions when trying to troubleshoot TCP/IP networks. For instance, is the address correct, is the configuration correct, which error message displayed, and so on? Additional questions include the following:

Does the problem happen in other applications on the host or only in one application?   If it's only one application, is it configured correctly?

Does the problem happen with one remote host or all remote hosts? Perhaps it occurs with only certain groups of remote hosts. If only one remote host is involved, the problem is likely with that host. A specific group of hosts involved means there's probably a routing problem. A problem with all hosts may mean there's a problem with the user's system.

Does the problem occur on other local systems?   If it's only a problem with the user's local system or host, then the problem is within that system. If it affects other systems, it's likely a router problem.

You should also keep a historical record of all problems, in case they reappear. Also, approach problems methodically so you don't waste your time trying to locate them. Test each possibility and systematically work through the next step. Watch error messages, talk to the user, but take what they say with a grain of salt; after all, most problems are caused by human error.

Following is some advice on how to proceed with specific problems:

If only one application on one host is having trouble, that program may be misconfigured.

If the application fails on multiple hosts when connecting to a specific remote host, the application may not be available on the remote host.

If an application fails from a different source than the TCP/IP protocol stack, it may not be compatible with the stack. This problem is seen mostly when an application is designed for a specific Winsock.dll but the stack is using a different one.

If the problem is on all local PCs, it originates from one of the devices that connects the network to the outside world.

If the problem is on one subnet, it originates from the device connecting the subnet to the rest of the network.

If the problem is on only one PC, the PC is likely misconfigured. If it's not misconfigured, use a laptop or other desktop to check the physical network link.

Unknown Host error means the problem is with the name server. If other computers can resolve the name, the PC is misconfigured. If no one can reach the host, the name may be wrong or misconfigured; try the numeric IP address.

Network Unreachable error means it's a routing problem. The remote host may be down or the path between the user's computer and the host may have a problem.

Cannot connect, No answer, or *Connection timed out* generally means the remote host isn't responding; it may be down or a link may be down. Do check the address, however, to make sure it is correct.

Terms and Definitions

Following are common definitions for terms associated with TCP/IP:

Address Resolution Protocol (ARP). AppleTalk protocol that enables the host to find the node's physical address on the same network when it only knows the local address. Under ARP, the NIC contains a table—address resolution cache—that maps logical addresses to hardware addresses. A node that needs to send a packet first checks the cache to see if the physical address is present. If the address is present, it is used and the traffic is reduced; otherwise, the ARP requests to determine the address.

Bandwidth. The capacity a communications channel has for transmission; stated in megabits per second (Mbps).

Checksum. A mathematical computation used to verify a packet has arrived intact.

Connectionless. Describes a communications model in which the source and destination addresses are included in each packet so direct connection between the nodes isn't required.

Domain Name. A name that represents a host; the name is easier to remember than the numeric IP address.

Domain Name Service (DNS). Also Domain Name System. The distributed database system that enables name mapping of hosts to numeric IP addresses.

Domain Name Service Server. The server containing the DNS database that enables name resolution.

Emulation. Using software to make a PC behave as though it were a terminal by altering the characteristics of the PC's interface.

Encapsulation. The procedure of interjecting header and data from a higher-level protocol into the data frame of a lower-level protocol.

File Transfer Protocol (FTP). Transfer protocol that divides information into smaller units so information can be conveyed from one computer to another, over a modem and phone line or over a network; FTP also handles error detection and correction. FTP supports a range of file transfer types and formats, including ASCII, EBCDIC, and binary.

Gateway. A hardware or software bridge, or shared connection, between a LAN and a larger system, such as a mainframe or the Internet. The gateway translates between two dissimilar protocols.

Host. The controlling computer in a network. The host provides services that other computers can access over the network.

Internet Control Message Protocol (ICMP). Protocol that provides functions used for the network layer management and control.

Internet Protocol (IP). Session layer protocol that regulates packet forwarding by tracking addresses, routing outgoing messages, and recognizing incoming messages. IP doesn't guarantee the delivery of a packet or specify the order of delivery.

Intranet. A corporate network that uses Internet technologies (TCP/IP, HTTP, and HTML) for distributing information and data to only the corporate network clients.

IP address. A set of four numbers, also called a *dotted quad*, that specifies the actual location of a computer on a TCP/IP-based network.

Local disk or resource. A disk or resource attached to a workstation rather than the network server; also known as *local drive*.

Multipurpose Internet Mail Extensions (MIME). An Internet standard that enables users to send multimedia messages; email applications that are MIME-enabled can send PostScript images, audio messages, and digital video over the Internet.

Network File System (NFS). Also Internet NFS. A distributed file-sharing system that enables a computer to use files and peripheral devices of another computer as if they were local. NFS can run on mainframes, RISC, diskless, and PCs.

Octet. Eight contiguous bits, or a byte.

Packet. A block of data sent over the network. A packet contains the sender, recipient, and error control information in addition to the message.

Packet filtering. Limiting the protocol-specific traffic to one segment of the network.

Packet switching. A method for routing and transmitting data packets simultaneously to make better use of the communications lines.

PING (Packet Internet Groper). A test for checking TCP/IP networks. PING uses ICMP to provide message packets to report errors and other information in IP processing.

Point-to-Point Protocol (PPP). A TCP/IP protocol that enables transmission over serial lines and telephone connections.

Port. A pathway for data to flow in and out from a computer or node.

Port number. The default I/O location identifier for an Internet application. HTTP, for example, is assigned a unique port number (usually 80) so the computer knows how to respond when it's contacted on a specific port.

Protocol. A specification that defines procedures to follow when transmitting and receiving data over a network. A protocol defines the format, timing, sequence, and error checking used on the network.

Protocol stack.   A set of protocols working together to provide various network services.

Remote File Service (RFS).   Distributed file system network protocol that enables programs to use network resources as if they were local.

Routing Information Protocol (RIP).   A TCP/IP protocol that distributes routing information on the network.

Server Message Block (SMB).   Distributed file system network protocol that enables the computer to use the files and resources of another computer as if they were local.

Simple Mail Transfer Protocol (SMTP).   Protocol for the exchange of email.

Simple Network Management Protocol (SNMP).   Protocol used to manage and monitor network nodes.

Subnet.   A logical network created from an IP address. Subnet uses a mask to identify bits from the host portion of the address to be used for the subnet address.

Telnet.   Terminal emulation protocol that provides remote terminal-connection services.

Terminal.   A device that enables you to send commands to a computer on a network. The minimum terminal is a keyboard, display screen, and simple circuitry. More than likely, you'll see terminal emulation software in a PC that allows the computer to be used as a terminal.

Transmission Control Protocol (TCP).   Connection-oriented, transport-level protocol.

Transmission Control Protocol/Internet Protocol (TCP/IP).   A set of communications protocols that enable media access, packet transport, session communications, file transfer, and more. TCP/IP is used by many vendors and computer systems.

TTL (Time to Live).   A designation of the number of seconds a datagram is able to stay on the wire before it is discarded, thus preventing a packet from endlessly looping around a network.

User Datagram Protocol (UDP).   Connectionless, transport-level protocol usually bundled with IP-layer software.

TECHNOLOGIES AND HARDWARE

This appendix covers common networking technologies and hardware. Included are telecommunications services, data communication devices, cabling, standards, topologies, and such.

Architecture and Infrastructure

Architecture defines what the system looks like, how it fits together, and the design of the network. *Infrastructure* describes the physical components of the network: wiring, routers, switches, operating systems, and so on. Both are needed for a network to function properly, and how they work together defines how efficient and effective the network will be.

Standards

Standards are important in networking and internetworking because they ensure interoperability of products and services from vendor to vendor. Data communications, telecommunications, and LAN hardware and software standards are governed by several international organizations, including:

IEEE (Institute of Electrical and Electronics Engineers). Establishes telecommunications standards.

CCITT (Consultative Committee of International Telegraph and Telephone). Develops worldwide data communications standards and publishes the standards every four years.

ISO (International Standard Organization). Establishes global standards for communications and information exchange.

ANSI (American National Standards Institute). Represents the United States in the ISO and is affiliated with CCITT; develops recommendations for programming languages, SCSI interfaces, and FDDI standards.

CCIA (Computer Communications Industry Association). Sets standards for commercial telecommunications.

EIA (Electronic Industries Association). Develops cabling standards to support multiproduct, multivendor environments.

Other standards are instituted because certain products become popular, such as IBM's PC (Personal Computer) or Microsoft's Windows. But most standards are developed to adhere to the ISO/OSI (International Standards Organization/Open Systems Interconnection) seven-layer network model. Most products, devices, software, and so on, will somehow work with and fit into at least one of the seven layers.

IEEE Standards

The IEEE (Institute of Electrical and Electronics Engineers) is a professional organization that develops computing and electrical engineering standards. IEEE 802 series are an example of these standards.

IEEE 802 is a set of standards that define LAN protocols, as follows:

IEEE 802.1 is the standard for network management and network bridging.

IEEE 802.11 is proposed for wireless Ethernet.

IEEE 802.12 is for 11VG-AnyLAN.

IEEE 802.2 is a standard for the portion of the LAN data-link protocols for use with 802.3, 802.4, and 802.5 networks.

IEEE 802.3 is the set of Ethernet standards.

IEEE 802.4 defines bus topology using token passing.

IEEE 802.5 is a standard for token-ring LANs.

IEEE 802.6 defines Metropolitan Area Networks (MANs).

IEEE 802.7 is the 802 technical advisory group on broadband.

IEEE 802.8 is the 802 technical advisory group on FDDI and fiber optics.

IEEE 802.9 is the 802 group on integrated data and voice networks.

IEEE 802.10 is LAN security.

EIA/TIA-568 Standard

The EIA/TIA 568 Commercial Building Telecommunications Wiring Standard specifies minimum requirements for cabling within offices, recommended topologies and distances, connectors and pin assignments, and the useful life of the cabling.

If you do your own cabling, you should have a handbook and follow these standards. If you're not going to do your own cabling, which is more likely, there are just a few things you should know about the standards. Following is a table of color coding for standard wiring. If your building is cabled to standard, then you can use the following tables to identify any cabling by its color.

Cross-Connect Field Colors

Color	Cable Function
Blue	Horizontal voice cable
Brown	Interbuilding backbone
Gray	Second-level backbone
Green	Network connections and auxiliary circuits
Orange	Demarcation point, telephone cable from central office
Purple	First-level backbone
Red	Key-type telephone systems
Silver or White	Horizontal data cables, computer and PBX equipment
Yellow	Auxiliary, maintenance, and security alarms

ISO/OSI Model

ISO/OSI is a networking reference model that divides network computer communications into seven layers, or *protocol stacks*. Each layer performs specific functions; each layer builds on the previous one.

Also, each layer communicates with its peer in other computers, via the other layers in its own computer. Information units each have a different name, depending on the layer. The Physical layer uses bits; the Data Link layer uses frames; the Network layer uses datagrams; Transport uses segments; and the Application layer uses messages. The term *packet* is often used to describe the information units in many of the layers.

> **NOTE**
>
> Packets, frames, cells—all are bits of data. *Packets* transfer data over low-speed, high-error–rate communications links. *Frames* are data sent over high-speed, low-error–rate communications links. *Cells* are small data bits with no error checking because they're transferred over fiber optics.

Layers

Figure E.1 shows a diagram of the seven OSI layers plus the two Data Link sub-layers.

Layer 1.   Physical layer defines the actual media used to transfer data over the network components, such as fiber optics, twisted pair cable, and so on. Some Physical layer protocol specifications include RS-232C, RS-449, V.24, V.28, and so on. Layer 1 covers speed and distance compatibility.

Layer 2.   Data Link layer describes the methods used to transfer data packets from device to device, such as tokens and codes, and controls the flow of the data. The Data Link layer organizes the Physical layer's bits into frames—a contiguous series of data. Layer 2 handles protocol compatibility. The Data Link layer contains two sublayers: MAC and LLC.

MAC (Media Access Control).   This sublayer describes how devices share access to the LAN. Since every LAN uses broadcasting, independent devices can send data at the same time, and thus corrupt the data and cause collisions. The IEEE 802 standards for LANs, specifically 802.3 to 802.5, describe the media access control: CSMA/CD, token bus, and token ring.

Figure E.1 Common representation of the OSI Reference model.

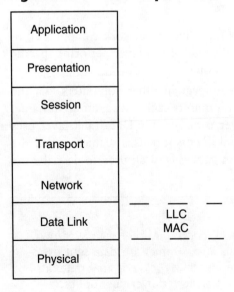

LLC (Logical Link Control). This sublayer provides transmission paths that appear error-free to the Network layer. LLC services are compatible with various MAC standards. IEEE 802.2 is a dominant protocol that implements the upper portion of the Link layer. It performs error control, flow control, and establishes logical connections.

Layer 3. Network layer defines the protocols for routing the data to the workstations or other node and then moves the information across the network segments. The Network layer enables switching and routing compatibility.

Layer 4. Transport layer defines the transport protocols and converts the data into a format for transmission; it also performs error checking. The Transport layer ensures reliable data delivery.

Layer 5. Session layer maintains a session and during the session performs security, logging, and other functions. The Session layer also handles upper-layer problems, such as lack of paper for the printer or inadequate disk space.

Layer 6. Presentation layer characterizes the way data is formatted, converted, and encoded so that the data can be understood by other computers. This layer may also compress, expand, encrypt, and decrypt data. The Presentation layer provides feature compatibility.

Layer 7. Application layer defines how an application interacts with the network and other applications, including file transfer, database management, and network control. Layer 7 covers operational compatibility.

Protocols

Different protocols characterize different OSI layers; some protocols span multiple layers, while others may span only one layer. Figure E.2 shows the OSI Reference model with several common protocols and components and the layers they fit into.

Infrastructure

A solid and sound infrastructure can mean a network with fewer system crashes, faster email, better bandwidth, and fewer problems. Building a strong infrastructure means you must invest money, time, and energy into optimizing the network. Employing industry standards, proven brands, and stable technologies will help you build a quality infrastructure for your network.

Figure E.2 Common components as they fit into the OSI layers.

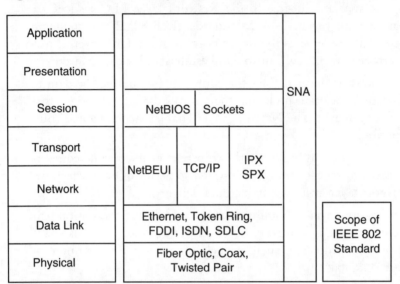

There are many types of networking hardware that you'll need to understand. You may choose to outsource the cabling and installation of the hardware, or you may supervise an inhouse employee or team. Either way, you should understand the basic concepts of networking hardware and how to fit the pieces of the network together for the most efficient performance and reliable service.

Fault Tolerance

Fault tolerance is a method of ensuring continued system operation, no matter if a server, a hard drive, or a LAN segment fails. This method may include redundant chips, circuits, hard drives, mirrored servers, and so on. Fault tolerance helps protect against the increasing costs associated with downtime. Following are some methods of fault tolerance.

RAID combines multiple hard drives so they function as a single unit, thus enhancing both performance and reliability by reading or writing multiple drives in parallel.

To use RAID with your network, you'll need a minimum number of disk drives, depending on the level of RAID you're implementing. Following are the minimum numbers of drives for each RAID level:

RAID Level	Description	Number of Drives
RAID 0	Striped Disk Array, no fault tolerance	2 drives
RAID 1	Mirroring	2 drives
RAID 2	Not applicable	
RAID 3	Byte striping with parity	3 drives
RAID 4	Segment striping with parity	3 drives
RAID 5	Segment striping with parity	3 drives

Clustered systems support an active configuration in which all servers in the cluster do useful work and provide failover services and load balancing for one another.

UPS is a battery power supply used to protect the server, router, or other equipment from power outages.

Redundant hot-swappable components—such as power supplies, fans, CPUs, switching modules, and so on—are similar to a mirrored server, taking over only if the primary device fails.

Some LAN topologies are inherently fault tolerant. FDDI is usually implemented as a dual fiber optic ring with a secondary ring providing backup to the primary one.

Hub-based topologies also offer fault tolerance. Intelligent LAN hubs can isolate failed clients, preventing a bad NIC from clogging the network, for example.

Routing protocols can address failures in routers, switches, hubs, or network links.

Different kinds of memory (RAM) supply different levels of performance and fault tolerance. Most memories are 60 nanoseconds; higher speeds aren't as critical when you can interleave them for greater bandwidth. ECC RAM provides error-correcting circuitry. ECC and Parity memory won't help or hurt system performance, but they will protect you from memory faults, including module failure.

Multihoming—a feature in UNIX, NetWare, and NT—means to run multiple network cards in a server to improve throughput and load balancing. Additionally, multihoming provides fault tolerance, since it spreads the client load over multiple cards and provides for the possibility of one card failing.

Topologies

Topologies are methods of arranging and connecting computers on a network. Each topology has advantages and disadvantages. Of the available topologies, spanning tree (star) and ring are the most efficient and reasonable for modern LANs. But there are also the bus and mesh topologies.

The physical topology is the design of the cables and hardware devices in the network. How are they connected? How does one relate to another? With physical topology, you want to consider your company's location or locations, the number of people you now employ and plan to add, and whether there will be moves from office to office or building to building in the near and distant future.

The logical topology is determined by the flow of messages and data. Considerations with logical topology include stability, scalability, fault tolerance, and security.

Bus

The *bus* topology is usually connected by a length of Ethernet cable along an open cable length or backbone. Use a bus topology for 30 users or less on a simple, low-traffic network. Installation and administration are simple and inexpensive; however, the bus topology sends only one packet at a time, thus slowing the network considerably. Also, if one workstation or cable along the line has trouble, the entire network goes down and finding the problem will be difficult. Finally, the bus topology limits future expansion in that you will likely need to replace the entire network topology if you want to add users.

Figure E.3 shows a simple bus network. The bus terminates at both ends of the medium.

Spanning Tree (Star)

The *star* topology connects computers through a central hub, and the hub distributes signals to all connecting cables. Servers and workstations are connected to the hub, each with a separate cable. The hub modifies transmission signals so each device receives input over the network.

10BaseT and 100BaseT use a modified star topology, or *spanning tree* (see Figure E.4). Each hub and its connections form a star, but you can connect to other hubs in a branching design. Use a hub to protect each cable connected to it from all other cables; if one cable is damaged, for example, only one computer on the network is affected. Different sizes of hubs are available—one hub

Figure E.3 Each node receives the same message through the network cable at the same time in a bus network.

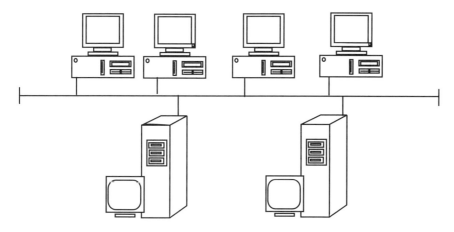

Figure E.4 Spanning tree topology uses hubs to extend the network.

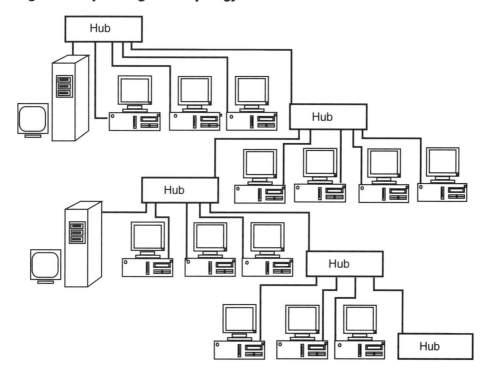

can connect 8 computers or hubs and another may connect 24 or 48 devices. Spanning tree is expensive since hubs cost so much, especially for 100BaseT networks.

Ring Network

In the *ring* topology, the computer sends a message, or token, that controls the right to transmit; the message is continuously passed from one node to the next in one direction only: in a ring around the network.

When a node has data to transmit, it captures the message, adds the message and destination address, and then sends the token on. If the address matches a node's address, the message is accepted; if not, the node regenerates the message and places it back on the network, where it travels to the next node in the ring.

Ring networks can cover greater distances than star networks; however, if there is a failure somewhere in the network—network card, wiring, or other hardware problem—the data cannot pass until the problem is fixed. Figure E.5 illustrates a ring topology.

Figure E.5 Each workstation is connected to two other workstations, forming a loop or ring.

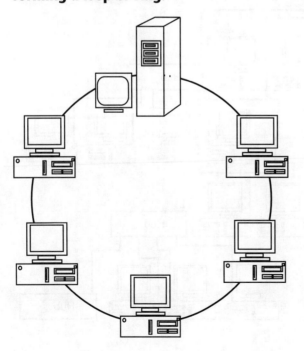

Mesh

A *mesh* topology is generally a Wide Area Network (WAN) that uses multiple paths to connect multiple sites (see Figure E.6). Routers are used to help determine the best path for the data, and it works very well as long as there aren't too many sites within the WAN. A mesh network with four or five sites, for example, is easy to create and manage; however, a mesh network with 50 or more sites may be impractical.

Mesh networks are stable and reliable because they offer redundant connections. Also, problem solving is diminished, and the problems you do encounter are easier to solve with a mesh network. The main disadvantage to this type of topology is that it would be expensive to reconfigure and replace with a different topology.

Figure E.6 A pure mesh network connects every node in the network.

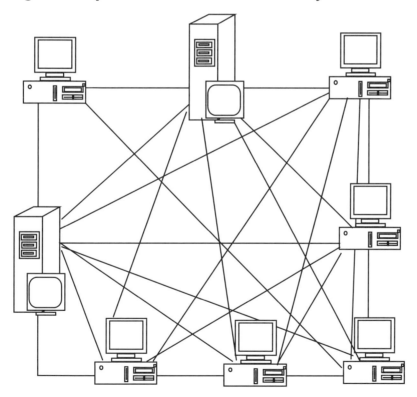

Network Cabling

The type of cabling, or wiring, you use can help to prevent bottlenecks as well as otherwise affect the network. The type of cabling you choose depends on the nature of your network, its functions, and its configuration.

As a brief overview, the most common type of cabling is twisted pair copper. Cat5 UTP is the most widely used type for commercial installations; Cat5 UTP supports transmissions up to 100MHz for up to 100 meters. Thin coaxial cable is flexible, relatively inexpensive, lightweight and effective for Ethernet and CATV networks. Thick coaxial cable is stronger but difficult to install and terminate. Fiber cabling (available in glass or plastic form) is easy to install, fast, and flexible, but expensive.

Telecommunications Closet Guidelines

You use a telecommunications closet to store cables, routers, and other equipment for easier troubleshooting, replacement and repair, and for a more organized approach to cabling. The room can contain infrastructure-related elements, such as cross-connects and interconnection equipment. Interconnection equipment includes main, intermediate, and horizontal cross-connects, patch panels (devices in which temporary or semipermanent connections can be made between incoming and outgoing lines), cable trays, raceways, and conduits.

When designing your telecommunications closet, consider the following guidelines:

Avoid cable stress from tight bends, cable ties, and tension.

Limit the length of patch cords and equipment cables on both ends of each link to no more than 30 feet or so.

Use only standard connecting hardware.

Use cross-connections for connections between cabling subsystems and for connections to equipment with multiport connectors.

Outlets should be securely mounted and marked.

All cabling should be labeled clearly.

Color code cross-connect jumpers.

Protect connectors from physical damage and moisture.

> **NOTE**
>
> For more information about cabling, see *LAN Wiring: An Illustrated Guide to Network Cabling* by James Trulove (Computing McGraw-Hill, 1997).

UTP/STP

UTP (Unshielded Twisted Pair) and STP (Shielded Twisted Pair) cabling are the most popular cabling used for LANs. So popular, in fact, that one or the other often comes preinstalled in office buildings. UTP can be used for most LANs; STP is more expensive but better for a LAN that needs protection from electrical interference.

UTP contains two or more pairs of twisted copper wires and is offered in both voice and data grades. UTP offers easy installation and inexpensive materials; however, the signaling speeds are limited and you must use shorter maximum cable segment lengths.

STP contains a foil shield and copper braid that surrounds pairs of wires. STP offers high-speed transmission over long distances; however, it is bulky to install and to hide. In both UTP and STP, the wires have a minimum number of twists per cable length; the greater the number of twists, the lower the crosstalk. Twisting wire pairs cancels out radiated energy from current flowing in any one wire by the radiated energy from the same current flowing back in the return wire of the same pair; twisting minimizes crosstalk and makes the wire pairs less susceptible to external noise. *Crosstalk* is interference from a physically adjacent channel that corrupts a signal or causes transmission errors. The channel carries the data from the sending device to the receiving device.

UTP/STP can support 10Mbps to 100Mbps, depending on whether you use Category 3 or 5 wiring. UTP/STP can be used in any network topology as well. Since this type of cabling doesn't cause harmful fumes when burned, it's recommended for use in all commercially zoned buildings because of fire laws.

Thinnet/Thicknet

Coaxial cables are generally already in place as a backbone for small- to medium-sized LANs. *Thinnet* is a coaxial cable used mostly with bus topology; it supports 10bps. Thinnet (thin Ethernet) connects coaxial cable on an Ethernet network. Distances range up to 1000 feet.

Thicknet (thick Ethernet) is a rigid coaxial cable that is used for more LAN backbones. Thicknet usually uses an AUI (Attachment Unit Interface) that's used by some Ethernet devices for adapting two different cabling types and wiring schemes. Distances range up to 3300 feet.

Cat 1 through Cat 5

Category 1–5 (often referred to as Cat1, Cat2, and so on) is a standard recommended by the Electronics Industry Association/Telecommunications Industry Association. All of these standards are set for use with UTP cabling, but at different speeds.

Category 1 is a standard set for unshielded twisted pair telephone cabling, which is not suitable for data transmissions.

Category 2 is for use at speeds up to 4Mbps.

Category 3 is for use at speeds up to 10Mbps; this is the minimum requirement used for 10BaseT.

Category 4 is for use with 16Mbps token ring.

Category 5 is for use at speeds up to 100Mbps.

Cabling and Topologies

Networks can be wired in various topologies. Coaxial cable, for example, can only be wired in a bus topology. A cable goes from one computer to the next, plugs in to one end of the T-connector and comes out the other end. The advantage of coaxial cable is it doesn't require a hub.

UTP does require a hub but the cabling is more expensive. UTP is wired in a star network with the hub at the center, which makes expansion easier. You can attach just two computers together with UTP and no hub, but you'll need to use a crossover cable instead of a normal cable.

Larger WANs and even backbones can be configured with UTP, fiber optic, or other cabling in a star or tree topology.

Fiber Optic

Fiber optic cabling transmits pulses of light through a glass or plastic core that's enclosed in a plastic shield. Each fiber includes a thin core that is immune to electrical interference. Transmission speeds begin at 100Mbps and span up to 6562 feet. Fiber optic is reliable, very fast, and offers great security; it's also very expensive. Fiber optic cables are also more expensive to repair than the other cables. Fiber optic makes a great high-speed backbone.

> **Fiber Installation**
>
> You must carefully plan the layout, support devices, and the termination components for fiber optic cable installation. Learn the fiber's operating specifications and characteristics—such as bandwidth, loss per kilometer at the operating wavelengths, the physical dimensions of the fiber and cladding, and the maximum force that can be applied to a fiber cable without damaging its internal strands—before you buy the cabling.
>
> Request that when the fiber cable is shipped to you, the factory test results accompany the shipment; don't accept a shipment of fiber cable without the factory test results. Tests are performed after the fiber cabling is assembled to make sure it meets specification requirements. Each reel of fiber cable should include its own factory test report that indicates the results of the test.
>
> Test the cabling after you receive it. Test again after installation. Terminate each cable in an enclosure designed to protect the backbone cable and provide optical connectors for each fiber in the cable. Test fiber termination equipment prior to installation.

Wireless Connections

Wireless LANs (WLANs) are employed in many vertical markets: retail, healthcare, finance, warehousing, and so on. Wireless technology provides an unobstructed link to the world network, enabling people to access all of the information their wired counterparts are accustomed to.

Wireless connections create a LAN, using technologies other than conventional cabling. Unbounded transmission media can transmit and receive electromagnetic signals without an electrical conductor; microwave, radio, infrared, and laser links are examples of this wireless media.

Speeds of 1Mbps to 10Mbps are the norm for WLANs; it's not the high speed of traditional wired network environments. There is currently a lack of standards to define how hand-held and portable end-user devices communicate with wireless access points. IEEE approved the 802.11 standard in 1997; that standard addresses various aspects of interoperability.

In a basic 802.11 wireless setup, a company's wired network would have wireless access points strategically located in areas where users want to connect wirelessly. Access points generally have 10BaseT Ethernet connections to the wired network. A wireless bridge can be used to connect two networks in situations where it is impossible to use traditional cable media.

Microwave

Microwave exists in terrestrial and satellite systems. Terrestrial links may be used to link separate buildings with limited areas for cable installation; they also provide high bandwidth. Microwave links are, however, susceptible to external interference and eavesdropping, and they require FCC licensing and approved equipment.

Satellite microwave links are also sensitive to external interference, but they provide links to extremely remote and underdeveloped areas. Providing high bandwidths, satellite microwave also supports narrow- or wide-beam paths, so transmission can be select or broad-based. The satellite microwave also requires FCC licensing, and long distances mean a noticeable delay compared to a direct line.

Infrared

Infrared line-of-sight is one method of wireless connection in which high-frequency light waves transmit data between nodes in an unobstructed path. Data rates are relatively high for infrared, but the light waves cannot penetrate obstacles, such as walls.

Advantages of infrared are high bandwidths and inexpensive technology. Disadvantages include interference from atmospheric conditions and a relatively short transmission distance.

Radio Signals

Another method is high-frequency *radio signals*. Radio signals can pierce some thin walls, but not heavy masonry. *Spread-spectrum* radio signals can pass through masonry walls, but data rates are slow. The lower the frequency of any wireless connection method, the lower the data transfer rates over longer distances. The higher the frequency, the higher the data transfer rates over shorter distances.

Spread-spectrum radio systems transmit data on multiple frequencies and are more secure than single-frequency radio systems. While terrestrial microwave systems allow communication over great distances, the sending and receiving stations must have a clear line of sight between them.

Advantages include radio is accessible to users throughout the world and the equipment is inexpensive. Disadvantages include FCC licensing and approved equipment, low to moderate bandwidths, and radio waves are susceptible to external interference.

Laser

A communication *laser* transmits a narrow beam of light that's modulated into pulses to carry the data. Laser technology is line-of-site but offers great bandwidth. No FCC license is required and laser is resistant to interference and eavesdropping.

Laser is also, however, sensitive to atmospheric disturbances and provides a relatively short transmission distance.

Network Interface Cards

A Network Interface adapter Card (NIC) plugs into the server or workstation to help the operating system control the flow of information over the network. A cable connects the card to the network, which in turn connects all the network interface cards in the network. You choose a network card depending on its speed, expense, and the topology of the network. You must make sure the NIC is compatible with the computer's operating system (OS) and the NOS. You must also match the network interface card to the topology of the network.

Common types of network cards include Ethernet 10Mbps, Fast Ethernet 100Mbps, FDDI, ATM, fiber, and wireless. 10Mbps is used with a 10BaseT Ethernet network. The 10Mbps technology is declining because of its slow speeds; it's okay for small office use, but still not recommended. 10Mbps is relatively inexpensive.

The *100Mbps card* is used with 100BaseT Ethernet network and is 10 times faster than a 10Mbps card. 100Mbps is perfect for using with large data files, video or sound files, images, and such. The 100Mbps card is more expensive than the 10Mbps, and installing the cabling also costs more because 100Mbps cable must be certified.

If you're on a tight budget, you can purchase 10/100Mbps cards that can attach to either a 10Mbps or a 100Mbps network. Use the 10Mbps hub to start with, and when you need it, you can add the 100Mbps hub to the system to make the network a 100BaseT.

Fiber cards use FDDI (Fiber Distributed Data Interface) networking and follow the ring topology. You'll need a PCI slot for the fiber card, fiber cabling, and fiber hubs. Because of the special equipment, fiber is very expensive to purchase and to install.

Wireless connections enable you to connect without using conventional cabling; instead, you use infrared or high-frequency radio signals for the connection. High-frequency light waves (infrared) transmit data between two computers up to 80 feet apart, using an unobstructed path. High-frequency radio signals transmit between two computers up to 130 feet apart.

Wireless LANs (WLANs) are employed in many vertical markets: retail, healthcare, finance, warehousing, and so on. Wireless technology provides an untethered link to the world network, enabling people to access all of the information their wired counterparts are accustomed to. This type of connection is better used for only special situations where nothing else will do. Wireless connections are expensive and not very dependable.

Logical Network Communications

Logical network communications determine how the computers transmit data over the physical media, or cables. The common logical networks are Ethernet, token ring, FDDI, and ATM. When you choose to use a 100BaseT network card and the unshielded twisted pair cabling, you've chosen by default to use Ethernet network communications. On the other hand, if you choose token ring cards, hubs, and topology, you're using the token ring network communications.

FDDI

FDDI (Fiber Distributed Data Interface) is a set of standards that include protocols, services, characteristics, and functions. FDDI is specifically for fiber optic networks and perfect for high-performance clients, such as engineering workstations, medical imaging, three-dimensional seismic processing, full-motion video, and so on. FDDI could, alternatively, use shielded and unshielded twisted pair cabling for shorter distances.

It is analogous to IEEE 802.2, 802.4, and 802.5 in relationship to the OSI model. FDDI provides high bandwidth and security for backbone networks for LANs, a frontend network for attachment of servers and workstations, or a backend network for high-speed peripheral connections.

FDDI uses a token-passing access method, can be configured in star topology, and can use fiber optic media. An FDDI network is made up of two rotating rings; traffic flows in one direction on one ring (primary) and in the other direction on the other ring (secondary). If all is working well, traffic flows on the primary ring only and the secondary ring acts as a fault-tolerant device. One ring can attach up to 500 stations reliably. A repeater is required at strategic points along the fiber optic cable.

FDDI supports the real-time assignment of network bandwidth, so it works well with today's applications. FDDI cites two types of traffic: *synchronous* and *asynchronous.* 100Mbps of bandwidth is used for continuous transmission—synchronous—for voice and video, for example. The remaining bandwidth can be used asynchronously by other stations.

Dual versus Single Connection

The FDDI standard is a dual ring of trees that offers fault tolerance. A typical FDDI network has one pair of counter-rotating rings and at least one tree of connections, although neither is technically mandatory. The FDDI network doesn't have to include a dual ring; you can customize the topology to suit your situation.

Figure E.7 shows both the dual rings of FDDI with a tree attached. The ring supplies fault tolerance to the mission-critical applications, and the tree offers only single connections to those devices.

A *dual ring* provides dual connections to other devices. If there's a failure on the ring, the token flow does an about-face and moves the other way. With a tree configuration, devices receive a single connection. This is cost effective, but a single failure fragments the ring so that segments cannot communicate.

If you want to configure the FDDI network to combine both dual and single connections, you can make some segments more fault tolerant than others. Following are some guidelines for making the decision:

Dual connections are useful for backbones, segments at risk from the environment, devices carrying critical data or large volumes of data, or for connections covering a large geographical area.

Single connections should be used if cost is important, in local network segments, desktop network segments, or where the wiring doesn't support dual connections.

Concentrators

When building your FDDI network, you'll want to consider the use of *concentrators*. Concentrators work similarly to the way 10BaseT hubs work, by providing additional attachment ports. Concentrators also route data; lower the cost for adapter cards by enabling you to use single-attached cards instead of dual-attached cards; and make the FDDI network more stable and reliable.

Token Ring

Token ring is more expensive than Ethernet because adapters and hubs for token ring are more expensive. Using the ring topology, token ring computers take turns sending data via a token that's passed between computers, one at a

Figure E.7 You can combine dual rings and trees in your FDDI network design.

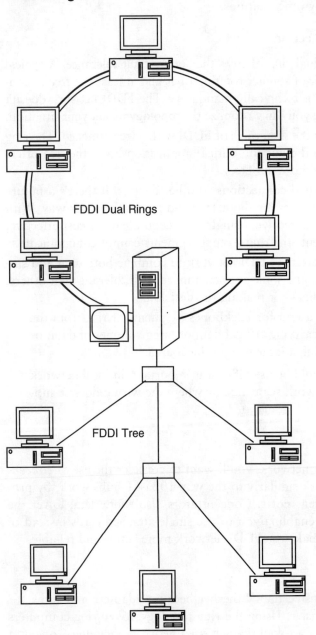

FDDI Dual Rings

FDDI Tree

time, around a ring. Removal of a node or cabling problems can keep the tokens from passing through the network unless the ring is maintained.

Workstations connect to central hubs, called *Multistation Access Units* (MAUs), and then multiple hubs are connected together to create the network. If a workstation fails, the MAU bypasses that station to continue the ring. A failed cable could cause the ring to revert back on itself, or loop back to reroute in the opposite direction.

The IEEE 802.5 standards for token ring state it's most appropriate for commercial and light industrial environments. Small frames, or tokens, circulate while stations are idle. As a token passes by, a station can catch it and begin a transmission of a data frame. While the station is transmitting, no token is on the ring and so no other station can transmit.

A new token is started on the ring when the station has finished its transmission and when a field in the token exists for a workstation to announce a priority for its transmission. When a new token is started, the next station can seize the token and begin transmission. If the traffic is light, token passing is weak because each station must wait its turn. However, if the traffic is heavier, the ring is more efficient and fair.

ATM

ATM (Asynchronous Transfer Mode) offers high-performance connectivity for LANs, WANs, and as a backbone for your network. ATM supports complex multimedia applications, like audio, videoconferencing, and advanced graphics. It offers scalability and compatibility with current technologies. ATM enables a nearly unlimited number of users to have dedicated connections with each other and with network servers. It also offers better management and control of enterprise-wide networks.

In other popular networks, users contend for access to the transmission medium; only one transmission can take place at a time. ATM provides each user with a dedicated media connection to a switch so that multiple connections can run in parallel. Even as more workstations are added to the network, the throughput remains constant. The maximum and average bandwidth for each connection are the same—155Mbps currently.

Also, ATM uses fixed-length cells as opposed to variable-length packets. Fixed-length cells mean hardware switching is possible; there is a simultaneous delivery of data. What this means is large file transfers don't clash with other traffic.

ATM is also connection oriented, which means a channel is built between the sender and receiver and the information is transmitted. Virtual channels provide multiple paths that enable load balancing and bandwidth allocation.

ATM Details

ATM is suitable for data and digitized voice and video, as well as streaming video transport. ATM can be used for both LANs and WANs, although it's often used as a high-speed backbone for WANs. Transfer rates range from 155.52Mbps to 622.08Mbps, even though the capabilities are quite a bit more.

An electronic switch designed to transfer data at high speeds is the basic component of ATM. A small switch can connect from 16 to 32 computers; the connection between the computer and the switch uses a pair of optical fibers. A host interface board plugs in to the computer's bus and uses LED (Light Emitting Diode) or laser to convert data into pulses of light that travel along the fiber to the switch.

Figure E.8 illustrates an ATM network using ATM switches between servers and workstations and between LAN segments.

Figure E.8 ATM speeds transmissions within the network.

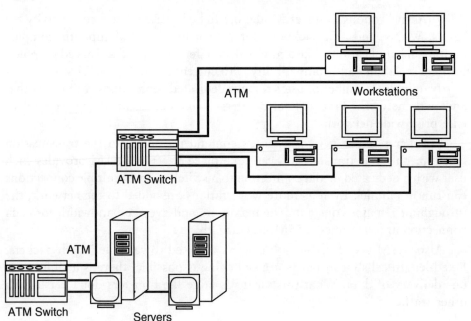

In the OSI model, ATM is considered Layer 2; but it doesn't really fit cleanly into the layered model because within ATM, end-to-end connection, flow control, and routing are all done at the ATM cell level. An ATM cell is 53 bytes.

ATM Performance

ATM can be used with multi-enterprise networks as a backbone, or as router-to-server connections, direct desktop connections, and so on. ATM can support a large number of subnets, even if they are not in the same physical location. High-end workstations that need bandwidth for multimedia, video productions, and such, can use ATM switches as hubs for 155Mbps dedicated bandwidth. Bottlenecks resulting from an overworked network server can be alleviated with ATM connections and switches.

ATM provides a variety of services, including telephony, online data retrieval, distributed data, multicasts for conferencing, and more. The performance of your ATM connection depends on the parameters specified at the time of setup, the quality of service request, whether bandwidth was reserved, and the load on the network.

Careful configuration and optimization are the only things that can guarantee high performance on an ATM network. To get higher performance from your ATM network, you can use PVCs and SVCs between end stations; the *Sonet* (Synchronous Optical Network) fiber optic transport standards; or ATM cell header information. VCI used to switch virtual channels and VPI used to switch virtual paths. It is extremely important that you seek technical help and guidance when installing and configuring an ATM network or backbone; ATM can be very difficult to implement.

Ethernet

Ethernet is one of the most commonly used networking technologies. Ethernet has a transfer rate of either 10Mbps or 100Mbps using the bus topology. Network nodes are connected by thick or thin coaxial cable, fiber optic cable, or by twisted pair wiring. Ethernet uses CSMA/CD (Carrier Sense Multiple Access/Collision Detection) to prevent network failures and collisions. CSMA/CD is a baseband protocol that detects collisions automatically. Nodes listen first and transmit only when the line is free; if two nodes transmit at the same time, a collision occurs. To prevent subsequent collisions, each node waits a different random length of time before transmitting again.

Ethernet packets are units of information that are transmitted on Ethernet networks. An Ethernet packet consists of a synchronization preface, a destina-

> **NOTE**
>
> The difference between Ethernet and 10BaseT is that Ethernet is an access method, or a set of rules, of how information travels over physical media, such as cable. Within Ethernet, there are cable specifications; 10BaseT is one of these specifications. 10BaseT uses unshielded twisted pair cable. Other physical media types are: thick coaxial cable (10Base5), Thin Ethernet or thin coaxial cable (10Base2), UTP super cable, shielded twisted pair, and fiber optic (10BaseF).

tion address, a source address, a type code indicator, a data field and a CRC (Cyclic Redundancy Check) that confirms the data's accuracy.

Fast Ethernet

Fast Ethernet provides 10 times the bandwidth (100BaseT) as Ethernet plus other features like full-duplex operation and auto-negotiation. Fast Ethernet also provides the following:

- Scalable technology

- Supports speeds of 10 and 100Mbps

- Retains the 802.3 frame format

- Supports twisted pair wiring (hub-to-hub maximum of 330 feet)

> **NOTE**
>
> *Full-duplex* refers to a channel with two ends, each serving as both a transmitter and a receiver; each can transmit and receive at the same time.

Fast Ethernet uses the CSMA/CD protocol that is standard for Ethernet, so it can offer reliability and economy. Fast Ethernet is the same foundation and standard (IEEE 802.2) as Ethernet as well. 100BaseT is the standard that lets Fast Ethernet run on Cat 3, 4, and 5 UTP cabling. The SNMP (Simple Network Management Protocol) application software can work with Fast Ethernet networks, as well as the Ethernet Management Information Bases (MIBs).

Switched Ethernet versus Fast Ethernet   Conventional bridges are often used to create logical boundaries between networks. But the Ethernet switch is also used for segmenting networks to maintain separate areas of bandwidth for small groups of workstations. Ethernet switching is a packet switching technology that provides a high-performance connection between multiple Ethernet networks.

Ethernet switching is inexpensive, easy to operate, offers high performance, and extends the throughput of the conventional Ethernet LANs. Use Ethernet switches to divide an Ethernet network into multiple parallel segments.

Switched Ethernet makes the entire 10Mbps bandwidth of Ethernet available to individual devices by creating dedicated paths. Fast Ethernet widens the data pipe to 100Mbps, which can be either shared or switched. Switched Ethernet is better for PCs with 10Mbps NICs and low-bandwidth ISA buses; Fast Ethernet is best for servers and newer PCs with 10/100Mbps NICs.

If you run ISA-based PCs with standard business applications and demand greater total bandwidth for continuous network loads, switched Ethernet would be more efficient. Switching dedicates the bandwidth to the desktop for this situation and takes the load off of the server. If you're running complex applications or transferring large files, Fast Ethernet would be the better choice because it offers greater peak bandwidth for higher throughput.

Remember, though, switched Ethernet doesn't really increase the maximum network bandwidth available to the desktop; it provides 10Mbps only. Fast Ethernet can supply 100Mbps to each node. Your choice depends on the type of applications you use and file sizes to be transferred.

Fast Ethernet Equipment   Fast Ethernet hardware includes network interface cards, switches, routers, and so on. With NICs, you can purchase dual speed cards that are 10/100Mbps, so that you can slowly ease your way into the Fast Ethernet technologies, if you want. Using these cards means workstations can remain on the 10Mbps network until you get all of your equipment in place; then they can transfer to 100Mbps when you're ready.

There are also Fast Ethernet hubs and switches that work with 100BaseT or 100BaseTX. Hubs supply 100BaseT ports for connections to various nodes. Switches also provide multiple 100Mbps ports as well as other features to improve bandwidth and promote easy network segmentation. Naturally, there are also stacked hubs and switches available that provide multiple ports in various configurations (such as fiber and UTP ports) for use with larger networks.

Terms

10Base2 is an IEEE 802.3 standard for thin Ethernet cabling for LANs using thin coaxial cable. It's also called Thinnet. You should not install this cable, but you may already be using it, say, as a backbone for hubs in a very small network.

10Base5 is a specification for thick Ethernet cabling for LANs using coaxial cable. 10Base5 was the backbone 10 years ago, and so there still may be some in use today; however, don't install it if you're planning a new network.

10BaseT uses unshielded twisted pair cable running at 10Mbps.

100BaseT is a set of standards for 100Mbps Ethernet, also 100BaseTX and 100BaseTF and 100BaseT4, a medium-independent interface and adapter.

100BaseT4 uses 8B6T encoding and 25 MHz clocking.

100BaseTF uses Ethernet framing and CSMA/CD but has physical characteristics of FDDI's multimode fiber PMD.

100BaseTX is similar to 100BaseTF but borrows FDDI's TP-PMD. 100VG-AnyLAN uses 100Mbps Ethernet with demand priority media access method.

The 1000BaseX standard is based on the Fibre Channel Physical Layer. Fibre Channel is an interconnection technology for connecting workstations, supercomputers, storage devices, and peripherals.

1000BaseT is a standard for Gigabit Ethernet over long-haul copper UTP. Allows up to 25-100M over four pairs of Cat5 UTP.

Gigabit Ethernet

Gigabit Ethernet operates at 1000Mbps; it's the next generation of Ethernet standard and it is fully compatible with existing Ethernet installations. Gigabit Ethernet retains the Carrier Sense Multiple Access/Collision Detection (CSMA/CD) as the access method. Additionally, Gigabit Ethernet supports the following:

- Full-duplex (frame-based flow control) as well as half-duplex modes of operation (supports CSMA/CD)

- Initially single-mode and multi-mode fiber and short-haul coaxial cable with twisted pair cable standards to be added in the near future

- IEEE 802.3 Ethernet frame format (meets IEEE 802 functional requirements)

- Start-wired topologies

- Simple forwarding between 10Mbps, 100Mbps, and 1000Mbps Ethernet

Gigabit Ethernet is used as a backbone for existing networks and for connecting Fast Ethernet switches, repeaters, routers, and such. It can also connect

> **NOTE**
>
> IEEE (Institute of Electrical and Electronics Engineers) sets telecommunications standards for bridges, Ethernet, bus topology, token passing, and so on. The 802.3 standards describe Ethernet standards.

workstations and servers for high-bandwidth applications like medical imaging or CAD. Figure E.9 illustrates a Gigabit Ethernet backbone that changes to a Fast Ethernet design between workstations.

As far as the OSI reference model goes, Gigabit Ethernet fits into the system well. All upper-layer protocols (TCP/IP, IPX/SPX, and so on) can run over Gigabit Ethernet. It also supports physical layer implementations for various media, including short copper links, horizontal copper, and single-mode fiber.

Figure E.9 Using Gigabit Ethernet as a backbone speeds transmissions to the workstations.

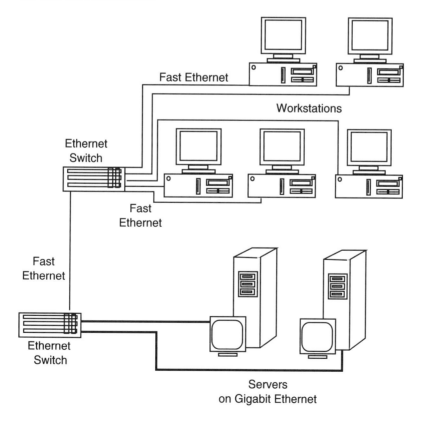

In full-duplex mode, a Gigabit Ethernet switch provides up to 2GB bandwidth to each node on the network. Frame-based flow control handles the congestion at the switch.

Network Speed

A 10Mbps network is slow, especially when users are doing more than small file transfers or using office productivity applications. When they begin to use graphics-rich multimedia applications, database and other data-rich applications, and collaborative groupware applications, more will be needed from the network.

100Mbps speed or more can help avoid network congestion and help network users get their jobs done. You can boost network performance by using Ethernet Switch, which gives a dedicated 10Mbps of traffic to each of its connected ports. But, even with switching, one is limited to 10Mbps throughput to any client.

100Mbps technologies can give sustained high-speed bursts to satisfy the bandwidth needs. Some of these high-speed technologies are:

- Asynchronous Transfer Mode (ATM)
- Fiber Distributed Data Interface (FDDI)
- Fast Ethernet
- 100VG-AnyLAN
- Fibre Channel

Telecommunications Services

Telecommunications can be used for remote access, Internet access, telecommuters, WAN connections, and such. Many services can use telephone wires to transmit data, voice, and even video on the same line. Each service has its advantages and disadvantages; each service has its specific uses.

ISDN

ISDN is a digital service that can transmit data, voice, and video on the same line. ISDN uses copper twisted pair cabling from the normal telephone system, so you can contact your phone company for information about ISDN services.

There are two types of ISDN lines: BRI and PRI. BRI is Basic Rate Interface and consists of two 64Kbps channels (B channels) and one 19.2Kbps signaling channel (D channel). PRI (Primary Rate Interface) consists of 23 B channels and one 64Kbps D channel (23B+D).

B channels provide:

- 64,000bps each

- Full-duplex so data can be sent and received simultaneously

- Circuit switching

- Digitized voice or data

D channels provide:

- 16,000bps for basic rate and 64,000bps for primary rate

- Full-duplex

- Both signaling and data

- Packet switching so each frame of data can go to a different destination

> **NOTE**
>
> ISDN had two standards: N-ISDN (Narrowband ISDN) and B-ISDN (Broadband ISDN). N-ISDN is the ISDN in common use now. B-ISDN is a high-speed data communications service that will support multimedia applications. B-ISDN is currently being developed.
>
> B-ISDN will use ATM technology and switching to support voice, video, and data. B-ISDN will represent a major technological break, because it affects services, protocols, signaling, and equipment.

Frame Relay

Frame relay is a standard for a packet-switching protocol that also provides for bandwidth on demand. Frame relay is ideal for a WAN backbone. It allows multiple subscribers to share the same backbone; every subscriber receives his or her fair share of bandwidth when needed.

The typical traffic generated by client/server applications is bursty, requiring large amounts of network bandwidth for short periods of time. Frame relay may be more cost-effective than leased lines for deploying client/server applications over a WAN. The major advantage of frame relay is that it handles bursts of data well while providing improved throughput.

Virtual Circuits

Frame relay is a connection-oriented protocol. A *virtual circuit*—either a PVC (Permanent Virtual Circuit) or a SVC (Switched Virtual Circuit)—must be set up before two nodes can communicate. PVC is a permanent connection between two nodes and cannot be torn down at any time. An SVC enables switched, on-demand frame relay service between two nodes.

PVC and SVC connections broaden frame relay's coverage to other types of applications, such as voice, video, and secure Internet applications. Currently, the SVC approach isn't widely used because it is so complex.

Each connection is identified by a Data Link Control Identifier (DLCI)—an identifier that pertains only to the local network. Different routers in the network can reuse the same DLCI, which enables the network to support a larger number of virtual circuits.

Advantages of Frame Relay

In a frame relay network, data is divided into variable-length frames, which contain addressing. Frame relay offers better performance than X.25, its predecessor. X.25 required acknowledgment and verification of packets and that slowed the throughput. Frame relay works with digital circuits and doesn't perform error detection and correction. Frame relay discards erred frames instead of sending them on or repairing them.

Also, frame relay doesn't use *flow control*, which means it's faster. Flow control governs the rate at which the originating router issues packets into a switch. When congested, for example, the switch notifies the originating router to stop sending packets until the congestion clears. Frame relay discards frames for which it doesn't have sufficient buffer space to continue. The originating router is left to recover from the data loss.

Frame relay offers the following advantages:

Reliability. Since a WAN connection is difficult to control and monitor, it must be highly fault tolerant. Frame relay provides dynamic rerouting when a PVC goes down and provides standby PVCs and backup PVCs, as well.

Availability. WAN connections should perform as quickly and reliably as LAN connections to support bursty traffic; frame relays provides for that.

Serviceability. Frame relay works with TCP/IP to provide flow control. TCP/IP was designed to work with WANs and provide flow control instead of the frame relay providing it; frame relay is flexible and accommodating.

WAN Management Frame Relay

You can manage frame relay or you can delegate it off premises to a carrier. Be careful of carriers; many subcontract to other firms because they're dealing with mergers, or their company is growing too fast to handle new business. Never outsource to a subcontractor unless you've done your research and know all you need to know about the firm. You may also find the services you need from a VAR (Value-Added Reseller) or a regional network systems integrator.

Watch the carrier who manages your WAN. Don't let it assert too much control over your network. You might want to limit read and/or write access on your router. Carriers should only take care of problems from the router out; you'll have to take care of problems from the router into your network.

T1

A *T1* line is a high-quality, long-distance communications circuit that you can lease, usually on a monthly basis. T1 provides 24 channels of 64Kbps for a total bandwidth of 1.544Mbps. Although expensive to install and maintain, T1 provides fast, reliable long-distance links to the Internet.

> **NOTE**
>
> When ordering T1, you may see a T1 line listed as having 1.544Mbps bandwidth or 1.536Mbps bandwidth. Also, generally a T1 channel is 64Kbps but sometimes only 56Kbps is delivered. Question the service to make sure you're getting what you're paying for.

To connect a T1 line, you need a CSU (Channel Service Unit), a DSU (Data Service Unit), perhaps a multiplexor, and a bridge or router. The CSU/DSU prevents faulty equipment from affecting the transmission systems and converts local area network signals to the T1 signaling formats. A multiplexor loads multiple channels of voice or data onto the T1 line; and the bridge or router provides the actual connection points between your LAN and the T1 system. Figure E.10 shows a WAN connected with a T1 line.

The basic 64Kbps channel is sometimes termed a *DS-0* in digital voice networking. A collection of 24 DS-0 channels is termed a *DS-1*. When DS-1 is delivered on copper wire, it's often called *T1*, which it isn't technically; however, T1 is generally accepted for any link with 1.536Mbps or more.

Figure E.10 CSU/DSUs attach the LAN segments to the T1 line via routers.

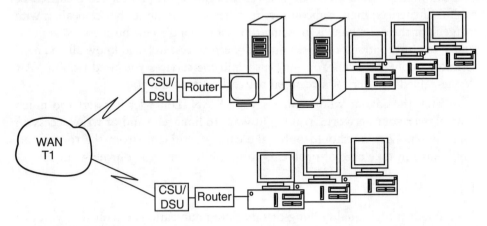

Fractional T1

A *Fractional T1* is a subchannel of a T1. You can purchase one or more fractional lines and add to that as your needs increase. Naturally, Fractional T1 lines are a small part of T1 so the speed is less, as well. A user pays for only the portion of the channel capacity and not the full channel. Fractional T3 services may also be available in your area. You might use a Fractional T1 service to evaluate your bandwidth needs without purchasing a full T1.

T3

T3 is equivalent to 28 T1 circuits and provides a bandwidth of 44.736Mbps. The T3 lines carry 672 channels of 64Kbps. T3 is specific to transmission over copper wires. Naturally, T3 lines are very expensive to maintain and install.

T3 is often referred to as *DS-3*. A DS-3 connection consists of 672 DS-0 circuits, for a total throughput of 43,008Kbps.

Hardware Devices

Hardware devices such as repeaters, bridges, and gateways are important additions to your network—for extension of services, transferring and interpreting data, and greater performance. Routers should, by rights, fit into the Hardware Devices heading because they, too, connect LAN segments and improve performance. However, routers are much different devices from repeaters or bridges, and there is so much more to know about routers. They're covered in the next section.

HDSL Saves T1 Lines

T1 is a core technology for voice, data, and video delivery. Ten years ago, T1 migrated to the local loop, which is the distance between the local telco office and the end users. Generally the local loop is about 2.5 miles and is the means of the customer's access to public and private networks.

This local loop is also referred to as *repeaters T1*. To enable high-speed transmission over copper wire, a set of repeaters is used. Copper wire distorts signal quality; repeaters restore signal quality. To work properly, repeaters must be installed at every 3000 to 4000 feet, which is expensive and time-consuming. Other disadvantages are as follows:

Using repeaters also yields poor signal quality when compared to fiber optics and HDSL.

Pairs for repeaters must be carefully selected to avoid crosstalk; often wire pairs must be reengineered.

Troubleshooting multiple repeaters is difficult.

This is where HDSL comes in. HDSL delivers high-performance and cost-effective methods of transmitting data of up to 2Mbps over copper cable. Using HDSL means no repeaters are needed, and no special line conditioning is needed.

HDSL has become the most cost-competitive method of establishing T1 links on copper for public and private networks. HDSL can maintain signal integrity, and it quadruples the distance a digital signal can travel without the need for amplification or a repeater.

HDSL decreases the cost of installing T1 lines and lessens the amount of time it takes to install the lines. HDSL enables connectivity extension over distances of up to five miles. HDSL is immune to crosstalk and is a reliable, high-performance technology.

Hubs

Hubs modify transmission signals so that a network can be extended to add more hubs and workstations. An *active hub* extends cable length, and a *passive hub* enables the additional workstations to be added. Hubs include a number of removable I/O and networking modules. I/O modules could be 10BaseT, 10BaseF, or FDDI, for example; networking modules might be bridges, routers, power supplies, and so on.

If a hub doesn't have the networking modules installed, it's simply a multi-port repeater. Signals are repeated across the hub by each I/O module. A concentrator is simply a hub without multiple kinds of I/O and networking modules.

Figure E.11 shows how a hub is used in a star topography network.

Repeaters

Repeaters function at the Physical Layer or the OSI Reference Model. Repeaters take packets from one network segment, boost the signal strength, and forward the signal on to another network segment. Repeaters deal only with electrical and optical signals and have no knowledge of the data or any addresses. Repeaters pass on everything they detect on the line, including noise, distortion, and the original signal.

Repeaters cannot be used to connect network segments with dissimilar architectures, such as token ring and Ethernet. Their main purpose is to extend the length of the network transmission beyond the normal maximum cable lengths.

Figure E.11 At the center of the star is a hub, or concentrator.

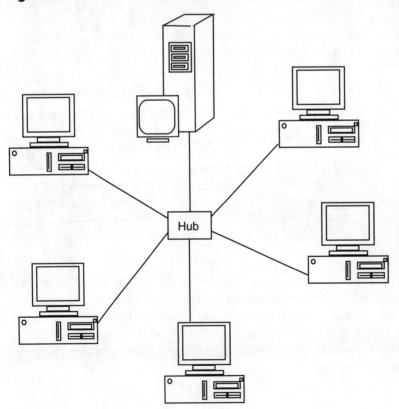

You can use more repeaters in a series to extend the LAN's length and topology. In an Ethernet LAN, you can only use a maximum of four repeaters to connect five segments. Figure E.12 illustrates repeaters between LAN segments used to extend the cable lengths.

Bridges

Bridges connect LANs, using different protocols; bridges can route between different media, such as Thinnet and fiber optic segments. Bridges operate at the Data Link layer of the ISO/OSI model and are used primarily to segment a network to reduce network traffic.

Bridges read the destination address of every packet and check it against the addresses it knows to be on the same network as the source. If the destination is not on the same network, the bridge forwards the packet. Note that the bridge

Figure E.12 Repeaters work only between similar network architectures.

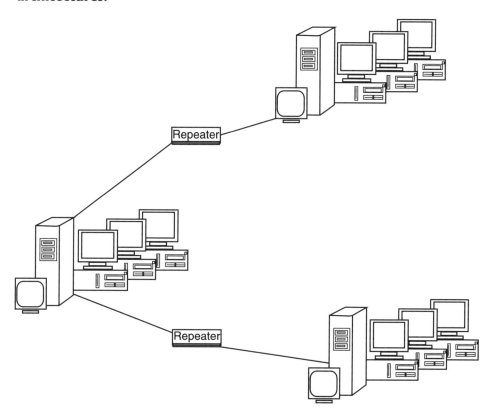

does not have to know that the destination address is, in fact, on the other segment. It only knows that the destination is not on the same segment as the source.

Bridges forward all broadcast packets. Additionally, when a bridge encounters an unknown destination address, its default action is to forward the packet to all network segments. Since most network protocols—IPX, NetBEUI, and TCP/IP—send broadcast frames that are addressed to every node on the network, a bridge will send these frames to every port, thus taking away bandwidth from actual network traffic. The larger the network, the more effect this will have on traffic.

Except for translating bridges, bridges don't connect networks with different architectures. Bridges are less expensive than routers and easier to install and configure. Avoid using bridges and routers together, since bridges are less discriminating than routers.

Switches

Switches extend a network by linking it to multiple separate, yet similar, types of LANs. A switch filters and speeds the flow of data between LANs. There are multiple modes for switches: cut-through/fast forward, cut-through/fragment free, or store-and-forward. Cut-through/fast forward and cut-through/fragment free enables the switch to examine the first few bytes of an Ethernet data packet for the destination address. Store-and-forward, also called *message switching*, enables the switch to examine the entire packet, check the address, search for errors, and then forward the data.

Advantages of using message switching include greater line efficiency because more devices share in the bandwidth and reduced traffic congestion because messages are stored en route, message priorities can be established, and one message can be sent to many destinations. Disadvantages include the fact that store-and-forward devices are expensive and message switching isn't compatible with most real-time applications.

Figure E.13 shows the use of a switch hub and a switch multiple LAN segments. Notice the servers have two network cards each.

Gateways

Gateways function at the Application and other upper layers of the OSI Reference Model to connect systems that use completely different protocols or data formats, such as a LAN and a mainframe or minicomputer. Gateways are slower than a bridge or router.

Generally, a gateway is a combination of hardware and software with its own processor and memory that it uses to perform protocol conversions.

Figure E.13 Use switches to speed the flow of data between LANs.

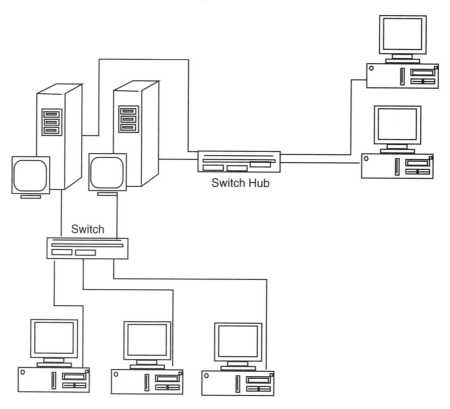

Switch Hub

Switch

> **NOTE**
>
> If you're looking to increase your bandwidth and connectivity, you might try moving from shared hubs to switched hubs. Switch store-and-forward mode screens for bad frames and errors, thus helping you avoid some network problems.

Routers

Routers connect networks through the OSI transport layer, which handles tasks such as addressing, connecting protocols, packet management, error detection, and routing. Since routers work on the transport layer, they can ignore differences in transport channels, such as Ethernet, FDDI, ISDN, and such. Routers must have common ground at the upper layers of the OSI model; so, if you want to connect an NT LAN to a mainframe, you must use a gateway as opposed to a router.

Routers read a data packet, remove its protocols and replace them with protocols the destination network needs, add routing information, and send the packet to the destination network. Routing protocols help the router decide which routes to use and how often to update routing information.

When purchasing a router, look for the following features or functions:

Find one that is flexible enough that you can control it by means of SNMP, through a Telnet session, and remotely through a modem.

Make sure it has a powerful processor (no less than 14,400Kbps).

It should offer connections to as many types of wire as possible—Ethernet, FDDI, token ring, and so on.

The router should allow you to swap out parts—such as CPUs and NICs.

Onboard memory should be from 2MB for small models to 8MB for larger, WAN devices.

It should be able to interpret IPX/SPX, TCP/IP, AppleTalk, and any other protocols you use.

For a TCP/IP network, find a router that includes RIP and OSPF. Don't buy a router that handles only one routing protocol, however.

Find a router that can handle power surges, excessive traffic, and traffic overloads.

Configuring a Router

Often switches and bridges can automatically configure themselves, but configuring a router is more complex. Router configuration involves setting the functions for perhaps hundreds of hardware interfaces, protocols, and parameters. Add to this vendor-specific methods and applications, and you have quite a job on your hands.

You must configure physical interfaces to LANs and WANs for most routers. On each interface, you need to enable support for traffic protocols, define routing tables or configure support for automatic routing tables, and define filters for each interface-protocol combination.

Most routers have at least two physical interfaces. LAN connections aren't generally difficult; however, WAN connections require more restricted information for configuration. For example, Ethernet interfaces that can handle either 10Mbit/sec or 100Mbit/sec links may need to be expressly configured to auto-negotiate the speed. The traditional approach is to connect individual subnets to discrete physical router ports.

WAN Connections

With WANs, there is generally a physical layer, or a line ending you don't control because it's terminated elsewhere, such as at a phone company. If a line isn't working properly, you have to trust that company if it says the problem isn't on its end.

If the link is a dial-up analog line, you set up modems on either end. You could create a script that issues AT commands to the modem and sends along a username and password to authenticate the session. ISDN modems easily dial the destination, but there are many decisions to make about the two BRI channels. Should the second channel be active all the time? Only when the first line is saturated? Or never? The decisions depend on your uses and requirements of the line.

Figure E.14 shows how routers might be used within a WAN.

Framing Protocols

Configure the link (whether dial-up or live) for one of the framing protocols—PPP, frame relay, LAP-B (Link Access Protocol-Balanced for X.25), HDLC (High-Level Data-Link Control), or other Layer 2 protocols (see Table E.1). You can get the information you need from your telecommunications service provider.

You must consider that routers are also bridges; multiple protocols on your LAN must be dealt with as each reaches the router. Some packets, such as NetBIOS, can't be routed because they don't have network layer source and destination addresses. If you wanted to use NetBIOS for, say, a peer-to-peer network, you can enable bridging between the two interfaces. You also can filter specific kinds of traffic so that every protocol that isn't routed will be bridged from one interface to the other. Some packet types—older IPX version and AppleTalk, for example—can be routed but they slow performance.

IP is the most common network protocol that you can link. Each router interface is assigned an IP address that is part of the same subnet as the other nodes on the segment. You also specify a subnet mask and usually a default gateway address. DNS server addresses are also specified with IP.

Figure E.14 Routers send messages to the appropriate addresses, even across a WAN.

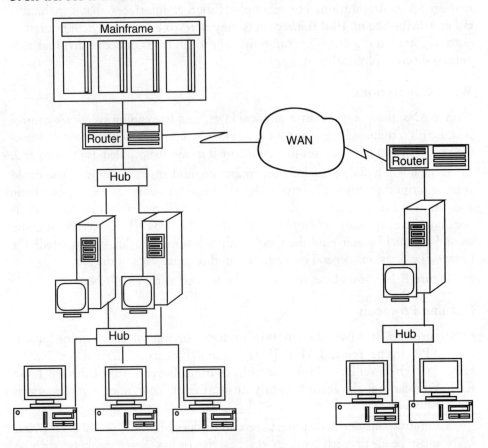

Table E.1 Framing Protocols

Protocol	Description
PPP (Point-to-Point)	Provides router-to-router and host-to-network connections over synchronous links.
Frame relay	A standard packet-switching protocol that runs very fast and supplies bandwidth on demand. Provides higher throughput than X.25.

Table E.1 *Continued*

LAP-B (Link Access Protocol-Balanced for X.25)	A bit-oriented, data-link protocol for packet-switched networks. Similar to HDLC, LAP-B enables a station to start a transmission without receiving permission from a control station.
HDLC (High-Level Data-Link Control)	A bit-oriented, synchronous protocol that provides error correction at the Data Link layer. Messages are transmitted in frames.
Layer 2	A simple protocol that provides end-to-end compression and encryption and is bidirectional in initiation.

> **NOTE**
>
> By default, NetWare and IntranetWare servers with multiple interfaces will route traffic between them. Assign a single network number to each interface for a router or a server acting as a router. If you're using IPX, you don't need IP addresses, subnet masks, and such; all you need is an interface and a network number for a new subnet.
>
> However, if you're using a combination of frame types—such as 802.2, 802.3, Ethernet II, and SNAP (Subnet Access Protocol)—a router may only route one frame type on an interface at a time.

Routing Protocols

A *router* keeps track of a packet's movements and how to move packets toward their destination. The tracking information is stored in the routing table, which associates network addresses with specific interfaces. There is a separate routing table for each enabled network protocol—one for IP, one for IPX, and so on. Some routing information protocols can automatically update routing tables. If there are several routing information protocols for each network protocol, you'll need to configure each manually. Defining static routes instead of using dynamic routing tables can save traffic but is more complex; you also can use a combination of static and dynamic routes.

For IP networks, the *RIP* (Routing Information Protocol) is widely used. RIP enables the exchange of routing information by periodic RIP updates; the information in the updates is what keeps the routing tables current. A routing table stores the network address, the number of ticks (delay time units), number of hops to an adjacent router, and the address of the next-hop node. Routers exchange request and response packets to maintain the routing tables. Each RIP packet can include as many as 50 route updates, but RIP broadcasts are limited to immediate segments to keep traffic down. With RIP, the best path is the shortest path (fewest hops).

RIP has a few weaknesses in that paths are rated by hop counts; realistically, 15 hops is the farthest a packet can hop to another host. Also, link speed and delay aren't counted into the best path the router calculates. Finally, each router's table is broadcast periodically (every 60 seconds in NetWare's RIP, for example), whether there are changes or not. This wastes WAN bandwidth.

Link-state is an improved method of determining the best path that improves on RIP (OSPF and IS-IS are examples of link-state). A routing algorithm uses the upper layer and type of service requested to determine the path. Only changes in routing tables and network connectivity are sent as they occur, which helps alleviate network congestion and traffic. Also routers using link-state share loads equally over shorter links (RIP uses only one of the links).

Of course, as the network size increases, the link-state router requires more CPU and memory. Also, if network changes occur quickly, before the router can calculate new paths, routing problems result.

> **NOTE**
> BGP, EGP, IGRP, OSPF, and RIP are all used with TCP/IP.

OSPF (Open Shortest Path First) protocol is used for large networks. A link-state algorithm enables the protocol to exchange routing information between IP routers. The OSPF routers synchronize their databases and then build the routing tables. OSPF presents a dynamic routing table that updates, using less network throughput capacity than RIP. Also, the configuration stabilizes after changes more quickly than RIP.

OSPF is one of the most widely used routing protocols. It can authenticate packets, and communicate with internal routers, border routers, and boundary routers. OSPF even offers *virtual links*—a method of bypassing broken links in backbones via border routers.

RIP and OSPF (also called *IGPs*—Interior Gateways Protocols) are designed for use with *autonomous systems*—areas with a common administra-

IP Routing

IP routers use routing protocols to learn transmission paths. The router discovers information about other routers and hosts on the network and keeps that information in a routing table. The router then selects the best path for any packet or datagram based on the information in the router's routing table. Each packet is processed separately.

The routing table directs routes for the router's network interfaces, static routes, and any routes learned from RIP, OSPF, BGP, and so on. Often, the routing table will contain different routes to the same location. IP uses a preference value as part of what determines which route to use.

External routes—OSPF, RIP, BGP, and such—usually have a preference value of 1 by default (least preferential); values range from 1 to 16. Static and direct routes as well as inter-area routes have a default preference value of 16. You can configure any value from 1 to 15 (16 is generally unreachable) for RIP, BGP, OSPF, and static routes. You cannot configure direct routes and inter-area routes.

There are also route weights that IP uses to help it select the best route and specific rules to define the routes it chooses, as well as IP routing policies and filters. All of these parameters work together to determine the routing of packets through the network.

tion and a common routing strategy. There are other routing information protocols that are best used between different autonomous systems.

EGP and *EGP-2* (Exterior Gateway Protocol) is one such routing information protocol. EGP is used to exchange network information between routers that serve as the end points of a connection between the two autonomous systems. The routers use information to maintain a list of gateways, the networks the gateways can reach, and the corresponding distances. EGP is used for communication between a number of government networks and other large backbone networks.

BGP (Border Gateway Protocol) is another such exterior gateway protocol that exchanges the network reachability information with other BGP systems. Current routing information is transmitted over a reliable transport layer connection so that periodic updates aren't necessary. Also, BGP guarantees transmissions free of loopbacks. When packets circle around a number of times, the protocol assumes there is a problem with the packet and then drops or discards it.

> **NOTE**
>
> You can manually add a route to another network and enter the route into the routing table (called a *static route*).

Finally, there are a few other routing protocols. *NLSP* (NetWare Link Services Protocol) works with IPX/SPX. IPX/SPX can address and route packets within a single network; however, it takes NLSP to accomplish the interconnection of IPX/SPX LANs. IGRP (Interior Gateway Routing Protocol) allows the user to configure many of its characteristics. IGRP recognizes interior and exterior routes as well as system routes. IS-IS (Intermediate System to Intermediate System protocol) is a dynamic routing protocol that can also work with IP. RTMP (Routing Table Maintenance Protocol) is AppleTalk's routing protocol.

Router Security

You can configure filters to help secure the network. When configuring a router, generally everything that is not explicitly permitted is prohibited, or everything not explicitly prohibited is permitted. Make sure you check the router documentation and carefully configure the security policies. You might filter all traffic except that which comes from a specific source address, or filter any characteristic transmitted in a packet—the source or destination addresses, protocol types, port IDs, specific data, and so on.

Some Configuration Possibilities

After setting up the router and performing the initial configuration—such as defining the router's address and name—you'll need to configure access control, server shutdown conditions, set up passwords, configure switching and scheduling priorities, and so on. Following are some configuration tasks that are part of initial setup of a router.

Enter and resolve the router's address

Specify a system image, configuration file, and buffer size for configuration files that the router loads at restart

Also, you'll need to configure the categories of interfaces and any special requirements for the interfaces. Following are some examples:

- ISDN basic rate switch type and whether to use caller screening

- FDDI timing parameters and address checking

- Asynchronous serial PPP or SLIP

- Token ring speed and early release of token options
- Dial-up interfaces require speed of transmission, start/stop bits, parity, control flow, and so on

Depending on the protocol you choose, the configurations will also be different. For example, AppleTalk requires you set a number of protocols, such as AppleTalk Address Resolution Protocol, Datagram Delivery Protocol, Routing Table Maintenance Protocol, Name Binding Protocol, and so on. IP requires addressing, address resolution, broadcast packet definitions, and so on. Read your documentation carefully and if in doubt, get some outside help from vendors, manufacturers, and/or consultants.

Backbones

The *backbone* is the part of the network that manages the majority of the network traffic. Usually, a backbone connects several buildings and networks by using a high-speed protocol and more applicable cabling from that used on the LAN segments. A *collapsed* backbone is a network backbone located in a single room; collapsed backbone could refer to a single router, multiport bridge, or a small LAN. Typically, a collapsed backbone refers to Ethernets in a number of buildings, each with a repeated fiber link into a central point where a router interconnects them.

The backbone system provides connections between telecommunications closets, server rooms, and entrance facilities. The system includes backbone cables, cross-connects, terminations, and patch cords used for backbone-to-backbone cross-connections. Backbones generally are limited in the number of cross-connects, total maximum distance, distance between terminations, and cable types. STP, UTP, and fiber optic cables work well as backbone cabling.

ATM and Gigabit Ethernet

ATM and *Gigabit Ethernet* both make an excellent backbone for an enterprise network. ATM offers better vendor and product support, price, flexibility in transmission media, and distances. Also, ATM supports the ability to handle different traffic types as a backbone. ATM also offers scalability and real-time traffic support.

Gigabit Ethernet is easier to incorporate as a backbone and is more backward-compatible with today's applications and software interfaces. Gigabit Ethernet uses 1000BaseSX; it's good for a single building but could be a problem for longer distances. Both ATM and Gigabit Ethernet handle network-layer switching the same. Although ATM may be better suited to IP switching, Gigabit Ethernet supports virtual LANs better. ATM is 155Mbps; Gigabit Ethernet is 1000Mbps.

Figure E.15 illustrates the use of ATM as a backbone, with Ethernet switching and Fast Ethernet switches added for certain workstations. The ATM backbone guarantees appropriate bandwidth to the servers; ATM is also used to provide more bandwidth to some workstations that need it. Notice some switches can switch both ATM and Fast Ethernet or ATM and Ethernet.

100BaseT and 100VG-AnyLAN

These two technologies are generally in competition because of their similarities. Both can operate at 100Mbps half-duplex, although 100VG-AnyLAN cannot operate at full-duplex. Both use UTP Cat 3, 4, and 5; STP; fiber cabling; and generally, share other specifications as well. 100VG-AnyLAN is better able to support a larger number of end systems, and distances aren't as limiting as with 100BaseT on copper. Following are the specifications on each technology:

> **NOTE**
>
> A *Virtual LAN* (VLAN) is a group of users that are grouped by function or job description rather than by physical location; yet packets are delivered as if it were a physical LAN. Members of a VLAN may be distributed across multiple sites. VLANs reduce network traffic and increase network efficiency by restricting broadcast messages.

Following are the specs on 100BaseT (Fast Ethernet):

- Operates at a speed of 100Mbps half-duplex and 20Mbps full-duplex
- Uses a CSMA/CD to access the media
- Uses star topology
- Can be switched or shared
- Supports hubs, adapters, routers, analyzers, and switches
- Uses UTP Cat 3, 4, and 5; STP, and fiber
- IEEE 802.3u specification

Disadvantages include flow-control problems, prioritization problems, and a bit of a distance problem if you're using Cat 5 copper cabling.

Figure E.15 ATM as a backbone in conjunction with backbone switches provides a high-performance, high-throughput network.

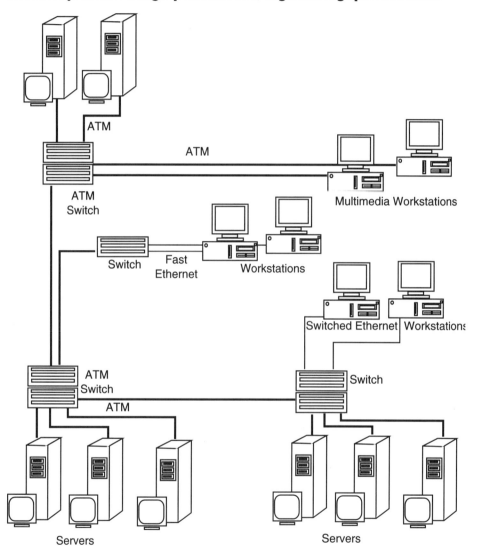

Following are the specs on 100VG-AnyLAN:

- Operates at 100Mbps half-duplex
- Can be shared or switched

- Works with star or ring topology
- Uses UTP Category 3, 4, and 5; STP; or fiber
- Supports adapters, hubs, routers, and switches
- IEEE 802.12 specification

100VG-AnyLAN doesn't support full-duplex. Only a few vendors manufacture switches for the backbone environment currently.

FDDI and FDDI II

Synchronous FDDI uses priority mechanisms to deliver tokens in a time-efficient method for use as a backbone. Operating speed is 100Mbps half-duplex and 200Mbps full-duplex. FDDI can be shared or switched, uses star and ring topologies and UTP Cat 5, STP, or fiber cabling. There are FDDI adapters, routers, hubs, and switches available as well as FDDI II adapters and hubs.

FDDI II divides the 100Mbps bandwidth into 16 channels, 6.144Mbps each. That is further divided into 96 channels that use ISDN protocols. FDDI supports various media types and is well-represented in the industry. One problem is that FDDI was originally designed as a shared-media technology, but there are vendors designing FDDI switches that make it workable as a backbone solution.

If you plan to use an FDDI as your network backbone, make sure you use *concentrators* to make the backbone stable and reliable. Concentrators protect the backbone from a multitude of problems by giving the administrator access to the logical data stream without requiring access to the physical connectors and cables of the backbone. Figure E.16 illustrates an FDDI backbone that also uses Fast Ethernet to some workgroup servers and Ethernet to the workstations.

> **NOTE**
>
> HIPPI (High-Performance Parallel Interface) presents gigabit speed, and isn't really suited as a LAN technology because PC-based bus architectures cannot make use of the technology.

Fibre Channel

Fibre Channel offers speeds of 100, 200, 400, and 800Mbps half-duplex with support for full-duplex. Supporting a ring or star topology and capable of being shared or switched, Fibre Channel provides high-speed LAN interconnectivity. While the technology supports both fiber and coaxial cabling, it doesn't support UTP.

Figure E.16 FDDI backbone and switched FDDI work well with Ethernet and Fast Ethernet.

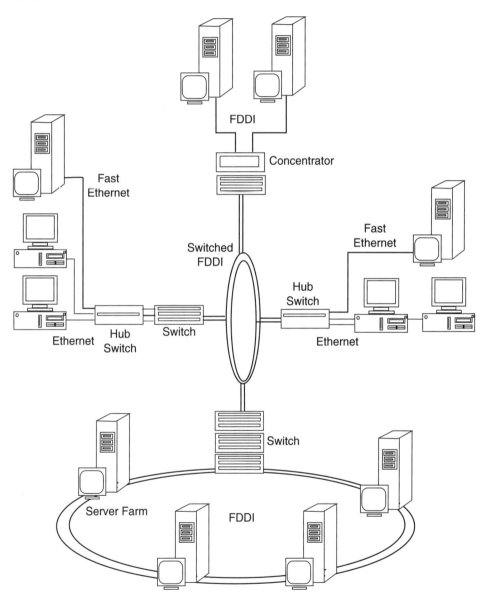

Backbone Switching

Most switches operate similarly to bridges in that they forward frames according to the destination MAC (Media Access Control) address. Dedicated connections, however temporary and virtual, provide more bandwidth than shared devices. Switches can help ease network congestion and at a lower cost than hubs, bridges, and routers.

> **TIP**
>
> Backbone routers are large and expensive; they route packets over networks with hundreds of servers and thousands of nodes. Get professional advice before purchasing one.

When you use switching within your workgroups to ease bandwidth deficiencies, you're simply moving the congestion to the backbone, which could be devastating to the entire network. If you add more users, applications, and so on, you'll need to address the backbone congestion you've created.

Be careful when you're choosing backbone switches. Some support only a single technology, while others support shared, switched, and serial technologies. An enterprise switching hub can provide connectivity across all three areas. Also, look for the following in a backbone switch:

- Provides fault-tolerant capabilities and flexibility with redundant components
- Possesses large address tables and supports numerous end-systems and segments
- Scalability in bandwidth in case you add more users and/or applications
- Large buffers and flow-control mechanisms
- Full-duplex support
- Levels of VLAN definitions, such as port, policy, and subnet/protocol
- SNMP compliance
- High-speed uplink
- Processors distributed rather than centralized

Telecommunications Devices

Communications over WAN connections, the Internet, an extranet, and so on, are often performed via telecommunications devices—analog modems, ISDN

Terminal Adapters, CSU/DSUs, and so on. Telecommunications services, including ISDN, telephone lines, and T1 lines, are used for these communications.

Table E.2 briefly describes the available devices and protocols. This section describes these devices in more detail.

Analog versus Digital Lines and Modems

Analog telephones transmit electrical impulses of varying intensity as a wave form. *Digital* systems carry bits; the intensity of the electrical signal doesn't change because all of the information is contained in numbers represented by 0s and 1s.

The process is as follows:

- Computer emits a series of digital 0s and 1s that go to your modem.

- Modem converts the binary digits into an analog wave form.

- Signal goes to the local phone company switch.

- Data is turned into digital form and transmitted at high speed to the nearest service provider.

Table E.2 Telecommunications Table

Connection	Description
PPP (Point-to-Point Protocol)	Dial-in connection at the speed of the modem
SLIP (Serial Line Interface Protocol)	Dial-in connection at modem speed
Dedicated PPP or SLIP	Dial-in connection at modem speed
56K line	Requires special equipment; connects at 56Kbps
DSL/ADSL	Modem that connects at 6 to 8Mbps; availability currently inconsistent
PPP ISDN	Requires special equipment; usage charges; connects at 128Kbps
Fractional T1	Uses a part of T1 line to provide varied speeds, depending on the size of the part
T1	Dedicated line connects at 1.5Mbps; price varies depending on distance
T3	Dedicated line connects at 45Mbps; price varies depending on distance

- Call is converted back into analog form and transmitted to the service provider's modem pool.

- Data is then converted back to digital again so the ISP's computers can deal with the information.

- Data may be corrupted during the conversions and so must be resent, causing delays.

> **NOTE**
>
> ISDN extends the *digital trunk lines*, or the lines between the switches, between your office and the telephone company switch so that you don't need a modem.
>
> To use ISDN, your area must have an ISDN-capable switch, which isn't available in all areas. If you live in an urban area, call and ask your phone company about ISDN. You must be within 3.5 miles of an ISDN switch. If you use ISDN, make sure your old analog phone and fax machines are upgraded to work on a digital line, or you can use a TA/NT1 with analog ports to support existing equipment.

A digital modem can be a CSU/DSU, ISDN TA/NT1, or a modem that can use both digital input and output. A regular modem takes analog signals in one side and outputs a digital bitstream on the other side. A true digital modem has both digital input and output with a brief analog modulation and demodulation being performed internally.

True analog modems run up to 33,000 bits per second over telephone lines. A CSU/DSU (Channel Service Unit/Digital Service Unit) is a device that powers the line to run faster than an analog modem. With CSU/DSU, the link is digital from end to end and there is no need for analog signal. A CSU/DSU is not really a true modem, but it looks like one and is often referred to as a *digital modem*.

TA/NT1 is sometimes called a *digital modem*. NT1 (Network Termination Unit One) provides power to the line and takes the two-wire ISDN line in through a U interface, converting it into a four-wire line. The Terminal Adapter (TA) takes the four-wire interface and connects it to a router or other device. If you are buying a router with a U interface, you can usually plug the phone line directly into it. TA also performs some control functions on the line.

28.8 and 33.6 Modems

Under ideal phone connections, 28.8 and 33.6 analog modems (V.34) will transmit 28,800 or 33,600 bits per second; if the modem uses data compression, however, those speeds can achieve higher throughputs. The V.34 standard is pretty mature and stable, so firmware upgrades should be few and far between (unlike the 56K V.90 standard that is new and will likely require a few upgrades).

56Kbps Technology

56Kbps analog modems (also called *V.90*) use the X2 or the K56 protocol. There are two competing standards for 56Kbps modem connections, both of which support downloading at speeds up to 53Kbps and uploading speeds of up to 33Kbps. The actual speed you get depends on the condition of the telephone lines and individual connections. However, because of data compression, the 56Kbps modems can achieve throughputs of two or more times the rate on compressible files.

56Kbps is affordable, easy to use, and provides good security. A problem with a 56Kbps connection is the local infrastructure may not support the speed.

ISDN Modems (Terminal Adapters)

An *ISDN* modem, or *terminal adapter*, is built to utilize the high speed available with ISDN BRI (Basic Rate Interface) connections. Each B channel can be considered a separate line, meaning you can download a file at 64K on one channel and talk to someone on the other B channel at the same time. You also could use both channels at the same time for a combined bandwidth of 128Kbps and even more with data compression.

With ISDN, you need a terminal adapter on your end of the line, and there must be a similar device on the other end. The distances for ISDN modems range up to 18,000 feet, although additional equipment can be used to extend the distance. Use ISDN modems for Internet or intranet access, remote LAN access, videoconferencing, frame relay, and so on.

xDSL

xDSL (Digital Subscriber Line) modems can be used over existing copper telephone wires; over clean telephone lines, xDSL can blast data at high speeds from site to site. Distance limitation for DSL devices is about 12,000 to 15,000 feet, although addition of a repeater may double a modem's maximum reach.

The repeater moves all packets from one network to another by regenerating, retiming, and amplifying the electrical signals to extend the length of the transmission beyond the normal maximum cable lengths.

When considering xDSL, you must realize that in addition to the limited distances, communications are often hampered by line impairments, such as white noise and near-end crosstalk generated by the presence of other ADSL, HDSL, ISDN, or T1 signals.

Guidelines

When searching for xDSL modems, be concerned with consistency as well as speed and distance. You might check for lab tests involving several modems to find one that delivers constant, dependable upstream and downstream speeds. *Latency*, or delay that the modem introduces before relaying the data, is another important factor. If latency is high, problems with streaming applications (such as video, interactive data, telephony, and so on) are more likely; when the stream is interrupted, the program can crash.

You must buy two modems to form the digital subscriber line. When looking for an xDSL modem, make sure it offers a graphical user interface for management applications, reports, configuration, and diagnostics. Also, check for standard protocol support (PPP and IP); easy upgrades; rate adaptivity (so it adjusts the data transfer rates to the highest speed possible); and a POTS splitter for voice-band support.

Transmission of Voice, Image, Data, and Video

To a communications network carrying and routing streams of bits, voice, images, and so on, the traffic looks the same; but there are differences in speed requirements.

Voice requires moderate transmission speeds, say, 64Kbps. With voice, the order of the transmission should be maintained.

Images or facsimiles use slow to moderate speeds with data compression (from 9600bps to 28.8Kbps). Data can, however, arrive in any order because it's reassembled upon arrival.

Data can use slow to moderate speeds (9600bps to 128Kbps) and can also arrive in any order.

Video requires high speeds (128Kbps minimum) because of the constant stream of images. Also, the order of transmission should be maintained.

DSL Types

There are different types of DSL; following is a description of each:

HDSL (High-bit rate DSL). Uses two or three pairs of copper wire to form a T1 or E1 connection; T1 is preferred. E1 is the European basic multiplex rate that carries 30 voice channels transmitted at 2.048Mbps. HDSL is symmetric, which means it provides the same bandwidth both upstream and downstream. Its speed is 1.544Mbps over two copper pairs and 2.048Mbps over three copper pairs. HDSL is an alternative to repeatered T1/E1 lines. HDSL has a 15,000-foot operating distance but signal repeaters can extend the range. HDSL is ideal for connecting PBX systems, POPs, Internet servers, and campus-based networks.

SDSL (Single-Line Digital Subscriber Line). Supports symmetrical T1/E1 transmissions using a single copper pair wire with a maximum operating range of 10,000 feet. SDSL is good for videoconferencing or collaborative computing.

ADSL (Asymmetric DSL). Allows more bandwidth downstream than upstream, which makes it ideal for applications such as video on demand, remote LAN access, and Internet access. It supports rates as high as 8Mbit/sec downstream (users typically download more than they send) and up to 16 and 640Kbps upstream. Also, it supports voice and data simultaneously and carries voice at lower frequency (as does HDSL) so it doesn't impact data throughout. ADSL transmits at distances of up to 18,000 feet over one wire pair and optimal speeds of 6 to 8Mbps are achieved at distances from 10,000 to 12,000 feet, using standard 24-gauge wire.

RADSL (Rate Adaptive DSL). A newer version of ADSL enables the modem to adjust the speed. RADSL operates at the same transmission rates as ADSL but adjusts dynamically to varying lengths and qualities of twisted pair access lines.

The cheapest, and slowest, is ISDN DSL (ISDSL), which provides end-to-end connectivity over the public switched telephone network.

VDSL (Very high speed DSL). Provides downstream speeds of 13 to 52Mbps and upstream rates of 1.5 to 2.3Mbps over a single copper pair wire. It delivers voice, video, and data for operating distances of 1000 to 4500 feet. VDSL is primarily used for high-definition television program delivery and multimedia Internet access.

CSU/DSU

A *CSU/DSU* (Channel Service Unit/Data Service Unit) is a digital circuit modem, of sorts. Other names for a CSU/DSU device include *digital sharing device*, *digital bridge*, *Multiple-Access Unit* (MAU), and *modem-sharing device*. A CSU/DSU provides the termination of a communications circuit from the telephone company into the users' equipment; generally, the circuit is carried over copper twisted pairs. The CSU terminates a digital circuit by performing line conditioning and equalization. The DSU converts the signaling protocol to and from the format used by the user's terminal equipment and the format used by a digital circuit or channel.

There are many types of CSU/DSU devices and each provides different services. You can buy a CSU/DSU that provides full SNMP management, or works over T1 or frame relay, or supports speeds of 2400 and 56,000, or maintains analog or digital.

> **NOTE**
>
> The X.25 protocol runs at 64Kbps, much slower than many newer technologies available today. As an older protocol, X.25 can't keep up with increased demands for voice and data switches, routers, multiplexors, and so on.

Network/Systems Management

Network/Systems management includes all activities and products to plan, configure, control, monitor, recover faults, tune, and administer computer networks and distributed systems. This management becomes more complex when you include diverse locations, NOSs, and hardware in your network.

Consider the number and variety of your network components, for example. You likely use different hosts, workstations, modems, concentrators, switches, routers, repeaters, and so on. The number of systems is probably diverse as well—operating systems, interfaces, protocols, and versions. Your network most likely spans several locations and uses a number of companies, vendors, operators, and service solutions.

Even if your network is small and you're using the same or similar hardware throughout, you probably use various services and distributed applications. Examples of distributed services include: file and print services, gateways, mail, accounting services, security, and multiple management systems services. How do you keep your eyes on all of these systems?

Network and systems management applications enable you to configure, control, monitor, and analyze your network. Matched to your operating system, the application normally lets you manage hubs, switches, routers, and remote access servers. Management systems let you monitor congestion and troubleshoot problems before they get out of control.

Along with network management applications are devices and utilities that help you test cables, sniff packets, and analyze your network. In the past, protocol analyzers were the primary network diagnostic tool, but there are so many more tools currently available for the network administrator.

Management Software

In order to manage a system or network, you must view the entire system. A global view lets you check configuration consistency and network equipment. There are many products available to let you view your system and network. Some products allow management of only one type of device and others allow management of multiple, dissimilar devices. If you use independent tools to manage your network, the tools likely will overlap in their control and maintenance areas and cause problems with consistency, alarms, and logging.

SNMP and RMON

SNMP and RMON are industry standards for managing remote devices and LAN segments. SNMP can poll devices through MIBs (Management Information Bases) and deliver information about the device, and RMON provides information about the LAN traffic but not the devices.

Most products use the services of the Simple Network Management Protocol (SNMP) to monitor the network. SNMP is a part of the TCP/IP suite and is used to manage and monitor nodes on a network. Multivendor management systems can manage devices from a central site by embedding SNMP within data communication devices, such as switches, routers, and so on.

There are three components of SNMP: *SNMP manager*, *SNMP agent*, and *MIBs*. Agents send and receive network management instructions. Managers run the network management software. SNMP also includes MIBs, which store information about devices in a network. The manager and the agent use SNMP commands to exchange information.

Devices that are SNMP manageable must supply information about their status, such as system information, interface information, and interface usage. Also, many hardware vendors are increasing the data that can be obtained by

SNMP as it relates to specific hardware devices—disk usage statistics, workstation activity, and memory mappings.

There are also limitations to SNMP. Although SNMP monitors and regularly polls devices, it doesn't monitor network traffic on a LAN segment. SNMP devices identify traffic as it applies to the device but not any transfers between devices, thus making troubleshooting more difficult.

The RMON (Remote MONitoring) standard enables a network device to collect data independently of a management station so that trends can be calculated. RMON supports the monitoring of the total traffic for remote LAN segments and analysis on network parameters for fault diagnosis, planning, and optimization.

RMON works through a set of MIBs that collect statistical information not available to SNMP and enable threshold setting for alarms. RMON supports network monitoring through the MAC layer, which means it's not capable of monitoring some protocol stacks (IP, FTP, and so on) as well as other problems with the upper OSI layers and their statistics. Enterprise RMON enables the monitoring of all seven OSI layers—any protocol traffic for any device or segment.

Network Management Products

You can find management software for UNIX, Windows NT, NetWare, VINES, and other popular network operating systems. Windows network management applications usually manage only one type of device; but there are exceptions. Some programs provide a range of tools, such as inventory management, software licensing, hardware monitoring, and remote access, including Intel Landesk and 3Com Transcend.

Novell has the NMS product that automatically records and maps network devices, monitors for network changes, manages alarm information, and so on. It also includes a LAN analyzer tool.

Two programs for UNIX—Solstice Site Manager and Hewlett-Packard's OpenView—provide graphical layouts of the network, using SNMP. Monitoring statistics for most network devices makes network management easier.

Network Diagnostic Tools

There are a variety of network diagnostic tools; hand-held devices are the most popular at the moment. The more complex a diagnostic tool is, the harder it is to read and interpret its findings. A cable tester's analysis, for example, is fairly easy to understand; however, a WAN tester's readings are complex and impossible to understand without a great deal of network knowledge.

3Com Transcend Enterprise Manager

Transcend is a management tool for Windows NT, or UNIX that works with 3Com devices. Transcend includes SNMP-based applications that enable network management of hubs, adapters, routers, and switches.

Transcend includes multiple versions and products, each with different jobs. For example, the Transcend Workgroup Manager is built for small networks, and the Transcend Enterprise Manager is designed for larger LANs and WANs. The management software includes the following tools:

- For network monitoring and analysis, agent-based statistics monitoring
- For VLAN management, ATM management capabilities
- Integration with HP OpenView by running on top of OpenView

Transcend enables you to build a network map of 3Com devices and manage those devices; you can also monitor devices and collect statistics. Transcend can detect broadcast storms and automatically disable offending ports before the rest of the network is affected. You can even configure the program to take action against certain events and traps on the network.

Transcend is scalable in that you can add more devices, and it maintains an even level of network surveillance. It also enables easier transfers of users' equipment and network reconfiguration after a move.

Transcend is difficult to set up and configure, as is any network management product. Also, you must use 3Com devices in order to benefit from the software, as is true with many network management applications.

Luckily, many devices are now shipping with what are called *expert systems*. Expert systems produce a diagnosis based on certain events or thresholds. Preconfigured with default parameters to conform to an average network, the administrator will most likely need to change defaults to analyze one segment at a time.

Cable testers are great troubleshooting tools; generally, half of all network problems result from the cabling. Cable testers can detect loose connections, faulty cables, incorrect configuration, and the wrong type of cable. You should use a cable tester to certify a new cable installation and recertify after a move, addition, or change to the cabling of your network. Standard cable testers locate errors in the cable, which is part of the OSI Layer 1.

A *network analyzer* is a cable tester with a processor, RAM, and instructions for SNMP, and enables you to diagnose problems from the wiring closet.

Some network analyzers locate problems in Layers 2 and 3 of the OSI reference model. A network analyzer can PING a device and measure round-trip delay, identify active servers and other components, and display data on error counts and network utilization. Many analyzers work over multiple network protocols—such as Ethernet, token ring, and TCP/IP—and link with other network management platforms.

WAN testers, network analyzers with an add-on board or external module enable testing of such elements as Fractional T-1 circuits. WAN testers are more complicated and require more skill and setup than a LAN tester because WANs have so many more interfaces and protocols. These network analyzers can locate problems on Layers 2 through 6 of the OSI reference model.

Protocol analyzers can be either hardware or software. The software versions are good for monitoring networks such as 10Mbps Ethernet segments. Hardware protocol analyzers that have dedicated memory and sometimes a coprocessor work well for high-performance networks such as FDDI or ATM.

There are software versions of most analyzers and testing devices. There are software analyzers for one LAN segment or for WAN connections. The problem with the software versions, however, is that they're not mobile as a hand-held tool would be.

> **NOTE**
> Packet sniffers are also called *network packet analyzers*. In addition to performing LAN and WAN diagnostics, such as monitoring traffic generation and troubleshooting, sniffers can capture every packet on a network and decode all seven layers of the OSI protocol model. Sniffers can also filter specified source and destination addresses of packets so you can interrupt and terminate attacks to your network. There are sniffers dedicated to ISDN, FDDI, and other network options.

Acronyms

ACL   Access Control List

ADSL   Asymmetric DSL

AIX   Advanced Interactive Executive

ANSI   American National Standards Institute

API   Application Program Interface

ARA   Apple Remote Access

ARAP   AppleTalk Remote Access Protocol

ARP   Address Resolution Protocol

ATM   Asynchronous Transfer Mode

ATMP   Ascend Tunnel Management Protocol

AUI   Attachment Unit Interface

BGP   Border Gateway Protocol

BIOS   Basic Input/Output System

B-ISDN   Broadband ISDN

BRI   Basic Rate Interface

CA   Certificate Authority

CAD   Computer Aided Drafting

CCIA   Computer Communications Industry Association

CCITT   Comité Consultatif Internationale de Téléphonie et de Télégraphie

CGI   Common Gateway Interface

CHAP   Challenge-Handshake Authentication Protocol

CISC   Complex Instruction Set Computing

COS   Client Operating System

CPU   Central Processing Unit

CRC   Cyclic Redundancy Check

CSMA/CD   Carrier Sense Multiple Access/Collision Detection

DAC   Discretionary Access Control

DAT   Digital Audio Tapes

DBMS   DataBase Management System

DDE   Dynamic Data Exchange

DDL   Data Definition Language

DES   Data Encryption Standard

DHCP   Dynamic Host Configuration Protocol

DLC   Data-Link Control

DLCI   Data-Link Control Identifier

DLT   Digital Linear Tape

DMA   Direct Memory Access

DNS   Domain Name System

DOS   Disk Operating System

DRAM   Dynamic RAM

DSL   Digital Subscriber Line

DSU/CSU   Digital Service Unit/Channel Service Unit

DUN   Dial-up Networking

DVMRP   Distance Vector Multicast Routing Protocol

ECC   Error Correcting Circuitry

EDO   Enhanced Data Output

EGP   Exterior Gateway Protocol

EIA   Electronic Industries Association

EIDE   Enhanced IDE

EISA   Extended Industry Standard Architecture

EMF   Enhanced Metafiles

FAQ   Frequently Asked Questions

FDDI   Fiber Distributed Data Interface

FTP   File Transfer Protocol

GUI   Graphical User Interface

HDLC   High-level Data-Link Control

HDSL   High-bit-rate DSL

HIPPI   High-Performance Parallel Interface

HPGL   Hewlett-Packard Graphics Language

HSM   Hierarchical Storage Management

HTML   HyperText Markup Language

HTTP   HyperText Transfer Protocol

I/O   Input/Output

ICMP   Internet Control Message Protocol

IDE   Integrated Drive Electronics

IE   Internet Explorer

IEEE   Institute of Electrical and Electronics Engineers

IGRP   Interior Gateway Routing Protocol

IMAP   Internet Message Access Protocol

IP   Internet Protocol

IPP   Internet Printing Protocol

IPSec   IP Security

IPX/SPX   Internet Packet Exchange/Sequenced Packet Exchange

IRQ   Interrupt Request

ISA   Industry Standard Architecture

ISDN   Integrated Services Digital Network

ISO   International Standard Organization

ISO/OSI   International Standards Organization/Open Systems Interconnection

ISP   Internet Service Provider

ITU   International Telecommunications Union

JNT   Java Network Terminal

L2F   Layer 2 Forwarding

L2TP   Layer 2 Tunneling Protocol

LAN   Local Area Network

LAP-B   Link Access Protocol-Balanced for X.25

LED   Light Emitting Diode

LLC   Logical Link Control

LPD   Line Printer Daemon

LPR   Line Printer Remote

LPQ   Line Printer Queue

MAC   Mandatory Access Control

MAC   Media Access Control

MAN   Metropolitan Area Network

MAU   Multistation Access Unit

MIB   Management Information Bases

MIME   Multipurpose Internet Mail Extensions

MIPS   Management Information System

MOSS   MIME Object Security Services

MPP   Massively Parallel Processing

MOSPF   Multicast Open Shortest Path First

NDIS   Network Device Interface Specification

NDS   Novell Directory Services

NetBEUI   NetBIOS Extended User Interface

NetBIOS   Network Basic Input/Output System

NFS   Network File System

NIC   Network Interface Card

N-ISDN   Narrowband ISDN

NLM   NetWare Loadable Module

NLSP   NetWare Link Services Protocol

NNTP   Network News Transfer Protocol

NOS   Network Operating System

ODBC   Open Database Connectivity

ODI   Open Datalink Interface

OLAP   Online Analytical Processing

OLTP   Online Transaction Processing

OS   Operating System

OSPF   Open Shortest Path First

PAP   Password Authentication Protocol

PBX   Private Branch Exchange

PCI   Peripheral Component Interconnect

PCL   Printer Control Language

PCMCIA   Personal Computer Memory Card International Association

PDL   Page Description Language

PGP   Pretty Good Privacy

PIM   Protocol Independent Multicast

PIN   Personal Identification Number

PING   Packet InterNet Grouper

PKI   Public Key Infrastructure

POP   Points of Presence

POP3   Post Office Protocol

POTS   Plain Old Telephone Service

PPP   Point-to-Point Protocol

PPTP   Point-to-Point Tunneling Protocol

PRI   Primary Rate Interface

PS   PostScript

PVC   Permanent Virtual Circuit

RACF   Resource Access Control Facility

RADIUS   Remote Authentication Dial-in User Service

RADSL   Rate Adaptive DSL

RAID   Redundant Array of Inexpensive or Integrated Disks

RAM   Random Access Memory

RAS   Remote Access Service

RDRAM   Rambus DRAM

RFS   Remote File Service

RIP   Routing Information Protocol

RISC   Reduced Instruction Set Computing

RMON   Remote network MONitoring

RNA   Remote Network Access

RPC   Remote Procedure Call

RTMP   Routing Table Maintenance Protocol

SAA   Systems Application Architecture

SAP   Service Advertising Protocol

SCSI   Small Computer System Interface

SDD   Solid-State Disk

SDRAM   Synchronous DRAM

SDSL   Single-Line Digital Subscriber Line

SET   Secure Electronic Transaction

S-HTTP   Secure HyperText Transfer Protocol

SIDF   System Independent Data Format

SLDRAM   SyncLink DRAM

SLIP   Serial Line Internet Protocol

SMB   Server Message Block

SMDS   Switched Multimegabit Digital Service

S/MIME   Secure MIME

SMP   Symmetric Multiprocessing

SMS   Storage Management Service

SMTP   Simple Mail Transfer Protocol

SNA   Systems Network Architecture

SNAP   Subnet Access Protocol

SNMP   Simple Network Management Protocol

SONET   Synchronous Optical Network

SPOOL   Simultaneous Peripheral Operation On Line

SQL   Structured Query Language

SSL   Secure Sockets Layer

STP   Shielded Twisted Pair cable

SVC   Switched Virtual Circuit

TA   Terminal Adapter

TCP   Transmission Control Protocol

TCP/IP   Transmission Control Protocol/Internet Protocol

TCS   Telecommunications wiring Standard

TDR   Time Domain Reflectometer

TSA   Target Service Agent

UDP   User Datagram Protocol

UPS   Uninterruptable Power Supply

URL   Universal Resource Locator

UTP   Unshielded Twisted Pair

VAR   Value-Added Reseller

VDSL   Very high speed DSL

VINES   VIrtual NEtworking Software

VLAN   Virtual LAN Networking

VPN   Virtual Private Network

VTP   Virtual Tunneling Protocol

WAIS   Wide Area Information Server

WAN   Wide Area Network

WINS   Windows Internet Name Service

WLAN   Wireless LAN

WORM   Write-Once-Read-Many

WWW   World Wide Web

NETWORK OPERATING SYSTEMS

There are many NOSs you might use. This appendix covers only the three most common and popular: UNIX, Novell NetWare, and Microsoft NT Server. For more information about other operating systems, you might try a third-party book or the Internet.

UNIX

UNIX is a 32-bit multitasking, multiuser operating system that was developed in the late 1960s and has been used as well as augmented over the years. UNIX is primarily used in networking servers because of the networking services it provides, especially its advanced security. UNIX is powerful, stable, and flexible as a network operating system; it is also extremely difficult to install, configure, and administer as it is primarily a command-prompt–oriented operating system (although you can use XWindows as a graphic-oriented operating system). UNIX uses the TCP/IP set of protocols.

There are many versions of UNIX available, including AIX, A/UX, Linux, Solaris, and so on. UNIX can run on a wide array of computational hardware, from the PC to a Cray supercomputer. Following are brief descriptions of common UNIX clones.

AIX (Advanced Interactive Executive). A UNIX version from IBM that runs on IBM workstations, minicomputers, and mainframes.

A/UX. A graphical version of UNIX that runs on Macintosh computers. A/UX is based on the System V release 2 of UNIX; it includes various Apple features that enable applications to use the Macintosh interface.

Linux. A UNIX clone that enables POSIX compliance. Linux employs true multitasking, virtual memory, memory management, TCP/IP networking, and so on.

Solaris.   A UNIX version from SunSoft that runs on Intel processors and supports a graphical user interface, email NFS (Network File System), and NIS (Network Information Services).

XWindows.   A graphical user interface that supplies a Windows-like interface between the UNIX operating system and the user.

There are other manufacturers who have developed their own versions of UNIX, such as Hewlett-Packard's HP-UX. Each version or clone has its own advantages and disadvantages, features and utilities, and compatibilities.

Solaris

There are multiple versions and uses for Solaris. Solaris 2 is more compatible with the rest of the UNIX industry than previous versions, for example. Trusted Solaris is for use with a distributed client/server network but offers strictly maintained security.

Solaris 2.x features a standard release of the XWindow system, is industry-standards compliant, and supports all Sun graphics hardware. Advantages of Solaris 2.x include OpenWindows standards, ANSI-C and POSIX compliance, multithreaded kernel, faster clock ticks, true multiprocessing, power management software included, and so on. Some disadvantages include a lack of migration support for previous versions and some missing functionalities, such as no C compiler.

Trusted Solaris is aimed more and more toward Internet and electronic commerce users. Trusted Solaris provides protection for company networks without impacting functionality. Features include data protection through MAC (Mandatory Access Control), policy enforcement over NFS, GUI tools for simplified management, customized system security, security profiles, and more.

AIX

AIX is a combination of System V and BSD, following various standards such as IEEE, POSIX, ANSI, and others. AIX stores most of its system management information in an object database, which is managed and administered by the Object Database Manager (ODM). The ODM is a set of library routines and programs that provide for basic object-oriented database facilities.

Linux

Linux is a UNIX clone that has many of UNIX's features, such as shared libraries, demand loading, shared copy-on-write executables, proper memory management, and so on. Linux usually runs on 386, 486, and Pentium-based computers and supports ports to other processors—PowerPC, DEC Alpha/AXP, RISC PC, and so on.

Before you implement Linux on an enterprise network, make sure it is totally compatible with all applications, hardware, protocols, and other features of your network. Linux is a free operating system; support may not be available for its use.

Linux supports XWindows as well as other standard UNIX utilities, TCP/IP, and hundreds of programs written specifically for Linux. It can share a disk with DOS, OS/2, and other operating systems on separate partitions. Linux is based on POSIX and UNIX APIs and supports both 32- and 64-bit hardware.

Linux is not UNIX, in that all UNIX trademarked systems must meet a complex set of X/Open standards; Linux doesn't meet those standards, but it is very close to the UNIX system. Linux uses Internet and industry-standard components and protocols for complete network integration.

XWindows

There are several types of UNIX operating systems for servers and networks; and UNIX can work with a variety of client operating systems. XWindows is an application that supplies a graphical user interface between the UNIX operating system and the user. Using XWindows, a user can open and run several applications at one time. You can use XWindows, for example, on a Sun Workstation or X terminal.

XWindows uses a mouse to cut, paste, and copy text within windows; minimize and maximize windows; and otherwise manipulate windows and document contents. An xterm provides a window where you can use a system prompt to enter normal UNIX commands; you can even move the mouse within the xterm window. XWindows provides menus of commands, such as common UNIX commands, window operations, and tools and applications. An intricate Help system also provides information about XWindows and XWindows programming.

Novell NetWare

NetWare is a series of multitasking network operating systems by Novell. NetWare runs on Intel computers and supports DOS, Windows, Macintosh, UNIX, and OS/2 clients. NetWare can use the IPX/SPX, AppleTalk Filing Protocol, TCP/IP, OSI, or the NetBIOS network protocols.

Novell has produced multiple versions and variants of its network operating systems. NetWare comes in versions 4.*x* and 5.*x*; there's also an IntranetWare available from Novell. Versions previous to 3.*x* are obsolete in today's networking environments.

NetWare 3.*x*

Although NetWare 3.*x* is still being used in limited environments today, it is outdated by more recent versions of the NOS; however, many people still use version 3.*x* in a small LAN or WAN and with older client systems. Version 3.*x* is a 32-bit NOS that runs on 386 processors and later.

Also, Novell offers an upgrade to NetWare 3.2 to improve reliability and enhance performance. A Windows-based SYSCON tool helps make administration easier, and updated client software means you can better use Windows 95 and 98 workstations with the NOS. The important part of the NetWare 3.2 upgrade is Internet access via Netscape Navigator and Year 2000 readiness.

NetWare 4.*x*

NetWare 4.*x* supports optical disks, CD-ROMs, data compression, and offers improved login security over previous versions. NetWare is suitable for large networks, including enterprises and WANs. It also includes utilities for management of both servers and clients. NetWare 4.*x* uses the proprietary IPX protocol that literally cuts off NetWare-based information and applications from the Internet. NetWare 4.*x* also introduces the use of NDS (Novell Directory Services) as a database for managing network resources.

NetWare 4.11 upgrades the previous versions by adding symmetric multiprocessing, integrated TCP/IP, a DHCP server, C2 security, migration tools, and improved performance over NetWare 4.1. NetWare 4.11 is the base for IntranetWare (see following section) that adds the Internet technologies to the operating system.

NetWare 5.*x*

Version 5.*x* will still use NDS for easy management and control of the networking environment. Additionally, IP and IPX are supported, as well as the DNS and DHCP industry standards. The key factor to NetWare 5.*x* is its integration with TCP/IP, with which Internet and intranet applications can be easily developed and run.

NDS

NDS (Novell Directory Services) is Novell's access, management, and control mechanism for any network operating system, beginning with NetWare 4. Using NDS, you can manage users and resources on the network in a secure and confident manner. You can assign rights and limitations through NDS-based management tools to design your security from the foundation up.

NDS provides a method of maintaining information about users, groups, printers, volumes, servers, and other resources on the network. NDS is based on a CCITT directory standard and replaces previous versions' bindery databases. The *bindery* was a system database that managed the operation of a single NetWare server as opposed to the entire network that NDS manages.

NDS reduces management and administration costs because it centralizes administration.

Building on NetWare 4, NetWare 5 offers a new file storage access system and print services. Also, additional security services include public-key cryptography and Secure Authentication Services. These services will help integrate Internet security across the corporate network.

IntranetWare

IntranetWare is built around the NetWare 4.11 operating system. IntranetWare is also compatible with NDS; enables compatibility with UNIX and NT, mainframes, and minicomputers; and supports open standards and Internet technologies. Management and administrative utilities are included for complete and easy control over applications and network integration.

The key to IntranetWare is its ability to access resources on the Internet and over your own intranet. A multiprotocol router is included to support frame relay, X.25, and ISDN connections. You can build your own web sites using Netscape FastTrack Server, included in the IntranetWare package. Also included are Netscape Navigator as a browser, CGI scripting, NetBasic, Java Virtual Machine, and other Java tools.

Web publishing and FTP tools are also included, as well as DHCP and DNS support. You can use either IPX or TCP/IP on your corporate intranet and network by use of an IPX/IP gateway.

IntranetWare for Small Businesses

Novell's IntranetWare for Small Businesses (IWSB) is an entry-level NOS friendly to new users. IWSB uses a friendly interface and it's easy to set up. A NetWare Easy Administration Tool makes installation and management easier than other versions of NetWare, and it offers a complete network system for sites using DOS, Windows 3.x, Windows 95, and Macintosh clients. IWSB also includes Novell's Web Server and NetWare Connect for users to connect to the network from a remote location via modem and phone line; users can share files, printers, and network applications.

Modified from full-blown IntranetWare, IWSB has no WAN features like the IP-to-IPX gateway; but it does use NDS. The use of NDS means IWSB could be migrated to a standard IntranetWare NDS at some point if the network grows or the administrator requires more from the operating systems. IWSB's NDS is, however, a flat directory instead of a hierarchical one. A hierarchical structure lets you organize a large network into smaller sections. With IWSB, you can't divide your network into smaller networks under the cover of one NDS umbrella. Also, IWSB is a standalone network; you can't include it as one branch of a larger NDS tree.

Windows Client/Server Networking

Microsoft has introduced several client/server applications to the networking world, including Windows NT 4, Windows NT Enterprise Edition, and the BackOffice Server Suites. Using Microsoft's products, you can build your entire enterprise network with confidence—system security, Web integration, mobile users, mainframe support, and much more.

Windows NT Server

NT Server has been around for a while, including version 3.51, which was a solid, 32-bit network operating system. However, with NT 4.x, Microsoft has hit on the perfect networking system for today's LANs and WANs. NT 4.x includes an authentication and security system to protect your users, auditing and accounting policies that give you control over the system, and resource permissions to help control access to your data. Also, NT provides print management capabilities, server management utilities, replication and backup tools, and more.

NT Server provides applications for helping you set up Web sites, manage content, and analyze usage patterns. You can use the Microsoft Index server, for example, to index text and HTML files on your intranet or Internet web server. FrontPage is program included in NT that enables you to design a Web site and create content for that site; you can also use its management features to organize your site(s). The Internet Information Server, a World Wide Web server included with the NOS, enables you to use NT's powerful auditing and security systems with your Web server, as well as provide a wide range of services to your users.

> **NOTE**
>
> NT Server 5.0, due for release in 1999, will include all of version 4's features plus a network directory services database to make user and resource management easier and more efficient.

Windows NT Server Enterprise Edition

The Enterprise Edition of NT Server extends the scalability, availability, and the manageability of NT Server 4. Use the Enterprise Edition for building and deploying large-scale distributed applications and enterprise networks. The Enterprise Edition includes a cluster-ready operating system that can provide higher availability for mission-critical data and applications. Clustering also provides automatic recovery from failures and centralized administration of the servers.

The Enterprise Edition of NT supports eight processors for symmetric multiprocessing, as opposed to NT 4's four-processor SMP. Adding processors to the server(s) means more fault tolerance, balanced server load, and more efficient services.

The Enterprise Edition also includes a built-in Transaction Server and Message Queue Server so you can more easily manage applications across thousands of machines in your enterprise while protecting transactions and ensuring delivery of messages.

BackOffice Server Suite

Microsoft also offers a host of servers that you can purchase separately or in the BackOffice bundle. These server applications are integrated with NT Server so that security, authentication, databases, and other features work together for seamless integration of services. BackOffice Server includes the following servers:

NT Server. The foundation of the network operating system and BackOffice suite.

IIS (Internet Information Server). A World Wide Web server.

Index Server.   A server for indexing content on the web server.

Certificate Server.   Management of licensing and authentication.

Transaction Server.   Provides distributed transaction services, manages security, and enables you to build applications quickly.

Message Queue Server.   Provides reliable delivery of messages and data across the network.

FrontPage.   An application for web content development and management.

Exchange Server.   A groupware application that provides messaging, calendaring, and other shared resource services.

Proxy Server.   Provides protection from Internet intruders and provides limits you can set for your users when accessing the Internet.

SNA Server.   Enables the exchange of data between PCs on the network and legacy systems—mainframes and minicomputers.

SQL Server.   A database management system for your network.

Site Server.   Enables you to control your Web sites, documents, addresses, and such, on the Internet.

Systems Management Server.   Provides a method of inventory to track software and hardware use on your network.

> **NOTE**
>
> There may be more or fewer servers in your BackOffice package, depending on the version you acquire.

Integration of NOSs

As you know, many networks are made up of heterogeneous platforms, hardware, and operating systems. It's common to begin a network with one operating system and then add to that system with other various NOSs to accommodate certain applications, corporate policies, new hardware or specifications, and so on. Most network operating systems can and do work well with other NOSs, either by features added to either or both NOSs or with the help from one or more third-party products. This section outlines a few common methods of integrating multiple NOSs.

OS/2 Warp

OS/2 Warp server, made by IBM, is a NOS that may be in place in your business. Although not as popular as the other NOSs mentioned here, OS/2 Warp server is popular in some banking and financial services' LANs and WANs. And, with IBM's newer version of OS/2—Aurora—more enterprise networks can make use of the operating system.

Aurora includes more backup capabilities and enterprise management utilities than OS/2 Warp did. One of the drawbacks of IBM's NOS is the lack of Java-based applications for OS/2 Warp server as opposed to the hundreds of applications available for Novell and Microsoft's NOSs.

Aurora does have its own Java Virtual Machine to speed performance; and it's year 2000 compliant. Aurora also includes a new command line GUI, automated backup for large networks, better performance, and enhanced Web server capabilities.

NOTE

As you know, most client operating systems—Macintosh, Windows 9X and NT, DOS, OS/2, and so on—work with most network operating systems. Integration is usually easy for sharing files, printers, and other resources.

NT and NetWare

NetWare and Windows have long worked together in a networking environment. Both products offer utilities to enable you to integrate the two systems, and many third-party applications are also available.

Novell offers many approaches to enable NetWare to work with NT Server. Multinetwork connectivity tools offer migration services between the two systems, Novell's add-ons for printer and file sharing, and so on. Both systems supply certain graphical utilities that you can use to manipulate NDS objects, file and print services, symmetric multiprocessing, telephony, multimedia, Internet and intranet browsing, and publishing capabilities.

Microsoft also furnishes utilities for NetWare file and print services, migration and gateway services, and such. NT provides the transport protocol software that enables servers to communicate with NetWare computers and a gateway service that enables servers and workstations on NT Server domain to use resources on NetWare network servers. The NT migration tool helps you transfer users, groups, and data files from NetWare to NT if you want to change over to an exclusive NT network.

Clients with or without NetWare client software can communicate with NetWare, using the gateway service provided by NT. Additionally, an NT add-on—File and Print Services for NetWare—enables an NT Server computer to function as a NetWare-compatible file and print server.

Also, various client operating systems— NT, Windows 95 and 98, Windows 3.x, UNIX, OS/2, Macintosh, and DOS—can share files and resources between the two systems. They both provide easy management on multiple servers.

Naturally, there will be problems between the two operating systems: slowed performance, user problems with operating between the two systems, and so on. However, you may be able to find some help with add-on products by Novell, Microsoft, or a third-party manufacturer. Following is an example of problems with multiple logons.

When you make changes to Novell's NDS, you must also make those changes again with NT domains, such as adding or deleting users. Users must then enter multiple passwords to log on to both environments. If you install Exchange to your NT Server, you make more problems for the administration and support staff, as well as confuse the users. Novell has an NDS for NT that integrates NT domains directly into the NDS tree and enables you to manage the NT Server domain through NDS. Only one login is necessary, and there is only one point of administration.

NT and UNIX

Currently, NT is out-shipping all UNIX systems combined for both desktop and server applications. UNIX is growing only at a small rate in comparison to the NT revolution.

Since Windows NT Server has entered the networking scene, some manufacturers have been working on a solution for using UNIX and NT in an integrated network approach. Using the two networks together can provide the administrator with many tools, features, and networking advantages.

UNIX provides some of the best networking features available, but it's hard to use; NT provides easier usage and lower costs. NT can provide file and print services for workgroups in large organizations. UNIX can provide a development platform for database applications and other high-end functions. Letting each NOS perform its strongest functions can give users the best of both worlds.

IBM, Unisys, and other high-end systems manufacturers are incorporating the two operating systems into Partitioned Symmetric Multiprocessing (PSMP) and clustered servers. These companies are trying to produce a server that can run multiple NOSs for true server consolidation. Unisys, for example, has created a cellular multiprocessing architecture that results in a 32-way Intel server partitioned into SMP cells separately running NT and UNIX in the same box.

Microsoft's Integration Tools

NT's use of TCP/IP enables a Windows NT Server system to be easily inserted into an existing UNIX network. Microsoft provides many other integration tools, including FTP and Trivial FTP as command-line utilities; Telnet for VT52; Finger for remote user lookups; Rexec and rsh for remote program execution; and other network commands like PING, netstat, route, and ipconfig that can be used from a command prompt in NT. NT also supports Gopher services, DHCP, and DNS. LPR/LPD printing is supported between NT and UNIX systems.

SNA Server for Host Integration

Although SNA Server is more of a BackOffice product than an NT feature, it works well with NT and enables host/PC integration. SNA Server enables an NT network client to communicate with an IBM mainframe or minicomputer, such as an AS/400, using a LAN-based protocol like TCP/IP. Then the SNA Server communicates with the IBM host via the SNA protocol.

SNA Server is perfect for an enterprise network. One server is capable of supporting 15,000 concurrent sessions and up to 15 SNA Servers can be active in one group at one time. SNA Server offers various features to further support the integration—load balancing, host print services, data-link encryption, single logon, and other features mean easy and effective integration with IBM host systems.

NetWare and UNIX

IntranetWare builds on NetWare 4.11, including directory, security, multiprotocol routing, messaging, management, Web publishing, and file and print services. IntranetWare also features a Web Server, Netscape Navigator Internet browser, File Transfer Protocol services for NetWare, Novell's IPX/IP Gateway, and IntranetWare Print Services for UNIX. The adoption of TCP/IP and other Internet technologies with IntranetWare has opened NetWare to the UNIX world, and vice versa.

Novell also produces a NetWare UNIX Print Services application that uses the set of TCP/IP services to provide connectivity between UNIX and NetWare environments. The NetWare/UNIX print services provide a bidirectional printing solution allowing both UNIX and NetWare users to share printers. Using NLMs, it also enables UNIX users to transfer files to and from the NetWare system.

AppleTalk

AppleTalk is a proprietary networking hardware and software solution offered by Apple Computer. AppleTalk is used mainly for Macintosh but also provides connectivity for IBM PCs, mainframes, and various UNIX computers.

AppleTalk protocols were designed for the Macintosh; they're easy to use and provide a seamless interface to the network, especially for small workgroups. The Macintosh's architecture is open enough to support third-party products and the AppleTalk protocols also support other technologies, including Microsoft, Shiva, Novell, and more.

Macintosh Clients and NT

Services for the Macintosh enables Macintosh clients and PCs to share files and printers. Computers using the Macintosh operating system can function with NT server clients without any additional software. There is an optional user authentication module software that provides secure logon to NT Server. Macintosh can send print jobs to any printer attached to the NT network, as well as to PostScript printers. Any Macintosh that can use AppleShare can use NT's Services for the Macintosh.

INDEX

Page references in *italic* type indicate illustrations.